ROYAL TAXATION
IN FOURTEENTH CENTURY
FRANCE

ROYAL TAXATION
IN FOURTEENTH CENTURY
FRANCE

The Development of War Financing
1322-1356

JOHN BELL HENNEMAN

PRINCETON UNIVERSITY PRESS
PRINCETON, NEW JERSEY
1971

Publication of this book has been aided
by a subvention from
the University of Iowa

This book is composed in Linotype Granjon
Printed in the United States of America
by Princeton University Press

To Charles Holt Taylor

with respect, affection, and gratitude

Preface

THE early history of royal finances in France may be divided into periods. Prior to 1356, taxes were temporary expedients for financing war, and there existed no special institutional machinery for administering them. Following the capture of the king at Poitiers in 1356, a new fiscal era began, as taxes were collected much more regularly, even in time of nominal peace, and a distinct administration for these revenues developed rapidly. The years immediately following 1356 are in need of restudy, but a certain amount of basic monographic literature is available for this period. Rather less is known about the period before 1356, when taxes were virtually synonymous with war financing. Recent studies and research still in progress answer many questions about the reigns of Philip IV and his first two sons (1285-1322), but the following thirty-five years have been seriously neglected. The purpose of this book is to explore the development of royal finances between 1322 and 1356, both to fill a gap in our knowledge and to suggest the background for the important institutional changes of the later fourteenth century.

Readers of this volume may find the title somewhat misleading, since "taxation," when applied to the fourteenth century, is an elusive term. I have defined it rather arbitrarily, placing little emphasis on some matters traditionally associated with taxation while devoting considerable attention to other problems which are not usually regarded as part of fiscal history. I have approached the subject as a student of French constitutional history, interested in the relationship of legal theory to actual practice and the influence of practical politics on the functioning of the state. Representative institutions have received considerable attention, but not administrative machinery or accounting methods. The latter have interested institutional historians like Adolphe Vuitry and Gustave Dupont-Ferrier, but their approach necessarily excluded certain peripheral problems which interested me a good deal. Such things as local particularism, economic and social change, war and diplomacy, political faction and dynastic feuds all influenced taxation in practice, and I have devoted considerable space to them here.

I have tried to focus on a number of basic questions: when and why did the king need money over and above his normal domainal revenues? From what sources did he seek the funds he desired? What methods and legal arguments did he employ? What was the response of his subjects to these methods and arguments? What factors influenced both the royal quest for revenues and the public response? Because the bulk of the royal financial archives have been lost, these questions cannot always be answered with complete confidence. Yet even the limited conclusions offered here will, it is hoped, shed light on the direction of French constitutional development in a critical century which witnessed the birth of many enduring institutions of the *ancien régime*. A second volume, now nearing completion, will examine the continuing evolution of royal finances after French taxation entered a new phase in 1356.

My approach to the problem of taxation has dictated a format or methodology which may be disturbing to some critics. Although no method is entirely satisfactory, I have adopted a strictly chronological approach rather than a regional or topical one. I have found that studies organized topically generally tend to obscure chronological development and the setting in which that development took place, thereby failing to deal with the questions which I find most important. In this study, royal fiscal activities will be found embedded in a welter of economic, social, political, and military developments which sometimes affected each other in bewildering ways. If this type of presentation happens to suffer somewhat in clarity, I may at least hope that it represents more accurately the way in which taxation actually developed. The struggle of the French crown to develop stable finances is seen as an unfolding narrative affected by all the irrational and unpredictable factors which have always influenced men's lives. While one of my purposes is to assemble a large amount of new or hitherto obscure data concerning royal taxation, I nevertheless hope that this data will always relate closely to the questions posed above and to the political history of the period. In a sense, it would have been more accurate to entitle this book "The Fourteenth Century French Monarchy Seen from the Point of View of Taxation." Yet this title also would have been rather misleading.

In referring to persons and places, and in citing sources, I have tried to follow the most common usage, with such deviations as seemed to be dictated by considerations of clarity. Complete consistency has been impossible to achieve but a few general rules have been followed. Names of places outside France I have generally anglicized unless conventional usage dictated otherwise. Names of places inside France have been left in French, usually the most modern form (thus Nîmes and Alès rather than Nismes and Alais). In the case of royalty and great persons closely connected to the crown, I have anglicized first names, while the names of lesser personages have been left in French. Here again I have tried to follow most common usage, despite certain difficulties and inconsistencies. Some readers may be disturbed to find Joan of Evreux and John of Armagnac in English while Godefroy d'Harcourt and Etienne Marcel are in French.

In the realm of official titles I have tried to anglicize wherever possible, hence "provost," "bailiff," "seneschal," and "viscount." In some cases, however, translation did not seem appropriate. *Viguerie* and *jugerie* were left in French because their English equivalents obscure the meaning of the terms. For the same reason I did not translate *Parlement* into "Parliament" although "Chamber of Accounts" and "Estates General" present no difficulty in English. I have used "bourgeois," "burgher," and "townsman" interchangeably for reasons of style, and for the same reason have used the words "crown," "government," and "king" as synonyms despite the distinctions between these terms which existed in medieval political theory.

The complex question of coinage and currency has been dealt with in a special appendix. In referring to money, I have used expressions like "pounds," *livres, l., l.t.,* or *l.p.,* but have deliberately avoided the symbol £. The latter is sometimes used by American writers, but it properly refers only to pounds sterling, a very different currency from that employed in France.

Because I have defined taxation and its context rather broadly, I have consulted a large number of sources not related to taxation, strictly speaking. My choice of works dealing with some peripheral topics was determined in part by their availability, and I cannot claim to have exhausted the literature on such subjects as coinage, economic and social history, and Anglo-French relations. A bibliography of all the works I have consulted would therefore not be of particular value to scholars referring to this volume, and I have decided to limit the bibliography of secondary sources to those actually cited in the footnotes. Most of the manuscripts listed in the bibliography I consulted in the archives or libraries where they are housed. A number were obtained on microfilm with the cooperation of local archivists, while I have been fortunate in obtaining copies and extracts of others from Raymond Cazelles, Charles Taylor, and Elizabeth Brown, who kindly made their notes available to me. Another valuable source of copies and extracts may be found in the Archives Nationales in Paris, cartons 2635 to 2643 of series AB xix. These are the notes of Jules Viard, who devoted half a century of research to the life of Philip VI.

No study of this type can be produced without the assistance of many persons, and it will not be possible to do them complete justice in a short preface. Four scholars in particular must be singled out because of their great and continuing contributions to this project: Charles H. Taylor, Elizabeth A. R. Brown, Raymond Cazelles, and Joseph R. Strayer.

A few words of dedication do not begin to express the author's debt to Professor Taylor, who originally inspired this study and supervised the Harvard doctoral dissertation from which the present volume is adapted. His articles, lectures, and graduate seminar have permeated my thinking about fourteenth century France and its institutions. As already mentioned, he allowed me to use the many useful extracts of documents he had collected in the course of his own research. My greatest debt to him, however, is one which I share with all his former students, for he has been an inspirational teacher of young scholars. It requires a special quality to teach sound research techniques and convey to students a love and respect for first-rate scholarship. In this exacting area of teaching, the name Charles H. Taylor is a symbol of excellence. The history department at Harvard suffered an irreplaceable loss when he retired in 1965.

Professor Brown has read most of this book in manuscript form at various stages of development. Her extensive suggestions and criticisms have been as valuable as the unflagging enthusiasm with which she has supported the entire project. She kindly allowed me to use her own unpublished dissertation and also made available to me the typescripts of several of her articles on French taxation before they appeared in print. Her exhaustive files of documents and bibliographical material have more than once rescued me from errors and omissions.

M. Cazelles, the foremost modern expert on French politics in the first half of the fourteenth century, has published an important book and numerous articles which show how the political rivalries and allegiances of the period affected institutional changes and governmental policies. My debt to him and to his approach will be apparent throughout the pages of this book. He has furnished me with valuable ideas in several letters, and showed the utmost kindness and hospitality when I solicited his aid on research trips to France. His notes and his great knowledge of the financial documents have been of the greatest help to me.

Professor Strayer is another scholar whose published research forms the essential background for this book. In addition, he has taken the trouble to read my doctoral dissertation and the typescripts of several of my articles and has made many helpful criticisms and suggestions. For more than six years, he has offered me continuing encouragement and given me useful advice on archives and source materials in France.

Without the assistance of these four scholars, this book could never have been written, but there are others who also provided indispensable aid. Chief among these are the unsung heroes of any American scholar performing research in France—the departmental and municipal archivists. Those who have been of particular help to me, either in person or through correspondence, are MM. J. Sablou (Gard), M. Gouron (Hérault), P. Bougard (Pas-de-Calais), J. Bousquet (Aveyron), R. Prat (Lot), and O. de Saint-Blanquat (Toulouse). In obtaining microfilms of documents, I am also indebted to the staffs of the departmental archives of the Tarn, Haute-Garonne, Dordogne, and Tarn-et-Garonne, as well as to the Bibliothèque Nationale and the Société Française du Microfilm.

Professors Thomas Bisson and Donald Sutherland read the entire manuscript of this book and provided me with detailed written criticisms which greatly facilitated the final revision for publication. A number of other scholars, friends, and colleagues have helped me in various ways. I should like to express my gratitude to the late Professor Robert Fawtier, and to Professors Philippe Wolff, Edouard Perroy, Robert Wheaton, Martin Wolfe, Gaines Post, Andrew Watson, Jan Rogozinski, Harry Miskimin, Charles Wood, and E. M. Beame.

Mrs. M. Parker, of the Mills Memorial Library, McMaster University, also deserves my thanks for her help in obtaining research materials via Inter-library Loan. The editor of *Speculum* kindly gave permission for me to reprint, with some revisions, portions of two of my articles which appeared in *Speculum* in 1967 and 1968. Miss R. Miriam Brokaw, Associate Director of the Princeton University Press, has patiently answered my many questions over the past year. I am also grateful to Ruth Babin and Andrea Green, who typed the manuscript of this book, and Diana Krejci and Joanna Hitchcock, who edited it for the press. My research assistants, Thomas Prest and Stephen Atkins, gave valuable help with the proofreading.

The research for this book was financed in part by a traveling fellowship from Harvard University in 1964 and grants-in-aid from McMaster University which made possible additional trips to France in 1966 and 1968. The University of Iowa furnished additional funds as a subvention in support of publication. I owe thanks to all these institutions.

Finally, my wife and children deserve to be saluted for their patient endurance of the years in which my work on this book seemed to dominate our family life.

All the persons and institutions mentioned above deserve a share of the credit for whatever merit this volume may have. I alone am responsible for its imperfections.

J.B.H.

Iowa City, Iowa
May 1971

List of Abbreviations

AB SHF	*Annuaire Bulletin, Société de l'histoire de France*
AD	Archives départementales
AESC	*Annales: Economies, sociétés, civilisations*
AHP	*Archives historiques de Poitou*
AHR	*American Historical Review*
AM	Archives municipales (communales)
AN	Archives Nationales, Paris
BEC	*Bibliothèque de l'Ecole des Chartes*
BIHR	*Bulletin of the Institute of Historical Research*
BPH	*Bulletin de philologie et d'histoire/Bulletin philologique et historique*
BN	Bibliothèque Nationale, Paris
CEH	*The Cambridge Economic History of Europe* (ed. M. Postan and E. Rich). 3 vols. Cambridge, 1941-1963
DF	*Historiens de la France, Documents financiers* series
Ec. HR	*Economic History Review*
EHR	*English Historical Review*
Foedera	*Foedera, conventiones litterae et cujuscunque generis acta publica inter reges Angliae et alios quosvis imperatores, reges, pontifices, principes vel communitates* (ed. T. Rymer, 3rd edition). 9 vols. The Hague, 1739-1745
Gr. Chartrier	*Archives de la ville de Montpellier, Inventaires et documents: Inventaire du Grand Chartrier redigé par Robert Louvet.* Vol. I (ed. J. Berthelet and F. Castets), Montpellier, 1895-1899. Vol. II (ed. O. de Dainville), Montpellier, 1955
HL	*Histoire générale de Languedoc avec des Notes et les pièces justificatives* (new edition, ed. A. Molinier et al.). 16 vols. Toulouse, 1872-1904
INV	*Inventaire sommaire des archives départementales/communales* (see Section II of Bibliography)
Isambert	*Recueil général des anciennes lois françaises depuis l'an 420 jusqu'à la Révolution de 1789* (ed. Decrusy, Isambert, and Jourdan). 27 vols. Paris, n.d. (18th c.)—1827
JEH	*Journal of Economic History*
JT Ch. IV	*Les journaux du trésor de Charles IV le Bel* (ed. J. Viard). Paris, 1917
JT Ph. VI	*Les journaux du trésor de Philippe VI de Valois suivis de l'ordinarium thesauri de 1338-1339* (ed. J. Viard). Paris, 1899
LC	*Lettres closes, lettres "de par le roy" de Philippe de Valois* (ed. R. Cazelles). Paris, 1958
MA	*Le Moyen Age*
Mignon	*Inventaire des anciens comptes royaux dressé par Robert Mignon* (ed. C. V. Langlois). Paris, 1899
NAF	Nouvelles acquisitions françaises
NRHD	*Nouvelle revue historique de droit français et étranger*
Ord.	*Ordonnances des roys de France de la troisième race recueillies par ordre chronologique* (ed. Laurière, Secousse, et al.). 21 vols. Paris, 1723-1849

P. J.	Pièces justificatives
P. O.	Pièces originales
P&P	*Past and Present*
PTEC	*Positions des thèses, Ecole des Chartes*
RBPH	*Revue belge de philologie et d'histoire*
RH	*Revue historique*
RHD	*Revue historique de droit français et étranger*
RQH	*Revue des questions historiques*
SPIC	*Studies Presented to the International Commission for the History of Representative and Parliamentary Institutions/Etudes presentées à la commission internationale pour l'histoire des assemblées d'états*
TRHS	*Transactions of the Royal Historical Society*

Contents

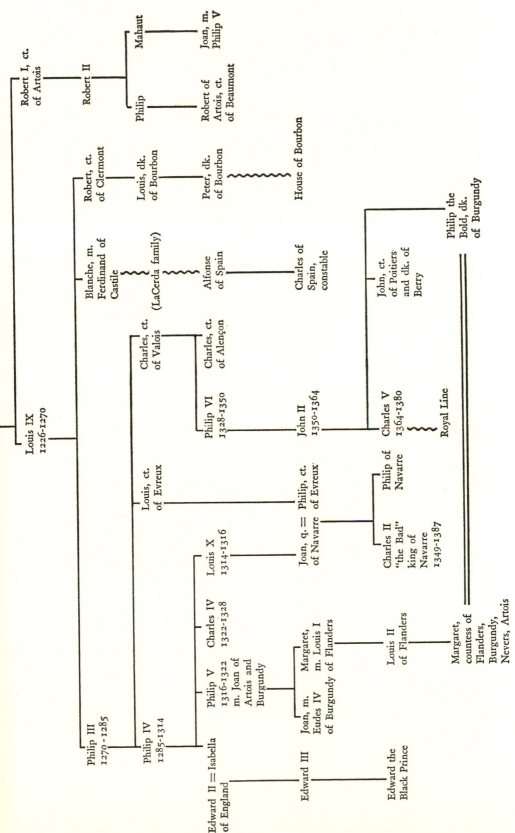

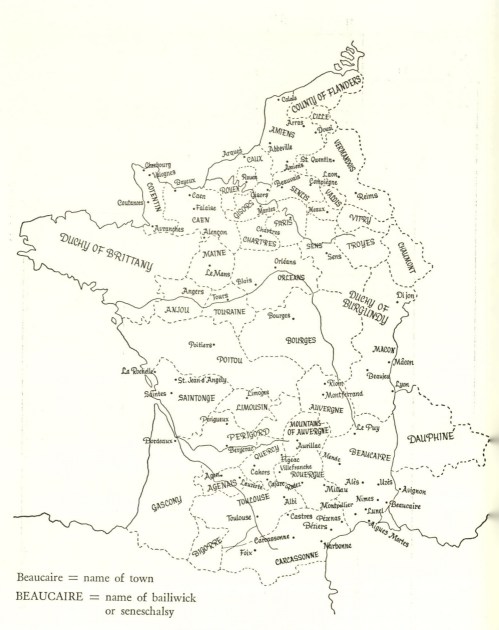

Beaucaire = name of town

BEAUCAIRE = name of bailiwick
or seneschalsy

FRANCE UNDER PHILIP VI

Showing approximate borders of administrative districts and the towns mentioned most frequentl
in this volume

ROYAL TAXATION
IN FOURTEENTH CENTURY
FRANCE

CHAPTER I

The French Crown and Its Finances at the
Beginning of the Fourteenth Century

To UNDERSTAND the financial position of the French monarchy in the first quarter of the fourteenth century, one first must be acquainted with the fiscal terminology and administrative geography employed in the documents. Of even greater importance are the economic, social, and political factors which conditioned the development of royal taxing powers at the beginning of this period.

1. Fiscal Terminology

The term "taxation" is used here to describe a set of late medieval practices which produced revenues but which often seem rather remote from "taxation" in the modern sense. The fourteenth century had no single word to describe these practices, but several which overlapped in meaning, each referring to the collection of money by a government. When a ruler canceled a tax or granted exemption, he usually used several words, such as "aids," "subsidies," "impositions," and *gabelles*, in order to be properly inclusive. All these words, however, seem to have had a preferred meaning.

Perhaps the most widely used term was *aide*, derived from the feudal concept of *auxilium*. By 1500, an "aid" in France usually meant an indirect tax, but two hundred years earlier, it was used for almost every type of tax at one time or another.[1] Four special circumstances under which a vassal owed his lord a payment are usually called "feudal aids" to distinguish them from other uses of the term. A lord could demand these payments when his eldest son was knighted, when his eldest daughter was married, when he was captured and had to be ransomed, and when he went on crusade.[2] When King John II had to be ransomed in the 1360s, certain sales taxes were levied as a feudal aid to raise the required sum. As these taxes became more or less permanent, the word

[1] G. Dupont-Ferrier, *Etudes sur les institutions financières de la France à la fin du moyen âge*, Paris, 1932, II, 2-22, discusses the meanings of the word "aid" as well as other questions of terminology. For the meanings in one region, cf. C. Hirschauer, *Les états d'Artois*, Paris, 1923, I, 111.

[2] A. Vuitry, *Etudes sur le régime financier de la France avant la Révolution de 1789 (nouv. série)*, I, Paris, 1878, 144. A. Callery, *Histoire du pouvoir royal d'imposer depuis la féodalité jusqu'au règne de Charles V*, Brussels, 1879, p. 24, mentions two other feudal aids of a more specialized nature.

"aid" gradually acquired its later, more restricted, meaning of indirect tax.

Sometimes a vassal might be asked to render pecuniary aid to his lord in a military emergency. These "aids for war" or "aids for the host" were not limited to royal vassals but usually were extended to most of the king's subjects. Despite royal efforts to associate wars with the public weal, the habit of considering them a sort of private venture—"the king's wars"—persisted well into the fourteenth century. Aids for these wars could be regarded as the public financing of a private undertaking, and were usually called "subsidies." It is almost redundant to say "war sub-sidy," but many documents do so, perhaps because even this word had other uses. Two "feudal aids"—for the knighting of the future John II in 1332-1335 and for his ransom thirty years later—are explicitly called "subsidies" in some texts.[3]

Another word, "subvention," was rather close in meaning to subsidy, generally referring to a tax whose proceeds were earmarked for some particular purpose, often war but not invariably so. "Imposition," on the other hand, increasingly tended to mean a particular form of tax—an indirect levy on exports or domestic sales. Two other terms, more re-gional in nature, seem to have been reserved exclusively for sales taxes. *Maltôte*, a term of opprobrium which enjoyed widespread use in the 1290s, was employed only in northern France in the middle fourteenth century. The term *gabelle* meant roughly the same thing in Auvergne and Languedoc, a tax on sales. First in the North and much later in Languedoc, *gabelle* gradually acquired its more restricted meaning, referring to the notorious tax on salt established first in 1341. We encoun-ter much more rarely the term *capage*, meaning "head tax."

An important fiscal term was *fouage* (*focagium* in Latin), which meant "hearth tax," whenever and wherever found. There has been much debate, however, about what was implied by the word "hearth." Originally, the hearth was a household or family unit, probably a mar-ried couple and their unmarried children, but in some places, perhaps, a larger patriarchal family. Official hearth counts were compiled for fiscal purposes and they presumably did not include tax-exempt persons, such as those with privileges or those who were very poor. The latter were normally those households possessing less than ten pounds.[4] A

---

[3] BN NAF 7603 (Fontanieu 72), fols. 141-142; BN *ms. lat.* 9175, fols. 24-26.

[4] P. Dognon, *Les institutions politiques et administratives du pays de Languedoc du XIIIe siècle aux guerres de religion*, Toulouse, 1895, pp. 620-621, argues that this meant ten pounds of capital, whereas some earlier writers understood it to mean income. If Dognon is right, some fourteenth century *fouages* must have been very

fouage was usually described as so much per hearth or per hundred hearths. It is probable that these taxes began quite early to be apportioned such that the wealthier units paid more and the poorer less. This was invariably the case in later centuries.

The difficulty concerning the word "hearth" arises mainly in the case of Languedoc, and indeed the *fouage* appeared only infrequently outside Languedoc until 1363. Many documents pertaining to hearth taxes in Languedoc required nobles or clergy to pay only for their *roturier* or urban property.[5] Some historians have inferred from these texts that the hearth in the Midi was a unit of real estate rather than a household unit as such. In the second half of the fourteenth century, moreover, we sometimes find taxes being assessed "according to the old number of hearths,"[6] and communities eagerly sought the privilege of being charged with fewer hearths for tax purposes.[7] These facts have led other scholars to conclude that the hearth was merely an administrative fiction. In the face of these views, Borrelli de Serres has argued persuasively that the hearth was still a family unit in the later 1340s and was treated as such long after this time. Beginning in 1348, a series of plagues, increased warfare, and economic depression greatly reduced the total number of households and may well have pushed many of the surviving ones below the minimum taxable income. Faced with rising fiscal needs, the monarchy tended increasingly to treat the *fouage* as an apportioned tax, assessing a given region, town, or diocese on the basis of a given number of hearths. In time, therefore, it appears that hearths did become an administrative fiction, although still tied in principle to the number of family units whose wealth exceeded a given minimum.[8]

Towards the end of the fourteenth century, the crown levied a series of taxes in the form of a *fouage* but called *grandes tailles*.[9] These gave rise to a gradual change of terminology, and the annual apportioned taxes from the fifteenth century onwards became known as *tailles*. Through most of the fourteenth century, however, the word *taille* had

---

onerous for the poorer taxpayers. A special application of the term *fouage* in Normandy is mentioned in Appendix 1.

[5] Examples are AD Hérault A 4, fols. 140r-v, 158v-159r.

[6] See J. Henneman, "The Black Death and Royal Taxation in France, 1347-1351," *Speculum*, XLIII (1968), 422.

[7] Dognon, *Institutions*, p. 624; *INV AM Montferrand*, I, 398-399 (CC 167).

[8] L. Borrelli de Serres, *Recherches sur divers services publics du XIIIe au XVIIe siècle*, Paris, 1905, III, 391-418.

[9] M. Rey, *Le domaine du roi et les ressources extraordinaires sous Charles VI, 1388-1413*, Paris, 1965, pp. 324f.

little or no connection with royal *fouages*. The term had once described an arbitrary seigneurial exaction, but by 1300, the *taille* in rural society was arbitrary only when applied to unfree persons described in the documents as "tallageable at will." Meanwhile, the word had experienced a different evolution in urban communities. Another complication arises from the use of inventories compiled in the seventeenth or eighteenth centuries when the *taille* was the royal tax apportioned unevenly over most of the kingdom. When the word appears in inventory descriptions of fourteenth century texts, it may refer to royal taxes which were not called by that name at the time.

Townspeople originally were tallageable in the same way as rural dependents, but the process of enfranchisement had gradually eliminated arbitrary urban *tailles* by 1200. Once enfranchised, the bourgeois might still be asked by the king or seigneur for voluntary payments.[10] These were a matter of negotiation, and in the fourteenth century they were called subsidies or impositions. For much of the thirteenth century, however, they were called *tailles* like their more degrading predecessor. By 1300, the word *taille* still had meaning in the towns, but it referred increasingly to taxes levied on burghers by their own municipal government. Municipal taxes also had other, less common names, like *socquet* and *barrage*, both found mainly in Languedoc and generally designed for the maintenance of fortifications.[11]

Although this study is concerned with royal, not municipal, taxation, the distinction was by no means as clear as one could wish. Towns frequently paid royal subsidies by means of a lump-sum payment. This money was raised through municipal taxes levied on the burghers, and a great many such levies were actually disguised royal taxes. Moreover, when a town collected a *taille* to finance repair of ramparts or to equip a contingent of sergeants, it was subsidizing a military operation which

[10] C. Stephenson, "The Aids of the French Towns in the Twelfth and Thirteenth Centuries," in his *Mediaeval Institutions: Selected Essays* (ed. B. Lyon), Ithaca, 1954, pp. 1-40. Cf. P. Timbal et al., *La guerre de Cent Ans vue à travers les registres du Parlement (1337-1369)*, Paris, 1961, pp. 217-218.

[11] *INV AM Montferrand*, I, 312 (CC 2); P. Wolff, *Commerces et marchands de Toulouse (vers 1350-vers 1450)*, Paris, 1954, p. 97. Another specialized tax found in upper Languedoc was the *commun de paix*, which will not be dealt with in this study. Aside from a series of documents in AD Aveyron G 471-473, it has left relatively few documentary traces from the fourteenth century. Its original purpose had been to finance the efforts of bishops to maintain the peace in their dioceses. See J. Poux, "Essai sur le commun de paix ou pezade dans le Rouergue et dans l'Albigeois," *PTEC*, 1898, pp. 107-116; T. N. Bisson, *Assemblies and Representation in Languedoc in the Thirteenth Century*, Princeton, 1964, pp. 106-134.

was ultimately a royal responsibility. In this way, urban taxes substituted for royal ones. The troubled 1350s witnessed a significant increase in locally financed military efforts as the weakened monarchy had difficulty mounting an effective campaign.[12] Urban *tailles* which substituted for royal taxes must be considered along with more direct forms of royal revenue. Moreover, many taxes, both royal and municipal, were in fact shared between the two governments. It had become established that municipal *tailles* could not be levied without the permission of the king (or the local seigneur if he was an important prince).[13] Sometimes the king obtained a part of the receipts in return for permitting a town to levy a tax.[14] Sometimes also, a town paying the king a subsidy was allowed to keep a portion of it for local needs.[15] Thus it is clear that municipal finance was closely connected to royal finance.

A final term which often meant "tax" in the fourteenth century was "loan." The crown frequently obtained loans, more or less forced, which simply were disguised taxes. Some were advances later repaid from slowly collected subsidy receipts, but many were never repaid and in some years loans formed a significant percentage of the king's revenue.[16]

[12] Thus some Norman communities actually equipped their own armies for local defense. See A. Coville, *Les états de Normandie, leurs origines et leur développement au XIVe siècle*, Paris, 1894, pp. 92-93.

[13] Timbal, *Guerre*, p. 227; H. Furgeot, *Actes du Parlement de Paris, deuxième série*, I, Paris, 1920, no. 3055; G. Post, *Studies in Medieval Legal Thought: Public Law and the State, 1100-1322*, Princeton, 1964, p. 275; A. Thierry (ed.), *Recueil des monuments inédits de l'histoire du tiers état, première série*, I, Paris, 1850, 530-531; G. Espinas, "Les finances de la commune de Douai des origines au XVe siècle," *NRHD*, 1901, pp. 413-415; S. Honoré-Duvergé, "Un fragment de compte de Charles le Mauvais," *BEC*, CII (1941), 294-297; P. Bertin, *Une commune flamande-artésienne: Aire-sur-la-Lys, des origines au XVIe siècle*, Arras, 1947, pp. 230-232; BN Moreau 227, fols. 166-167.

[14] For some examples, see *Ord.*, XII, 484-485; E. Le Maire (ed.), *Archives anciennes de la ville de Saint-Quentin*, II, Saint-Quentin, 1910, 287.

[15] For a case of this sort, see J. Henneman, "Financing the Hundred Years' War: Royal Taxation in France in 1340," *Speculum*, XLII (1967), 287.

[16] On loans, see *ibid.*, pp. 276, 278, 284; Timbal, *Guerre*, pp. 66-67; J. R. Strayer and C. H. Taylor, *Studies in Early French Taxation*, Cambridge (Mass.), 1939, pp. 19-21; H. Miskimin, *Money, Prices, and Foreign Exchange in Fourteenth Century France*, New Haven, 1963, pp. 45-46; Borrelli de Serres, *Recherches*, II, 442-443. The tables compiled by R. Fawtier, *Comptes du trésor*, Paris, 1930, pp. lix-lx, indicate that Charles IV borrowed 200,000 *livres parisis* more than he repaid during the first four years of his reign. In *JT Ch. IV*, no. 10005, one finds repayment in 1326 of a loan dating back to 1292! An important occasion for the use of loans occurred in 1360, when a vast sum had to be raised quickly for the first payment on King John's ransom. The crown sought heavy loans from the wealthy, who were to be repaid from the receipts of the aid levied for the ransom. See J. M. Richard,

2. *The Geographic and Administrative Framework*

The king deemed it advisable to invoke the expression "defense of the realm" when seeking to obtain subsidies, but the precise meaning of the term "realm" was not always completely clear. Even if we assume a fairly well-accepted frontier separating France from Spain and from the Holy Roman Empire, the fact remains that the French king exerted considerable authority in some regions outside this kingdom while having little effective control of certain regions within it.[17]

From a legal standpoint, the lands within the kingdom may be classified as royal domain, *apanages*, and fiefs. The fiefs may be reclassified only with the greatest difficulty because of variations in power, wealth, and jurisdiction. In these lands, the effective authority of the king depended on many factors. Feudal/seigneurial power often involved rights or revenues which cannot be described in geographical terms. Even if we confine ourselves to the territorial aspect of royal authority, we must remember that fiefs of comparable legal status might vary considerably in size. They might be compact in nature or consist of scattered holdings; located near a frontier or close to Paris. With respect to both fiefs and *apanages* a vital personal element could be involved. A given king might be on friendly terms with some lords, indifferent or hostile to others. Some great magnates were related by marriage to the king; others guarded a strategic border; certain ones might be strong or weak personalities; others were minors or women or clergy.

Bearing in mind all these complexities, we can make certain generalizations concerning the period 1322-1356. Among the great fief-peerages, Flanders had so successfully defied the king in the period 1302-1320, that it was, from the fiscal point of view, virtually a foreign country. The same can be said for Aquitaine or Guyenne, whose duke was king of England. Brittany enjoyed considerable independence by virtue of its geographical position. Besides these three, Burgundy and Blois were in practice freer from royal control than the other lay fiefs, but

---

"Instructions données aux commissaires chargés de lever le rançon du roi Jean," *BEC*, xxxvi (1875), 81-90.

[17] The late Capetians exerted great influence in some parts of the empire and actually controlled Navarre, but their authority was largely theoretical in Brittany and Gascony. On the problem of defining the realm, see C. Wood, *"Regnum Francie*: A Problem in Capetian Administrative Usage," *Traditio*, xxiii (1967), 117-147; J. R. Strayer, "France: The Holy Land, the Chosen People, and the Most Christian King," in *Action and Conviction in Early Modern Europe* (ed. T. Rabb and J. Seigel), Princeton, 1969, pp. 5-7; B. Guenée, "Etat et nation en France au moyen âge," *RH*, ccxxxvii (1967), 24-27.

their respective lords enjoyed a close personal relationship with Philip VI. A strategic location enabled the count of Foix to obtain fiscal privileges, while his enemy the count of Armagnac rose to a position of great power because of his marriage connections with the royal house.[18] Among the *apanages,* Artois was ruled by women throughout the fourteenth century and their close connections with Philip V and Philip VI helped the crown exercise considerable authority in the county up to 1348. Two other princes, Bourbon and Alençon, usually cooperated closely with the crown, but the Evreux branch of the Capetians were far less friendly to the Valois and their lands virtually became enemy territory in the generation after 1354. All these factors, as well as the political circumstances of a given year, affected royal taxing power, and the crown usually had to negotiate special subsidy arrangements with these magnates.

In the winter of 1327-1328, when the royal domain achieved its greatest territorial extent of the later Middle Ages, the crown conducted a census of hearths and parishes in the kingdom, presumably for fiscal purposes. The only lands excluded from this census were the remaining *apanages* (Alençon, Artois, Bourbon, Evreux) and a few great fiefs (Blois, Brittany, Burgundy, Flanders-Nevers, Guyenne). It has been argued that these territories were the only parts of the kingdom in which royal fiscal officers did not have the power to act.[19] It does not follow, however, that all the rest of the realm constituted royal domain. Royal accessibility to the many other fiefs varied according to time, place, and political circumstances. Even when not a part of the royal domain, they were attached to one of the bailiwicks or seneschalsies of the domain for administrative purposes.

These administrative districts, of which there were about three dozen, form the territorial framework for considering taxation in our period. In the absence of a regular administration for collecting non-domanial revenues, the crown employed existing local officers or special commissioners. These were always assigned to one or more of the bailiwicks or

[18] On the position of the count of Foix, see BN *Coll. Languedoc* 84, fols. 144r-v, and documents in AD Basses-Pyrenées E 406 which are cited in subsequent chapters. On John of Armagnac's marriage to a great granddaughter of Louis IX, see M. de Gaujal, *Etudes historiques sur le Rouergue,* Paris, 1858, II, 165. Armagnac's daughter later married a brother of Charles V; F. Lehoux, *Jean de France, duc de Berri: Sa vie; son action politique (1340-1416),* Paris, 1966, I, 140-141.

[19] F. Lot, "L'état des paroisses et des feux de 1328," *BEC,* xc (1929), 51-107, 256-315, and especially Lot's comments on pp. 286-288; cf. M. Nortier, "Le sort des archives dispersées de la Chambre des Comptes de Paris," *BEC,* cxxiii (1965), 463-465.

seneschalsies.[20] The five bailiwicks of Normandy and the four of Champagne were sometimes treated collectively because these regions had enjoyed a certain historic unity. More important in our period was the lieutenancy of Languedoc, comprising the seneschalsy of Périgord and those lying south of the Dordogne river. The royal lieutenant in this large region wielded such powers that he has been called a veritable viceroy.[21] Languedoc came to have an administration quite different from that of the North, particularly in the 1350s.

The central administration of the royal government consisted of five main branches whose personnel and functions were somewhat ill-defined and overlapping. These were the royal household, chancery, treasury, Chamber of Accounts, and *Parlement*. Together with the important prelates and lay magnates, these bodies formed the personnel pool from which was staffed the royal council. The main lines of governmental policy were established by the king and council. The king still traveled a good deal, as did the chancellor, and this practice helped create disordered procedures in the chancery.[22] The treasury, which had long been run by the Templars, retained the organizational structure of a bank. The Chamber of Accounts, still in the process of development, supervised and audited the collections of domainal revenue. The records of these two financial bodies have largely been destroyed or dispersed,

[20] The Norman bailiwicks were Rouen, Caux, Gisors, Caen, and Cotentin. Those of Champagne were Meaux-Provins, Chaumont, Vitry, and Troyes. The other districts in the region of the Languedoil were Paris, Amiens, Vermandois, Senlis, Sens, Valois, Touraine, Anjou, Maine, Lille, Auvergne, Mountains of Auvergne, Orléans, Chartres, Bourges, Mâcon-Lyon, Poitou, Limousin, and Saintonge. The districts were often changed or combined, and their boundaries were long uncertain. See G. Dupont-Ferrier, "Ignorances et distractions administratives en France aux XIVe et XVe siècles," *BEC*, c (1939), 145-156. For their situation in the early fourteenth century, see the convenient summary by E. Perroy, *The Hundred Years War* (Eng. tr. W. B. Wells), London, 1951, p. 41. The basic reference work on this subject is G. Dupont-Ferrier, *Gallia Regia, ou état des officiers royaux des bailliages et des sénéschausées de 1328 à 1515*, 6 vols., Paris, 1942.

[21] R. H. Bautier, "Recherches sur la chancellerie royale au temps de Philippe VI," *BEC*, cxxii (1964), 103-105, and notes. The seneschalsies of Languedoc, besides Périgord, were Quercy, Rouergue, Agenais, Gascony, Bigorre, Beaucaire-Nîmes, Toulouse, and Carcassonne.

[22] Bautier, "Chancellerie," pp. 165-167. On the institutions of the monarchy, the most recent work is F. Lot and R. Fawtier, *Histoire des institutions françaises au moyen âge*, ii, Paris, 1958. On the political factors affecting the king's council, see R. Cazelles, *La société politique et la crise de la royauté sous Philippe de Valois*, Paris, 1958; R. Cazelles, "Les mouvements révolutionnaires du milieu du XIVe siècle et le cycle de l'action politique," *RH*, ccxxvii (1962), 279-312; P. Lehugeur, *Philippe le Long, roi de France 1316-1322: Le mécanisme du gouvernement*, Paris, 1931 (hereafter cited as *Mécanisme*).

and those which survive are hard to use because of coinage fluctuations.[23] Most of the documents express figures in money of account at the value current when the receipts or expenditures were made. This system was based on *livres* (pounds), each consisting of twenty *sols*, each consisting of twelve *deniers*. *Livres parisis* (*l.p.*) were used in the Ile-de-France and the bailiwicks farther north. Four of these equaled five of the *livres tournois* (*l.t.*) used in the rest of the kingdom.

The bailiffs and seneschals in their respective districts were assisted by judges and "receivers," as well as the ubiquitous but unpopular sergeants who enforced executive orders. Administrative subdivisions, like the viscounties in Normandy and the *jugeries* or *vigueries* in Languedoc, were sometimes used as the basis for tax collection.[24] The most powerful and flexible figure in French field administration was the special commissioner. The famous *enquêteurs-réformateurs* sent by St. Louis to remedy the abuses of rural officials were such commissioners. Limited money and personnel increasingly led the crown to name as commissioners persons who were already in the field as bailiffs, judges, etc. Armed with extraordinary powers, such men proved to be formidable fiscal agents, and this function sometimes overshadowed their role as reformers of abuses.[25]

Through the first half of the fourteenth century, the royal administration was designed primarily to exploit domainal resources and preserve public order. Derived from an earlier, simpler era, it was really not equipped to supervise an efficient system of taxation. Despite the domain's steady growth in the thirteenth century, its revenues were becom-

[23] See Nortier, "Archives dispersées," pp. 46of.; Borrelli de Serres, *Recherches*, ii, 104-142; J. Viard, editor's introduction to *JT Ph. VI*, pp. xiv-xx; cf. the discussion in Appendix i.

[24] These subdivisions and their officers are indicated in Dupont-Ferrier, *Gallia Regia*, passim. They were especially important in Normandy and Languedoc, two regions which influenced French administrative development in important ways. See J. R. Strayer, "Normandy and Languedoc," *Speculum*, xliv (1969), 1-12; J. R. Strayer, "Viscounts and Viguiers under Philip the Fair," *Speculum*, xxxviii (1963), 242-255; J. Rogozinski, "The Counsellors of the Seneschal of Beaucaire and Nîmes, 1250-1350," *Speculum*, xliv (1969), 421-439. On provosts and farmers of taxes, see Dupont-Ferrier, *Institutions*, ii, 71-96. On the evolving functions of the crown's local officers, see J. Fesler, "French Field Administration: The Beginnings," *Comparative Studies in Society and History*, v (1962), 76-111.

[25] Fesler observes, *ibid.*, p. 99, that "there was a blending of functions supported not only by tradition but by a logic whose force is likely to be overlooked." For the application of this practice to commissioners, see J. Henneman, "*Enquêteurs-Réformateurs* and Fiscal Officers in Fourteenth Century France," *Traditio,* xxiv (1968), 309-349.

ing inadequate to support the needs of the state. This growing deficiency may be associated in part with changing economic and social conditions.

3. Economic and Social Change

The great expansion of the Capetian royal domain had occurred during a period of general economic and demographic growth. This boom had been marked by rising prices, a matter of concern to rural landlords whose income was relatively stable. Although expansion of the domain increased the king's resources, it also increased his commitments. Consolidation of power throughout Europe meant that feudal buffer states no longer effectively separated French royal lands from those of the emperor, the count of Flanders, the king of Aragon, and (in Gascony) the king of England. By 1300, a new era of confrontation and war had succeeded the peaceful thirteenth century, and at this moment the economic boom lost its force.[26]

The prosperity of the thirteenth century had not been equally advantageous to all. The bourgeoisie could profit from expanding markets and improved business methods, but the profits were distributed unequally. Some peasants could benefit from rising grain prices and other opportunities, but the condition of many began to suffer when the great land clearances ended.[27] The lords, whose changing tastes played an important role in stimulating the economic boom, were in a position to benefit from commercial expansion. Yet in time they began to suffer from the rising prices if they depended mainly on fixed manorial dues, and some lesser seigneurs found it increasingly difficult to maintain status. Inflation became the enemy of the seigneurial class, and the great landed interests were quick to oppose inflationary royal policies like coinage debasement.

Nobles began to worry about their finances to a greater degree than in the past. They found that powers arising from justice and monopolies were more lucrative than those they enjoyed as landlords,[28] yet the growth of royal authority and jurisdiction was undercutting this source of wealth. The greater peace and public order provided by the thirteenth century monarchy reduced the opportunity for plunder, ransoms,

[26] On the pattern of consolidating powers and loyalties, see J. R. Strayer, "Laicization of French and English Society in the Thirteenth Century," *Speculum*, xv (1940), 82-84. Coville, *Etats Norm.*, p. 27, believed that the prosperity of the royal domain was what permitted the crown to avoid making demands for taxes in the thirteenth century.

[27] G. Duby, *Rural Economy and Country Life in the Medieval West* (Eng. tr. C. Postan), London, 1968, p. 116.

[28] *Ibid.*, pp. 224f.

and military salaries. To meet his own financial needs, the king began tampering with the coinage, levying fines on non-noble acquirers of fiefs, and seizing the assets of Jewish and Italian moneylenders. These policies created higher prices, lower property values, and more restricted credit, all of which complicated further the economic position of the aristocracy.[29] Their financial difficulties directed the attention of the French nobility towards one occupation in which they could engage profitably without fear of losing status: warfare. In the fourteenth century, Anglo-French hostilities dragged on endlessly, as neither side could marshal the resources needed for total victory. There were doubtless many reasons for this, but it seems clear that economic conditions had given an important part of the European nobility a vested interest in war.

The period of growth, moreover, came to an end in the fourteenth century, and an overpopulated Europe began to experience famines as climatic disturbances and the exhaustion of marginal lands reduced the food supply.[30] Grain became less profitable and some landed proprietors began to raise grapes instead of cereals because wine prices remained high longer. Carpentier has suggested that the worst harvest periods were the decades 1310-1320 and 1340-1350. Duby has described a weakening of the domainal economy in the period 1320-1340 and again in 1350-1360, with an intervening leveling-off period. Evidently higher prices accompanied the bad harvests but generally lower prices followed.[31] Europe was undernourished and already experiencing eco-

[29] M. E. Carreau, *Les commissaires royaux aux amortissements et aux nouveaux acquêts sous les Capetiens (1275-1328), PTEC*, 1953. The late Prof. Robert Fawtier very kindly made available to me a typescript of this unpublished thesis. Cf. Henneman, "Enquêteurs," p. 313; J. R. Strayer, "Italian Bankers and Philip the Fair," *Explorations in Economic History*, VII (1969), 115-118; J. Henneman, "Taxation of Italians by the French Crown, 1311-1363," *Mediaeval Studies*, XXXI (1969), 30-40.

[30] H. Lucas, "The Great European Famine of 1315, 1316, 1317," *Speculum*, V (1930), 343-377; G. Fourquin, *Les campagnes de la région parisienne à la fin du moyen âge*, Paris, 1964, pp. 191f.; M. Larenaudie, "Les famines en Languedoc aux XIVe et XVe siècles," *Annales du Midi*, LXIV (1952), 28-32; E. Carpentier, "Autour de la peste noire: Famines et épidémies dans l'histoire du XIVe siècle," *AESC*, XVII (1962), 1075f.; Duby, *Rural Economy*, pp. 306-307. A different view of the fourteenth century economy is presented by W. Robinson, "Money, Population, and Economic Change in Late Medieval Europe," *Ec.HR*, XII (1959), 68, 73, but this author seems to have some serious misconceptions about the period, as pointed out by M. Postan, *ibid.*, pp. 77f.

[31] Duby, *Rural Economy*, pp. 319f.; Carpentier, "Peste noire," p. 1075; Fourquin, *Campagnes*, pp. 194-195, 199-206. On the depression in Europe generally, see J. Heers, *L'Occident aux XIVe et XVe siècles: Aspects economiques et sociaux*, Paris, 1963; R. Lopez and H. Miskimin, "The Economic Depression of the Renaissance," *Ec.HR*, XIV (1961-1962), 408-425.

nomic depression when the Black Death appeared in 1348. This disaster caused a drastic depopulation of the towns and a labor shortage. High urban prices and wages, coupled with a sharp decline in the demand for footstuffs, stimulated a migration of peasants from country to town. The result was a new shortage of rural labor, while the contracting market for urban products tended to create an unemployed proletariat in the towns.[32]

It is not easy to assess the depression's effect on taxation. Town governments complained chronically of local impoverishment when they wished to avoid royal taxes. Yet communities which used this argument to resist moderate taxation in the reign of Philip VI were able, despite a reduced population, to pay much larger sums a generation later when convinced of the necessity of doing so.[33] The effects of the Black Death were considerable, and these will be discussed in a later chapter. Otherwise, it was not so much the depression itself as a broad social malaise which may have had the greatest effect on royal tax-raising efforts.

A series of tragedies and disturbances upset French society in the early fourteenth century, contributing to an atmosphere in which men fell back upon privileges and sought security in the narrow interests of locality or class. The nobility, whose mounted warriors long dominated European warfare, suffered humiliating defeat at the hands of Flemish burghers in 1302, the first of several famous disasters for cavalry at the hands of infantry during the century. The papacy, symbol of European spiritual unity, was humiliated by Philip IV in 1303, and for the next three generations, the pontiffs were Frenchmen, living at Avignon, who struggled with mixed success to keep their holy office independent from the pressures of the French crown. The order of the Knights Templar, accused of sordid and extravagant practices, was destroyed by Philip IV. Famine and epidemic gripped northern France in 1315 and 1316. In 1320, the South was troubled by the quasi-religious uprising of the Pastoureaux. A year later, there were wild rumors that the Jews had induced the lepers to poison the wells.[34] Within the royal family, the

[32] Duby, *Rural Economy*, pp. 298-309; Carpentier, "Peste noire," p. 1086; G. Prat, "Albi et la peste noire," *Annales du Midi*, LXIV (1952), 18-24.

[33] A convenient example is Montpellier, which paid 2,000 *l.t.* in 1328 with great reluctance after alleging local impoverishment. Forty years later, the town paid taxes amounting to four or five times that much, despite economic decline, military disasters, and two serious plagues in the intervening decades. See *HL*, x, cols. 676-680; *Gr. Chartrier*, nos. 3596, 3604.

[34] See H. Johnstone, "France: The Last Capetians," in *The Cambridge Medieval History*, Cambridge (Eng.), 1932, VII, 312f.; Lucas, "Famine"; *HL*, x, cols. 613-615; *Ord.*, XI, 481-482; AD Hérault A 4, fol. 56r-v; J. Viard (ed.), *Les grandes chroniques*

descendants of St. Louis were involved in a shocking adultery scandal. Philip IV, still in his mid-forties, died a few months later amid a general revolt. He was soon followed to the grave by Louis X, the infant John I, Philip V, and Charles IV, all of them young and without male heirs. Philip VI, who established the Valois dynasty in 1328, was clearly uneasy in his conscience about the title which he had inherited.[35]

Among these disturbing events, all classes of French society found reasons for insecurity and lack of confidence. The nobles, no longer invincible in battle and troubled economically, sought to safeguard their status. They went to court to defend the obligation of vassals to serve in the army under their own lords.[36] They stoutly resisted royal taxation of those dependents who still were tallageable serfs.[37] The clergy waged a losing struggle to protect its declining revenues from royal and municipal taxation.[38] The peasants found life more precarious as the level of warfare increased. As they began to discover that the king and nobility could not always protect them from brigandage and enemy invasion, they became increasingly bitter at the financial exactions they were forced to bear.[39]

The reaction of the towns was more complex because many interests were represented in these communities. The economic and social problems of the fourteenth century surely accentuated the internal tensions and rivalries which determined municipal politics. Urban unrest and class struggle were rather common in the later Middle Ages, but beyond this generalization we are not well-informed about the politics of individual French towns. The particular interests of those who controlled urban governments must have influenced the form taken by royal taxes in these towns and the way in which they were negotiated. In many communities of Languedoc, a continuing dispute divided the rich, who

---

de France, VIII, Paris, 1936, pp. 358-359; A. Hellot (ed.), "Chronique parisienne anonyme de 1316 à 1339," *Mémoires de la Société de l'histoire de Paris*, XI (1885), 56.

[35] R. Fawtier, *The Capetian Kings of France* (Eng. tr. L. Butler and R. Adam), New York, 1960, pp. 36-41, 53-54. On Philip of Valois and his title, see P. S. Lewis, *Later Medieval France: The Polity*, London, 1968, pp. 37, 79, 110-111. Lewis would doubtless agree with Fawtier, who argued in a conversation in Paris in 1964, that the Valois were deeply disturbed about the question of their legitimacy. This concern was a factor in the fearful, erratic behavior of several of the Valois kings.

[36] Inventoried by Furgeot, *Actes*, II, no. 4753; published by Timbal, *Guerre*, pp. 16-17. Perhaps equally important was the way in which the nobles became increasingly anxious for pitched battles. See Perroy, *The Hundred Years War*, p. 115.

[37] See below, note 50.   [38] See Chapter IX.

[39] See Duby, *Rural Economy*, pp. 332f.; R. Delachenal, *Histoire de Charles V*, Paris, 1909, I, 349f.

wished to base municipal finances on indirect taxation, and the poor, who preferred to have taxes assessed on property.[40] The *populares*, however, were not always synonymous with the poor, for the term could describe an opposition party of any financial position.[41]

The king and his officials became involved in the affairs of the towns at an early date. Urban political and social strife presented them with opportunities to collect money. Royal officers frequently were prone to side with the *populares*, who posed a lesser threat to the king's rights and powers than did the nobles and the bourgeois patricians who usually dominated town governments. Moreover, royal investigation of abuses by the wealthy bourgeois could yield profitable taxes and fines, and yet be viewed as a reform in the best tradition of St. Louis. The king's *réformateurs* and tax commissioners therefore posed a threat to the *haute bourgeoisie* and were in a strong bargaining position when negotiating a subsidy. Because the crown usually needed money quickly, however, the commissioners often struck a bargain with the patricians. The town would pay a lump sum in lieu of a tax, while the royal officers would confirm the town's privileges, suspend investigation of local abuses, and help the municipal government enforce collection of whatever *taille* was employed to raise the promised sum. Such arrangements must have perpetuated many local injustices. The interests of the *populares* were being sacrificed to the financial needs of the crown.[42] The urban *populares* probably felt the main weight of royal taxation prior to 1350, and in the second half of the century, violent insurrections became more numerous. When these occurred, the crown usually joined with municipal governments in suppressing the disorders.

[40] P. Wolff, "Les luttes sociales dans les villes du Midi française, XIIIe-XVe siècles," *AESC*, II (1947), 443-454.

[41] J. Rogozinski, "Social Conflict in the Urban Communities of Lower Languedoc during the Fourteenth Century," unpublished paper presented at the Midwest Medieval History Conference, Omaha, 1967.

[42] Besides the works cited in the last two notes, Timbal, *Guerre*, pp. 208-218; and Lewis, *Later Medieval France*, pp. 255-263, discuss aspects of municipal politics, taxation, and royal officers. The tactics of the latter are discussed by Henneman, "Enquêteurs," pp. 315, 325-342. In terms of local politics, an interesting bargain was that made in early 1346 between royal representatives and the *capitouls* of Toulouse. The latter were excused from the obligation of military service for their noble fiefs, but all other fief holders were to be prepared to serve: *INV AM Toulouse*, p. 39 (AA 3, no. 250). Also interesting is J. Richard, "Finances princières et banquiers au XIVe siècle: L'affaire des Bourgeoise et la Réformation de 1343 en Bourgogne," *Annales de Bourgogne*, XXVII (1955), 25-27, where the *échevins* of Dijon saw ducal *réformateurs* as a threat to their privileges and were prepared to appeal to the king against them.

Throughout French society, therefore, the fourteenth century was a troubled time. It was against a background of increasing economic difficulty and social unrest that the crown sought to develop its taxing powers.

4. Royal Fiscal Power in Theory and Practice

The king might call himself "emperor in his own kingdom," and his advisers might expound impressive theories of sovereignty based on Roman law, but actual royal power was determined mainly by the legacies of the earlier Middle Ages. The Franks could not conceive of the state as an abstraction, with public officers collecting taxes for the common welfare. They considered the old imperial fisc to be the private property of the king. The confusion of public power and private rights became even more pronounced after the Carolingian monarchy disintegrated and authority became fragmented among many feudal lords. Long after the crown began to regain power in the twelfth century, many attributes of government were seigneurial rights treated as private property. The feudal/seigneurial structure still determined the assumptions of most Frenchmen in the early fourteenth century and it therefore formed the framework within which the monarchy had to act.

Royal revenues were based on powers derived from several different sources. The king was an important landlord with seigneurial powers over manors and towns, and revenues which were subject to the same economic factors affecting other landlords. He was a feudal lord with many vassals over whom he had jurisdictional rights and from whom he collected feudal incidents and aids. Even more important, he was supreme suzerain, the ultimate overlord of all the seigneurs in the kingdom. This suzerainty, effectively established only in the thirteenth century, enabled the king to exploit profitably the concept of *abrégement du fief*, collecting important fines from clergy and non-nobles who acquired fiefs. It also enabled royal justice to achieve far greater scope than that of the great feudatories. Above all, perhaps, the king's suzerainty facilitated a gradual revival of the concept of sovereignty. An increasing number of persons were being trained in Roman and canon law. They were prepared to assert what earlier feudal society had not been able to grasp—that the ruler was not a *dominus*, but a *curator* or guardian, to whom were entrusted an office, a domain or fisc, and certain public responsibilities, all of which must be preserved and handed on intact to his successor.[43] Only after this notion gained wide acceptance could the term "state" be employed without anachronism.[44]

The royal domain consisted of many scattered pieces of territory and numerous rights which produced revenue. Some domainal revenues were collected by special agencies and were usually listed separately in the king's financial records. These included chancery fees, certain judicial fines, taxes on commerce ("ports and passages"), fines for acquisition of fiefs, revenue from the royal waters and forests, and mint profits. The other, more miscellaneous proceeds of the domain were collected under the supervision of the bailiffs and seneschals and used for local expenses, with any surplus being sent to Paris.

It has been customary to call these the "ordinary" revenues of the crown, as opposed to the "extraordinary" revenues such as the clerical tenth and war subsidies.[45] The "ordinary-extraordinary" distinction is not very satisfactory. The clerical tenth was collected so regularly in the fourteenth century as to lose much of its extraordinary character. Certain seigneurial and jurisdictional rights, technically belonging to the domain, produced greatly fluctuating income because they sometimes were stretched to extortionate proportions. Among these were mint profits, judicial fines, and taxes levied on foreign businessmen like Jews and Italians. Most ambiguous, perhaps, were the four feudal aids. They

[43] P. Riesenberg, *Inalienability of Sovereignty in Medieval Political Thought*, New York, 1956, p. 3; cf. E. Kantorowicz, *The King's Two Bodies: A Study In Medieval Political Theology*, Princeton, 1957, pp. 166f.

[44] On the emergence of the state see Guenée, "Etat et nation," pp. 25-27. A much broader, if not entirely convincing, definition of the term "state," with applicability to the whole feudal period, has been suggested by S. Ehler, "On Applying the Modern Term 'State' to the Middle Ages," in *Medieval Studies Presented to Aubrey Gwynn*, Dublin, 1961, pp. 497f. See also W. Ullman, *The Medieval Idea of Law as Represented by Lucas de Penna*, London, 1946, p. 204; O. Gierke, *Political Theories of the Middle Age* (ed. and trans. F. Maitland), Beacon edn., Boston, 1958, pp. 87f; and Post, *Studies*, Chapters v, vi, and viii.

[45] Most historians have employed this distinction, but they differ on matters of detail. J. Declareuil, *Histoire générale du droit français des origines à 1789*, Paris, 1925, pp. 702-703, divided "domainal" revenues into three sub-categories: seigneurial, feudal (including feudal aids and agricultural profits), and special revenues from natural resources. A. Esmein, *Cours élémentaire d'histoire du droit français*, Paris, 1903, pp. 545-546, subdivided domainal income into more types, but excluded feudal aids from the resources of the domain. Callery, *Hist. du pouvoir*, pp. 10-16, wrote of ordinary domainal, extraordinary domainal (including feudal aids), and seigneurial "taxes" (which include some items which no other scholar has considered a tax). Still another variation is that of Hirschauer, *Les états d'Artois*, I, 114, who said that "the aid granted to the king was called 'ordinary,' that of the count, 'extraordinary.'" Most satisfactory, perhaps, is the classification used by Vuitry, *Régime financier*, passim. He called feudal aids, clerical tenths, and war subsidies "extraordinary" revenues and treated all others as part of the domain.

were ordinary in that they were regulated by custom and restricted to largely forseeable situations. The situations themselves, however, were extraordinary and non-recurring. Historians have differed as to how these aids should be classified, and because of their peculiar feudal character it has been said that they were insignificant in the development of true taxation.[46] Yet one of the most important taxes of the fourteenth century, the ransom of John II in the 1360s, was, in principle, a feudal aid, and even the earlier feudal aids played a role in the theory and practice of taxation when the king tried to extend them beyond his direct vassals.[47]

In the analysis of treasury receipts in Appendix 1, those tabulated as "ordinary" are those which were collected on a regular, annual basis. I have applied the label "extraordinary" quite broadly, including not only aids, subsidies, and the tenth, but also other revenues which fluctuated widely because they were exploited as fiscal expedients.

Except for the clerical tenth and the war subsidy, all the revenues described so far were derived from the king's seigneurial power or his feudal suzerainty. Even a war subsidy could be based on these if the king successfully asserted the moral obligation of a vassal to render extraordinary pecuniary aid when his lord faced an emergency. This principle, however, was not suitable for dealing with the sort of prolonged warfare which became common after the mid-1290s. A more promising basis for taxation was the commutation of military service owed by vassals and towns. Money raised in this way could be used to pay the experienced mercenaries which increasingly formed the nucleus of royal armies.

Commutation of military service could be generalized by appealing to the old Germanic custom which required military service from all free men. This obligation was invoked by the *arrière-ban*, a general summons addressed to all who were capable of bearing arms.[48] Because of the long dependence on heavy cavalry, military service had for several centuries been the monopoly of the seigneurial class, which alone could

---

[46] Minimizing the significance of feudal aids were Callery, *Hist. du pouvoir*, p. 21; and H. Prentout, *Les états provinciaux de Normandie*, Caen, 1925, I, p. 68. Declareuil, *Droit français*, pp. 702-703, listed feudal aids with purely domainal resources (last note).

[47] On the ransom and its importance, see Esmein, *Cours*, p. 568; Delachenal, *Histoire de Charles V*, II, 264-265.

[48] On the *arrière-ban* and commutation of military service, see P. Guilhiermoz, *Essai sur l'origine de la noblesse en France au moyen âge*, Paris, 1902, pp. 284, 293, 296-297, 466f.; Lot and Fawtier, *Institutions*, II, 221, 531-532; B. Lyon, *From Fief to Indenture: The Transition from Feudal to Non-Feudal Contract in Western Europe*, Cambridge (Mass.), 1957, p. 251.

afford the equipment of a knight. Nevertheless, the reviving importance of infantry and the greater use of mercenaries made it appropriate in the thirteenth century to reintroduce the general obligation, this time purely as a fiscal device. The *arrière-ban*, followed by fines in lieu of personal service, became an important basis for royal taxation in the early fourteenth century. In issuing the summons, the king usually excluded those who were in critical occupations or were unable to bear arms by reason of age or sex, but he still insisted that they had an obligation and required them to send substitutes. Besides these, many of those who were included in the summons doubtless did not wish to serve in person. All these people were expected to pay money in lieu of service, and throughout the period up to 1356, a military summons must be regarded as evidence of a tax demand unless the particular circumstances show that the king really did desire armed men.[49]

Employment of the *arrière-ban* for fiscal purposes created problems. Nobles often wished to serve in person for reasons of status, and they expected their subjects to contribute heavily to their expenses. They wished to preserve their revenues by keeping these subjects exempt from royal military summonses, while the king's officers sometimes tried to extend the *arrière-ban* to unfree subjects of nobles.[50] The towns were most concerned with their own defense, and many poured large sums into the rebuilding of long-neglected ramparts. They too were often irritated by royal calls to arms, especially if the projected campaign did not involve the defense of their immediate locality.[51]

The government developed various ways of using the *arrière-ban*, depending on the circumstances. For a single campaign, there would usually be a military summons in the spring or early summer, followed by the dispatch of commissioners to collect fines or negotiate some other form of subsidy locally. In time of more continuous war, taxes might be

---

[49] For different uses of the military summons in 1340, see Henneman, "Financing," pp. 289-290.

[50] On the nobles' concern about taxation of their subjects, see Vuitry, *Régime financier*, II, 52-53; E. Delcambre, *Les états du Velay des origines à 1642*, Saint-Etienne, 1938, pp. 6-49. At times, the king rebuked his officers for attempting to levy taxes on these men: BN NAF 3653, no. 102; AD Hérault A 4, fol. 230.

[51] Disputes with towns about taxation will be encountered throughout this book and summarized in Chapter IX. Royal officers were accused of encroaching on the privileges of *bastides* (AN JJ 74, no. 49; BN Doat 157, fols. 96v-100r). Even towns which lacked special privileges usually bore the major burden for their own defense (Timbal, *Guerre*, p. 172). For a variety of reasons, political, military, and economic, the crown often extended special favors to communities located at or near a critical frontier: Le Maire, *St. Quentin*, II, no. 554; AD Hérault A 1, fols. 89r-90r; *INV AM Limoux* AA 28.

sought first, with the actual military musters being saved to employ selectively against recalcitrant communities. When war was being waged on several fronts, still another procedure might prevail, with regional commanders sometimes issuing the *arrière-ban* independently of the crown. At times, multiple and overlapping summonses created confusion and resentment.[52]

The close connection between taxation and military needs was emphasized by the occasional practice of expressing a tax grant in military units—"a certain number of sergeants" or "four hundred horsemen for four months." Sometimes a town actually might recruit, equip, and pay its own contingent of men, rather than paying the money as a tax to royal officers, but this practice seems to have been exceptional.[53] After 1345, critics of the government wanted guarantees that tax revenues would be used only for defense and not be squandered or embezzled. As a concession to this sentiment, and perhaps also in hopes of by-passing the time-consuming procedures of the *arrière-ban*, the crown encouraged the grant of subsidies expressed as so many men-at-arms. They became more frequent in the next decade.

Once taxes were computed in military units, the salary scales for soldiers became an important issue. Bourgeois taxpayers wished to keep these low, while the nobles, from whose ranks most men-at-arms were recruited, wanted higher salaries. Military wages fluctuated, but under Philip VI, the standard scale established a daily wage of 20 *sols tournois* for a knight banneret, 10 *s.t.* for a knight bachelor, 6 *s.t.* for a mounted squire, and one *s.t.* for a sergeant. According to a higher rate, known as *grands gages*, these four kinds of soldier were paid 30, 15, 7½, and 2 *s.t.* respectively.[54] The king frequently had to pay *grands gages*, and to prevent brigandage it was necessary to pay mercenaries for their travel between their homes and the battle zone. Surviving military payrolls show clearly the high cost of maintaining a modest army. The defense of his kingdom, even in times of truce, placed a serious burden on the king's resources.[55]

[52] An example of this problem, involving upper Auvergne in 1346, will be discussed in Chapter vi. Similar difficulties had already arisen in lower Languedoc in 1339 and 1340 (Chapter iv). Cf. Henneman, "Financing," pp. 277-281.

[53] Ord., i, 602-603; Strayer and Taylor, *Studies*, pp. 71, 118-122.

[54] On military pay scales, see, among other places, J. Viard, "La France sous Philippe VI de Valois. Etat géographique et militaire," *RQH*, lix (1896), 377-378; AN P 2291, p. 189; M. Jusselin, "Comment la France se préparait à la guerre de cent ans," *BEC*, lxxiii (1912), 222-223.

[55] A typical payroll is BN *ms. fr.* 7877, fols. 1-22. The mercenaries employed for a minor siege in 1339 cost 30,000 *l.t.*, about 10% of what a war subsidy in the same

The *arrière-ban* was hallowed by ancient usage and could be employed without reference to the kind of sovereignty implied by Romano-canonical law. Taxes raised by this technique could be considerable, but it was a cumbersome procedure to follow when large amounts of money were needed quickly. A general military summons was credible only in a genuine situation of war. Long before he collected the tax, the king had to pay his troops. Some military forces had to be maintained during truces or in times of peace. Unable to employ the *arrière-ban* at such times, the government had to rely on the feudal and seigneurial revenues of the domain, and these were proving inadequate. Continually short of money, the king had to consider two possible remedies: one was the use of fiscal expedients which might provide a temporary windfall; the other was to find a different basis for taxation, some principle that would enable the government to levy taxes when needed.

To the legal experts of the royal entourage, the desired principle was conveniently at hand. They invoked the Romano-canonical theory of royal sovereignty. To them, sovereignty meant, above all, the right of the monarch to take whatever actions were dictated by the common profit and to require his subjects to make the sacrifices necessary to meet the sorts of emergency which were recurrent in the fourteenth century. By the first years of the century, a mass of legal literature was available, including the work of the post-glossators, who had done much to interpret the Roman civil law in a way adaptable to feudal Europe.

The fundamental maxims of Romano-canonical theory may be summarized as follows: The king has the obligation to preserve the *status regni* and act for the common profit, and the right to declare when there exists an emergency which threatens the common welfare and requires defense of the realm. In such a situation of "evident necessity," private rights must yield to the superior right of the public welfare and the king may levy general taxes.[56] This suspension of rights, however, involves

---

period might yield in one year. These men were paid *grands gages*, and in some cases they spent more time traveling than actually fighting.

[56] The considerable literature on this subject is headed by Post, *Studies*, pp. 310-332 (on *status regni, utilitas publica*, and common profit); also 15-19, and 436f. See also Ullmann, *Lucas de Penna*, pp. 166-170; Kantorowicz, *The King's Two Bodies*, pp. 235f. and 284f.; Gierke, *Political Theories*, pp. 79-81; M. Wilks, *The Problem of Sovereignty in the Later Middle Ages*, Cambridge, 1963, pp. 209, 212, 217, 218; C. Bayley, "Pivotal Concepts in the Political Philosophy of William of Ockham," *Journal of the History of Ideas*, x (1949), 200-202; G. de Lagarde, "La philosophie sociale d'Henri de Gand et Godefroid de Fontaines," *Archives d'histoire doctrinale et littéraire du Moyen Age*, xviii (1943-1945), 88-127; F. M. Powicke, "Reflections on the Mediaeval State," *TRHS*, xix (1936), 7; J. R. Strayer, "Defense of the

another legal principle, that "what touches all must be approved by all." That is, those whose rights were affected had to be given a hearing and express their consent, at least in some procedural way.[57] This doctrine did not necessarily impose limitations on royal power. Consent could be given by persons having full power to represent those whose rights were affected. Gaines Post has argued that an assembly of such representatives resembled a court of law. If the proctors failed to attend, they were in default and could be regarded as having given procedural consent to the decisions reached at the assembly. If they did attend, their full powers ought to imply sufficient instructions to preclude "reference back" to local constituents and make it difficult, if not impossible, to withhold consent.[58] Taken as a whole, these legal maxims offered a king sweeping powers to levy necessary taxes.

It was one thing to assert such principles, but to put them into practice was quite another. Rarely does a society absorb a body of theory completely intact without changes in emphasis, and it was not yet clear how these legal maxims fitted into the outlook of most Frenchmen. Did "defense of the realm" and *pro patria mori* imply a sense of *status regni*, incipient nationalism? Or did people associate *patria* merely with the *pays* or local region?[59] If "necessity knows no law," might not the right to consent itself be overridden in a true case of necessity?[60] Were people convinced that the maxim *quod omnes tangit ab omnibus approbetur*

Realm and Royal Power in France," *Studi in onore di Gino Luzzatto*, Milan, 1950, I, 289-296. Philippe de Beaumanoir, *Coutumes de Beauvaisis* (ed. A. Salmon), Paris, 1899, II, arts. 1510, 1512, 1515, invoked necessity and the common profit as a justification for extraordinary measures on the part of the king, but Esmein, *Cours*, p. 341, doubted that Beaumanoir was drawing upon Roman legal concepts in this case.

[57] Y. Congar, "Quod omnes tangit ab omnibus tractari et approbari debet," *RHD, 4e série*, XXXVI (1958), 210-259; Post, *Studies*, pp. 113, note 96; 123, note 118; 170-172, 209, 231-232; Ullmann, *Lucas de Penna*, p. 183; Lagarde, "Philosophie sociale," pp. 119-120; Wilks, *Sovereignty*, pp. 204-205; Gierke, *Political Theories*, pp. 64, 78; A. Marongiu, "Q. o. t., Principe de la démocratie et du consentement au XIVe siècle," *SPIC*, XXIV (1961), 101-115.

[58] See Post, *Studies*, pp. 91-162.

[59] On *pro patria mori*, see Kantorowicz, *The King's Two Bodies*, pp. 236-257. According to Post, *Studies*, p. 447, "the French legists held that the common or public utility of the realm was a higher end than that of any part thereof, and the common *patria* of the kingdom therefore superior to any local *patria* of city or province." Strayer, "Laicization," passim, implies that the ordinary man increasingly tended to think along similar lines. Nevertheless, both writers would be quick to admit the continuing importance of local particularism which, as we shall see, had a great effect on the development of royal fiscal institutions.

[60] The legists were not completely unanimous on this point. Some claimed that in an emergency the king could act without obtaining consent. See Post, *Studies*, p. 478.

gave them the right to consent when their rights were affected by royal taxation? What did such consent entail, and how might it be given? Who had the right to speak for a community? Did proctors called to an assembly consider it comparable to a civil court proceeding? How much advance information did constituents require in order to send proctors who would not refer back? Although not always unanimous, the legal theorists had answers to most of the questions, but there is no certainty that the taxpaying population understood things in the same way.[61]

One ancient philosophical maxim, for instance, was given a practical application which had the effect of limiting the freedom of action which the doctrine of "necessity" conferred upon the king. This principle, *cessante causa cessat effectus*, is illustrated in the writings of Pierre Dubois in the early fourteenth century. Dubois attributed wide powers to the monarch "in case of necessity for the defense of the realm—which is beyond the law." Then he observed that "exaction beyond necessity would be a mortal sin unless the needless exaction be restored."[62] Thomas Aquinas, whose political principles are said to have enjoyed "sensational popularity" in the fourteenth century,[63] was willing to condone extraordinary taxes not merely for the common profit but even for the financing of a prince's ordinary needs if his domainal revenues were insufficient. Yet he was equally explicit in condemning unjust extortion, the penalty for which was eternal damnation. When the need for an extraordinary tax ceased to apply, the tax itself must cease.[64]

[61] See R. S. Hoyt, "Recent Publications in the United States and Canada on the History of Representative Institutions before the French Revolution," *Speculum*, XXIX (1954), 370, and Post's not altogether satisfactory reply (*Studies*, p. 4, note 2). Although he believes that constituents did not need to know how much tax the king would request at an assembly (*ibid.*, p. 147), Post does indicate that *plena potestas* could be limited by the constituents' knowledge of the issue to be discussed (*ibid.*, p. 107). A fully empowered proctor could be limited by qualifying instructions, according to E. Brown, "Philip the Fair, '*Plena Potestas*,' and the *Aide pur fille marier* of 1308," *Historical Papers Read at Bryn Mawr College, April 1968, SPIC*, XXXIX (1970), 1-27.

[62] P. Dubois, *The Recovery of the Holy Land* (ed. and trans. W. Brandt), New York, 1956, pp. 184-185. The background, practical employment, and principal bibliography for *cessante causa cessat effectus* are found in an important forthcoming article by E. Brown, "*Cessante causa* and the Taxes of the Last Capetians: The Political Applications of a Philosophical Maxim."

[63] Wilks, *Sovereignty*, p. 119.

[64] E. Brown, "Politics, Taxation and Discontent: Philip the Fair's Legacy to his Sons," unpublished paper first delivered before the annual conference of the Society for French Historical Studies, Ann Arbor, 1966; E. Brown, "Taxation and Morality in the Thirteenth and Fourteenth Centuries," unpublished paper delivered before the American Historical Association, Washington, 1969.

This principle was not, in itself, a limitation on royal power in time of necessity, for it merely stated that emergency measures should not continue after the emergency ended. But it did impose serious responsibilities on the ruler, who had to be able to justify his decision that the common profit called for extraordinary measures. In part this was a political matter, requiring that taxpayers be persuaded that their self-interest was at stake, but it was also a moral question for the king who had to face his confessor. Philip IV has long been a symbol of cynical ruthlessness, but he never forgot that he was the grandson of St. Louis. The moral prestige inherited from Louis IX would also be a valuable asset to the Valois monarchs whose title to the throne was uncertain.[65] Kings who exploited the moral legacy of their sainted ancestor were forced to pay the price—the possibility that their conduct would be judged by the standards established by Louis IX in his lifetime.

Whether for reasons of conscience or propaganda, kings could not ignore moral considerations, but these could conflict with reasons of state. Philippe de Beaumanoir suggested that the king could levy taxes in time of war or even when war merely threatened, subject to certain conditions.[66] Faced with a threat of war, he was obliged to raise an army and could legitimately levy a tax. If he then averted war by negotiation, he might be serving the common profit, but according to *cessante causa*, he had to halt tax collections. If collection had been slow, however, this cancellation might leave him without the funds to pay the army he had assembled. The king often faced this very dilemma. To resolve it he might, for financial reasons, avoid a negotiated peace or be forced to adopt some ruthless fiscal expedient in order to pay his troops. Neither of these alternatives was really consistent with the common profit. Thus the theories of sovereignty and royal responsibility were fraught with contradictions which limited their usefulness. These were not merely questions for scholastic disputation. They involved political decisions which the king and his council could not avoid.

A major purpose of this study is to relate the legal theories to actual practice, and in doing so we must look for guidance to the institutional historians. Their most valuable contributions have concerned representative institutions and the mechanism of consent. Consent to taxation had two dimensions. According to the maxim *quod omnes tangit*, those whose rights were affected had to consent to any extraordinary measures for the common profit which overrode these rights. On a more practical

---

[65] See above, notes 35, 64.
[66] Beaumanoir, *Coutumes de Beauvaisis*, art. 1510.

level, no tax could be collected without considerable cooperation from those who were taxed, so their acquiescence was needed.[67] This acquiescence amounted to consent, but it had nothing to do with *quod omnes tangit*. A representative assembly, whether central, regional, or local in nature, might give consent for either or both of these reasons. On the other hand, consent did not have to be given in an assembly, and assemblies could be used for purposes other than consent. If we are to understand the constitutional implications of taxation in this period, we must relate taxation to the use of assemblies and relate both to the question of consent. To what extent did taxes receive formal consent, rather than merely being imposed? To what extent, and at what level, were assemblies employed as consenting bodies? Was the giving of consent their primary function or were they normally convened for other reasons? In a recent study of early French assemblies, Gavin Langmuir made a contribution of great importance when he stressed the distinction between consent and counsel. The latter, which occurred far more frequently, was advice in the feudal sense and did not involve the suspension of private rights for the common welfare.[68] Langmuir's distinction raises the question of which was meant by Beaumanoir, who never used the word "consent," but declared that the king could make new *établissements* only *par grant conseil*.[69] If he thought that the king merely had to take counsel in the traditional feudal manner, Beaumanoir could not have taken *quod omnes tangit* very seriously.

Langmuir has also shown that the Latin terminology for different types of assembly in the thirteenth century was used with greater precision than scholars formerly believed. Meetings which dealt with important matters of policy and political decisions were called *concilia* and were distinct from those dealing with judicial matters (*curiae*). The distinction was less clear after vernacular usage became more common, but in any case the type of meeting called a *concilium* fell into disuse in the last two-thirds of the thirteenth century. When the crown resumed major consultations on political questions after 1300, both the government and the representatives were lacking in experience and had to experiment a

[67] Strayer, "Laicization," p. 80; Strayer and Taylor, *Studies*, pp. 21-22; Bisson, *Assemblies*, p. 273.

[68] G. Langmuir, "Counsel and Capetian Assemblies," *SPIC*, xviii (1958), 28: "A superior might seek counsel to ensure the wisdom of any kind of decision, but he had to seek consent only when the execution of a decision would infringe the rights of others. . . . Any attempt to understand royal consultations should, therefore, differentiate between the very many occasions on which the king sought counsel and the remarkably rare occasions on which he also sought consent."

[69] Beaumanoir, *Coutumes de Beauvaisis*, art. 1515.

good deal.[70] The Estates of the fourteenth century would continue to be plagued by inexperience arising from lack of continuity.

In the end, it was regional assemblies which acquired greater continuity, and some of these had an important history in the thirteenth century. Those of Languedoc are particularly interesting because Roman law was deeply rooted in the customs of southern France. Studying thirteenth century assemblies there, Thomas Bisson found frequent use of terminology like "necessity" and "urgent cause" but he also found that legal theories had relatively little influence on practice. Despite many situations in which *quod omnes tangit* seemed relevant, those called to the southern assemblies made little use of it and seemed more conscious of a duty to give counsel than a right to give consent.[71]

In short, it appears that institutions were poorly developed by the late thirteenth century and had, as yet, made little contact with theory. It was at this point that the monarchy under Philip IV sought to remedy a difficult financial situation by putting into practice the legal theories of royal sovereignty.

5. *Politics and Taxation under the Last Capetians*

Philip the Fair did not invent new taxes, but he generalized older ones, collected them more frequently, and stretched "ordinary" revenues to extraordinary lengths, while his legal advisers claimed sovereign powers for the monarch.[72] It is generally agreed that his reign (1285-1314) was an important one for French royal finances. The military and diplomatic pattern of the fourteenth century was established in these years as a result of the continued expansion of the royal domain.

This expansion had involved a penetration and gradual absorption of the great fiefs. Few important fiefs remained at the end of the thirteenth century, but two of them stoutly resisted royal encroachment. The duke of Guyenne was king in England and he found it irritating to be the vassal of another king for his continental holdings, especially since the French relentlessly pressed their jurisdictional rights and forced him to maintain a permanent legal staff in Paris.[73] Equally threatened by en-

---

[70] G. Langmuir, "Concilia and Capetian Assemblies, 1179-1230," *SPIC*, xxiv (1961), 58-63; G. Langmuir, "Politics and Parliaments in the Early Thirteenth Century," *SPIC*, xxix (1966), 53-58.

[71] Bisson, *Assemblies*, pp. 296-297. For a similar sentiment in northern France, see Hirschauer, *Les états d'Artois*, i, pp. 52-53.

[72] Strayer and Taylor, *Studies*, p. 7.

[73] G. Cuttino, *English Diplomatic Administration 1259-1339*, London, 1940. Other important works relating to the problem of Guyenne and Anglo-French relations in

croaching royal jurisdiction, was the count of Flanders, whose wealthy fief on the northern frontier was tied to England economically because of the wool trade. In 1294, France and England went to war. The English sought to raise money by means of an embargo on wool, and this policy created economic depression in Flanders. The count, with grievances of his own against his suzerain, was now impelled to join the English.[74] In Britain, meanwhile, the king of England was trying to expand his own power. He subdued the Welsh with considerable difficulty, but Scotland still resisted and in the process became a natural ally of France.

The war, which began in 1294, was easily won by the French, who overran Guyenne and Flanders. Philip IV, however, could not hold these conquests. A struggle with the papacy diverted him, and in Flanders, a rebellion of cloth workers expelled the French and their sympathizers. A punitive expedition was crushed by the Flemings at Courtrai in 1302, and Philip found it politic to make peace with England and restore most of Guyenne. By 1305, he had defeated the papacy and the Flemings, but the latter retained their independence and a strong will to resist French encroachment.[75] The monarchy, meanwhile, found its moral and material resources seriously depleted.

With certain variations, this military and diplomatic pattern would be repeated in the years after 1322. The English king resented giving homage for Guyenne, and French pressure on that duchy continued. England still supported anti-French elements in Flanders and the Low Countries, while France continued to aid Scotland. With such support, both Flanders and Scotland preserved their independence and Anglo-French relations remained hostile.

---

this period are L. de Bréquigny, "Mémoire sur les différends entre la France et L'Angleterre sous le règne de Charles le Bel," in C. Leber, *Collection des meilleures dissertations, notices et traités particuliers rélatifs à l'histoire de France*, Paris, 1838, xviii; P. Chaplais, "Règlements de conflits internationaux franco-anglais au XIVe siècle, 1293-1327," *MA*, lvii (1951), 269-313; P. Chaplais, "English Arguments Concerning the Feudal Status of Aquitaine in the Fourteenth Century," *BIHR*, xxi (1948), 203-213; G. Cuttino, "The Process of Agen," *Speculum*, xix (1944), 161-178; Y. Renouard, "Les Papes et le conflit franco-anglais en Aquitaine de 1259 à 1337," *Mélanges d'archéologie et d'histoire*, li (1934), 258-292; J. Le Patourel, "Edward III and the Kingdom of France," *History*, xliii (1958), 173-189; E. Perroy, "Franco-English Relations 1350-1400," *History*, xxi (1936-1937), 148-154. On the diplomatic activities of the 1330s, see E. Déprez, *Les préliminaires de la guerre de Cent Ans: La papauté, la France, et l'Angleterre (1328-1342)*, Paris, 1902; H. Jenkins, *Papal Efforts for Peace under Benedict XII*, Philadelphia, 1933.

[74] F. Funck-Brentano, *Philippe le Bel en Flandre*, Paris, 1897, pp. 133, 157-160.
[75] *Ibid.*, pp. 233-504.

War or threat of war became increasingly common, and the French crown had to find the money to support growing military commitments. Even before 1294, Philip IV had levied a feudal aid and a general sales tax of a *denier* per pound, while extorting money from Jews, Italians, and acquirers of noble fiefs. He also collected clerical tenths authorized by the pope.[76] When the war began, he soon turned to forced loans and alteration of the coinage.[77] He also had his first altercation with Boniface VIII over taxation of the clergy without papal consent. By 1297, the pope had backed down and agreed that taxation for "defense of the realm" did not require his consent.[78] Ironically, Philip soon found it easier to obtain papal consent than to negotiate with his own clergy.

More important for our purposes here, was Philip's approach to the taxation of laymen. From 1295 to 1300, he levied general taxes almost annually without going through the formality of calling out the army. The subsidies were not large, being small assessments of 1 percent or 2 percent on property. They also met some opposition and Philip had to sacrifice uniformity and permit individual regions to substitute other forms of payment. Nevertheless, the levy of these taxes marked a brief triumph for the Romano-canonical theory that a king could declare an emergency and collect a tax for the defense of the realm.[79] Philip did not attempt to invoke the common profit in time of peace, but he found a more efficient basis for war subsidies than any system founded on military service.

In the second half of his reign, however, Philip IV ran into difficulties which undid some of his earlier achievements and left the monarchy in a less advantageous position to develop a system of taxation. His relations with the papacy entered a new crisis in 1301, and the following spring the Flemings revolted and defeated the French army. For the rest of 1302, the king's position was difficult and he desperately needed money and moral support. Theories of sovereignty had to be relegated to the background as Philip tried to enlist the backing of his clergy and a nobility badly shaken after Courtrai. In 1303, royal domestic policy was characterized by conciliation, charters of reform, and assemblies to promote the royal cause.

In this situation, the king abandoned the promising basis for taxation established up to 1300. It was less controversial to invoke the obligation of military service, and beginning in 1302, Philip's taxes for war were

---

[76] Strayer and Taylor, *Studies*, pp. 7-19, 43, 95.

[77] *Ibid.*, pp. 19-20; R. Cazelles, "Quelques réflexions à propos des mutations de la monnaie royale française (1295-1360)," *MA*, LXXII (1966), 86.

[78] Strayer and Taylor, *Studies*, pp. 24, 29-42.

[79] *Ibid.*, pp. 45-56.

preceded by the *arrière-ban*. This system was slow, but it still could yield impressive results, and in 1304, the crown collected a subsidy of perhaps 735,000 *l.t.*, a figure not to be equaled in the next half-century.[80]

Circumstances would never permit Philip IV to resume his earlier practice of levying taxes directly for the defense of the realm. In 1305, peace was made, and for eight years Philip had no basis for seeking a subsidy. The monarchy proved unable to live on domainal revenues in peacetime, even when these were supplemented by frequent clerical tenths granted by Clement V. Philip turned to fiscal expedients such as heavy extortions from the Jews, Lombards, and Templars, as well as feudal aids for the marriage of his daughter and the knighting of his son.[81] The last of these was being collected in 1313 when a new Flemish crisis broke out. The king called out the army and began collecting a war subsidy, but the Flemings agreed to negotiate and no campaign occurred. Hoping perhaps to facilitate collection of the feudal aid, Philip IV cancelled the war subsidy. Not only that, but he ordered his officers to return what had been collected. This remarkable action gave explicit royal endorsement to the principle of *cessante causa* and set an ominous precedent.[82]

A year later, in 1314, another Flemish war scare ended in negotiation, but this time Philip IV continued to levy a war subsidy. Wrathful at the king's attempt to ignore his own precedent, the nobility rose in revolt after forming leagues against the crown. Philip IV died of a stroke in November and his son Louis X quickly ordered return of the subsidy and issued charters of privileges to the principal malcontents. Gradually the realm was pacified, but the royal ability to levy taxes had suffered seriously. Philip IV's legacy of discontent would influence the course of royal taxation in succeeding decades.[83]

Historians of Philip IV's reign have generally remarked upon the great influence of his more prominent advisers, especially those who were lawyers.[84] It is only with the fourteenth century that documentation permits us to know enough about such men to consider their impact on policy.

---

[80] *Ibid.*, pp. 59-75.

[81] C. V. Langlois, in *Histoire de France* (E. Lavisse, ed.), Paris, 1900-1911, III pt. 2, pp. 180-230; Strayer and Taylor, *Studies*, pp. 17-20, 42-43, 77-78; Henneman, "Italians," pp. 26-27; Brown, "Aide of 1308"; Lot and Fawtier, *Institutions*, II, 227-261.

[82] Brown, "Politics and Taxation."

[83] *Ibid.*; Brown, "Taxation and Morality."

[84] F. Pegues, *The Lawyers of the Last Capetians*, Princeton, 1962, esp. introductory section.

Their influence would be important throughout our period. A comprehensive study of royal officials and their interests has not been made, but the work of Raymond Cazelles, supplemented by that of other scholars, suggests a rough pattern of political change after 1314.[85] Each short reign brought a new king and new counselors to power and a limited purge of those who had served the preceding monarch. Cazelles has detected two main political groupings among the men who served Philip of Valois. One faction, associated with the Chamber of Accounts, tended to draw its inspiration from the aggressive and imaginative government of Philip IV, in which fiscal experts necessarily played a great role. The second group was associated with the *Parlement*, and tended to place greater emphasis on justice and reform in the tradition of St. Louis. Both groups were usually represented in the royal council, along with other prominent figures not clearly aligned with either faction. At times, however, one faction or the other would predominate, with noticeable effects on royal policy.

The careers of a few important men offer some indications of the changes. Mile de Noyers headed the Chamber of Accounts in the 1330s and had a strong voice in the government. Previously he had served Philip IV and Philip V but had less influence under Louis X and Charles IV.[86] Etienne de Mornay, however, apparently belonged to the opposing party. A follower of Charles of Valois, he became chancellor for Louis X, fell from power under Philip V, but regained importance under Charles IV.[87] It appears that the Valois princes and Robert of Artois were on good terms with Louis X and Charles IV, but not with Philip V. The latter, however, was favorable to many of the old fiscal advisers of Philip the Fair and established marriage connections with Burgundy and Flanders.[88]

The "Chamber of Accounts party" probably took shape among Philip IV's financial experts. These men strove to establish what Pegues has

---

[85] Cazelles, *Soc. politique*; Cazelles, "Mouvements"; Lehugeur, *Mécanisme*.

[86] Cazelles, *Soc. politique*, pp. 113-129; Lehugeur, *Mécanisme*, pp. 30-33, 51, 215; H. Jassemin, "Les papiers de Mile de Noyers," *BPH*, 1918, p. 176.

[87] F. Guessard, "Etienne de Mornay, chancelier de France sous Louis Hutin," *BEC*, v (1843-1844), 374-382.

[88] J. Viard, "Philippe de Valois avant son avènement au trône," *BEC*, xci (1930), 310-311; J. Richard, *Une petite-nièce de Saint-Louis, Mahaut, comtesse d'Artois et de Bourgogne (1302-1329)*, Paris, 1887, p. 16; J. Petit, *Charles de Valois (1270-1325)*, Paris, 1899, pp. 147-154, 169, 173, 197f., P.J. 15; Cazelles, *Soc. politique*, p. 42. See also *ibid.*, pp. 75-105, for the downfall of Robert of Artois after 1330.

31

called "fiscal absolutism" for the crown. They were notable for their habit of going into the field to supervise personally the execution of policies they had helped to formulate.[89] The accession of Louis X in a period of crisis and rebellion was followed by a purge of the late king's more unpopular fiscal advisers.[90] The important princes, most of whom sympathized with the *Parlement* party," played a greater role under Louis X, although it is misleading to speak of a "feudal reaction."[91] When Louis died suddenly in 1316, his brother Philip seized the regency and then the crown as Philip V. Prudence dictated the retention of many of Louis' policies and advisers at the outset. By 1319, however, the king was relying heavily on men of his own choosing, most of them former servants of Philip IV and linked to the Chamber of Accounts faction.[92] Philip V died in 1322 and a new reaction swept many of these men from power. For a decade, the Chamber of Accounts exercised a diminished influence and conservative policies dominated the government. In the 1330s, however, the fiscal experts returned to power, led by Mile de Noyers.

The short reign of Louis X was marked by political unrest, war in Flanders, and widespread famine. With the utmost tact, Louis levied a modest war subsidy in 1315 and tried to exploit other expedients while posing as a reformer.[93] In preparation for the campaign of 1316, he held a number of large assemblies of burghers and nobles, but he died before the new tax could be collected.[94] His successor resumed this line of policy in 1318-1319. Philip V's goal was to use central assemblies to obtain endorsement of a subsidy in principle at a time when renewal of the Flemish war seemed probable but had not taken place. In effect, the assemblies were to give counsel on the question of whether a tax was

[89] Pegues, *Lawyers*, pp. 226-228, for fiscal absolutism; pp. 118, 131, for going into the field. Cf. Bautier, "Chancellerie," pp. 103-105 and notes.

[90] Pegues, *Lawyers*, pp. 61f.; J. Favier, *Un conseiller de Philippe le Bel, Enguerran de Marigny*, Paris, 1963, pp. 191f.

[91] Petit, *Charles de Valois*, p. 157; Lot and Fawtier, *Institutions*, II, 559; E. Brown, *Charters and Leagues in Early Fourteenth Century France: The Movement of 1314 and 1315*, unpublished doctoral dissertation, Harvard University, Cambridge (Mass.), 1960.

[92] Lehugeur, *Mécanisme*, pp. 115-123.

[93] Brown, *Charters*, pp. 471-473; Brown, "Politics and Taxation," pp. 12-13. For the subsidy of 1315, see Mignon, nos. 1646, 1647, 1651, 1654, 1657, 1658, 1660, 1664-1666, 1668, 1670-1672, 1678, 1680, 1682, 1683, 1688-1692.

[94] C. Taylor, "Assemblies of French Towns in 1316," *Speculum*, XIV (1939), 275-299; C. Taylor, "The Composition of Baronial Assemblies in France, 1315-1320," *Speculum*, XXIX (1954), 435. Cf. an important forthcoming article by E. Brown, "Assemblies of French Towns in 1316: Some New Texts," to appear in *Speculum*, XLVI (1971).

justified. Many of the nobles were very reluctant to do so, but the towns generally promised aid in the event that war should actually break out.[95]

Philip V ultimately did levy a war subsidy in 1319, receiving lump-sum payments from the southern towns and funds for the upkeep of "a certain number of sergeants" from northern communities.[96] In the same year, his daughter married Eudes IV, duke of Burgundy, and he levied a feudal aid.[97] Both taxes aroused some opposition, but they represented the most successful royal fiscal effort in fifteen years. When the Flemish campaign ended quickly, Philip found it politic to return half the subsidy, much as his father had returned the subsidy of 1313 when a feudal aid was being levied at the same time.[98] Given the apparent weakening of royal authority since 1313, Philip V may be credited with a successful fiscal policy. Philip IV had sometimes used large representative assemblies for obtaining counsel and support. Philip V began to develop their role in connection with taxation.

Finally making peace with the Flemings in May 1320,[99] Philip V was able to concentrate his attention on what seems to have been his primary interest—improving the efficiency of governmental administration. Philip's administrative enactments codified and systematized the changes which had occurred in half a century of ad hoc measures and experimentation. A series of royal ordinances regulated the *Parlement*, Chamber of Accounts, royal household, waters and forests administration, and procedures for taxing wool exports. The crown looked into the acquisition of fiefs by non-nobles and established a high scale of fines for *amortissement*. A systematic inquiry into the state of the domain aimed at recovery of alienated royal rights.[100]

---

[95] Taylor, "Baronial Assemblies," pp. 441-448; Strayer and Taylor, *Studies*, pp. 116-136, 144-145; C. Taylor, "An Assembly of French Towns in March, 1318," *Speculum*, XIII (1938), 295-301.

[96] Mignon, nos. 1643, 1644, 1652, 1653, 1655, 1659, 1662, 1669, 1674, 1684, 1687, 1692, 1693; LeMaire, *St. Quentin*, I, no. 293; BN Moreau 223, fol. 41; *INV AM Toulouse*, p. 454 (AA 34, no. 84); BN NAF 7599, fol. 220r; BN *Coll. Languedoc* 83, fols. 107, 111; *Coll. Languedoc* 159, fol. 14r; AM Millau CC 505 (2 unnumbered pcs.).

[97] Mignon, nos. 1694-1721.

[98] A. Mahul (ed.), *Cartulaire et archives des communes de l'ancien diocèse et de l'arrondisement administratif de Carcassonne*, Paris, 1857-1882, III, 256; *HL*, IX, 413; D. Haigneré, *Les chartes de Saint-Bertin*, Saint Omer, 1891, II, no. 1484; BN *Coll. Languedoc* 83, fol. 137; BN *ms. lat.* 9174, fols. 34-35.

[99] BN NAF 7599, fols. 272-275.

[100] These enactments are found in *Ord.*, I, 656-688, 703-712, and 727-734. The important ordinance regulating the Chamber of Accounts is found on pp. 703-706.

It is evident that Philip was surrounded by energetic administrators who believed in systematic government. Mostly associated with the Chamber of Accounts party at court, they seem to have been a remarkable group. The dominant personality in the government was Henri de Sully, who headed both the treasury and the Chamber of Accounts, played an important role in the *Parlement*, directed royal negotiations with the pope, supervised the inquest into alienated domain, and found time to play a major part in negotiating taxes in 1319 and 1321.[101] Mile de Noyers was also active in the royal entourage, as were such men as Raoul Rousselet, Hugues de la Celle, Martin des Essars, Giraud Gueite, and Guillaume Flote.[102] Most of them had served Philip IV but had played a less prominent role under Louis X. Those who still were active in the 1330s would reappear in high places when the Chamber of Accounts again became dominant at court. Working under Philip V, these men helped give institutional character to the advances in royal administration since the reign of St. Louis. From the financial standpoint, however, their most interesting project involved the assemblies of 1321.

For most of the reign, the government engaged in efforts to recover alienated domain and buy up seigneurial coinage rights. Completion of these projects would strengthen the crown's domanial resources and reduce the need for extraordinary fiscal measures. The plan would cost money, but Philip V argued that it served the common profit and that his subjects should help him pay for it.[103] He scheduled two large assemblies of barons, prelates, and towns to meet at Poitiers and Paris respectively during the summer of 1321. In the spring, royal officials traveled through the country proposing to preliminary regional assemblies an attractive series of reforms—recovery of domain, suppression of baronial currency, revaluation of the royal coinage, and standardization of weights and measures. At these local meetings, the government stressed the value of

---

On wool exports, see also *Ord.*, XI, 478-481, and J. L. Moreau de Beaumont, *Mémoire concernant les impositions et droits en Europe* (2nd edn.), Paris, 1787-1789, III, p. 353. On *amortissement* and acquisitions of fiefs, see *Ord.*, I, 745, and AN JJ 58, no. 451 (transcribed in Carreau, *Commissaires*, pp. 291-292). On the effort to recover alienated domain, see also C. V. Langlois, "Registres perdus de la chambre des comptes," *Notices et Extraits des Manuscrits*, XL (1917), 106-151, 219-224.

[101] Lehugeur, *Mécanisme*, pp. 215, 223; E. Boutaric, *Actes du Parlement de Paris*, *première série*, II, Paris, 1867, no. 6144; Langlois, "Registres perdus," pp. 144-146; Henneman, "Enquêteurs," p. 316, note 24; C. Taylor, "French Assemblies and Subsidy in 1321," *Speculum*, XLIII (1968), 227, 237.

[102] *Ibid.*, p. 227; Henneman, "Enquêteurs," p. 316, note 24, and p. 319, note 37; Lehugeur, *Mécanisme*, pp. 115-123, 147; and citations notes 86 and 89, above.

[103] Taylor, "1321," pp. 228f.

the reforms and hinted that their accomplishment would enable Philip to undertake a long-delayed crusade. What was really at stake, however, was the precedent of a subsidy in time of peace, and few of the king's subjects failed to perceive this.[104]

Despite the efforts to prepare public opinion, only the clergy agreed to support the royal plan when the Estates convened at Poitiers and Paris during the summer. The nobles showed little interest, while the towns postponed their answer "and presumably took refuge in the plea of reference back to their constituencies."[105] Philip tried more persuasion at a new round of local assemblies, but at Orléans in October, town representatives reconvened and returned a negative answer, apologizing for giving such *petit conseil*.[106] A strenuous effort on the part of the government thus failed to gain results, and the crown abandoned its experiments with central assemblies. Such meetings were infrequent in the next twenty years, and not until the Estates of 1343 would a large central assembly again be asked to consider a tax.

The royal disappointment of 1321 deserves careful examination because it seems to have influenced future royal policy towards assemblies. One important question still appears unresolved: did the king assume the reforms to be popular and begin by demanding representatives with full power to consent to the proposal? Or did he merely wish to receive counsel on the utility of the proffered reforms? He seems to have pursued the latter course after his rebuff at the Poitiers-Paris meetings during the summer. If his earlier efforts were directed at obtaining consent, they clearly failed and may have been a tactical error.[107] Philip's

---

[104] *Ibid.*, pp. 228-230, 236.   [105] *Ibid.*, p. 235.

[106] *Ibid.*, pp. 239, 244. Cf. Vuitry, *Régime financier*, II, 4, where it is stated that those who had the right to oppose an arbitrary or useless tax also had the obligation to "vote" a necessary and just one. Sentiments like this may have caused the apologetic tone of the towns' refusal.

[107] In a forthcoming article, Elizabeth Brown will argue that the king assumed the reforms to be popular and began by seeking consent to the tax, but that he changed his position after the midsummer assemblies and later merely asked for counsel. This conclusion suggests that consent was less important in the eyes of the townsmen than the issue of whether or not the common profit would be served. There is reason to believe that this was the case (see below, Chapter IX, part 3), but it is far from clear that Philip V did begin by seeking consent in 1321. Taylor's inference that the king sought proctors with full powers is not completely established by the documents he cites. It appears that the king requested *avis et conseil* from those summoned to the meeting at Paris (Taylor, "1321," p. 224), and that he had sought *conseil et deliberation* at the bailiwick assemblies held earlier (*ibid.*, p. 227). If Langmuir's distinction between counsel and consent holds true (above, note 68), Philip V may have sought nothing more than counsel in 1321.

previous assemblies in 1318-1319 had been willing to offer counsel on the need for taxes but not to consent to a specific subsidy. In any case, the government found that it could not get a central assembly of town representatives to commit itself without referring back to constituents, even when preparatory meetings were held first.

There were other lessons to be learned from the experience of 1321. It became clear that the kingdom could not be persuaded to pay a subsidy in time of peace, even if offered extensive reforms which promised to serve the common profit. Moreover, the assemblies were no longer effective even as a propaganda forum. Wild rumors of an extortionately high tax demand began to circulate, creating a kind of "credibility gap" between the king and his subjects.[108]

Under these circumstances, the entire policy of using assemblies must have appeared bankrupt, and it is not surprising that they were abandoned. It is doubtful that many Frenchmen regretted their eclipse, for one detects a reaction against the whole approach to government which was associated with them. The kingdom had wearied of men like Sully and Noyers who practiced such aggressive financial policies. Assemblies, taxes, royal propaganda, and administrative innovation all characterized a régime which had grown unpopular. After years of turmoil, subsidy demands, and experimentation in government, France was ready for a breathing spell, the kind of pause which often follows a period of change. Perhaps, as the chroniclers assert, the death of Philip V early in 1322, spared the country a serious crisis.[109] In any case, it brought to the throne a man of very different outlook.

The new king of France was Charles IV, Philip the Fair's last son. Charles had been among those in Philip V's council who were aligned against the Chamber of Accounts party. On his accession, power quickly changed hands. Sully went into exile and Gueite died a terrible death, while Noyers exerted much less influence and the presidency of the Chamber of Accounts was left vacant for four years.[110] Former members of Louis X's government, such as Etienne de Mornay, now regained influence.[111] In the financial sphere, aggressiveness gave way to conservatism, some of this made possible by certain revenues and administrative improvements inherited from Philip V. Peace with Flanders was another valuable legacy. There remained the recurrent issue of English homage

---

[108] Taylor, "1321," p. 242.   [109] *Ibid.*, note 174.
[110] Langlois, "Registres perdus," pp. 144-146; Lehugeur, *Mécanisme*, pp. 224-225; *Foedera*, II pt. 2, pp. 58, 63, 66-68; Cazelles, *Soc. politique*, pp. 430-431.
[111] Guessard, "Etienne de Mornay."

for Gascony, but Charles IV escaped for the moment the awkward problem of seeking war taxes from an unwilling nation.

Somewhat more embarrassing, perhaps, was the matter of a crusade. All the prominent French princes having taken the cross some years earlier, Charles fell heir to this long-delayed expedition and at least went through the motions of supporting it. The pope was sufficiently encouraged to grant him a two-year tenth in June of 1322.[112] In 1323, a meeting of barons and prelates heard appeals for help from Christian rulers in the Levant, and the viscount of Narbonne was placed in charge of the project. Money was sought from the population of Languedoc,[113] but the effort appears to have been rather halfhearted, and nothing more was heard of it after 1324 when troubles with England diverted the king's attention.[114]

From the outset, Charles IV was unable to live on the resources of the domain alone, judging from the heavy borrowing recorded in his treasury journals.[115] He managed to supplement his income by exploiting the least controversial sources of revenue. The clerical tenth normally provided more than 20 percent of the annual treasury receipts, although its relative importance varied from year to year.[116] The customs duties included a *denier* per pound on goods exported through Burgundy,[117] a 6 *d./l.* tax on cloth and 1 *d./l.* on other products leaving the port of

[112] AN P 2290, pp. 547-548. Another tenth was granted in December 1324, also for two years (*ibid.*, pp. 573-584).

[113] H. Hervieu, *Recherches sur les premiers états généraux et les assemblées représentatives pendant la première moitié du XIVe siècle*, Paris, 1879, pp. 175-176; "Chron. parisienne," p. 77; *HL*, x, cols. 621-624; AD Hérault A 4, fol. 74v; BN *Coll. Languedoc* 83, fols. 138-139, 147r-v; *Ord.*, I, 810f.; Isambert, IV, 306-309.

[114] Existing studies on fourteenth century crusading schemes are A. S. Atiya, *The Crusade in the Later Middle Ages*, London, 1938; A. de Boislisle, "Projet du croisade du premier duc de Bourbon," *AB SHF*, XIV (1877), 230-236, 246-255; and J. Delaville de Roulx, *La France en l'Orient au XIVe siècle*, Paris, 1886, I, 78-85. All these works are rather disappointing. When war broke out with England (see below, next chapter), Charles IV ordered that all crusading funds accumulated by Amalric of Narbonne be surrendered. See E. Martin-Chabot, *Les archives de la cour des comptes, aides et finances de Montpellier*, Paris, 1907, no. 606, 12 November 1324. It was believed that this sum came to 30,000 *l.t.* Besides those texts cited in the last note, other sources of the crusading scheme of 1323 are BN *Coll. Languedoc* 83, fols. 151r-v, 156r; BN NAF 7600, fols. 130r-136v; BN NAF 7373, fols. 5r-17v; AN P 2289, pp. 714-719; AN JJ 62, no. 355; AN K 41, no. 22; Petit, *Charles de Valois*, P.J. nos. 19-20. Cf. M. Lot, "Projets de croisade sous Charles le Bel et sous Philippe de Valois," *BEC*, XX (1859), 503-509.

[115] See the tables of Fawtier, *Comptes du trésor*, pp. lix-lx.

[116] The tenth produced 17% of receipts at the treasury in 1325 and 33% a year earlier, but usually fell between these extremes. See tables in Appendix I.

[117] *JT Ch. IV*, nos. 22, 889, 967, 1427.

Aigues Mortes,[118] and a 12 *d./l. gabelle des draps* on finished cloth exported from the Carcassonne district.[119] The most widespread customs duty was a system of licenses to export wool, known as *haut passage*.[120]

Charles IV also benefited from two legacies from his brother's reign. Philip V's indefatigable *réformateurs* in Languedoc, Raoul Rousselet and the count of Forez had, in 1319, negotiated a transaction with towns of the Carcassonne district, whereby the communities in question bought up certain royal salt rights for the large sum of 150,000 *l.t.* payable in six annual installments by means of a heavy tax of 3 *l.t.* per hearth.[121] In 1321, the government had exploited the widespread rumors that the Jews had induced the lepers to poison the wells. Already vulnerable as usurers, the Jews were assessed a fine of 150,000 *l.t.* Those of Languedoc were to pay 47,000 pounds of this total, the great bulk of which was assessed on the seneschalsies of Beaucaire and Carcassonne where most of the Jews in the Midi evidently resided.[122] By the end of 1321, 15,837 *l.t.* had reached the treasury,[123] but most of the collections occurred in the reign of Charles IV. For collection of the fine and sale of confiscated Jewish property, special commissioners were assigned to various parts of the kingdom.[124] When it was found that the Jews could not pay the full sum demanded, the fine was reduced by 20 percent, but even the reduced figure was impossible to collect. Viard calculated that the crown received 53,400 *l.p.* in 1322 and 1323, but less than 5,000 pounds thereafter.[125] Even if receipts did not measure up to expectations, they provided Charles with a convenient windfall at the beginning of his reign.

[118] *Ibid.*, no. 9409 and note of Viard, pp. xx-xi. The *denier*-per-pound *claverie* of Aigues Mortes was part of a vain attempt to maintain this port which was gradually silting up (see below, Chapter III). For evidence of its collection, see *JT Ch. IV*, nos. 424, 2163, 2760, 5326-5328, and 9979. Cf. A. Germain, *Histoire de la commerce de Montpellier antérieurement à l'ouverture du port de Cette*, Montpellier, 1861, I, P.J. no. 89.

[119] Originating under Philip V, this cloth *gabelle* became a contentious matter under Philip VI. See below, Chapter III.

[120] G. Bigwood, "La politique de la laine en France sous les règnes de Philippe le Bel et de ses fils," *RBPH*, xv (1936), 79-102, 429-457; xvi (1937), 95-129; Henneman, "Italians," p. 18.

[121] AN JJ 59, nos. 309 and 555, the latter being published in *Ord.*, I, 724-727. Cf. *JT Ch. IV*, nos. 122, 496, 623, 2715, 4378, 9309, 9310.

[122] "Chron. parisienne," p. 56; *HL*, x, col. 617.

[123] BN NAF 21857, fol. 177r.

[124] *HL*, IX, 415. Citations of this volume will be to Vaissete's text unless the notes of Molinier are specified.

[125] *JT Ch. IV*, p. xxiv. In all, 118 entries in this register deal with the fine on the Jews: for 1322, forty-four entries between no. 28 and no. 2284; for 1323, forty-six entries between no. 2308 and no. 4378. The remaining twenty-eight entries are in the years 1324-1326, and I have found none in *JT Ph. VI*. The total collected under Charles IV, added to that obtained in 1321, came to 88,587 *l.t.* in all.

Charles also collected money from the Italians in the kingdom. They paid a small sum to celebrate the king's "joyous accession" in 1322, and those frequenting the fairs of Champagne offered another 5,300 *l.t.* in November 1323.[126] Two regular taxes were also paid by Italians in France, a *denier* per pound on business transactions known as the *boîte aux Lombards* and an annual 5 percent property tax for which they enjoyed bourgeois privileges.[127] The crown also realized important revenues, especially in times of peace, by selling privileges or negotiating fines and "compositions" with persons or communities accused of "excesses."[128]

The reign of Charles IV thus commenced with two years of peace. The king pursued a conservative policy, avoiding costly commitments and relying on revenues that were politically safe. Yet it is noteworthy that he still was unable to live on the receipts from the domain and a few regular taxes. Heavy borrowing and short-run fiscal expedients were necessary. As in the first two decades of the century, the years after 1322 were marked by a permanent royal need for funds, even in those rare years when the kingdom was at peace. This chronic shortage of adequate revenues would soon be aggravated by a new Anglo-French confrontation.

---

[126] Henneman, "Italians," p. 24.   [127] *Ibid.*, pp. 21-24.

[128] These large payments were very miscellaneous in nature, sometimes involving urban privileges or the settlement of litigation, sometimes clearly in the nature of fines. Their importance to this study lies in the fact that they always became much more numerous in times of peace, not only in 1322-1323, but also in such periods as 1327, and 1330-1336. See Henneman, "Enquêteurs," pp. 331, 336. Several large amounts were levied by Charles IV in 1322 for "excesses": 50,000 *l.p.* on the bishop of Langres (*JT Ch. IV*, p. xxiv, and nos. 2549, 3402, 3982, 4625, 5119, 10071, 10079, 10286) and 12,000 *l.t.* on the archbishop of Rouen (*ibid.*, nos. 2191, 5131, 5728). So-called "compositions" from towns are mentioned a good many times: *ibid.*, 481, 899, 1347, 2419, 2569-2571, 2614, 2736, 2844, 2845, 3153, 3708, 3983. Some of the larger ones obtained in 1322 were 5,000 *l.t.* from Lauran (AN JJ 61, no. 140), 8,000 *l.t.* from Carcassonne (AN JJ 61, no. 127), 3,000 *l.t.* from Limoux (AN JJ 61, no. 117), 4000 *l.t.* from Montpellier (AN JJ 61, no. 113), 4,000 *l.p.* from Dunois (*JT Ch. IV*, no. 2845), and 6,000 *l.t.* from Saint-Quentin (Le Maire, *St. Quentin*, 1, no. 300). Thus from six towns and two prelates the crown obtained over 100,000 *l.t.* in 1322. Even if these sums were payable over a few years and never fully collected, the amount remains impressive in terms of annual royal receipts. Other transactions in 1323 and 1324 further swelled the total (AN JJ 61, no. 159; JJ 62, no. 110).

CHAPTER II

The War Subsidies for Gascony and Flanders, 1324-1329

1. The War of Saint-Sardos

IN ACCORDANCE with his generally cautious policy, Charles IV did not even bring up the matter of English homage for Guyenne until the latter part of 1323. Historians have credited him with an accommodating attitude on this question,[1] but domestic politics probably were a factor. After the suspicious and hostile reaction to Philip V's fiscal program of 1321, Charles doubtless wished to postpone the day when he might have to seek new war subsidies.

In July of 1323, he finally summoned Edward II to render homage at Amiens between 2 February and Easter 1324.[2] Edward responded with delaying tactics, claiming that the treachery of the Scots would make this a bad time to cross the channel.[3] In November, he tried to bargain with Charles, formally requesting a delay of the homage while seeking redress of English and Gascon grievances against the encroachments of French officials.[4] Unfortunately for Edward, these proposals coincided with events in Gascony of which he was not yet informed. For several years, the abbey of Sarlat had proposed to convert its priory at Saint-Sardos into a *bastide* to be held in *paréage* with the French crown. English interests in Gascony, led by the lord of Montpezat, opposed the plan because it would place French officials in a strategic fortress in their vicinity, but the *Parlement* had ruled that the *paréage* could be accomplished.[5] The crown was to take over its new rights there on 16 October 1323, but just before the appointed day, the lord of Montpezat destroyed Saint-Sardos and hanged the French officer who had arrived there. Ralph Basset, Edward's seneschal of Gascony, was in the vicinity and

---

[1] Bréquigny, "Mémoire," pp. 368-369, 377; P. Chaplais, *The War of Saint-Sardos (1323-1325): Gascon Correspondence and Diplomatic Documents*, London, 1954, p. ix. Chaplais states that Charles did not want to press Edward over the homage and embarrass him when he was embroiled with the Scots. At the same time, however, the two kings were corresponding over the perennial problem of alleged abuses on the part of French seneschals in the Southwest. See *Foedera*, II pt. 2, pp. 49, 67, 79.

[2] Bréquigny, "Mémoire," p. 368; Chaplais, *St. Sardos*, p. ix.
Scottish conflict, see *Foedera*, II pt. 2, pp. 55 and 60.

[3] *Ibid.*, pp. 176-177. On some of Edward's fiscal and military preparations for the

[4] Bréquigny, "Mémoire," pp. 370-371.

[5] Chaplais, *St. Sardos*, pp. ix-xi, 179-180. For the judicial proceedings, see Boutaric, *Actes*, II, nos. 5466, 6498, 6980. The last of these is the *arrêt* of 4 December 1322 which finally ordered construction of the *bastide*.

40

had recently received Montpezat's homage. He failed to investigate the raid and was accused by the French of being involved.[6]

Edward disavowed the act when he finally learned of it, and ordered an investigation.[7] Charles accepted this action in good faith and also agreed to postpone the homage until July of 1324. He nevertheless proceeded with plans to punish the offenders himself, and did not inform Edward that he was doing so. Montpezat and the English seneschal were summoned to court, and the English proctor at Paris was arrested. The offenders ignored the summonses, and after the final one (9 February 1324) they were declared banished from the realm. Failing to eject the lord of Montpezat from his castle, the French prepared for war, placing Aimeri de Cros, seneschal of Périgord, in charge of the local preparations.[8]

Edward II tried to avert a crisis by removing the offending seneschal and offering reparations to the French, but Charles was determined to maintain his superior feudal position. He considered himself the judge in this case, not merely one party to it.[9] He was therefore in no mood for Edward's next action, which was to request a new delay in rendering the homage.[10] When the July deadline passed, Charles of Valois led a French army through Agenais and besieged La Réole. After capturing this town in September, he agreed to a truce until 14 April 1325.[11] Both sides evidently expected the war to resume at that time,[12] but the pope and the queen of England (Charles IV's sister) intervened in the dispute. A

[6] Chaplais, *St. Sardos*, pp. xi-xii; Bréquigny, "Mémoire," pp. 372-375, whose account is based largely on Rymer's *Foedera* and therefore differs in emphasis from those of the chroniclers. The latter stress the Saint-Sardos incident and largely ignore the homage question. Cf. *Gr. Chron.*, ix, 31-33; *Cont. Nangis*, ii, 55.

[7] Bréquigny, "Mémoire," p. 376; Chaplais, *St. Sardos*, p. xi.

[8] *Ibid.*, pp. xii-xiii; Bréquigny, "Mémoire," p. 379.

[9] Chaplais, "Règlements," p. 258. In March and July 1324, the pope wrote to Edward, urging him to render homage and preserve the peace, but between these two appeals Edward complained to the pontiff of the French "excesses" in Gascony. *Foedera*, ii pt. 2, pp. 93-94, 98-99, 102.

[10] Chaplais, *St. Sardos*, pp. xiii, 182-184, for the confiscation of the English fiefs; *Foedera*, ii pt. 2, pp. 96, 102-103, for Edward's continuing discussions with his Gascon officials and the naming of persons to represent him in dealings with France.

[11] Bréquigny, "Mémoire," pp. 394-406. The homage seems to have been the main issue for the French, who used the border incident as an excuse for taking action. On the assembling of troops in August by the count of Valois, see BN *Coll. Languedoc* 83, fol. 170. Cf. *HL*, ix, 432-433; *Cont. Nangis*, ii, 57-60.

[12] Bréquigny, "Mémoire," p. 409f; BN NAF 7600 (Fontanieu 67), fols. 93r-v. In July, Edward II had ordered the arrest of French subjects in England and had written the pope that he had no intention of giving up Gascony merely in order to have peace: *Foedera*, ii pt. 2, pp. 105-107. For Edward's continuing military preparations in the early months of 1325, see *ibid.*, pp. 131, 133.

treaty was concluded at the end of May and ratified in England on 13 June.[13]

The eighteen months preceding this settlement had been marked by little actual fighting. In southwestern France, however, war seemed imminent through the first half of 1324, while during the winter of 1324-1325, the whole kingdom anticipated major hostilities in the spring. Under these circumstances, Charles IV felt justified in seeking war subsidies. In 1324, he directed his efforts only to the threatened regions nearest to Gascony, but early in 1325, he attempted to levy a general tax throughout the kingdom. Before collecting this subsidy, however, he made use of other sources of income which were less controversial because they were based upon unchallenged royal rights. In doing so, he followed the same basic policy which he had already employed in augmenting domainal resources in 1322 and 1323.

In the second half of 1324, Charles directed his attention to the Italians in the kingdom and also to the export trade. Beginning in September, the crown collected a large number of small loans *in subsidio guerrarum*. In most cases, the treasury journals identify the lender as an Italian,[14] but the king seems to have borrowed money on a more general basis. In March 1325, royal notaries in the Périgord-Quercy region were raising loans for the "host of Montpezat,"[15] and similar operations in the Toulousain produced 3,407 pounds during the first half of the year.[16] The king also obtained a large loan secured by the revenues of Auvergne and borrowed additional funds from several cardinals.[17] In the case of the Italians, these loans were but a small part of their contributions to the Anglo-French war in Gascony. Between March and May 1325, they presented a "gift" for the war.[18] They also paid annual *finances* in lieu of two small regular taxes, but in 1325, these *finances* involved vastly more money than usual. The sums paid by the Italians in January 1325 and again in the last quarter of the year amounted to a major extortion.[19]

With respect to external commerce, Charles IV generalized practices which were already being applied to wool. In June 1324, as the deadline for Edward II's homage approached, Charles issued an ordinance reaffirming an earlier prohibition of certain exports.[20] Six months later, on

[13] Bréquigny, "Mémoire," pp. 420-428; *HL*, ix, 436; Perroy, *The Hundred Years War*, pp. 65-66; *Foedera*, ii pt. 2, p. 132.

[14] Henneman, "Italians," p. 29.

[15] F. Maillard, *Comptes royaux 1314-1328*, Paris, 1961, nos. 8378-8386.

[16] *Ibid.*, nos. 4823-4857.   [17] *JT Ch. IV*, nos. 7279, 9294-9297.

[18] Henneman, "Italians," p. 30.   [19] *Ibid.*, pp. 25-26.

[20] Bigwood, "Politique," p. 85; *Ord.*, xi, 487-492.

13 December, an important new ordinance extended the list of forbidden exports to even more articles, but the government set up a regular tax which would buy exemption from the rule. On most things the tax was to be an *ad valorem* levy of 4 *d./l.*; the main exception was wine, which was assessed according to a separate schedule of rates.[21] This tax on exports, known as the *droit de rève*, was another enlargement and extension of a seigneurial right, made possible by the growing maturity of the royal ports and passages administration.[22] Both the timing of the ordinances and the wording of treasury journal entries support Viard's conclusion that this tax was mainly a war measure.[23] Mignon's inventory suggests that it was seen in this way by contemporaries. It was suspended in some parts of the kingdom when peace was made in June 1325, but was reinstated as soon as the country was again at war.[24] Collection of it began before the end of 1324 in some districts and was under way everywhere before 1325 was well-advanced.[25]

Another resource available to the monarchy was the coinage, which had occasioned considerable debate since Philip IV had begun to alter it in the 1290s. Charles IV held cautious deliberations with assemblies of coinage experts from the towns and raised the price of silver in 1322. He did not realize significant coinage profits until 1324, but then they began to soar as Charles stepped up his alterations in order to increase revenue. In time, the policy antagonized important interests, but not in Charles' lifetime.[26]

[21] Vuitry, *Régime financier*, I, 133-134; Borrelli de Serres, *Recherches*, II, 451; *Ord.*, I, 783-784, II, 148-149; AN P 2289, pp. 362-366.

[22] See J. R. Strayer, "Pierre de Chalon and the Origins of the French Customs Service," *Festschrift Percy Ernst Schramm zu seinem siebzigsten Geburtstag von Schulern und Freunden zugeeignet*, Wiesbaden, 1964, I, 334-339.

[23] *JT Ch. IV*, no. 7293, and Viard's introduction, p. xxi. Cf. Moreau de Beaumont, *Mémoire*, III, 353-354, and Henneman, "Italians," p. 19.

[24] Mignon, nos. 1730-1788, grouped the accounts for the export tax under a single heading with those for the war subsidy. Suspension of the *droit de rève*, coinciding with the English treaty, occurred on 8 July 1325 in the bailiwicks of Chaumont and Mâcon and the seneschalsy of Carcassonne, resuming on 12 December after war had broken out with Flanders (*ibid.*, no. 1748). It was suspended in Vermandois on 24 June (*ibid.*, no. 1736). For the Beaucaire district, the texts indicating suspension in the early summer are in AM Montpellier G-6, nos. 3407-3408. Mignon's inventory indicates, however, that the tax was not interrupted in the bailiwicks of Senlis and Caux, two regions in which exports were not an important part of the economy. The treasury journals contain entries indicating collection from Paris in every month except September and October, so if a suspension occurred there it must have been brief.

[25] Mignon, nos. 1734, 1736, 1741-1743, 1748, 1750, 1761, 1771-1775, 1778, 1785.

[26] See the discussion in Appendix I.

In his effort to minimize subsidy demands as such, Charles found another useful device in the fines called *franc-fief* and *amortissement* which were levied on non-nobles who acquired noble fiefs. Philip V had investigated these acquisitions and had instituted a schedule of fines which raised the former rates.[27] His ordinance had not been applied in practice, but Charles IV made use of it soon after naming commissioners to seek a general war subsidy at the beginning of 1325. The commissioners were given additional powers, generally the right to investigate acquisitions of fiefs and levy fines, but sometimes the broader investigatory and punitive powers of an *enquêteur-réformateur*. Equipped with such authority, they were able to apply heavy pressure when negotiating a subsidy for war yet remain active in times of peace when they could collect important fines. Being based upon acknowledged royal powers, the pressure they exerted could not be attacked as a novel invasion of rights.[28]

Charles IV's first war subsidy was confined to the districts nearest to English Gascony. Once it appeared that force was needed against the lord of Montpezat, the seneschals of Toulouse and Périgord were ordered to assemble troops at Lauzerte on 15 March 1324. The mustering date was twice postponed, and the campaign did not actually take place until Charles of Valois arrived in the summer.[29] Meanwhile, the seneschal of Limousin ordered the inhabitants of his district to be in arms "each according to his ability," but when he attempted to levy a subsidy on this basis he encountered opposition at Limoges. The viscount of Limoges protested to the king when he tried to force recalcitrant inhabitants to serve.[30]

Much more is known about what transpired farther south at Périgueux. This town received a letter from the seneschal, Aimeri de Cros, ordering that 100 sergeants be raised for the force that was to assemble at Lauzerte. This summons was read at an assembly of the inhabitants on 1 March, and the mayor and consuls were told to designate burghers who would furnish these sergeants. Evidently, those wealthy enough to do so were to supply the salary of one sergeant, while those with fewer resources would join in groups and take joint responsibility for supply-

[27] *Ord.,* I, 745; AM Gourdon CC I, no. 3.

[28] Henneman, "Enquêteurs," passim, and especially pp. 325-327.

[29] *Ibid.,* pp. xiii, 22-23, 187; J. N. Moreau, *Mémoire sur la constitution politique de la ville et cité de Périgueux, avec Recueil de titres et autres pièces justificatives employés dans le Mémoire sur la constitution politique,* Paris, 1775 (the two volumes in one hereafter cited respectively as *Mémoire* and *Recueil*), pp. 207-208.

[30] BN Doat 243, fols. 14r-20v.

ing a sergeant. The response to this order was dilatory and the seneschal applied pressure by ordering seizure of arms in the town with which to equip sergeants. When a new town meeting was poorly attended, royal agents named the persons who, individually or in groups, would be responsible for presenting sergeants at a muster on 9 March. Some of the men still did not appear, and those sergeants who had been recruited began to commit "excesses" in the town when the successive postponements of the muster at Lauzerte delayed their departure.[31] Eventually, sergeants from Périgueux did join the royal army besieging La Réole, after being sent in two companies to Lauzerte.[32]

Details of this sort are only rarely available. We are provided here with a valuable glimpse of the procedure whereby a town might supply a contingent of armed men. A tax for military purposes was being apportioned among the inhabitants on the basis of wealth, a practice which seems to have been fairly common. What was more distinctive about the case of Périgueux was the requirement that individuals or groups were to be directly responsible for a specific sergeant. It made very clear the close relationship between taxation and military defense. In all probability, most towns which granted subsidies of "sergeants" did not go through such a procedure, but merely expressed their tax in military units. The experience of Périgueux certainly suggests why many communities preferred to pay lump sums.

Less is known about the process of recruiting sergeants from other towns of southwestern France in 1324, but by the summer a good many of them had sent contingents to the army. Cahors sent 200 sergeants, Millau fifty, and Cajarc twenty.[33] The crown obtained some additional aid from Rouergue[34] and possibly from Auvergne as well,[35] but evidently did not try to tax lower Languedoc or parts of the realm that were distant from Gascony.

In the course of 1324, a punitive expedition against the lord of Montpezat had been transformed into an Anglo-French war. Despite the truce concluded in September, Charles IV expected a resumption of hostilities

---

[31] Moreau, *Recueil*, pp. 196-209.   [32] *INV AM Périgueux*, p. 67 (CC 45).

[33] G. Lacoste, *Histoire générale de la province de Quercy*, Cahors, 1875, III, 36-37; E. Dufour, *La commune de Cahors au Moyen Age*, Cahors, 1846, p. 92; AM Millau CC 345, fol. 10r, EE 118, no. 234; AM Cajarc, EE *supp.*, nos. 65-66.

[34] AN K 41, no. 10, indicating that *mineurs* were sent from Rouergue; AD Aveyron 2E 178, no. 2, fol. 184r-v, indicating negotiations for sergeants at Najac.

[35] In February 1324, Charles IV confirmed certain guarantees extended to Auvergne by Philip V in 1319 on the occasion of a subsidy grant (AN JJ 62, nos. 41-42). At the end of March, he ordered the bailiff of Auvergne not to violate the privileges of Montferrand in levying taxes (*INV AM Montferrand*, I, 5 [AA 10]).

in the spring, and to be ready for them he prepared to tax the entire kingdom. Military preparations were announced as early as December 1324, when the king ordered Charles of Valois to be at Bergerac on the following first of May, with 400 men-at-arms and 1,000 crossbowmen.[36] The seneschal of Carcassonne was told to provide 300 of the crossbowmen.[37] In preparing for the campaign five months ahead of time, the king was merely laying the groundwork for a war subsidy, and several other fiscal measures occurred at about the same time. The 4 *d./l.* export tax was established, and the king named new commissioners to investigate the Jews in Languedoc.[38] In January 1325, the Italians paid their first heavy *finance*.[39] Against this background, the crown issued commissions on 18 January for the levy of a tax throughout the kingdom. The royal agents were ordered to approach the communities and towns for a "pecuniary subsidy for men-at-arms," because war was "imminent" and "touches each and all." They were to promise that such aid would prejudice no rights,[40] and were also authorized to "compose" with ecclesiastics owing service, to pardon crimes committed under the king's predecessors, to deal with usurers, to diminish the excessive number of royal notaries and sergeants. Many of these extra instructions were added two days later when new royal letters authorized investigation of fief transactions and empowered some of the commissioners to act as *enquêteurs-réformateurs*.[41] The fiscal-military preparations of 1324-1325 thus represent a well-coordinated program, involving many potential sources of revenue and the promise of reforms. The claims of military necessity were reinforced by careful exploitation of undisputed royal

[36] BN NAF 7600 (Fontanieu 67), fol. 131, describing a text in AN J 164A, no. 50.

[37] BN *Coll. Languedoc* 83, fol. 168; *HL*, ix, 435.

[38] *HL*, x, col. 631.   [39] See above, note 19.

[40] For this commission, see *HL*, x, cols. 632-634, whereby the head of the customs service, Pierre de Chalon, was ordered to join the seneschal of Carcassonne in levying taxes in that district. He was also to serve in the seneschalsy of Toulouse, where his associate was Raoul Chaillot, royal *réformateur* (AN JJ 64, no. 55). Some of the other commissions are in BN Doat 146, fol. 172; AM Millau, EE 118, no. 3; BN NAF 7600 (Fontanieu 67), fols. 153-162; and AM Cordes CC 29, no. 267, partly published by C. Portal, *Histoire de la Ville de Cordes 1222-1799*, Albi, 1902, P. J. 5. Cf. *HL*, ix, 435. In *JT Ch. IV*, no. 7273, there is an entry of 27 March indicating payment to a notary for fifteen letters to commissioners for the Gascon war subsidy.

[41] BN *Coll. Languedoc* 83, fols. 177r-v; *AHP*, xi, 296-302; AN JJ 62, no. 352, JJ 64, no. 58. Another text, published in *Ord.*, i, 786-787, clearly states that the fines for new acquisitions are to be collected for the war. On this whole money-raising effort, see *HL*, ix, 435, and Henneman, "Enquêteurs," pp. 325f. and notes.

rights, and commissioners in some regions possessed so many powers that they were extremely well-equipped to bargain for money.

Negotiations of the war subsidy in the Toulouse district serves to illustrate the way in which such commissioners might conclude a sort of "package deal" that could be very lucrative for the crown. Six communities representing the *jugerie* of Albigeois agreed to pay the government 13,700 *l. petits tournois*. The transaction specified that this payment not only met their subsidy obligations but also excused them from investigation of various "excesses," fines for using illegal currency, and fines for fief alienations. In return, the crown ordered that royal sergeants and notaries stop extorting from the populace and that judges enforce this ruling.[42] While we have no information on how this payment was apportioned, one town of the region, Cordes, made specific arrangements with the royal *réformateur* which seem to define that town's conception of "evident necessity." In lieu of a proposed direct tax, the consuls of Cordes agreed to an indirect levy on such commodities as cattle, grain, wine, skins, etc., for as long as the king maintained 2,000 horsemen and 6,000 foot soldiers in the field. This agreement was reached on 3 April 1325.[43]

In the other parts of the seneschalsy of Toulouse we find subsidy agreements that were similar in nature to that made with the towns of Albigeois. Eight communities of the *jugerie* of Rivière agreed to pay a tax of 10 *s.t.* per hearth over a four-year period, under virtually the same terms as the Albigeois—an end to war-subsidy demands and pardon for certain abuses and fief alienations.[44] The *jugeries* of Lauragais and Villelongue preferred lump sums and paid 13,000 *l.t.* apiece.[45] All these transactions were made between royal commissioners and certain named consuls of specified towns, who were described as acting "for themselves and their communities" in the appropriate *jugerie* "and its *ressort*." Presumably, lesser communities in the *jugeries* were to pay their shares of the promised sums, but precise evidence on this matter is lacking.

In the seneschalsy of Beaucaire, the crown seems to have negotiated with larger groups than in the Toulousain. The prior of La Charité, acting as royal commissioner, sent letters to the *baylies* of the district, ordering that representatives come to Nîmes.[46] One town sent proctors to a meeting scheduled there for 15 April.[47] Alès, however, sent three

[42] AN JJ 64, no. 58.
[44] AN JJ 64, no. 36.
[46] A. Bardon, *Histoire de la ville d'Alais*, Nîmes, 1891, I, p. 94.
[47] *Ibid.*, note 1.

[43] AM Cordes CC 29, no. 267.
[45] AN JJ 62, nos. 523-524.

consuls to represent the town and *viguerie* at an assembly of bishops, abbots, barons and towns, to be held on the 29th.[48] It thus appears that there was no single meeting for the whole seneschalsy, but two or more small assemblies which included all three orders and not merely townsmen. Nothing is known, however, about the process of negotiating the taxes, and it appears that each town may have made its own bargain with the king. Alès agreed to pay 400 *l.t.* which would be apportioned among the various towns of the *viguerie*.[49] Nîmes and Saint-Gilles promised 1,000 and 44 *l.t.*, respectively.[50]

Montpellier seems to have been treated separately from the other communities of the Beaucaire district. Taxation of this town was always a contentious affair because the king of Majorca was direct seigneur of much of the town and French fiscal officers were perennially accused of infringing on his rights. In 1325, the subsidy negotiations took so long that peace had been made before the tax was finally arranged. During the spring, Montpellier complained of "excesses" on the part of royal commissioners who were tallaging the Jews and investigating usury.[51] It is possible that such agents were particularly zealous during the time that a subsidy was under discussion. The town consuls experienced further difficulties when clergy with urban property sought to escape municipal taxation.[52] Perhaps the king's support of the municipality on this point facilitated the subsidy negotiations. Finally, Montpellier consented to pay 1,500 *l.t.* for the war in Gascony on condition that the sum would not be payable for four months. This agreement was dated 18 June,[53] however, and ten days earlier, Charles IV had written to his officers in Languedoc announcing an end to taxation.[54] Although no reason was given for this order, it obviously coincided with the Anglo-French treaty which ended the war, and it must have reached Mont-

---

[48] *Ibid.*, notes 1 and 2; AM Alès 1 S-3, no. 5.

[49] *Ibid.*, nos. 6-8. [50] *HL*, IX, p. 435.

[51] *Gr. Chartrier*, nos. 1217, 1941. Presumably the commissioners on Jews were those named in December (above, note 38). The usury commissioners, who seem to have been different persons, had been arresting wealthy Majorcan subjects.

[52] *Ibid.*, nos. 3295-3296. Clergy with property or engaging in trade were ordered in April and May 1325, to contribute to a "subsidy." Since Montpellier had not yet granted the king a war subsidy, the tax in question must have been a municipal levy.

[53] *HL*, X, cols. 646-648.

[54] AM Montpellier G-6, no. 3406 ordered that no inhabitant of Montpellier be forced to pay *"tailles,* impositions or subventions for reason of our said war of Gascony." Albi received a similar letter also dated 8 June, as did Agde (BN *Coll. Languedoc* 83, fol. 172), so we can conclude that the tax cancellation in Languedoc was general.

pellier just a few days after the grant of 18 June.[55] Two weeks after halting the subsidy, Charles revealed the extreme caution which characterized his approach to taxation: he instructed the seneschals of Beaucaire
and Carcassonne to cease collection of the 4 *d./l.* export tax (23 June).[56]

Both of these cancellations seem to have been ignored by the crown's
local officials at Montpellier. Although the subsidy was not to have been
levied at all for four months, the commissioners who had labored so long
to obtain the grant evidently attempted to collect it immediately, and in
September, the king had to reissue, forcefully, his order that nothing be
levied.[57] As for the report tax, it too seems to have been levied in the face
of the royal prohibition, for on 8 October, still another letter from the
king repeated cancellation of the subsidy and added that merchants
could export their goods from Montpellier without paying a tax.[58] This
correspondence not only reveals the difficulty in getting zealous local
officers to execute royal orders, but also shows how closely the export tax
had been tied to the war.

Once the crown had finally brought a halt to the collection of war
taxes at Montpellier, the citizens encountered an intensified round of
investigation and extortion from assorted royal commissioners charged
with looking into usury, levying fines for *franc-fief*, and collecting the
debts owed to Jews.[59] It was this sort of harassment which the towns of
the Toulousain had sought to avoid by agreeing to pay large lump sums
for a package of royal concessions.[60] The tax negotiations of 1325 in
Languedoc illustrate very well the unpopularity of royal commissioners
of "reform" and inquiry, and the coercive role which they could play.
Complaints against their activities were also heard from the seneschalsy
of Carcassonne. Within a single week in June, Pézenas had obtained
from Paris one document ordering commissioners not to seek fines from
any person who was not an avowed usurer or clearly the possessor of a

---

[55] J. Petit, M. Gavrilovitch, et al., (eds.) *Essai de restitution des plus anciens
mémoriaux de la chambre des comptes de Paris*, Paris, 1899, pp. 188-189, shows times
normally required to travel to Paris from certain parts of the realm in this period.
It was a thirteen-day trip from Paris to Beaucaire, and a letter sent on the eighth
should have reached Montpellier two weeks later.

[56] AM Montpellier G-6, no. 3407. *INV AM Pézenas*, no. 1623, mentions suspension
of this tax also.

[57] *HL*, x, cols. 653-654.   [58] Germain, *Commerce*, I, P.J. no. 93.

[59] *Gr. Chartrier*, nos. 1216, 1942-44, 1946, 2081. Cf. Henneman, "Enquêteurs," pp.
327-328. In all cases, the king acceded to the complaints of the citizens and ordered
the commissioners to desist.

[60] See above, notes 42-45.

noble fief, and a second letter forbidding seizure of sums owed by local citizens to Jews.[61]

Taxation in the Carcassonne district seems to have consisted of lump-sum payments by the towns. Carcassonne and Trèbes paid the subsidy in this manner,[62] while the consuls of Narbonne engaged in lengthy debate with the crown as to whether they should do the same. The issue at Narbonne was whether or not a war was in progress. Following the treaty of peace, Charles IV had ordered cancellation of taxes, but the treaty was not ratified in England until five days after this order (13 June).[63] It took time for news to travel southward, and the king's officers at Béziers claimed to have understood only that the truce was extended to 15 July. On 22 June, having doubtless learned of the treaty's ratification, the king ordered that collection of the subsidy in the Carcassonne district cease because the reasons for the tax no longer applied.[64] This document may have been concealed or ignored by his officials. On 15 July, they called to arms all inhabitants of Narbonne who had not fined. The consuls protested to Paris, not to challenge the expiration of the truce, but to argue that this expiration did not in itself mean that a state of war existed.[65] Narbonne, like Cordes, evidently had ideas as to what kind of situation justified a tax, and the consuls were prepared to challenge the king's officers on the matter. This dispute also illustrates the selective use of a local military summons as a pressure tactic to speed collection of a tax.

Documentation from upper Languedoc for 1325 is much more scanty. The inhabitants of Millau were under pressure from royal commissioners levying *franc-fief*,[66] while those of Najac negotiated with the government over payment of a war subsidy.[67] Saint-Antonin agreed to pay 240 *l.t.* subject to a letter of non-prejudice, provided that other towns of Rou-

[61] *INV AM Pézenas*, nos. 1619-1620.

[62] *HL*, IX, 435. Both Vaissete and Mahul, *Cartulaire*, I, 383, claimed that Trèbes had only forty hearths but paid 200 *l.t.* This is an obvious error, and if the hearth figures for Trèbes are correct the actual payment was probably 20 *l.t.*

[63] See above, notes 13 and 54.

[64] Martin-Chabot, *Cour des Comptes*, no. 615. In all probability, however, the king hoped to resume collection of this tax at the earliest opportunity. In September, he asked for a list of those at Narbonne who had not paid: *ibid.*, no. 617; BN *Coll. Languedoc* 83, fol. 185r.

[65] BN Doat 52, fol. 134r; BN *Coll. Languedoc* 83, fol. 185r.

[66] J. Artières, *Documents sur la ville de Millau* (*Archives historiques du Rouergue*, VII), Millau, 1930, nos. 145, 148, this series hereafter cited as *A. H. Rouergue*. Perhaps the crown obtained money for affirming Millau's exemption from *franc-fief*, but there is no other evidence of a subsidy there.

[67] AD Aveyron 2E 178, no. 2, fols. 192r-193v.

ergue also paid. If any of them received remission of the tax, Saint-Antonin was to be included, and no other aid for the war would be requested.[68] The crown sought subsidies from the important towns of Quercy and received 500 *l.t.* from Cahors for the support of 100 sergeants. Here again, however, the commissioners aroused opposition by trying to continue collecting after the war ended, and their levies for *franc-fief* and usury were equally unpopular.[69] At Périgueux, the government raised a contingent of sergeants as in 1324 and evidently had to seize the municipal revenues in order to force compliance.[70]

The subsidy in Poitou, Limousin, and La Marche was collected under the direction of another of those commissioners who had received extensive powers in January 1325, including the title of *réformateur*.[71] Because partial financial accounts have survived, we know that the crown levied slightly more than 2,200 *l.t.* from the various sergeantries and *châtellenies* of this region for the Gascon war subsidy of 1325.[72] In the same period, the same officials received over 4,100 *l.t.* for fief alienations and another 380 pounds from usurers, sergeants and notaries.[73] In other words, less than one-third of the total receipts from this area was provided by the war subsidy. It was their other powers which made the commissioners' errand a lucrative one.[74]

Of all the subsidy grants in 1325, the earliest actually came from Paris, where there was no problem of distance to delay the negotiations. Before the end of January, the capital promised to support 200 men-at-arms for six months if the king led the army personally, and for four months if he did not. The money would be raised by means of a *denier*-per-pound sales tax on merchandise to commence on 1 February. While it was levied, the king was not to seek any other *aide* or proclaim the *arrière-ban*.[75] Depending on the troops' salary and their duration of service, the total grant probably came to between 9,000 and 18,000 *l.t.*[76]

[68] BN Doat 146, fol. 172.

[69] E. Albe, "Cahors: Inventaire raisonné et analytique des archives municipales," pt. 2, *Bulletin de la Société . . . du Lot*, XLI (1920), nos. 314-315; Dufour, *Cahors*, pp. 92-93; Lacoste, *Quercy*, III, 39-40; AM Cajarc EE supp., no. 69.

[70] *INV AM Périgueux*, p. 67 (CC 46).   [71] *AHP*, XI, 296-302.

[72] Maillard, *Comptes*, nos. 10152-11263.   [73] *Ibid.*, nos. 8782-10151.

[74] Again, see Henneman, "Enquêteurs," pp. 324f., for a more detailed discussion of the role of commissioners with multiple powers in 1325.

[75] *Ord.*, I, 785-786; BN NAF 7373, fols. 193-195v. Cf. Vuitry, *Régime financier*, II, 168-170; Moreau de Beaumont, *Mémoire*, III, 230.

[76] Paris usually supported mounted troops rather than foot sergeants. In 1315, such a grant had been based on a daily salary of 7½ *s.t.* (*Ord.*, I, 602-603). By 1335, an ordinary knight would be paid 10 *s.t.* daily (AN P 2291, p. 189). Assuming that

Among those contributing were the tallageable dependents of the Paris cathedral chapter. Always jealous of their rights, the canons obtained a letter of non-prejudice in March, and a later royal letter ordered the king's officers to stop collecting from these persons and turn over what they had levied to those who normally collected *tailles* from them.[77] This text suggests a new agreement between crown and chapter whereby the latter would levy the subsidy from their own men and possibly retain part of it.

Vuitry found it noteworthy that Paris agreed to a sales tax, since the capital had paid a very large sum in 1292 to be excused from just such a levy. By 1325, however, France had become more accustomed to tax requests, and wealthy interests may well have decided that indirect taxes were preferable to other forms. Furthermore, the Parisians received additional guarantees in 1325 which made the levy more palatable. They were promised that no rights would be prejudiced, while in the event of peace, collections would be halted and two-thirds of any unspent tax receipts would be turned over to the municipal government.[78]

Other seigneurs besides the Paris chapter were concerned with the exactions on their tallageable men, and in April, the king ordered that subjects of nobles in the *villes bateices* of Normandy were not to be subject to the municipal *tailles*, but only to a sales tax of 2 *d./l.* granted by the towns.[79] The conditions and duration of this grant are not known, but a fragmentary unpublished account for the bailiwick of Caen has survived.[80] A curious case is that of Abbeville, in the county of Ponthieu, dowry possession of Queen Isabella of England. This town gave 2,000 pounds to Charles IV for the Gascon war and received in return certain concessions regarding municipal finances.[81] The crown also received a grant in early 1325 from the bailiwick of Senlis. The commissioners had executed the mid-January instructions promptly, visiting the towns of Senlis, Beauvais, Chaumont, Pontoise, Beaumont, and Chambli, and calling before them the "most sufficient" people for subsidy discussions.

---

the salary estimated in 1325 lay between these two figures, the contingent supported by Paris would have cost between 2250 and 3000 *l.t.* per month.

[77] AN K 41, nos. 11 *bis* and 12.

[78] See the citations note 75 above, and especially Vuitry, *Régime financier*, II, 168-169.

[79] *Ord.*, I, 787-788. This must be the document referred to by Moreau de Beaumont, *Mémoire*, II, 4-5.

[80] BN NAF 21155, no. 8, a document now almost completely illegible. See also *JT Ch. IV*, no. 7653.

[81] E. Prarond, *Histoire d'Abbeville avant la guerre de Cent Ans*, Paris, 1891, p. 318, citing document CC 8 in the now-destroyed Abbeville archives. Perhaps the town's generosity was a manifestation of the hostility of Isabella to her husband, Edward II.

They obtained a sales tax on many products, to be paid by the seller, with a reduced rate for outsiders (*forains*) selling wares in the towns.[82] The town of Provins in Champagne engaged in considerable negotiation at Paris during 1325, including the habitual complaints about royal sergeants. The town accounts mention an "imposition made for the year 1325."[83]

The rather limited documentation from northern and western France for 1325 is supplemented by financial texts, notably Mignon's inventory of accounts, which indicates that the 4 *d./l.* export tax and a 1 *d./l.* sales tax were the principal sources of support for the war.[84] Beyond this general statement, Mignon is regrettably vague. We have seen that lump-sum payments by towns or *vigueries* predominated in the Beaucaire district, while a 2 *d./l.* sales tax was levied in Cotentin. Yet Mignon described the accounts from both these districts simply as a subsidy levied "on certain towns."[85] Besides Paris and Senlis, the bailiwick of Troyes is known to have paid a 1 *d./l.* sales tax.[86] A sales tax was also used to pay the subsidy in five other districts (Amiens, Vitry, Vermandois, Sens, and Caux) but the actual rate is not known.[87] The inventory mentions taxes of unspecified type in seven other districts.[88] Mignon also indicated the dates at which collection began in certain areas and, not surprisingly, these show that the crown began to receive the subsidy much sooner in the North than in Languedoc.[89] We also have evidence of when the tax was halted following the treaty with England in June, i.e., on 19 June in the bailiwick of Caux and three days earlier in that of Sens.[90] In some places, however, it appears that collections continued through the year.[91]

---

[82] BN NAF 7600 (Fontanieu 67), fols. 153-162.

[83] M. Prou and J. d'Auriac (eds.), *Actes et comptes de la commune de Provins*, Provins, 1933, pp. 268-283, especially p. 275.

[84] Mignon, no. 1730.

[85] *Ibid.*, nos. 1764, 1787.

[86] *Ibid.*, nos. 1766-1767, for Troyes. *JT Ch. IV* entries indicating the sales tax of 1 *d./l.* are nos. 7607 (Troyes), 7396, 7469 (Senlis), 7561 and 7712 (Paris).

[87] Mignon, nos. 1740, 1815 (Amiens), 1768-1769, 1855-1856 (Vitry), 1736 (Vermandois), 1745 (Sens), and 1759 (Caux); *JT Ch. IV*, no. 7397 (Amiens), 9268 (Vitry), 7552, and 8997 (Sens).

[88] *Ibid.*, nos. 7587 (Orléans), 7657, 7748 (Touraine), 7689, 7970, 8329 (Gisors), 9173 (Bourges), 8720, 8743 (Meaux); Mignon, nos. 1770 (Chaumont) and 1779 (Périgord-Quercy).

[89] Mignon indicated the following dates for the beginning of specific accounts of collection: Senlis, 2 February (nos. 1732-33); Caux, 18 February (no. 1759); Sens, 3 March (no. 1745); and Vermandois, 11 March (no. 1736).

[90] *Ibid.*, nos. 1759, 1745. For the halting of collection in Languedoc, see above, note 54.

[91] Treasury journal entries indicating collection from Paris are scattered through the year with no apparent interruption. Mignon, nos. 1732, 1736, indicated no interruption of collection in the bailiwicks of Senlis and Vermandois.

One other type of tax levied through much of the kingdom in 1325 and 1326 was raised from royal notaries and sergeants. On various occasions, notaries were required to pay the crown a mark of silver. Throughout our period, the payment of this fee is badly documented, but in 1325, there seems to have been a particular effort to collect it. At the same time, the crown obtained money from royal sergeants, and since the commissioners had been empowered to reduce the number of these unpopular functionaries, one infers that they paid in order to retain their positions.[92] Their willingness to pay suggests that the post of sergeant could be lucrative. The many complaints against them generally arose from their alleged extortions and malpractices.

Certain documents of 1325 describe these levies on royal officials and connect them with the war in Gascony. One of them, referring to Périgord and Quercy, indicates that marks of silver were received from royal notaries and couriers, and subsidies of 40 *s.p.* from each horse sergeant and 20 *s.p.* from each foot sergeant.[93] An account of the receiver of Toulouse for the first half of 1325 mentions two silver marks for the Gascon war paid by notaries, 60 *s.p.* by each horse sergeant and 20 *s.p.* by each foot sergeant.[94] More cryptic references by Mignon indicate levy of the subsidy on sergeants in 1326 in the bailiwick of Vitry and "marks of silver" on sergeants in the Cotentin district.[95] The tax was also collected in Poitou and Saintonge.[96] These regions are so widely distributed that these taxes must have been levied throughout the realm subject to regional variations in amount.

If the treaty ratified by Edward II on 13 June 1325 brought an end to the collection of war subsidies in France, it did not end Anglo-French tensions or relieve Charles IV from his military commitments. The treaty provided that Edward II's son, the future Edward III, would render homage to Charles and be invested with Guyenne, while the French would receive 60,000 *l.p.* Pending the execution of these provisions, the French would hold the principal strong places in Gascony.[97] In charge of Gascony during the summer was Henri de Sully, who had already

---

[92] Certain special offices like royal notary were required to pay a silver mark on many occasions, not merely for wars but at other times when the king needed money. Presumably, such a payment justified certain fiscal privileges for the holders of these offices. For a succession of texts on this subject, see *INV AM Toulouse*, pp. 77-78 (AA 5, no. 124). See also the discussion of fiscal privilege in Chapter ix, pt. 2; and references to the tax on sergeants in *HL*, ix, 435.

[93] Mignon, no. 1779. [94] Maillard, *Comptes*, nos. 5117-5200.
[95] Mignon, nos. 1764, 1771. [96] Maillard, *Comptes*, nos. 12155-12169.
[97] Bréquigny, "Mémoire," 428-429; *Foedera*, ii pt. 2, pp. 141-142.

played a prominent role in the negotiations between the two kings.[98] In England, the formal cession of Guyenne to the younger Edward was accomplished at the beginning of September and the prince crossed the channel and performed homage on the 14th. Although Charles IV directed Sully to relinquish Gascony on 24 September, it was November before the French evacuation took place. We can hardly say that the régime of the younger Edward in Guyenne began in an atmosphere of good will. The settlement was made doubly shaky by the fact that it had been engineered largely by Queen Isabella of England, who had remained on the continent with her favorite, Mortimer, and who now was able to influence the younger Edward. Edward II rightly distrusted Isabella and therefore also the French treaty. His effort to force her return to England would keep Anglo-French relations in a state of tension.[99]

2. The Later Taxes of Charles IV

No sooner had he received homage for Guyenne than Charles IV had to concern himself with a new crisis in Flanders. Franco-Flemish relations underwent a change in 1322 with the accession of Count Louis I, who had been brought up in France and was married to a daughter of Philip V. The pro-French party (mostly wealthy patricians) at last regained political significance, the influence of Ghent supplanted that of Bruges, and the recent comital policy of independence (widely supported in Flanders) was reversed. Louis was devoted to his suzerain, unlike his predecessors, and French wars in the county after 1322 were not struggles between king and count but rather royal efforts to help the count suppress rebellions.[100]

Hostility to the new count produced a rebellion in 1323 which encompassed Bruges, Ypres, and maritime Flanders. Count Louis appealed to Charles IV for aid, and once the Gascon question appeared settled, the king responded. According to earlier treaty arrangements, the Flemings incurred a papal interdict by their rebellion against the crown, so warfare against them acquired a certain religious sanction. In the winter of 1325-1326, Charles IV prepared a punitive expedition, but in fact the

[98] *Ibid.*, pp. 102-103; Bréquigny, "Memoire," pp. 403f. Since the death of Philip V, Sully had been in the service of Edward II, but he remained a great officer of the crown in France.

[99] *Ibid.*, pp. 432-434. For Edward II's correspondence on the subject of Isabella in France, see *Foedera*, II pt. 2, pp. 147-148, 153, 154, 159.

[100] H. Lucas, *The Low Countries and the Hundred Years' War (1326-1347)*, Ann Arbor, 1929, p. 46 and passim.

crisis proved short-lived. After a brief military demonstration, Charles concluded the treaty of Arques in April 1326.[101] This agreement only postponed the day of reckoning for two years, but it did permit Charles IV to avoid his predecessors' pitfall of extended commitments in Flanders.

The efforts to finance this brief Flemish war are poorly documented. The crown certainly levied a subsidy, but it is not clear that the whole kingdom was taxed nor is there much basis for assessing the public reaction to royal tax-raising efforts. As with the recent Gascon war, the government made use of additional fiscal measures besides a war subsidy. The second group of large *finances* from Italians swelled treasury receipts in the final months of 1325,[102] and by the end of the year the 4 *d./l.* export tax had been restored in those regions where it had been canceled the previous June.[103] In some districts, collection of the earlier subsidy may have continued despite the June treaty; while in others, the Flemish conflict provided an excuse to resume levying taxes granted for the Gascon war but suspended when it ended.[104] Finally, some commissioners with multiple powers had never ceased to levy fines for acquisition of noble fiefs and violation of usury or monetary ordinances.[105]

The usually informative archives of lower Languedoc reveal nothing of taxation for the Flemish war, and possibly the seneschalsies of Beaucaire, Carcassonne, and Toulouse were not taxed at all.[106] Yet Béarn and Bigorre, which were even further from Flanders, were assessed 1,000 foot sergeants.[107] The crown also raised money in Périgord, which had contributed twice to the Gascon conflict, but collections were halted in the spring of 1326.[108] Mignon's inventory furnishes rather little informa-

[101] Langlois, in Lavisse, *Histoire*, III pt. 2, p. 310; F. Lot, *L'art militaire et les armées au moyen âge*, Paris, 1946, I, p. 275; A. and E. Molinier (eds.), *Chronique normande du XIVe siècle*, Paris, 1882, pp. 34-35, hereafter cited as *Chron. norm.* AN JJ 64, no. 154, is an act pardoning the Flemish rebels, dated 19 April 1326. A copy of the treaty, dated 26 April, is in AN P 2290, pp. 663-668.

[102] Henneman, "Italians," p. 29 and note 58.

[103] Thus Mignon, no. 1748, indicates that collections in three districts, which were halted on 8 July 1325, were resumed on 12 December.

[104] See above, notes 90-91.

[105] See above, note 59; Mignon, nos. 1859-1861; *Ord.*, I, 787; *INV AM Aurillac*, II, 88 (FF 47); BN Doat 103, fols. 137r-v, 153r-154r.

[106] Dognon, *Institutions*, p. 166, mentions one text at Montpellier which alluded briefly to the Flemish campaign in connection with a dispute between the *populares* and the municipality over taxation.

[107] *JT Ch. IV*, no. 9681.

[108] Prof. C. H. Taylor very kindly furnished me with excerpts of AM Périgueux CC 47. This register, on fol. 29v, indicates a gift made to the royal commissioner who

tion about a subsidy for the Flemish expedition. A tax was collected in the bailiwick of Orléans and "on certain towns" in Saintonge, Angoulême, Poitou, Limousin, and La Marche. Collections from the northern town of Douai ran from November 1325 to 24 June 1326.[109] Tournai also contributed to this war.[110] Besides his explicit references to the Flemish war, Mignon listed some accounts under his general rubric of war subsidies without making clear which war of 1325-1326 was involved. The bailiwicks of Senlis, Troyes, and Touraine are in this category.[111]

The surviving account for Poitou and Limousin shows total collections of around 4,700 pounds, more than double what had been collected there a year earlier for the Gascon war.[112] Yet the account also states that more than 40 percent of this total was collected *after* it had been ordered that the tax cease.[113] It is not clear whether these last sums were used, returned, or credited on the next subsidy. By this time, at any rate, the crown was embroiled in new troubles in Gascony.

Edward II's well-founded distrust of his queen had been extended to their son and heir who, as duke of Guyenne, was effectively under the tutelage of Isabella and Mortimer. On several occasions in the early months of 1326, the English king had taken action against those believed to be carrying seditious letters to England from Isabella,[114] and he continued his unremitting efforts to effect her (and Mortimer's) return to England. As a means of forcing their return, he began to reassert his old rights in Guyenne, with the result that the two Edwards were soon giving conflicting orders in the duchy, those of the prince no doubt reflecting the wishes of Isabella and Mortimer.[115] If the French court was scandalized by the behavior of Isabella and Mortimer,[116] it was no less concerned at the meddling of Edward II in his son's Gascon *apanage*, and military preparations began in France in the spring of 1326. The king

---

was levying the Flanders war subsidy. The consuls later received a letter halting subsidy collections (fol. 25v), and we must presume that the tax was stopped because of the treaty with the Flemings.

[109] Mignon, nos. 1744, 1746, 1777, 1861.

[110] A. d'Herbomez, "Notes et documents pour servir à l'histoire des rois fils de Philippe le Bel," *BEC*, LIX (1898), 698.

[111] Mignon, nos. 1732-33, 1751, 1766. Another ambiguous case is that of Saint-Quentin in Vermandois: Le Maire, *St. Quentin*, I, no. 340.

[112] Maillard, *Comptes*, nos. 11264-12154.

[113] *Ibid.*, nos. 11860-12154. It is not stated when the tax was halted, but about 2,050 pounds appear in the accounts after the cancellation order.

[114] See the documents cited by Hellot, "Chron. parisienne," p. 105, notes 152-154.

[115] Bréquigny, "Mémoire," pp. 433-436. See above, note 99, and H. Kervyn de Lettenhove (ed.), *Oeuvres de Froissart*, Brussels, 1876-1877, XVIII, 7-12.

[116] Perroy, *The Hundred Years War*, p. 58.

dispatched his cousin, Alfonse of Spain, lord of Lunel, to the Southwest as royal lieutenant in Languedoc,[117] and early in the summer, hostilities were reopened when Anglo-Gascon pillagers attacked various French installations with the knowledge and connivance of Edward II.[118] If any declaration of war was needed, it was provided by the latter's letter of 19 June to Charles IV, which accused the French of deliberately harboring the treasonous Mortimer.[119] More serious was Edward's seizure of the property belonging to the priories of French religious establishments located in England.[120]

In this crisis, Charles IV held the only central assembly of his reign, although it scarcely merits the term "assembly." No towns were involved, and it appears that the barons and prelates who assembled at Meaux were a fairly restricted group whose presence constituted little more than an enlargement of the royal council. The date of the meeting is not known, but it probably occurred towards the end of July or the beginning of August if we are to believe a usually reliable chronicler. According to his account, the king was acting with the advice of this assembly when he ordered that on 16 August 1326, the persons and property of all Englishmen in the kingdom be seized in reprisal for the action of Edward II.[121] The assembled magnates promised the king "certain aid" from themselves and from their subjects, and on the basis of this response the king dispatched tax commissioners, although apparently not immediately.[122] While these events were taking place, Isabella and the younger Edward were in the Low Countries, where on 25 August, a marriage contract was drawn up between Edward and Philippa, daughter of the count of Hainault-Holland.[123] It was in Hainault that an attack on Edward II was planned, and the ensuing invasion of England resulted in the arrest of Edward II in November and his deposition in favor of Edward III in January 1327.[124]

---

[117] HL, IX, 439.

[118] Ibid.; Cont. Nangis, II, 78.

[119] Bréquigny, "Mémoire," p. 437.

[120] "Chron. parisienne," p. 105.

[121] Ibid., pp. 105-106.

[122] Strayer and Taylor, Studies, pp. 198-200, and commentary on pp. 175f. The date of this document, 20 October, presumably marked the beginning of tax negotiations in Burgundy.

[123] Lucas, Low Countries, p. 55; J. Viard and E. Déprez (eds.), Chronique de Jean le Bel, I, Paris, 1904, 77-81, describes the actual marriage, which followed Edward's accession as king.

[124] The struggle between Edward II and his wife and son is documented by correspondence in Foedera, II pt. 2, pp. 162, 167-169. See also Lucas, Low Countries, pp. 55-56; Jean le Bel, I, 13-32; Cont. Nangis, II, 70-72.

Against this background of internal and external politics, the French crown undertook to collect a new war subsidy, the third in two years and, for some regions, the fourth since February 1324. Because the king had been approaching taxation in such a cautious manner, the negotiations in some places may have gone more smoothly than in 1325. In Languedoc, new hostilities along the Gascon border had broken out by early summer so the South was confronted by outright war, not merely the expectation of war as in the winter of 1324-1325. We are told that most of the nobles of Languedoc rendered personal military service under Alfonse of Spain.[125] In much of Languedoc, moreover, little had been collected in 1325 because of the June suspension of taxes, so the tax of 1326 was less a new subsidy than reinstatement of the older one.[126] As already indicated, it appears that lower Languedoc had escaped taxation for the intervening war in Flanders.

Least fortunate were the regions of upper Languedoc which had been raising and maintaining their own sergeants rather than promising subsidies in money. Perhaps this practice was less costly than paying a royal tax, and it certainly preserved the principle that military service was as good as money when it came to meeting a town's defense obligations. However, once such sergeants were assembled and armed, the town had to pay them, and it is doubtful that towns employing this method ever derived much benefit from the suspension of taxes when peace was made. The most frequently taxed region in France during this period seems to have been Périgord, which had provided sergeants for Gascony in two different years and also had been approached for the Flemish campaign. The municipal accounts of Périgueux show that the crown had ended its earlier seizure of that community's revenues. The mayor and consuls were allowed to raise a local tax to pay for repair of the walls, and received help from royal officers in making recalcitrant inhabitants contribute.[127]

There was considerable resistance to paying at Périgueux in 1326, for the accounts speak of "rebels in the matter of the sergeants,"[128] and one inhabitant was subsequently imprisoned for attacking a royal tax collector.[129] It appears that no sooner had the Flemish war subsidy been canceled, than the royal treasurer at Cahors approached Périgueux for aid

---

[125] Molinier, *HL*, IX, 440, note 4, discussing *HL*, X, cols. 662-667.

[126] *Gr. Chartrier*, no. 2355, is quite explicit in saying that the tax of the year before was simply reinstated at Montpellier.

[127] *INV AM Périgueux*, p. 68 (CC 47).   [128] AM Périgueux CC 47, fol. 23r.

[129] *INV AM Périgueux*, pp. 298-299 (FF 198).

in the new Gascon crisis. The request was for 600 *l.t.* to support 100 sergeants for 60 days of service. This time the crown seems to have wanted
the money directly rather than a contingent of men as in the past two
years, for the treasurer had mentioned a definite sum and a royal notary
later arrived to demand money. This notary was bribed 100 *s.* to avoid
any repetition of the seizures of the year before, and the accounts mention messages from the town to the seneschal,[130] but we do not know how
the sum was to be raised. However, on 25 August, Alfonse of Spain
urgently requested the town to send 60 fully armed sergeants to him,[131]
thus apparently abandoning the proposed pecuniary subsidy and accepting the traditional contingent in order to obtain the troops quickly. But
although he was asking for a smaller number of sergeants than in the
past and had promised non-prejudice of local rights, the town still resisted compliance. On 20 September, Alfonse ordered that all inhabitants
of Périgueux contribute to the cost of the sergeants or be compelled to
do so *per captionem et venditionem bonorum suorum*.[132] Besides war
subsidies, there were pressures from usury and fief commissioners, to
whom a single bourgeois of Périgueux had to pay 1,000 pounds (probably as a result of the 1325 investigations).[133] Such evidence as we have
suggests that individuals had to deal separately with these *enquêteurs*
and that there was no effort to combine such fines with the subsidy at the
town level.

Investigation of usury and fiefs certainly played a role in the tax negotiations at Cahors, where the royal effort to obtain a subsidy had begun
in May. Early in June, Charles IV wrote to the subsidy commissioners at
the request of the consuls of Cahors, ordering them to place certain limitations on *franc-fief* and usury collections.[134] Although possibly over-
zealous, they accomplished their fiscal mission, for by July, Cahors had
sent 100 sergeants to the war and had fined for an additional 500 *l.t.*
which released the town from any other military payments during the
year.[135] The town of Gourdon also contributed to the subsidy of 1326,
judging from a reference in a much later document.[136] At Cajarc, the

---

[130] *Ibid.,* p. 68; AM Périgueux CC 47, fols. 16r, 24v.

[131] Moreau, *Recueil,* pp. 213-214.   [132] *Ibid.,* pp. 257-258.

[133] Boutaric, *Actes,* II, no. 7852. Another such fine, larger than the annual war
subsidy paid by most towns, had been levied in 1325 by *réformateurs* in Périgord
and Quercy against a person accused of violating a royal safeguard. Originally 1200
l.t., it was reduced to 500 pounds by royal order (AN JJ 62, no. 495).

[134] BN Doat 119, fol. 57. Lacoste, *Quercy,* III, 40, stated that the commissioner
raising money in Quercy exercised his powers with "blind severity."

[135] BN Doat 119, fol. 60; Albe, "Cahors INV," no. 318; Lacoste, *Quercy,* III, 40.

[136] AM Gourdon CC 47, no. 34.

crown attempted to levy sergeants as in 1324 but encountered a distinct lack of enthusiasm. The consuls called for volunteers, but after six days of repeated proclamations they had found only two persons willing to serve. Finally, on 9 July, ten more sergeants were enrolled and Cajarc finally was able to send a contingent to Bergerac, paid for forty days' service.[137]

In nearby Rouergue, Alfonse of Spain had more difficulty than elsewhere in obtaining aid for the war. Negotiations at Najac were accompanied by the appearance of royal *réformateurs*[138] who may have had to apply some pressure. Resistance to taxation in Rouergue induced King Charles in July to order the suspension of collections pending new instructions.[139] His lieutenant in Languedoc, however, needed money with which to pay troops. On 9 August, therefore, Alfonse ordered his men to collect from those immediately subject to the king, notwithstanding any royal letters, past or future, which might say otherwise.[140] Saint-Antonin, which had already been excused in May from contributing to the Flemish expedition,[141] had received during the summer the sort of letters Alfonse had in mind. One ordered suspension of fines for usury and *franc-fief*, while another suspended the subsidy as well.[142] In September, Alfonse issued urgent new orders: necessity dictated that the subsidy be collected immediately from everybody, directly subject to the king or not, including the men of the barons and prelates. Soon thereafter, however, he again suspended collection,[143] perhaps on orders from Paris. On 5 October, he instructed the seneschal of Beaucaire to cease using force on the subjects of the king of Majorca.[144]

Documents from Millau indicate a grant amounting to 1,000 *l.t.*, half of it being a subsidy in money, while the remainder was in the form of a contingent of sergeants whose salaries came to 500 *l.t.* This tax was obtained by commissioners who combined the functions of *réformateur* with their responsibility for raising subsidies. They agreed to various conditions which the consuls of Millau attached to the grant; there must

---

[137] AM Cajarc EE 3, no. 290; EE 4, no. 352.

[138] AD Aveyron 2E 178, no. 2, fols. 201-203.

[139] BN Doat 146, fol. 177.

[140] *Ibid.*; de Gaujal, *Etudes*, II, 164; *HL*, IX, 440; BN *Coll. Languedoc* 83, fol. 198r-v.

[141] J. L. Rigal and P. A. Verlaguet, *Notes pour servir à l'histoire de Rouergue*, Rodez, 1913, I, 300, note 1. This royal letter of 31 May may be only a cancellation of taxes because the Flemish war had ended, but it also could mean that Saint-Antonin was given special treatment not accorded to other communities in Rouergue.

[142] BN Doat 146, fol. 177.   [143] *HL*, IX, p. 440; de Gaujal, *Etudes*, II, 165.

[144] *HL*, IX, 440. These subjects were at Montpellier.

actually be a war in progress and other towns directly subject to the king must similarly contribute; payments would be in installments and no more taxes would be requested for a year; nothing would be paid if the king canceled subsidies because of peace. This arrangement was not concluded until the end of January 1327, although negotiations had been underway for some time.[145]

The crown was more successful in taxing lower Languedoc in 1326, although opposition was not lacking. The *capitouls* of Toulouse furnished men-at-arms and 2,000 foot soldiers, but only for thirty days, after which the troops might return home without permission. It appears that the town actually intended to provide men rather than money, and this non-prejudicial "gracious gift" may have been a mixed blessing to the crown.[146] Montpellier, which had evidently paid none of the 1,500 *l.t.* promised the year before, now agreed to contribute this sum and 500 pounds more, payable in two installments in July and September 1326. To raise the money, the consuls levied municipal taxes—a sales tax on wine, 6 *d./l.* on revenues, and another levy on capital. They had to request royal help in enforcing payment, as opposition continued for two years.[147] A subsidy was also collected from the *viguerie* of Alès,[148] but in Velay, the nobles and clergy insisted on the exemption of their tallageable men, and the seneschal's lieutenant ordered an investigation of the claims.[149]

The entire effort to obtain money from Languedoc, while meeting with some success, was complicated further by the fact that the pope, involved in a struggle with the Emperor Louis IV, was taxing the French clergy at this time to support his own military operations against the Ghibellines in Lombardy. On 12 October, Charles IV ordered a halt to this levy, but it apparently continued to be collected well into 1327.[150]

Outside Languedoc, we have much less evidence of Gascon war subsidy collections in 1326. Mignon mentions the existence of such taxes in the five bailiwicks of Senlis, Vitry, Vermandois, Orléans, and

---

[145] Artières, *A. H. Rouergue*, VII, nos. 151, 152; AM Millau CC 345, fol. 23v, EE 118, no. 113, EE 1 (this last is a roll of municipal tax collections).

[146] *INV AM Toulouse*, p. 29 (AA 3, no. 162).

[147] *Gr. Chartrier*, nos. 2355, 3410, 3524, 3298, 3300. The last two of these texts belong to 1328, when the town was still requiring royal assistance to compel some citizens to pay the money.

[148] AM Alès 1 S-12, no. 8.   [149] Delcambre, *Etats Velay*, P.J. 1.

[150] *Ord.*, I, 798-799; BN *ms. lat.* 11016, fol. 86r-v; *HL*, IX, 440. Despite the royal order, the pope continued to collect the tax in 1327 and acknowledged receipt of 250 pounds from one abbot in the fall (BN *Coll. Languedoc* 83, fol. 26or). According to *Cont. Nangis*, II, 77, the king agreed to tolerate the pope's tax as a condition for the new clerical tenth granted in 1326.

Troyes,[151] and in the county of Eu in Normandy.[152] That a subsidy was solicited from towns and nobles in the duchy of Burgundy and in the bailiwicks of Mâcon and Lyon is proven by the October document which mentions the midsummer assembly at Meaux.[153]

This meeting of barons and prelates was probably confined to important magnates of Languedoil and intended to lay the groundwork for the subsidy in the north and center of the kingdom. Farther removed from the Gascon front, these lands had paid the war subsidy of 1325 and a second tax for the Flemish campaign. It was doubtless considered necessary to test public opinion before asking them for still another tax, especially since the Gascon conflict appeared to be local in nature and not a direct threat to the northern part of the realm. If collection everywhere in Languedoil began as late as it did in Burgundy (i.e., October), the crown must have exercised considerable caution even after the midsummer assembly, and it is probable that little money was collected prior to the end of 1326. In calling together these barons and prelates, Charles IV had before him Edward II's hostile letter of mid-June and could also point to the English seizure of French property in pleading the justice of reopening the war.[154] On 18 July, moreover, Charles issued an ordinance on fief alienations which reduced the fines for new acquisitions by about two-thirds, to the level of 1275.[155] Given the accumulating opposition to these fines, the gesture must be seen as a concession to public opinion on the eve of a new subsidy request.[156] Having convened at Meaux, the barons and prelates, as we have seen, endorsed retaliatory measures against English property in France and approved the subsidy in principle.[157]

Actual negotiations got underway slowly, and most of the resultant subsidy grants are known to us mainly because of their subsequent cancellation. In Poitou and Limousin, a tax in lieu of military service in Gascony was collected for a time, but on 6 March 1327, Charles IV ordered the money returned.[158]

[151] Mignon, nos. 1804 (Senlis); 1768-1769, 1855-1856 (Vitry); 1736 (Vermandois); 1746 (Orléans); and 1766 (Troyes).

[152] *Ibid.*, no. 1760. D'Herbomez, "Notes," pp. 698-699, indicated that the king approached Tournai for the subsidy for Gascony, but received only an evasive reply to the effect that the citizens were willing to serve the king loyally as in the past.

[153] See above, note 122.   [154] See above, notes 119-120.

[155] *Ord.*, I, 797-798; *INV AM Aurillac*, I, 429 (CC 26); AN P 2288, pp. 1122-24, 1128-30; Carreau, *Commissaires*, p. 40.

[156] Henneman, "Enquêteurs," p. 329.   [157] See above, notes 121-122.

[158] *AHP*, XLIV, 387-388. In *JT Ch. IV*, nos. 9730, 9832, are references to subsidy collections in Poitou and Limousin in 1326.

Another tax levied and then canceled was a *maltôte* in the county of Boulogne.[159] The town of Provins did not even grant a tax until February 1327 and then only with great reluctance. Proctors of the town made three trips to Paris in the course of month-long negotiations before agreeing to pay 1,000 *l.t.*[160] Paris itself did not agree to any subsidy until 12 February, when it finally granted 200 men-at-arms under conditions similar to those established two years earlier. All inhabitants of the town and its suburbs who were free or occupying non-servile land would be required to pay, and the money was to be levied by the Parisians themselves and paid into the royal treasury on a monthly basis beginning 1 May. The tax would end in the event of peace.[161]

Warfare in this period tended to be characterized by summer campaigns and winter truces. In reviewing the known tax grants which followed the Meaux assembly, we may conclude that Charles IV was less interested in money for 1326, than in having a strong basis for negotiating a general subsidy in time for a conclusive Gascon campaign in 1327. The government was prepared to minimize friction by holding rather leisurely negotiations.

The king's policy in 1326-1327 was evidently based upon an important memorandum drawn up by royal advisers. According to this document, the crown would plan on a standing army of 1,000 mounted men and 4,000 foot sergeants for nine months prior to 1 May. On that date, the king would arrive to take direction of the war, and the army would be increased to 5,000 men-at-arms and 20,000 sergeants who would serve for a five-month campaign. The standing army would cost 21,000 *l.t.* per month, or 189,000 *l.t.* prior to May. The five-month summer army was expected to entail a total cost of 525,000 *l.t.*[162] This document explains why Paris planned to defer collection of its tax until May.[163] The fact that the nine-month preparatory build-up would begin on 1 August (about the time of the assembly at Meaux) suggests that these royal plans for reducing Gascony were discussed and approved by the magnates at the midsummer meeting.

[159] *INV AD Pas-de-Calais*, p. 358 (A 462).

[160] Prou and d'Auriac, *Comptes*, pp. 284-285. Like Montpellier, the town government had to obtain royal help in forcing payment from some citizens.

[161] AN JJ 64, no. 231; BN NAF 7601 (Fontanieu 68), fols. 99-101r. In "Chron. parisienne," p. 111, Paris and several other towns are said to have made a *grant subside* to the king in the latter part of 1326 (old style).

[162] Jusselin, "Comment la France . . . ," p. 220.

[163] See above, note 161. A text in AM Millau CC 505, indicates that taxes levied there in 1327 were to be held until 1 May and returned in case of peace.

Although we have seen that some tax negotiations began late in 1326, the comprehensive royal program really did not get underway until 23 January 1327. On that date, Charles IV issued a number of important orders. Among these were instructions sent to commissioners who would negotiate the proposed general subsidy. Their tone suggests a careful and conciliatory approach, with the king sounding almost apologetic about asking for a new tax. The commissioners were told to convene regional assemblies of the nobles and of the towns (who were to send two to four representatives with *tout pouvoir*). At such meetings, they were to enumerate the iniquities of the English and to stress that the matter touched everybody. They were to ask the nobles to assess their subjects at the rate of four foot sergeants per 100 hearths for six months because the crown had suspended the raising of war subsidies in the lands of the nobles. The towns were to furnish sergeants at the same rate or "sums of money of the [same] value." Letters of non-prejudice would be granted if desired, and the assemblies were to be informed that *réformateurs* had been named to redress grievances.[164]

On the same date in January, the government issued other enactments, two of them devoted to *franc-fief* and *amortissement*. These fines for fief acquisitions, which had been decreased dramatically the preceding summer, were now raised again, although not to the high level of 1321-1325. Given the use of these fines in subsidy negotiations during 1325, the increased rates of 1327 were not coincidental, but formed an integral part of the royal fiscal program.[165] Another act of 23 January concerned the execution of cartage services owed for the Gascon war.[166] These also were an important part of the royal program, since the government memorandum on the war estimated that such services would cost 85,000 *l.t.*[167] Besides these various circulars to local officers of the crown, Charles IV also named a new military commander in the Southwest.[168]

---

[164] Petit, *Essai de restitution*, pp. 203-204; BN Dupuy 673, fol. 8r-v. These texts are undated, but Jusselin, "Comment la France . . . ," p. 213, and Lot, *L'art militaire*, I, 332, both indicate that they are part of a larger document dated 23 January 1327 and printed by Funck-Brentano in *De exercituum commeatibus*, which I have been unable to locate. The text cited above, note 162, belongs to the same group of documents. Another document, dealing with the taxation of sea-borne merchandise, has been summarized by Petit, *Essai de Restitution*, p. 63.

[165] *Ibid.*, pp. 27, 87; *Ord.*, XI, 501-502; Henneman, "Enquêteurs," pp. 329-330.

[166] AN P 2289, pp. 934-958.

[167] Jusselin, "Comment la France . . . ," p. 221. Another text, *ibid.*, p. 222, deals with the naval aspect of the planned royal war effort.

[168] BN Doat 8, fols. 135-137. Two weeks later a new lieutenant was named in Poitou and Saintonge (*AHP*, XI, 274-275).

In making all these plans, the crown presumably did not anticipate the swift overthrow of Edward II by his wife and son. The events in England at the start of 1327 did not automatically guarantee a change in Anglo-French relations, but they placed Charles IV's sister in the dominant position at the Plantagenet court. Isabella and her son doubtless realized that only prompt conciliatory action would save England's remaining foothold in Gascony. Edward III soon released the French property which had been seized in England[169] and began negotiations with France. At length, a treaty was concluded (31 March) which ended the Anglo-French troubles for the rest of Charles IV's reign.[170]

This treaty brought an end to the ambitious war preparations undertaken in France, and it explains the various tax cancellations alluded to above.[171] It also explains why a chronicler reported that the grant by Paris *tantost aprez fut du roy rappellé*.[172] In some places, royal officials were reluctant to halt the proceedings. A grant by Narbonne, on 19 February 1327, seems too early to have resulted from negotiations started in January. It must have been a very belated tax for 1326, agreed upon only after extended bargaining. Like most subsidy grants, Narbonne's was conditional upon the actual existence of war, and although the war soon ended, the crown's commissioners probably felt that it should be collected to help pay for the war of 1326. In any case, it appears that they concealed word of the treaty, as in 1325, for on 26 April, they ordered the town to pay within two weeks. Narbonne refused to pay, claiming to have heard from the pope that peace had been made. The decision on the tax was deferred, pending official word from Paris.[173] In due course, the town must have escaped paying.

If the peace with England ended all hopes for a French conquest of Gascony and a war subsidy to support this campaign, it must have also left Charles IV embarrassed with debts and military expenditures which somehow had to be met. It became necessary to exploit sources of revenue which were traditionally regarded as "ordinary." One such revenue came from coinage profits, and these reached a high level in 1326 but may have fallen off in 1327.[174] There remained, however, the resourceful

---

[169] Lucas, *Low Countries*, p. 56.

[170] *HL*, IX, 446; AN K 41, no. 16; *Foedera*, II pt. 2, pp. 185-187. The treaty was ratified in England on 11 April.

[171] See above, notes 158-160.   [172] "Chron, parisienne," p. 111.

[173] BN Doat 52, fol. 161r; BN *Coll. Languedoc* 83, fol. 202r. In *HL*, IX, 445, it seems to be assumed that these negotiations at Narbonne had begun in 1327 and were part of the new year's tax drive.

[174] See Appendix 1; Miskimin, *Money*, p. 43.

réformateurs and investigatory commissioners, whose powers permitted them to levy a variety of fines. Large fines and sales of privileges which had swelled the treasury receipts in earlier peacetime years now became important again.

Commissioners looking into fief acquisitions were able to enforce the higher rates established for the fines in January 1327, even though these no longer had relevance to negotiation of subsidy. As in 1325, the seneschalsy of Toulouse provided a lucrative arena for their operations. On 18 June 1327, communities in the *jugerie* of Rivière concluded a transaction with persons called *réformateurs* in the districts of Carcassonne, Toulouse and Bigorre, with special responsibility over fief acquisitions. This arrangement set up a levy of 15 *l.t.* on every inhabitant who had acquired a noble fief, but the sum was to be raised by the consuls and then turned over to the crown. It was stipulated that this levy was to acquit the towns of all obligations for new acquisitions, that the consuls could use force in collecting it, and that payment would cease if the king should in the future excuse the whole seneschalsy from paying these fines.[175] Not only is the war ignored here, but the tax was to be levied only on those who had acquired fiefs, as opposed to the tax levied in the same *jugerie* two years earlier which affected everybody. The new tax was intended to produce only 1,500 *l.t.* Towns of another Toulousian *jugerie* (that of Verdun) paid the crown a 10 *s.* hearth tax in 1327, to satisfy commissioners who were investigating alleged "excesses."[176] Some 3,000 *l.t.* were obtained by the same *réformateurs* from seventeen communities in Bigorre to cover both fief alienations and "excesses."[177] Elsewhere, the crown obtained large sums from Limoges, Lautrec, and Montolieu on a variety of pretexts,[178] and commissioners charged with finding money were active throughout the kingdom.[179]

Thus the grandiose scheme for making an end to the Gascon problem had given way to the traditional policy of peacetime fiscal expedients. The swift deposition of Edward II and his son's timely concessions to France had saved Guyenne for England. Because the elaborate fiscal-military plans evolved in France in the winter of 1326-1327 were interrupted at such an early stage, there is no way we can evaluate their chances for success. The lesson of 1321 did not have to be learned again, and Charles IV studiously avoided peacetime subsidies. As a result, his

---

[175] AN JJ 65A, no. 99.   [176] AN JJ 64, no. 548.
[177] AN JJ 65A, no. 83.
[178] AN JJ 67, no. 85; JJ 65A, no. 62; Mahul, *Cartulaire*, I, 136.
[179] Henneman, "Enquêteurs," pp. 331-332; BN NAF 7373, fol. 297; AD Aveyron 2E 178, no. 2, fol. 211v; Molinier, in *HL*, IX, 446-448, note 6.

financial position was not very satisfactory in 1327 and irregular expedients had to be used in order to find money for the government.

On the other hand, the general position of the government appears to have improved during the reign of Charles IV. He was a militarily successful king, having apparently ended the trouble in Flanders and twice defeating the English in Guyenne. These victories were achieved quickly and with rather light taxation. Opposition to subsidies was inevitable after the reign of Philip V, but Charles IV appears to have kept it at a minimum by his generally conservative approach. Moreover, the territorial acquisitions in Guyenne were valuable ones, judging from the treasury records. Domainal receipts in 1328-1330 were substantially higher than in 1322-1325.[180]

The greater domainal receipts may also have been due to more efficient administration of the domain, for it was in the winter of 1327-1328 that Charles IV held the great census of hearths and parishes which has been referred to previously. As already pointed out, this inquest was probably conducted for fiscal purposes, and it is interesting that royal officers were able to carry it out in so much of the kingdom.[181] This fact alone may be some measure of the king's political strength in the final months of his life. A final factor, which may have influenced both the success of the census and the political strength of the monarchy under Charles IV, is the fact that Charles had a more legitimate and uncontested title to the throne than either his predecessor or his successor.

Both the political strength and the legitimacy of title were not enduring assets, however, for towards the end of 1327, Charles IV fell ill. Two months later he was dead, leaving a pregnant queen but no sons or brothers.[182] Although the Hundred Years' War would give notoriety to the succession of 1328, the matter was actually resolved with less difficulty than in 1316. When Charles became seriously sick, the oldest of his three cousins, Philip of Valois, was accepted as regent. He was to hold this position if the king died and left a posthumous son, but the magnates agreed that he would become king if the queen gave birth to a daughter.[183] When this latter event occurred in April, Philip's accession was unopposed. Although lacking in personal distinction, he was the son of

---

[180] Appendix 1, Table 3.

[181] See above, Chapter 1, note 19. Three 17th century inventories offer evidence of the inquest while it was in progress: BN NAF 7430, fol. 211r; BN Doat 254, fol. 1129r-v; BN Doat 255, fol. 371v.

[182] J. Viard (ed.), *Les grandes chroniques de France*, IX, Paris, 1937, 65.

[183] *Ibid.*, pp. 71-73; Cazelles, *Soc. politique*, pp. 47-48, 71.

a distinguished father and brought into the royal domain the greatest *apanage* in the kingdom.

3. Philip VI's First Year as King

The fact that Philip VI's title to the throne was open to challenge would be important for the entire reign. Where women had been excluded from the throne since 1316, the decision of 1328 had the effect of denying their right even to transmit a claim to their male heirs. Yet if the concept of legitimacy was to have any future at all, this step may have been a necessary consequence of the earlier female exclusion. Cazelles has pointed out that Edward III's claim lost much of its validity after a son was born to Joan of Evreux (Louis X's daughter) in 1332.[184] Permitting women to transmit a claim would leave room for serious future complications, and the Valois succession was therefore dictated by practical politics. Nevertheless, the French were not accustomed to changes of dynasty and the Valois would long be preoccupied with the question of legitimacy and afflicted by a certain lack of confidence.[185]

Of considerable immediate importance was the fact that Philip VI was politically indebted to the great magnates for sanctioning his accession to the regency and then the throne. Early enactments of the new reign, pleasing to the nobles but unpopular with the clergy, have suggested to Cazelles that Philip was to some extent the prisoner of his bargains with the lay magnates.[186] In any case, the conservative fiscal stance of Charles IV's reign would have to be continued for the present, and the Chamber of Accounts faction would have to wait for several more years before regaining influence at court.

[184] *Ibid.*, p. 51. It was decided in 1328 to return Navarre to Joan as her rightful inheritance. The other important lands belonging to her paternal grandmother were Champagne and Brie, and these the crown was not willing to surrender. They were to be administered by the king pending some later settlement (Cazelles, *Soc. politique*, pp. 49-50). This settlement was finally concluded in 1336 (AN JJ 70, no. 152). The Evreux were to receive Angoulême and Mortain and certain annuities in return for renouncing the counties. See J. Viard, "Philippe de Valois. Le début du règne," *BEC*, xcv (1934), pp. 270-272. As executed, this settlement did not prove satisfactory to Joan's son, Charles, who revived the question of Champagne and Brie in the 1350s. See D. F. Secousse, *Mémoires pour servir à l'histoire de Charles II, roi de Navarre et comte d'Evreux, surnommé le Mauvais*, II, Paris, 1758 (hereafter cited as *Charles II*), pp. 23-27.

[185] See above, Chapter I, note 35. Cazelles, *Soc. politique*, p. 193, notes Philip VI's preoccupation with the future of his own dynasty, and Bautier, "Chancellerie," pp. 125-126, makes the interesting point that the Valois were so solicitous of their legitimacy that they refrained from using the great seal until after their coronations.

[186] Cazelles, *Soc. politique*, pp. 56, 71-72, 424.

Among Philip's strong supporters was Louis of Nevers, count of Flanders, whose loyalty to the crown had been repaid by Charles IV's assistance against the Flemish rebels in 1325-1326. Now Louis needed help again, for the rebellion in maritime Flanders had flared up once more. In supporting the new king, Louis doubtless expected some royal assistance in suppressing the rebels once and for all.[187] The experiences of the past quarter-century could hardly have made the French nobility enthusiastic about another Flemish campaign, but in an assembly held after the coronation at Reims they were persuaded to support the venture when the aged and highly respected constable, Gaucher de Châtillon, spoke in favor of it.[188] Within three weeks after the coronation, the arrière-ban was proclaimed, with the military mustering point to be Arras on 31 July.[189] There followed the short and glorious Flemish campaign which had eluded Philip's predecessors. The rebel forces were destroyed in the battle of Cassel late in August[190] and Louis regained full control of Flanders. The French crown claimed a war indemnity and a systematic inquest was undertaken after the victory to arrange for the confiscation of rebel property which was to be divided between the count and the king.[191]

This short campaign naturally involved a new war subsidy, beginning with the military summons of 18 June. Two letters addressed to the seneschal of Beaucaire on this date indicated the procedure to be used. The shorter document[192] ordered the seneschal to have proclaimed throughout his jurisdiction the summons of all non-nobles "of whatever estate they may be" to come to the king at Arras on 31 July armed "each according to his power and estate." But "if by chance" any could not come they might substitute a money payment that would permit others to go in their place. The seneschal was to forward all funds collected in this way to the treasury at Paris as soon as possible so the money could be used to pay the troops being sent. The second letter[193] reviewed the

---

[187] Viard, "Début," p. 280; Jassemin, "Papiers," pp. 201-206, publishes letters of Louis I of Flanders complaining to his towns about violations of the treaty of Arques. See also *Gr. Chron*, IX, 78; and Cazelles, *Soc. politique*, p. 54.

[188] *Ibid.*, p. 55; Viard, "Début," p. 281.

[189] *HL*, X, col. 674. Some chroniclers and later historians were misled into thinking that the army was to convene earlier, on 22 July. On the confusion over dates and the general nature of the summons, see J. Viard, "La guerre de Flandre (1328)," *BEC*, LXXXIII (1922), 364-365 and notes.

[190] Lucas, *Low Countries*, pp. 84-89; *Jean le Bel*, I, 93-94; *Gr. Chron.*, IX, 88-91.

[191] Viard, "Guerre," pp. 381-382. For litigation over the apportionment of the indemnity, see Furgeot, *Actes*, I, no. 1501.

[192] *HL*, X, col. 674.　　　　　　　[193] *Ibid.*, cols. 674-676.

crown's grievances against the Flemings and added that the king would be at Arras on the appointed day to take action against them. The summons to all non-nobles was repeated and the seneschal ordered to assemble before him the "notable persons" and specifically explain to them the king's intentions. This letter was clearly intended for public consumption, while the one accompanying it would seem to have been in the nature of private instructions to the seneschal, stressing as it did the financial aspects of the summons not mentioned in the longer missive.

A document listing the sums collected for this subsidy of 1328 indicates that in five southern districts the tax "*fut imposé par villes.*"[194] As in previous years, the towns of Languedoc, either individually or in small groups, negotiated payment of lump sums to the crown. The seneschal of Beaucaire obtained 400 *l.t.* from proctors representing the town and *viguerie* of Alès.[195] The *viguerie* of Uzès paid 1,400 *l.t.*, although some of its communities escaped contributing because of various hardships.[196] Montpellier offered 1,500 *l.t.* to one royal commissioner, the prior of La Charité. His colleague, the seneschal of Beaucaire, refused to accept this offer, however, perhaps because he was more familiar with the local situation and knew the consuls could be persuaded to pay more. They finally agreed to pay 2,000 *l.t.*, but did so with ill-grace, complaining that piracy and other royal taxes had impoverished the region. The tax was to be paid by November, but the final installment was four months late, as the consuls met determined resistance from the *populares*, who accused them of inequities in levying the required municipal *taille*.[197] Nîmes agreed to pay 800 *l.t.*, but the crown did not receive the first installment until 1329.[198] Many of the towns in the Beaucaire district were convened to an assembly at the beginning of July, but reluctance to pay was strong. The consuls of Lunel tried to claim that the town was not accustomed to send troops to the army and was under no obligation to do so since it was not directly subject to the crown. The summons to the assembly, however, was so explicit that they had to empower their proctor to "com-

---

[194] Dureau de la Malle, "Document statistique inédit (quatorzième siècle)," *BEC*, II (1840-1841), 172-173.

[195] AM Alès 1 S-12, nos. 9, 10; Bardon, *Alais*, I, 95.

[196] AD Hérault A 4, fols. 83v-84v.

[197] *HL*, x, cols. 676-680; *Gr. Chartrier*, nos. 3530, 3870, 3871. On the controversy between the *populares* and the municipal government, see *ibid.*, nos. 3233, 3299, 3531, 4061, and the paper by Rogozinski cited above in Chapter I, note 41.

[198] L. Ménard, *Histoire civile, ecclésiastique, et littéraire de la ville de Nismes*, Paris, 1751, II, *preuves*, 63-64. For a controversy in Nîmes over whether doctors should contribute to the tax, see *ibid.*, pp. 67-69. These texts are from AM Nîmes NN 1, nos. 11-14.

pose" for men-at-arms if other arguments failed.[199] The nobles and clergy of Velay again protested the taxation of their tallageable men.[200]

In the Toulouse district, the crown negotiated with the different *jugeries* as in the past. Seven letters of non-prejudice have survived,[201] and while they do not indicate the amount of subsidy, the whole seneschalsy paid only about 21,000 pounds, according to Dureau de la Malle.[202] Compared to the figures for 1325 (when the *livre tournois* was worth more), this was a very small tax. Unlike 1325, the government could not exploit fief alienations and usury, since the towns of the Toulousain had paid for these things in 1327. It seems clear that a subsidy by itself produced much less money in this period than a "package deal" negotiated with one of the dreaded *réformateurs*. Dureau de la Malle's figures are doubtless incomplete, yet his total receipts for the Beaucaire and Toulouse districts are in about the same ratio as the number of hearths in these two regions. These two seneschalsies seem to have produced an average tax of only about 3 *sols* per hearth. The seneschalsy of Carcassonne, on the other hand, apparently paid a hearth tax of 10 *s.*, which yielded more than 42,000 *l.t.* in all.[203]

Dureau de la Malle's text gives no receipts from Rouergue, probably because opposition to the subsidy there delayed its collection. The consuls of Najac sent emissaries to Villefranche to see the seneschal *del fag de Flandres*. Then a commissioner visited Najac on the same errand and several more trips back and forth were necessary before the question of a subsidy was resolved.[204] The subsidy in question was to be expressed as a given number of sergeants. Saint-Antonin also resisted stubbornly, finally making an offer in 1330 which the commissioners rejected as inadequate. As in 1326, the consuls of this town wanted a letter of non-prejudice and a promise that they would not be taxed if the other towns in Rouergue did not make comparable payments.[205]

---

[199] *HL*, x, cols. 671-676; BN *ms. lat.* 9174, fols. 78-80; Molinier, in *HL*, ix, 452-453, note 7.

[200] Delcambre, *Etats Velay*, pp. 52, 57.

[201] *HL*, x, cols. 683-684; AN JJ 65B, nos. 94, 120, 134, 157; JJ 79B, no. 42.

[202] Dureau de la Malle, "Document," pp. 172-173.

[203] *Ibid.* It appears that the seneschalsies of Beaucaire and Toulouse each paid about 14 pounds for every hundred hearths. Borrelli de Serres has noted discrepancies between Dureau's figures and the Common Receipts of the treasury in AN KK 2 (*Recherches*, II, 457). He has also argued that subsidy receipts were in a definite ratio to the number of hearths and that Carcassonne paid at 10 *s.* per hearth (*ibid.*, III, 399).

[204] AD Aveyron 2E 178, no. 2, fols. 218r-221v.

[205] BN Doat 146, fol. 211; de Gaujal, *Etudes*, II, 167.

Elsewhere in upper Languedoc, Moissac agreed to a 1 *d./l.* indirect tax for the war in Flanders, but not until early February 1329.[206] In Quercy, the crown sought a modest 6 *s.* hearth tax which was resisted by seigneurs when levied on their men. Cahors also resisted and sent two proctors to Paris, where they arranged a lump-sum payment of 700 pounds.[207] Périgueux was also reluctant to pay. A royal sergeant had to make four different trips to the town, receiving on his first visit what amounted to a bribe of 44 *s.* Here too, the negotiations were in progress months after the battle of Cassel and the town gained a further delay in paying until November 1329.[208]

At Poitiers, a tax of 400 *l.t.* was still being apportioned in May 1329. Contributing with some reluctance were suburban areas which normally were not subject to the town's municipal taxes.[209] We have some information also from Provins where the sum was brought together in piecemeal fashion,[210] and from Reims, which was allowed to pay only 500 *l.* because of the great coronation expenses just incurred.[211] The wide regional variations in the form taken by the payments in 1328 are already evident, although the summons of 18 June was a general one. Dureau de la Malle's document, which indicates the mode of taxation in only ten districts, suggests that six different methods were used in these regions.[212]

Three of these were Norman bailiwicks and a slightly different procedure was used in each. In Rouen, the tax appears to have taken the form of a lump sum promised by the whole bailiwick and apportioned among the parishes on the basis of ability to pay. In Caen, the payment was spread over two and a half months, again being apportioned among the parishes. In a third Norman bailiwick, Caux, the tax was apportioned among the towns. In the bailiwick of Sens, still another method was used. Each 100 hearths was to pay 10 *sols* per day for four months. Presumably this was the daily wage of a knight. In the bailiwick of Troyes the tax

---

[206] A. Lagrèze-Fossat, *Etudes historiques sur Moissac*, Paris, 1870, II, 124, quoting the municipal cartulary.

[207] Lacoste, *Quercy*, III, p. 56; Dufour, *Cahors*, p. 95.

[208] AM Périgueux CC 49, fols. 2v-4v. The first three visits of the sergeant occurred before the beginning of February, 1329, too early to have been related to the later subsidy request for a new Gascon war scare.

[209] *AHP*, XLVI, 7-12.   [210] Prou and d'Auriac, *Comptes*, p. 290.

[211] P. Varin (ed.) *Archives administratives de la ville de Reims*, II, Paris, 1843, 556-557. Coronation expenses were normally paid by Reims, and in 1328 they amounted to over 13,430 *l.p.* (*ibid.*, p. 489). Resistance to taxation in 1328 was reflected by a court decision against certain bourgeois who had attacked and wounded a royal tax collector (Furgeot, *Actes*, I, no. 475).

[212] Dureau de la Malle, "Document," pp. 170-173.

was graduated on the basis of wealth and restricted to those with at least ten pounds in income. The individual rates varied from a minimum of 7½ *sols* to 4 *l.* 10 *s.* for those whose fortune exceeded 500 pounds.[213] This rather limited information suggests that negotiations in much of France were at the bailiwick level and may have entailed some assemblies of local notables.

Dureau's figures give a total of around 230,000 *l.t.* for this subsidy of 1328, with no receipts reported for the districts of Paris, Rouergue, Amiens, Chaumont, Senlis, or Agenais-Gascony. Since the totals given for Carcassonne and Toulouse indicate wide disparity in the average tax paid per hearth, it is perhaps unwise to extrapolate. Nevertheless, some adjustments must be made if we are to estimate the total actually collected. Between Dureau's figures and actual treasury receipts there are discrepancies, and if the former are incomplete the latter must be still more so, since their total is smaller.[214] Some of the tax proceeds must have been spent without being sent to Paris. If we assume that Paris contributed 18,000 *l.t.*, and that the other unreported districts paid at about the same average rate as the rest of the kingdom, the total collections would amount to about 293,000 *l.t.*[215] This figure is probably conservative, but we are doubtless safe in saying that the tax of 1328 produced less than half the 735,000 *l.t.* estimated to have been collected in 1304.

Paris agreed to support 400 *hommes de cheval* for three months. The Parisians would raise the money themselves and begin paying it to the treasury on 1 August 1328. The tax was to end in the event of peace and no further aid would be demanded from Paris for this war. If a salary of 10 *s.* per day was used for computing the tax, Paris owed 18,000 *l.t.* in all.[216]

Exemptions and claims of privileges hindered the royal effort to raise money for the subsidy of 1328, and Philip VI's desire not to antagonize those with influence may have kept receipts low. The nobles were concerned about taxation of their subjects. The census taken in 1327-1328 implied that royal fiscal officers could act in the lands of all but the greatest magnates. Philip VI's concessions implied that royal authority was

---

[213] *Ibid.*

[214] Borrelli de Serres, *Recherches*, II, 456-457, and notes.

[215] Dureau de la Malle's total of about 230,000 pounds represents collections from about 1,900,000 hearths. Aside from Paris, the areas not included in this total contained about 373,000 hearths, which would have produced around 45,000 *l.t.* if they contributed at the same average rate. The total arrived at here conforms rather well to the totals recorded at the treasury in 1328 and 1329. See Appendix 1, Table 2.

[216] *Ord.*, II, 20. On the question of salaries of troops, see above, note 76.

actually much less extensive, but we may infer that the king had political reasons for seeking the goodwill of the seigneurial class. In 1328, many lords who accompanied Philip on the Flemish campaign, including some who did not even possess high justice, were allowed to collect the tax in their own lands, although royal officials attempted to ignore this privilege.[217] Of the great fiefs, the duke of Burgundy and the counts of Blois and Foix were permitted to raise the subsidy in their own lands.[218] It is doubtful that the king ever received any of this money, but these magnates must have paid the contingents they brought.[219] In the principal remaining *apanage*, Artois, the countess Mahaut collected a subsidy and sent troops on the Flemish expedition.[220]

Since the pope had followed his customary practice of granting a new two-year tenth in 1328,[221] the French clergy were already being taxed. However, they were also involved with the war in other ways. Localities raising money to pay the royal subsidy expected the clergy to contribute to these levies if they owned property in the community.[222] The important cartage services were largely the responsibility of monastic establishments, and these too were a form of contribution to the war.[223] Above all, however, there were ecclesiastical corporations who owed military services much as did vassals or towns. From these, the royal commissioners hoped to obtain an equivalent money payment. The abbey of St. Maxence in Poitou, called upon to furnish 50 foot sergeants, resisted on the grounds that its military obligation was limited to 40 days' service and then only for campaigns waged between the Loire and Dordogne rivers. After much argument, a 200-pound fine was agreed upon in return for a letter of non-prejudice.[224]

[217] Viard, "Guerre," p. 366, noted that Tournai escaped royal taxation in order to prepare local defenses. The inhabitants of Clermont-en-Beauvaisis, part of an *apanage*, argued that the bailiff of Senlis was trying to force them to pay the subsidy, contrary to their privileges (AN J 167, no. 2). On the nobles generally, see *Ord.*, II, 27.

[218] U. Plancher, *Histoire générale et particulière de Bourgogne, avec des notes, des dissertations, et les preuves justificatives*, Dijon, 1741, II, no. 248; AN K 42, no. 4; AD Basses-Pyrénées E 404, no. 123.

[219] Viard, "Guerre," p. 365, note 2, evidently believed otherwise, but it seems most unlikely that great feudatories who had been allowed to collect the subsidy in their lands were excused from supporting their own troops.

[220] *INV AD Pas-de-Calais*, I, 364 (A 478, 479).

[221] AN P 2290, pp. 785-817.

[222] *INV AM RIOM*, p. 62 (CC 8). As late as 1334, some inhabitants of Auvergne still owed arrears of the subsidies of the 1320s (AM Riom CC 10, no. 958).

[223] Petit, *Essai de restitution*, pp. 191-200; AD Pas-de-Calais, *Coll. Rodière*, ms. 106, pp. 587-589. I am indebted to P. Bougard, departmental archivist, for sending me excerpts of the latter text.

[224] AN JJ 67, no. 72.

The short campaign in Flanders was probably not a severe drain on royal finances, but as always the costs of the war had to be met before any significant sums from the subsidy were available. In this situation, Philip resorted to the time-honored expedients of borrowing and confiscation. Italian companies, wealthy French bourgeois, and prelates of the church all provided money in the form of loans.[225] Philip also profited from the arrest and execution of Pierre Remi, a leading treasury official under Charles IV, whose confiscated wealth was used to repay certain debts which Philip had incurred previously.[226]

The new monarch also maintained his predecessor's policy of exploiting *abrégement du fief* for fiscal purposes. In March, when still regent, he had confirmed Charles IV's commission to Robert de Condé, who would zealously scrutinize property transactions in the Champagne bailiwicks until 1332.[227] Even more significant was Philip's action of 18 June. On the very day that he issued his military summons for the Flemish expedition, the king ordered commissioners to investigate property transactions and levy fines for *franc-fief* and *amortissement* at the rates established by Charles IV in January 1327. As in 1325 and 1327, therefore, the crown ordered fief investigations and subsidy negotiations simultaneously. Commissioners dealing with fief acquisitions would be busy throughout the kingdom in 1328 and 1329. On the other hand, there was a sharp decline in the large fines and sales of privileges which had proven lucrative in the non-war year of 1327.[228]

Having disposed of the Flemish problem so speedily, Philip VI had strengthened himself politically, and his next concern was the perennial question of English homage for Gascony. Charles IV had been able to delay this matter for nearly two years after becoming king, but Philip's debatable title to the throne made it politically essential to secure the prompt recognition of his most formidable potential rival. The homage question therefore carried with it a particular urgency on this occasion. Since Edward III had dynastic reasons for wishing to delay the homage and avoid a formal act of liege homage, Philip VI expected trouble.[229]

---

[225] AN KK 2, fols. 61v-62v; J. Viard, "Les ressources extraordinaires de la royauté sous Philippe VI de Valois," *RQH*, XLIV (1888), 215; L. Delisle (ed.), *Actes normands de la chambre des comptes sous Philippe de Valois*, Rouen, 1871, p. 1.

[226] Viard, "Début," pp. 263-268; *Gr. Chron.*, IX, 74; *Cont. Nangis*, II, 85; AN JJ 65B, nos. 2, 66, 142; JJ 66, no. 66.

[227] Longnon, *Documents*, III, xxii; Henneman, "Enquêteurs," pp. 331-332.

[228] *Ibid.*, pp. 332-333, notes 101-103, 106.

[229] As early as 19 September 1328, Edward had ordered the seizure of French goods at Southampton because of alleged acts of piracy: *Foedera*, II pt. 3, pp. 18-19.

Early in 1329, he ordered that the French army muster at Bergerac in the spring.[230] This early summons might serve two purposes; putting pressure on Edward and preparing France for a new war subsidy.

A genuine crisis did not develop until Edward actually refused homage in March. Then it was that Philip ordered his bailiffs and seneschals to seek a war subsidy from the towns and *châtellenies* of their respective jurisdictions. The royal instructions, while conciliatory in tone, were quite explicit. Although regional variations in the mode of paying were permitted, the tax was to be tied closely to the support of the army. If a district paid by installments, the first was due by Ascension. If payment took some other form, the total must be ready by Pentecost in order to pay the troops assembling at Bergerac. By way of guaranteeing that the money would be used only for military purposes, Philip promised that all collections would be stored locally until war was a certainty.[231]

Philip thus was admitting that only an actual state of war could justify this subsidy. Charles IV had implicitly conceded the same principle, and in the prevailing mood of the 1320s no king could do otherwise. Philip VI, whose political position was less secure than that of his predecessor, evidently felt it necessary to be more specific on this point. Under existing conditions, it did not seem wise to invoke Beaumanoir's dictum that a tax could be levied when war merely threatened. Moreover, Philip was careful to carry out his promises. On 6 June, Edward capitulated and rendered homage at Amiens.[232] The same day, a royal letter was dispatched to the seneschal of Beaucaire (and no doubt to other local jurisdictions also) ordering the seneschal not only to inform all nobles that the summons to Bergerac was canceled, but also to halt collections of all "impositions and aids" for the war and return what had been collected thus far.[233] A royal ordinance of 18 June reaffirmed the king's determination to return what had been collected.[234]

Viard, in noting Philip's caution at this time, suggested that the king had reason to expect opposition to any subsidy not justified by urgent

---

[230] Viard, "La France," p. 379, stated that the nobility had been summoned to war even before the homage was refused. On war preparations, see also Jusselin, "Comment la France . . . ," pp. 222-226.

[231] Varin, *Reims*, II, 585-587; *HL*, x, cols. 686-687; Le Maire, *St. Quentin*, II, no. 476.

[232] *Foedera*, II pt. 3, pp. 23, 27; *Gr. Chron.*, IX, 99-104; Déprez, *Préliminaires*, pp. 38f.

[233] *HL*, x, cols. 694-695; *Gr. Chartrier*, no. 3143.

[234] AN JJ 79B, no. 19; *Ord.*, II, 29.

considerations of defense.[235] There were, of course, many precedents for such opposition, but on future occasions, Philip would not be deterred by it. Other considerations must have dictated his cautious tactics of 1328-1329: the political realities of the Valois dynasty's first year in power. Despite the backing of the magnates and his quick victory over the Flemings, Philip's position was not yet secure. His title to the throne was still subject to dispute and he seems to have seen his own position as weak. In fact, he excused his failure to return to Edward III certain Gascon lands occupied by the French under his predecessor on the grounds that he was not strong enough to enforce such a restoration. An Englishmen writing to Edward further affirmed that Philip lacked the power to keep royal officials from meddling in English Gascony.[236] Concern over the excessive zeal of royal officials is suggested by the tone of his order to cancel the subsidy in June. It stressed that the money was to be returned so quickly that there would be no complaints to the king and that none of it was to be used for meeting expenses.[237]

Little is known about the manner in which the Gascon war subsidy of 1329 was negotiated or to what extent it may have been collected (or at least granted) before the levy was halted. In Reims, which we know had paid the subsidy for Flanders, the bailiff of Vermandois executed the royal writ by holding an assembly of the leading men of the community.[238] Apparently, therefore, the procedure employed for the previous tax (that is, the use of small local assemblies as a starting point for negotiations) was being attempted again. Whether Reims actually made a grant for the Gascon crisis is another matter entirely, and I can find no clear instance of any region or community which *granted* a second subsidy within this first year of Philip VI's reign. Montpellier objected to the tax request because the king of Majorca had not consented first,[239] and at Périgueux, the cryptic nature of the town accounts makes it very difficult to sort out the negotiations of the two subsidies (for Flanders and Gascony, respectively).[240]

In slightly more than five years, a series of difficulties in Gascony and Flanders had made necessary a number of different war subsidies, all of them supplemented by other fiscal expedients. The way in which these

---

[235] Viard, "Ressources," p. 171.

[236] Cazelles, *Soc. politique*, p. 413.

[237] *HL*, x, cols. 694-695.

[238] Varin, *Reims*, ii, pp. 585-587.

[239] *HL*, x, cols. 688-692.

[240] See above, note 208. AM Périgueux CC 49 mentions a tax for Gascony throughout, but the earlier negotiations could only have been for the Flemish campaign. Probably the town was approached for money for a Gascon campaign in the spring of 1329 but escaped paying when the homage was rendered.

expedients were used and the scope of the subsidies themselves illustrate the care with which the monarchy sought to minimize controversy when levying taxes. Both the succession question and the events and precedents of 1313-1321 compelled the French crown to pursue limited fiscal objectives in the 1320s. Thus when war broke out in 1324 and 1326, Charles IV began by seeking aid only from the regions most directly affected. In 1325 he used fiscal expedients to augment revenues and apply pressure on reluctant taxpayers, then canceled taxes with the coming of peace and reimposed them on a selective basis when war broke out with Flanders. Philip VI, who depended on the backing of the magnates, felt compelled to risk a new Flemish campaign, but he was rewarded by a victorious pitched battle and emerged from the expedition with greater strength. The general subsidy for this brief war entailed endless negotiations, and Philip understandably showed great moderation in preparing for the Gascon war scare of 1329.

Despite the consistently cautious approach employed by the crown, subsidy negotiations were often protracted and acrimonious, privileges were tenaciously defended, and letters of non-prejudice were in great demand. The subsidies were carefully tied to the principle of military service, sometimes being expressed in terms of sergeants or knights, sometimes being described as a *finance* to avoid personal service. Despite this fact, the only clear case of a general *arrière-ban* we have encountered was in 1328. Both the subsidy of 1325 and that planned in 1329 were preceded by somewhat vaguer orders to military commanders to have the army at a certain place at a certain time, but not a general summons to all communities in the sense usually associated with the *arrière-ban*. Instead, an explicit military summons was sometimes saved until a later stage of subsidy negotiations, when it would be directed at a certain community to speed up the grant of a tax.

The monarchy's care in relating taxation to warfare and military service was a necessary consequence of its experiences in 1313-1321. It left unanswered the question of how the government might regularly sustain its finances in time of peace. Prior to the Hundred Years' War, the kings were usually spared the need for a strong standing army in time of nominal peace, but even without this burden they seem to have been unable to live on their ordinary domainal resources. In such periods, Philip IV and Charles IV had found it necessary to employ loans, fines, extortions, and other expedients in order to finance the royal household and government. Now, in 1329, Philip VI entered a period of peace which would last for nearly eight years. He would soon find it necessary to draw upon the precedents established by his uncle and cousin.

CHAPTER III

The Fiscal Policies and Feudal Aids of Philip VI, 1329-1336

1. Fiscal Expedients and Court Politics

IN SEEKING to analyze the principal sources of Philip VI's revenue during the early 1330s, we are severely handicapped by the destruction of the Chamber of Accounts' records in the eighteenth century. Where local archives are often rich in material dealing with subsidy negotiations or taxes which threatened privileges, they are far less informative about the more prosaic sources of income available to the king in time of peace. The same is true of representative assemblies. Of those held in the 1330s, some were apparently quite large in size, but the surviving documents tell us virtually nothing about them.[1] Fortunately, some initial information about this period is furnished by the treasury's book of Common Receipts for 1328-1330 which has fortuitously survived. Otherwise, we must rely on inventories or imperfect restorations of destroyed financial registers.[2]

Two previous kings, Philip IV and Charles IV, had been able to supplement their revenues considerably by manipulation of the coinage. This source of income was not available to Philip VI for two reasons. First, the magnates, on whom his position depended, demanded a reform that would restore the sound money of St. Louis' time. Secondly, a shortage of silver bullion appears to have curtailed the amount of currency which could be issued.[3] The rather modest debasement of the currency which occurred in 1311 had occasioned considerable agitation for reform in the following decade, and when Charles IV's policies created an even sharper increase in the price of silver, resentment built up rapidly. In his war years of 1324-1326, Charles realized substantial coinage profits, but in time the government had to pay a higher price for the metal in order to attract it to the mints. By Philip's VI's accession, therefore, the debased currency was not really yielding much revenue, and mint profits made up only 5.4 percent of the royal treasury receipts in 1329.[4]

---

[1] Cazelles, *Soc. politique*, pp. 127-128, summarizes these meetings briefly, but see the discussion of some of them in the following pages.

[2] The Common Receipts, AN KK 2, are described in Appendix 1 and analyzed in Table 2. The restored memorials of the Chamber of Accounts are in AN, series P. The inventory of original texts used here is AN PP 117.

[3] See Appendix 1, and the important article by A. Watson, "Back to Gold—and Silver," *Ec.HR*, xx (1967), 15f.

[4] Miskimin, *Money*, p. 43; and Appendix 1.

The great seigneurs, many of whom had fixed incomes and feared inflation, were traditionally most hostile to coinage alterations, and this class was the one to which Philip VI felt politically obligated. Even before he was assured of peace with England, Philip had to convene an assembly (March 1329) to discuss the coinage, and at this meeting it was decided to return to sound money in two steps. The first reduction in the price of silver would occur in December 1329, the second at Easter 1330. Together they represented a revaluation of about 50 percent, and Philip promised not to take any profit from the new coinage.[5] Thereafter, until the Hundred Years' War broke out in 1337, coinage was not a significant source of royal revenue.

Philip VI therefore had to rely on other fiscal expedients. One of these was provided by the continuing inquest into acquisition of fiefs by clergy and non-nobles. Although the rates for *franc-fief* and *amortissement* has been changed at times, the investigation of these property transactions had been underway with little or no interruption since early in 1325. By the 1330s, it is very likely that this activity was beginning to yield diminishing returns. Nevertheless, we have continuing evidence of fief commissioners at work in most parts of the kingdom through 1332.[6] By this time, the documents indicate a slackening of activity, and thereafter references to these fines are only sporadic. Despite brief new flurries of activity in 1337 and 1344, the chancery registers of the next thirty years reveal nothing approximating the thorough investigations carried out in 1325-1332.[7] While this great seven-year campaign lasted, it provided useful additions to the king's revenue and served as a valuable lever in negotiating war subsidies. Nevertheless, fief acquisitions, like coinage manipulation, seem to have been largely exhausted as a source of royal income by the early 1330s.

With these expedients declining in value, and a new crisis with England beginning to develop late in 1330,[8] Philip VI turned to the Italian moneylenders for his next important fiscal measure. As wealthy foreigners, many of whom were carrying on an illegal business (usury), the Italians were always vulnerable, notwithstanding the bourgeois privileges they had been compelled to purchase some years before. We have seen that the crown exploited them for loans, gifts, and heavy fines at the time of the Anglo-French war of 1324-1325. Since then, they had escaped a

---

[5] *Ibid.*; *Ord.*, II, 27, 43; "Chron. parisienne," pp. 127-128; *Gr. Chron.*, IX, 131; AN P 2289, pp. 300-312.

[6] Henneman, "Enquêteurs," pp. 334-335.

[7] *Ibid.*, and notes.   [8] See below, notes 40-42.

major extortion, except in the case of isolated individuals.[9] Beginning late in 1330, however, the crown undertook the most comprehensive exploitation of the "Lombards" hitherto attempted. Normally a "lombard" was a petty loan shark or pawn broker, the nature of whose business made him a "manifest usurer," who could not conceal the interest on his loans as effectively as the large international companies of merchant bankers.[10] The royal action of 1330, however, seems to have been directed at international companies as well, if their principal business was the lending of money.[11] The fines now levied on the Italians certainly exceeded those of 1325. A Chamber of Accounts inventory indicates a payment of 18,000 pounds by "Sienese and others" in 1331 and a *finance* of 120,000 *l.p.* apportioned among "Italians of the province of Lombardy" in 1332.[12]

These fines, which may represent only part of the total, were doubtless the result of the arrests carried out late in 1330, when Lombards were held captive for three weeks before being released on the promise of a large fine.[13] This method of extortion was not an innovation, having been employed in 1311 and probably on other occasions.[14] What followed, however, seems to have been a new departure for royal policy towards the Italians. The government early in 1331 sought to recover the vast sums they were owed by debtors. Since usurious loans were illegal contracts, the crown declared them canceled. All debtors were released from paying interest, but they were to repay the principal to the crown.[15] It was decided in January 1331 to seek three-quarters of all outstanding debts, as a fair approximation of the principal, but collection was deferred for four months.[16] Soon afterwards, the same arrangement was extended to those owing debts to Jews.[17] After the four-month period had elapsed, Philip VI took other measures to bolster his revenues, one of which was a general inquest into usury in the kingdom. Although usury had not been neglected in preceding years, royal commissioners of in-

---

[9] Henneman, "Italians," pp. 22, 28-30. Early in Philip VI's reign, however, the crown did collect impressive sums from the confiscated property of one important financier, Mache des Maches: AN KK 2, fol. 123v.

[10] R. de Roover, *Money, Banking, and Credit in Mediaeval Bruges*, Cambridge (Mass.), 1948, pp. 99-100.

[11] Henneman, "Italians," note 3, and p. 30.

[12] *Ibid.*; AN PP 117, pp. 418, 443-444. The king followed his seizure a year later by a new ordinance on the Champagne fairs, establishing the rules of credit to be followed there: *Ord.*, II, 73f.

[13] "Chron. parisienne," p. 143.   [14] Henneman, "Italians," pp. 26-27.

[15] *Ibid.*, p. 31; *Ord.*, II, 59-61.   [16] *Ibid.*

[17] *Gr. Chartrier*, nos. 3341-3343.

quiry had concentrated on fief alienations. With fiefs gradually ceasing to supply the crown with lucrative fines, the emphasis now shifted to usury, which would remain a major concern of royal commissioners for several years.[18]

The absence of documentation prevents any estimate of the actual amounts collected from debtors to the Jews and Lombards in this period,[19] but for other types of fiscal expedient some figures are available. As in 1322-1323 and 1327, the peacetime years of the early 1330s were notable for some very large judicial fines, and the crown gained other large sums from the sale of rights or privileges.[20] In two of the more spectacular cases, Arras was assessed 15,000 pounds for misdeeds dating back two decades,[21] while Toulouse, in 1335-1336 had to promise 50,000 *l.t.* for the recovery of its privileges after the *capitouls* were found guilty of exceeding their jurisdiction.[22] Meanwhile, the king's waters and forests administration busily looked into usurped royal rights.[23]

Related to the sale of privileges was a royal tax in the Laonnais region which actually was the commutation of a domainal right. The king obtained a 2 *sol* hearth tax from this locality when he revoked the so-called *appels volages*. Long a matter of great contention in Laonnais, the *appels volages* were a judicial procedure which permitted the by-passing of the seigneurial courts. In revoking this system the king not only realized some revenue but also managed to please the local nobility.[24]

The crown obtained a much larger *finance* as the result of a change in the system of wool customs in the seneschalsy of Carcassonne. The ex-

[18] AN JJ 79 B, no. 39, indicates a general inquiry into usury in the kingdom, ordered on 2 May 1331. Other documents relating to the pursuit of usurers in this period are AN JJ 66, no. 1471; BN Doat 146, fols. 214r-v. Philip VI was not able to live on his ordinary revenues. At the end of May 1331, he ordered that all debts owed to the crown were to be recovered, notwithstanding any letters of remission which had been issued: *Ord.*, II, 65-66. In the same month, he had all customs revenues and the small regular taxes on Italians applied to the expenses of the royal household. See Jassemin, "Papiers," pp. 178-179.

[19] Our only estimate of this kind belongs to late 1347, when the government expected to collect 1,200,000 pounds as the principal of Lombard debts, according to *Ord.*, II, 418. It is not known whether a comparable sum was anticipated in 1331 or whether such an enormous total was ever a realistic estimate. The budget memoranda submitted to the king by his advisers in the 1330s are regrettably silent on the matter.

[20] Henneman, "Enquêteurs," notes 125-127.

[21] *Ibid.*, note 128.   [22] *Ibid.*, note 129.

[23] AN JJ 66, nos. 386, 887, 942, 967, 1026, 1098, 1130; JJ 67, no. 34.

[24] *Ord.*, II, 444-445. A discussion of this jurisdictional question is in Lot and Fawtier, *Institutions*, II, 324-325. Additional documents, belonging to the later 1330s, are AN JJ 70, nos. 87, 106, 128, 140, 181.

port of wool was normally governed by the system of licenses known as *haut passage,* but since 1317, a different system had prevailed in the Carcassonne district, Albigeois, and the county of Foix. In this part of the kingdom, as elsewhere, the export of wool and associated raw materials was prohibited, but instead of selling export licenses, the government collected a 12 *d.* tax on each piece of finished cloth, this tax being known as the *gabelle des draps.* This system of protection evidently was popular at Carcassonne and Béziers, where the clothmakers were glad enough to pay the tax if they no longer had to compete with Italians for their raw materials.[25] Those who found the Italian trade desirable or who did not profit from the *gabelle des draps,* preferred the older system of *haut passage.* They were strongest at Narbonne, but their leader was actually an inhabitant of Béziers named Pierre de Brenac.[26]

Brenac seems to have enlisted the support of royal officers during the 1320s, for by August 1329, the king's commissioners were looking into a possible revocation of the cloth *gabelle.* Opinion remained divided and the economic stakes were high, judging from a royal letter of March 1330. Those wishing to revoke the tax offered 150,000 *l.t.* to indemnify the crown for its loss of revenues. Their opponents who favored the *status quo* were prepared to pay 40,000 pounds as well as remaining subject to the tax. In a period of peace and sound currency, these were impressive sums, and the king ordered an investigation to determine which course of action would be most profitable.[27] The consuls of Narbonne acted with a narrow self-interest which typified the whole proceeding. They wished an end to the *gabelle des draps* but were unwilling to pay for it unless assured that all other inhabitants of the region, including nobles, did the same.[28] The consuls of Carcassonne, on the other hand, declared

---

[25] In BN Doat 157, fols. 31v-33r, the cloth interests described the background of the tax and its value to the region. Regions given for retaining the arrangement are listed *ibid.,* fols. 50v-57v.

[26] Summarizing the discontent, Molinier, *HL,* ix, 466-468, note 3, dealt mainly with BN Doat 157 and did not consider other documents, but his analysis of the conflicting interests seems sound. That Béziers and Carcassonne preferred the cloth *gabelle* and export prohibitions is made clear by the objections of their consuls against the proposed change. These are in BN Doat 157, fols. 27v-57v, and 11v-14v, respectively. Narbonne, however, was prepared to pay for the revocation as early as 31 August 1329 (BN Doat 53, fols. 79v-80r; 157, fols. 36r-37v). For Brenac's activities, *ibid.,* fols. 37v-49r.

[27] *Ibid.,* fols. 15v-17r; BN *ms. fr.* 7327, no. 31.

[28] BN Doat 53, fols. 79v-80r.

that the proposed revocation was damaging to the king and asked that their community not be included in the transaction.[29]

Assemblies were scheduled to meet at Narbonne and Pamiers in 1330 to debate the issue,[30] but we possess no documents for the following eighteen months. By March 1332, the government seems to have decided on revocation of the *gabelle des draps*, and new commissioners were sent to arrange collection of the 150,000 *l.t.*[31] The consuls of Béziers, who wished to retain the tax, protested strongly, claiming that the commissioners were acting in a ruthless and violent manner and were abetted by Pierre de Brenac and his partisans. They declared that the "better part" of the communities opposed the transaction, and demanded Brenac's punishment.[32]

Late in February 1333, the commissioners ordered that the tax be revoked in return for 150,000 *l.t.* payable over five years by the towns, nobles, and clergy, including those living in the county of Foix.[33] Narbonne had already agreed to its share, an annual payment of 5,111 *l.t.*, of which 2,227½ pounds were owed by the *cité* and the rest by the *bourg*. The crown promised that Narbonne would not be assessed an additional amount if the nobles or clergy should fail to pay.[34] The gov-

---

[29] BN Doat 157, fols. 11v-14v.   [30] BN Doat 157, fols. 18r-27r.

[31] A text of 22 January, now evidently lost, may have shed further light on royal policy (AN PP 117, p. 510). The main surviving document on the revocation of the cloth *gabelle* is that cited below, note 33.

[32] BN Doat 157, fols. 39r-50v. It was said that Brenac enlisted the aid of various barons and prelates who committed numerous "excesses" and violations of royal safeguard.

[33] AN JJ 66, no. 1231; JJ 68, no. 41; JJ 69, no. 324 (published in *Ord.*, 11, 88-81); JJ 70, no. 51; JJ 71, no. 15. This text, which was copied into five different registers of the *Trésor des Chartes*, is a royal confirmation dated 5 April 1333. Enclosed are the letters empowering the commissioners (11 March 1332), and their order of 24 February 1333 that the *gabelle* be revoked in return for 150,000 *l.t.* The same text appears in corrupt copies or extracts in BN *Coll. Languedoc* 84, fols. 46r-47v, 101r-v; BN NAF 7603 (Fontanieu 71), fols. 246r-258v; *INV AM Narbonne, sér. AA*, p. 34, note. On the assessment of the tax, see also AN P 2291, pp. 753-754; *Ord.*, XII, 14-15. In July 1333, the *Parlement* agreed to hear the objections of towns in the county of Foix (Furgeot, *Actes*, 1, no. 779). In 1338, the king declared that these communities would not have to pay (AN JJ 66, no. 1278).

[34] Dated 16 October 1332 in *INV AM Narbonne, sér. AA*, p. 34 (AA 99, fol. 346v), and 17 October in BN Doat 53, fols. 93v-95v, this act seems to have been misinterpreted by Mouynès in the Narbonne inventory. He suggested that an original assessment of 5,111 pounds was reduced to 2,227 pounds. It is clear in the Doat copy that the large sum was payable by the consuls of the *bourg* and *cité* together, while the lesser sum was the part owed by the *cité* alone. This is confirmed in a second copy, BN Doat 52, fols. 181r-182v, and Narbonne's eventual payment of 17,000 pounds (BN Doat 53, fols. 56-59) seems to rule out any possibility that the final

ernment later specified that subjects of the nobles and clergy should pay only if they were normally liable to municipal *tailles*.[35] The long debate over the *gabelle des draps* was thus resolved by the spring of 1333. Except for one text of 1338, we hear nothing more of it until the crown tried to collect arrears in 1344.[36] The entire episode illustrates the difficulty of getting group action on a fiscal matter, even at the seneschalsy level, when communal rivalries and conflicting economic interests were involved.

The crown had other customs revenues in the 1330s besides the *gabelle des draps*. The 4 *d./l.* export tax or *droit de rève* was collected regularly from late 1325 until it was canceled for a time in 1333.[37] The system of licenses governing most exports of wool, *haut passage*, continued in force despite diminishing receipts owing to shifting trade routes.[38] One rather specialized duty affected imports as well as exports. The various cities and kingdoms bordering on the western Mediterranean perpetually accused each other of piracy and in the 1330s, the communities of Languedoc were especially aggrieved at Genoa and Savona for alleged depredations on French commerce. After some rather involved legal proceedings, Philip VI instituted a tax of 3 *d./l.* on all goods imported or exported by the Genoese and their subjects. This tax was based on letters of marque issued against the Genoese and it remained in effect from 1335 until 1351 when Genoa paid the French crown a large lump sum to abolish it. Legally, this tax was imposed solely to reimburse private persons for their losses to Genoese shipping, but in practice much of the money probably found its way into the royal coffers.[39]

The foregoing discussion has dealt with rather miscellaneous sources of royal revenue. Some of these were purely fiscal expedients, while others arose from applying certain "ordinary" revenues in a broader and more systematic way. All these fiscal activities must be considered with reference to the political framework within which they occurred. The

---

1332 assessment was only 2,227 pounds. The promise not to raise Narbonne's assessment is in BN Doat 53, fol. 81r. The town's payments began to fall behind almost immediately, judging from the receipt *ibid.*, fol. 79r, and *INV AM Narbonne, sér AA*, p. 34 (AA 99, fol. 347v).

[35] AN P 2291, pp. 753-754.

[36] The text of 1338, mentioned in BN Doat 53, fol. 80r, and Doat 253, fol. 646v, is probably that in AN JJ 66, no. 1278, cited above, note 33. According to BN Doat 53, fols. 56-59, Narbonne in 1343 admitted having paid 17,000 *l.t.*, whereas it owed 25,555.

[37] See below, note 83.   [38] Henneman, "Italians," p. 18 and notes.

[39] *Ibid.*, pp. 20-21, and below, Chapter VII.

transitional period at the beginning of Philip VI's reign was followed by several years of political turmoil in France during the early 1330s. Both domestic and international politics in this period would have important effects on the development of royal taxation, paving the way for the outbreak of the Hundred Years' War and the return to power of the Chamber of Accounts party at the French court.

Edward III's homage in 1329 was of great importance to Philip VI because it carried with it a recognition of the Valois succession. There remained, however, important unsolved problems in Anglo-French relations, including the status of certain Gascon territories occupied by the French in the reign of Charles IV. More serious from the French point of view was the conclusion of Philip VI's advisers that the homage of 1329 did not constitute the liege homage required of the English king. Controversy over these matters threatened to produce a new crisis between the two countries in 1330,[40] and the French undertook to apply pressure on Edward by staging a military demonstration against Saintes. At length, Edward III and Philip VI met in April 1331 and a serious crisis was averted.[41] Having reached agreement on the question of homage, the two countries made a final effort to resolve their territorial disputes, but the so-called Process of Agen in 1333 ended in failure. The French remained inflexible on jurisdictional matters and continued to aid the Scots against Edward III.[42]

In this period of troubled relations with England, the French court was also disturbed by domestic political upheavals in the 1330s. During the reign of Philip V, the Valois princes and the future Charles IV had been the leading opponents of the Chamber of Accounts faction at the royal court. Charles IV's accession had brought an end to their influence and Philip VI, who shared Charles' views, inaugurated no significant changes in 1328. The conservative style of Charles IV's advisers was suitable, if not essential, to a king of Philip's uncertain political position. Philip introduced into the government some of his own men, long affiliated with the Valois family, but he retained most of the important figures who had worked with Charles IV. A highly influential prince under Philip VI was his cousin and brother-in-law, Robert of Artois, count of Beaumont-le-Roger. Robert's aspirations in Artois were blocked by his

[40] Déprez, *Préliminaires*, pp. 71f. For documents dealing with the homage, see also *Foedera*, II pt. 3, pp. 36, 56.

[41] Déprez, *Préliminaires*, p. 76; *Foedera*, II pt. 3, pp. 61, 63; *INV AM Amiens*, I, 28 (AA 4); AN JJ 66, no. 779.

[42] Déprez, *Préliminaires*, pp. 83f.; Cuttino, "The Process of Agen," passim; Chaplais, "Règlements," pp. 285-286; *Foedera*, II pt. 3, pp. 67-68, 108-110.

aunt, the countess Mahaut, whose daughter and heiress had married Philip V. The Artesian succession dispute had made Robert implacably hostile to Philip V, and therefore friendly to Charles IV and the Valois. Of the great magnates on whose support Philip VI relied, Robert of Artois was especially important, as a leading Capetian prince. Yet Robert's claims to Artois, which he pressed again late in 1328, proved to be a serious embarrassment to the new king. Countess Mahaut's two granddaughters (who naturally opposed Robert) were married to the duke of Burgundy and the count of Flanders respectively. These two peers of France were also close to Philip VI, whose queen was the sister of Eudes IV of Burgundy. Thus the claims of Robert of Artois created a serious division among the great lords of France and within the royal family itself.[43]

Late in 1329, Mahaut of Artois died, followed to the grave less than two months later by her daughter. The counties of Artois and Burgundy now devolved upon Joan, duchess of Burgundy. At this point, the government proposed a solution to the Artesian dispute which would have been very beneficial to the monarchy as well. Following Mahaut's death, the county had been taken temporarily into royal hands, and a considerable party in Artois evidently desired to remain under crown control. Provided with sufficient funds, the king could buy up the rights of those who claimed the county and return it to the royal domain permanently. Hence, on 25 April 1330, Philip VI ordered his officials to assemble the "prelates, clergy, nobles, communes, good towns, and others," and ask them for the "great and suitable aid" he would need for the purpose. The event would be a notable one for the emergence of the provincial estates of Artois, but the assembly proved unwilling to supply the requested subsidy and the crown was unable to reacquire the county.[44] The failure to gain a subsidy in this case, from a region whose own interests were very much involved, illustrates the continuing hostility to peacetime taxation and also underscores the fact that the crown needed additional revenues in such periods in order to exploit opportunities of this sort.[45]

When this project failed, the duchess of Burgundy received her inheritance, and the embittered Robert sought to build up allies among any magnates who had reasons for being hostile to Burgundy. Fearing

[43] Cazelles, *Soc. politique*, pp. 75-78.

[44] *Ibid.*, pp. 79-80; Hirschauer, *Les états d'Artois*, i, 12, ii, 147-148.

[45] The crown did make one acquisition at this time, buying John of Bohemia's rights to Lucca. See P. Gasnault, "Nouvelles Lettres Closes et 'de par le roy' de Philippe VI de Valois," *BEC*, cxx (1962), 176-177. Far less important than acquisition of Artois would have been, this purchase cost the government 35,000 *l.t.*

Robert's strong position at court, Eudes of Burgundy and Louis of Flanders made their own alliance and sounded out Edward III for possible assistance. This step coincided with the brief Anglo-French war scare of 1330-1331, and it may have persuaded Philip VI that Robert of Artois was a less dangerous enemy than Burgundy, and therefore expendable. Cazelles has linked the Anglo-French settlement of April 1331 to Robert's fall from power and the accompanying rise to prominence of Eudes IV of Burgundy.[46] In any case, the crown abandoned Robert, drew closer to Burgundy, and late in 1331, held an assembly of peers who pronounced against Robert.[47] Now a rebel, Robert went into exile, eventually to become an anti-Valois agitator at the English court. The political turmoil accompanying his fall from favor continued through much of 1332, and it may explain the assembly convoked for the spring of that year. On 13 February, the seneschal of Beaucaire was ordered to have seven major towns of his jurisdiction each send two or three men to Paris on 15 April with powers to consult with the barons and prelates on a delicate matter touching the royal person, the laws and liberties of the kingdom, etc.[48] If southern towns were summoned all the way to Paris, the assembly probably included the estates of the whole kingdom, and if other towns of comparable size were convoked, around 200 communities must have been represented. Nothing further is known about this assembly, but a month after it was to meet, the king confiscated the lands of Robert of Artois. Given his insecure hold upon the throne, Philip VI may have wished to enlist broad public support before taking such action against a royal prince.[49]

In terms of court politics, the fall of Robert and the rising influence of Eudes IV of Burgundy were important events. A growing number of Burgundians acquired influence at court, among them Mile de Noyers, the "sovereign" of the Chamber of Accounts, whose influence had been minimal since the death of Philip V. Son-in-law of Philip V and brother-in-law of Philip VI, the triumphant Eudes of Burgundy provided the patronage through which the administrators and fiscal experts would return to power after their long eclipse. Their victory did not come at once, however, despite a growth in influence during the early part of 1332. Philip VI installed a new chancellor, Guillaume de Sainte-Maure, who remained the government's leading figure until his death in 1335. A

---

[46] Cazelles, *Soc. politique*, pp. 81-91, especially p. 90.

[47] Isambert, IV, 395-396.

[48] Cazelles, *Soc. politique*, pp. 96, 128; AN K 166B, no. 160, as transcribed by Viard in AN AB xix 2636.

[49] For the confiscation, AN JJ 66, no. 659.

long-time servant of the Valois, Sainte-Maure was linked to the "feudal" or *Parlement* faction, and the Chamber of Accounts did not really dominate the government while he lived. From 1335, however, their ascendancy was assured, and for the next eight years Mile de Noyers would play the decisive role in the royal council.[50]

During the three years of Sainte-Maure's leadership, the government directed considerable energy towards a crusade. Philip VI's father had long nursed political ambitions towards the eastern Mediterranean, and Sainte-Maure was probably in sympathy with this tradition. Yet the interest in a crusade coincided with an unusually difficult period for royal finances. The sound coinage established in 1330 proved increasingly hard to maintain in the face of a growing shortage of silver at the mints.[51] The profitable investigation of fief acquisitions had come to an end, and it is likely that the sums confiscated from the debtors to Jews and Italians had largely been collected by the end of 1332. The government had to search for other sources of money, and the largest judicial fines levied in the 1330s belong to the Sainte-Maure years.[52] Through most of the period 1332-1335, however, the crown's financial policy involved a concentrated effort to levy general feudal aids on the entire realm. These aids form the most important phase of Philip VI's peacetime financing in the 1330s.

2. *The Feudal Aids*

The feudal aids of the 1330s can be viewed in several different ways. In the first place, they were another peacetime fiscal expedient like those levied by Philip IV a generation before. In addition, the aids had some relation to the steadily increasing tension between England and France. Successful collection would give Philip VI greater resources for helping Scotland and developing French defenses. Moreover, the marriage aid of 1332-1333 was the direct outgrowth of an alliance with Brabant aimed at checking the progress of English diplomacy among the Netherland princes. Finally, and perhaps above all, the aids may be seen as part of the royal effort to finance the crusading venture which Philip hoped to lead. These different factors help explain Philip's ambitious attempt to collect three feudal aids within a very short period.

When he fled France late in 1331, Robert of Artois had taken refuge in the Netherlands. Robert's enemy, the count of Flanders, was embroiled with Brabant over the disputed possession of Malines. Perhaps

[50] For the foregoing discussion, see Cazelles, *Soc. politique*, pp. 91-121.
[51] See Appendix I.   [52] See above, notes 21-22.

for this reason, John of Brabant welcomed Robert, but in doing so he antagonized France. French influence had been strong in the Low Countries in the early fourteenth century, but Edward III's marriage had gained him the valuable friendship of the count of Hainault-Holland. Philip VI could ill-afford to see Brabant also slip away from the French sphere of influence in a time of worsening relations with England, and French diplomacy therefore moved swiftly. Philip cemented his ties to Count John of Luxemburg (who was also king of Bohemia), and John quickly assembled a league hostile to Brabant. Having threatened the duke with a show of force, Philip then stepped in with diplomatic inducements—a marriage alliance with Brabant and French mediation of the Malines dispute with Flanders.[53]

Philip's diplomatic activities helped make "a continual celebration of the year 1332."[54] The heir of the French throne, John, was invested with the *apanages* of Normandy, Anjou, and Maine in February.[55] Then he married Bona of Luxemburg, daughter of the Bohemian king. In the autumn, Marie of France married the duke of Brabant's heir, and at the same time the new duke of Normandy was knighted. The twin ceremonies for the marriage of a royal daughter and the knighting of the king's son were naturally the occasion for a splendid feudal assemblage. Following the celebrations on 2 October 1332, Philip asked the magnates to swear to serve his son loyally while he was on crusade, and to have John crowned king if Philip should die while on the expedition.[56]

Both the marriage and the knighting provided the occasion for feudal aids, as did the crusade, although the latter had not been the basis for a general aid since before the time of Philip IV and may have lost some credibility in the intervening decades because of unfulfilled crusading promises. Philip VI had taken the cross in 1313, along with his three predecessors, at the time when all the Capetian princes had been knighted.[57] We have seen that Philip V invoked his crusading plans when he found it useful, but otherwise showed little interest, while Charles IV made stronger gestures towards the scheme, only to abandon it when

[53] Cazelles, *Soc. politique*, p. 101. Documents relating to the Franco-Brabançon negotiations are BN *ms. fr.* 7374, fols. 191-204; BN NAF 7603 (Fontanieu 71), fols. 156-182; Jassemin, "Papiers," pp. 211-213.

[54] Cazelles, *Soc. politique*, p. 101.

[55] BN NAF 7603 (Fontanieu 71), fols. 48-49v.

[56] M. Félibien and G. Lobineau, *Histoire de la ville de Paris*, Paris, 1725, I, p. 757; Cazelles, *Soc. politique*, p. 128; BN NAF 7603 (Fontanieu 71), fol. 185; *Gr. Chron.*, IX, 133; *Cont. Nangis*, II, 134.

[57] AN AB xix 2636. Both Delaville le Roulx, *France en l'Orient*, I, 88, and Atiya, *Crusade*, p. 95, argued that Philip took the cross a second time in mid-1332.

war broke out with England.[58] Philip VI seems to have been much more sincere, but perhaps this impression is created by the fact that he had a longer period of peace in which to indulge in crusading dreams. John XXII had granted Philip tenths in 1328 and 1330,[59] promulgated indulgences for the crusade at the end of 1331[60] and renewed the tenth the following summer. In naming commissioners to collect this tax, Philip had stated that it would be used only for the crusade, and he arranged for storage of the money until his departure.[61] In June 1332, he gave 10,000 florins to the king of Armenia.[62] In understanding the feudal aids of the 1330s therefore, the crusade is every bit as important as the king's Netherland diplomacy and the need for additional revenues. At the very least, energetic plans for the crusade would help safeguard the clerical tenth as a vital part of the royal peacetime budget.[63]

Direct vassals of the crown owed their lord aid when his son was knighted and daughter married. Those who attended the assembly of October 1332 did not need to consent to these taxes. For the aid to be profitable, however, it had to be generalized, and herein lay the issue which had made such taxes controversial under Philip IV and Philip V. Besides extending these taxes to rear vassals, the crown wished to levy them on non-nobles, especially the towns. The bulk of our documentary evidence involves these last. Some towns had paid feudal aids in the past, while others had resisted them tenaciously.

One criterion for liability to the aids might be whether or not persons were directly subject to the king. Non-nobles who customarily aided their direct lords in the "four cases" might resist paying the king if he was not their direct lord. However, "direct lord," like "domain," is difficult to define with precision. The census of 1327-1328 left the impression that royal fiscal officers had access to all but the greatest fiefs in the realm, but a feudal aid was a special kind of tax, not related to a national emergency, and earlier efforts to generalize these had met great opposition. Legal writers, while claiming that kings could levy aids from persons other than direct vassals, also cautioned them against exacting these taxes unjustly or excessively.[64] The documents of the 1330s leave

---

[58] See above, Chapter I, at notes 112-114.   [59] AN P 2290, pp. 837-887.

[60] Delaville le Roulx, *France en l'Orient*, I, 86; Atiya, *Crusade*, p. 96. Philip VI had been negotiating with the Venetians over transport services since 1331: *LC*, no. 39.

[61] AN K 42, no. 12; Delaville le Roulx, *France en l'Orient*, I, 86. See also J. Viard, "Les projets de croisade de Philippe VI de Valois," *BEC*, xcvii (1936), 308.

[62] Viard, "Ressources," p. 211.

[63] Appendix I, Tables 2 and 3, for the importance of the tenth in the royal finances.

[64] Brown, "*Aide* of 1308."

many questions unanswered, for they rarely indicate exactly what categories of person were taxed. When objections were raised by townspeople, however, they were almost always founded on privilege and precedent rather than status or jurisdiction. The *Parlement* finally did define the criterion for liability to feudal aids, but only after lengthy litigation.[65]

Efforts to collect the aids must have begun soon after the ceremonies of early October, for the crown was receiving complaints by the first week of November. Aside from those claiming specific privileges granting exemption, these complaints were based almost exclusively on one argument—that the district in question had never paid such aids in the past. A lesser irritant, undoubtedly, was the simultaneous levy of two aids. For this there certainly was no precedent, and the government capitulated first on this point.

In the bailiwick of Caux some persons claimed, for instance, that previous kings had not levied such aids on them. In Auvergne, the town of Riom claimed that its privileges and the customs of the region made it exempt from both aids. For every protest, the crown had an answer— words of concession. Riom was still required to pay, but new instructions delayed collection of the aid for the marriage of the king's daughter until June 1333.[66] A similar order sent to Anjou and Maine on 9 November 1332[67] suggests that this suspension must have been universal, and when the bailiff of Caux received instructions on 20 December these dealt with the knighting aid but ignored that for the marriage. The bailiff was told to collect only from those who traditionally had paid this aid, and then only in the same manner as was customary. He was to start in the duke of Normandy's own domains, where opposition presumably would be at a minimum. If anyone presented privileges and claimed exemption, a copy of such documents must be forwarded to Paris for scrutiny by the Chamber of Accounts. In the meantime, no constraint was to be used.[68] A similar sort of letter to the bailiff of Senlis expressed displeasure at attempts to extort money from unwilling payers in this region.[69]

Although the crown from the outset was displaying a spirit of moderation, it was nevertheless determined to collect the feudal aids from as many people as possible. Every bailiwick and seneschalsy of the kingdom received basically the same royal letter in the winter of 1332-1333. Besides those just cited, we have instructions sent to Chartres, Carcas-

[65] For earlier efforts to define the scope of feudal aids, see *ibid.* For *Parlement's* decision of 1334, see below, note 123.

[66] AM Riom CC 9, nos. 783, 1304.   [67] AN P 2291, p. 749.

[68] AN P 2291, pp. 751-752; BN Moreau 227, fols. 125r-126r.

[69] AN P 2291, pp. 755-757.

sonne, Toulouse, and Rouergue, and others dealing with the subjects of certain intermediate seigneurs.[70] The aid was to be levied only on those who traditionally paid, but those claiming exemption were to present written privileges, a copy of which was to be sent to Paris. The burden of proof was thus placed on the taxpayers and the inference is that those without documents to support their position were expected to pay. Moreover, written privileges were no guarantees of exemption, for several towns in the seneschalsy of Carcassonne, having sent documents to Paris, were at length ordered to pay anyway (6 December 1333).[71] It is significant also that inhabitants of the château of Lautrec, receiving a confirmation of their privileges in March of 1333, were declared exempt from all subsidies *except* the four feudal aids.[72]

In lands not directly under the authority of the king, the subjects of intermediate seigneurs did not receive entirely uniform treatment. Too few documents have survived to permit generalization, but at this stage of the proceedings, the crown evidently hoped to collect what it could, and based its actions toward these subjects on considerations of practical politics.[73] Subjects of Pierre de Pascy, like everyone else in the kingdom, were to pay the tax unless they had documents justifying their claim to exemptions. If they presented such documents, the latter would have to be forwarded to Paris for scrutiny by the Chamber of Accounts. This rule applied to persons subject to both high and low justice.[74] Inhabitants of the county of Foix were made subject to the same general rule in letters of 25 March 1333, but three days later, the king ordered the seneschal of Carcassonne not to tax them at all.[75]

By March of 1333, nearly half a year had passed since the knighting and marriage ceremonies. In seeking to collect two aids, the crown had received protests almost immediately, had suspended the second one until June, and had ordered that all objections to paying either tax be forwarded in writing to Paris. The bold step of trying to levy two aids at once was justified by the circumstances but not by precedent. Perhaps

---

[70] AN P 2291, pp. 743-747; BN *Coll. Languedoc* 84, fol. 73r-v; BN NAF 7603 (Fontanieu 71), fols. 200-202, 242-243; BN Doat 146, fol. 79; AD Basses-Pyrénées E 404, no. 121.

[71] BN NAF 7603 (Fontanieu 72), fols. 24r-25v; AN AB xix 2640, Viard's copy of the text in Bibliothèque de Rouen ms. 3402, fol. 177v. This ruling applied specifically to those directly subject to the crown.

[72] BN *Coll. Languedoc* 84, fol. 76; AD Basses-Pyrénées E 490, no. 65.

[73] See above, Chapter I, part 2, for a discussion of the way in which royal taxation of indirect subjects was affected by different practical factors.

[74] BN NAF 7603 (Fontanieu 71), fols. 242-243.

[75] AD Basses-Pyrénées E 404, nos. 121-122.

it was no more than a tactic, permitting the government to appear conciliatory by making an early retreat, while setting the stage for a heavier tax than would have appeared justified by one of the "four cases" alone. At any rate, the desire to examine all documents in Paris suggests that the Chamber of Accounts wished to formulate a set of uniform rules which would make as many people as possible subject to the aids without blatantly violating privileges. In some instances, town proctors came to Paris, as in 1309, to argue against paying the tax. Nîmes sent such a delegation in the winter of 1334.[76] In the Carcassonne district, the royal order to forward documents to Paris could not have been received much before mid-February, and the local officials commanded Béziers to send a proctor to Paris on 5 March, rather than simply dispatching documents.[77] This action must have been taken on their own initiative, perhaps because they felt Béziers had a strong case and wished to force the town to make some *composition* rather than undergo the expense of sending persons all the way to Paris. There is, in short, no evidence that the government actually wished to deal with proctors in Paris.

The king, in fact, was not in Paris between February and April 1333, but in the Loire valley. Guillaume de Sainte-Maure, occupied with a diplomatic mission, was not with Philip, except for a brief time late in March when the chancellor joined the king at Orléans.[78] An important piece of business brought them together on this occasion, but our only direct information comes from a coinage ordinance of 25 March, issued after consultation with *plusieurs de noz prelates, barons et des bonnes villes et autres saiges cognoissans du fait des dites monnoies*. The major problem dealt with in this enactment was the shortage of silver coming to the mints. Those with silver plate were asked to sell the crown one-third of what they possessed. The king, in return, promised to take no profit from the transaction.[79] Three months later, the crown issued a new coinage which raised the value of silver and thus violated Philip's commitment of 1329-1330 to maintain the sound money of St. Louis' day.[80] This action must have been discussed at the assembly, perhaps being endorsed as a last resort which might attract more silver to the mints.

It seems equally clear that the assembly did not restrict itself to the

---

[76] Ménard, *Nismes*, ii, *preuves*, 84f.

[77] AM Pézenas layette 10, liasse 4, no. 1120. I am indebted to Mrs. Brown for furnishing me with a transcript of this text, which is misdated in the archive inventory.

[78] Bautier, "Chancellerie," p. 158.

[79] *Ord.*, ii, 83-88; AN P 2291, pp. 87-101; Ménard, *Nismes*, ii, *preuves*, 81-84.

[80] Appendix i, Table i, and notes; Miskimin, *Money*, p. 166.

bullion crisis. Another ordinance, dealing with the general welfare of the kingdom, attracted the attention of contemporaries because it authorized the lending of money at interest up to 21⅔ percent per annum.[81] Having squeezed what he could from both usurers and their debtors, Philip now legalized interest to this extent. It is very likely that this measure was requested by the assembly, since nobles and town governments were frequent borrowers and must have suffered from the debt confiscation of 1331. Still other important measures were timed in such a way as to coincide with the March assembly. The crown issued letters revoking usury and *franc-fief* commissions. These were dated 22 March, when the assembly was probably in session.[82] Several days earlier, the 4 *d./l.* export tax was canceled, no reason being given.[83] Molinier's statement that this revocation was connected with the negotiations over the Carcassonne cloth *gabelle* is unsubstantiated and implausible.[84]

It thus appears, from a number of sources, that the assembly of Estates at Orléans in March 1333, coincided with a wide range of fiscal matters, yet remarkably little direct evidence of this meeting has survived. A procuration from Cahors dated 1 March, makes it clear that coinage was the principal business for which the king had called the meeting by letters of 18 February.[85] The word *plusieurs* in the ensuing ordinance may mean the barons were not represented in large numbers,[86] and the lack of more municipal documents leads one to conclude that the towns represented were not numerous either. Perhaps the meeting was restricted to episcopal cities. Regardless of the assembly's size, however, the evidence just cited indicates a number of royal concessions, some made before the meeting as if for propaganda purposes, others made later, as if they were requested at the assembly. The king canceled the export tax, recalled unpopular commissioners, legalized lending at interest, and promised various reforms. All he appears to have gotten in return was a questionable promise of support in coping with the bullion shortage.

---

[81] *Ord.*, XII, 16-18; "Chron. parisienne," p. 151.

[82] AM Alès 1 S-23, no. 1; AM Montpellier G-5, nos. 3341-3342.

[83] *Ibid.*; de Gaujal, *Etudes*, II, 169-170, note 1; BN Doat 8, fols. 147-149v.; AD Gard, 18th cent. ms. inventory of AM Beaucaire, fol. 161r.; AN P 2291, p. 781; AD Basses-Pyrenées E 404, no. 10; AN PP 117, p. 523; *HL*, IX, 469-470. The revocation seems to have been ordered originally in mid-March, although these various texts bear a number of different dates.

[84] Molinier, *HL*, IX, 466-468, note 3.

[85] BN Doat 119, fol. 69.

[86] Taylor, "Baronial Assemblies," p. 451, has suggested that the king maintained a list of about 300 barons who were normally summoned to central assemblies and that the term *plusieurs* indicated a more restricted group of barons.

As it stands, this does not seem to be a very equal bargain. What else could Philip have obtained, or at least hoped to obtain, from this meeting of the Estates? The most likely answers concern the feudal aids and/or the crusade.

The assembly was not followed by any dramatic change in collection of the feudal aids, but since the tax for John of Normandy's knighting was encountering such opposition, Philip could have been content to gain an endorsement of his plan to have the Chamber of Accounts examine all claims of exemption and pronounce on their validity. However, Philip did not invite towns to send proctors to Orléans with power to discuss the objections to the aid. It is therefore more likely that what the king sought from the Estates was an endorsement of the crusade. Royal letters of 20 March, endorsed two days later by the duke of Normandy, set forth certain fiscal arrangements for the projected expedition. Not only did the king reiterate that the clerical tenth would be employed exclusively for the crusade, but he also named persons who would travel through the kingdom inducing individuals to swear oaths pledging them to go on the crusade.[87] From another text, it is known that such persons would then have to pay a "gift" to be released from their oath.[88] Acceptance of this scheme by an assembly would have been valuable to the king, and the timing of his letter of 20 March suggests that he may have sought such endorsement.

What remains unclear, of course, is the precise connection between the knighting aid and the crusade. If Philip seriously intended to undertake the crusade, the knighting aid would be a vital source of revenue for the project. If he was really not sincere and merely wanted to obtain money, the crusading scheme might serve the purposes of propaganda and facilitate collection of the knighting aid, as Philip V had hoped it would in 1321.[89] In all probability, Philip VI was sincere about the crusade, but one suspects that some of his advisers, like Mile de Noyers, were aware of its propaganda possibilities also. Whether or not this question can ever be fully resolved, there seems no doubt that the royal government in 1333 was engaged in a complex fiscal program which combined three of the "four cases" in which a feudal aid might normally be sought. For two years following the Orléans assembly, it was the aid for John's knighting which received by far the greatest emphasis.

[87] AN JJ 66, no. 1502. See also AN INV *sér* 1, no. 68, describing a fragmentary document in AN J 1029, no. 5.

[88] AN P 2289, pp. 700-703. See also the remarks of J. Brundage, *Medieval Canon Law and the Crusader*, Madison, 1969, pp. 69-70, 175.

[89] Taylor, "1321," pp. 222-223.

The laborious effort to collect this aid is well-documented in Langue-doc, where aids for the "four cases" were not so well entrenched in custom as in the North. Only in scattered *seigneuries* were these aids traditionally paid.[90] During 1332 and 1333, royal commissioners obtained offers of a 20 *s.t.* hearth tax from a few towns in the seneschalsies of Toulouse, Beaucaire, Rouergue, and Bigorre, but the great majority claimed to be exempt.[91] In the Carcassonne district, the crown sought 10 *s.t.* per hearth for each of the two feudal aids but encountered opposition from the consuls of Narbonne.[92] One argument against the tax was that it was payable only to direct seigneurs and not to the king as overlord.[93]

The aid was opposed in upper Languedoc on various grounds. Claiming to have never paid such aids in the past, Najac received a temporary suspension, but then had to defend its claims of exemption before local officers of the crown at Villefranche.[94] The county of Rodez had a tradition of feudal aids and they had a rather wide application. The count could collect for his own knighting and for the marriages of his daughters and sisters.[95] Whether the king had any right to collect the present aid was far from certain, however. At Millau, collection of the tax had been ordered in December 1332. For the next two years, the consuls sent a succession of letters to Paris and proctors to Villefranche and Rodez in a strenuous effort to avoid paying. Informed that all towns in the royal domain would have to contribute, they tried to pretend that Millau was a rear fief, then argued rather feebly that the king possessed no fiefs in the town's dependencies.[96] The towns of Agenais may have paid,[97] and a 1 *d./l.* sales tax was levied at Moissac in the face of considerable opposition.[98] At Cahors, resistance was based on the argument that the

---

[90] See the comments of Molinier, *HL*, ix, 469, note 3.

[91] *HL*, ix, 468.　　　　　　　　　　[92] *Gr. Chartrier*, no. 3872.

[93] *HL*, ix, 468. But see above, at note 72. Some towns of the Carcassonne district did contribute to the aid: BN NAF 7603 (Fontanieu 72), fols. 24r-25v.

[94] BN Doat 146, fol. 79; de Gaujal, *Etudes*, ii, 168; AD Lot F 271, AD Aveyron 2E 178, no. 2, fol. 248.

[95] *INV AD Aveyron*, iv, 1045 (G 964). In AD Aveyron G 965 *bis*, fol. 42r, is an indication that a *taille* had been levied at Rodez in order to contribute to the royal aids. One suspects that when the crown decided not to tax indirect subjects the municipality retained what it had raised and did not return money to the taxpayers.

[96] AM Millau CC 508, nos. 123, 129; CC 345, fol. 76r-v; CC 512, no. 150; CC 509, several unnumbered documents.

[97] G. Tholin (ed.), *Chartes d'Agen se rapportant au règne de Philippe de Valois*, Bordeaux, 1898, pp. 40-43.

[98] Lagrèze-Fossat, *Moissac*, ii, 124.

town was subject to Philip only by virtue of a *paréage*, and the crown finally halted the tax.[99] Albi paid a hearth tax of 20 *s.*, but not without some brutality on the part of a royal officer who imprisoned a consul of the town for recalcitrance when the latter requested a delay in which to appeal to the king.[100] When an official at Cordes tried to enumerate hearths in order to impose the tax, he encountered bitter protests based on privileges formerly issued by the count of Toulouse.[101]

The pattern was much the same in the Beaucaire district. Nîmes obtained a delay by sending representatives to Paris in March of 1334, but when the crown still demanded payment, the consuls submitted a legal brief to the *Parlement* asking for a ruling.[102] As part of the royal domain, Nîmes was finally declared to be liable, but the consuls faced a new obstacle when clerks who practiced law or engaged in commerce tried to avoid contributing. The seneschal of Beaucaire had to overrule these claims, and it was June 1335 before the town had completed its payment of 500 *l.t.*[103] The king was only partial seigneur at Alès and Montpellier. The consuls of Alès underwent an extended imprisonment before agreeing to pay,[104] and the tax was levied at Montpellier only after the royal council had considered and overruled the town's objections.[105]

The controversy over payment of the aids had originally revolved around the question of whether or not a given town had ever paid in the past. By the second half of 1334, however, a new point of contention had begun to assume importance—whether or not a community was directly subject to the king. The fact that privileges and claims of exemption were, in most cases, to be sent to Paris indicates that the government hoped to find some principle which might justify collection in the face of such claims. The crown did not have a strong case with respect to subjects of an intermediate lord, for here the rights of the lords might be prejudiced as well as those of their subjects. Direct royal subjects, however, were much more vulnerable, unless their privileges very

---

[99] Albe, "Cahors INV," no. 343; Dufour, *Cahors*, p. 103.

[100] AM Albi CC 54.

[101] AM Cordes CC 30, no. 161; Cf. Portal, *Cordes*, p. 46.

[102] AM Nîmes NN 1, no. 15; Ménard, *Nismes*, II, *preuves*, 84-92. Viard, "Ressources," p. 175, cited this document as evidence of an aid for the crusade. It clearly refers to the knighting aid, however.

[103] Ménard, *Nismes*, II, 75-76, and *preuves*, 94. According to an anonymous work, *Nouvelles recherches pour servir à l'histoire de la ville de Beaucaire*, Avignon, 1836, p. 70, Beaucaire also contributed to the aid.

[104] AM Alès 1 S-12, no. 11; Bardon, *Alais*, I, 96-97.

[105] AM Montpellier G-4, no. 3301.

explicitly exempted them from the aids of the "four cases." Until the middle of 1334, Philip VI continued to press for payment by indirect subjects as well, but on 30 July, under the mounting pressure of petitions and protests, he finally suspended the aid in Languedoc pending action by the *Parlement*.[106] This order was not well-executed, for as late as mid-October the crown issued orders to halt collection in the seneschalsy of Beaucaire and the *viguerie* of Uzès.[107'] While the suspension was in force, most of the important southern towns presented legal arguments for consideration by the *Parlement* in Paris.[108]

Collection of the tax in northern France has largely been obscured by the loss of the royal financial archives. An inventory of one lost register indicates that Saint-Quentin owed 6,000 pounds for the knighting aid, Montdidier 2,000, and Soissons 4,000.[109] The archives of Saint-Quentin reveal that the town was permitted to levy a municipal *taille* for six years in order to make up the required sum. This tax met opposition, especially from the clergy. Saint-Quentin had paid the crown 3,000 pounds by June 1335.[110] The government sought both feudal aids in the county of Artois, but it is not clear that either was actually levied there.[111] The tax was certainly levied at Péronne, Amiens, and Bourges.[112] Although one writer has stated, without proof, that Saintonge paid the aid, La Rochelle was explicitly excused from contributing.[113] Paris made a substantial payment, judging from what was later returned to the town, but the subjects of the abbot of Saint-Denis were not required to pay.[114] The towns of Lille, Douai, and Seclin were declared to be part of the royal domain and therefore liable to contribute.[115]

---

[106] *HL*, ix, 496.   [107] AD Hérault A 4, fols. 82v-83v.

[108] *INV AM Pézenas*, no. 1630, and above, note 102.

[109] AN PP 117, pp. 516-517. Oddly, Soissons had privileges granting exemption from paying such an aid (AN JJ 62, nos. 106, 108), but these must have been disallowed because the town was in the royal domain.

[110] Le Maire, *St. Quentin*, nos. 511, 512, 519, 527.

[111] AD Pas-de-Calais A 530, indicating payment for letters on the subject of the aids.

[112] AN JJ 70, no. 169; AN PP 117, p. 438; BN NAF 7603 (Fontanieu 72), fols. 159-160v; Furgeot, *Actes*, I, no. 2030. The last of these texts excused Italian merchants from contributing to the tax at Bourges.

[113] Bardon, *Alais*, I, 95; Furgeot, *Actes*, I, no. 985.

[114] "Chron. parisienne," p. 165, indicates that 10,000 pounds returned to the town was not the full amount. A list of amounts to be returned is in BN Clairambault 471, pp. 247-283. For the exemption of subjects of Saint-Denis, see AN PP 117, p. 520.

[115] Furgeot, *Actes*, I, no. 1032.

Although the aid for the marriage of the king's daughter, Marie, had been suspended early, Montferrand was one community with a precedent for paying this aid, having done so for the marriage of Philip V's daughter and that of his sister, Isabella. In 1334, as collection of Philip VI's feudal aids dragged on, the bailiff of Auvergne was asked to verify this precedent and the town's apparent claim that nothing was owed for knighting the king's son. Should the latter aid be owed, the crown would credit to it that sum paid for the now-suspended marriage aid.[116] We know that by the end of 1333, at least 70 of the 300 pounds demanded for this aid had been paid.[117] Montferrand was a close neighbor of Riom, whose claim to exemption from both aids has already been noted. The fact that custom and precedent, as interpreted by the various localities, could vary in this way from town to town in the same geographical region and political jurisdiction, illustrates the difficulty of the crown in generalizing any tax. In the archives of Riom are several documents dealing with royal efforts to collect. The claim of exemption was followed, as we know, by the suspension of the marriage aid until the following June.[118] There is no indication that the effort to collect this aid was ever resumed. As a matter of fact, the princess herself died on 22 September 1333,[119] and this tragedy may have influenced the king's thinking in 1335 when John of Normandy (then his only male heir) fell dangerously ill. At any rate, our next document in the Riom series is a royal order of 15 July 1335, following John's recovery, which halted the collection of the aid for that prince's knighting, ostensibly because of the prayers which had been offered for his recovery during the recent illness.[120]

This cancellation of the aid at Riom was no isolated instance. On the same date (15 July), Philip VI sent identical letters to the receiver of Paris, and we must conclude that the same orders were sent throughout the kingdom. Not only did Philip halt the tax, but he also ordered its return, subject to the understanding that no royal rights would be prejudiced. To facilitate this process, all collections to date were to be reported in detailed accounts to be presented at Paris in the first week of August.[121] In the case of Riom, a sum of 300 l.t. already collected for the knighting aid, was to be returned in three installments. Typically, the royal receiver delayed in executing these orders, claiming that he was re-

---

[116] INV AM Montferrand, I, 311 (CC 1).

[117] Ibid., II, 1 (CC 303).   [118] See above, note 66.

[119] "Chron. parisienne," p. 154.   [120] AM Riom CC 9.

[121] BN NAF 7603 (Fontanieu 72), fols. 141-142.

quired to send the money to Paris, but eventually he agreed to return it.[122]

For nearly two years, the crown had collected documents giving reasons why different communities should not pay the aids. The protests from Languedoc were finally brought before the *Parlement*, which reached a decision on 20 December 1334. The *arrêt* stated that persons in the royal domain directly subject to the king were liable to pay the feudal aids. Those outside the domain, even if partly under the king's jurisdiction by reason of *paréage* arrangements, would not be required to pay. Communities partially outside the domain would pay proportionately—that is, to the extent that they were directly subject to the crown.[123] Molinier called this document the first financial ordinance applicable to the whole kingdom and having a legislative character, but he clearly exaggerated. Earlier decisions had set forth the same basic principle, and it only applied to feudal aids, which would be rare for the rest of the century.[124]

The decision of March 1334 did, however, mark the culmination of a strenuous royal effort to collect the knighting aid from as many people as possible. The government had devoted considerable time to this effort and clearly was serious about the aid. Yet just seven months after the *arrêt* of the *Parlement*, Philip VI was willing not only to halt collection but even to return the tax. How are we to explain this action, so astonishing to the modern observer? Both the documents and the narrative sources give but a single reason for the return of this money—the recovery of John of Normandy from his illness.[125] Elizabeth Brown has linked Philip's action to a broader medieval phenomenon—the feelings of guilt about taxation which afflicted various monarchs from Merovingian times until the Renaissance.[126] Yet this was not a typical case of allegedly un-

[122] AM Riom CC 9, no. 60. The royal receiver's argument was correct as far as domainal revenues were concerned, and it is likely that the aid receipts were being incorporated into domainal profits for convenience.

[123] Furgeot, *Actes*, I, no. 986; *HL*, x, cols. 748-749; BN *Coll. Languedoc* 84, fols. 88r-89r; BN Doat 185, fols. 268-270r; BN NAF 7601 (Fontanieu 68), fol. 278v. The original text of this important document is in AN X 1a 7, fol. 11. The litigants were southern towns: those of Bigorre, the Toulouse *jugeries*, and such major centers as Carcassonne, Nîmes, Alès, Montpellier, Narbonne, Moissac, as well as other smaller places.

[124] Molinier, *HL*, ix, 469, note 3. For earlier decisions, see Martin-Chabot, *Cour des Comptes*, no. 359; *HL*, x, col. 248.

[125] BN NAF 7603 (Fontanieu 72), fols. 141-142, 159-160v; *Gr. Chron.*, ix, 148-149; "Chron. parisienne," p. 165; *Cont. Nangis*, ii, 146-147; Félibien and Lobineau, *Paris*, i, 591.

[126] Brown, "Taxation and Morality."

just taxation. The king was not trying to levy a war subsidy in defiance of the doctrine of *cessante causa*. He was proceeding, with careful legality, to collect one of the feudal aids which had long been enshrined in custom. If Philip VI was troubled in his conscience about this tax, he must have had reasons peculiar to his own personality and situation.

It is probable that the illness of his son was a particularly traumatic experience for Philip VI, who was not entirely certain of his right to the throne and was anxious to secure the future of his dynasty.[127] At this time, John was his only son. Philip had sought to collect two feudal aids, each associated with one of his children. His daughter had died in 1333; his son had been narrowly spared. Did these events touch Philip's conscience and make him doubt the justice of this tax-raising effort? His will suggests that he was concerned about the rightness of his taxes, particularly those levied for crusades.[128] If the feudal aids were closely linked to the crusading project, as seems to have been the case, Philip may have had reason for a tender conscience. His four predecessors on the throne had promised to go on crusade and had profited financially from clerical tenths based on this promise. Yet none of them had gone, and all had died relatively young. However great his own sincerity about crusading, Philip VI may have realized in 1335 that the expedition might not take place. Under these circumstances, the illness of his son could have appeared as a warning of divine displeasure requiring some act of retribution.

Philip had not neglected the crusade, however, and plans for the expedition accelerated for a time after the assembly of March 1333. In July of that year, Pope John XXII published a statement of the privileges and indulgences which would be conferred on crusaders.[129] The current clerical tenth was to be collected for a six-year period and used for the expedition.[130] In September, Philip VI held an assembly of towns to discuss the crusade and perhaps explore the prospects of levying another aid to support it.[131] After this meeting, the king renewed his arrangements for the levy and storage of the crusading tenth.[132] In the last months of 1333, he was corresponding with the Venetians to seek their aid against the Turks. In a similar effort to promote the crusade, Philip

---

[127] Cazelles, *Soc. politique*, p. 193.

[128] AN J 404A, nos. 32, 33. Mrs. Brown, who cites these documents in "Taxation and Morality," has kindly furnished me with copies of them.

[129] Delaville le Roulx, *France en l'Orient*, 1, 87; Atiya, *Crusade*, p. 96; Petit, *Essai de restitution*, pp. 169-170; Félibien and Lobineau, *Paris*, 1, 586.

[130] Viard, "Ressources," p. 210.

[131] *INV AM Périgueux*, pp. 72-73 (CC 52).   [132] AN K 42, no. 22.

attempted to help resolve conflicts between Aragon and the Genoese.[133] Most essential to the expedition, of course, was an understanding with England, and Anglo-French discussions of the crusade occurred until as late a date as July 1336.[134]

In 1334, John XXII died, to be succeeded by Benedict XII. Philip dispatched Mile de Noyers to Avignon to confer with the new pontiff about certain matters which were important to the French king—the benefices which might be at royal disposal and the availability of ecclesiastical sanctions against any who rebelled against Philip. On this occasion, the king seems to have wanted merely to regulate his relations with the new pope and perhaps gain Noyers' assessment of Benedict's personality. In 1335, however, Noyers was back at Avignon to obtain permission to continue the collection of the six-year tenth.[135] Perhaps it was at this time that Philip began to doubt that the crusade would take place. The Chamber of Accounts was again influential at court and the king's advisers were pressing for a more aggressive foreign policy towards the empire and increased aid to Scotland.[136]

Philip did try to levy an aid specifically for the crusade. Some towns had been approached earlier,[137] but it was only in 1335-1336, when the knighting aid had been abandoned, that a crusading aid was seriously discussed. Of the four feudal aids, that for a crusade was of more recent origin than the others and may not have been so widely incorporated into feudal custom. On the other hand, it had been sought several times by the monarchy between the reigns of Louis VII and Louis IX.[138] In the next half-century it had not been levied, even though the crown had made use of many other different kinds of tax. There is no evidence that Charles IV's brief effort to collect a tax for crusading purposes in 1323 had affected any laymen. For most of the country, therefore, this type of aid had become an unfamiliar thing by the 1330s, just as enthusiasm for the crusading movement had waned considerably in the preceding century.

When the citizens of Reims were asked to contribute to the crusade,

---

[133] LC, nos. 46, 50, 51, 53, 61.

[134] Foedera, II pt. 3, pp. 77, 130-131, 149; Viard, "Ressources," p. 175.

[135] Jassemin, "Papiers," pp. 213-214, 216-217.

[136] See section 3 of this chapter.

[137] Viard's notes in AN AB xix 2638, drawn from the town accounts of Lille for 1333 (fol. 44v) and 1335 (fol. 19v). Reims may have been approached earlier, since Varin, Reims, II, 664-665 has been assigned the date of 1332 by the editor. He had no apparent reason for doing so, however, and the date is suspect.

[138] The occasions are discussed by Callery in Hist. du pouvoir.

they replied that no municipal tax could be levied for this purpose because of the shortage of currency, the costs of royal coronations, and other "damaging and grievous accidents." The *échevins* did suggest that wealthy individuals might be able to aid the king.[139] The town of Périgueux seems to have recognized an obligation to render token assistance, and it agreed to pay a mere forty pounds if Philip actually went to the Holy Land.[140] In Rouergue, four priests were seeking funds for the royal crusade during November 1335, and some money must have been collected.[141] Niort promised eighty pounds if the king went in person, and Beaucaire also made a contribution.[142] Some barons undertook to supply troops, and in August 1335, the king published a list of salaries payable to different kinds of fighting men.[143] The town of Aurillac offered 350 *l.t.* in three installments, provided that the voyage actually took place, and other towns of comparable size contributed at the same rate.[144] Paris is said to have offered an impressive sum, 40,000 *l.p.*, but the chronicler may have had in mind the knighting aid rather than that for the crusade.[145]

There is, in short, very little documentation for the crusading aid, and one infers that the crown had tried much harder to collect the knighting aid. Whatever may have transpired at the assembly of 1333, the kingdom was decidedly skeptical about the crusade and the king's sincerity. Perhaps Philip had decided that he would appear more forthright if he returned the knighting aid and then appealed for funds to support the crusade. By 1335, however, Guillaume de Sainte-Maure was dead and Mile de Noyers dominated the royal council. This change in power at

[139] Varin, *Reims*, II, 664-665.

[140] *INV AM Périgueux*, pp. 55 (CC 9) and 74 (CC 54). The date of the grant is not clear except that it fell in 1335, old style. Since, however, the annual town accounts began in November, it probably occurred after January 1.

[141] *HL*, IX, 484; AD Aveyron C 1519, no. 17.

[142] Hervieu, *Recherches*, p. 200; Molinier, *HL*, IX, 484, note 4.

[143] A. Huillard-Breholles, *Titres de la maison ducale de Bourbon*, Paris, 1867, I, no. 2083, BN NAF 7603 (Fontanieu 72), fols. 145-146; AN P 2291, p. 189.

[144] *INV AM Aurillac*, II, 11-12 (EE 3). An undated text in AM Riom CC 7, requesting relief from a crusading subsidy, may indicate a royal effort to obtain money from this town also.

[145] "Chron. parisienne," p. 165, mentions this grant, apparently made in September 1335. This was the time at which the crown was attempting to have the knighting aid returned. Unreturned portions of the latter were still being deducted from the war subsidy of 1337, but one finds no further mention of the crusade. Perhaps Paris agreed, provisionally, to apply the proceeds from the knighting aid to the crusade. If, however, the two aids were closely associated in the public mind (as suggested above in the discussion of the assembly of 1333) the chronicler may simply have confused one aid with the other.

court must have been accompanied by a declining interest in the crusade. The effort to obtain an aid for this project in 1335 and 1336 appears to have been halfhearted, while the kingdom's response was equally lukewarm.

The evident lack of enthusiasm for the crusade may have strengthened Philip's determination to return the money collected for the knighting aid.[146] The process of doing so was an arduous one, and it was never fully completed.[147] On 22 May 1336, the *gens des comptes* had to be commanded once again to take this action.[148] In the case of Paris, a group of prelates and royal officials deliberated on the subject in October 1335, ordered that the amounts assessed and collected be reported in detail in the Chamber of Accounts so that it could be determined what sums should be returned to whom. The entire sum was to be returned, minus expenses incurred, and the same action was to be taken with respect to all towns in the kingdom.[149] Evidently the accounting which was to have been made in early August[150] had not been made, and in all probability much of the money received by the crown had already been spent. On 14 March 1336, the treasurer at Paris again was ordered to return the money and allow no one to be molested, evidence that even in the capital some officers still were trying to collect.[151] At length, a royal receiver was fined 7,000 pounds and this sum was to be used in repaying the Parisians (8 August 1336).[152] But it was still necessary to deduct 10,000 *l.p.* from the next war subsidy paid by Paris in order to effect return of the knighting aid.[153] The difficulty of repayment at Riom has already been recounted.[154] Several small communities of the Beaucaire district complained about the tax early in 1336 and the crown directed letters to the receiver of Nîmes in February and March ordering return of the money.[155]

[146] The king reiterated this intention in September 1335: Le Maire, *St. Quentin*, II, no. 528.

[147] The money had still not been fully returned in 1344. See below, Chapter v, note 166.

[148] AN PP 117, p. 441.

[149] *Ibid.*, p. 439; AN AB xix 2639, copy of a document from Bibliothèque de Rouen ms. 3398, fol. 19r.

[150] BN NAF 7603 (Fontanieu 72), fols. 141-142.

[151] BN NAF 20025, no. 128.   [152] AN PP 117, p. 442.

[153] "Chron. parisienne," p. 165. BN Clairambault 471, pp. 183-227, records sums to be paid for the war subsidy of 1337, with an accompanying figure showing how much was to be deducted from these subsidy payments because of the unreturned knighting aid.

[154] See above, note 122.   [155] BN *ms. fr.* 25698, nos. 57, 59.

The return of the knighting aid and the indifferent response to the proposed crusade marked the final stages of Philip VI's unsuccessful effort to exploit the feudal aids for profit during the peaceful 1330s. By invoking three of the "four cases" more or less simultaneously, holding several assemblies, canceling unpopular taxes and commissions, and making unusually determined gestures towards actually organizing a crusade, Philip VI may have hoped to gain an unusually large tax in time of peace as well as a long-term grant of the clerical tenth. The government showed that it was serious about the money-raising effort when it insisted on collecting in writing all objections for scrutiny by the Chamber of Accounts and legal judgment by the *Parlement*. Successful collection of a large sum would have augmented domainal revenues and eased the financial difficulties faced by the crown during the Sainte-Maure years. It would have made the crusading project substantially more realistic, if this expedition really was a serious royal objective.

By 1336, however, all was in ruins. Afflicted by personal tragedy in his family, the king lost his confidence and resolve, perhaps even doubting that he had the right to exploit the decision of the *Parlement* in the face of established rights and precedents. The knighting aid was canceled and returned. The bullion crisis finally came to a head and the mints were forced to close in 1335 for lack of silver.[156] Anglo-French relations deteriorated over Scotland. The final blow fell when Philip visited Benedict XII early in 1336. The pope decided to abandon the crusade until a definitive Anglo-French settlement should be made, and he canceled the clerical tenth.[157] For the first time in nearly thirty years, the French crown was deprived of this important source of revenue, at the very moment when all signs pointed to an imminent new war with England.

3. Financial Preparations for War

As pointed out above, one of the factors creating doubts about Philip VI's crusading intentions was the continuing stance of intransigence which France displayed towards England. This policy was reflected in two ways—the refusal to give up supporting Scotland against Edward III, and the refusal to make any concession in the negotiations over

[156] Appendix 1, note 23. It appears that there were continuing efforts to head off this crisis. *Gr. Chartrier*, no. 3411, indicates a summons of representatives from Montpellier to an assembly on the coinage late in 1333, and forty-four northern towns met in February 1335 (AN P 2291, p. 845), while towns from farther south also convened about this time (INV AM Périgueux, pp. 73-74).

[157] Viard, "Ressources," p. 213; Déprez, *Préliminaires*, pp. 123-124; Perroy, *The Hundred Years War*, p. 90.

Gascony which might appear to prejudice the position of the French king as feudal suzerain and *souverains par dessus*.[158] Cazelles has argued that Philip hoped to adopt new approaches towards England after the homage of 1331 but that he was frustrated when the "war party" came to power at court.[159] This group evidently cut across other party lines, but was probably strongest in the Chamber of Accounts faction if we are correct in associating the rise of Mile de Noyers with more aggressive policies. The latter's position of pre-eminence in the government was assured when Guillaume de Sainte-Maure died early in 1335.

Well before 1335, the French were thinking in terms of possible war with England. The war scares of 1329 and 1331 had both ended when Edward III capitulated on the matter of homage. The second of these crises had been marked by actual military clashes, as Philip VI's brother, Charles of Alençon, led an attack on Saintes. As in 1324, this expedition was the occasion for a subsidy from those localities closest to the fighting. The government sought aid from Quercy, Périgord, and perhaps Saintonge.[160] Our only detailed information, however, comes from Périgueux, where an assembly of townspeople on 6 March 1331 arranged for the contingent of sergeants requested by Alençon. On the tenth, these troops departed for Saintes under the leadership of two of the burghers.[161] The end of this crisis did not lead to a relaxation of vigilance in France. Government officials drew up estimates of what a large-scale war might cost.[162] A commissioner was in Normandy in 1333 to examine naval defenses,[163] and in the same year, the bailiffs and seneschals were told to inspect the fortresses of the kingdom and report on their condition.[164]

Upon assuming power in 1335, Mile de Noyers displayed an interest in expanding French influence towards the lands of the empire. Perhaps his Burgundian background gave him a particular interest in the eastern frontier, but the French crown had pursued aggressive policies in this direction on previous occasions when the Chamber of Accounts had been influential. In 1335, Noyers went into the field to take personal

[158] See the discussion by Déprez, *Préliminaires*, pp. 113-142; Chaplais, "Règlements," pp. 285-286. On *souverains par dessus*, see Beaumanoir, *Coutumes*, art. 1043.
[159] Cazelles, *Soc. politique*, p. 413.
[160] AN F2 1, 1464, describing AM Gourdon EE 6, the original of which I have been unable to locate; BN Clairambault 471, fols. 171-172, indicating an "imposition" at La Rochelle without giving further information; AN JJ 66, no. 535, a renewal of privileges at Saint-Jean d'Angély which could have been connected with tax negotiations. See also next note.
[161] AM Périgueux CC 50, fol. 4v.
[162] Jusselin, "Comment la France . . . ," pp. 226f.
[163] AN JJ 66, no. 1257.   [164] AN P 2291, pp. 767-769.

charge of a project to seize the stronghold of Sainte-Colombe, across the imperial frontier near Vienne. This place had long harbored brigands who menaced trade routes. The Dauphin Humbert II advanced claims to Sainte-Colombe, but Philip VI announced that the "public good" and "defense of the realm" justified its occupation by France.[165] A garrison was installed, and the crown undertook to raise money by issuing a military summons in the seneschalsy of Beaucaire. On 11 April 1335, the seneschal ordered all persons at Montpellier capable of bearing arms to muster at Tournon on 1 May.[166] The summons was not obeyed, so it was ordered that the richest citizens report within six days or be fined 100 marks (over 400 *l.t.*). After some negotiation, this pressure proved effective, and Montpellier agreed to pay 500 pounds at Christmas and another 500 pounds at Easter 1336. In time, the money was paid, but the town seems also to have been assessed a fine for "disobedience" committed in the army.[167] Our only other information on taxes for this campaign comes from Mende, whose bishop exercised temporal power in the county of Gévaudan and protested a royal effort to raise 200 men there.[168]

The generally more aggressive tone of French policy in 1335-1336 was reflected in a strenuous effort to improve port facilities and naval defenses. When applied to Mediterranean harbors, the effort was also justified by crusading plans, which were still under discussion as late as 1336. Aigues Mortes, St. Louis' old embarkation port, was silting up in this period and would soon be at the end of its usefulness. In 1336, the crown attempted to restore this harbor and develop an alternate facility farther west.

Two taxes already were being levied for the purpose of maintaining the harbor at Aigues Mortes. The first of these was the so-called *claverie*, a *denier*-per-pound tax on goods exported from the port.[169] The other was a tax of 6 *d.* on cloth, which by 1335 was being levied at other southern ports as a general export tax.[170] The extension of this levy is evidence that the government realized the need for additional resources to check

---

[165] Cazelles, *Soc. politique*, pp. 115f.; BN *ms. fr.* 7374, fols. 266r-268r; BN Clairambault 11, nos. 48-49; Clairambault 31, no. 153; and notes of Viard in AN AB xix 2638, 2639.

[166] AM Montpellier G-1, nos. 3115-3118.

[167] *Ibid.*, no. 3119; *Gr. Chartrier*, nos. 552, 3873, 3874.

[168] R. Barroux, "Procès des évêques de Mende avec la royauté (1336-1369) au sujet de la réparation du port d'Aigues Mortes," *BEC*, LXXXV (1924), 85-87.

[169] See above, Chapter I, note 118, and Furgeot, *Actes*, I, no. 160.

[170] See above, Chapter I, note 118, and *Gr. Chartrier*, no. 3754.

the deterioration of the harbor at Aigues Mortes. In 1336, an assembly of the nobles, clergy, and towns of the seneschalsy of Beaucaire decided that the matter was one of general concern in Languedoc. Those present agreed that the seneschalsy of Beaucaire would raise 10,000 *l.t.* for port repairs, a figure representing one-third of the total sum required. Of this, only 700 *l.t.* were to be sought from the nobles and clergy; the rest would come from a hearth tax graduated from one to three *sols*. Montpellier's share (3,000 *l.t.*) was payable in installments, spread over two years.[171] Apparently there was less enthusiasm for the tax at inland towns like Nîmes and Alès than there was at Montpellier.[172] The nobles and clergy of Velay again protested efforts to include their tallageable men in the levy, denying that this was a case of *evidens utilitas*.[173] The bishop of Mende also raised lengthy objections when the king's commissioners sought to levy the graduated hearth tax on Gévaudan, but the tax was collected notwithstanding the appeal.[174] This controversial levy did not, however, succeed in arresting the decline of Aigues Mortes.[175]

Montpellier's willingness to pay so large a portion of the assessment for Aigues Mortes may perhaps be explained by a fear of the rivalry of other towns farther west, for at this very time an effort was underway to develop a new seaport in the seneschalsy of Carcassonne. The towns of the latter region, however, who ought to have profited from such a port, helped to wreck the enterprise by their own inability to present a united front. As in the dispute over the cloth *gabelle*, conflicting interests seem to have divided the communities. Narbonne favored the new port, but wished it to be at Leucate, where its merchants already enjoyed certain privileges. An assembly of towns was held on 25 March 1336 but the other communities could not agree with Narbonne to underwrite the cost. Narbonne still offered 10 *sols* per tallageable person but attached numerous conditions. When the commissioners rejected these, the town dropped half of the conditions but significantly retained one, which demanded that everyone, of all social classes, living between Leucate and Bordeaux, who stood to profit from the new port, be obliged to con-

---

[171] *Ibid.*, nos. 3755, 3823, 3829, 3831. The hearth tax was to be apportioned on the basis of capacity to pay.

[172] Ménard, *Nismes*, II, *preuves*, 95-96.

[173] Huillard-Breholles, *Bourbon*, I, no. 2137, indicates this document, which is published in A. Jacotin (ed.), *Preuves de la Maison de Polignac*, Paris, 1898, I, pp. 425-426.

[174] Barroux, "Procès," passim, and especially pp. 97-105.

[175] Germain, *Commerce*, I, P.J. nos. 115, 120. These texts of 1339-1340 show that Philip VI had to authorize navigation of the lagoons near Montpellier because of the silting of Aigues Mortes.

tribute. The commissioners agreed to report to the crown on the matter, but nothing further was done.[176]

The interest in Mediterranean port facilities may be attributed in part to the royal hopes for a crusade. Many communities of the North and West, however, were also engaged in negotiating royal taxes of a regional nature, and these could only have been justified by deteriorating relations with England. One example is afforded by Saintonge, where a well-prepared French navy could menace the shipping lanes between Britain and Bordeaux, but where an unprotected coast would be vulnerable to the ravages of Anglo-Gascon mariners. Late in 1335, royal commissioners were sent to this region and were able to secure from the towns of La Rochelle and Saint-Jean d'Angély a grant of 4 d./l. on sales to finance local fortifications; the tax to be returned in the event there was no war.[177] Not long afterwards, on 9 January 1336, the town of Amiens made a grant for fleet maintenance.[178] Normandy was another region particularly concerned with the "army of the sea." The three bailiwicks of Rouen, Caen, and Cotentin produced over 10,500 pounds for fleet maintenance in 1336-1337.[179]

Besides these various royal taxes which were local in their application, there was another kind of tax which often served the same basic function although it was actually not a royal levy at all, but a municipal tax. Town governments were expected to obtain royal permission before levying municipal taxes. To obtain this permission, they sometimes had to promise the king a portion of the proceeds. Shared municipal taxes of this type were certainly not uncommon in Languedoil, but there is evidence of a sharp increase in their number during the period 1335-1337. The documents are often vague, usually saying merely that the town in question needs to pay its debts. The largest urban expenditures, however, were usually for their fortifications, walls, or bridges, and the majority of the shared municipal taxes of the late 1330s were in communities near the important northern frontier. We may probably regard these levies as another aspect of French war preparations, with most of the money

---

[176] BN Doat 52, fols. 224-231v; BN *Coll. Languedoc* 84, fols. 107r-108r. C. Port, *Essai sur l'histoire du commerce maritime de Narbonne*, Paris, 1854, pp. 199-201, discusses this project, which was reopened in 1359 without any result.

[177] AN P 2291, pp. 197-200 (La Rochelle) and 193-196 (Saint-Jean d'Angély). Vuitry, *Régime financier*, II, 11, and Viard, "Ressources," p. 175, are somewhat confused in their citations of the texts.

[178] AN P 2291, pp. 219-229, published by Thierry, *Recueil*, I, 459-461.

[179] Delisle, *Actes*, pp. 155-158, publishing BN *ms. fr.* 25996, no. 143. Of the total, Rouen produced over 5,100 pounds.

doubtless being applied to strengthening ramparts. The king's share of these taxes was a source of revenue which augmented his income in time of peace when other forms of extraordinary revenue were not easily available.

A municipal tax of 1 *d./l.* on merchandise, levied at Douai from 1334 to 1336 to repair the fortifications, yielded 10,791 *l.p.* in two years, of which Philip VI's share was one-fifth, or 2,158 *l.p.*[180] He received one-fourth of the municipal *maltôtes* levied at Seclin and Orchies, and one-third of a sales tax levied for three years at Miraumont with royal permission.[181] The king received a similar share (one-third) of taxes authorized at Crécy, Montreuil, and Crotoy in 1337.[182] Similar arrangements prevailed at Saint-Quentin, but there, the king relinquished his third of the tax late in 1335 as a means of repaying the knighting aid.[183] Another shared tax of the same type was the *maltôte* regularly levied at Tournai.[184]

All these local taxes, whether royal or municipal, whether for port maintenance, naval defenses or repair of town walls, collectively indicate a greater French concern with military preparedness in 1335-1336. These measures came at a time when the French crown's finances were in their worst condition of the reign. Although he still talked about a crusade until March of 1336, Philip had obligated himself to return the sums collected for the knighting aid, and when Benedict XII halted the crusade plans he also discontinued the tenth. Thus Philip was without an important source of peacetime revenue at the same moment when he was forced to tap his domainal resources in order to return the aid. The result was to leave him with drastically diminished treasury receipts in a year or badly deteriorating relations with England.[185] The desperate state of royal finances probably helps to explain the very local orientation of the war preparations of 1335-1336. The inhabitants of each region

---

[180] Viard, in AN AB xix 2636, copying extracts from AM Douai CC 2 and CC 684. Another text, in Jassemin, "Papiers," pp. 189-192, indicates the royal concern with the defensive posture of the northern towns. It lists provisions ordered for the garrison of Lille.

[181] Viard, in AN AB xix 2640, citing texts from Menant's Chamber of Accounts extracts in Bibliothèque de Rouen ms. 3404, fol. 7r.

[182] AN J 384, no. 1.

[183] Le Maire, *St. Quentin*, II, no. 529.

[184] *LC*, no. 52; A. d'Herbomez, "Philippe de Valois et la maletôte à Tournai," *MA*, xx (1907), 57-81.

[185] The extremely low treasury receipts indicated in AN KK 5 for 1336 are shown in Appendix I, Table 4.

were, in effect, being asked to support such preparations as were in their own immediate interest and conformed to their rather parochial criteria for "evident necessity."[186]

If the king was appealing for aid on this basis, even at so local a level, he had to have some justification for doing so. In fact, there was every reason to fear a new outbreak between France and England after 1335. Not only did the French show little real desire for a settlement of the Gascon question in 1333, but they seemed determined to thwart Edward III's effort to subdue Scotland. Following Edward's victory at Halidon Hill in July of 1333, the supporters of David Bruce needed French assistance in order to continue an effective struggle, and this assistance Philip VI was willing to provide.[187] Benedict XII rightly perceived that Philip was incapable of arbitrating impartially the Anglo-Scottish dispute, but the pope himself was too uncompromising to negotiate an Anglo-French settlement.[188]

Determined to save his inheritance in Guyenne from French absorption, Edward III, like his grandfather before him, saw that France might be vulnerable to attack from the North. There the frontier was relatively close to Paris; Edward's father-in-law controlled the three counties of Hainault, Holland, Zealand; and there was a strong anti-French party in Flanders.[189] Throughout the Low Countries, but especially in Flanders, the economic importance of England's wool gave Edward a valuable diplomatic tool. The pope found most disquieting the efforts of the English king to build a network of alliances in the Netherlands, but because these treaties often took the form of economic and commercial agreements it was hard to attack them as inimical to peace.[190]

The greatest complication in the effort to gain an Anglo-French settlement was created by the excommunicated emperor, Louis IV. The pope regarded him as a heretic and refused to countenance French efforts to draw closer to Louis and plead his cause at Avignon. Edward III needed Louis' friendship since it would greatly enhance his diplomatic schemes in the Netherlands if Louis were to name him imperial vicar there. The alleged papal partiality for France, which Edward suspected and re-

---

[186] See above, for instance, for the resistance of inland places to paying for the upkeep of Aigues Mortes. Montpellier, on the other hand, had been ready to pay rather generously for this project.

[187] Déprez, *Préliminaires*, pp. 92, 126-127. See also *Foedera*, II pt. 3, pp. 114 and 146.

[188] Jenkins, *Papal Efforts*, pp. 9-17.   [189] Lucas, *Low Countries*, Chapter VI.

[190] Jenkins, *Papal Efforts*, p. 22.

sented, helped bring him and the emperor into closer relations. When Edward and Louis finally concluded their alliance, in mid-1337, the pope compromised his subsequent efforts as peacemaker by allowing his anti-imperial sentiments to get the better of him. He authorized Philip VI to levy a tenth on the clergy for defensive warfare against the German "heretic." While Edward remained allied with Louis, Philip was able to claim that he was waging a holy war,[191] and while this argument made little impression on French laymen, it permitted Philip to tax the clergy and enroll the bishops as propagandists without any pangs of conscience.[192]

Although the Anglo-Imperial alliance may have helped the French propaganda position eventually, it was not concluded until the middle of 1337. In the meantime, Philip's relations with Benedict XII were little better than Edward's, thanks to the pope's change of position regarding the crusade, his cancellation of the tenth, and his mediation efforts which Philip regarded as interference.[193] Since Benedict's policy had antagonized both France and England, it "ended by precipitating the very conflict which it aimed at avoiding."[194]

The immediate area of Anglo-French confrontation was, as always, Gascony. As early as 1335, Cordes had fortified itself against Anglo-Gascon "brigands."[195] English raids occurred in 1336, especially in Béarn, and in July, the French retaliated by taking the town and castle of Puymirol.[196] The count of Foix assumed command of French forces in the southwest, and in October 1336, the king increased the number of troops under his direction on the Gascon frontier.[197] Despite local resistance, some money for troops was raised from Cahors, and doubtless from other places near to the sensitive border.[198] Increasing royal attention was devoted to strengthening *château* garrisons.[199]

As fighting began to break out in the southwest, and Edward III increased his diplomatic activity in the Netherlands, Philip VI increased his aid to the Scots.[200] When the English coalition in the Low Countries became more ominous in May 1337, Philip responded by ordering the

[191] *Ibid.*, pp. 36f.

[192] See below, Chapter IV, note 91, for the king's effort to enlist the bishops as propagandists. For England's position, see *Foedera*, II pt. 3, pp. 195-196.

[193] Jenkins, *Papal Efforts*, p. 28.

[194] Perroy, *The Hundred Years War*, p. 90.

[195] Portal, *Cordes*, p. 47.   [196] *HL*, IX, 489, note 3.

[197] BN Doat 164, fol. 146.

[198] Dufour, *Cahors*, pp. 103-104; AM Millau EE 3 (tax roll for raising troops).

[199] AN JJ 70, no. 78.   [200] Déprez, *Préliminaires*, pp. 127f.

confiscation of Guyenne.[201] Thus began the newest phase of the Anglo-French conflict, later called the Hundred Years' War. It was to bring about a critical new phase in the fiscal and constitutional history of the French monarchy.

[201] Perroy, *The Hundred Years War*, p. 92.

CHAPTER IV

The Beginnings of the Hundred Years' War, 1337-1340

1. Early Resistance to Tax Requests

WITH war a virtual certainty, Philip VI had already proclaimed the *arrière-ban* throughout the kingdom on 30 April 1337.[1] This order was clearly a fiscal device. As in 1328, the war subsidy was to be based squarely upon the obligation of personal military service. Three weeks later, on 20 May, the count of Foix was ordered to have French troops muster at Marmande on 8 July.[2] This summons was doubtless aimed at those lords who were expected to serve in the army personally. From the outset, Philip expected to wage a two-front war, for his northern subjects were to muster at Amiens on the same date (8 July).[3]

Within a week following the *arrière-ban*, the city of Paris had agreed to supply a subsidy of 400 horsemen, to be supported for six months if the king went to battle in person and for four months if he did not.[4] It was anticipated that 18,000 *l.p.* would support the force for four months, and Paris was subsequently permitted to levy a sales tax to raise this sum. All inhabitants would be required to contribute.[5]

In Languedoc, the *arrière-ban* of 30 April was not executed locally for several weeks because of the delays inherent in medieval communications.[6] The crown sought to facilitate collection of a subsidy by establishing a uniform mode of payment for those who fined in lieu of rendering personal military service. The rates were based on the hearth, which was the traditional unit of assessment in Languedoc. Non-nobles were to pay a total of 20 *s.t.* per hearth over a four-month period (25 *l.t.* for every hundred hearths for each of four consecutive months). This rate would apply also to non-noble lands held by nobles. Fiefs, whether held by nobles or non-nobles, would be assessed at 20 percent of a year's income.[7]

Having ordered the application of this set of rates in Languedoc and

---

[1] *HL*, x, cols. 764-765, and the discussion by Molinier, *HL*, IX, 490, note 3. For a sketch of the military preparations, see Déprez, *Préliminaires*, pp. 154, note 1, and 157, note 1.

[2] *LC*, no. 71.   [3] Varin, *Reims*, II, 781-784.

[4] J. Viard, *Documents parisiens du règne de Philippe VI de Valois*, I, Paris, 1899, 291-293; *Ord.*, XII, 39-42.

[5] *Ibid*. It will be recalled that sums still to be refunded from the knighting aid were deducted from the subsidy of 1337 (BN Clairambault 471, pp. 183-227).

[6] *HL*, x, cols. 764-765.   [7] *Ibid*., col. 773.

Auvergne, the royal government almost immediately began to back down. On 23 May, before any protests could have reached Paris from lower Languedoc, the king instructed his tax negotiators to collect first from the towns and lands of the royal domain and the clergy before trying to raise money from possessions of the nobility.[8] Already, therefore, some resistance by the nobles was anticipated. On 10 June, additional instructions deferred payment of the first monthly installment until the end of that month and spelled out details of the rates the king had established.[9] A new letter of the same date, received in Languedoc two days later than the first one,[10] sharply modified the rate of the hearth tax.

The king doubtless was receiving information which led him to make conciliatory gestures, for by 10 June, the earliest protests against taxation could have reached Paris from Languedoc. The crown now reduced by one-fifth the tax to be collected monthly from each hundred hearths in royal and church lands. Moreover, "men of the barons and other nobles" not only had their assessment similarly reduced but in addition were to pay each month only two-thirds of the new rate (or 13 *l.* 6 *s.* 8 *d.* per 100 hearths), the remainder to be paid at the following Easter and then only if the war continued. Those subjects of nobles who were tallageable at will would not be taxed.[11] In less than three weeks, the crown had therefore retreated considerably from its original demands.

Before these concessions had been made public in the south of France, there arose the wave of protests which the government must have hoped to avert. They are illustrated by three documents dated 27 June 1337,[12] two of these embodying protests by members of the nobility. Those of the *cité* of Carcassonne, complaining to the tax commissioners, presented privileges dating from 1304 and asked that they not be forced to pay.[13] The nobles of the *cité* of Narbonne also presented privileges three decades old and their argument is worthy of notice as an unusual one. They claimed that they were tallageable by the *bourg* and *cité* of Narbonne and were thus subject to the hearth tax that the town was to pay for the subsidy. They were therefore protesting the revenue tax on nobles as a

---

[8] *Ibid.*, col. 770. [9] *Ibid.*, cols. 770-771.

[10] Local officials gave their *vidimus* to the first letter on 3 July and to the second letter (*ibid.*, cols. 771-774) on 5 July.

[11] *Ibid.*

[12] Cited in the next four notes, these letters are the earliest of which we have record, but they come from the parts of the kingdom furthest from Paris. Some regions nearer to the capital probably had complained before the king's letters of 10 June.

[13] BN Doat 52, fols. 259-269.

double taxation which had been explicitly forbidden by Philip IV in 1303.[14] It appears from a subsequent text that some nobles of the seneschalsy of Carcassonne did in fact pay a fifth of their revenues for not going to war and that royal tax commissioners had tried to obtain the same from some who did answer the summons.[15]

Objections to the subsidy were by no means limited to the nobility. In the third protest of 27 June, the town of Narbonne found the hearth tax itself too high (news of the reduced rates not yet having arrived). It was claimed that the inhabitants were being taxed by commissioners who had not obtained the town's agreement and were probably acting in a manner of which the king was not aware. There followed the argument that the town was impoverished as a result of piracy, poor crops, and earlier royal taxes.[16] On 10 July, it was Montpellier which protested, claiming that the town was under no obligation to pay a subsidy.[17] Meanwhile, however, the crown received and acted upon Narbonne's complaint, ordering collection of only so much as had been levied for the last general war subsidy in 1328. This decision resulted in a payment of 1,250 *l.t.* by Narbonne.[18] In 1328, the entire seneschalsy had paid at an average of 10 *sols* per hearth, so a reversion to the rate of that year would mean a tax in 1337 of only half the amount originally demanded.

The clergy in the south were as reluctant to pay as were the nobles and towns, and the government showed a conciliatory spirit while at the same time seeking to keep up pressure until some sort of tax was negotiated. On 7 July, Philip VI ordered that clergy of the diocese of Nîmes were not to be forced to pay extraordinary levies on non-noble property in their places of residence.[19] Since scores of other royal enactments in these years gave exactly the opposite order, this was a special case and was evidently intended to avoid the sort of double taxation which had induced the nobles of Narbonne to protest. The clergy were being freed for the moment from contributing to the payments of their own localities because the king was hoping to collect a tax from them as a class. The effort to gain this aid was inaugurated in July. On the 21st, Philip ordered a commissioner to enter the seneschalsy of Carcassonne, assemble

---

[14] BN *Coll. Languedoc* 84, fols. 120r-121v.

[15] *Ibid.*, fol. 118r-v, a statement in September to the effect that certain nobles had paid.

[16] BN Doat 52, fols. 251-257. Two days earlier (*ibid.*, fols. 247-249), on 25 June, the consuls of Narbonne had demanded that the tax be returned if there were no war, presumably equating "war" with "invasion."

[17] *HL*, x, cols. 775-776; *Gr. Chartrier*, no. 1015.

[18] BN Doat 52, fol. 283.   [19] AD Hérault A 4, fols. 86v-88.

the clergy, remind them of the iniquities of the king of England and point out that those accustomed to living in peace under royal protection ought to aid in the defense of the kingdom. The response to this appeal must have been evasive, for on 1 September, a new royal letter asked for an "agreeable response" and specifically requested a tenth for two years, which would prejudice no rights and would cease if the war did. At length, some sort of favorable response seems to have been received, but opinion was divided and one abbot, who obtained a further delay in order to consult the pope, eventually was cited before the royal court.[20]

For the most part, the story in Languedoc in 1337 was one of negotiations with individual towns, once the government had had to retreat from its proposed general hearth tax. Lunel apparently escaped the subsidy by virtue of the exemption accorded to its seigneur, Charles of Spain.[21] Le Puy, whose commerce had suffered seriously, could only pay very little.[22] The town of Beaucaire provided a "loan" of 400 *l.t.*[23] A somewhat unclear local history indicates that Alès paid its tax by equipping and sending a contingent of sergeants to the Gascon front.[24] Montpellier, which had protested that it owed no subsidy, received a royal letter in August suspending the taxation of all citizens who were subjects of the king of Majorca.[25] In the Gévaudan region, subjects of the Bishop of Mende also escaped paying the war subsidy.[26]

Royal efforts to collect money in 1337 met with disappointment in two districts that were close to English Gascony—the seneschalsies of Toulouse and Quercy. There is no evidence of tax grants by the *jugeries* of the Toulousain, although Cordes was certainly approached for money. This community rejected a modest hearth tax of 6 *s.t.*[27] In Quercy, a local

[20] BN *Coll. Languedoc* 84, fols. 125-128v; BN Baluze 390, no. 32.

[21] BN Clairambault 212, no. 75. Also exempted were subjects of the viscount of Narbonne, for lands held of him: BN NAF 7430, fol. 151.

[22] E. Delcambre, "Le paréage du Puy," *BEC*, XCII (1931), 325, citing *HL*, x, cols. 940-942, a letter of 1344 from Philip VI acknowledging a long series of economic miseries which had afflicted the Velay region.

[23] AD Gard, ms. inventory of AM Beaucaire (1772), fol. 165v, indicating a high municipal sales tax to raise the money for both the war subsidy and the earlier tax for the repairs at Aigues Mortes.

[24] Bardon, *Alais*, I, 98, gave an incorrect date (8 June) for the mustering of the army and stated that Alès formed a contingent of troops on 30 June only to be asked for more men in mid-July. The town archives do not amplify Bardon's statements.

[25] AM Montpellier G-4, no. 3304; G-5, no. 3345.　　[26] Barroux, "Procès," p. 88.

[27] Portal, *Cordes*, p. 47, citing AM Cordes CC 30. The detailed municipal accounts of Toulouse (AM Toulouse CC 1845) indicate collection of large sums to pay the fine incurred in 1335-1336 (above, Chapter III, note 22) but they say nothing about a war subsidy in 1337.

assembly of nobles and consuls of towns evidently convened to discuss a subsidy, but royal commissioners ran into violent resistance when they tried to collect.[28] After considerable negotiation, the crown obtained small sums from Martel, Cajarc, and Gourdon.[29]

In Rouergue, the seigneurs and towns usually supplied their own contingents of troops. The nobles put into the field an army of nearly 6,000 men, 500 of them mounted. John of Armagnac, count of Rodez, personally raised a force of 363 mounted men and 5,133 sergeants.[30] To support this army, he requested a subsidy from his own subjects and ran into opposition. He finally accepted 400 pounds from the *bourg* of Rodez as a loan deductible from the annual *taille* owed him by the burghers.[31] This seigneurial tax substituted for a royal one in that it supported the French army in Gascony. The inhabitants of Rodez seemed no more willing to support their own count than to aid the king. Millau, a royal town, sent forty mounted men to the seneschal at Villefranche in June, and levied a municipal tax for their upkeep.[32]

The crown may have been willing to reduce friction by letting individual lords and towns actually raise the money for the army in Rouergue. Nevertheless, the king claimed the right to tax the subjects of an intermediate lord, and in September 1337, four commissioners arrived to collect a tax of 3 *s.* per hearth.[33] The amount was so small that the ensuing debate must have revolved around principle. The subjects of the count of Rodez, led by the clergy, made bitter protests. They claimed that the count was responsible to the king for supplying armed men and that they were responsible to the count and owed nothing to the king once they contributed to the count's army. If the king taxed them he would be impairing the count's ability to render service, for "no man can serve two

[28] Lacoste, *Quercy*, III, 86, mentioned an assembly and subsequent uprising which are placed between 1336 and 1338.

[29] AM Martel BB 3, fols. 2-7; AM Cajarc CC supp., no. 73 (indicating a partial payment on 16 September); AD Lot F 208 (extracts of AM Gourdon BB 2, which is no longer extant).

[30] C. Sibertin-Blanc, "La levée du subside de 1337 en Rouergue et l'Hôpital d'Aubrac au début de la guerre de Cent Ans, à propos d'un mandement inédit de Philippe de Valois," *BPH*, 1953-1954, p. 317, note 3. De Gaujal, *Etudes*, II, 173-174.

[31] *Ibid.*, p. 317. The protest of Rodez and the subsequent agreement ratified by the count are in AD Aveyron G 965 *bis*, fols. 28v-29v, 32r-v.

[32] AM Millau EE 3; EE 118, unnumbered text. Either to support these sergeants, or perhaps in addition to them, Millau was required to pay the sum of 500 *l.t.*, much of which was still unpaid in 1343 when the crown remitted half the total: *ibid.*, CC 508, no. 139.

[33] Molinier, in *HL*, IX, 491, note 1; Sibertin-Blanc, "Levée," pp. 322-324; BN Doat 186, fols. 145r-153v.

masters."[34] To these arguments the commissioners replied that they were only doing their job. They would not accept an appeal, nor would they transmit one to higher authority.[35] We are left uninformed as to the final disposal of these appeals. Proctors of the hospital of Notre-Dame d'Au-brac were still in heated debate with the commissioners in mid-January 1338.[36] Clergy of the dioceses of Vabres and Rodez claimed that they could not pay without the permission of the pope, but the commissioners said that they did not have the authority to grant the necessary delay.[37] Whatever may have resulted from these particular controversies, it is likely that Rouergue, by sending its own military contingents to the war, gave the king more aid in 1337 than did the neighboring seneschalsies of Toulouse and Quercy. Even in Rouergue, however, the right of the king to seek a subsidy in money from other than his direct subjects, had been bitterly disputed.

For Languedoc, a war with England inevitably focussed attention on Gascony, but the government in Paris probably felt greater concern over the much closer northern frontier. Alarmed over Edward III's growing system of alliances in the Low Countries, Philip VI had ordered his northern vassals to muster at Amiens in July. Meanwhile, he undertook to counteract the English king's effort to draw Flanders into an alliance against France. Eventually, Edward would succeed when his economic pressure on the Flemish cloth interests proved stronger than Count Louis' loyalty to Philip.[38] In 1337, however, Philip still hoped to buy support, and he acceded to a Flemish request and canceled the large unpaid remainder of war indemnities which the Flemings owed him.[39]

A major problem for the French king in the first years of the war was created by the absence of large-scale fighting. If southern districts near to Gascony were reluctant to contribute to the war, the regions farther north must have been even more dubious about the need for taxes when the summer wore on without any invasion from the Netherlands. Easily victorious over England in the 1320s, the French had little reason to perceive a case of "evident necessity" in 1337.

The existence in 1337 of what we could now call a "phony war" is well documented by Philip's correspondence with one of his important mili-

---

[34] *Ibid.*; Sibertin-Blanc, "Levée," pp. 320, 324-325, 329-330.

[35] *Ibid.*, p. 325.   [36] *Ibid.*, p. 331.

[37] AD Aveyron G 10, no. 67, fol. 62v.

[38] Lucas, *Low Countries*, pp. 200f., 240-278, 328f.

[39] AN JJ 71, no. 16; PP 117, p. 524. On the magnitude of the unpaid indemnity, see Jassemin, "Papiers," pp. 180-182. It had been the subject of considerable litigation among the Flemings (Furgeot, *Actes*, 1, no. 1501).

tary allies, the count of Savoy. In mid-June, the king was still unsure
where the danger would be greatest and could not yet decide whether
the count should go to Amiens or Marmande. Two months later, the
threat was most evident in the North and the count was asked to be at
Amiens on 23 September.[40] Yet the summons was postponed to 8 October
and then to 1 November. By early October, the danger from the north
seemed so grave as to warrant summoning not only the count of Savoy
but also the lord of Albret in the distant southwest, at the head of a sizeable body of troops, to Amiens on 15 November.[41] With the tax collections so closely tied to calling out the army and the existence of an actual
state of war, we may well imagine how such uncertainties tended to
complicate the already difficult problem of negotiating a subsidy.

With regard to the taxation of northern France in 1337, the case of
Normandy presents serious problems because the narrative sources are
far from clear. Both Coville and Prentout, the historians of the Norman
Estates, have said that the first true meeting of this assembly took place
in 1337.[42] According to one chronicler, the barons, prelates, and towns
of Normandy were assembled and asked to grant a tax. Led by the
counts of Eu and Harcourt, the assembly refused until given a renewal
of Norman privileges, after which it offered the king a *grant somme*. The
account goes on to say that soon afterwards, the king went back on his
promises and instituted *maltôtes* and *gabelles*.[43] This report, and that of
a second chronicler cited by Prentout, both actually seem to be referring
to the assembly of 1339 and the indirect taxes subsequently established
in 1340 and 1341.[44] As sources for a Norman assembly in 1337, they are
highly suspect. One Norman source for 1337 which is not a chronicle indicates that the mayor and *échevins* of Rouen made a grant patterned
after that of Paris, offering to support 200 mounted troops for the four
months of June to September.[45] This text suggests a certain amount of
local bargaining rather than an assembly.

The only source which really indicates Norman assemblies in 1337 is
an unpublished Rouen chronicle which appears to differentiate between
the circumstances of 1337 and those of 1339, although not very clearly.
The writer speaks of several meetings of barons, prelates, and towns at

[40] *LC*, nos. 72, 76.   [41] *Ibid.*, nos. 77-78, 80-81.
[42] Coville, *Etats Norm.*, pp. 43-44; Prentout, *Etats Norm.*, I, 92-93, citing S. Luce
(ed.), *Chronique des quatre premiers Valois (1327-1393)*, Paris, 1862, pp. 8-9.
[43] *Ibid.*
[44] C. de Beaurepaire (ed.), *Chronique normande de Pierre Cochon*, Rouen, 1870
(hereafter cited as *Chron. Cochon*), pp. 56-57. On 1339, see below, notes 177-180.
[45] BN NAF 20025, no. 131.

Pont Audemer and Rouen and letters to the king defending their liberties.[46] If several such meetings did occur in 1337, they must have occurred in the spring, before Rouen's grant of troops for the summer
months. Perhaps the crown did hold assemblies, encounter baronial opposition and decide to negotiate individually with the towns. To have
done all this before June, however, would have required a very early effort to raise money from the Normans. In short, the available evidence
leaves serious doubts as to whether there really were Norman assemblies
in 1337. Even if there were, the important meeting, in terms of the history of the Norman Estates, was that of 1339.

Scattered information from other parts of the kingdom indicates collection of varying amounts of taxes in 1337. The town of Poitiers granted
500 pounds, to be collected not only from inhabitants but also from those
living in the suburbs. The assessment seems to have been based on the
individual's capacity to pay.[47] Reims was granted permission to delay
payment of the subsidy until 29 September, but then it became necessary
to obtain a royal letter halting sergeants of the king who had been seizing the property of the burghers to enforce payment.[48] In Auvergne,
Montferrand had paid a part of the subsidy by mid-September. The form
of the tax is not stated, and the payment in question was but 41½
pounds.[49] The crown augmented revenues from this region by threatening to levy fines for acquisitions of noble fiefs. Investigations of property
holdings were called off in 1338 only after a 400-pound "loan" had been
granted to the king.[50] In Auvergne, as in Languedoc, a 20 s. hearth tax
had been sought originally from non-nobles who did not serve in the
army, only to be reduced by one-fifth before collection could have been
well-advanced.[51] Aurillac is known to have paid the tax of 1337 but there

---

[46] *Chronicon Rothomagensis apud Labbe Nova Bibliotheca*, ms. I, pp. 386-387,
quoted by A. Cheruel, *Histoire de Rouen pendant l'époque communale, 1150-1382*,
II, Rouen, 1844, pp. 10-11: *Praelati, barones, et communiae Normanniae apud Pon-
tem Audomari et Rothomagi pluries se congregant et pluries miserunt ad regem
pro suis, et propriis et communibus, libertatibus defendis.* The same chronicle, pp.
387-388, follows immediately with what is clearly a discussion of the events of 1339.
Cheruel saw these years as a running debate between the Normans and the crown
over Norman privileges, probably a fair assessment, but even this chronicle does
not make it absolutely clear that Norman assemblies at Pont Audemer and Rouen
occurred in 1337.

[47] *AHP*, XLVI, 52-62.   [48] Varin, *Reims*, II, 772-773.

[49] *INV AM Montferrand*, II, p. 1 (CC 333).

[50] *Ibid.*, I, 312 (CC 1), for Philip VI's order of April 1338, canceling investigations after receipt of the loan. The original order to obtain declarations of fief
holdings is in *Ord.*, XII, 37-38.

[51] AM Riom CC 10, no. 1338.

is no indication as to the bargaining process which may have been involved.[52] Farther west, municipal accounts indicate that Périgueux paid a subsidy (or portion of a subsidy) totaling 335 *l.* 18 *s.* 3 *d.*[53] La Rochelle and Saint-Jean d'Angély paid by means of an indirect tax ("imposition") on wine and grain, but they attached conditions to the grant, notably the demand that the other towns of Saintonge also pay. It was mid-October when this tax was finally negotiated, and royal confirmation did not come until November.[54]

Various factors affected the collection of the subsidies granted by the different regions. A persistent complication was the higher nobility. Philip VI deemed it wise to conciliate this class, while some of his zealous officials tended to put fiscal pressure on them. Eudes of Burgundy, count of Artois (an *apanage*), complained to the king about musters of Artesian nobles by tax commissioners in the bailiwick of Amiens. On 23 July, Philip VI acceded to Eudes' request and ordered that the nobles of Artois not be compelled to muster.[55] One month later, he directed the commissioners to provide an exact count of the nobles who had answered the summons in the bailiwick of Amiens. Included were orders on publishing the summons, and no noble was to be excused from mustering.[56] Presumably this order was not intended to include the nobles of the county of Artois, but its apparent ambiguity was sufficient to cause some disregard of the earlier orders. On 10 September, the king somewhat impatiently reiterated his command that Artesian nobles not be forced to muster.[57] That this entire correspondence about musters was actually concerned with taxation seems clear. The governor of Artois, in declaring that the subsidy would not be levied in the county,[58] was certainly referring to the royal orders just described.

Arrangements made with certain other lay lords also diminished the tax totals reaching the treasury. While it is tempting (and in some cases doubtless accurate) to treat these tax concessions as part of an effort to placate the nobility, it is equally possible to regard some of them as a means of paying faithful royal servants their salaries. By December 1337, the royal expenses had so exceeded tax collections that Philip VI ordered the withholding of part of the salaries of his officials. This move met great opposition from the very persons on whom the king most de-

---

[52] *INV AM Aurillac*, II, 12 (EE 3).   [53] *INV AM Périgueux*, p. 75 (CC 55).

[54] AN P 2291, pp. 445-450; PP 117, pp. 458-459; Viard, "Ressources," p. 178; Vuitry, *Régime financier*, II, 12.

[55] BN NAF 7604 (Fontanieu 73), fols. 70-71; BN *ms. fr.* 20685, pp. 231-232.

[56] *Ibid.*, pp. 175-176.   [57] *Ibid.*, p. 232.

[58] AD Pas-de-Calais A 563.

pended, and it thus enjoyed very limited success.[59] If, however, the government lacked the funds with which to pay its officials, it was possible to compensate them by means of tax exemptions. Thus Savary de Vivonne, seneschal of Toulouse, was permitted to have all the subsidy which the crown collected from his subjects.[60] Pierre Trousseau, the royal chamberlain, received the right to tax his own subjects who had 50 *l.* or more in property.[61] These grants were made early in 1338, and hence after the withholding of salaries had been ordered. The privileges, however, were not limited to those holding special positions in the government. The viscount of Thouars received by "special grace" the same right given to Savary de Vivonne (i.e., to have for himself the subsidy raised from his men).[62] Both these seigneurs agreed that the action would not prejudice any royal rights in the future.[63] In these cases, therefore, the crown's legal right to tax subjects of an intermediate seigneur was recognized and protected. However, certain ecclesiastical seigneurs obtained exemption for their tallageable subjects. The subsidy commissioners were forbidden to collect the war subsidy from tallageable subjects of the chapters of Saint-Père and Saint-Etienne[64] in Troyes. In October, it was ordered that those subject to the jurisdiction of the Paris cathedral chapter, in the bailiwicks of Chartres and Gisors as well as Paris, be excused from paying the tax until 15 November.[65] Eventually, those in Paris probably did pay, because the king ordered in December that all inhabitants of the capital contribute to the city's subsidy payment.[66]

Royal efforts to tax the French kingdom in 1337 thus produced mediocre results. The crown collected money in most parts of the realm, but the promise to return the knighting aid made necessary some deductions from the totals. Moreover, the whole fiscal effort encountered opposition from the nobility and from the southern towns. Facing such resistance, Philip VI retreated, permitting nobles and clergy various concessions regarding the taxation of their subjects and scaling down the tax rate imposed on the towns. Although Paris and Rouen granted fairly sub-

---

[59] Viard, "Ressources," pp. 181-183. For the order withholding salaries, see *Ord.*, XII, pp. 38-39; BN NAF 7604 (Fontanieu 73), fols. 137-139. A later ordinance (*Ord.*, XII, 42, 20 February 1338), exempted officers of the treasury and Chamber of Accounts from this tax, suggesting that the king may have been under pressure to modify his earlier ruling.

[60] AN J 384, no. 6.

[61] AN P 2291, p. 461.

[62] *AHP*, XIII, 137-138.

[63] Texts cited above, notes 60-61.

[64] BN *ms. fr.* 25698, nos. 73, 75.

[65] AN K 42, no. 43.

[66] Texts cited above, note 4.

stantial sums, returns generally must have been disappointing and probably were collected slowly. Given the difficult position in which the treasury found itself in 1336, the monarchy was ill-equipped financially to meet the expenses it incurred in 1337.

Unquestionably, these expenses were considerable. Even without an active campaign, the guarding of French frontiers had been estimated to cost 29,000 pounds a month in 1327. In 1339, when the alloy of the coinage was the same, these costs were estimated at 57,000 pounds per month.[67] At such rates, the salaries of troops during the last seven months of 1337 may have equaled the entire subsidy of 1328. Yet subsidy receipts in 1337 probably did not approach this figure because so many Frenchmen evaded payment or denied that a genuine war was underway.[68] Troop salaries, moreover, were only part of Philip VI's military expenses. In October, he arranged for naval assistance from the Genoese admiral, Antoine Doria, who promised to serve with twenty galleys for 900 florins per month.[69] None of these figures include logistical expenses, which also could be considerable. In May 1337, the king incurred another expense which was unrelated to the war but which amounted to more than the combined subsidy payments of Paris and Rouen. He purchased a castle and barony from the count of Dreux.[70]

Mounting expenses and lagging receipts were not new experiences for the French crown. As in the past, the government tried to remedy the situation by various fiscal expedients. In 1337, the mints began offering a higher price for silver and were able to resume operations. Philip VI began to overvalue the *gros tournois*, and thereby inaugurated a new period of coinage alterations which would prove extremely unpopular after 1340.[71] The crown also undertook a new investigation of usury, which aroused complaints as early as April 1337.[72] Soon thereafter, the

[67] Above, Chapter II, notes 162, 167. In 1339, when the money was of the same alloy as in 1327-1328, royal advisers believed that it now would require 37,700 *l.t.* per month to guard the Gascon frontier and another 7,200 *l.t.* for Saintonge. Jusselin, "Comment la France. . . ," pp. 228-229.

[68] The estimate cited *ibid.* said that an offensive campaign for four months would cost 900,000 pounds. This figure should be compared with the highest war subsidy collected up to this time: 735,000 *l.t.* in 1304. The tax of 1328 had produced about a third of what the campaign was estimated to cost. The high costs of war may in part be due to the widespread use of the high *grands-gages* salary scale for troops. In any case, Philip lacked funds, and in 1338, he had fallen 29,000 pounds in debt to the count of Foix and had to cede him half the viscounty of Lautrec as partial repayment. Lacoste, *Quercy*, III, 94.

[69] AN JJ 71, no. 21; BN *ms. fr.* 20691, p. 788; BN *Coll. Languedoc* 84, fol. 168r-v.

[70] BN NAF 7374, fols. 304-309.   [71] Appendix I, Table I.

[72] Germain, *Commerce*, I, P.J. no. 112.

property of Lombards was seized to finance the war, and on 19 May, the government confiscated the principal of usurious debts as in 1331.[73] It is possible that Philip VI also reinstituted the 4 *d./l.* export tax in 1337.[74] A special tax was also imposed on lawyers.[75] Finally, the crown began a new inquiry into the acquisition of fiefs by clergy and non-nobles. We have seen that this investigation persuaded Montferrand to make a loan to the king,[76] and commissioners for *franc-fief* were also active in Normandy, the Ile-de-France, and Montpellier.[77]

The most important use of fief investigations, however, was in southwestern France, where the crown overcame resistance to taxation by means of tactics similar to those employed in 1325. On 13 November 1337, Philip VI appointed two captains-general for Languedoc, the master of crossbowmen, Etienne le Galois de la Baume, and Simon d'Erquery. These officers were given complete authority to supervise military operations in Gascony and Agenais and to perform a wide variety of other functions, such as raising money, investigating abuses, and instituting reforms.[78] Once on the scene, they put to use their multiple powers, naming commissioners late in December who were to negotiate subsidies, investigate usury and monetary violations, correct abuses and levy fines for fief acquisitions.[79] These commissioners proceeded immediately to the districts which had most vigorously resisted taxation in 1337—Rouergue, Quercy, and the Toulousain. Rodez was fined 1,000 *l.t.* for usury violations, far more than the war subsidy it had resisted the year before.[80] Millau paid 1,200 *l.t.*, more than double its usual war subsidy, in order to be excused from the subsidy and pardoned for various offenses.[81] The communities of the viscounty of Caraman, late in 1338,

---

[73] C. Piton, *Les Lombards en France et à Paris*, Paris, 1892, I, 37, note 1; E. Cabrol, *Annales de Villefranche de Rouergue*, Villefranche, 1860, I p. 208; Ord., XII, 35-36; Henneman, "Italians," p. 33.

[74] Officials were certainly supervising exports from Languedoc in 1337, according to BN Doat 52, fol. 245r-v. See the comments in Henneman, "Financing," p. 294, note 120.

[75] BN Colbert (*Cinq Cents*) 64, pp. 109-110, for the tax in Burgundy. For the Beaucaire district, see Ménard, *Nismes*, II, *preuves*, 101.

[76] See above, note 50.

[77] AN JJ 70, no. 340; BN Clairambault 471, pp. 229-247; AM Montpellier G-5, no. 3346.

[78] Their commission is included in a number of different documents, among them BN Doat 186, fols. 131v-143v; AN JJ 71, no. 151; JJ 72, no. 4. See also the discussion by Molinier in *HL*, IX, 498-499, note 1.

[79] *Ibid.*; BN Doat 186, fols. 131v-143v.   [80] *Ibid.*

[81] AN JJ 71, no. 251. For a fuller discussion of this entire mission, see Henneman, "Enquêteurs," pp. 337-339, especially note 139 regarding Millau.

made a similar agreement, offering 400 pounds as a combined war subsidy and fine.[82]

Throughout the seneschalsy of Toulouse the fiscal transactions of 1338 closely resembled those of 1325, as towns paid large lump sums to satisfy commissioners with multiple powers. Thus, in March 1338, the towns of the *jugerie* of Albigeois offered 5,000 pounds and some sergeants as well in order to be quit of the war subsidy, escape fines for monetary violations and fief acquisitions, and receive certain reforms and privileges. Through comparable transactions, the commissioners obtained 9,000 *l. petits tournois* from the *jugerie* of Villelongue, a 10 *s.* hearth tax from the *jugerie* of Rieux, and a 5,000-pound lump sum from the *jugerie* of Verdun. At Toulouse itself, one citizen paid the large fine of 1,000 *l.t.* for violating the usury laws and on 24 April, the *capitouls* offered the crown 12,000 *l.t.* by way of paying the subsidy and receiving a pardon for other offenses which the commissioners were investigating. Once again, it becomes evident that royal commissioners with multiple powers were the most successful subsidy negotiators because they could exert multiple pressures.[83]

The authority to sell privileges and levy fines was not invariably tied to subsidy negotiations in 1338. The crown obtained 5,000 *l.t.* from Narbonne in a completely separate transaction uniting the *bourg* and *cité*.[84] The inhabitants of Auch paid 1,200 *l.t.* to be pardoned for "excesses."[85] In Quercy, the town of Cajarc seems only to have been concerned with the war subsidy and not with other levies. This community sent twenty sergeants to the army in the fall of 1338, paying them to serve forty days.[86] Cahors, on the other hand, was certainly the object of multiple pressures. Erquery demanded the money to support 200 sergeants, had difficulty collecting it, and then sent usury commissioners who fined the Cahorsins 6,000 *l.t.* The town borrowed money to pay one installment of 3,000 *l.t.*, then obtained a 10 percent reduction in the total fine as well as a confirmation of privileges and royal letters confirming the Cahorsins' exemption from fines for *franc-fief*.[87]

[82] *Ibid.*, note 147.

[83] *Ibid.*, pp. 338-339, and notes 140-145. Such pressures did not, however, eliminate opposition to the subsidy in Rouergue. Protests against taxation were sent to the king by Villefranche (Cabrol, *Villefranche*, I, 209) and by Najac, Millau, and Saint-Antonin, which apparently acted together (unnumbered document in AM Millau CC 512). Philip VI also permitted Villeneuve-en-Rouergue an exemption from paying fines for fief acquisitions (AD Aveyron C 1519, no. 14).

[84] AN JJ 71, no. 89; *INV AM Narbonne, sér. AA*, pp. 9-10, 28.

[85] AN JJ 72, no. 386.

[86] AM Cajarc, CC *supp.*, no. 76; EE *supp.*, no. 71.

[87] Albe, "Cahors INV," nos. 352, 353, 358; Lacoste, *Quercy*, III, 89, 91.

The tax-raising effort during the winter and early spring of 1338 actually took place during a period of truce. Edward III's diplomatic arrangements were still incomplete and his finances were far from satisfactory so he had no difficulty agreeing to the winter truce which the pope's envoys had been trying to arrange.[88] This truce was to last until June, but the Gascon frontier was never entirely quiet and the French continued to maintain important forces in Agenais.[89] In preparing for a year of anticipated large-scale hostilities, Philip VI had to find ways to obtain a better response to his tax requests than in 1337. We have already considered his use of pressure tactics by investigatory commissioners. He also hoped to gain the utmost propaganda advantage from the English alliance with the excommunicated emperor. Late in March, Benedict XII granted Philip a two-year clerical tenth for use in repelling any attack by Louis IV.[90] On 4 May, as the expiration of the truce drew closer, Philip sent letters close to the bishops of France, ordering them to hold processions, special masses, and deliver sermons dealing with the need to defend the kingdom and restore peace. They were even told what things to stress in the sermons: the willingness of king and princes to risk their lives to defend the kingdom, the alliance of Edward III with a heretic, the fact that the English threat had prevented the crusade, and the intention of Edward to invade France.[91]

Even before embarking on the propaganda campaign, the crown had called out the army.[92] This time, Philip clearly viewed the threat from the Low Countries as most serious, and the host was first ordered to assemble at Amiens on 31 May 1338. Once again, however, the problems of the English and their allies brought about postponements.[93] The Gascon front was all but neglected, for not only did a contingent of troops from L'Isle-sur-Tarn pass through Rodez en route to Picardy in June,[94] but such powerful Gascon lords as Foix and Albret were summoned to Amiens.[95]

The seneschal of Beaucaire was ordered to lead a contingent of mounted troops and crossbowmen from his district, to rendezvous with Count Gaston of Foix en route to Amiens. The consuls of Nîmes ob-

---

[88] Jenkins, *Papal Efforts*, pp. 37-40; *Foedera*, II pt. 3, p. 198; II pt. 4, pp. 3-4.

[89] AD Lot F 11; *INV AM Agen*, describing EE 54.

[90] AD Aveyron G 35, no. 34; Viard, "Ressources," p. 214; Vuitry, *Régime financier*, II, 206-207; Jenkins, *Papal Efforts*, p. 43.

[91] Ménard, *Nismes*, II, *preuves*, 103-104; *LC*, no. 87.

[92] *AHP*, XLVI, 67-69.   [93] *LC*, nos. 88-89, 92-94, 96-97, 99-100.

[94] AD Aveyron G 965 *bis*, fol. 63v, attributed to 1337 by Sibertin-Blanc, "Levée," p. 316.

[95] *LC*, nos. 89, 92-94.

jected bitterly to the effort to tax their town to support these troops, claiming among other things that they were impoverished by the exactions of royal *réformateurs*. Even before receiving this protest, Philip VI called off the *enquêteurs*, and Nîmes finally made a reluctant grant of 450 *l.t.* The consuls claimed they were not obligated to do so, and they made payment dependent upon the actual arrival of Edward III in France. When the English king failed to cross the frontier, Nîmes protested the continued levy of the tax.[96]

A similar pattern of resistance prevailed in other parts of lower Languedoc. Montpellier offered its tax in the form of a 2,000 *l.t.* "loan" and then bitterly protested when a local officer of the crown issued a military summons to the citizens.[97] Philip VI ordered commissioners who were levying fines for false appeals to halt their activities at Montpellier.[98] The consuls of Alès were subjected to intimidation and imprisonment before consenting, on behalf of the whole *viguerie*, to pay their usual war subsidy of 400 *l.t.* plus an added fifty pounds for the maintenance of Aigues Mortes. Lesser towns of the *viguerie* then negotiated with the consuls of Alès to determine their shares of the tax.[99] Narbonne, in the Carcassonne district, paid a tax of at least 1,100 *l.t.* in 1338.[100]

It seems clear, from such documentation as we possess, that the towns of lower Languedoc stoutly resisted taxes based on military service in 1338, denying any obligation to contribute and indicating doubts as to whether in fact a war was in progress. It appears that the king's right to declare an emergency and levy extraordinary taxes in time of war or threat of war was not acknowledged by his subjects or else was not believed to apply to the circumstances of 1338. These circumstances may in fact offer some clue as to the practical interpretation of the terms "necessity" and "defense of the realm" in this period. A state of war certainly existed: Edward's Netherland alliance was directed against Philip; Philip had confiscated Edward's fiefs; and the truce had expired in June of 1338. Yet the towns of lower Languedoc did not feel threatened. They had not been called upon to defend the nearby Gascon frontier but had been summoned to Amiens, at the opposite end of the kingdom, to wage

---

[96] Ménard, *Nismes*, II, *preuves*, 107.   [97] *Gr. Chartrier*, no. 1017.

[98] *Ibid.*, no. 1189. Commissioners investigating other matters seem to have been busy at Montpellier in 1338 (*ibid.*, nos. 1948, 3567).

[99] AM Alès I S-11, no. 3; I S-12, nos. 12-15.

[100] *INV AM Narbonne, sér, AA*, p. 73 (AA 103, fol. 113), indicating Narbonne's presentation of the royal letter of the year before which limited the town to a contribution of 1,250 *l.t.* as in 1328. BN Doat 53, fols. 18-25, makes it appear that in 1338 Narbonne's payment took the form of 1,100 *l.t.* plus some sergeants.

purely defensive war against an enemy who never crossed the frontier. It was, moreover, the second consecutive year in which the English had failed to attack. Although subsidy grants often were made conditional upon an actual state of war, it appears that what these towns had in mind was an emergency affecting them directly. Philip VI, moreover, was prepared to agree with them. On 9 November 1338, he ordered a halt to collections in the seneschalsies of Beaucaire and Carcassonne because war had not taken place. Not only that, but the money was to be returned.[101] Like his uncle in 1313, Philip thus honored the principle of *cessante causa*, but he extended it further. In 1338, the cause for maintaining readiness had not ceased to apply. The war was not over and the pope himself had authorized a tenth to support it. Yet Philip VI, like his subjects, seemed to equate war with invasion. For tax purposes, "war" was not defined by royal proclamation, but had to be an actual clash of arms which threatened the region being taxed.

If the absence of a visible military threat created hostility to taxes among the towns, the nobility posed an even greater problem. Although treated with considerable deference by Philip VI, the seigneurial class remained hostile to taxation and worried by economic and social matters.[102] No doubt some had been embarrassed financially by the resumption of coinage alterations and the confiscations of debts owing to usurers. The nobles had two principal concerns—to maintain military wages at a high level and to avoid taxation of their subjects.[103]

At Montpellier, royal officers tried to tax the subjects of the king of Majorca in 1338, but were repeatedly told not to do so and to return

[101] BN Clairambault 212, no. 26; AM Montpellier, G-5, no. 3351; AM Nîmes NN 1, no. 19; BN *ms. lat.* 9174, fols. 140r-v. The commissioners were recalled from Quercy on 2 January 1339 (AM Cajarc EE 6, no. 390). Return of the money was still underway the following spring (AM Alès 1 S-12, nos. 16-17), and in the spring of 1340, Philip had to issue another order to complete the process (AD Hérault A 4, fols. 119v-120). Despite the king's repeated admissions that war had not taken place, the French had raided Southampton in September 1338 (AD Lot F 11).

[102] See above, notes 14-15. Many of the grievances of the nobility in this period were expressed in an undated list belonging to the early years of the Hundred Years' War: HL, x, cols. 880-884. A case before the *Parlement* early in 1339 involved the lord of Bazillac in Bigorre, who had provoked illegal assemblies of nobles and had prevented his subjects from lending money for the support of troops going to Flanders (Furgeot, *Actes*, 1, no. 2330).

[103] See below, note 106, and above, Chapter 1, part 3. According to Cabrol, *Villefranche*, 1, 209, a famine occurred in 1338 and the shortages were aggravated by the need to keep troops supplied. The restlessness of the nobles thus may have been related to difficulties afflicting the manorial economy.

what had been taken.[104] On 5 May, Philip VI ordered suspension of collections from all subjects of barons and nobles.[105] In June, he issued a lengthy ordinance to the nobles of Languedoc, promising them that pecuniary aids for the support of war would not be levied on their men, that nobles rendering personal service would receive a salary advance for travel expenses, and that salaries would be at the level of 1329 and 1335 (i.e., 10 *s.* per day for a knight bachelor).[106]

Certain great lords throughout the kingdom received particular fiscal privileges in 1338. One of these was the count of Foix, who had long been able to enjoy some fiscal independence and who now was a royal creditor. Cancellation of taxes in his lands was one way by which Philip VI could repay some of the debt.[107] Because the diversion and cancellation of taxes were used in this way to discharge financial obligations the king could not otherwise meet, it is clear that no figures giving actual receipts and expenditures of the royal treasury are complete in this period. Another great feudatory receiving a tax concession in 1338 was Eudes of Burgundy and Artois. On 20 April, the commissioners assigned to collect war subsidies in his territories were ordered to suspend the tax on lawyers until 1 November and return what had been taken up to that time.[108] Taxes were also halted in the French possessions of the count of Bar.[109]

[104] *Gr. Chartrier,* nos. 1016-1018, 3347, 3350.

[105] AM Montpellier G-5, no. 3348. Ménard, *Nismes,* ii, *preuves,* 107, and BN Clairambault 212, no. 27 are other texts indicating that subjects of nobles in the Beaucaire district were not to be taxed for the war in Picardy.

[106] *Ord.,* ii, 120f. At about the same time, the king issued another reform ordinance largely devoted to the clergy: AN JJ 68, no. 43. On 28 July, Philip sent circular letters to the southern seneschals indicating that the ordinance dealing with the nobles had been drafted after consultation in Paris with two representatives from each seneschalsy, that the nobles and their vassals had been mainly concerned at the efforts to pay lower military salaries, and that the new ordinance, along with earlier ones of Louis IX and Philip IV, was to be enforced strictly. See BN *ms. lat.* 9174, fols. 137-138v, evidently the same text described in AN PP 117, pp. 460-461.

[107] By the end of 1339, Philip VI admitted owing the count of Foix nearly 50,000 *l.t.* (AN AB xix 2636, note from AN J 893), and a number of documents indicate the efforts at repayment and the fiscal privileges obtained by the count: BN *Coll. Languedoc* 84, fol. 144r-v; BN Doat 186, fols. 231r-232r, AD Basses-Pyrénées E 406, no. 33, E 404, no. 39. On 9 April 1339, Philip ordered the receiver of Agenais to pay the count 13,000 *l.t.* to support the army of 500 men-at-arms and 2,000 foot-soldiers he was to have in the field: BN Doat 186, fols. 270r-271r. Lists of troops serving in Gascony under his command are in AD Lot F 155.

[108] BN Colbert (*Cinq Cents*) 64, pp. 109-110.

[109] Viard, in AN AB xix 2636, copying a document of 10 November 1338.

Philip also heeded the complaints of the lesser nobility of the North. On 5 September 1338, the bailiffs of the Champagne bailiwicks—Meaux, Troyes, Vitry, and Chaumont—were ordered to suspend taxation of tallageable subjects of the nobility pending a royal investigation into claims that they were exempt from host service and subsidy payments.[110] As in Languedoc, there were also complaints by nobles about fines for non-service. On 8 September, Philip decided that nobles from Champagne who came personally to the army by the 20th need fear no fine. The king further promised that there would be no more summonses or subsidy requests until the following May.[111] By the end of September, he canceled the tax on persons subject to the *taille* and justice of a noble in the Chaumont district.[112] Nobles seem to have enjoyed similar privileges in the bailiwick of Sens.[113]

Despite these various concessions, the government did collect money from most of Languedoil, usually as fines in lieu of personal service. Military muster rolls listing such payments have survived for the bailiwicks of Chaumont, Chartres, Amiens, Senlis, Vermandois, and Gisors.[114] The nobles of Artois paid fines for host service to Count Eudes rather than to the king.[115] Péronne and Saint-Quentin escaped with reduced taxes because they were frontier towns.[116] Reims paid a lump sum by mid-September.[117] A series of municipal taxes in Paris may indicate that the capital paid a subsidy in 1338.[118] Collections in Auvergne took the form of fines for the *arrière-ban* at Aurillac and a loan at Riom.[119] In Poitou, the crown ordered confiscation of the property of wealthy persons who did not join the army. This threat soon led to a "loan" of 500 pounds.[120] The government sought loans as a fairly widespread substitute for taxes, but some money which had been borrowed was returned in the fall.[121]

---

[110] Lognon, *Documents*, III, 237.   [111] *Ibid.*, pp. 237-238.

[112] BN Moreau 229, fol. 27r.   [113] Note of Viard in AN AB xix 2640.

[114] Longnon, *Documents*, III, 237-265; BN Clairambault 229, pp. 1261-1318; 472, pp. 1-97.

[115] *INV AD Pas-de-Calais*, II, 23-24 (A 571).

[116] BN Moreau 229, fol. 33r-v; Le Maire, *St. Quentin*, II, nos. 541, 545, 548.

[117] Varin, *Reims*, II, 793-794.

[118] BN Clairambault 472, pp. 157-229, is an account for collection of municipal taxes at Paris. They were levied for nearly two years and could have helped to pay two consecutive war subsidies.

[119] *INV AM Aurillac*, II, 12 (EE 3); AM Riom CC 7, no. 55.

[120] *AHP*, XLVI, pp. 71-76.

[121] BN NAF 7604 (Fontanieu 73), fols. 177r-178v, indicating a repayment of 6,300 *écus*. Evidence that the crown sought loans on a fairly general basis is in AN PP 117, p. 461, in addition to the examples of Montpellier and Aurillac (already cited).

The royal fiscal effort in 1338 had, in general, succeeded best in those northern districts nearest to the threatened frontier or in those southern regions where royal reform commissioners employed their multiple functions as a coercive device. Taxes based on the commutation of military service were resisted in part because the attack which justified the military summonses never actually materialized. Large-scale concessions to the nobility and the decision to return taxes in parts of Languedoc seriously depleted royal treasury receipts.[122]

In the winter of 1338-1339, the French government feared the possibility of an English attack from Gascony. Philip's principal ally from the empire, King John of Bohemia, was named royal lieutenant in Languedoc on 30 November 1338.[123] His mission was to obtain funds by every possible means in order to prosecute a successful campaign, and he gave his subordinates sweeping orders to this effect on 8 January 1339.[124] To obtain a loan from the consuls of Nîmes, his commissioners seem to have engaged in the usual highhanded and extortionate methods. Eventually made to disgorge 700 *l.t.*, the indignant consuls appealed to the king. In February 1339, the new royal lieutenant, who had succeeded John of Bohemia in the South, excused them from paying and the money was returned.[125] At Montpellier, the continued harassment of his subjects led James of Majorca to protest to Philip, who ordered his commissioners to desist. They were accused of extorting a forced loan from the hundred richest citizens and withholding money owed to those who brought silver bullion to the mints.[126] Officials at Figeac and Cahors also employed pressure in their efforts to raise money.[127]

The coming of spring in 1339 meant a repetition of the now familiar pattern: Edward III and his coalition in the Low Countries seemed ready at last to launch their long-heralded invasion from the North,[128] while Philip VI in May again summoned the army to repel the danger, intending that summons to have a fiscal as well as military purpose. The first date for assembling the French army seems to have been Ascension (May 6), when the nobles and non-nobles were to be at Amiens. As so often in the past, however, the date was postponed several times.[129]

---

[122] Appendix I, Table 4.
[124] *Ibid.*

[123] Molinier, *HL*, IX, 509-510, note 7.
[125] Ménard, *Nismes*, II, *preuves*, 108.

[126] *LC*, no. 104. From AM Montpellier G-5, no. 3352, it appears that the consuls of that town were being harassed over various charges made against them, until the crown ordered a halt to such proceedings.

[127] AN JJ 71, no. 260 (regarding Figeac's complaint); BN Doat 119, fol. 72r-v (revocation of a military summons used against the Cahorsins).

[128] Perroy, *The Hundred Years War*, pp. 102-103.

[129] Varin, *Reims*, II, 819, note 1.

In Languedoc, however, the Gascon front was nearer, even if the real invasion was expected to come from the Netherlands. Each year, the crown had to assess the relative importance of the two fronts and to decide whether it was worth the difficulty and expense involved to have troops from the South report to the northeastern mustering point. Local particularism being what it was, the southern taxpayers were always more cooperative when the danger lay in Gascony.[130] In 1339, the French government faced a real dilemma on this matter, and appeared quite uncertain as to where the danger was most imminent.

Jean de Marigny, bishop of Beauvais, arrived in Languedoc in mid-May as royal lieutenant in Saintonge and Languedoc (i.e., the Gascon theater of war). He immediately called upon the towns to send contingents to Marmande.[131] As in other years, the towns, which were summoned for fiscal purposes, were called earlier than the nobles, who were not ordered to Marmande until 29 June.[132] Among the places receiving the May summons, Périgueux sought to obtain a delay in sending money equal to one armed man per hearth.[133] Narbonne paid 1,200 *l.t.* in lieu of 150 sergeant-crossbowmen, but only with great protest. The commissioners rejected a lesser offer and arrested the consuls.[134] Other southern towns sent sergeants to the Gascon front: Cajarc, twenty men; Nîmes, ninety-five; and Alès, one for every forty hearths.[135]

These arrangements, however, were confused by the arrival of a new order, this time from the king, who commanded the southern seneschals to lead their forces to Compiègne by 22 July.[136] After some delay, the seneschal of Beaucaire issued orders for contingents from the towns to be at Nîmes early in July.[137] The towns immediately protested. Beaucaire had already sent forty men to the Gascon front and now complained when told to furnish one additional armed man per hearth.[138] On 7 July,

[130] The unhappy experience of 1338, when the Gascon front was almost ignored and the southerners balked at serving in Picardy, made this fact clear. Military summonses were still not purely fiscal in intent, because nobles who were to serve in person were involved. If they had been designed exclusively to raise money, the crown would have probably tried to cultivate a local sense of crisis by establishing mustering points that were not too distant.

[131] Molinier, *HL*, ix, 514, note 1. [132] *HL*, ix, 514.

[133] *INV AM Périgueux*, p. 76 (CC 57).

[134] BN Doat 53, fols. 5, 9, 18-25; *HL*, ix, 517; *INV AM Narbonne, sér. AA*, p. 73.

[135] AM Cajarc CC supp., no. 78; EE 7, no. 386; Bardon, *Alais*, i, 100; Ménard, *Nismes*, ii, *preuves*, 109.

[136] *Ibid.*, pp. 110-112; *LC*, no. 107; BN *ms. lat.* 9192, fol. 22v. There is some confusion about the various summonses in *HL*, ix, 516.

[137] *Ibid.*, p. 516, Molinier's note 3; Ménard, *Nismes*, ii, *preuves*, 110-112.

[138] AD Gard, unsigned ms. inventory of AM Beaucaire (1772), fol. 131v.

Alès made similar objections.[139] Despite the grumbling, most towns in the district seem to have answered the summons,[140] but Montpellier and Lunel proved very stubborn. The seneschal started north with the men he had collected, but was still at Le Puy on 21 July. Throughout July and August, he ordered various punitive measures against the recalcitrant communities,[141] and the latter countered with arguments of their own.[142] Eventually, 300 citizens of Montpellier were arrested and royal sergeants were installed in the houses of the consuls, but when some subjects of James of Majorca became involved, Philip VI ordered a halt to the proceedings. His letter of 14 August implied that Montpellier had made some sort of contribution, perhaps following the earlier summons to Marmande.[143]

Nobles and clergy in the Beaucaire district who claimed exemption from taxes were required to contribute to common expenses insofar as they held non-noble property,[144] but exclusion of royal sergeants from seigneurial lands was still enforced in the possessions of the viscount of Uzès.[145] In the diocese of Mende, the royal judge ruled against improper alienation of fiefs subject to the king and several communities were required to pay taxes levied for the *arrière-ban*.[146] In September, however, the bishop of Mende, one of Languedoc's most tireless litigants, obtained suspension of the subsidy in his temporalities pending a new investigation of his rights.[147]

In the seneschalsy of Toulouse, the crown also raised crossbowmen to be sent to Compiègne.[148] A subsidy payment of 132 *l.t.* (one installment of a larger one) was obtained from Albi.[149] *Réformateurs* were still active in this region in 1339, collecting fines for new acquisitions[150] and obtaining from Gaillac a 2,000 *l.* subsidy payment in return for exemption from the Compiègne summons and a pardon for certain abuses with which the town was charged.[151]

[139] AM Alès 1 S-16, no. 12; cf. Bardon, *Alais*, I, 100.

[140] T. Millerot, *Histoire de la ville de Lunel depuis son origine jusqu'en 1789*, Montpellier, 1879, p. 129.

[141] *HL*, IX, 516, note 3, and x, cols. 844-845; Ménard, *Nismes*, II, *preuves*, 111-112; BN *ms. lat.* 9192, fols. 23v-24r; AM Montpellier G-2, no. 3145; Millerot, *Lunel*, p. 130. Lunel escaped paying because of its lord's privileges, not, as Millerot supposed, because it had not paid in the past.

[142] *Gr. Chartrier*, nos. 3108-3110.

[143] Ménard, *Nismes*, II, *preuves*, 112; *Gr. Chartrier*, no. 422.

[144] AD Hérault A 4, fol. 134.   [145] *Ibid.*, fols. 136v-137.

[146] BN Doat 255, fol. 437v; AD Hérault A 4, fols. 105v-106r.

[147] *Ibid.*, fols. 87v-88; BN *Coll. Languedoc* 83, fol. 132.

[148] AN K 43, no. 6 (first two pieces).   [149] AM Albi CC 58 (first piece).

[150] AN JJ 71, nos. 297, 299.   [151] AN JJ 72, no. 45.

In the county of Rodez, the inhabitants were caught between the demands of both king and count for military service. In 1337, they had resisted both demands. In 1339, when the count asked them to support the contingent he was leading to the army, they refused, claiming that the king had asked them directly for contributions to the war. On 20 July 1339, the count reached an agreement with the *bourg* of Rodez, which henceforth would be excused from rendering him any military service but would pay him 150 *l.t.* whenever he was summoned to the army. If, however, the king taxed the town, it would not owe the count the 150 *l.t.*[152] This transaction illustrates why so many lords wished to avoid royal taxation of their subjects or at least share the sums which the crown collected. These subjects were a resource on whom the lord depended for financing his own military service. When the king taxed them, their capacity to aid their direct lord was thereby diminished.

In the royal parts of Rouergue this problem did not exist. Millau was forced to pay 1,100 *l.t.* to *réformateurs* in April 1339 for transgression of usury and monetary ordinances, and then had to send sergeants to Picardy during the summer.[153] Villefranche underwent a similar experience, and actually sent a few men both to Gascony and to Picardy.[154] In July, the bishop of Beauvais made a special arrangement with the consuls of Villefranche. They paid 1,200 *l.t.* for the construction of a fortress and in return were declared exempt from all military service whatever during the next four years.[155]

In central France, commissioners sent to the bailiwick of the Mountains of Auvergne were collecting lump sums from individual communities, Aurillac's share being 320 *l.t.*[156] On 8 May, the king ordered collection of a subsidy in Poitou and Limousin, but he had to repeat this order in October.[157] The misdeeds of the English were stressed, and the commissioner was to persuade the towns of the region to pay not a loan as in the previous year but a "simple subsidy" as in 1337. The money was to be rushed to the royal treasury at Paris. In Saintonge, the king renewed an earlier authorization for Saint-Jean d'Angély to levy a municipal tax on wine. Although not a royal tax, it was applied to the upkeep of important port facilities and thus spared the treasury an expense.[158]

[152] E. Baillaud (ed.), *Coutumes et privilèges de Rouergue*, Toulouse, 1910, I, pp. 128-133; de Gaujal, *Etudes*, II, 176; BN Doat 186, fols. 310r-316v.

[153] *A. H. Rouergue*, VII, 78-79; AM Millau EE 4, EE 5, EE 118 (unnumbered text).

[154] Cabrol, *Villefranche*, I, 210-211.

[155] AN JJ 72, no. 65; BN NAF 7374, fols. 377-378v.

[156] *INV AM Aurillac*, II, 12 (EE 3).   [157] *AHP*, XLVI, 77, 82-84.

[158] AN JJ 71, no. 208.

The city of Paris in 1339 offered a large subsidy based, as usual, on the salaries of a given number of troops, provided that the king or his son personally went on the campaign. According to one source, the grant was for 800 mounted men paid 6 *s.p.* daily but only for forty days.[159] This was much less than Paris usually paid, and the figure may be incorrect. Another text, which certainly seems to deal with 1339, reports that municipal taxes in Paris were expected to raise 32,000 pounds granted for the *arrière-ban*. In general, the town raised the money by a 4 *d./l.* sales tax on merchandise,[160] but certain municipal taxes levied since early 1338 also contributed to the total.[161] The canons of the Paris cathedral chapter received a letter of non-prejudice and the right to collect the sales tax from their own men.[162] Another cathedral chapter, that of Beauvais, paid 500 *l.p.* to the crown.[163] The inhabitants of Artois supported the war only indirectly, paying an aid to the count and countess.[164]

In Vermandois, the towns were very concerned with local defense in 1339, because they were located near the likely invasion route from the empire.[165] The inhabitants of Reims called attention to the needs of local defense in their effort to avoid having to answer the military summons to Amiens that summer.[166] By 24 August, a royal order instructed commanders at Amiens not to force Reims to send troops, because local defense was more important. They were to return whatever they had seized from the burghers to force compliance with the *arrière-ban*.[167] The crown must have had in hand an earlier, undated, petition from the town asking that it be excused from furnishing any aid beyond that which it always gave to the archbishop.[168] A month later, however, the king wrote to the bailiff of Vermandois, indicating that the contingent from Reims was not due until late September, and canceling the town's military service in return for a payment equal to that made the year before.[169] Thus, although the town had asked to avoid all royal service except as might be required for local defense, the royal letter which purported to grant this request actually required substitution of the usual money payment. The earlier letter of 24 August may be evidence that the *échevins* had agreed to negotiate the *finance*, but the documents are not entirely clear.

[159] Félibien and Lobineau, *Paris*, v, 319; BN *ms. fr.* 8605, fols. 28-29.
[160] Furgeot, *Actes*, i, no. 2622; Timbal, *Guerre*, p. 56.
[161] BN Clairambault 471, fols. 175-179. Also see above, note 118.
[162] AN K 42, no. 43 *bis*; Timbal, *Guerre*, pp. 54-57.
[163] Note of Viard from Bibliothèque de Beauvais, in AN AB xix 2640.
[164] Hirschauer, *Les états d'Artois*, i, 15.
[165] See Le Maire, *St. Quentin*, ii, no. 556, for defense arrangements there.
[166] Varin, *Reims*, ii, 819, note 1. [167] *Ibid.*, p. 816.
[168] *Ibid.*, p. 819, note 1. [169] *Ibid.*, pp. 818-819.

We have seen that certain clergy were concerned about taxation of their subjects in 1339.[170] The same was true of the nobility, whom Philip VI still treated with consideration. He restricted the activities of royal sergeants in seigneurial lands,[171] and excused the subjects of many nobles from paying the subsidy.[172] Philip assisted another noble, Guy de Sévérac, by requiring that his subjects contribute to his war expenses.[173] Evidently nobles, like towns, sometimes needed royal help in getting their subjects to pay.

Military action finally took place in 1339, but Philip VI's army, so laboriously assembled, did not engage in major fighting. Edward III ravaged Thiérache in October but withdrew without significant gains when the French declined battle.[174] In the light of later French experience, this strategy may have been sound, but it meant another year of frustration for those who yearned for combat. For five years there had been incessant talk about crusades or English invasion, but the opportunity for glory and booty had never come.[175] The nobles, even those who fined in lieu of serving, closely associated their obligations in wartime with personal service and actual fighting, doubtless to a far greater extent than did other groups in the kingdom. Perhaps the absence of a major chance for military prowess affected their morale and thereby gave the crown an additional reason (besides those already considered) for humoring this class with concessions in precisely the area which tied in so closely with their military role—taxation.

Considerations of this sort may have influenced the government's decision to propose a more aggressive policy when approaching the Normans for taxes in 1339. Apparently believing France to have sufficient command of the sea,[176] the crown suggested that Normandy support an invasion of England. Only Normandy possessed a royal charter which restricted taxation, and this region had contributed little to the support of the war since paying taxes for the navy in 1336. Now, in 1339, the Nor-

---

[170] See the cases of the bishop of Mende and the chapter of Paris, above notes 147 and 162.

[171] Huillard-Breholles, *Bourbon*, I, nos. 2232, 2240; above, note 145.

[172] Among these were the viscount of Melun and (for the second year in a row) the nobles of Champagne. *HL*, x, cols. 854-855; Varin, *Reims*, II, 812; AN P 2291, pp. 483-484.

[173] BN Doat 186, fol. 322r-v.

[174] Perroy, *The Hundred Years War*, p. 103; *Jean le Bel*, I, 153-165; *Cont. Nangis*, II, 164.

[175] Perroy, *The Hundred Years War*, p. 115, writing of 1343, describes what must have been a common sentiment among the nobles: "the knights of the two camps . . . found themselves robbed of the great pitched battle for which they longed."

[176] Lot and Fawtier, *Institutions*, II, 540.

mans demanded and received a new charter which made more explicit the limitations on the king's right to proclaim the *arrière-ban* and demand their aid for military ventures. This charter did not, of course, prevent the king from *asking* aid on other occasions or the Normans from granting it if they chose, but it may have helped to institutionalize the process of seeking consent from assemblies representing the important interests.[177] The count of Harcourt led the nobles in demanding the new charter at an assembly of the three orders of the duchy. Then the Normans agreed to a generous aid for the purposes of financing an invasion of England. The troops were to be paid at the higher rate known as *grands gages*,[178] a fact of some economic importance to the nobility. Yet it was specified that even if conditions should prevent an attack on England and require a defensive war instead, Normandy would still maintain a large body of men for an eight-week period, so the grant in all its aspects was more substantial than most of the reluctant offers which the crown had been obtaining in these years. Best of all, perhaps, from the king's standpoint, was the flexibility of the Norman grant, for if a truce should occur before use could be made of the troops, it was stipulated that the Normans would provide 3,000 men-at-arms for three months at the outset of the king's next war.[179] The promise of a vigorous and potentially glorious campaign, not to mention the second Norman charter, had opened the purses of this region's leading inhabitants. In preparation for the projected descent on England, the government issued the first of the ordinances governing the "army of the sea," even going into some detail concerning tactics.[180] The invasion scheme, however, was doomed before it could be launched. French command of the sea, already questionable in view of Edward's unopposed passages to the Low Countries, was utterly shattered on 24 June 1340 by the disastrous defeat at the hands

[177] Coville, *Etats Norm.*, pp. 50-51; *Ord.*, vi, 549. In March, John of Normandy had already reissued the charter of 1315 (AN JJ 71, no. 253). The transaction with the Norman Estates seems to be that mentioned in *Chron. Val.*, p. 8. It is certainly described in *Cont. Nangis*, ii, 162-163; and *Chron. Cochon*, pp. 56-57.

[178] For *grands gages*, see above, Chapter i, at notes 54-55.

[179] BN *ms. fr.* 21023, pp. 305-319. Other versions are in AN J 210, nos. 4 and 7. For the proposed invasion, the duke of Normandy himself was obliged to furnish the large force of 1,000 men-at-arms, but if he did so, the Normans would supply an additional 3,000 mounted men and 2,000 footsoldiers. Inhabitants of the Evreux and Alençon *apanages* were to contribute, and they may have resisted the effort to make them do so, for in October, Philip VI expressly ordered that they pay their share: AN JJ 73, no. 14.

[180] BN *ms. fr.* 21023, pp. 305-319. Cf. the discussion of Coville, *Etats Norm.*, pp. 48-49; and Lot and Fawtier, *Institutions*, ii, 540.

of the English in the Battle of Sluys. The French seem to have kept a lingering hope that the expedition was possible, for as late as 9 September 1340, Philip VI sought a 1,000 *l.t.* loan for invading England.[181] By this time, however, an invasion of France from the North was a more serious possibility.

2. The Widely Varied Taxes of 1340

Although Edward III had finally attacked French soil in 1339, his campaign, as we have seen, had been brief and ineffectual. A much heavier blow was to come in 1340. Just as the war intensified, so also did the fiscal efforts of the French crown, and some scholars have seen 1340 as the beginning of a period in which the king levied taxes with greater success and frequency.[182] Certainly the documents suggest that 1340 was a much better tax year for the king than 1338, especially with regard to the nobility, who proved far more generous now that they were promised some military action. The most striking characteristic of 1340, however, was the great variety of different taxes, for local differences as to form were at their height in this period. Mile de Noyers and his associates addressed themselves to the task of raising money with a persistence and ingenuity reminiscent of Philip V's reign. The year began auspiciously when, in February, Benedict XII granted Philip a new two-year tenth,[183] but the pope continued to demand an accounting for the earlier crusading tenths which the king had long since spent, and this dispute was clearly a source of worry and embarrassment to Philip.[184]

The effort to levy a war subsidy began very early in 1340, starting at Montpellier, where the crown had encountered such bitter opposition in 1339. In a letter of 29 January, Philip VI ordered the seneschal of Beaucaire to complete collections of fines from those who had not served the year before, and to have all royal vassals stand in readiness for an imminent new military summons.[185]

The seneschal decided to apply this order to Montpellier, and late in

[181] AD Lot F 14.

[182] Henneman, "Financing," notes 1 and 2, citing Vuitry and Perroy. The rest of this chapter is a condensed version of the portions of that article which appeared in *Speculum*, XLII (1967), 277-295, reprinted here by permission.

[183] Viard, "Ressources," p. 214; Vuitry, *Régime financier*, II, 206-207.

[184] *LC*, no. 119.

[185] Ménard, *Nismes*, II, *preuves*, 113-114; AD Hérault A 4, fols. 85v-86. Even earlier, on 12 January, Philip had ordered the recruitment of crossbowmen in Languedoc, evidence that the government was quite serious in its intention to be prepared for fighting earlier than in the past few years. BN NAF 7604 (Fontanieu 73), fols. 200r-201v.

February, he ordered a subordinate to muster each head of family in the town.[186] The consuls of Montpellier argued that the seneschal was exceeding his powers in ordering them to muster, since they did not owe personal service. They were still required to pay a subsidy, however, and were threatened with an enormous fine if any of them should fail to appear before the seneschal. The usual complaints of poverty arising from local economic conditions failed to move the royal officials, and late in March, they began to ask each of the wealthier inhabitants to furnish a sergeant for forty days' service.[187] At length, Philip VI received the consuls' complaint and responded with his usual order not to molest the subjects of the king of Majorca.[188] Then, in mid-May, he canceled the military summons and the subsidy at Montpellier, and sent new commissioners to seek a "loan" as in 1338.[189] Negotiations for this loan in lieu of a tax took most of the summer, but in September, Montpellier offered 2,000 l.t., their usual subsidy grant.[190] A month later, the consuls ordered collection of a municipal *fouage* to raise this sum, and the crown finally received the money in November.[191] While the negotiations were in progress during the summer, Montpellier paid another 2,500 l.t. to receive a letter of safeguard and a pardon for various offenses then under investigation by royal *enquêteurs-réformateurs*.[192] The crown thus obtained 4,500 l.t. from Montpellier, none of it in the form of a war subsidy. The effort had taken many months and it seemed to prove that it was easier to obtain concealed taxes derived from municipal *tailles* than royal subsidies based on military obligations.

In seeking money from the rest of Languedoc in 1340, the crown followed a more conventional pattern. In April, Philip VI issued the *arrière-ban*, calling the host to Picardy,[193] and early in May, commissioners went to the seneschalsy of Beaucaire with orders to explain the urgency of the situation and to collect, notwithstanding privileges, from

---

[186] Ménard, *Nismes*, II, *preuves*, 113-114.

[187] AM Montpellier G-1, no. 3111; G-2, nos. 3146-3148; Ménard, *Nismes*, II, *preuves*, 114.

[188] *HL*, x, cols. 859-860.

[189] AM Montpellier G-2, no. 3152; *LC*, no. 125. Any subsidy already collected was to be returned.

[190] AM Montpellier H-6, no. 3880.

[191] The receipt of 14 November is in *Gr. Chartrier*, no. 450, the October commission to collect the *fouage, ibid.*, no. 319.

[192] *Ibid.*, nos. 96, 2916-2917; AN JJ 68, nos. 97-98; JJ 72, nos. 327-328; Furgeot, *Actes*, I, nos. 3018, 3075. Under investigation were the levy of an illegal municipal tax and the failure to contribute to the repairs at Aigues Mortes.

[193] AD Hérault A 4, fols. 97v-98v.

all who had ever paid before.[194] While negotiations for money were in progress, the English launched a diversionary attack from Gascony and besieged Condom. Jean de Marigny eventually forced them to raise the siege on 18 August, but we are told that his military summons to the inhabitants of Languedoc received a poor response.[195] Certain of the towns reacted with hostility when his commissioners approached them for money. In a mid-September protest, the consuls of Montpellier pointed out that they had just paid the king the 2,000-pound loan. They also stated that the rights of the nobility were being violated by the agents sent out by Marigny and his commanders.[196]

The claim that noble privileges had been violated was a general one, in no way limited to Montpellier. In apparent violation of the ordinance of 1338, Marigny had sought to levy a fiftieth on the subjects of nobles who had not reported to the army. This action had aroused complaints and Philip VI agreed on 8 August that all money collected contrary to privileges was to be returned.[197] As in 1337, an effort to collect in the face of privileges was defeated. A second and more explicit royal letter to his officers in the seneschalsy of Beaucaire on 18 September forbade the molesting of nobles who had failed to serve or pay in connection with the Condom campaign.[198] Evidently, the nobles were able to force recognition of their privileges in this way throughout lower Languedoc.[199]

The Condom campaign complicated the royal fiscal effort, but it served to emphasize that this year the emergency was genuine. Having rejected an earlier offer, the crown collected 400 *l.t.* from the town of Beaucaire.[200] Nîmes made two payments totaling 600 *l.t.*, but resisted additional demands to send help to Condom and obtained a *vidimus* of fiscal privileges granted by Louis X in 1315.[201] Alès resisted a demand for

---

[194] *HL*, IX, 520; BN *Coll. Languedoc* 84, fols. 183-185; AD Hérault A 4, fols. 127v-129v.

[195] *HL*, IX, 522. The military summons of 4 August ordered all persons over fourteen to report to the army (AD Hérault A 4, fols. 131r-133v).

[196] *Gr. Chartrier*, nos. 424, 427, 3135, 3882-83.

[197] *Ibid.* Some nobles who had not answered Marigny's summons may, of course, have rendered service with the king in Picardy.

[198] *Ibid.*, no. 3354. From documents in AD Hérault A 4, fols. 140v-145r, it is clear that a fiftieth (2%) had been sought from nobles generally. A noble who sent a contingent of men was considered exempt even if he did not personally go to war.

[199] Huillard-Breholles, *Bourbon*, I, no. 2247, indicates a similar development in Velay. See also *INV AM Toulouse*, p. 532 (AA 45, no. 8).

[200] *HL*, X, cols. 870-873.

[201] AD Hérault A 4, fol. 100v, excusing Nîmes from service, was followed by the payments indicated in AM Nîmes NN 1, no. 22. The letters of Louis X which were confirmed in 1340 (NN 1, nos. 7, 8) stated that the consuls could decide whether

money capable of supporting forty men, but by August, the *viguerie* had granted 400 pounds and was apportioning it among the various communities. This payment was complete by mid-September.[202] Lunel, also pressed for a subsidy and also reluctant, made a 100-pound payment by October.[203]

Farther west, the evidence becomes more miscellaneous and a less complete picture is possible. At Toulouse, the citizens had been classified according to the military equipment they could afford.[204] When, however, the crown tried to tax them on the basis of military service, the *capitouls* negotiated a familiar sort of "package deal" with the government. Toulouse would pay 6,500 *l.t.*, not only for the war subsidy but also to obtain pardons for monetary violations and a confirmation of their exemption from military service.[205] The Albigeois towns paid for troops sent to the Condom campaign,[206] while Albi itself paid a finance for violations of ordinances, perhaps a disguised tax.[207] Narbonne's lump-sum payment of 1,250 *l.t.* replaced a 5 *s.* hearth tax which was levied throughout the seneschalsy of Carcassonne. There is no evidence that the crown obtained consent to this tax, and it only produced 15,000 *l.t.*, much less than an average of 5 *s.*[208] In Bigorre, both direct and indirect subjects of the king fined to avoid personal service, apparently after an assembly of some sort agreed upon the rate.[209] The bishop and chapter of Rodez refused an urgent request to send a dozen horsemen to the army in Gascony,[210] but the crown did collect fines for *amortissement* from the clergy of Rouergue.[211] The king's lay subjects in Rouergue resisted a military summons at first, but a delegation consisting of a proctor of the barons and one consul each from Villefranche and Millau

---

they wanted to send men or money for an aid, and that any sum paid after cessation of hostilities was to be returned.

[202] AM Alès 1 S-16, no. 14; 1 S-12, nos. 19-21.

[203] AM Lunel CC 60, nos. 2215-2216; *INV AM Lunel* (ms.), II, 51, describing EE 1, no. 1968 (the original is now largely illegible).

[204] *INV AM Toulouse*, p. 81 (AA 5, no. 161).

[205] *Ibid.*, pp. 41, 532 (AA 3, no. 258; AA 45, no. 8).

[206] Portal, *Cordes*, p. 48; C. Compayré, *Etudes historiques et documents inédits sur l'Albigeois, le Castrais, et l'ancien diocèse de Lavaur*, Albi, 1841, p. 395.

[207] AM Albi CC 61. In the same year, the crown prohibited further extortions by sergeants who had been abusing the town's privileges (CC 63). Such a document was often issued in connection with tax negotiations.

[208] *AM Narbonne, sér. AA*, p. 73 (AA 103, fol. 113v). Molinier, *HL*, IX, 524, note 6, basing his figure on the receiver's account in AN K 498, no. 1.

[209] *HL*, IX, 524. Dognon, *Institutions*, p. 203.

[210] AD Aveyron G 28, no. 26.   [211] BN Doat 157, fols. 93-95.

finally granted some sergeants on behalf of the whole district.[212] The crown seems to have used investigation of fief acquisitions as a pressure tactic in Quercy, where grants of subsidy were not obtained until late in the year.[213]

In Auvergne, the only indication of a subsidy in 1340 is a reference to a conference of royal financial officials at Clermont concerning "the *arrière-ban* and several other things."[214] In the nearby bailiwick of the Mountains, commissioners assigned "for the matter of the *arrière-ban*" were ordered not to force payment of a *finance* by any person for fiefs having less income than 10 pounds each, if such a person had paid the subsidies of 1337 and 1338.[215] This order would apply to both noble and non-noble fiefs and it suggests that the basis for subsidy payment in this region was real property, that the king was trying to ease the burden on small property holders, and that collections of the subsidies of 1337 and 1338 were lagging.

In the region of Périgord, the documents indicate that many different fiscal pressures might be faced in one year by the citizens of a single community. At the end of March 1340, well before any formal *arrière-ban* had been proclaimed, the government sent instructions to the receiver of Périgord, telling him to float a loan but to keep the matter secret.[216] Enclosed were letters to various prelates, chapters, and other clergy, presumably soliciting loans from them directly. Also enclosed were unaddressed form letters which the receiver was to give to the wealthy men of the seneschalsy requesting money from each according to his resources. These letters cited the crown's heavy expenses and the good financial state of the addressee and went on to promise repayment.[217] Loans from all sources were to be collected by the receiver and

---

[212] At Millau, the transaction was ratified on 29 August: AM Millau EE 118, no. 289. Cabrol, *Villefranche*, I, 211-212, reported that Villefranche paid 600 pounds for the upkeep of a contingent of 100 men. Such a grant would seem to have been contrary to the arrangement concluded earlier with Marigny (above, note 155).

[213] AM Cajarc CC supp., no. 81. Albe, "Cahors INV," no. 276, a letter of Louis X exempting the citizens of the principal towns of Quercy from *franc-fief* was presented by the citizens to the royal judge. As at Nîmes (above, note 201), bourgeois being harassed by royal commissioners seem to have sought protection in privileges now twenty-five years old.

[214] AD Côte-d'Or B 11891, copied by Viard in AN AB xix 2636. The conference involved the treasurer of the county of Auvergne and other persons.

[215] *INV AM Aurillac*, II, 12 (EE 3).

[216] *LC*, no. 120. A list of commissioners "to make loans for men-at-arms" is indicated in AN PP 117, p. 555, perhaps an indication of a more general effort to float loans in 1340.

[217] *LC*, no. 121.

forwarded to Paris. There is no clear statement as to how these loans were to be repaid; perhaps the royal collectors promised to use eventual tax receipts for this purpose. Only a partial record of sums collected has managed to survive.[218] The municipal archives of the town of Périgueux mention various direct involvements with the war along the Gascon frontier. Within the town, a *taille* was levied for fortifications and produced 766 *l.t.* In the same year, the town paid a *finance* of 6,400 pounds to the crown to recover jurisdictional rights.[219] It is not clear whether this transaction involved extortion on the part of the government, but it certainly resembles a familiar type of fiscal expedient. Meanwhile, the seneschal of Toulouse (one of the commanders on the Gascon front) had to be cautioned not to molest the inhabitants of Périgueux for levies of money or supplies since they were already burdened with heavy war expenses.[220] Then in December 1340, the king issued a letter releasing the town from penalties incurred for civil disturbances ("excesses") committed many years earlier.[221] Thus in 1340, the population of this region faced a number of demands: a royal request for a loan, levies for local defense, a large payment to buy back rights, charges of misconduct, and additional demands of a logistical nature from local royal officers. All of this was in addition to a war subsidy of at least 400 *l.t.* promised to the royal lieutenant, Jean de Marigny.[222]

We may compare the experience of Périgueux with that of Poitou in the same year. On 6 February, the king assigned a royal captain in this region the task of raising money by a variety of methods. He was to levy fines on persons who had acquired fiefs, to investigate usury violations, to collect all sums owing to the crown including marks of silver from those officeholders who owed them, and to raise a war subsidy, the latter to be employed only for the upkeep of men-at-arms.[223] On 23 February, he named subordinate commissioners to carry out these orders. They were to order all nobles, under pain of being regarded as traitors, to

[218] BN *ms. fr.* 25997, no. 283.

[219] AM Périgueux CC 58, fol. 11, for the payment to recover jurisdiction rights. The *taille* for fortifications, recorded at the back of the same register, has been published by A. Higounet-Nadal, *Les comptes de la taille et les sources de l'histoire démographique de Périgueux au XIVe siècle*, Paris, 1965, pp. 106f.

[220] *INV AM Périgueux*, pp. 55-56 (CC 10).

[221] AN JJ 73, no. 234. The incident in question is described by N. Zacour, *Talleyrand: The Cardinal of Périgord (1301-1364)*, Philadelphia, 1960, p. 9.

[222] *INV AM Périgueux*, p. 78 (CC 59); Higounet-Nadal, *Comptes*, pp. 30-31. A good deal of pressure had to be applied before the subsidy, part of it called a "loan," was collected.

[223] *AHP*, XIII, 165.

hold themselves in readiness for an imminent military summons, and were to pursue vigorously the collection of fines for fief alienations. This document suggests the aggressive methods of the zealous provincial officer. It seems clear that the combination of a military summons and fief investigations was being used to extract a subsidy from Poitou. The *arrière-ban* was greeted with protests from Poitiers, and the fines for *franc-fief* eventually produced over 5,000 pounds.[224] Before the year was out, the inhabitants of Poitiers also had to pay a 2 percent tax to put their walls in order.[225]

The city of Paris agreed to maintain 450 men-at-arms for four months at 6 *s.* per day (for a total grant of 20,250 *l.t.*) if the king or his son John personally went to war. It was specified that all inhabitants of whatever status, even those living subject to an ecclesiastical establishment, would contribute "according to their abilities." Rights, however, would not be prejudiced for the future, and it was promised that no other aid would be asked before June 1341.[226] In Normandy, meanwhile, a tax based on commutation of military service (a "*taille* for the army") was levied following a new guarantee of Norman privileges in March.[227]

The towns of northeastern France were most threatened by Edward III's army in Flanders, and Philip VI decided to make use of assemblies in seeking aid from this region. A memorandum drawn up by royal officials in 1339 had suggested that the crown might find it preferable to use national or regional assemblies to obtain money, instead of time-consuming local negotiations.[228] Men like Mile de Noyers, who had gained experience with assemblies twenty years before, may have favored their reintroduction, especially in view of the generous grant by a Norman assembly in 1339. In any case, the crown needed speedy grants of money from northern France in 1340, for the military situation there was deteriorating rapidly. Edward III now claimed to be king of France and was calling on the French to rally to his cause. An invasion from the North seemed imminent.[229]

---

[224] *Ibid.*, pp. 168-172; XLVI, 89.   [225] *Ibid.*, XLVI, 90-91.

[226] Viard, *Docs. par.*, pp. 81-83.

[227] Delisle, *Actes norm.*, pp. 264-268, a fragmentary account of this tax. The renewal of Norman privileges is found in *Ord.*, VI, 549.

[228] Jusselin, "Comment la France . . . ," pp. 229-230.

[229] Hirschauer, *Les états d'Artois*, I, 13. The intensified military activity is readily observable in the entries in *INV AD Pas-de-Calais*, II, 29f. See also A. Guesnon (ed.), "Documents inédits sur l'invasion anglaise et les états au temps de Philippe VI et de Jean le Bon," *BPH*, 1897, pp. 222-233. On Edward III's claims and his exchange of negotiations and defiances with Philip VI, see *Foedera*, II pt. 4, pp. 61, 64-67, 77, 80-81.

The government began convening assemblies in the northern districts early in the year. The three Estates of the *apanage* of Artois met on successive days at the end of February to name and instruct proctors who would represent Artois at a larger regional assembly at Amiens on 5 March.[230] This latter meeting contained representatives from the three bailiwicks of Amiens, Senlis, and Vermandois (Artois being included in the first of these). One surviving text lists thirty-two towns which granted taxes at this meeting. Each town made a slightly different bargain with the king, but in general, the subsidy was to be a 4 *d./l.* sales tax, of which some fraction would be retained by the towns for their own purposes, notably fortification.[231] It was unusually early in the year for the king to receive a definite subsidy grant, and to this extent the assembly must be pronounced a success for the crown. On the other hand, it is clear that the town representatives did not act together in any corporate sense. Moreover, many communities which were represented at Amiens took no action there. Among these were the more important towns of Artois.[232]

The towns of Vermandois which did not make a grant at Amiens were called to a new assembly. They were to send three or four notable citizens with full powers to Pontoise on 21 March.[233] This meeting in the royal presence still failed to convince Reims to pay. The town's proctors listened to the king's request for a sales tax and then returned home with a letter from him. Representatives from the town seem to have made three more trips to the royal court by mid-June, still without making a grant acceptable to the king.[234] Finally, Reims was visited by a pair of tax commissioners who apparently arrived during the summer and seem to have remained in the town for a rather long period.[235] It is quite possible that their arrival corresponded with the issuance of the *arrière-ban*, for

[230] Hirschauer, *Les états d'Artois*, II, 149, P.J. II.

[231] AN P 2291, p. 809f. The towns are listed in Viard, "Ressources," p. 187; and Henneman, "Financing," p. 287, note 81. Even before the assembly, taxes for local defense had been established or renewed in a number of towns. See *ibid.*, note 83, and AN PP 117, p. 553.

[232] Conspicuously lacking from the list were such important towns as Reims, Saint-Quentin, Arras, and Saint-Omer. Yet it is clear that Reims was represented at the assembly (Varin, *Reims*, II, 835) and the Artesian towns must also have been.

[233] Le Maire, *St. Quentin*, II, no. 567.

[234] Varin, *Reims*, II, 830-831, 835-836. For a more detailed analysis of these Reims accounts, see Henneman, "Financing," pp. 288-289. As indicated there, I feel that Viard ("Ressources," pp. 187f.) has not given a satisfactory description of the tax negotiations in the northern part of France in 1340.

[235] Varin, *Reims*, II, 831. The commissioners, who were in Reims *pour cause de la male-taute*, remained long enough to collect a salary of 72 pounds.

the inhabitants were ordered to be in arms on 29 July.[236] This summons may have been for the entire bailiwick, for Saint-Quentin was ordered to the same rendezvous by a royal letter of 4 July. The bailiff of Vermandois was to have all nobles and non-nobles between the ages of 18 and 60 muster at Arras on the 29th. Those who could not come (such as women) were to send substitutes, and only very poor people who were legitimately occupied with manual labor were to be excused.[237]

Now there was at this time a very genuine military threat, but there had been one for some months. The *arrière-ban* was therefore probably a device to hasten tax collections. Saint-Quentin may have been as stubborn as Reims; we know only that it had refused to grant a subsidy at Amiens in early March, had been called to the later assembly, and finally agreed to the 4 *d./l.* sales tax.[238] At Reims, the resistance continued, and after another royal letter, there arrived a receiver-general "to have levied the *maltôte*."[239] Finally, two representatives in Paris were instructed to set a figure payable to the king as a lump sum in lieu of a sales tax.[240] While there is some uncertainty regarding the precise order of these last events, it is nevertheless clear that in 1340, when a major invasion of the kingdom was underway from the North, a subsidy could be levied at Reims only after the greatest expenditure of time, travel and correspondence.

Throughout the North, taxation was complicated by the endless military operations of 1340. Payrolls indicate that a large army of knights was active in Artois and the Low Countries through the first nine months of the year, and that these were paid the high daily wage of 15 *s.t.* for a knight bachelor.[241] Periodic local emergencies forced royal commanders to impose upon the towns, demanding that they send crossbowmen or stripping them of war machines needed for local defense.[242] It is not always possible to distinguish clearly between a military summons for fiscal purposes and one aimed at assembling urban militias to repel a local attack. Thus the summons to Saint-Quentin and Reims on 4 July, to

---

[236] *Ibid.*, p. 839. [237] Le Maire, *St. Quentin*, ii, no. 575.

[238] A later sales tax granted at Saint-Quentin in 1342 renewed one which had run for a year and a half (*ibid.*, no. 589). This means that a 4 *d./l.* imposition had been collected in the town since shortly after the middle of 1340, but the timing of the levy with respect to the July *arrière-ban* cannot be determined.

[239] Varin, *Reims*, ii, 832. On this individual, see BN Clairambault 33, no. 189, and Henneman, "Financing," note 97.

[240] Varin, *Reims*, ii, 840. It is not at all clear when this trip occurred, but the two proctors had been to Pontoise during an early stage of the negotiations.

[241] The salaries are indicated in BN *ms. fr.* 7858, fols. 55-184v.

[242] Le Maire, *St. Quentin*, ii, nos. 568, 571.

have all citizens in arms by the 29th, seems to be a fiscal device. A week later, Saint-Quentin received a new summons, this one ordering the town to have as many well-supplied men as possible at Arras on 22 July (a week before the original mustering date).[243] Was this but another effort to extort a subsidy from reluctant burghers? Perhaps so, but the urgency conveyed by the text makes one hesitate to classify it as a purely fiscal document.

This sort of ambiguity seriously hinders our assessment of the fiscal situation in Artois, where the documentation consists almost entirely of bailiwick accounts which rarely suggest a clear link between military measures and royal taxation. An account of 1341 mentions an assembly of Artesian towns which convened at Hesdin on 1 June 1340. This was three weeks before the disaster at Sluys and five weeks before the *arrière-ban* was proclaimed in Vermandois.[244] Since no major towns in the county of Artois had joined in the tax grants made at Amiens in March, it is very likely that this meeting was a follow-up assembly comparable to that held at Pontoise for the towns of Vermandois. Eventually, the crown seems to have obtained a tax, at least from the town of Arras. We learn of it from an account showing how Arras paid for repair of fortifications. The bulk of the money was raised by a tax on heritable real property collected "by mandate of the king." In accordance with a royal mandate, the sum applied to local fortresses was to be a fourth of the total sum owed for the tax. This town, like those which made their grants in the Amiens assembly, was subject to a royal tax of which a portion (in this case a quarter) was reserved to the town for its own defenses. Arras paid a tax on property instead of the *maltôte* on merchandise which was universal among the other towns. The amount allocated to local defenses came to nearly 1,700 pounds, and it is reasonable to suppose that the crown's share of the levy was triple that sum, or more than 5,000 pounds.[245]

Thus, with widely varying degrees of difficulty and with considerable negotiation at the local level being necessary despite the assemblies, the government was able to levy a tax throughout the towns of the Northeast. The clergy and nobility of the same regions also granted a tax, and it is probable that these two classes of society were similarly convened in assemblies at the time that the towns met at Amiens. The chapters of

[243] *Ibid.*, no. 576; BN Moreau 229, fols. 211-212; AD Lot F 11.

[244] *INV AD Pas-de-Calais*, II, 36 (A 604); Hirschauer, *Les états d'Artois*, I, 13-14.

[245] *INV AD Pas-de-Calais*, II, 31 (A 593). I am indebted to P. Bougard, departmental archivist, for calling my attention to this account and verifying that the portions quoted in the inventory are the only ones bearing on royal taxation in this year.

Laon and Senlis granted a half-tenth to support troops going to Picardy. The tax was to be collected from their benefices, while their subjects would also pay a sales tax on their merchandise, and the king promised to take action on certain grievances. Both these grants were tied to a grant made by the nobles of their respective bailiwicks (Vermandois and Senlis) and would be collected as long as the nobles paid.[246] We are fortunate in possessing additional information about this subsidy offered by the northern nobility. Acting as a group, those of the bailiwicks of Amiens, Vermandois, and Senlis agreed to a sales tax of 4 *d./l.* on sales of one pound or more, with a lower rate for smaller transactions, and a special rate for wine, along with other special modifications. Collectors were to be appointed by the nobles from among the "most sufficient" persons in their lands. These collectors were not to have any dealings with local royal officials but were subject to the discipline of their immediate lords who guaranteed their accountability to a special royal receiver. The tax raised in this way was to be used only for payment of the *gens d'armes de ladictes pays*. Collection was to begin on 17 April 1340 and was to continue for a year and a half, and receipts were not to exceed the salaries for the men-at-arms (their number not specified) at the *grands-gages* rate. All nobles who desired them were to receive letters of non-prejudice, and other extraordinary revenues were not to be collected from this region unless there were "such great necessity that one cannot suffer" from new levies in the opinion of the local "men of estate."[247] The fact that the northern nobility was willing to grant a tax of eighteen months' duration equal to that offered by the towns, does suggest that the king was in a stronger fiscal position. One reason for this success was perhaps the propaganda value of an assembly, held in advance of the military summons and offering a way in which the unpopular musters by subsidy commissioners might be avoided. But it is also significant that the sense of crisis was much greater in 1340, especially in the regions nearest to the Low Countries. There was not, of course, a uniformly satisfactory response. Besides the resistance of towns like Reims, some ecclesiastical establishments failed to join in the grant. The abbey of Notre Dame at Soissons, for instance, customarily owed either 100 foot sergeants or 200 *l.t.*, and on 30 March, Philip VI had to order force used to obtain this contribution.[248] Nevertheless, the fact remains that the gov-

[246] BN Moreau 229, fols. 124r-v, 192r-v.

[247] Text inventoried in AN PP 117, pp. 470-471, and published by Jusselin, "Comment la France . . . ," pp. 230-232.

[248] BN Moreau 229, fol. 187r. Doubtless the places granting the half-tenth had their customary obligations waived in return for making this grant.

ernment had obtained, at an earlier date than usual, a grant from all three orders of society in this three-bailiwick region.

The nobles of central France, like those of the North, were also responsive to royal fiscal demands in 1340. Those of the bailiwicks of Orléans, Tours, and Bourges granted the crown a fiftieth (2 percent).[249] It is entirely possible that here too, the government had tried an assembly of three bailiwicks at once. A fiftieth was probably the general basis on which the crown had tried to tax the nobility in 1340, for it had been sought in Beaucaire and apparently also was levied in the bailiwick of Sens.[250]

Despite the evidence of grants by the nobility of several regions in this year, it continued to be politic for the king to deal cautiously with the great magnates. He agreed to return to Raoul of Eu the *imposition* levied on his subjects in Poitou following the *arrière-ban* in 1339.[251] The count of Blois received favorable treatment of a sort which hardly suggests that the crown was enjoying a freer hand. Not only were royal officials forbidden to extort money from the count's tallageable subjects (as they had apparently been attempting to do) but, in addition, the tax collected from his non-tallageable dependents was to be divided equally between the king and the count.[252] The same arrangement governed royal taxation of the duke of Bourbon's subjects in Clermont, where the 4 *d./l.* granted by the northern towns would be collected, but one-half the proceeds turned over to the duke.[253]

Again, it becomes evident that the French war subsidy in 1340 could take an almost infinite variety of forms. It might be called a loan or a fine or even a *taille*; it might be an income tax, sales tax, hearth tax, levy on real property, or lump-sum payment raised by some local or municipal tax. Both assemblies and local negotiations at the town level, employed in different combinations, could be used to obtain the desired sums. The bargaining might involve considerations of local defense, or the rights of a great seigneur, or some locality's desire to escape investigation of fief alienations, monetary violations, "excesses," etc.

---

[249] We know of this grant indirectly, through privileges extended to the count of Blois with respect to it: AN K 43, no. 9; BN NAF 3653, nos. 99, 100. An account of the collection of the 50th in the *banlieu* of Blois is in BN Clairambault 471, pp. 287-325.

[250] For Beaucaire, see above, note 198. The tax in the bailiwick of Sens is indicated in a subsequent court decision: Furgeot, *Actes*, I, no. 3462.

[251] *AHP*, XIII, 164-165. One should not discount the possibility that the king was employing this device in order to pay part of the constable's salary.

[252] BN NAF 3653, nos. 99-100, 102.

[253] See Henneman, "Financing," note 118.

Sums levied upon foreigners or upon commerce were another royal resource of 1340. The connection between the 4 *d./l.* export tax and the war was maintained by Philip VI in 1340, and early in the year he sought to increase returns from it by canceling the right of certain prelates to have merchandise taken outside the kingdom free of the *droit de rève*.[254] That the export tax remained a valued source of revenue was made clear by Philip's formal re-enactment of it in October 1340.[255] The government also tapped the Italian merchants and moneylenders as in 1337. In the spring, the king took one of his periodic steps against foreign usurers. Debtors were not to pay back their creditors, but were to consider the interest canceled and pay the principal to the crown, or more specifically to make *composition* with the *gens des comptes* for as much as the latter could recover from them.[256] The Italians also remained subject to the basic taxes on their commerce which had been in effect for some time; a 5 percent property tax and a levy of 1½ *d./l.* on sales.[257]

The foregoing discussion suggests that royal taxation, while still arousing some opposition, proved markedly more successful in 1340 than in the three preceding years. This impression is borne out by the Book of the Changer, which indicates that over a million *livres parisis* reached the king's account at the treasury, perhaps 40 percent more than in 1339, even though some receipts were paid directly to the troops without reaching Paris.[258] Much of this difference, however, is eliminated when one adjusts the figures to compensate for coinage changes. Since the crown extorted large sums from the Italians and their debtors in 1340, and also collected *monnayage* at an increased rate, the actual subsidy receipts may not have exceeded those of 1339. In both these years, however, treasury receipts far exceeded those of 1336, 1337, or 1338. In 1341, receipts again declined significantly, and did not regain the level of 1340 for some time.[259] Thus, even if the crown did collect impressive sums in 1340, this achievement did not mark the beginning of a new period of greater financial strength. Instead, it was the last year in which revenues rose, and was followed by a period of financial difficulty which would haunt the last decade of Philip VI's reign.

---

[254] AD Hérault A 4, fols. 90v-91v, where the necessity of the Gascon war is given as the reason for this action.

[255] *Ord.*, ii, 147-150.

[256] *Ibid.*, pp. 143-145; BN NAF 7389, fol. 276r; AD Hérault A 4, fols. 122r-v.

[257] *Ibid.*, fols. 89r-v, 154r-156r, 172r-175r. Henneman, "Italians," pp. 21-24.

[258] Viard, introduction to *JT Ph. VI*, pp. xli-xlvii.

[259] See Appendix 1, with reference to Table 4.

CHAPTER V

The Fiscal and Political Difficulties of Philip VI, 1341-1345

1. The Establishment of More Uniform Taxes

ALTHOUGH the first real military action of the war had occurred in 1340, the failure of the English to capture Condom and Tournai left the situation deadlocked. Late in September, the truce of Esplechin was concluded,[1] the first of many truces which would cause the French government no end of financial embarrassment. As a step towards peace, the truce accomplished little. The southwest remained unsettled because of private warfare, largely the feud between the counts of Foix and Armagnac which would drag on through most of the century. The count of Foix had been an important French commander, but John I of Armagnac had married into the Bourbon branch of the royal family and his fortunes were on the rise. At this time, he made peace with Edward III in order to concentrate on his local struggle,[2] but in time, his ties to France would prevail and his adversary, Gaston Phoebus, count of Foix (1343-1391), would become alienated from France. Their continuing duel in the Midi would have important influence on the tax burden of this region.[3]

Another important struggle was soon to open in Brittany, where a succession dispute would cause civil war from 1341 to 1365. This conflict also was, to some extent, a purely private war, largely unaffected by Anglo-French truces and treaties. Yet both kingdoms quickly took sides in the quarrel and Brittany soon provided Edward III with a far better base for operations on the continent than did his costly alliances in the Netherlands. The presence of English troops in this duchy would prove a serious threat to the peace and prosperity of Normandy, and here too, the history of French taxation would be affected in important ways.[4]

---

[1] *Foedera*, II pt. 4, pp. 83-84.

[2] BN Doat 187, fols. 114-115, 194. Edward III responded by ordering his lieutenant in Aquitaine to punish any incursions by the count of Foix: *Foedera*, II pt. 4, p. 89.

[3] The Foix-Armagnac struggle was particularly important for the taxpayers of Languedoc in 1360. See Lehoux, *Jean de France*, I, 147f.

[4] For the deterioration of the French crown's position in Normandy and the diplomatic role of the Breton situation in the 1350's, see Chapter VIII. On Brittany, see Perroy, *The Hundred Years War*, pp. 114-117; *Chron. Norm.*, pp. 52-53; *Jean le Bel*, I, 244-272. On 16 May 1341, Edward III ordered seizure of the English possessions of the late Breton duke (*Foedera*, II pt. 4, p. 99). On 7 September 1341, the French

Finally, the truce in no way ended English influence in the Netherlands, where Van Artevelde still dominated Flanders and opposed France. At three corners of the kingdom, therefore, but above all in the west, Philip VI found himself confronted by warfare or hostility.[5] These conflicts could threaten the peace of the realm and imperil the prosperity of important regions, yet the truce with England deprived him of the excuse to call out the French army and levy a large subsidy. The crown did levy a subsidy in many parts of the kingdom during 1341, as will be seen below, but no large grants were received and treasury receipts fell sharply from their level of 1340.[6] It was unquestionably the existence of a truce which prevented Philip from making the large tax-raising effort which adequate military defenses would require.

Continuing financial need, and awareness of the difficulties involved in any effort to negotiate a new subsidy, doubtless influenced the government's decision to introduce a new indirect tax early in 1341. By an ordinance of 16 March, Philip VI established for the first time the celebrated *gabelle* (or sales tax) on salt. This levy was to have a relatively short life under Philip VI, but its reappearance in the next reign would inaugurate a period of nearly four and one-half centuries in which the tax would be one of the best known revenues of the French monarchy, to the extent that the term *gabelle* would eventually come to mean, simply, the salt tax. Taxes on salt had been known in Italy in the twelfth century and had been fairly widespread in Provence by the middle of the thirteenth. The thirteenth century had in fact seen wide variations from one part of France to another in the way in which salt was handled by local seigneurial authority: it might be free, or subject to a special tax, or simply taxed like other commodities. In the case of the royal domain, *droits* had been paid by salt merchants but the actual commerce in salt had been free. Although there had been nothing precisely like the new *gabelle* in either domainal revenues or extraordinary impositions,[7] the expansion of royal power had led to the acquisition of salt pans in southern France which the crown normally exploited as a seigneurial right.[8] This effort, however, was largely local in scope, and the first royal ordinance on the

---

Parlement pronounced in favor of Charles of Blois, the French candidate for the Breton succession (Furgeot, *Actes*, I, no. 3669).

[5] On the situation in Flanders, see Lucas, *Low Countries*, pp. 438f.

[6] See Henneman, "Financing," pp. 297-298; and Appendix I, Table 4.

[7] G. Perousse, "Etude sur les origines de la gabelle et sur son organisation jusqu'en 1380," *PTEC*, 1898, pp. 90-91.

[8] Molinier, *HL*, IX, 527-528, note 6. There were royal *salins* at Toulouse and Carcassonne.

subject of salt, that of Louis X in 1315, was actually nothing more than a price-fixing measure aimed at protecting the populace against unscrupulous salt dealers.[9] Only in salt-producing regions such as Carcassonne and Agenais, had the citizens been obliged to buy salt prior to 1341.[10] What made the royal *gabelle* on salt instituted by Philip VI a really new departure, was the generalizing of the requirement of forced purchase.[11]

The ordinance of 16 March 1341 established commissioners who were to go through each part of the kingdom, seizing all salt, paying the merchants for it, and storing it in royal warehouses where it would be sold by *gabelliers*. Beyond this the orders were somewhat general, to be executed by the officers "as will seem best."[12] The commissioners assigned to this task at the bailiwick level were for the most part existing royal officials who merely received an extra assignment.[13]

Although the new tax was proclaimed in mid-March and copies of the ordinance were distributed to the towns in the seneschalsy of Beaucaire,[14] there was evidently some variation from place to place as to when the royal orders were executed. In Velay, there was an instantaneous reaction to an early effort to set up a proposed salt *grenier*. Led by the *sauniers* of Le Puy, the inhabitants of that town drew up protests which were sent to the crown by the end of March. The *gabelle* was opposed on the grounds that it would prejudice the privileges of the *sauniers* as well as the rights of both the bishop of Le Puy and the viscount of Polignac. It was denounced as a dangerous novelty; town privileges of 1226 and 1307 and the *paréage* agreement of 1307 were invoked against it, as was the written (i.e., Roman) law. It was claimed that the *gabelle* was not for the common profit and constituted a deprivation of seisin without the proper judicial procedure.[15] In the face of these arguments, the king yielded and ordered on 21 April that the salt *grenier* be transferred elsewhere.[16]

[9] E. Meynial, "Etudes sur la gabelle du sel avant le XVIIe siècle en France," *Tijdschrift voor Rechtsgesiedenis*, III (1922), 122; *Ord.*, I, 607.

[10] Viard, "Ressources," p. 190.   [11] Lot and Fawtier, *Institutions*, II, 224.

[12] Perousse, "Gabelle," p. 92; *HL*, x, col. 890; AM Alès I S-12, no. 18; BN NAF 7604 (Fontanieu 74), fols. 42r-43r; AN PP 117, p. 541. Commissioners were named for Normandy, Picardy, the Loire region, and Poitou-Saintonge besides Languedoc (AN AB xix 2636). In Quercy, the royal commissioner was the prior of Saint-Martin des Champs: Lacoste, *Quercy*, III, 97.

[13] From *HL*, x, cols. 887-888, it seems clear that most of the persons charged with organizing the *gabelle* were existing local officials of the crown who had been given this assignment as a special commission.

[14] One is in Alès I S-12, no. 18.   [15] Jacotin, *Polignac*, I, 441-443.

[16] AD Hérault A 4, fol. 17or-v. Cf. Molinier, *HL*, IX, 527, note 4; Delcambre, "Paréage," pp. 325-326.

Perhaps the swift hostile response of Le Puy induced the royal commissioners to delay the execution of the *gabelle* ordinance for several months. No other document appears on the subject until orders were published by the commissioners on 26 July directing that all persons having salt were to declare the quantity in their possession to the royal receiver of the *gabelle* and bring it to the appropriate warehouse.[17] By this time, the towns were ready with protests, and we have documents from Montpellier, Nîmes, and Lunel.[18]

Two general lines of argument were used—the poor economic state of the region and the fact that the proposed tax was without local precedent. In terms of Romano-canonical theory, the argument of Le Puy was fairly typical—the assertion that the tax was for the common utility was denied, and the king was accused of failing to consult those whose rights were touched. Montpellier complained that the seigneurs of the *salins* should have been consulted, and that the commissioners were acting contrary to their instructions since their action did not work toward the profit of the people nor did it "seem best."[19] Three days later, the commissioners indicated that they would proceed as planned.[20] Nîmes also protested vigorously, stating, among other things, that an inquiry into the possible harm involved should have preceded action by the commissioners. When the proclamation was renewed, Nîmes and Lunel made a new protest, only to be turned down again.[21]

In time, however, the government had to take cognizance of local objections to the new tax, and on 23 September 1341, there came a letter from Paris which praised the *gabelle* as a wise and necessary measure and urged the crown's officials to use diplomacy and endeavor to persuade people in the seneschalsy of Beaucaire of the utility of the tax while at the same time taking every step to make it work smoothly with a minimum of injury to individuals.[22] The irate consuls of Nîmes were not so easily mollified, however, and on 8 January 1342, the town made another protest to the effect that the salt tax violated rights and impoverished the land. These complaints the harassed commissioners sent on

---

[17] Ménard, *Nismes*, II, *preuves*, 117-118; Bardon, *Alais*, II, 4; Viard, "Ressources," p. 191.

[18] AM Montpellier B-2, nos. 597-601; *HL*, x, cols. 888, 891; Ménard, *Nismes*, II, 100-102, and *preuves*, 117-118; *INV AM Lunel* (ms.), II, fol. 49 (HH 2), no. 1938.

[19] AM Montpellier B-2, nos. 597-601; *HL*, x, col. 888.

[20] *Ibid.*, col. 691; Ménard, *Nismes*, II, *preuves*, 117.

[21] *Ibid.*, pp. 118-120; AM Nîmes CC I, nos. 9, 10; *INV AM Lunel*, II, fol. 49 (nos. 1937-38).

[22] Ménard, *Nismes*, II, 103-110, and *preuves*, 120-121.

to Paris.[23] There, they did not sway the determination of the crown to go through with the salt tax, for on 24 February, new royal orders were issued which reaffirmed the tax and further defined the powers of the commissioners.[24] We have evidence of *gabelle* officials at Lunel and Lodève in 1342.[25]

Significantly, these protests came from the seneschalsy of Beaucaire, and not from those of Carcassonne and Toulouse, where royal *salins* had already been operated as a seigneurial right[26] and the *gabelle* was not a startling innovation. The Beaucaire region, however, had long enjoyed unusual freedom in salt commerce and the imposition was more in the nature of a sovereign than a seigneurial action. As a result, it was much resented.[27] Although the salt tax was being imposed in many other parts of the kingdom, the only region besides Beaucaire for which protests at this time are recorded, is the county of Artois, where we are told that the opposition approached revolutionary proportions.[28]

Although the *gabelle* was to have a long and notorious future, its appearance in 1341 was fully in keeping with the recent French tradition of fiscal expedients in time of truce. It was, in effect, a levy based on a seigneurial right which now was generalized and stretched to "extraordinary" proportions. It was accompanied by some of the other measures which we have encountered in earlier periods of peace or truce. The crown made an extensive investigation of abuses of the royal waters and forests rights, beginning in Languedoc.[29] A reform commission with broader powers toured the seneschalsies of Toulouse, Carcassonne, and Bigorre, sometimes instituting genuine reforms,[30] but also seeking to raise money for the king.[31] The most lucrative of their operations involved Pamiers, where the count of Foix was co-seigneur with the bishop. The bishop's officers were accused of violating royal and comital

---

[23] *Ibid.*; AM Nîmes CC 1, no. 11.   [24] AD Hérault A 4, fols. 184v-185.

[25] *INV AM Lunel*, ii, no. 2218 (CC 60); AM Lodève AA 2, no. 170.

[26] See above, note 8.   [27] Molinier, *HL*, ix, 527-528, note 6.

[28] Hirschauer, *Les états d'Artois*, i, 15.

[29] AN JJ 68, no. 434; JJ 72, nos. 250, 368, 382; JJ 74, no. 580; Furgeot, *Actes*, ii, nos. 5155, 6506.

[30] *HL*, ix, 533; *INV AM Toulouse*, p. 561 (AA 56), indicates a reform ordinance.

[31] The documents show a sharp increase in the number of fines and compositions arising from a wide variety of individual or community misdeeds, although the size of these fines did not approach the level of those collected in earlier years of peace like 1322, 1327, and 1334-1336, which have been described above in Chapters ii-iii. Texts for 1341 include AN JJ 72, no. 374; JJ 74, no. 107; JJ 75, no. 227; BN Doat 109, fols. 239v-243r; Furgeot, *Actes*, i, no. 3713; AN PP 117, p. 555. An indication of fines for *francs-fiefs* is in AD Tarn E 2298, but the text is rather mutilated.

jurisdiction and were ordered to desist.[32] The town, however, had also been guilty of misdeeds and had lost its consulate. Rather than restoring it for a price, as the crown often did in such cases, the commissioners accepted 20,000 *l.t.* from the count and bishop, who claimed that the "greater and wiser part" of the citizens did not wish restoration of the consulate. The hapless citizens probably were taxed by their seigneurs in order to raise this sum.[33] Other fiscal expedients included a new usury commission established in Languedoc in July,[34] and a request for "subsidies" from Florentines in the kingdom.[35]

All these expedients, the *gabelle* included, were scant substitute for war subsidies, and the crown still tried to levy these whenever and wherever the military threat was sufficient to open the purses of local inhabitants. Both private war and border skirmishing were creating military necessity in Languedoc in spite of the truce, and the latter was, in any case, expected to end fairly early. As a result, the crown issued military summonses before the spring of 1341 in hopes of collecting some much-needed money. On 27 March, the seneschal of Beaucaire sent a subordinate to Montpellier to require the inhabitants, whether subject to the king of France or the king of Majorca, to furnish one properly equipped sergeant per household for forty days' service. The order evidently was aimed primarily at the wealthier citizens as in 1340, and Montpellier protested.[36] The crown must have collected in due course, for a document of 19 July made reference to those at Montpellier who had contributed.[37] It is not clear whether or not Lunel paid a subsidy, but royal officers classified the citizens according to what arms they could afford, and this effort was met by protests.[38]

Late in May, Jean de Marigny summoned the nobles of Carcassonne and Rouergue to muster on 1 July.[39] Those from the county of Rodez were permitted to serve under their own count and perhaps he, rather than the king, collected a war subsidy from some of them.[40] Direct royal subjects in Rouergue, however, were taxed by the crown, which imposed a 2,000-pound assessment to cover both the subsidy and fines for mone-

[32] BN Doat 93, fols. 120r-132v.

[33] *Ibid.*, fols. 118r-119v, 134-178; Molinier, *HL*, IX, 531-532, notes 3-4.

[34] *HL*, x, cols. 885-887.   [35] AN PP 117, p. 472.

[36] *HL*, x, cols. 884-885; *Gr. Chartrier*, nos. 3112, 3149-3151.

[37] *Gr. Chartrier*, 3305.

[38] *INV AM Lunel*, II, nos. 1968, 1970-1973 (EE 1).

[39] *HL*, IX, 533-534; BN Doat 187, fols. 202r-204v.

[40] *Ibid.*, fols. 204v-206v. The document is not too clear. It merely authorizes John of Armagnac to lead his own vassals in the campaign.

tary violations.[41] After negotiating with royal officers at Montpellier, Millau paid its *finance* in July from the proceeds of a municipal property tax which produced 560 pounds.[42] Villefranche raised a contingent of sergeants and paid another 300 *l.t.* to obtain confirmation of its privileges.[43] In all, ninety-three communities in the royal part of Rouergue sent a total of 339 sergeants to the war, Millau sending the largest number (forty).[44] Meanwhile, an enemy force occupied a fortress on the Aveyron and the seneschal of Rouergue ordered the bishop of Rodez to raise troops to recapture the place. When the bishop tried the less expensive device of excommunicating the offenders, the seneschal seized his temporalities.[45] The towns of Albi and Cajarc also paid subsidies in 1341,[46] but in general, the crown seems to have realized less from taxes in Languedoc than from *finances* levied by *réformateurs*.

Auvergne was a region lying between Languedoc and Languedoil, and this location gave rise to some jurisdictional debate in the 1340s. Although upper Auvergne (the bailiwick of the Mountains) asserted that it had always been subject to written law like Languedoc,[47] the entire region tended increasingly to be subject to the fiscal administration at Paris rather than the royal lieutenant in the Midi. Thus in 1341, the two bailiwicks of Auvergne paid a sales tax of 4 *d./l.* (1⅔ percent), like most of northern France. After ordering the bailiff and receiver of Auvergne to collect this tax, the government reversed itself and forbade royal and seigneurial officers from taking part in the collection.[48] One infers that the communities of this region had obtained the right to supervise farming and levying of the subsidy. At Aurillac, in the bailiwick of the Mountains, royal officers did oversee collection, however.[49]

The sales tax of 4 *d./l.* was rather widespread in northern France. Paris granted such a tax for one year beginning in the spring of 1341.[50]

[41] AM Millau CC 516, unnumbered document.

[42] AM Millau CC 512, unnumbered document, indicates a payment for the war, while BN *Coll. Languedoc* 84, fol. 211r, indicates the bishop's order to the commissioners to stop their oppressions. Tax negotiations are in AM Millau CC 345, fol. 81v and the tax roll is in AM Millau, second series, ee 9.

[43] Cabrol, *Villefranche*, p. 213; AN JJ 76, no. 168.

[44] L. Constans (ed.), *Le livre de l'épervier, cartulaire de la commune de Millau*, Montpellier, 1882, pp. 192-195.

[45] AD Aveyron G 473.

[46] AM Albi CC 58, the *vidimus* of a receipt dated 23 July 1341; AM Cajarc CC no. 423; CC *supp.*, no. 85.

[47] *INV AM Aurillac*, i, 20 (AA 8).

[48] AM Riom CC 10, nos. 81, 99; *INV AM Montferrand*, i, 312 (CC 1).

[49] *INV AM Aurillac*, i, 398-400 (CC 3).

[50] AN P 2291, p. 667; AN PP 117, p. 470; *Ord.*, xii, 64-66. The continuing dispute between the tax farmer and the cathedral chapter was before the *Parlement* in

So also, did the towns of Normandy, where the levy began in August and produced 8,759 *l.t.* at Rouen.[51] Reims agreed to pay it for eighteen months, beginning in September, and the other towns of Vermandois did the same. As in 1340, the towns were to retain a portion of the tax (about 25 percent) for local fortifications. The military action of 1340 had probably persuaded these communities near the Netherlands that a genuine danger existed despite the truce. In addition, Reims was under pressure from royal *enquêteurs*.[52] The sales tax was also levied in the bailiwicks of Amiens,[53] Sens and Mâcon,[54] and in Anjou, Maine and Touraine, where the clergy substituted a half-tenth and some nobles resisted any taxation in their lands.[55] The count of Blois permitted the levy in his lands subject to a letter of non-prejudice.[56] Thus the sales tax employed in 1340 was now extended through most of Languedoil and renewed with a minimum of controversy. In northern France, taxation achieved a greater uniformity than the kingdom had known for over forty years.

This documentation suggests that the government was having greater success in levying money than in the past. Nevertheless, treasury figures make clear that this was not the case.[57] The sales tax was very small, was paid only by non-nobles, and was not as lucrative as fines levied in lieu of military service. The *gabelle*, barely established and still the object of considerable opposition, could not have produced much revenue initially, and we have seen that Languedoc produced very little in subsidies. The truce of late 1340 made it difficult to justify an *arrière-ban*, yet the crown had to cope with new dangers from Brittany while maintaining a watchful stance on the Flemish and Gascon frontiers. It is probable that most tax receipts and a good portion of the domainal revenues were applied to military requirements in these localities, thus depleting the totals which actually reached the treasury.

Meanwhile, the government continued to alter the coinage, striking an overvalued *gros* which helped raise the price of silver about 50 percent in 1341. The rate of royal coinage profits was somewhat less than in 1340, as the mints were forced to pay steadily higher prices to attract silver.

February 1342 and was resolved on a legal technicality which did not prejudice the claims of the chapter: Furgeot, *Actes*, I, no. 3985.

[51] AN JJ 72, no. 230; BN *ms. fr.* 25997, no. 349; Viard, "Ressources," p. 188; Vuitry, *Régime financier*, II, 19; AN P 2291, p. 789; AN PP 117, p. 553.

[52] Varin, *Reims*, II, 857-858.   [53] Thierry, *Recueil*, I, 553.

[54] Plancher, *Bourgogne*, II, 212.

[55] B. de Brousillon, *Documents inédits pour servir à l'histoire du Maine au XIVe siècle* (*Archives historiques du Maine*, V), Le Mans, 1905, 27-29, publishing AN P 2291, p. 565.

[56] AN K 43, no. 18.   [57] Appendix I, Table 4.

The alterations and the rising price of silver would continue through 1342, provoking a growing amount of discontent.[58]

The war resumed in 1342, and increased fighting made it possible for the crown to collect greater amounts in taxes. Yet even in the feeble currency of 1342, treasury receipts did not approach those for 1340.[59] Such taxation as occurred in 1342 was more general and uniform than in the past, thus continuing the trend which had begun to appear in Languedoil during 1340 and 1341. Despite the crown's continuing inability to levy really large subsidies, this greater uniformity may be seen as progress, of a sort, for the monarchy. The tendency for taxes to vary in form from one locality to another, which had first appeared in 1296 and had reached its greatest extreme in 1339-1340, had been the direct result of the crown's desire to obtain money quickly. Yet the practice had encouraged extreme localism in outlook. More uniform taxation might encourage (and result from) a less parochial view of the common profit and a less cumbersome and costly process of tax negotiation.

One important tax in 1342 was a 20 s. hearth tax (*fouage*) which would have produced a large amount if applied uniformly throughout the realm. Some historians have greatly exaggerated its extent, stating that it was in fact levied everywhere.[60] On the face of it, this claim is doubtful, because the *fouage* would have overlapped the sales taxes being collected in Languedoil, thereby violating the main condition under which most of these had been granted.[61] A scrutiny of the documents indicates that this hearth tax was really confined to Languedoc, where it proved a good deal more successful than the similar levy attempted in 1337. Once again, there were reductions and changes in form for various localities, but these were less numerous than five years before.

On 6 April 1342, Philip VI gave sweeping new powers to Jean de Marigny, bishop of Beauvais, his royal lieutenant in Languedoc and Saintonge. He also ordered collection of a subsidy of 20 *s.t.* for each hearth for the next year because the kingdom was in danger and all were obliged to help defend it.[62] In the next few days, Philip ordered the royal

---

[58] *Ibid.*, Table 1.

[59] *Ibid.*, Table 4. On the resumption of military activity in 1342, see below, notes 64, 83, and Froissart, IV, 1-121.

[60] Viard, "Ressources," p. 188, who has been followed uncritically by most subsequent writers.

[61] See, for example, the grant by Paris, above, note 50.

[62] BN *Coll. Languedoc* 84, fols. 237-238; Ménard, *Nismes*, II, *preuves*, 126. It was this document which led Viard and others to conclude that the whole realm was to be taxed 20 s. per hearth, but actually it proves nothing of the kind. Addressed to the seneschal of Beaucaire, the letter merely established that the tax was not to be

host to muster at Arras on 24 June, when the truce with England was to end.[63] The documents cited thus far hardly prove that the proposed levy was national in scope, but they certainly leave open the possibility. All other documents on this subject, however, relate to southern France.

Writing from Cahors on 21 May, the bishop of Beauvais issued letters indicating that the *fouage* was being imposed in the bailiwick of the Mountains of Auvergne and in the seneschalsies of Toulouse, Carcassonne, Beaucaire, Périgord and Quercy, Bigorre, and Rouergue. Although the king's military summons had called for some southern troops to go to Arras, the Gascon frontier had to be defended and Marigny issued his own summons to Marmande.[64] Nothing was neglected in the effort to raise money, and on 3 June 1342, the bishop named new commissioners to investigate fief alienations and other matters.[65]

Although Marigny had listed eight districts in which the 20 *s.* hearth tax was applied, one of these, upper Auvergne, was not normally in the lieutenancy of Languedoc, and we have seen that in 1341, this region paid a sales tax like most of the other districts governed from Paris.[66] There was apparently still some uncertainty, however, as to which part of France had jurisdiction over the Mountains of Auvergne, and in January 1342, the king had written Marigny stating that this bailiwick was part of Languedoil and exempt from exactions by the bishop's officers.[67] Yet Marigny still tried to levy the hearth tax there in 1342. In November, Philip wrote to him again, saying that his commissioners were to cease making demands on this region which, as part of Languedoil, had paid the 4 *d./l.* sales tax.[68] By this date, the imposition of 1341 would have expired, and we may conclude that upper Auvergne (with other parts of Languedoil), had renewed this tax while the 20 *s.* hearth tax was limited to the seven seneschalsies of Languedoc.[69]

The levy of the tax in the Midi was preceded by local bargaining with

---

confined to that district. The important passage, from the document in the *Coll. Languedoc*, is as follows: "... *et ad ipsius regni et nostri ac ipsorum subditorum juris conservationem dictum posuit negotium uni dei auxilio feliciter consummari, ipsis subditis pro singulis focis, videlicet 20 s.t. pro foco duximus pro anno presenti et pro nunc incendum.* ..." The differences in Ménard's version are minor.

[63] AD Hérault A 4, fols. 181-182; Cf. *LC*, nos. 148, 151.

[64] *HL*, IX, 540-541.

[65] Molinier's summary of the work of these commissioners is in *ibid.*, pp. 541-542, note 5.

[66] See above, notes 47, 49.

[67] *INV AM Aurillac*, I, 20-21 (AA 8).   [68] *Ibid.*, p. 21.

[69] The previous sales tax, granted for a year, dated from August 1341. If such a tax was in force at Aurillac in November 1342, it must have been a renewal of the previous one.

towns seeking a reduced rate or wishing to commute the hearth tax to a lump-sum payment. The town of Pézenas would pay only 4 *s.* per hearth initially, treating this amount as a loan, until assured that other towns of the Carcassonne district were also paying. Pézenas agreed to pay the remaining 16 *s.* per hearth if the rest of the region did so.[70] In time, this seneschalsy paid over 73,000 *l.t.*, somewhat less than 20 *s.* per hearth.[71] For its share, Narbonne offered 3,500 pounds provided that no more would be sought during the year, either for the upkeep of sergeants or in the form of a loan.[72] Royal receipts in this region were reduced by tax exemptions[73] but augmented by *finances* collected by the crown's commissioners.[74]

In Quercy, the hearth tax of 20 *s.* gave rise to great protest and the king had to order that nothing be collected beyond what was customary.[75] The two districts of Périgord and Quercy produced the feeble total of 24,526 *l.t.*, an average of about 4 *s.* per hearth. One reason for these low net receipts is that nearly 9,000 pounds had to be deducted from the gross receipts for expenses, while the important town of Périgueux was excused from paying altogether.[76] In Rouergue, the nobles rendered personal military service, and one town is known to have sent some sergeants to the army.[77] The seneschal of Beaucaire was ordered

[70] AM Pézenas, B, 3, I, 25, no. 1643.

[71] Molinier, *HL*, ix, 540, basing the figure on AN K 498, no. 2.

[72] BN Doat 53, fols. 45-46; *HL*, ix, 451. This payment was much larger than Narbonne had contributed in the past, and indeed the 20 *s.* per hearth was double the tax paid in 1328 and other years. The difference, however, was completely wiped out by the effects of coinage alterations. The figures in Appendix I, Table I, indicate that the mark of silver had risen in price from 5.4 *l.t.* in 1328 to 12.5 *l.t.* in the summer of 1342. If prices followed a similar curve, the crown was actually obtaining less money in 1342 than in 1328.

[73] Two documents which are certainly misdated but which may refer to exemptions in 1342 are AM Pézenas, B, 3, I. 21, no. 1639 (excusing notaries from the tax), and Mahul, *Cartulaire*, v, 347 (excusing "sergeants and other inhabitants").

[74] Three different fines in Languedoc which each produced 2,000 *l.t.* for the crown are indicated in BN *Coll. Languedoc* 84, fol. 235r; AN JJ 68, no. 431; JJ 75, no. 83.

[75] Albe, "Cahors INV," no. 382; Lacoste, *Quercy*, iii, 99-100.

[76] BN *ms. lat.* 9194, pp. 1-13; Molinier, *HL*, ix, 540, note 1, quoted the gross receipts, which came to more than 33,500 *l.t.*, but this total was depleted by very high expenses of nearly 9,000 pounds (BN *ms. lat.* 9194, pp. 14-25). These were apparently caused by the fact that Anglo-Gascon marauders were making the roads dangerous, for a troop of horsemen had to be maintained in order to protect those who levied and transported the collections.

[77] Rigal and Verlaguet, "Notes," iii, no. 2989; Cabrol, *Villefranche*, i, 214-216. The town finally did send Marigny a few archers. Our only evidence from Millau, AM Millau CC 60, is a "roll of contributions" to a municipal tax, which may indicate

to have the first half of the hearth tax raised immediately and the rest collected when further word should be sent.[78] Montpellier agreed, as a compromise, to pay 15 s. per hearth subject to letters of non-prejudice. Then, in return for a revocation of all loans and subsidies, the consuls offered 3,000 l.t. in lieu of the fouage.[79] Lunel, the fief of Charles of Spain, escaped the tax,[80] and so did Aigues Mortes, on the grounds that it was a vital fortress and seaport.[81] The earlier tax to sustain the facilities of this old harbor was still a cause for acrimony and debate.[82]

Late in the summer of 1342, Jean de Marigny and the military forces of Languedoc were occupied with besieging the English at Sainte-Bazeille.[83] It is in connection with this siege that we learn about the subsidy contributed in this year by the seneschalsy of Toulouse, which according to a chronicler, was taxed 33,000 pounds for war expenses. This sum probably represents the proceeds of the hearth tax.[84] Albi paid 1,333 pounds for the hearth tax and another 600 l.t. for jurisdictional rights.[85] Marigny's force at Sainte-Bazeille included 124 sergeants from Narbonne, although this town had just paid its largest tax of the reign on condition that the crown demand no more sergeants during the year.[86] It is noteworthy that Narbonne was prepared to waive this guarantee so promptly. In all probability, the consuls regarded the campaign as sufficiently important to warrant an extra effort. A local military action of this sort may have impressed them as a case of "necessity" more "evident" than those earlier occasions when the king had declared the kingdom to be in danger. For the consuls of Narbonne, the critical question evidently was not whether an emergency justified special measures or suspension of privileges, but rather, whether or not a given situation could really be called an emergency.

---

a war subsidy, but the first folio is torn and it cannot be determined what the tax was for.

[78] AD Hérault A 4, fols. 185-186; Ménard, Nismes, II, preuves, 126.

[79] Gr. Chartrier, nos. 3113, 3357.

[80] AM Lunel CC 60, no. 2217; BN ms. lat. 9174, fols. 166-167.

[81] AD Hérault A 4, fols. 240v-242r.

[82] Gr. Chartrier, no. 2581; AN AB xix 2636, Viard's note from AN x 1a 8847, fol. 246v.

[83] Molinier, HL, IX, 526, note 1, correcting the error of a chronicler (HL, x, col. 43), who placed the siege in 1340 and was followed in this by Mahul, Cartulaire, v, 347 (see above, note 73).

[84] HL, x, col. 43, a chronicler whom Molinier was prepared to accept on this point while Vaissete was not (HL, IX, 525-526, and notes).

[85] AM Albi CC 58; BN Doat 103, fols. 239v-254v.

[86] HL, IX, 542; BN Doat 53, fol. 47; see above, note 72.

Poitou was subject to the *arrière-ban*, and the king sought taxes from those who did not wish to muster at Arras, but in May, the order was canceled.[87] In general, it appears that the sales tax of 4 *d./l.* was renewed in Languedoil. Rouen received a letter of non-prejudice in August, after granting it for another year.[88] It was also levied in the possessions of the count of Blois, for the receivers of Tours and Orléans were ordered to turn over to the count either half the tax receipts or 3,000 *l.t.*, whichever was smaller, to reimburse him for his military expenses.[89] In the bailiwick of Senlis, the sales tax was being levied even in the lands of those with high justice.[90] In Vermandois, Saint-Quentin granted the tax for a year beginning 1 February 1342. One fourth of the proceeds were applied to the town's own expenses, and we are told that the same arrangement had been in force for the past year and a half.[91] The count of Forez received a letter of non-prejudice in October for the levy of the sales tax in his possessions,[92] and we have seen that it was collected also in Auvergne.[93] Although this tax was general through most of Languedoil, the justiciable subjects of the bishop of Chartres provided one exception, for they paid the crown a fiftieth.[94]

Despite variations, the trend towards uniformity seemed established in 1342, with the South paying a hearth tax while the North and Center of the kingdom paid a tax on sales. France was thus divided into two main fiscal areas, but there were other taxes which applied everywhere —the *gabelle*, the 4 *d./l.* export tax,[95] the *haut passage* on wool exports,[96] and the clerical tenth.[97]

These different taxes failed to produce enough revenue to put the kingdom's finances and defenses on a sound footing. Local officers with troops to pay had to borrow or extort the funds they needed.[98] Under these circumstances, the French government was increasingly subject to

---

[87] *AHP*, XLVI, 101-105.   [88] AN JJ 74, no. 315.

[89] BN NAF 3653, no. 108; 3637, no. 49.   [90] Furgeot, *Actes*, I, no. 4567.

[91] Le Maire, *St. Quentin*, II, no. 589.   [92] AN JJ 74, no. 341.

[93] See above, notes 67-69. See also *INV AM Montferrand*, I, 312 (CC 1).

[94] BN Clairambault 473, pp. 15-25.

[95] On the farming of this export tax, see Cazelles, *Soc. politique*, p. 277; and BN *ms. fr.* 25698, nos. 104, 111-113; AD Hérault A 4, fols. 180r, 192v-195r; Le Maire, *St. Quentin*, II, no. 601.

[96] The regulations governing this tax of declining value were altered in 1342 in an effort to make it more efficient and lucrative: Henneman, "Italians," p. 18, note 8; AD Hérault A 4, fols. 183v-184.

[97] Vuitry, *Régime financier*, II, 206. BN Moreau 230, fol. 94r-v, shows that by 1343, the tenth was regarded as a tax for the support of the war.

[98] Viard, "La France," p. 393. This problem continued well into the next reign. See Timbal, *Guerre*, pp. 65-66.

criticism. The bad harvests of the 1340s were a source of misery and un-rest. The coinage debasement had reached seriously inflationary propor-tions. Taxes continued and even seemed to proliferate, yet the crown was still short of money, and the war no nearer a satisfactory conclusion. The king had avoided pitched battles and his nobles could not take satisfac-tion in victory, spoils or honor. Important interests and regions felt ex-cluded from political power at court. This combination of factors pro-ducing discontent would come to a head in 1343 and present Philip VI with a serious political challenge.

2. The Crisis of 1343

The latest flare-up of Anglo-French War in 1342 had involved three fronts but the real trouble spot was now in Brittany. The new pope, Clement VI, strove to bring about a settlement before this succession dis-pute could lead to a serious escalation of the war. His efforts ultimately failed, but they were rewarded briefly in 1343 when the two monarchies accepted the truce of Malestroit late in January.[99] Ironically, this truce hastened the internal crisis which was brewing in France, for the crown ran into bitter opposition when attempting to continue levying taxes in Languedoc.

At Le Puy, an uprising occurred when commissioners tried to obtain a subsidy in February 1343 (i.e., after the truce). The government soon brought the disturbance under control by taking a conciliatory posi-tion.[100] In Périgord, resistance to taxation required the personal attention of the bishop of Beauvais on his way south in February.[101] It is not clear whether the tax at issue was a new one or merely the old *fouage* which was still being collected.[102] The town of Toulouse seems to have made a "gracious" offer of 3,000 *l.t.* in 1343 before the truce was con-cluded. This arrangement was ratified by Agout de Baux, the seneschal, who had relieved Marigny as royal lieutenant in Languedoc for the three winter months. The money was to be the equivalent of a full year's tax, and there were to be no fines by commissioners of inquiry or additional requests for men or money during the year *unless the kingdom should be invaded*.[103] Consuls of five towns in the *jugerie* of Albigeois offered to

[99] Perroy, *The Hundred Years War*, p. 115.
[100] Delcambre, "Paréage," p. 326.
[101] Molinier, *HL*, IX, 546, note 5, citing the third of several letters of Marigny in AN JJ 74, no. 174.
[102] BN *ms. lat.* 9194 indicates that collection of the tax in Périgord and Quercy ran from the spring of 1342 until the end of April 1343.
[103] *INV AM Toulouse*, pp. 461 (AA 35, no. 52) and 532 (AA 45, no. 11).

pay 5,333⅓ *l.t.* in lieu of a 15 *s. fouage* which Agout de Baux's commissioner had requested.[104] This grant was probably made after the truce, for at the request of these towns, Philip VI ordered cancellation of all "subsidies, loans, *fouages*, or *finances*" granted for the war after the truce.[105]

In the Beaucaire district, a new hearth tax of 15 *s.t.* was canceled on 2 March 1343, because of the truce.[106] Montpellier was already having difficulty in raising money because the king of Majorca challenged the consuls for levying a municipal *taille* without his permission.[107] Millau, in Rouergue, was also paying *finansa subsidi* in lieu of a 15 *s.t.* hearth tax in 1343,[108] while the seneschalsy of Carcassonne was only contributing half as much—a *fouage* of 8 *s.t.*[109] On 6 May, the day he canceled subsidies in the Albigeois, Philip VI also canceled those in the Carcassonne district,[110] and by this date taxes must have been halted throughout Languedoc.

The truce was not well kept by the antagonists along the Gascon border, and even if it had been, the crown faced a problem which would become severe in later decades—the menace of unemployed soldiers who were engaging in brigandage following the truce. Philip VI had to order action against those in Agenais.[111] The bishop of Beauvais felt that the military situation justified a new tax, and on 10 April, he sent a military summons to the seneschalsy of Beaucaire.[112] Other parts of Languedoc seem not to have been affected by this call to arms. Montpellier paid the bishop 3,800 *l.t.* to satisfy his demands and gain a new cancellation

[104] AD Tarn E 1402. The towns were Gaillac, Cordes, Rabastens, Lisle, and Cahoussac.

[105] Compayré, *Etudes*, p. 425.

[106] *HL*, x, cols. 924-925, dated 12 March which is probably an error, since this document is taken from the copy in BN *ms. lat.* 9174, fol. 163. Two contemporary versions in AM Montpellier (G-5, no, 3323; H-6, no. 3884) are dated 2 March. The tax in question certainly appears to be a new one, not an installment of that granted in 1342. It was canceled because of the truce, and there was no allegation that it was being wrongfully collected after its expiration.

[107] *Gr. Chartrier*, nos. 263-264.   [108] AM Millau CC 345, fol. 87r.

[109] BN *ms. fr.* 26001, no. 498; 26003, nos. 1020, 1023, 1024. The last three texts are undated accounts placed with documents belonging to 1360. One of them mentions Agout de Baux, however, and M. Cazelles has pointed out to me that they probably belong to 1343. The fact that they deal with a *fouage* of 8 *s.t.* makes it far more probable that they belong to 1343 than to 1360.

[110] BN Doat 53, fols. 54-55, cited incorrectly in Cazelles, *Soc. politique*, p. 163.

[111] Tholin, *Agen*, pp. 62-64, a letter of 1 August.

[112] AD Hérault A 4, fols. 186v-187.

of the *fouage* Agout de Baux had been levying earlier.[113] At this point, the royal government, which had canceled taxes in Languedoc, sought to find money in the Midi by levying arrears from earlier subsidies. Montpellier protested this action and the king called off his commissioners when he learned of the town's recent arrangement with Marigny.[114] Nîmes, which was said to owe 600 pounds from the taxes of 1338 and 1339, may also have escaped paying at this time, but the matter would be revived there in 1344.[115] The entire incident illustrates the lack of coordination between the king and his southern lieutenant.

The cancellation of subsidies because of the truce put Philip VI in a difficult financial position, and he sought other means of obtaining money besides collecting arrears. Several weeks after the truce was concluded, Philip took action to improve the organization of the *gabelle* on salt. An ordinance of March 1343 was intended to give this tax a more permanent administration and help increase the revenues it would provide. The king named seven commissioners who were placed in charge of the whole *gabelle* administration. Their responsibilities were divided up on a regional basis but a minimum number of them were to be in Paris at all times. They were to deal with litigation arising from the tax,[116] so they may be regarded as judicial as well as fiscal officials. Their appointment replaced the earlier, less centralized arrangement which had employed a mixture of regular royal local officers and occasional commissioners. Now the salt tax was to be administered by a special arm of the royal service. This first great effort to organize and institutionalize the *gabelle*[117] could only have been regarded as clear evidence that the crown was seeking to make the tax permanent.

Whether or not the *gabelle* was causing discontent at this time, there is no doubt that the coinage had become a burning issue. Continuing financial need had led the king to alter the coinage frequently in the early 1340s, and by 1343 the price of silver had risen nearly fivefold in a decade.[118] In Languedoil, where the truce seems to have had no effect on the prevailing 4 *d./l.* sales tax, the coinage was a major factor in the crown's effort to renew this imposition. A letter of non-prejudice issued

[113] BN *ms. lat.* 9174, fols. 168r-169v; AM Montpellier H-6, no. 3885.
[114] *Ibid.*, nos. 3885-3886; *Gr. Chartrier*, nos. 472-473.
[115] Ménard, *Nismes*, ii, *preuves*, 128-130.
[116] *Ord.*, ii, 179-182.
[117] Meynial, "Gabelle," pp. 122-123. In September 1343, a salt *grenier* was set up at Millau over the objections of the town consuls (de Gaujal, *Etudes*, ii, 180).
[118] Appendix i, Table i.

to Joan of Navarre in July, indicated that the continued levy of the sales tax in the Evreux family's lands was conditional upon a royal promise to reform the currency.[119] The crown had been authorized to levy this tax by an agreement with Joan in May.[120]

Other arrangements with great magnates do not mention the coinage but they do make clear that once again a sales tax of 4 *d./l.* was being collected in much of Languedoil. Both the count of Blois[121] and lord of Pousauges[122] agreed to share equally with the king the proceeds of this tax in their lands, thus apparently continuing an arrangement which had been followed the year before. A similar tax was levied at La Rochelle in 1343, with the crown and municipal government sharing the receipts.[123] It was also being collected in Vermandois, and the archbishop of Reims agreed to have it raised in his lands as in the previous year, again on the understanding that none of his rights would be prejudiced.[124]

These documents all suggest that much of northern France merely continued to pay the sales tax as it had for several years, notwithstanding the conclusion of the truce. As with 1341, however, this apparent evidence of greater royal success in the fiscal sphere is rather misleading, for the government was faced by widespread disaffection in 1343. An influential Norman baron with a strategic fief, Godefroy d'Harcourt, lord of Saint-Sauveur, refused to answer a royal summons based on charges of illegal private war. He now launched a thirteen-year career of chronic rebellion against the house of Valois and soon became the leader of disaffected elements in Normandy and other western districts.[125] Cazelles has pointed to the general restlessness of the nobility of the West, men who were closely interrelated, had many ties with England, and were largely excluded from power at court. Led by Mile de Noyers, the Chamber of Accounts party had dominated the government for eight

---

[119] AN JJ 74, no. 132; Viard, in AN AB xix, citing AD Basses-Pyrenées E 513.

[120] AN P 2291, p. 599; BN Moreau, fol. 68r-v.

[121] Cazelles, *Soc. politique,* p. 163; and Vuitry, *Régime financier,* II, 21, both citing AN P 2291, p. 791, an undated text which has been assigned the date of 1344 by the copyist. It renewed an agreement which had been in effect the year before, so if the document does belong to 1344, it is evidence for 1343 as well.

[122] BN *ms. fr.* 25997, nos. 362-363. A number of towns produced a total of 680 *l.t.* of which the seigneur received half.

[123] AN AB xix 2640, note to BN *ms. fr.* 27319.

[124] AN P 2291, p. 793.

[125] L. Delisle, *Histoire du château et des sires de Saint-Sauveur-le-Vicomte,* Valognes, 1867, pp. 52f. and P.J. nos. 67, 76; Froissart, IV, 310-311.

years and was beginning to encounter opposition. Regional feeling may well have been involved, since a preponderant influence was exercised by Burgundians and Auvergnats.[126] In any case, the year 1343 was troubled by outbreaks of rebellion,[127] as well as discontent at the *gabelle* and coinage and the opposition to taxes in Languedoc already described.[128]

In order to pacify this opposition, Philip VI ordered certain reforms in the spring and may at that time have discussed the coinage with the magnates.[129] By June, in any case, he had resolved to offer the kingdom a sweeping reform of the coinage if, in return, he might obtain a tax. This decision led to a most important assembly—the "Estates General" of 1343.

Our only direct evidence of this meeting is furnished by two documents from Narbonne. On 12 July 1343, the consuls named two proctors to attend the assembly, indicating that Béziers and other towns in the area had been ordered to send two persons each to Paris with sufficient instructions to consider both a coinage reform and a 4 *d./l.* sales tax which the king hoped to levy on the whole kingdom for one year. Narbonne had not received this summons (which must have been sent in June), but the consuls regarded this as an oversight and evidently assumed the right to send representatives anyway. These representatives were instructed to resist the tax vigorously on the grounds of local impoverishment and a long succession of other burdensome taxes in recent years.[130] The second Narbonne document is dated 3 December, nearly five months later. It contains royal instructions to commissioners indicating that the assembly had met and agreed to coinage reforms and that the 4 *d./l.* sales tax was to reimburse the king for the expense of improving the currency. The commissioners were to assemble the inhabitants of their assigned districts and negotiate the form and amount of subsidy.[131]

These documents suggest, first of all, that the crown had issued an unusually explicit summons, offering a specific reform to the whole kingdom. Secondly, Narbonne assumed a right to send proctors to Paris even though the town had not actually received a summons. To these apparent novelties, we must add a third inference from the documents—that

---

[126] Cazelles, *Soc. politique*, pp. 132, 151f.

[127] *Ibid.*, p. 152-155, 157.   [128] Viard, "Ressources," p. 192.

[129] Cazelles, *Soc. politique*, p. 167. For reforms issued in the spring, see *Ord.*, II, pp. 171-173.

[130] BN Doat 53, fols. 56-59.   [131] *HL*, x, cols. 933-935.

the crown still had to negotiate locally before it could obtain the desired tax. Thus Viard and Hervieu would seem to have been wrong in stating that the Estates "voted" the tax.[132]

This last problem—the question of whether or not the king had to negotiate locally after the assembly—is much more complicated than it appears, however. The document of 3 December makes no mention of any desire by the representatives to "refer back" to local constituents. Nor does it explain why the crown should have waited so many months before instructing its commissioners. The ordinances executing the coinage reforms are dated 22 August,[133] so the assembly must have convened no later than the middle of that month. To reconstruct what really happened at the Estates we must turn to a variety of fiscal documents which do not mention the assembly.

In the first place, Philip VI was not in Paris at all when the assembly met, but in the Loire valley.[134] Perhaps he was detained there by bad health, but it is entirely possible that he did not feel his presence was needed at the assembly. If so, the meeting was not intended as a propaganda forum which would require a ceremonial appearance by the king, but was to be a working session at which hard bargaining would take place. Philip's letter of non-prejudice to the queen of Navarre, well before the assembly, mentioned coinage reform in connection with the sales tax.[135] It seems reasonable to conclude that the king had already discussed the scheme with the princes and magnates, and had obtained their approval and support before having drafted his very specific summons to the Estates General.

Once the latter convened in August, an important factor in the negotiations must have been the different fiscal histories of North and South in recent years. For Languedoil, the sales tax of 4 *d./l.* was familiar, hav-

---

[132] Strayer and Taylor, *Studies*, pp. 171-172, note 29. Taylor rightly took exception to these two authors, but may have leaned too far in the opposite direction, not being immediately concerned with the fiscal documents of 1343 which are discussed below.

[133] *Ord.*, II, 182-188; *Gr. Chartrier*, nos. 429-430.

[134] J. Viard, "Itineraire de Philippe de Valois," *extrait de la BEC*, LXXIV (1913), 84. The consuls of Cahors, who had other business with the king, were to meet with him at Orléans, but late in July he told them to appear before the bishop of Beauvais in Languedoc instead: BN Doat 119, fols. 140r-141v. The change was ostensibly ordered as a convenience to the consuls, but it may indicate that Philip was in poor health.

[135] See above, note 119, and J. Henneman, "The French Estates General and Reference Back to Local Constituents, 1343-1355," *Historical Papers Read at Bryn Mawr College, April 1968, SPIC*, XXXIX (1970), pp. 30-52.

ing been levied on a widespread basis since 1340. In Languedoc, however, hearth taxes or lump-sum payments were traditionally preferred, and there was considerably more sensitivity about taxation in time of truce. Under these circumstances, the two regions of the kingdom might have been expected to act somewhat differently when confronted by the royal proposal. Documentation from Languedoil is quite scanty, but it is very probable that these northern districts agreed at Paris to renew the sales tax. Our source for the tax in Vermandois is dated 20 August, about when the assembly must have ended.[136] Soon afterwards, Rouen received a letter of non-prejudice and the sales tax was levied there for another year beginning in September.[137] Besides these documents and those cited previously, we can also point to evidence of the tax in the districts of Sens, Anjou, and Maine.[138] It is not clear, however, whether Paris participated in the levy. The capital received certain privileges during August and seems to have paid a *finance* for the *arrière-ban*.[139] The king must have found it more profitable to conclude a "package deal" with the kingdom's largest city before the Estates convened.[140] In general, however, we may say that the sales tax of 4 *d./l.* was again levied throughout Languedoil in 1343 and that most districts agreed to this arrangement at the August Estates in return for the coinage reform.

The towns of Languedoc quite obviously did not make final agreements for the sales tax at Paris, but the more important ones did so rather soon thereafter. They all substituted a lump sum for the proposed sales tax and they all received certain other royal concessions, but agreement on these matters was reached so quickly that most of the arrangements must have been concluded in Paris at this assembly.

Before the end of September, Philip VI had already ratified a transaction with Toulouse, whereby the *capitouls* were to pay 12,000 *l.t.*, half at Christmas and half on 2 February 1344. In addition, the crown granted

---

[136] AN P 2291, p. 793.

[137] AN JJ 74, no. 250. There are brief references to the "new imposition" in Delisle, *Actes Norm.*, pp. 288-289. Cf. Coville, *Etats. Norm.*, p. 58.

[138] Furgeot, *Actes*, II, no. 7027; *JT Ph. VI*, no. 1363. AM Lyon OC 368, no. 2 also indicates a tax at this time.

[139] Viard, in AN AB xix 2636, cites AD Côte-d'Or B 11477, no. 1905, which seems to belong to 1343, and according to which the town agreed to pay a *finance* but asked for a royal renewal of privileges. Philip responded favorably on 27 August. Cazelles, *Soc. politique*, p. 165, cites Félibien and Lobineau, *Paris*, v, 319 for a tax grant in 1343, but the document in question is almost certainly misdated, since it corresponds exactly with BN *ms. fr.* 8605, p. 25, which deals with the tax of 1345.

[140] According to "Chron. parisienne," p. 62, the crown had blamed Paris for leading opposition to the crown at the last great fiscal assembly in 1321.

a pardon for a variety of transgressions of the type regularly investigated by royal *enquêteurs*.[141] Once again, the work of these investigatory commissions was closely linked to taxation as such and the king was
able to realize pecuniary profit by calling off these agents. An account of
receipts collected from the seneschalsy of Toulouse ("*finances* for the reform of the currency") indicates that the six *jugeries* paid a total of
16,500 *l.t.*, while another 300 pounds were obtained from the temporalities of the bishop of Toulouse.[142]

Another early agreement to the tax for reforming the coinage came
from Nîmes. By 5 October 1343, Philip VI had accepted this town's offer
of 1,000 *l.t.*, granting in return that fines levied for monetary infractions
were to be returned, and excusing Nîmes from paying the rest of a
fouage levied by Agout de Baux.[143] A receipt in the Nîmes archives indicates that this sum had been paid by 20 January 1344.[144] At Montpellier,
agreement was reached by October. Here too, the final transaction was
made after the consuls drew up a list of grievances and demanded redress. A royal letter issued in October accepted an offer of 4,000 *l.t.* in
lieu of the sales tax and pardoned the town for monetary infractions,
usurious loans, unjust apportionment of municipal taxes and illegal debts
to Jews.[145] Here, however, the commissioners inquiring into these
offenses do not seem to have halted their operations, for although payment was made,[146] their continued harassments led the consuls to seek
local confirmation of their transaction with the king and their earlier
3,800 *l.t.* grant to the bishop of Beauvais. The seneschal's *vidimus* was
obtained in April 1344.[147]

Finally, several other towns are known to have ratified this tax rather
early in the fall. Lunel's 250 *l.t.* contribution was released by the king to
the town's seigneur.[148] Limoux obtained a jurisdictional concession before paying the sum of 740 *l.t.*[149] The *bourg* of Carcassonne paid 800 *l.t.*;
Béziers, 1,500 *l.t.*; Le Puy, 4,000 *l.t.*; and Bragerac, 250 *l.t.*; all being excused from the sales tax and all receiving letters of remission for various

---

[141] AN JJ 72, no. 339; *INV AM Toulouse*, pp. 460-461 (AA 35, no. 50), and 82
(AA 5, no. 169); BN *Coll. Languedoc* 159, fol. 19.

[142] BN *Coll. Languedoc* 159, fol. 20v.

[143] BN *ms. lat.* 9174, fols. 171-172.   [144] AM Nîmes CC 1, no. 12.

[145] AN JJ 74, no. 127; *Gr. Chartrier*, nos. 2356-57, 3327-28; BN *ms. lat.* 9174, fols.
173-178v. A list of grievances drawn up by Montpellier is in AM Montpellier G-3,
no. 3176.

[146] BN *ms. lat.* 9174, fols. 173-178v.

[147] *Ibid.*; *Gr. Chartrier*, nos. 2356-57, 3327-28.   [148] Molinier, *HL*, ix, 562, note 3.

[149] AN JJ 74, no. 517. Cazelles, *Soc. politique*, pp. 165-166, has cited most of these
transactions, but the notes are out of order.

offenses by their inhabitants.[150] In each case, however, the reform of the coinage was given as the principal reason for the payment. Not one of these towns was prepared to accept the *form* of a 4 *d./l.* sales tax, and as far as our evidence goes, it appears that every southern town, in paying a lump sum to avoid the sales tax, extended the bargain to include extra concessions from the king. Thus as far as Languedoc was concerned, the coinage reform was not the only concession made by Philip VI, and additional demands had to be satisfied before money was forthcoming.

Most of these transactions were concluded very rapidly, being ratified in Paris by October, long before the instructions were issued to commissioners on 3 December. Given the time required to travel between Paris and Languedoc,[151] there could have been very little time for local bargaining. Moreover, the basic similarity of these various agreements suggests that most of the negotiations had taken place at Paris.

The royal directive of December 3rd was therefore limited to towns like Narbonne, which had instructed their proctors to oppose the sales tax. Having obtained prompt agreement to its proposal from most of the realm, the crown was ready, by this date, to approach those towns which had not been willing to engage in bargaining at Paris. Besides Narbonne, they were relatively few in number. Narbonne finally agreed to pay a mere 1,100 *l.t.* on 12 February 1344.[152] Even so small and late a grant as this was hotly opposed when the municipal government imposed a *taille* to raise the money, for on 29 September 1344, it was necessary for Philip VI to order the seneschal of Carcassonne to force certain privileged persons to contribute.[153] The *viguerie* of Alès held out until July 1344 before offering 500 pounds in return for certain royal concessions.[154] Albi

---

[150] AN JJ 74, no. 469; *HL*, x, cols. 930-932; BN *ms. fr.* 25997, no. 382; AN JJ 75, no. 547.

[151] Petit, *Essai de restitution*, p. 188. A round trip was close to four weeks in length.

[152] *HL*, x, cols. 933-935. The sum was small compared with the 3,500 pounds contributed by Narbonne for the war in 1342, but not when one recalls the intervening coinage reform.

[153] BN Doat 53, fol. 62. Although the major towns compounded for lump sums, the Carcassonne district as a whole seems to have paid a hearth tax instead of the 4 *d./l.* on sales. Borrelli de Serres, *Recherches*, III, 408, said that this was a 20 *s.* *fouage*, but the documents suggest a much smaller tax of only 5 *sols.* per hearth: AM Pézenas B, 3, 1, no. 26, and BN P.O. 1210, *dossier* Foucault. The latter reference was very kindly furnished by M. Cazelles.

[154] Of this sum, 141 pounds were paid by the outlying communities of the *viguerie*. The money was evidently raised by a local hearth tax. Bardon, *Alais*, II, 8; AM Alès 1 S-12, nos. 22-23; 1 S-23, no. 2.

paid a *fouage* of 8 *s.t.* for the coinage reform,[155] and subjects of the bishops of Vabres and Rodez finally made a payment in the second half of 1344.[156] Most towns in Quercy refused to accept the royal plan at the Estates and were visited by commissioners executing the instructions of 3 December 1343. Among these were Cahors, Cajarc, and Gourdon.[157] The nearby community of Figeac may have been the last of all the southern towns to agree to pay for the coinage reform. It offered a "free gift" of 725 *l.t.* on 20 September 1344.[158]

Despite the evidence that negotiations in some areas dragged on through most of 1344, we must not lose sight of the fact that most of the important southern towns had reached firm subsidy agreements very soon after the August assembly. After October 1343, only a handful of communities, all of them in Languedoc, had failed to make a firm commitment on the proposed tax. Under these circumstances, the Estates must be regarded as a great success for the monarchy. In a year of truce, complicated by widespread disaffection and revolt, Philip VI had obtained a subsidy from almost the whole realm with unusual rapidity. The crown was able to mollify opposition, reform the coinage, and gain tacit acceptance of the *gabelle*. By consulting the magnates first and then issuing a most explicit summons to the Estates, Philip had obtained more profitable results from a central assembly than any of his predecessors.

Oddly enough, the coinage reform, which formed the keystone of the royal program in 1343, proved to be no easy matter to effect. To cushion the economic shock inherent in a 76 percent reduction in the price of silver, the government originally planned to return to sound money in a series of steps.[159] By October, however, it was found that speculators were trying to capitalize on the proposed timetable, and a new royal ordinance of the 26th ordered immediate completion of the reform.[160] This "brutal revaluation," as Cazelles has called it, meant that the mints were paying 3.2 *l.t.* for a mark of silver in November 1343, as against 13.5 *l.t.* just three months earlier. The resultant drop in prices proved quite unpopular and effectively brought an end to forty years of agitation for

---

[155] AM Albi CC 58.

[156] AD Aveyron G 31, no. 28. Protracted negotiations by the *bourg* of Rodez with the royal officers at Villefranche are indicated in AM Rodez (*bourg*) CC 125, fols. 36-38.

[157] Dufour, *Cahors*, p. 107; Lacoste, *Quercy*, III, 101; AM Cajarc CC, no. 296; AM Gourdon CC 1, no. 12.

[158] AN JJ 75, no. 344.   [159] See Appendix I, at note 26; *Ord.*, II, 182-188.

[160] *Ibid.*, pp. 191-194.

a return to the coinage of St. Louis.[161] The landed interests and creditors who disliked inflation were presumably satisfied with the change, however.

3. Declining Revenues in Time of Truce

The truce of early 1343 lasted more than two years despite mutual accusations of violation and harsh French punishment of Norman rebels linked with Godefroy d'Harcourt and the pro-English faction.[162] Scattered military action along the frontiers continued, however, and the Flemings remained hostile. Royal finances soon proved quite inadequate, just as in earlier periods when the crown had lacked the justification for a war subsidy. The northern sales tax was apparently renewed, as it had been during the earlier truce of 1340-1341, but the king was in no position to levy fines in lieu of military service, tax the nobility or negotiate subsidies in Languedoc. Nor could he now fall back upon the convenient expedient of coinage manipulation.

These considerations made the middle 1340s a very difficult period for the monarchy. Truces and lulls in the fighting may have reduced royal expenditures, but income suffered an even greater reduction in these periods. The only response available was to adopt coercive fiscal expedients and seek to prolong the existing indirect taxes. Yet both these tactics aroused antagonism which would inhibit the collection of subsidies when the war resumed. Because of the truce, we find very few documents dealing with taxes between the end of 1343 and the spring of 1345. On the other hand, there has survived one of those rare but valuable summaries of royal finances prepared for the king by his advisers. Several of these documents exist for the reign of Philip VI, and it is perhaps significant that all of them belong to years of truce or peace and sound money, in which the king could not hope for revenue from subsidies or coinage profits.[163] These were the years when the king would be most interested in a detailed report on his fiscal position, but the historian interested in extraordinary revenues regrets the lack of such documents for years in which a war subsidy was levied.

One measure taken by royal officers to augment revenues in 1344 was to pursue the collection of unpaid arrears from earlier taxes. Such an effort had been launched in 1343 but had been suspended when the king

---

[161] Cazelles, "Quelques réflexions," pp. 94-95; and Appendix 1, Table 1.

[162] Froissart, IV, 206-213, and notes, pp. 453-455; Delisle, *St. Sauveur, preuves*, pp. 99-100.

[163] The budget memoranda are cited in Lot and Fawtier, *Institutions*, II, 201, note 1. That of 1344 is published in *BEC*, LIII (1892), 111f.

sought to negotiate the sales tax for the coinage reform. Now the consuls of Nîmes were again approached for those sums declared to be owing from 1338 and 1339. The crown claimed 600 pounds from this community and collected two sums totaling about 280 *l.t.* After protesting vigorously, the consuls seem to have escaped paying further, but the dispute continued for a decade.[164] Because our sources are limited to the seneschalsy of Beaucaire, it is possible that this effort to claim arrears was not a royal policy but represented an initiative on the part of local officials.

In the same district, the king's men actually attempted to resume collection of the knighting aid which had been canceled and supposedly returned in 1335. Philip VI had to order a halt to these proceedings.[165] On the other hand, when the consuls of Alès tried to obtain the rest of the money owed to them as a result of the return of this aid, the receiver of Nîmes reported an empty treasury.[166]

Another sum uncollected from earlier years was a portion of the 150,000 *l.t.* promised by the seneschalsy of Carcassonne for revocation of the cloth *gabelle* in the 1330s. Expenses of the commissioners levying this tax had added 8,000 pounds to the original total.[167] Since the outbreak of the war, the crown had evidently been too concerned with war subsidies to pursue the matter, but now on 6 November 1344, the government claimed that over 21,000 *l.t.* were owed, and ordered collection from Albi and Narbonne.[168] That these payments had fallen behind seems incontestable, for on the basis of the original annual assessment, the two parts of Narbonne should have paid over 25,000 *l.t.* for the five-year period.[169] They had admitted that they had paid only 17,000 *l.t.*,[170] but resistance to paying more dragged through the following year before the case was closed in 1346.[171]

It was also in 1344 that we find, for only the second time since 1332, numerous mentions of commissioners for *amortissement* and *francs-fiefs*.

---

[164] Ménard, *Nismes*, II, *preuves*, 128-130. The protests of Nîmes are in AM Nîmes NN 1, no. 23.

[165] BN Clairambault 212, no. 90. [166] AM Alès 1 S-12, no. 24.

[167] BN Doat 53, fols. 90v-91v. Most of the expenses had evidently been incurred during the inquest of 1330-1331 when the merits of the transaction were being disputed. See above, Chapter III.

[168] BN Doat 53, fols. 90v-91v; AM Albi CC 65. The fact that payment had to be made in the sound money of 1333 probably made it difficult for some towns to meet their obligations.

[169] It will be recalled that the annual assessment on the *bourg* and *cité* of Narbonne was 5,111 pounds (BN Doat 52, fol. 181; 53, fol. 93v).

[170] *Ibid.*, fols. 56-59. [171] *HL*, x, cols. 989, 993.

Scattered investigations of fief alienations had occurred throughout this period, especially in Languedoc where a single commission would cover a wide range of investigations. Now, however, fines for new acquisitions were sought on a general basis[172] and evidently not simply to force contributions to another sort of tax. Hospitals caring for the sick were explicitly excused from such fines.[173] The government also conducted other investigations of a more punitive nature, proceeding against delinquent tax farmers[174] and violators of monetary ordinances,[175] offering pardons to other kinds of offenders,[176] and selling privileges or offices.[177] By this period, the commissioners charged with making reforms were given such wide powers of a fiscal nature that they were regarded with great suspicion. The consuls of Montpellier said that they "always sought a thousand pretexts for troubling them," and obtained the promise that they would conduct their investigations only in the presence of the seneschal or his lieutenant.[178] In addition to these makeshift sources of revenue, the crown also floated loans,[179] and continued to levy the clerical tenth, having finally obtained from Clement VI a dispensation from repaying the earlier crusading tenths.[180]

Because a truce was in effect, the military operations of 1344 were very local in nature and war taxes necessarily had to be equally local in scope. The king continued to pay considerable attention to urban defenses in Picardy, although the cost of these was largely borne by the individual towns.[181] Military preparations in this region enjoyed a high priority because an English raid on the French coast was believed imminent.[182]

---

[172] AD Hérault A 4, fols. 344r-350v; AN PP 117, pp. 480-481; AN JJ 68, nos. 124, 125; JJ 75, nos. 184, 228; JJ 81, no. 547; BN Moreau 230, fols. 158r-162v, 180r.

[173] BN NAF 7605, fols. 139-140; BN Moreau 230, fol. 180r.

[174] AN JJ 74, no. 25; JJ 75, no. 214.

[175] AN JJ 75, nos. 131, 242. Cf. Bautier, "Chancellerie," p. 104, note 4.

[176] AN JJ 75, no. 45; Furgeot, *Actes*, II, no. 5786.

[177] *Ibid.*, nos. 7778, 7929, 8959, 9552 (relating to a division of the *viguerie* of Béziers); INV AM Limoux, describing AA 13, fols. 1-7; Delcambre, "Paréage," p. 328; Lacoste, *Quercy*, III, 104.

[178] *Gr. Chartrier*, nos. 185, 3355. Commissioners also caused resentment in the county of Foix (BN Doat 189, fols. 56r-57v).

[179] *INV AM Pézenas*, nos. 1645, 1646.

[180] AN J 719, no. 18, cited by Viard, "Ressources," p. 213. Cf. M. Faucon, "Prêts faits aux rois de France par Clément VI, Innocent VI et le comte de Beaufort," *BEC*, XL (1879), 570f.

[181] AN PP 117, p. 560; Thierry, *Recueil*, I, 503-504; Le Maire, *St. Quentin*, II, no. 609. Cf. Timbal, *Guerre*, pp. 185-187.

[182] BN P.O. 1675, *dossier* 38,869, no. 4.

At the other end of the kingdom, in Gascony, the French conducted operations along the Gironde. Small numbers of armed men were sent to the army by Cahors and Villefranche,[183] and a local assembly in Rouergue discussed an "imposition."[184] It appears that a hearth tax of 20 *s.t.* was collected in parts of Languedoc to finance the local campaign.[185] The count of Foix, to whom the crown still owed large sums for his earlier military expenses, complained about incursions by royal officials and obtained relief in a series of directives issued at the beginning of July 1344.[186] Among the favors extended to Foix was an order issued in January 1345, which suspended royal fiscal activities until Pentecost of that year. These included the subsidy for coinage reform, the export tax, and all fines for fief alienations levied on the count's subjects. The king's sergeants were also told to stop holding military musters,[187] evidence that royal officials had been trying to levy a war subsidy in this county.

Still another region close to the Gascon frontier was Agenais, where the towns had an ancient tradition of mutual consultation. Here, a group of sixteen towns requested permission to meet together to discuss matters dealing with the *communem utilitatem patrie Agennensis*. It is possible that financial arrangements for local defense arose from this meeting, the holding of which was authorized by the seneschal on 4 August 1344.[188] Our only other trace of a new tax in this year is at Beaucaire, where the inhabitants of a *bastide* were claiming early in 1345 to be exempt from *tailles* levied to pay "royal *deniers*."[189] In the same seneschalsy, Philip VI ordered nobles at Bernac and Schandalac to contribute to "*tailles* and *impositions*,"[190] but there is no evidence that these were new taxes.

A text of early 1345, indicates collection of a 500-pound subsidy from Poitou, as well as a levy of 1,000 pounds arising from the *arrière-ban*.[191] It is not known what was meant by this distinction, unless the former tax was for the coinage reform of 1343. In general, the sales tax of 4 *d./l.* seems to have continued in Languedoil during 1344, although the docu-

---

[183] Dufours, *Cahors*, p. 111; Cabrol, *Villefranche*, I, 218.

[184] AD Tarn-et-Garonne A 207.

[185] Borrelli de Serres, *Recherches*, III, 408; Albe, "Cahors INV," no. 382.

[186] See above, Chapter IV. In April 1344, the king ordered payment of 11,000 pounds to the count: AD Basses-Pyrénées E 406, no. 33. See also *ibid.*, nos. 29, 35; BN Doat 189, fols. 53-55.

[187] AD Basses-Pyrénées E 406, nos. 30, 35.

[188] AM Agen BB 15, no. 35.

[189] AD Gard, ms. inventory of AM Beaucaire (1772), fol. 132.

[190] AD Hérault A 4, fol. 36v.

[191] *AHP*, XLVI, 109, a résumé of a no longer extant document.

mentation is extremely scanty. The duke of Bourbon agreed to the continued levy of this tax in his county of La Marche, from June 1344 to June 1346, in return for half the proceeds.[192] The count of Blois may have made a similar arrangement.[193] Royal taxes were collected elsewhere in Languedoil[194] and by the end of 1345, widespread fear was voiced that the 4 *d./l.* sales tax and the *gabelle* on salt were becoming customary and that the crown was trying to make them a permanent part of the domain.[195]

It was in the South, where subsidy collections were most irregular and were difficult to collect in time of truce, that the truce was most shaky. In 1345, with the French monarchy woefully unprepared, the earl of Derby arrived in Gascony to launch the most serious incursion into French soil up to that time, and when the military summons was issued to deal with this attack, the need for taxes was greater than ever.[196]

Peace talks at Avignon having broken down, the French government began to seek money late in March for the expected renewal of fighting. Although Edward III did not formally break the truce until late in May,[197] the French subsidy-raising effort had made only small headway by that date. As in 1337, Philip VI began by obtaining a subsidy grant from Paris. Letters addressed to the rest of the kingdom on 4 April (Easter Monday), stated that Paris and some other towns had granted funds to pay "a certain number of men-at-arms" for six months.[198] Dom Vaissete stated that collection of this tax would begin in six months time (i.e., not until the end of September). The surviving copies of the letters of 4 April do not include this provision, but these letters were sent by the king, while Vaissete referred to letters of the same date from the duke of Normandy.[199] Despite the lack of explicit corroboration, there is some evidence that Vaissete was correct, at least insofar as the grant by Paris is concerned. Details of this subsidy are set forth in a document of

---

[192] AN P 2291, p. 823.   [193] *Ibid.*, p. 791, but see above, note 121.

[194] AN K 43, no. 33; K 45.

[195] *Ord.*, II, 238-241 (February 1346) makes clear this resentment. See also Furgeot, *Actes*, II, no. 6476, for a case involving "excesses" against tax collectors.

[196] Molinier, *HL*, IX, 572, note 4.   [197] *Foedera*, II pt. 4, pp. 177-178.

[198] BN *Coll. Languedoc* 84, fols. 290-291; Varin, *Reims*, II, 949-951.

[199] *HL*, IX, 572. Cazelles, *Soc. politique*, p. 225, seems to have been misled into thinking that Paris paid two subsidies in 1345. From the documents, it seems clear that Paris granted money in the spring and made a payment in the fall (see next note). If Vaissete was correct, the money paid in the autumn was that granted in the spring and deferred for six months, an explanation which seems far more appropriate to the context of 1345 than a second grant.

6 October, six months after the king claimed to have received the grant. Not until December were the first collections recorded at the treasury.[200]

The text of 6 October indicated that Paris offered 500 troops at a salary of 6 *s.p.* per day. The total subsidy would thus amount to 33,750 *l.t.* (27,000 *l.p.*), to be raised by a sales tax on wine and grain, and subject to guarantees of non-prejudice to local rights. It was specified that no other tax would be levied on Paris, nor would the burghers be required to render any other service, except in the case of an *arrière-ban*, when the service might be rendered but the present tax would cease.[201] The subsidy seems to have been collected very slowly, although treasury receipts may be misleading if some of the money was paid directly to troops. Less than 10,000 *l.p.* had reached the treasury by the beginning of 1347, and the next recorded payment was in 1349.[202]

These difficulties were far in the future, however, when Paris made its offer towards the end of March 1345. Compared to earlier grants, it was an impressive sum, and Philip VI was encouraged to use the generosity of Paris as a model which he hoped the rest of the realm would follow. His letters of 4 April urged his subjects to emulate Paris and grant a certain number of troops for six months subject to the same conditions. Each region was invited to choose its own mode of payment and name the persons who would supervise collection.[203] The king's letters indicated that other towns besides Paris had made such an early grant. It is not known which communities had done so, but the earliest collections of a new subsidy occurred in Normandy. Accounts have survived for collections in the three viscounties of Rouen, Pont Audemer, and Pont l'Arche, which paid a total of 8,523 *l.* in the year ending 30 April 1346. The unit for computing the tax was, as at Paris, the man-at-arms, and the sums collected indicate the number of men-at-arms supported by each town.[204] Only about 7 percent of the total resulted in *compositions*,[205] presumably lump-sum payments in lieu of the salaries of men-at-arms. Except for these, it would seem that a given number of hearths were intended to support one mounted man.[206] In addition, the abbot of Saint-Denis, who was conducting the taxation of Normandy, floated loans (from forty-three persons in the three viscounties under discussion)

---

[200] BN *ms. fr.* 8605, pp. 25-26; *JT Ph. VI*, no. 196.

[201] BN *ms. fr.* 8605, pp. 25-26. [202] *JT Ph. VI*, no. 2582.

[203] Texts cited above, note 198. [204] BN NAF 20026, nos. 1-7.

[205] *Ibid.*, no. 7. These came to just under 600 pounds.

[206] This conclusion seems probable since the document gives the shares of some places as fractions of a knight.

but these were subsequently canceled by order of the Chamber of Accounts.[207]

Evidently, Normandy did not insist on delaying six months before starting to pay, and Philip did not mention that Paris had done so when he asked the seneschalsy of Carcassonne to follow the capital's example. He did stress the offer to let each district choose its own collectors, noting that royal commissioners and sergeants had been oppressive in the past, which "much displeases us."[208]

On the whole, the king's position seems to have been conciliatory and flexible, yet it produced very disappointing results in Languedoc. On 29 April, the *arrière-ban* was proclaimed throughout France, all nobles and non-nobles being summoned for the defense of the kingdom.[209] The *viguerie* of Alès was subsequently told to provide 141 crossbowmen to go to Agen,[210] where full-scale hostilities broke out in June.[211]

Montpellier was approached for money at the end of May,[212] but negotiations there lasted for half a year. Perhaps an ordinance of reform issued by the seneschal of Beaucaire in August[213] improved the government's bargaining position, but one suspects that the consuls were more impressed by the English capture of Bergerac.[214] They were adamant, however, in resisting the royal plan for supporting a number of men-at-arms, and by September, the crown was ready to accept a lump sum raised through a municipal tax. Two more months passed before the town agreed to pay the modest sum of 2,000 *l.t.* After some debate, the consuls established certain indirect taxes to raise this money, but they could not enforce collection. At the end of December, the crown had to order coercive measures to obtain payment.[215] Other towns in the seneschalsy of Beaucaire were somewhat more cooperative. By the end of the summer, Nîmes had paid 500 *l.t.*[216] and Alès 400 *l.t.*[217]

Although less distant from Gascony, the seneschalsy of Carcassonne bitterly resisted taxation for most of 1345. The royal proposal of 4 April, calling for a grant in men-at-arms, produced little response, and in June, the king sent out another letter, this one urging his commissioners in

---

[207] BN NAF 20026, no. 8.

[208] BN *Coll. Languedoc* 84, fols. 290-291.

[209] AN PP 117, p. 561.

[210] BN Doat 255, fol. 323.

[211] Molinier, *HL*, ix, 572, note 4; M. Bertrandy, *Etude sur les chroniques de Froissart: Guerre de Guienne, 1345-1346*, Bordeaux, 1870, pp. 20-25.

[212] *HL*, x, cols. 969-972.

[213] BN *ms. lat.* 9174, fols. 181-189.

[214] See below, note 226.

[215] *HL*, x, cols. 969-972; *Gr. Chartrier*, nos. 454, 513, 1780, 3155, 3887-3888. It appears (*ibid.*, nos. 468, 469, 528) that the town paid on 31 December.

[216] AM Nîmes NN 1, no. 26.

[217] AM Alès 1 S-12, no. 26.

Languedoc to step up their search for money and to resort to new measures such as floating loans.[218] Funds were needed quickly and the immediate grant of a loan rather than the slowly collected subsidy might well prove profitable to all concerned. Additional commissioners went south and a new assembly was held. This time, a number of small communities in the lands of the count of Vendôme and his brother, agreed to pay 2,500 *l.t.* but no other grants were made.[219] On 26 August, Philip VI sent still another letter, this one persuasively written and surely intended for public consumption. Philip described the measures he was taking for the conduct of the war both at home and abroad. He ordered military musters of the nobles and townsmen of the seneschalsy and again demanded payment of sufficient subsidy from each person, according to his ability, to support for six months a number of men-at-arms in the manner of Paris and other towns. In short, the old conditions were restated. One community finally did offer a 10 *s.* hearth tax, but in September, the commissioners had to report that no other offers were forthcoming and that the effort had failed. Only in the final months of the year did more contributions come from this region.[220] It is not surprising that French commanders in the South found themselves lacking the money with which to pay troops.[221]

This lack of resources and an inadequate army in Languedoc proved disastrous in 1345, for Edward III was now ready to make a serious new effort in the war. Having announced his defiance in a letter to the pope in May,[222] Edward ordered his lieutenant in Gascony, the earl of Derby, to take the offensive.[223] In England, meanwhile, he accepted the homage of a very valuable ally, Godefroy d'Harcourt, exiled from France since 1343, and the lord of the important Norman fortress of Saint-Sauveur. The English king promised not to make peace with Philip VI without protecting Harcourt's interests.[224] Despite these ominous developments, the French should have had time to make preparations in Languedoc, for Derby was still at Southampton as late as 6 July.[225] This respite, however, may actually have worked against the efforts of the French crown

---

[218] *Ibid.*, fols. 291v-292r.   [219] *Ibid.*, fols. 292-296.

[220] *Ibid.*, fols. 296v-299. The commissioners reported the failure of their mission on 7 September 1345, but the following spring the Carcassonne district claimed to have furnished loans and troops in the last quarter of 1345 (*HL*, x, cols. 988-996, art. 21). Obviously the region was frightened by Derby's raid. Evidence of a tax payment late in the year is in AM Albi CC 64, second piece.

[221] Viard, "La France," p. 393.   [222] *Foedera*, II pt. 4, pp. 177-178.

[223] Bertrandy, *Etude*, pp. 20-25.

[224] *Foedera*, II pt. 4, p. 179; BN Moreau 699, fol. 132r-v; Delisle, *St. Sauveur*, p. 60.

[225] Bertrandy, *Etude*, p. 28.

to raise money in the South, for there was as yet no real sign of danger, no visible evidence that a genuine emergency existed. By August, however, the calm was rudely shattered, as Derby occupied Bergerac on the 24th and spent the next two months conquering Périgord.[226] On 21 October, he defeated the French at Auberoche and then besieged La Réole. Following the capture of this place, he took the important fortress of Aiguillon at the confluence of the Lot and Garonne rivers, towards the end of November.[227] In one brilliant campaign of less than four months' duration, the earl had stripped Languedoc of its natural defenses and had completely reversed the military situation in the Southwest. After a century of French encroachment on Aquitaine, the Plantagenets now began to recover much of the land formerly held by their ancestors.

It is of course an exaggeration to attribute these defeats entirely to the failure to raise taxes in Languedoc, but it is equally clear that lack of funds hindered French efforts to assemble a strong army. The difficulty in raising money must have sorely disappointed the king's advisers, since the crown had offered such wide latitude to the different regions in controlling the tax they would pay. Local control of tax collections, however, was not really a great concession to the towns of Languedoc, which had customarily apportioned taxes among themselves and paid lump sums raised by whatever means they chose. In the North, the king's proposal actually did offer relief from unpopular royal fiscal agents. Insofar as it was adopted, the system of locally designated tax collectors may be seen as the beginning of the *élus*.[228] In Languedoc, however, where the proposal was not really a new departure, it was not a strong inducement to pay new taxes, and the king offered no other concessions as attractive as his coinage reform of 1343. Above all, however, it is probable that the absence of a sense of danger played an important role in delaying tax contributions. The usual summer campaigning season was nearing its end when the earl of Derby captured Bergerac, and for weeks thereafter he concentrated on Périgord, not lower Languedoc.

Not every region was as stubborn about taxes in 1345 as Montpellier and the Carcassonne towns. The seneschalsy of Toulouse, which would be gravely threatened by the enemy, contributed a *fouage* with collec-

---

[226] *Ibid.*, pp. 33-83. Cf. *INV AM Périgueux*, p. 186 (EE 10).

[227] Bertrandy, *Etude*, pp. 122-187.

[228] *Elus* were not widespread until 1348 (Henneman, "Black Death," pp. 409-412), but Viard ("Ressources," p. 195) believed that a system of local collectors was accepted in parts of Languedoil in 1345, notably in Vermandois, where some precedent had been established in 1340. See above, Chapter IV, note 247, and Henneman, "Financing," note 97.

tion beginning in July, and totaling 34,226 *l.t.*[229] The town of Toulouse was permitted to levy another hearth tax on its citizens in order to repair fortifications.[230] The communities in the *jugerie* of Albigeois ultimately paid 2,000 *l.* but only with great reluctance and after long complaints about bad harvests, the need for all the money and men to be devoted to local defense, etc.[231] Albi itself seems to have agreed to a tax somewhat earlier, but was not able to pay by 24 June as required, and obtained permission to delay until 15 August. At Albi, the clergy and laity were engaged in prolonged wrangling about privileges and the obligation to contribute to defense.[232]

In Quercy, the citizens of Cahors made a loan of 1,000 *l.t.* for the war, but objected to paying a small municipal tax for the repair of fortifications.[233] The citizens of Gourdon paid a lump sum in lieu of a 15 *s.* hearth tax, but they too came under great pressure from the seneschal before taking action to repair their defenses, despite the fact that the enemy was not far from this town.[234] Cajarc had paid only 58 *l.t.* as a subsidy by 26 September, and soon thereafter the town obtained from the king a suspension of collection.[235] In Rouergue too, the crown seems to have had trouble raising funds. The royal lieutenant resorted to the now-familiar step of sending out *réformateurs* to extort money when the military situation grew critical in the fall. Fines for *franc-fief* were levied at Villefranche and drew protests elsewhere.[236] Bertrand de Pibrac, prior of Saint-Martin des Champs, who was to play an important role in Languedoc for a decade, arrived at Millau in October and obtained a subsidy. Two tax rolls indicate collection of more than 600 pounds at Millau in the last quarter of the year.[237] Another grant from Rouergue was

---

[229] I am indebted to M. Cazelles for this reference. The account of this *fouage* is among the documents preserved at the Bibliothèque Saltykoff-Schredrine in Leningrad.

[230] *INV AM Toulouse*, pp. 461-462 (AA 35, no. 62). Razed at the time of the Albigensian crusade, the walls of Toulouse had to be rebuilt hurriedly in the 1340s. See B. Darmaillacq, "Le Prince Noir contre le comte d'Armagnac, expédition de 1355," *Revue de Gascogne*, LV (1914), 12.

[231] Portal, *Cordes*, pp. 48-49; AM Cordes CC 32. Over half the sum contributed was paid by Cordes (1,054 pounds).

[232] AM Albi CC 64, EE 5.

[233] BN Doat 119, fols. 163r-167.

[234] AM Gourdon CC 1, no. 13; EE 6.

[235] AM Cajarc CC supp., nos. 91, 92.

[236] AD Aveyron 2E 212, no. 1; Molinier, *HL*, IX, 578, note 3; Cabrol, *Villefranche*, I, 220.

[237] *A. H. Rouergue*, VII, 82; AM Millau CC 347, fols. 2r-9v. The municipal tax rolls are *ibid.*, EE 63, EE 64.

a 1,000 *l.t.* contribution from the lord of Rubrac,[238] but here, as in the Carcassonne district, the general pattern was for new commissioners to apply pressure in the fall after tax negotiations begun earlier had broken down.

Difficulties in collecting money may well have extended beyond Languedoc. Although the crown did levy a 4 *d./l.* sales tax in the bailiwick of Auvergne,[239] we know only of local taxes at Aurillac and Limoges, where some groups objected to paying. There is no evidence that the crown received any portion of these.[240] In the seneschalsy of Poitou, an assembly was held in order to negotiate taxes with the towns and nobles, but on 26 July, the royal commissioners had to report failure.[241] Three weeks later, however, the royal lieutenant imposed a subsidy of 800 *l.t.* on Poitiers and its *banlieu*.[242] The abbot of Vendôme also agreed to a subsidy on his dependencies in Poitou at the end of July, and it appears that this tax began to be paid promptly and resembled in form the grant by Paris—a number of men-at-arms to be supported for six months at a salary of 6 *s.*[243] In Anjou and Maine, a 4 *d./l.* sales tax was in force. The viscount of Beaumont, lord of Mathefelon, and other seigneurs of this region, permitted its levy in their lands, and in July, Philip VI made a similar request of the lord of Laval. This letter had a slightly threatening tone which implied that Laval had been stubborn. Philip stated that a reply was awaited, and that meanwhile the seigneur was to hold himself ready in arms for a military summons.[244] An entry in the treasury journal of 1349 mentions a subsidy also in the bailiwick of Orléans during 1345.[245] Not only in this region but in Touraine as well, were lands of the count of Blois, whose tallageable subjects were again excused from paying.[246] The tax in question was probably the sales tax which was becoming familiar in northern France.

There remains the case of Reims, which did not grant money until late in the year. On 4 April, the king ordered his commissioners in Vermandois to seek a subsidy in men-at-arms for six months, with both the form of tax and its collectors to be chosen locally.[247] Five years earlier, the nobles of Vermandois had granted a tax subject to collection by local

---

[238] Molinier, *HL*, IX, 578, note 3.

[239] M. Boudet, "Les états d'Issoire de 1355 et leurs commissaires royaux," *Annales du Midi*, XII (1900), 35.

[240] *Ord.*, XII, 74; *INV AM Aurillac*, I, 435-437 (CC 28); II, 44-45 (FF 9).

[241] *AHP*, XLVI, 110. [242] *Ibid.*, pp. 112-115.

[243] *Ibid.*, pp. 110-112; *AHP*, LII, 225. [244] *LC*, no. 173; *JT Ph. VI*, no. 1781.

[245] *Ibid.*, no. 2464. [246] BN NAF 3653, no. 133.

[247] Varin, *Reims*, II, 949-951.

appointees, and Viard argued that the entire bailiwick adopted such *élus* in 1345.[248] There is no clear evidence, however, that such was the case. Six months passed following the original request for money. On 3 October, about the time that Paris was beginning to pay its subsidy, Philip wrote to the *échevins* of Reims, reminding them again of the military situation and the grants made by other communities. They were ordered to send two or three proctors "having power for this" to Paris on the fifteenth to tell the king or his *gens des comptes* what aid the town would like to make.[249] At length, the town agreed to the 4 *d./l.* sales tax, for which it received a letter of non-prejudice in December.[250]

Despite the fragmentary nature of surviving documents, the royal effort to obtain subsidies in 1345 must be pronounced a failure. It is true that Paris made a large grant, that Normandy made an early grant, that most parts of Languedoil ultimately paid the 4 *d./l.* sales tax already levied for several years, and that much of Languedoc finally made some kind of contribution. Nevertheless, the kingdom as a whole seemed remarkedly insensitive to the English threat and rather unimpressed by the king's concession to local particularism. In many regions, the negotiations were long and arduous, and resistance to paying, stubborn. Even the Parisians, whose grant of money the king advertised so widely, seem to have demanded a six-month delay before starting to pay. As will be seen in the next chapter, the basic proposal advanced by the crown in 1345 would be presented a year later to the Estates General. This fact raises a very important question: why did the government not choose to call a central assembly in 1345? Those historians who have seen assemblies as a form of popular control of the monarchy and a check on royal power would immediately reply that the king deliberately avoided such a meeting. Perhaps he did so, but his decision still requires an explanation. Philip VI had employed regional assemblies in Normandy in 1339 and in other regions the following year. He had held a central assembly in 1343. On each occasion, the political and fiscal results had been more satisfactory than those obtained through local negotiations. An assembly in 1345 might have served to persuade the country that a serious renewal of hostilities was indeed in prospect. It might have made the offer of local control over the form and collection of the subsidy appear more attractive. Even if followed by local negotiations, it might have ensured larger and speedier grants, permitted a redress of grievances, and avoided coercive expedients, given the precedents of the preceding dec-

[248] See above note 228. [249] Varin, *Reims*, II, 962-963.
[250] *Ibid.*, pp. 976-977.

ade. Yet the crown did not convene assemblies except on the local level in some regions.

It may never be possible to reach an accurate explanation of royal policy in 1345. One possible answer, however, is suggested by the findings of Cazelles. To overcome the crisis of 1343, the crown had had to pay a price. One consequence of 1343 was a decline in the influence of the Chamber of Accounts in royal policies. The most imaginative use of assemblies up to this time had been made when the fiscal experts were in power. Now, however, their influence was on the wane, and the retirement of Mile de Noyers in 1344 marked the end of an era.[251] Continuity with the preceding years was certainly not broken, but it is entirely possible that the royal council in 1345 did not share the belief, so typical of the Chamber of Accounts party, that large assemblies might be useful instruments of royal fiscal policy. It is hard to escape the conclusion that the government made an error in judgment in 1345. When it turned to assemblies in 1346, it had lost the initiative and was in the position of desperately seeking counsel on ways to overcome a grave fiscal crisis.

Failing to obtain satisfactory taxes in 1345, the French government once again had to employ fiscal expedients. Communities like Pézenas might resist taxation but were willing to buy rights and privileges.[252] In October 1345, the difficult financial position of the crown forced it to suspend the salaries of officials, but this action met such opposition within the government that it was soon rescinded.[253] The king also levied another tax on lawyers,[254] taxed cattle brought into the kingdom to pasture,[255] and extorted money from the Italian moneylenders. The latter were ordered in the spring to appear before their respective bailiffs or seneschals to "hear certain things" from the Chamber of Accounts. The crown probably hoped for some sort of forced loan or gift.[256] Besides these miscellaneous sources of revenue, the 4 *d./l.* export tax, the salt *gabelle*, and small regular payments by Italian merchants all continued to bring in certain sums.[257]

Loans also played an important part in royal finances in 1345. On 15 June, the government issued a general order to borrow money.[258]

---

[251] Cazelles, *Soc. politique*, pp. 170-171. [252] *INV AM Pézenas*, no. 265.

[253] *JT Ph. VI*, no. 288 and pp. 71-72, note 1; *LC*, no. 177.

[254] *JT Ph. VI*, nos. 192, 195, 246, 3021.

[255] *Ord.*, II, 233; BN NAF 7389, fol. 253r. [256] Henneman, "Italians," pp. 33-34.

[257] For the export tax, BN *Coll. Languedoc* 84, fol. 270. For the *gabelle*, *JT Ph. VI*, nos. 656, 657, 910, 914, 915, 922, 914, 1053, 1054, 1345, 1365, 1867; AD Hérault A 4, fols. 222v-223. For the taxes on Italians, *ibid.*, fols. 236-240.

[258] BN Doat 119, fols. 163r-164v; BN *Coll. Languedoc* 84, fols. 292-296.

Treasury journal entries indicate loans for the war received from the districts of Anjou and Maine, from a citizen of Paris, and from assorted members of the clergy.[259] Philip VI ordered still another round of loans early in 1346.[260]

As in other years, fiscal weakness in 1345 meant more than military weakness. It was also a reflection of political frailty, and Philip VI found it wise to conciliate the nobility on the subject of taxation. Nobles rendering personal service obtained tax relief for their subjects,[261] and some seigneurs even managed to have their tallageable men excused from paying the tax for the coinage reform of 1343.[262] The lord of Tournon obtained revocation of a war subsidy in his lands.[263] These examples are all from the seneschalsy of Beaucaire, a region quite remote from the war fronts and perhaps not typical of other districts. Yet Philip VI may well have faced some disaffection among the nobles. The lord of Saint-Sauveur, who had joined the English cause, had sympathizers in Normandy, and a reluctance of the nobles to pay taxes is indicated by the reaction of the bourgeois during the next few years, when a great effort was made to have privileged persons pay subsidies.[264]

Philip VI was thus in trouble both financially and politically by the end of 1345. What appeared to be a flexible and conciliatory royal proposal had not produced the needed taxes. The government had been forced to vacillate between coercive fiscal expedients and concessions to the privileged or influential. For the better part of five years, it had been very difficult to raise money, especially among those of the king's subjects who did not feel a sense of danger. Coinage manipulation had been abused, challenged, and temporarily repudiated. The one new tax of this period, the *gabelle du sel*, was increasingly unpopular. Finally, the English had scored their first really impressive gains in Gascony, and an influential Norman lord had defected. The leadership provided under Mile de Noyers was no longer present, and the government seems to have been uncertain as to what policy to pursue next. Under these circumstances, it is not surprising that Philip VI once again turned to a central assembly.

[259] *JT Ph. VI*, nos. 182, 183, 296, 1463, 5009.
[260] BN NAF 7606, fol. 6; Viard, "Ressources," p. 217.
[261] BN *Coll. Languedoc* 84, fol. 330; AD Hérault A 4, fol. 226r-v.
[262] *Ibid.*, fol. 203; *HL*, x, cols. 968-969.
[263] AD Hérault A 4, fols. 220r-221v.   [264] See next chapter, parts 3 and 4.

CHAPTER VI

Military Disaster, The Estates, and the Plague, 1346-1348

1. The Estates of Languedoil

THE years 1346 to 1348 are of great importance in French political and constitutional history, but they were given little serious study before Raymond Cazelles published his important book in 1958. Cazelles has pointed to a number of interesting parallels between these years and the more famous crisis of 1355-1358, and his findings can be supported and amplified by comparing the fiscal documents for the two periods, which he did not stress.[1] It was in this period that the Estates of Languedoc first played an important role. At the same time, Languedoc became increasingly separate from the North in its fiscal and military administration, partly because Anglo-Gascon conquests enhanced the geographical separation of the two main parts of the French kingdom. The years 1346-1348 were also notable for the fact that external and largely unforeseen factors dramatically affected French fiscal and constitutional development at crucial moments. Such factors were the Crécy campaign and the Black Death.

In 1343, the crown had chosen to summon an assembly and had used it skillfully to escape a serious crisis. In 1345, the government had developed a tax proposal that would seem to have made an assembly appropriate, yet none was called. By 1346, the financial and military position of the crown was so serious that there seems to have been no choice but to hold an assembly. As opposed to 1343, it was to be held in two parts, the representatives of Languedoc to meet at Toulouse and those of Languedoil at Paris. There are other differences between 1343 and 1346 to be noted at the outset. In the latter year, the whole approach of the government conveys a picture of urgent royal need rather than of royal initiative. The summonses of 1346[2] were strikingly different from 1343, containing no mention of a specific subsidy request, and speaking of many grievances without suggesting specific reforms. It thus appears at the outset that the meetings of 1346 were intended to give counsel and

---

[1] Cazelles, *Soc. politique*, pp. 253-261; Henneman, "Black Death," and "The French Estates."

[2] For the summons to the South, see *HL*, x, cols. 976-978. Extant copies of the summons to the northern towns are in Varin, *Reims*, II, 977; AM Riom AA 21; and AM Arras AA 5, no. 23, this last being published in Guesnon, "Documents," pp. 233-234.

air grievances. They were not being asked to consent to some previously announced proposal as in 1343, even though the king may have had some definite plan in mind. Hence the government returned to the unspecific summons of earlier reigns and abandoned the approach of 1343.

Perhaps because of the distances involved, the summons to the southern assembly was issued first, on 31 December 1345.[3] This meeting, which convened before the duke of Normandy at Toulouse in mid-February, will be considered in the next section of this chapter. The northern assembly was summoned on 4 January and was to meet at Paris on 2 February. It evidently included representatives from all but the six seneschalsies south of the Dordogne, since deputies are known to have come from as far as Auvergne.[4]

The letter of 4 January stated that the assembly was to include "the prelates . . . , barons and other nobles, the communes and good towns of our kingdom." The towns were to send two or three of "the best instructed and advised." The king was not specific about the action to be requested from the Estates. He did acknowledge the existence of widespread discontent over the conduct and number of royal officers and a growing suspicion that the *gabelle du sel* and the 4 *d./l.* sales tax were assimilated into the permanent revenues of the domain. In the light of these and other grievances, Philip expressed a desire to have deliberation which might be profitable to the kingdom.[5] Doubtless everyone knew that the crown needed money for an army, but the failure of his proposal of the year before left Philip VI and his advisers without any sure idea of how to obtain such funds in 1346. In these circumstances, he desired merely to take counsel. With no specific plan to offer, he did not demand full powers for those who attended as representatives.

Several weeks after the summons must have been received, the town of Arras acknowledged it (27 January).[6] The next day, the *échevins* named and instructed their proctors. Given the vague nature of the summons, it is hardly surprising that these representatives were told merely to "hear and report" what the king should "say and ordain."[7] Just as the king's summons was much less specific than in 1343, so also were the instructions to the urban proctors who came to Paris.

The representatives from Lille departed for Paris on 28 January 1346. Because town proctors claimed expenses on a *per diem* basis, they were expected not to waste time traveling, so it is probably safe to assume that

---

[3] *HL*, x, cols. 976-978.   [4] AM Riom AA 21, no. 766.
[5] Varin, *Reims*, II, 977; Guesnon, "Documents," pp. 233-234.
[6] *Ibid.*, p. 234.   [7] *Ibid.*, pp. 234-236.

a five-day trip from Lille was required in order to reach Paris on the appointed day. These representatives were home again on the eleventh, bearing two documents, "the counsel and reasons answered to the king on the part of the good towns" and "the response of the prelates and barons."[8] It thus appears that the proctors from Lille remained until the end of the meeting, and that they left Paris on 6 February or early on the 7th. An assembly of five days' duration was not unusual in the first half of the fourteenth century.[9] The fact that Lille's deputies returned with two replies suggests that the town representatives deliberated separately from the barons and prelates.

The two replies seem to have been similar in substance, however, judging from Philip VI's ordinance of 15 February, which made no distinction between them.[10] This document is one of the earliest of those comprehensive reform ordinances which in later years would often be issued after an assembly of the Estates. Like its many successors in the century to follow, this ordinance is a valuable source for the assembly itself, a catalogue of the grievances presented to the king. Philip ordered a reduction in the number of local royal officers and restrictions on their activities, abolition of forced loans (which had been used extensively the year before), and a series of regulations aimed at curbing abuses of the right of *prise* (requisition). The war's logistical problems had led to some rather dubious practices by royal officers who needed to obtain supplies quickly.[11] The crucial question in 1346 was, of course, taxation, and the king declared that he had no intention of making the *gabelle* and the sales tax permanent royal rights. He went on to point out, however, that the defense of the kingdom required money, and that elimination of existing taxes would depend upon agreement to support the necessary number of troops. In short, the king was willing to abolish unpopular taxes if his subjects would devise some less objectionable way of raising and maintaining an army. It was the same proposal offered in 1345 with the important addition of sweeping reforms and a promise to cancel

[8] *Ibid.*, p. 236, note 1, an excerpt from the accounts of the Hanse of Lille for 1346.
[9] If anything, a five-day meeting was longer than usual, for what little we know about these early assemblies suggests that they were usually very short. Cazelles, *Soc. politique*, pp. 174-175, used the royal ordinance of 15 February rather than the Lille document in determining the length of the assembly, thereby concluding that the meeting lasted a good week after the Lille delegation must have left Paris. However, since these deputies brought home with them written copies of the replies of the Estates, I believe that Cazelles is incorrect here.
[10] *Ord.*, II, 238-241; Furgeot, *Actes*, II, no. 6957.
[11] For litigation which might arise over the right of *prise*, see Timbal, *Guerre*, pp. 81-103.

existing taxes if the necessary troops were provided. The same basic approach would be used in 1347-1348 and adopted by the Estates themselves in 1355. It offered a way of meeting criticisms of royal squandering, rapacious commissioners and tax farmers, and unpopular forms of tax, while still providing for that "evident necessity" which justified royal taxation.

The royal ordinance stated that the Estates had made a "good and gracious response," but the representatives did not agree to anything specific. They expressed a desire to "refer back" to their constituents, which is understandable if all the deputies had received instructions as vague as those from Arras.[12] Thus when the assembly ended, the king had promised reforms and had offered to replace existing taxes with some alternative arrangement for raising troops as soon as this should be agreed upon locally.

The royal ordinance was published more than a week after the assembly ended. During this intervening period, the king's brother Charles, count of Alençon, whose *apanage* lay in Normandy, issued a document of some importance. Dated 12 February 1346, this text has been the subject of much debate and misinterpretation. Alençon stated that "each estate according to its ability, and among the others those of the said estates . . . of Normandy have granted . . . or are in the process of granting" an aid which would pay the salaries of a certain number of men-at-arms for six months for each of the next two years, in return for which the existing indirect taxes would be canceled. The count agreed to let his lands contribute to this aid "in case and in the manner that the said prelates, barons, nobles, and communes of Normandy" granted it, but the tax would be "imposed, assessed, and collected by our own people."[13]

This document was published ninety years ago by Hervieu, who read it very carelessly and supposed that *les diz gens d'armes par les diz six mois* meant that Alençon offered to furnish ten men. Hervieu saw the text as evidence that the "Estates General" had been followed by a meet-

---

[12] *Ord.*, II, 238-241; Varin, *Reims*, II, 1009-1010. Cf. Henneman, "The French Estates."

[13] *Chascune nation et estat selonc sa faculté et entre les autres, ceuls des diz estatz de la langue de Normendie, lui aient accordé ou soient en voie d'accorder touz en commun, aide à leurs propres fraiz, gages et soudés de certain nombre de genz d'armes. . . .* This important text has been published by Hervieu, *Recherches*, pp. 244-245, from a copy in AN J 384, no. 7. Other extant copies and excerpts are in AN JJ 76, no. 259; BN *ms. fr.* 20684, pp. 202-203; BN *ms. fr.* 21043, p. 633; AN AB xix 2636.

ing of "provincial Estates."[14] Viard believed that the document proved that the "Estates General" deliberated by "province" rather than by order.[15] Each of these scholars was hampered by an excessive tendency to apply the institutional terminology of a later period to the fourteenth century in an imprecise way. Coville concluded that the Norman Estates met separately from those of the rest of the kingdom, but he did not elaborate further.[16] Among these historians, the consensus was that only Normandy was prepared to grant money at this time. Vuitry, on the other hand, took note of the "good and gracious response" mentioned in the royal ordinance, and the undeniable fact that the sales tax and *gabelle* continued to be levied in some regions. He concluded that there was a reluctance to grant men-at-arms and so the assembly in effect sanctioned continuation of the existing taxes. Vuitry felt that Alençon's document proved that a separate caucus of the Norman delegation took place while the Estates were still in session.[17] Cazelles, unlike the earlier scholars, knew of the Lille document, but did not use it to determine the length of the assembly. He assumed the meeting to have lasted until the royal ordinance was issued, with the Normans holding a separate meeting during this period. But unlike Vuitry, he believed that the Estates actually endorsed the principle of men-at-arms in lieu of the existing indirect taxes.[18]

As indicated above, the evidence from Lille seems unmistakably to show that the Estates General concluded deliberations on 6 or 7 February. The ordinance of the 15th was clearly drawn up at the behest of the assembly, but there is no need to infer that the assembly remained in session until the date of its publication. Alençon's document in no way indicates a new or separate Norman meeting. Like the royal ordinance, it shows that the tax negotiations were not yet concluded. It furnishes the valuable additional information that a grant of men-at-arms for two six-month periods had been actively discussed at Paris. The king's brother merely stated that the Normans, among others, had agreed in principle to furnish men-at-arms. He singled out Normandy because his lands were in that region. He agreed to permit the levy in his lands of whatever tax the Normans should decide upon, provided that his own people collected it. As an important apanaged prince, the count was trying to assist the king by publicly supporting a royal tax proposal which was still under negotiation.

---

[14] Hervieu, *Recherches*, pp. 218-219.
[15] Viard, "Ressources," p. 196.
[16] Coville, *Etats Norm.*, p. 59.
[17] Vuitry, *Régime financier*, II, 25-27.
[18] Cazelles, *Soc. politique*, pp. 174-175.

The nineteenth century historians of this assembly were all somewhat troubled by the fact that the *gabelle* continued to be levied.[19] It seems to be assumed that the salt tax continued without interruption from 1341 onwards. In 1898, however, an *Ecole des Chartes* thesis by Gabriel Perousse argued that the tax was eliminated in the course of regional and local tax negotiations during 1346 and 1347,[20] just as proposed in the royal ordinance and the Alençon document of February 1346. Information on this point is extremely scanty, but Perousse is supported by negative evidence. I have found no mention of the salt tax in tax negotiations after early 1347, and no evidence of it at all in the period 1348-1355. In December 1355, it was clearly being reinstituted, not simply continued.[21]

The success of the Estates of 1346 can be measured only when we examine the follow-up assemblies which were to be held at the regional or bailiwick level to consider grants of men-at-arms. It will be seen below that a crisis of external origins disrupted the work of these assemblies. In the immediate perspective of February 1346, however, the central assembly seems to have accomplished as much as the king could expect. Uncertain how to proceed after his failure of 1345, Philip VI made no specific proposal in summoning the meeting and did not ask for an assembly with full powers. He wanted simply to take counsel, reduce discontent, and plan whatever steps were needed to raise the urgently needed money for troops. His vague summons meant vague instructions for those who came to the meeting. They would hardly do otherwise than refer the royal proposal and reform promises to their constituents for subsequent action. The assembly evidently agreed in principle that the king needed money for an army, and this agreement was the "good and gracious response" which Philip mentioned.

The government seems to have had a definite idea as to its military needs when the time came to approach the follow-up assemblies, judging from instructions issued to commissioners sent to the bailiwick of Sens.[22] It is quite possible that the formula contained in these instructions was presented to the Paris assembly for discussion. The commissioners were to obtain from every 200 hearths the salary for one man-at-arms for six months. The salary was to be 5 *s.p.* per day, and it was therefore esti-

---

[19] Viard, "Ressources," p. 191, noted the continuing existence of the *gabelle*, and one chronicler gives the impression that the old taxes were still in effect in some areas after the battle of Crécy: R. Newhall (ed.), *The Chronicle of Jean de Venette* (tr. J. Birdsall), New York, 1953, p. 44.

[20] Perousse, "Gabelle," p. 92.

[21] *Ord.*, III, 19-37, is the enactment which re-established the salt tax in 1355.

[22] AN P 2292, pp. 55-58.

mated that each hearth would pay 2 *d.* per week. In the case of impoverished and servile persons, 300 hearths were to support one soldier, paying a weekly hearth tax of three *oboles.* Communities with fewer hearths than these would be grouped together for purposes of computing the tax. Each provostship would administer its own tax collections. The king hoped to collect this tax each year that the war continued, although the count of Alençon had indicated that the Estates were discussing only a two-year levy. The commissioners charged with obtaining this subsidy were instructed to make sure that the February ordinance was executed in all respects.

Such was the bargain which the crown hoped to conclude. Its execution would have associated the taxpayers with the government in assuming responsibility for financing the war. It represented a trade of troops for reforms through the use of assemblies, yet it left room for variations in the form of tax which individual districts might prefer. The scheme was an ambitious one, with interesting constitutional possibilities for the future. The unexpected intervention of the Crécy campaign would prevent its orderly implementation, but it formed the basis for further experiment in 1347-1348 and 1355-1356.

While awaiting action on the proposed subsidy of men-at-arms, Philip VI was rescued from serious financial embarrassment by the generosity of Clement VI, who appears to have been more sympathetic to the French crown than any other Avignon pope. Beginning late in 1345, Clement and his brother, Guillaume Roger, count of Beaufort, provided Philip with loans totaling 622,000 florins, an enormous sum.[23] The first loan, for 30,000 florins, had been made on 26 November 1345. During the first four months of 1346, the crown obtained another 125,000 florins,[24] and it is quite possible that the royal fiscal policy in 1346 was influenced by the availability of these resources. With papal assistance to help him meet short-term needs, the king was in a less desperate bargaining position as he sought the grant of troops from his subjects. He may therefore have been more willing to use the central assembly for propaganda purposes and then approach later local assemblies in the hope of obtaining a sizeable sum.

In Normandy, the existing tax for supporting men-at-arms would terminate late in April 1346. There is no surviving evidence of the Nor-

---

[23] Faucon, "Prêts," p. 571, included a 30,000-florin loan of 1345 in his total of 592,000 florins borrowed from the papacy, but his addition seems wrong. The 592,000 florins were borrowed after 1345.

[24] *Ibid.,* p. 572.

man assembly which was to have dealt with the proposals for supporting men-at-arms. If such an assembly did meet, it may have secured cancellation of the *gabelle*, but the tax levied in Normandy to support troops in 1346 was none other than the much maligned 4 *d./l.* sales tax which had grown familiar in recent years. It was being collected as early as 5 May and was still being levied in the fall.[25] Collection of this subsidy may, of course, indicate that a Norman assembly had not met or had declined to adopt a new method for raising men-at-arms. It may also mean that the Normans actually preferred indirect taxes as long as their right of consent was explicitly acknowledged by the king.

The effort to establish a tax for men-at-arms, as proposed in February, had not been completed when the English invaded Normandy. Then the king was forced to suspend proceedings and resort to the *arrière-ban* in order to collect men and money quickly. The documents from Reims illustrate the difficulty of reconstructing precisely the taxes of 1346. On 4 March, the king wrote to Reims announcing a new assembly for the towns of Vermandois to be held at Noyon, on 3 April, to act upon the proposals discussed at Paris. The *échevins* of Reims were to send persons "sufficient to report . . . your deliberation and opinion."[26] The meeting was postponed for some reason, for it was a month before the king instructed the bailiff to attend and set forth the royal viewpoint.[27] The new convening date was 29 April, and on the appointed day the assembly met, with representatives from Reims in attendance.[28] There are no further documents, however, until the end of July, when the bailiff was ordered to proclaim the *arrière-ban*, excluding from service only those in essential occupations.[29] This order was a typical military summons for fiscal purposes, but it is uncertain how we should relate it to the assembly held at Noyon three months before. If it was intended merely to coerce the citizens into making a grant, one would expect it to have been issued earlier.[30] It therefore seems probable that the Noyon assembly did agree to support men-at-arms. Perhaps, as in Normandy, the 4 *d./l.* sales tax was retained for this purpose.[31] Whatever the form of tax decided on,

[25] BN NAF 20026, no. 10; Delisle, *Actes norm.*, pp. 345-346.

[26] Varin, *Reims*, ii, 1009-1010. [27] *Ibid.*, p. 1019.

[28] *Ibid.*, p. 992. [29] *Ibid.*, p. 1124, note 1.

[30] By the end of July, nearly three months had elapsed since the regional assembly at Noyon. With no evidence of coercive measures against Reims in that period, it seems likely that some agreement was reached at that assembly. There is some evidence of a sales tax at Noyon (Furgeot, *Actes*, ii, no. 7394) and Corbie (BN *ms. fr.* 25698, no. 152).

[31] Reims, of course, had only renewed the earlier sales tax in December 1345, so its action at the Noyon meeting may have been little more than a ratification

however, very little could have been collected by the end of July. Faced with an English invasion, Philip VI had no choice but to employ the *arrière-ban* in order to raise men, money, or both.

Confronted with this military summons, the *échevins* of Reims seem to have been very anxious to avoid paying fines in lieu of service, possibly because these taxes were usually based on capacity to pay and therefore weighed more heavily on the wealthy. In any case, a mission was dispatched to the king on 3 August to arrange a lump-sum payment for "a certain number of men-at-arms." The trip took eighteen days,[32] partly, no doubt, because Philip was on the move with the army, but perhaps also because of lengthy bargaining with the king's advisers. There are no documents to indicate what these negotiations achieved. One might expect the king to have welcomed a large lump-sum payment at this time, whether for the *arrière-ban* only or to supersede the existing tax as well. In any case, the next military summons received at Reims (on 21 September) was restricted to the holders of fiefs.[33]

If the situation in Vermandois evolved in this way, it was probably somewhat similar in other bailiwicks. Little is known about the assemblies which were to have been held in the spring, except for the apparent cancellation of the *gabelle* over the course of the next year. In all cases, however, the timing of the English invasion was such that the grandiose scheme proposed in February did not have time to be tested properly. Encouraged and aided by his Norman ally, the lord of Saint-Sauveur, Edward III had been preparing his invasion at Portsmouth since early spring. Nevertheless, his landing in Cotentin on 11 July seems to have been a surprise to the French. Capturing Caen and St. Lô, Edward was able to threaten the environs of Paris early in August before moving northwards in an effort to cross the Somme. Philip's hastily assembled army finally cornered the invaders at Crécy, only to suffer a disastrous and bloody defeat on 26 August 1346. Finally permitted the pitched battle for which they had longed, the French nobility suffered humiliating losses.[34]

Throughout Languedoil, the fiscal documents for the second half of 1346 are hopelessly complicated by this military crisis. In Poitou, for in-

---

and extension of that agreement to meet the royal estimates of needed troops. See above, note 25, for the apparent Norman retention of a sales tax in 1346.

[32] Varin, *Reims*, II, 993.   [33] *Ibid.*, p. 1124.

[34] J. Viard, "La campagne de Crécy, juillet-août 1346," *MA*, XXXVII (1926), 1-84; Froissart, IV, 375-434, and notes, 483-494; *Jean le Bel*, II, 63-79; Lot, *L'art militaire*, I, 348; Perroy, *The Hundred Years War*, p. 119.

stance, an *aide* for the royal host was collected from late July onwards, but the timing, as well as the fact that it was levied by royal commissioners, suggests that it consisted of the traditional fines for non-service, levied following the *arrière-ban* of midsummer.[35] There is no evidence of any local assembly in Poitou. Lyon paid 1,000 *l.t.* in August in return for a letter of non-prejudice. Here too, the grant was evidently in response to the military summons, but since the *gabelle* was canceled at Lyon on 16 September, it is possible that some new tax arrangement was made with this community after Crécy.[36]

There is no evidence of any tax in Paris in 1346, but a series of ordinances in March granted or renewed various privileges,[37] and it is quite possible that some subsidy for men-at-arms was obtained at this time. Here too, a military summons was received late in July, but it was restricted to the bishop and his vassals, perhaps another indication that the non-nobles of the capital were already paying a tax.[38] Documents relating to the bailiwicks of Sens and Senlis cannot be considered reliable evidence of taxation in 1346,[39] while the only recorded subsidy in the Chaumont district was paid in lieu of military service.[40] Evidence of a 4 *d./l.* sales tax in Picardy has already been cited,[41] and late in the summer, the king's lieutenant in this region obtained troops from the abbot of Corbie and from Artois.[42] Indeed, the later summer and fall of 1346 present a picture of feverish military activity, with few indications of the fiscal program discussed the winter before. All efforts were directed towards rebuilding the forces shattered at Crécy and protecting northern France from the incursions of the Flemings or of the English army now besieging Calais.[43] At Saint-Quentin, the *gabelle* was canceled in September and the town received other privileges at about the same time, but

---

[35] *AHP*, LII, 229-236.

[36] AM Lyon AA 2, fols. 15v-16r. There is, however, no evidence of any bargaining over taxes at this time.

[37] AN JJ 75, nos. 481-485.

[38] BN NAF 7375, fols. 58r-59v; NAF 7606, fol. 40r-v.

[39] For Sens, our only text is the set of instructions cited above, note 22, which says nothing about actual negotiations or collections. Cazelles, *Soc. politique*, p. 176, cites a document from the Senlis district in connection with 1346, but this text has been given the date of 1348 by the copyist and the later year seems far preferable. See Henneman, "Black Death," notes 23 and 44.

[40] Timbal, *Guerre*, p. 64.

[41] Above, note 30. Cf. Vuitry, *Régime financier*, II, 26.

[42] BN Moreau 231, fol. 32r-v; Viard, in AN AB xix 2638, citing a text in AD Pas-de-Calais.

[43] J. Viard, "Le siège de Calais," *MA*, XL (1929), 137-168; AN P 2291, p. 779; Le Maire, *St. Quentin*, II, nos. 621, 622, 626.

there was no mention of any grant of men-at-arms and these concessions may have been an effort to bolster the loyalty of a critical frontier town.[44]

Auvergne is one region which did hold a local assembly to act on the plan discussed by the Estates General in February. Here, however, the military crisis created particular problems because Auvergne was nearer to Gascony than to Picardy and was subject to fiscal demands by the royal lieutenant in Languedoc as well as the king.[45] The three Estates of the bailiwick of Auvergne were to meet at Clermont on 17 April.[46] The municipal accounts of Montferrand do not mention this assembly, but they contain many entries dealing with military summonses. Ordered to send troops to Toulouse on 1 August, Montferrand complained to the king. Before an answer was received, the *arrière-ban* was proclaimed in Auvergne, and Montferrand sent a second envoy to Paris to arrange a *finance*. While these negotiations were in progress, the bailiff held musters and applied pressure until Montferrand sent another protest to Paris. In due course, the king canceled the summons to Toulouse and by November, a series of local assemblies had agreed to an "imposition" on the towns and clergy. Perhaps this was to implement the king's original request for men-at-arms, but we cannot be certain. By this time, the towns of Auvergne were trying to drive the English from Tulle. The accounts mention a *gabelle*, but it is not clear whether the revocation of the salt tax was at stake or whether the term simply referred to the "imposition" or some local sales tax.[47]

The complication caused when both Paris and the southern commander asked for aid was also a factor in the adjacent bailiwick of the Mountains. John of Normandy, besieging Aiguillon, issued a military summons to the barons, prelates, and towns of upper Auvergne early in August, to render service on 8 September. Yet at the beginning of September, a contingent of sergeants from this region was being equipped to go to Paris.[48] There is no information as to assemblies in this bailiwick in 1346. The situation in Auvergne generally resembled that prevailing farther north. Local assemblies met in some regions but their work was disrupted or obscured by the military crisis. The assemblies

---

[44] *Ibid.*, nos. 622-624; BN Moreau 231, fols. 19-20.

[45] Thus Riom had been summoned in January to the Paris assembly (AM Riom AA 21, no. 766) but later was asked to send persons to a southern assembly at Toulouse (*ibid.*, AA 15, no. 97).

[46] *Ibid.*, AA 16, no. 358.

[47] *INV AM Montferrand*, I, 367-370 (CC 162).

[48] *INV AM Aurillac*, II, 7-8 (EE 1); BN *ms. fr.* 7877, fol. 301. By this time the siege of Aiguillon had been raised.

in Languedoil probably had mixed results: some did not meet, some met but produced disappointing responses, and some may have acted as intended. In all cases, however, collections were slow and the English landing in Normandy produced a crisis not anticipated in February. Troops and money now were needed quickly, and the earlier effort to raise a force of men-at-arms was sidetracked. Lack of documentation frustrates our efforts to fill in details, but it is evident that the English invasion halted a promising royal program.

2. The Estates of Languedoc

As mentioned before, the king had issued a summons to the Estates of the southern seneschalsies to meet at Toulouse rather than make the long journey to Paris. This letter was transmitted through John of France, duke of Normandy and heir to the throne, who had gone to Languedoc as royal lieutenant.[49] Under the nominal authority of this prince, Jean de Marigny continued to exercise administrative functions and the duke of Bourbon retained the military command which he had held in Languedoc in 1345.

Conditions in Languedoc differed from those in the North in two important respects, one of them military, the other fiscal. Except for Picardy and Brittany, northern France had not yet encountered serious military action when the Estates of 1346 met. When the crisis came, it was a sudden invasion which briefly threatened the seat of government and ended in the destruction of a French army. Languedoc, however, had not only known a more continuous threat along the Gascon frontier but had already undergone the sobering experience of a major military setback at English hands. The second main point of difference between the two regions lay in the fact that Languedoc had upheld more successfully its claim to escape taxes in time of truce. There was no general sales tax in Languedoc comparable to that which had aroused criticism in the North.

Following Derby's successes of 1345, the French crown was finally able to collect subsidies in Languedoc towards the end of the year, but the reluctance shown earlier had not entirely dissipated. The seneschalsy of Carcassonne was paying a hearth tax and contributing both mounted troops and foot soldiers to Bourbon's army.[50] The seneschal, however, was careful to order that the mustering of these troops should not create

[49] *HL*, x, cols. 976-978.
[50] *HL*, IX, 583; Borrelli de Serres, *Recherches*, III, 408.

added expenses for the communities where they were assembled.[51] In the Beaucaire district, nobles of the viscounty of Creyssels remained lukewarm about supporting the war. They wished assurances that they would have to serve only if the other nobles of the seneschalsy did so.[52] When the consuls of Montpellier refused to furnish crossbowmen, their houses were occupied by royal sergeants, until the duke of Normandy ordered a halt to this coercion.[53] The disaffection in Languedoc had not been silenced by the English raid, and special royal action was called for if the crown wished to hold the loyalty and tap the resources of this region.[54] Thus despite the differences between North and South, the need for an assembly was equally evident in each region. Although the history of Estates in the two regions would begin to diverge significantly after February 1346, the meeting at Toulouse on the seventeenth amounted to a separate section of the Estates General, held apart from the main assembly for convenience.[55] The king's summons to the southern assembly was identical with that sent to the Estates who met at Paris. It indicated no awareness of problems peculiar to Languedoc and mentioned discontent with the sales tax although this was not even being levied in the South.

Indeed, our analysis of the Estates of Languedoc in 1346 is continually hindered by the fact that nearly all correspondence from the king in Paris referred to the program discussed at the northern assembly and made no reference to issues peculiar to Languedoc. A careful review of the documents suggests that the time-lag in communications and the apparent royal ignorance of conditions in the South created confusion in 1346 as well as confusing modern historians.

Although all three orders were summoned to meet at Toulouse on 17 February, the only surviving answer is that given by the towns *aut . . . majore parte earundem*, which promised a 10 *s.* hearth tax to be collected in installments during the months of April, May, and June.[56] Then, on 10 April, John of Normandy issued a summons to the clergy, nobility, and towns of the six southern seneschalsies, to convene at Toulouse on

---

[51] BN Doat 53, fols. 103-104.

[52] Molinier, *HL*, ix, 585, note 5, citing BN Doat 189, fol. 231.

[53] *Gr. Chartrier*, no. 3156.   [54] Cazelles, *Soc. politique*, p. 177.

[55] Molinier, *HL*, ix, 584, note 3. In speaking of central assemblies, one should bear in mind Charles Taylor's definition of this term: ". . . not merely assemblies that included delegations from all of France, but assemblies that were 'central' in the sense of drawing from a large regional area" as opposed to *viguerie* or bailiwick assemblies. Strayer and Taylor, *Studies*, p. 110, note 4.

[56] *HL*, x, col. 978.

31 May as a result of a decision taken "by our great council, being in Toulouse by our special mandate." The purpose of the new meeting was made quite clear. It would discuss the proposals for men-at-arms which had been considered at Paris in February. The language of the summons resembled closely Philip VI's ordinance of 15 February, a copy of which had certainly reached John by April.[57]

Most authorities have assumed that the February assembly at Toulouse received the same proposals as the meeting at Paris and granted the hearth tax purely as a stop-gap measure pending reference back to local constituents.[58] Implicit in this assumption is the belief that the *magnum consilium* mentioned by John on 10 April was actually the assembly of 17 February, which disbanded with the intention of reconvening later to take more definite action. Molinier offered another reason for the second assembly. Since surviving documents indicate only the reply of towns, he argued that the barons and prelates were not present in February and that their presence and consent would be necessary for any large tax to be binding.[59] Many subsequent meetings of the southern Estates were indeed restricted to towns, but Molinier's conclusion is a dangerous one to draw from purely negative evidence, since all three estates had been called to the first assembly. Moreover, the assemblies of later years, which did contain town representatives only, were able to grant important taxes and were in no way inhibited by the absence of the other two estates.

Whatever the composition of the February assembly at Toulouse, there is really no basis for assuming that it acted like its Paris counterpart. The king's summons to the two assemblies, besides betraying ignorance of conditions in Languedoc, also indicated considerable uncertainty as to what action to propose at the meetings. The deliberations which occurred at Paris were entirely appropriate to current conditions and recent fiscal history in Languedoïl, but it is most unlikely that similar discussions took place at Toulouse. With such an experienced man as Marigny to advise him, the duke of Normandy would hardly have proposed a plan which Languedoc had recently rejected, nor would he have offered to cancel a tax which was not even current in the South. Notwithstanding the identical summonses sent from Paris, the southern Estates must have dealt with matters relevant to their own region.

[57] *Ibid.*, col. 979. Philip's ordinance (*Ord.*, II, 238-241) has been cited above, note 10.

[58] Cazelles, *Soc. politique*, p. 175; Vuitry, *Régime financier*, II, 26; Molinier, *HL*, IX, 584, note 3; Viard, "Ressources," pp. 197-198.

[59] Molinier, *HL*, IX, 584, note 3.

In all probability, therefore, the assembly at Toulouse was approached for money on the basis of military necessity in Languedoc. Given the need to recover some of the losses to Derby's raid of 1345, the assembly responded with a far-from-generous offer of 10 *s*. per hearth. Then the duke of Normandy received word of what had transpired at Paris. Evidence suggests that copies of the king's ordinance of 15 February were sent to all the major towns of Languedoc but that they were not received until the second half of March.[60] Still ignorant of affairs in Languedoc, Philip VI wished the South to emulate the North and hold assemblies to determine how many men-at-arms would be granted in return for cancellation of other taxes. Upon receipt of royal orders to this effect, John of Normandy had to take counsel with his advisers on how best to implement the plan in the light of conditions in Languedoc. The likely place for such discussions was Toulouse, where the duke had his headquarters. Thus the *magnum consilium* to which he later referred was probably a fairly restricted meeting with senior advisers during March, rather than the assembly of Estates in February. The fact that John did not summon the second assembly until 10 April, supports this conclusion. Not until 4 June, after the second assembly, did John formally reissue Philip's February ordinance.[61]

The hearth tax of 10 *s*. which was to be collected during the spring had evidently been granted to meet the local military situation. The particular objective of the French command in Languedoc was recovery of the fortress of Aiguillon in Agenais, which Derby had captured the preceding autumn.[62] On 2 April 1346, the duke of Bourbon proclaimed the *arrière-ban*, signal for the serious beginning of the campaign.[63] Three days later, the duke of Normandy ordered collection of the hearth tax to begin and empowered his commissioners to employ any constraint necessary to ensure prompt payment.[64] Even so, the tax was a small one, spread over three months, and it would be some time before significant

---

[60] The ordinance was received at Cahors on 17 March (BN Doat 8, fol. 183), at Cajarc on 18 March (AM Cajarc CC no. 247), at Toulouse on 30 March (*INV AM Toulouse*, p. 462 [AA 35, no. 63]), and at Narbonne in April (*INV AM Narbonne, sér. AA*, p. 339). Other indications that this ordinance was widely circulated are in *Gr. Chartrier*, no. 431; and BN Doat 255, fol. 444v.

[61] *HL*, x, col. 988.

[62] According to *HL*, ix, 586, an army began to be assembled at Toulouse by the French late in the winter of 1346. On Aiguillon, see Bertrandy, *Etude*, p. 187; Perroy, *The Hundred Years War*, p. 118.

[63] AD Hérault A 4, fols. 204v-205. It is interesting that the summons occurred at the beginning of the month in which the first installment of the hearth tax was to be collected, for the call to arms might help speed collection.

[64] *HL*, x, col. 978.

sums would be in hand. Even fines from persons who did not wish to join the army would take time to collect, and no new tax from the towns could be obtained until the assembly of 31 May convened and took action. Extensive borrowing[65] brought in some money, but by 19 April, it was evident to John of Normandy (then besieging Aiguillon) that much more was needed quickly. He therefore named three special commissioners, giving them power "to procure and amass all the money to be had from each and every person of the said seneschalsies."[66] Among the specific actions falling under their cognizance were to be jurisdictional disputes, seizures of rebel property, granting of privileges and liberties to persons of all three classes, granting of letters of nobility and legitimizing of bastards, making *paréages*, dealing with civil and criminal cases for which fines could be levied, receiving fines for fief alienations, hearing complaints, and imposing "the subsidy or *fouage* newly ordered by our people at Toulouse."[67] As in previous years, therefore, the government employed commissioners with sweeping powers to find money from all possible sources and to speed collection of the hearth tax.[68]

The crown continued to assemble troops for the Aiguillon campaign. Agen, asked to produce 1,000 men, sent no more than 100 crossbowmen and then was called upon to supply some equipment.[69] Towns obtained permission to raise municipal taxes for local defense and the crown claimed one-fifth of that levied at Le Puy.[70] Jean de Marigny supervised the levy of the subsidy and he was able to speed up collection by accepting lump-sum payments from some towns in lieu of the hearth tax.[71] One such community was Montpellier, which made a payment of 1,000 *l.t.* on 22 May.[72] Another was Millau, which offered a lump sum and then raised the money by means of a municipal property tax.[73] Castres, and other towns in the lands of the count of Vendôme, paid a total of 2,191 *l.* 10 *s.*,[74] while in many places the hearth tax itself was collected, a slow

---

[65] For loans from the pope and others, see Vuitry, *Régime financier*, II, 211; above, notes 23-24; and below, notes 136-138.

[66] *HL*, X, col. 980.　　　　[67] *Ibid.*, cols. 981-982.

[68] Henneman, "Enquêteurs," pp. 342-343.　　[69] AM Agen BB 16, fols. 30-36v.

[70] AN JJ 75, no. 414. For more on urban fortifications, see below, note 103.

[71] Molinier, *HL*, IX, 588, note 2.

[72] *Gr. Chartrier*, no. 451. Also embroiled with the king of Majorca over the latter's desire to raise a sales tax in the town, Montpellier obtained the aid of Philip VI in evading this tax (*ibid.*, nos. 687, 1713-1720).

[73] AM Millau CC 65.

[74] BN *Coll. Languedoc* 85, fol. 37v. This sum was paid as a *finance* with the commissioners whom John of Normandy had appointed in April (above, note 66).

process but one which promised to yield more money, in some cases, than the payment of lump sums.[75]

Meanwhile, the commissioners who were exploring other sources of revenue spent an active month of May, collecting money from two moneychangers of Toulouse,[76] extorting money from Albi for usury and monetary violations,[77] and exerting pressure to recover nearly 1,000 pounds in arrears from the export tax of the preceding year.[78] Forced requisitions at Cahors gave rise to opposition and the duke of Normandy had to order moderation.[79]

The costly siege of Aiguillon may have compelled the government to employ these fiscal expedients to supplement tax revenues, but the activities of the commissioners were hardly calculated to foster a generous mood in the assembly which convened on 31 May. The Estates by now were well aware of the deliberations taken at Paris in February, and they had far more advance information than had the northern representatives four months earlier. However, the king's plan for replacing existing taxes with a long-term grant of troops had far more potential appeal to northern France, where the existing taxes were more onerous and there was no strong tradition of lump-sum payments by towns. Moreover, John of Normandy had not indicated how many troops he wished Languedoc to promise. Consequently, the southern Estates now did what their northern counterparts had done in February. They demanded and received a long reform ordinance and promised to refer the matter of men-at-arms to their constituents. On 4 June, the duke issued letters announcing the results of the meeting. A grant of men-at-arms, to be collected only in time of war, would be considered locally by the towns, who would reconvene on 15 July to give a definite answer.[80] This letter enclosed two other documents, one of them being a copy of Philip VI's ordinance of 15 February. The other was a roll of instructions for implementing the measures discussed by the Estates. From Languedoc,

[75] As will be seen below, a second tax of 10 s. was granted in June, and in the Beaucaire district it seems that the entire 20 s. was entered in a single account, summarized in BN Coll. Languedoc 159, fols. 24-25. Collections were slow, but many communities came much closer to producing 20 s. per hearth than did Montpellier, whose finance was for a much smaller sum.

[76] Molinier, HL, IX, 588, note 2.

[77] BN Doat 103, fol. 285r. John of Normandy ordered them to halt the exaction from Albi when it appeared that the town had already paid 150 pounds for these offenses to another commissioner late in 1345.

[78] AD Hérault A 4, fols. 242v-243.

[79] Albe, "Cahors INV," no. 407. John later confirmed the privileges of Cahors in June (ibid., no. 408).

[80] HL, x, col. 983.

the crown hoped to obtain one man-at-arms for every hundred hearths, paid for one year at a daily wage of 7 s. 4 d.t. In effect this would mean a heavy new hearth tax of 26 s. 4 d., although, as always, the communities could choose their own way of raising the money. The crown estimated that its formula would produce an army of 20,000 to 30,000 men if applied throughout the kingdom. The hearth figures, probably based on the census taken nearly two decades earlier, were subject to challenge, so the duke of Normandy promised a new hearth count. There seems, however, to have been little confidence that the Estates would give a favorable reply when they reassembled. They agreed to a second 10 s.t. hearth tax for the war in Languedoc, to be collected after 15 July if the new assembly failed to grant the desired men-at-arms.[81]

It was this last provision which permits us to say that the southern Estates accomplished more than their northern counterparts. Two successive assemblies representing a large region had now granted taxes binding on their constituents. In taking this action, the assemblies of 1346 may have played a critical role in assuring the continued use of the Estates in Languedoc, although their emergence as an essential institution really belongs to the period after 1356. The tax negotiations of 1346 in Languedoc were vastly more successful from the royal point of view than those of 1345. We should, of course, remember that the subsidies in question were not large and that Languedoc, unlike the North, had experienced a serious military incursion in the intervening year.

As in 1343, the communities of Languedoc were not content with the royal reforms promised to the North. Having published his father's ordinance, John of Normandy then issued another long document of thirty-two articles which dealt with the grievances of Languedoc.[82] As pointed out elsewhere, this ordinance reflected the royal fiscal practices which had aroused resentment during the preceding decade.[83] Most of its provisions dealt with the raising of taxes, the mustering of troops, and the activities of royal commissioners. It is clear that royal taxation and the oppressions of the king's *réformateurs* (*reformatores . . . ad extorquendum pecunias*) were the major causes of southern discontent.

In issuing this ordinance, John has been accused of a rather quick "surrender," perhaps a symptom of his great financial need.[84] Possibly it can be seen as an early indication of his characteristic lack of self-confi-

---

[81] *Ibid.*, cols. 983-988, is the version sent to the Carcassonne district. For the comparable document sent to Beaucaire, see *Gr. Chartrier*, D-viii, no. 1.

[82] *HL*, x, cols. 988-996.   [83] Henneman, "Enquêteurs," p. 343.

[84] Molinier, *HL*, IX, 590-591, note 2.

dence. Cazelles regards the ordinance as a belated attempt to moderate disaffection caused by French rule in Languedoc which appeared much harsher than English rule in Guyenne.[85] Certainly the timing of the ordinance (June), raises the question of John's tactics in negotiating for money. If there was any chance of obtaining the large proposed grant of men-at-arms, might it not have been more effective to withhold the ordinance and send commissioners to the various localities armed with concessions which might secure a binding agreement? In 1343, despite general agreement in Paris on the reforms to be instituted, the southern towns had made firm grants only after receiving specific concessions at the local level. Perhaps, however, the general discontent of 1346 made necessary an immediate reform ordinance. Having just experienced in April and May an exhaustive effort by commissioners to obtain money locally, the Estates may have insisted on royal concessions as a precondition for considering the men-at-arms proposal. In any case, the assembly showed some shrewdness in promising the second 10 s. hearth tax. If the local meetings were to conclude that a large grant of troops was too high a price to pay for abolition of the *gabelle*, they could do so in good conscience and argue that they had already promised 20 s. per hearth in 1346 for the defense of the realm.

During June, the siege of Aiguillon continued, as did collection of the first 10 s. hearth tax. The duke of Normandy halted the levy of both this tax and fines for the *arrière-ban* in the county of Foix, which succeeded in escaping most taxation during Philip VI's reign.[86] Meanwhile, the crown attempted to obtain money for men-at-arms from the clergy of Languedoc. At the assembly of 31 May, some clergy of the province of Narbonne had agreed to furnish an aid, and those of the provinces of Toulouse and Auch did the same. The clergy were ordered to reconvene on 8 July, a week earlier than the towns and nobles, in order to make a definite grant.[87] The military activity of the summer may have delayed this meeting. In any case, the clergy proved unable to agree on common action. By the latter part of August, those of the province of Toulouse made a grant of 8,000 *l.t.* in return for exemption from certain logistical services they found onerous.[88] The clergy of Albi granted 1,100 *l.t.* subject to the pope's consent, perhaps hoping that Clement VI would give them an excuse to avoid paying. In December, the pontiff finally ap-

---

[85] Cazelles, *Soc. politique*, p. 177.   [86] AD Basses-Pyrénées E 406, no. 17.

[87] BN *Coll. Languedoc* 84, fols. 342r-343v; *HL*, IX, 591.

[88] *Ibid.*, p. 592, note 2; BN Doat 157, fol. 122r. The grant was made with papal consent, which Molinier did not make entirely clear in his note.

proved the grant but attached certain conditions, some of which Philip VI would not accept. The affair dragged on for nearly three years before the crown finally collected 927 *l.t.* in March of 1349.[89]

The long struggle to obtain this relatively modest sum illustrates the difficulty faced by the monarchy in its attempts to finance the Hundred Years' War. The clergy, of course, were being pressed for taxes from different quarters, since they were already paying the clerical tenth granted for three years in 1344,[90] and were subject to taxation by towns raising money for both war subsidies and their own defenses.[91] In addition, they had paid heavy fines for *amortissement* during the preceding decades. No effort seems to have been made in 1346 to relieve them of multiple taxation as was done when a special tenth was desired in 1337.

The nobles were, on the whole, rather better treated, as they had been throughout the reign. The exemption from taxation accorded to the county of Foix was a special case, but nobles, in general, were able to avoid payment of any subsidy by rendering personal service, and some of them were given portions of the tax receipts from their own lands. The viscount of Lautrec, for instance, received 1,000 *l.* from the 10 *s.* hearth tax, and many nobles with high justice escaped taxation during the year.[92] *Hommes de corps* and tallageable-at-will subjects of nobles throughout Languedoc were considered exempt from the hearth tax, but when some lords abused the privilege and tried to tax them for their own benefit, John of Normandy ordered that all persons who had formerly paid royal taxes would do so on this occasion.[93] In keeping, however, with the generally sympathetic attitude towards the great vassals, John finally allowed the king of Majorca to collect a controversial tax he wished to levy on Montpellier, provided that it did not exceed 6,000 *l.t.* for each of two years.[94]

The assembly scheduled for 15 July, at which the Estates were to have given their answer to the royal request for men-at-arms, seems never to

---

[89] BN Doat 109, fols. 303v-310r (the pope's qualified approval of the grant on 5 December); fols. 311-319 (Philip VI's qualified acceptance); fols. 327-329v (order to use constraint against the bishop of Albi); fols. 331r-332v (Philip's order of 13 June 1347 to the bishop, telling him to have his clergy immediately pay the money as a loan). See the discussion of the episode by Molinier in *HL*, IX, 592, note 1.

[90] *JT Ph. VI*, no. 2595.

[91] BN *ms. lat.* 9174, fols. 222-223v. On the clergy and municipal taxes, see the discussion in Chapter IX, part 2.

[92] *HL*, IX, 592; AD Hérault A 1, fols. 79v-80v; BN *Coll. Languedoc* 84, fols. 345-346.

[93] *HL*, IX, 593. [94] *Gr. Chartrier*, no. 1721. See above, note 72.

have met. As with the bailiwick assemblies scheduled in Languedoil, it appears that the midsummer military crisis may have been a factor. Although the long and futile siege of Aiguillon was not actually lifted until late in August, it had been necessary to start sending troops northward a month earlier.[95] In any case, the May-June Estates did not display much enthusiasm for the royal proposal, if we except the clergy. As already pointed out, the provisional grant of a second hearth tax afforded the towns an excuse for taking no further action. All evidence points to the collection of this second 10 s. per hearth, proof that the grant of men-at-arms was not forthcoming.[96]

As in April, the duke of Normandy proclaimed the *arrière-ban* before undertaking collection of the hearth tax. On rather short notice, he ordered the men of Languedoc to muster with him before Aiguillon on 8 July. The consuls of Millau declared themselves willing to serve, but not on the appointed day, since they had not received the summons until the 6th.[97] The communities of Rouergue then sent representatives to Villefranche to arrange a *finansa*.[98] The towns of Quercy also did not receive the military summons until 6 July. John excused them for failing to muster on time, and then collected either the hearth tax or a fine in lieu of service.[99]

The two hearth taxes of 10 *s.t.* proved difficult to collect in the seneschalsy of Beaucaire. An incomplete account indicates receipts of 47,744 *l.t.*, including 400 from Alès, 773 from Lunel, 3,000 from Montpellier, and 1,139 from Beaucaire. The last three of these towns resisted paying and had to be coerced. With 2,033 hearths, Beaucaire paid much less than its share, and Montpellier's total contribution seems to have equaled only about half of what it should have paid for a 20 *s. fouage*.[100] In other parts of Languedoc, Moissac and Castres evidently fined to avoid the hearth tax,[101] while Pézenas sent crossbowmen to the army.[102] A great

---

[95] Molinier, *HL*, IX, 593-594, note 4.

[96] *Ibid.*, p. 593, note 1.   [97] AM Millau EE III, no. 6.

[98] AM Millau, *archives non classées*, a fragmentary account of consular expenses showing a ten-day trip to Villefranche for this purpose.

[99] AM Cajarc EE 9, no. 400; EE supp., no. 75; and CC supp., no. 75 *bis*; Albe, "Cahors INV," no. 409. The seneschal of Quercy had to be ordered to respect the newly confirmed privileges of Cahors (*ibid.*, no. 410).

[100] AD Gard, ms. inventory of AM Beaucaire (1772), fol. 132v; BN *Coll. Languedoc* 159, fols. 24-25; AM Lunel CC 60, no. 2221.

[101] BN Doat 127, fols. 178-179. It is not clear whether the 10 s. hearth tax at Castres mentioned at the bottom of fol. 37v, BN *Coll. Languedoc* 85, belongs to 1346 or 1347, but it would seem to be the second 10 s. levied in 1346.

[102] *INV AM Pézenas*, nos. 1648-1649.

effort was made throughout the Midi to speed the fortification of major towns.[103]

When the duke of Normandy abandoned the siege of Aiguillon and hurried back to Paris late in the Crécy campaign, he was replaced as royal lieutenant in Languedoc by John I, count of Armagnac and Rodez.[104] The latter displayed considerable energy, collecting troops from Languedoc and Auvergne to repulse the English advances and recapture Tulle.[105] Montpellier sent 2,000 *l.t.* to equip troops being sent to the count of Armagnac at Agen,[106] but in general, tax collection dragged on interminably. On 5 November, Armagnac had to send a letter of encouragement to the collectors of the *fouage* which was now several months overdue.[107] The government turned once again to fiscal expedients, seizing the property of "rebels," assessing marks of silver on the notaries, and selling royal letters of privilege or non-prejudice.[108] These were merely stop-gap measures, like the *fouage* itself, and the crown remained in dire need of funds because the unsuccessful siege of Aiguillon had been costly. Armagnac, therefore, called a new assembly of towns, this one to meet at Moissac on 8 November.[109] Three weeks before the meeting was scheduled, the count issued another reform ordinance, this one for the benefit of the towns in the Toulouse district. Aside from one jurisdictional clause, the matters dealt with in this decree were entirely fiscal and military. Extortions of war subsidy commissioners were to end; foodstuffs were not to be seized to force payment; taxes contrary to custom and privileges were to be revoked; the remission of the old subsidy levied by Agout de Baux was to be accomplished with deductions from the present tax if necessary. Because the towns had sent troops to the

[103] *INV AM Toulouse*, pp. 462, 533 (AA 35, no. 64; AA 45, nos. 21, 23). As pointed out above, Chapter v, note 230, rebuilding the walls of Toulouse had become an urgent matter. The crown permitted the *capitouls* to levy sales taxes intended to raise 12,000 pounds annually for this purpose. See *HL*, ix, 594 and 596, note 4; AD Hérault A i, fols. 86-87, 90-92. Similar efforts were in progress at Albi (BN Doat 109, fols. 278v-286v, 294f.). For Montpellier, see *Gr. Chartrier*, nos. 1781, 1784, 2365, 2367-2370.

[104] *HL*, ix, 594.

[105] *Ibid.*, pp. 595-598. See also *INV AM Montferrand*, i, 369; *INV AM Périgueux*, p. 80.

[106] *Gr. Chartrier*, no. 2366. Although the duke of Normandy said that the payments were complete (*ibid.*, D-viii, no. 57), these 2,000 *l.t.* seem only to have completed the 3,000 mentioned above, at note 100. It was later decided that Montpellier should pay more. See below, note 120.

[107] BN *Coll. Languedoc* 84, fol. 354r-v.

[108] *HL*, ix, 596-597; BN *Coll. Languedoc* 84, fol. 322r. AD Hérault A i, fols. 87v-89r.

[109] *HL*, ix, 597.

bishop of Beauvais the previous March, they were permitted another de-
duction from the current subsidy. However, in response to a request that
the hearth tax be returned because of expenses incurred in repairing
town walls, Armagnac would agree to no more than a suspension.[110]
Even after the Crécy disaster, Languedoc remained unimpressed with
the difficulties of the crown in distant parts of the realm. By this time,
Derby had shifted his headquarters to Bergerac and was menacing
Poitou rather than Languedoc.[111]

Armagnac tried to minimize the cost of the new concessions by canceling various assignments of money made to the nobility through the ir-
responsible generosity of the duke of Normandy; here, however, he was
overruled by the king.[112] Despite the great distance separating him from
Languedoc and the earlier indications that he did not fully comprehend
the situation there, Philip VI had his own ideas about fiscal policy in the
South. He ordered John of Armagnac to remit the unpaid portions of the
fouage in Rouergue.[113] The count was understandably reluctant to halt
or return this tax if he could avoid doing so. At Nîmes he suspended the
levy for a month in response to royal orders, but his subordinates,
equally reluctant to comply, seem to have delayed for several weeks in
executing this order,[114] Receipt of the king's correspondence must have
created some confusion for Armagnac and his advisers, and doubtless
persuaded them to cancel the proposed assembly at Moissac. There is
certainly no evidence that it met, and Armagnac himself was busy with
the siege of Tulle.

Following his defeat at Crécy, Philip VI was necessarily occupied with
emergency military measures for a number of weeks. In addition, the
need both for scapegoats and for more efficient government dictated
some administrative reorganization.[115] For most of the autumn of 1346,
these concerns occupied the government and left it unable to take decisive action in the fiscal sphere. Nevertheless, Philip never lost sight of
his original scheme for obtaining a nationwide grant of men-at-arms in
return for the reforms already issued and a cancellation of existing taxes.
At no time do we find any indication that the king considered Languedoc

---

[110] *HL*, x, cols. 1002-1007; AD Hérault A 1, fols. 8ov-85r. Royal confirmations of
the ordinance are found *ibid.*, fols. 96v-104r. Molinier, *HL*, ix, 597, note 3, incorrectly
associates these texts with the preceding winter (1345-1346). Vaissete (*HL*, ix, 597)
wrongly understood this ordinance as a promise to return the current tax. Later, the
king did in fact call for its return (see below, note 116).

[111] Molinier, *ibid.*, p. 595, note 4; *Jean le Bel*, ii, 120-125.

[112] *HL*, ix, 598.   [113] Cabrol, *Villefranche*, i, 222.

[114] AN Nîmes NN 1, no. 28.   [115] Cazelles, *Soc. politique*, pp. 178f.

to be different from the North in fiscal matters. Undoubtedly, this thinking influenced his effort to have the count of Armagnac cancel and return the second 10 *s. fouage* levied in the South.[116] This tax was to have been collected only if the towns failed to grant the larger sum required to support one mounted soldier for every hundred hearths. The Crécy campaign had disrupted efforts to obtain this grant in Languedoil and Philip evidently attributed to the same source the failure of the southern towns to convene in July and make a favorable response. If he showed good faith by halting and returning the *fouage*, the southern towns might be prepared to support the large number of troops which the king desired. A document in the archives of Millau makes clear what the king had in mind. On 15 December 1346, he wrote to his commissioner, Bertrand de Pibrac, summarizing the royal plan, describing the deliberation at Paris in February, and taking note of the assembly held by John of Normandy for the same purpose in May. He described the proposal for a grant of men-at-arms as unfinished business and ordered Pibrac to seek such grants from the seneschalsies of Rouergue and Beaucaire in return for cancellation of the *gabelle* and the sales tax. The commissioner received representatives from Millau at Najac and imposed on the town "a certain number of sergeants."[117] Despite Philip's plan to obtain a comprehensive grant from the whole kingdom, this text suggests rather local negotiations which, in Millau's case, produced only a reluctant grant of foot soldiers as in other years.

Poor documentation prevents us from reaching firm conclusions about taxation in Languedoc during the winter of 1346-1347, but it appears that Millau's experience may have been typical, as scattered local negotiations produced grants of men or money. Perhaps Pibrac convened small assemblies, but they have left no evidence. The commissioner seems to have adapted his instructions to local realities in the Midi, using the cancellation of the *gabelle* as a bargaining device to obtain small grants at a local level. Even the disappearance of the *gabelle* is established only by negative evidence.[118] The government obtained 2,300 pounds as a war subsidy from the bishops of Vabres and Rodez.[119] Commissioners de-

---

[116] AD Hérault A 1, fols. 103v-104, shows that Philip finally ordered a sweeping cancellation of the second *fouage* of 1346 throughout Languedoc.

[117] AM Millau EE 121, no. 228.

[118] Molinier, *HL*, IX, 605, note 2; *HL*, X, cols. 1021-1022. A text in BN NAF 7606, fols. 94-95, calling for an accounting of the *gabelle* in June 1347, gives no indication as to whether or not this tax had been canceled by that date, although it probably had been in most places.

[119] AD Aveyron G 31, no. 29. In return, their privileges were confirmed.

manded more money from Montpellier, arguing that the 3,000 *l.t.* paid thus far amounted to no more than a single *fouage* of 10 *s.* Montpellier finally agreed to pay another 2,000 pounds plus 150 *l.t.* for the expenses of the commissioners, provided that the second *fouage* be collected from other towns of the seneschalsy.[120] No doubt the crown's officials were glad to have a pretext for resuming collection of this tax where it had been halted. Later in the winter, Pibrac imposed a new hearth tax on the Beaucaire district, with collection to begin in April 1347. Montpellier's share was to be 3,000 *l.t.*, and receipts have survived for two-thirds of this sum. Nîmes contributed 600 *l.t.* by 5 May and the tax was also imposed at Lunel. Receipts from the whole district, however, came to less than 24,000 pounds.[121] A new *fouage* was also levied in the seneschalsy of Carcassonne,[122] and in Quercy various towns agreed to raise two men-at-arms and fifty-nine sergeants in May.[123] At Rodez, a subsidy was payable in widely spaced installments, the last payment not being due until 30 November 1347.[124] Languedoc may also have sent troops to aid the king in his effort to relieve the besieged port of Calais,[125] but in general it appears that the crown obtained very little in the South from the last quarter of 1346 through the end of 1347.

Most of the money paid by the southern populace in this period was devoted to local defense and urban fortifications. Toulouse was permitted to extend its heavy local taxes for this purpose,[126] and the king contributed 2,000 pounds of his ordinary revenues to help secure Périgueux against English forces and their local sympathizers.[127] It was necessary, throughout Languedoc, to compel privileged persons to contribute to these levies for local defense.[128]

---

[120] BN *ms. lat.* 9174, fols. 204r-205v; *Gr. Chartrier*, nos. 4005-4009. Perhaps to hasten a favorable response from the consuls, the rector of Montpellier demanded 150 crossbowmen from the town and the consuls protested the action: AM Montpellier G-1, nos. 3129-3131.

[121] *Gr. Chartrier*, no. 4004; AM Nîmes NN 1, no. 29; BN *Coll. Languedoc* 159, fol. 25v; *INV AM Lunel*, describing EE 1, no. 1974, which now appears to be lost.

[122] Molinier, *HL*, IX, 605, note 2; BN *Coll. Languedoc* 85, fols. 37v-38v.

[123] AM Cajarc EE 10, no. 349; EE *supp.*, no. 245; AD Lot F 188; Lacoste, *Quercy*, III, 116.

[124] AM Rodez (*cité*) CC 371, no. 9.

[125] *HL*, IX, 603-604; Viard, "Ressources," pp. 199-200.

[126] *INV AM Toulouse*, pp. 462-463. See above, note 103.

[127] *INV AM Périgueux*, pp. 55-56, 81-82 (CC 10, CC 62); Moreau, *Recueil*, pp 251-253.

[128] AD Hérault A 1, fols. 95v-96v; A 4, fols. 177v-178; BN Doat 53, fols. 130r-131v; AM Gourdon CC 1, no. 14. At Montpellier, however, nobles who regularly paid

The crown also sought a tax from the clergy of the southern ecclesiastical provinces, obtaining 12,000 *l. petits tournois* from those of Narbonne and a delayed grant from the province of Bourges which the king wished to replace with an immediate loan.[129] Like Edward III, Philip seized the prebends of prelates and other clergy not residing in the kingdom, but through the queen's intervention, he modified the order to exclude those who lived at the papal court at Avignon.[130]

In Paris, meanwhile, Philip VI still clung to some hope of a large grant of men-at-arms from the kingdom. On 12 March 1347, he ordered Narbonne to send two well-instructed representatives to Paris for an assembly of towns which would discuss the common profit. The proctors were duly empowered on 24 April,[131] but nothing more is heard of this meeting. Far from being a contemplated "Estates General,"[132] it probably represents a final effort on Philip's part to implement in Languedoc the plan discussed at the Paris Estates in 1346. Perhaps the king hoped to bring the plan to fruition by a personal appeal to the southern towns. However, he continued to be preoccupied with the struggle for Calais and by April, was deeply involved in raising men and money in Picardy.

3. Fiscal Confusion and the Siege of Calais

From mid-1346 until the fall of 1347, Philip VI's government struggled ineffectively to cope with several different problems. One of these, of course, was financial, and Philip seemed determined to carry out the plan of early 1346, whereby a large grant of men-at-arms would replace all other taxes. We have seen that this proposal did not meet with much enthusiasm in Languedoc, where it seemed little relevant to existing conditions and merely confused an already difficult fiscal situation. In Languedoil, however, it was a different story, and in all probability, the northern bailiwicks would have been prepared to adopt the plan had they not suddenly been interrupted by an external factor—the English invasion of Normandy.

The Crécy campaign necessarily suspended orderly procedures and the crown busily sought to levy troops by such conventional means as a

---

municipal taxes were not to have to fine for military service as well: *Gr. Chartrier*, no. 1234; BN *ms. lat.* 9174, fols. 224-225.

[129] *HL*, ix, 603. Molinier, however, questioned the grant of the province of Bourges, believing that Vaissete has confused it with the loan discussed above, note 89.

[130] *LC*, p. 126, note 3 to no. 185.   [131] AM Narbonne AA 172.

[132] Molinier, *HL*, ix, 603, note 3, merely accepted the faulty analysis of Hervieu, *Recherches*, p. 225.

general call to service. Following the disastrous battle, the situation became still more chaotic. The king sought to isolate Edward III by diplomatic means and devoted great attention to short-term military and fiscal needs and to reorganizing his government. While never losing sight of his goal of obtaining a large grant, Philip could pursue it only sporadically and indecisively. In this atmosphere of confusion, the government not only neglected long-term objectives but also failed to meet its primary short-term objective, which was to prevent Edward III from capturing Calais. Men and money were always in short supply and Philip seemed incapable of a sustained military effort to break the siege, perhaps out of reluctance to face a new pitched battle.[133]

To ease his financial woes, Philip VI had remarkably little room in which to maneuver. Coinage manipulation, abandoned in 1343, was still unpopular and could be undertaken only with the greatest tact.[134] Fief alienations and usurped royal rights had been exploited thoroughly in 1344 and were unlikely to yield much profit. As long as Philip wished to keep alive the prospect of a long-term grant of men-at-arms, he had to honor his reform ordinance of 1346 which, among other things, forbade the use of forced loans. Even the papacy, which had been so generous early in 1346, provided little aid during the Crécy and Calais campaigns. Except for a loan of 5,000 florins, in April 1347, the Roger brothers did not make available any more funds until the final week of 1347.[135] Robert de Lorris, Philip's principal negotiator of papal loans, was also charged with borrowing from other clergy,[136] and, in fact, the crown did manage to obtain loans from some prelates. The abbot of Saint-Denis advanced 1,000 *l.p.*,[137] and a number of much larger sums were borrowed from other prelates, including 20,000 florins from Talleyrand, cardinal of

---

[133] Guilhiermoz, *Noblesse*, p. 297, note 117, accepted Froissart's statement that the king was resolved to employ nobles only in his military campaigns. Perroy, *The Hundred Years War*, p. 120, indicates that Philip lost confidence in his army. It is not clear whether these factors were more important than Philip's obvious lack of funds, and in any case Edward had assembled a very large force for the siege of Calais. Whatever the reasons, the failure to launch a serious sustained attack on the English army during this long siege is very striking and must have affected public opinion late in 1347.

[134] See Appendix 1, note h to Table 1. Philip VI seems to have ordered a reduction in the price of silver in the spring of 1347 while negotiating with assemblies for taxes, but the reform was not put into practice, and an unpopular debasement undertaken in the winter continued in force until after the Estates General of late 1347.

[135] Faucon, "Prêts," p. 572. For other loans, however, see *HL*, x, col. 1019.

[136] *Ibid.*; G. Mollat, "Clément VI et le chancelier Firmin de Cocquerel," *BEC*, CXXII (1964), 257-261.

[137] *JT Ph. VI*, no. 290.

Périgord.[138] These loans, however, could have done relatively little to alleviate the critical shortage of money afflicting Philip VI during the months that Calais was being besieged.

From the English point of view, the great value of the victory at Crécy lay in the fact that the French were so paralyzed by defeat that an early counter-offensive could not materialize. Edward's position was still precarious in the following weeks and for a time the French fleet was able to prevent him from receiving reinforcements.[139] Philip did issue a new military summons in September 1346, but it failed to produce the men and money needed for a successful attack on Edward.[140] It was difficult for the French to assemble forces for this purpose in Artois and Picardy because Edward's Flemish allies threatened these districts from another direction. The English king may have been disappointed at the failure of the Flemings to assist materially in the siege of Calais, but their forays into French territory disrupted efforts to organize a campaign against Edward,[141] and the towns of northern France were distracted by the need to see to their own defenses.[142] Eudes IV, duke of Burgundy, had apparently not made much effort to fortify his wife's county of Artois, and as a close associate of Philip VI and the men who had advised the king for the preceding fourteen years, he became a scapegoat following Crécy. In December, the French crown took over the government of Artois.[143]

These French distractions gave Edward III a valuable breathing spell, and in time, he assembled before Calais an army of more than 30,000 men, an enormous force by medieval standards.[144] Philip's successes during this period were confined to the diplomatic sphere. The count of Flanders having died at Crécy, England and France courted his young successor, Louis II, each king hoping to buy Louis' support by a marriage alliance. Louis' strong desire to re-establish himself in Flanders and gain the support of his disaffected subjects may have given England a

---

[138] Zacour, *Talleyrand*, p. 20; *HL*, x, col. 1019; BN Doat 243, fols. 163r-178r.

[139] Viard, "Le siège de Calais," pp. 134f.

[140] AN P 2291, p. 779; Le Maire, *St. Quentin*, II, no. 621; AN AB xix 2638 (copied from BN NAF 9241, fols. 95-99v).

[141] Viard, "Le siège de Calais," pp. 138f.

[142] Several northern towns received permission to levy taxes for fortifications or were given other fiscal concessions: Thierry, *Recueil*, I, 530-531; *AHP*, xiii, 343-346; AN JJ 68, no. 168.

[143] Cazelles, *Soc. politique*, pp. 196-200; *INV AD Pas-de-Calais*, I, 116 (A 83).

[144] BN Moreau 699, fols. 161-164, enumerates the different categories of fighting men at Calais and gives a total of 30,492 men. The total of 32,000 is given by K. McFarlane, "England and the Hundred Years War," *P & P*, xxii (1962), 4.

diplomatic weapon, but France was in a position to promote an alliance with Brabant and to ensure that Louis' mother would inherit the county of Artois. In the end, French policy triumphed with a Flanders-Brabant marriage, although Flemish politics determined that Louis would never espouse the French cause with the enthusiasm shown by his father.[145] The French crown also reached a reconciliation with the Norman turn-coat, Godefroy d'Harcourt, lord of Saint-Sauveur. Crécy had given this baron his revenge, but his brother, the count of Harcourt, had died there on the French side. Godefroy became disenchanted with Edward early in the siege of Calais, and made his peace with Philip VI, receiving a letter of remission for his past offenses in December 1346.[146] By the following summer, he was in charge of French forces in lower Normandy, with wide powers to raise troops and taxes.[147]

A pressing task for Philip VI in the fall of 1346 was to restore public confidence in his government. Three abbots were placed in charge of royal finances, terminating the long and close association between the royal council and the Chamber of Accounts. Appointment of the abbots was a temporary emergency measure, but the eclipse of the Chamber of Accounts party was now assured for a long period.[148]

Shortly after the beginning of 1347, the French government resumed efforts to obtain war subsidies in Languedoil. On 20 January, Philip wrote to a commissioner charged with raising men-at-arms in the Norman bailiwick of Gisors. Referring to popular distrust of local officials and to an alternate plan for obtaining troops which the Great Council had supported, he ordered the commissioner to proceed in accordance with certain secret instructions. He was to impose a tax on the towns and collect it in baronial and princely lands as well as the domain.[149] The wording of this document suggests the scheme for raising men-at-arms which had been discussed by the Estates nearly a year before. The secret instructions, which have not survived, could be the same as those sent to the bailiwick of Sens in 1346. In 1346, Normandy was discussing a subsidy which would support troops for six months in two consecutive years, and we have seen that the duchy did pay a tax during the summer. The king's order of January 1347 seems more concerned with collecting a tax than with negotiating a new one. It seems possible to conclude, there-

---

[145] For some of the diplomatic correspondence, see *Foedera*, III pt. 1, p. 8; BN *ms. fr.* 21023, pp. 621-659.

[146] Delisle, *St. Sauveur*, pp. 64-66, 109-111.

[147] *Ibid.*, pp. 68-69, 113-114; Coville, *Etats Norm.*, p. 60.

[148] Cazelles, *Soc. politique*, pp. 179f., 432.   [149] BN NAF 7606, fols. 57r-6or.

fore, that Philip was now proceeding with collection of the second installment of a subsidy in men-at-arms promised the year before.

This document is unique, for all other evidence of taxes in Languedoil during 1347 belongs to the spring and summer. It is therefore possible that Normandy had been unique in 1346, agreeing to spread its grant of men-at-arms over two years. Elsewhere, the subsidies of 1346 may have been for one year only. By the spring of 1347, such taxes would be expiring, whether they were grants of troops by bailiwick assemblies in 1346 or a one-year renewal of the 4 *d./l.* sales tax in default of such grants.

With the government so anxious to regain public trust and with the Chamber of Accounts now thrust into the background, Philip may have deemed it wise not to seek new subsidies before the expiration of the current taxes. Nevertheless, his financial situation remained difficult and the English around Calais were proving steadily stronger. The king's need for money may have been complicated by the position of the nobility. Throughout his reign, Philip had found it wise to cultivate this class, especially in times when his position was weak. Nobles had generally succeeded in obtaining guarantees of their privileges and support for their claims of tax exemption. As recently as 1346, those of Languedoc had received such sympathetic treatment.[150] The battle of Crécy, however, had been a major disaster for the French nobility, not merely in terms of casualties, but also in terms of prestige. The king's position in the winter of 1346-1347 was far from enviable, but if scapegoats were desired, the nobility as a class was extremely vulnerable. Their military role was the major theoretical basis for their social status and their claims of fiscal privilege. Moreover, despite their economic difficulties during the past century, the nobles still controlled an important part of the wealth of France. On previous occasions when Philip VI had been politically weak or financially embarrassed, his difficulty generally had been due to the fact that his subjects questioned the justification for taxes. Such occasions arose when there was little or no military action and the kingdom did not feel threatened. Frugal burghers dominated by a sense of local self-interest could make common cause with nobles desirous of booty and glory. The political importance of the latter dictated conciliatory measures. At Crécy, however, the nobles finally had their chance for a pitched battle and were found deficient, while the bourgeoisie of northern France began to learn the meaning of *evidens necessitas*. The increased vulnerability of the aristocracy becomes apparent in the fiscal documents beginning in 1347. Grants of subsidies by the towns increasingly included the requirement that all persons, of what-

[150] See above, notes 92-94.

ever status, contribute to the tax. In his orders to the tax commissioner in the Gisors district, Philip gave an early indication of the changing sentiment by making it clear that the subsidy was to be collected in everybody's lands.

There is additional evidence that Philip was prepared to deal more sternly with the nobility. His next fiscal expedient was a massive confiscation of debts contracted with Italian moneylenders in defiance of the usury laws. There were several precedents for such action, but in the case of 1347-1348, there are indications that the crown sought particularly to tap the assets of the noble class. According to one chronicler, the crown extorted *ingentes pecunias* to succour the town of Calais.[151] Another contemporary reported that Philip took action against the Lombards around mid-Lent of 1347.[152] Documentary evidence substantiates these reports. On 12 February, Philip VI secretly ordered his bailiffs and seneschals to arrest Italian moneylenders, seize their property, and annul their contracts. On the 20th, the crown ordered Lombards banished from the kingdom, a step which had sometimes preceded a large extortion in the past.[153] On this occasion, the banishment order may have been genuine, but restricted to a few Italian companies accused of "excesses." In any case, the government soon began to collect from debtors the principal they had borrowed at usury from certain Italian moneylenders.[154] These proceedings were already underway on 19 March, when the *Parlement* issued a judgment against usurers. According to this document, they had so oppressed the king's subjects, noble and non-noble, as to prevent "the said nobles and others from aiding us in our wars." Consequently, the king was seizing the debts owed to culpable Lombards.[155]

This judgment of the *Parlement* is worded in such a way that it appears to stress nobles. One infers, moreover, that nobles had complained of the oppressions of usurers when seeking to avoid paying subsidies. There is little doubt that many nobles were indebted to the Lombards, including such an important man as Robert de Fiennes, future constable of France.[156] By confiscating the principal of these debts, Philip VI could

[151] J. Lemoine (ed.), *Chronique de Richard Lescot, moine de Saint-Denis (1328-1344). Continuation de cette chronique (1344-1364)*, Paris, 1896, pp. 74-75.

[152] *Gr. Chron.*, IX, 291.

[153] Cazelles, *Soc. politique*, p. 279; *HL*, IX, 602; BN *ms. fr.* 7222, p. 103.

[154] Henneman, "Italians," p. 35. The Scarampi seem to have been the crown's main target in the next few months (*ibid.*, notes 85-86).

[155] AN x 2a 5, fol. 97.

[156] E. Garnier, "Biographie de Robert de Fiennes, connétable de France (1320-1384)," *BEC*, XIII (1852), 27. Another important debtor, also a well-placed royal military commander, was Jean de Nesle (AN AB xix 2643, note on BN *ms. fr.* 6212, no. 6). On the nobles as debtors generally, see Henneman, "Italians," note 95.

pose as a reformer while collecting large sums from the nobility without making an issue of their privileges. Viewed in this light, the debt seizure of 1347 appears to be one of the more ingenious fiscal expedients of Philip's reign.

The king's profit, moreover, was not restricted to the collection of the debts. A curious feature of the confiscation of 1347, which distinguishes it from earlier actions of this type, is the fact that many of the transactions with debtors were registered at the royal chancery. There are nearly seventy such entries for 1347 and 1348, almost half of them before the end of April 1347, at the very time that Philip was busily trying to raise money for an army which might rescue Calais. The typical transaction was one in which the king accepted less than the actual debt (sometimes less than one-third) and declared the debtor quit of his obligations. Where the social class of the debtor can be determined, the overwhelming majority are nobles. In an effort to gain money quickly, the government often accepted much less than what could be claimed as the principal of the loan,[157] but it reaped substantial profits from chancery fees. A letter patent sealed with a double *queue* cost nearly 64 *sols*, which equaled the price of a cow in the fourteenth century. Charters sealed in green wax cost nearly triple this amount. A significant number of debtors to the Lombards were prepared to purchase expensive formal documents of this type to spare themselves future harassment.[158]

The many transactions recorded at the Chancery, provide much more documentation than is available for earlier seizures of debts to Lombards. This cannot have been an accident. Unquestionably, the government did what it could to encourage wealthy debtors to protect themselves by purchasing expensive charters. Many of the debtors, however, were probably not wealthy, and for these, the confiscation must have posed a grave hardship. The crown, however, had no reason to impoverish or antagonize the nobility. Its objective was purely fiscal—to obtain money with which to raise an effective army. This allowed considerable flexibility in approaching the debtors. Therefore, the king permitted some nobles to discharge the principal of their debts in a manner fully consistent with their social values. They were merely to render a certain amount of military service at their own expense.[159]

Thus the usury laws furnished Philip VI with a highly effective and

---

[157] *Ibid.*, p. 37. [158] Bautier, "Chancellerie," pp. 375, 380.

[159] *LC*, no. 182, and note 1 to this document. Cazelles states that this method for discharging the debts proved inconvenient and was not generalized. That the method was used at all is an indication of the awkward financial circumstances of some nobles.

politically safe devise for exploiting the financial resources of the aristocracy. It is likely that the nobility contributed far more to the royal war effort in 1347 than in any previous year of the reign.[160] Besides the sums obtained from them through the debt confiscation, the government also persuaded them to participate more fully in war subsidies.

When the crown next took up the question of subsidies, it was mid-March, and the documents which have survived deal primarily with regional assemblies in those parts of the kingdom closest to Calais. The king obviously felt that his best chance of obtaining money for an army to raise the siege lay in appealing to those subjects who would feel most seriously threatened by an English occupation of Calais.

On 18 March, Philip VI wrote to the town of Reims asking that two to four of the "best advised" persons be sent to consult with him without delay, and that the letter be answered as soon as received.[161] For some reason, this document was not received in Reims until 1 April, the day when representatives of Picard towns met at Amiens and agreed to reconvene on the 16th to take action regarding Calais. The king ordered the *échevins* of Reims to have a reply ready at this second meeting.[162] About the same time, the towns of the Oise valley were called to a meeting which appears to have met at Montdidier around the first of May.[163] The towns of Artois were ordered on 14 April to send representatives to still another assembly, this one on 1 June.[164]

It appears that Reims did not grant a tax at the assembly of Picard towns, perhaps because the citizens were worried about their own defense. On 11 May, the king's lieutenant in Vermandois requisitioned a war engine over the protests of the local clergy, while the king reassured the *échevins* about their own defense and ordered the bailiff to enforce the *arrière-ban*. It is not clear in this case whether the king was applying pressure to obtain a subsidy or whether he actually wanted reinforcements. The royal lieutenant in Vermandois had been told to raise men and equipment for a local military operation.[165] Since Crécy, the north-

---

[160] The largest contribution from the nobles in the quarter-century preceding 1347 was the fiftieth collected from them in parts of the kingdom in 1340. It will be seen below that the nobility of one region paid 2½% in 1347, and when one includes personal service, the debt confiscation, and the growing taxation of tallageable dependents of seigneurs, it seems clear that the aristocracy contributed much more than usual in the year after Crécy.

[161] Varin, *Reims*, II, 1145. Cf. Viard, "Ressources," p. 200, and Vuitry, *Régime financier*, II, 27.

[162] *LC*, no. 181; Varin, *Reims*, II, 1151.   [163] *Ibid.*, p. 1145; *LC*, no. 185.

[164] AN AB xix 2638, note from AM Arras AA 2, no. 52.

[165] *LC*, no. 186; Varin, *Reims*, II, 1153-1154, and notes.

ern towns had suffered a loss of confidence and were fearful of a possible English attack.[166]

After the assemblies of northern towns, Philip VI issued an ordinance of reform in May, indicating that he had been granted a subsidy. The tax was to be collected by a group of five commissioners who were to make sure that all nobles and non-nobles contributed.[167] The tax appears to have been expressed as a number of men-at-arms, but at Saint-Quentin it took the form of a 4 d./l. sales tax, which met some clerical resistance.[168] Collection of the money in Vermandois was reinforced by the *arrière-ban*. On 27 April, all inhabitants were called to arms, and Philip ordered the bailiff two weeks later to enforce the summons.[169] The *échevins* of Reims sent a contingent of troops, but their equipment and behavior was evidently not up to standards. In June, the crown ordered stern measures against citizens who owed service but had not rendered it, while those who had left the army were to return immediately or be pronounced traitors.[170] It appears that even during a major military campaign, Philip VI was encountering obstacles, not only in raising men and money but in enforcing essential orders.

The nobles of Vermandois had been summoned to the army as early as 12 March, but the response was mediocre and Philip had to issue a new call to arms six weeks later.[171] In June, the king ordered seizures of the property of those who failed to come, and took steps to counter various kinds of evasion.[172] The government was taking a much stronger position towards the nobles than it had in the years before Crécy. It is clear that it wanted money from them rather than personal service. The king's German and Spanish mercenaries had to be paid, and he had found it necessary to send an urgent request to the queen at Paris for funds with which to pay them.[173] The queen may have been charged with negotiations with the nobles of the Ile-de-France, for while Philip was still at Montdidier, he wrote her a second letter rejecting the suggestion that these nobles serve at their own expense.[174]

---

[166] Guesnon, "Documents," pp. 236-240.

[167] *Ord.*, ii, 262-263; Moreau de Beaumont, *Mémoire*, iii, 231. The five royal commissioners were to be the bishop of Laon, the abbots of Saint-Denis and Marmoutier, and two lay councillors of the king.

[168] Le Maire, *St. Quentin*, ii, no. 633.

[169] Varin, *Reims*, ii, 1124, note 2; see above, note 165.

[170] Varin, *Reims*, ii, 1153, note 2, and 1154, nos. 566 and 568. It is possible (*ibid.*, p. 1166) that Philip VI did eventually obtain a levy of 4 d./l. at Reims.

[171] *Ibid.*, p. 1124, note 2.

[172] *Ibid.*, pp. 1124, note 2, and 1154, no. 567 and note 2.

[173] Gasnault, "Nouvelles lettres . . . ," pp. 177-178.   [174] *LC*, no. 184.

By 18 June, nobles of the Ile-de-France "graciously granted" a subsidy of 2½ percent of the value of their landed property. Wealthy non-nobles, with property worth more than 100 pounds, would pay at the same rate for their property outside towns, including movables and inheritances. The non-nobles were excused from host service and from any other aid in the present year except for *arrière-ban après bataille*. The money was to be collected by local men who would pay the troops directly. The king authorized these *élus* to use coercion against subjects of nobles or clergy who might resist paying.[175] It seems clear that the government was determined to tap the resources of wealthy persons who had escaped large taxes in the past when 4 *d./l.* sales taxes had been the rule in Languedoil. It is also clear that these taxpayers were determined to specify the kind of emergency which would justify new tax requests— an *arrière-ban* such as had followed the disaster at Crécy, not simply an "ordinary" *arrière-ban*, which had been so overworked as to lose credibility.

Vuitry and Viard thought the king had been so encouraged by the assemblies of the spring that he had simply ordered this direct tax on all the nobles and non-nobles of the kingdom.[176] In fact, however, the tax was regional in character, was limited to certain kinds of property, and was evidently granted after negotiations and not merely imposed. It paralleled whatever taxes had been granted by the towns. The long succession of threats, summonses, and royal letters which proved necessary in Vermandois suggests that the response of the towns had not, in fact, been very encouraging at all. The crown obtained a new clerical tenth in July when the previous three-year tenth had expired,[177] but levied no other subsidies on the northern clergy. Such assemblies as occurred in the first half of 1347, appear to have been local in nature, restricted to a single class, and concerned with taxes of a stop-gap nature. The original plan of 1346, which would have disassociated subsidies from the *arrière-ban* and tied them to long-range military needs, was not pursued. It remained available, however, as a precedent for the future.

In Auvergne, the towns engaged in extensive consultations concerning the *gabelle* during the first two months of 1347. Montferrand sent envoys to other towns and to the king, finally obtaining a sealed document from Paris. The man who accomplished this mission then attended an assembly at Riom, in April, which concluded a transaction with the crown re-

---

175 AN AB xix 2636, a text copied from Bibliothèque de Rouen which described a grant from those of the *cort de France et de Dunoys.*

176 Viard, "Ressources," p. 200; Vuitry, *Régime financier*, II, 27-28.

177 AN P 2292, p. 69.

garding the *gabelle*.[178] Since the sources do not mention salt, the *gabelle* could mean any sales tax, but it is probable that these discussions involved repeal of the tax on salt. While they were in progress, certain nobles, clergy, and bourgeois granted a sales tax of 6 *d./l.* to royal commissioners.[179] This tax must be the "imposition for men-at-arms" being levied at Riom in May in the face of opposition.[180] It is not clear whether Montferrand was subject to this tax, but the town did contribute troops after agreement was reached on the *gabelle*. Supporting five men-at-arms for six months, Montferrand paid 342 *l.t.*, beginning with a first installment of 200 pounds late in July.[181] In the adjacent bailiwick of the Mountains, Aurillac was to pay a *finance* of 500 florins for the *arrière-ban* but the sum was not paid four years later when the king agreed to reduce it if payment was made immediately.[182]

In Normandy, where the king had made his earliest attempt to raise money in 1347, the tax is called an imposition in one text and a *fouage* in another.[183] It is entirely possible that the Normans were paying for men-at-arms as they had in 1345, with each parish and group of hearths being assessed a certain amount. In another document, however, the king ordered two Norman bailiffs to have everybody with land and revenues contribute to "the two impositions" for the war.[184] Assuming that the first of these was the *fouage*, the second tax was probably a levy on the property of nobles such as that being collected in the Ile-de-France.[185]

It is clear that these taxes were not sufficient to supply the military needs of the crown. Godefroy d'Harcourt, now French commander in lower Normandy, had such difficulty paying his troops that he had to use the domainal revenues held by the receiver of Caen, to prevent desertions.[186] One reason for his difficulty was that Philip VI, in Picardy, was absorbing subsidy receipts as fast as they accumulated. The receiver of Gisors was ordered to send Norman *fouage* receipts to Amiens.[187]

---

[178] *INV AM Montferrand*, I, 370 (CC 162).

[179] AM Riom CC 10, no. 640. The crown guaranteed non-prejudice.

[180] *Ibid.*, CC 7, no. 812.

[181] *INV AM Montferrand*, I, 370-371 (CC 162); and II, 1 (CC 333), for the receipt for 200 pounds.

[182] *INV AM Aurillac*, I, 403 (CC 8).

[183] Delisle, *Actes norm.*, pp. 353-354; BN *ms. fr.* 25699, no. 69.

[184] Coville, *Etats Norm.*, p. 50, citing Delisle, *Actes norm.*, pp. 351-352.

[185] See above, note 175. The royal order that those in Normandy with land and revenues contribute to the imposition surely suggests that one of them was a tax on land and revenues like that in the Ile-de-France.

[186] Viard, "La France," p. 393. See also *LC*, no. 197.

[187] Delisle, *Actes norm.*, p. 352.

Despite such efforts, however, the laboriously acquired tax grants produced sums which trickled in much too slowly to accomplish the payment of the army to relieve Calais. When, in July, Philip VI finally decided to make a last desperate attempt to save the town, he once again had to ask the local towns for men rather than money. Abbeville was asked to rush men to the king by 19 July, when he was to undertake the relief of the city in accordance with the recommendations of the barons, prelates, and bourgeois.[188] The town's normal military obligation was 50 sergeants and 50 crossbowmen, but on this occasion they responded with a contingent of 200 men, and Philip declared them exempt from any subsequent *arrière-ban*.[189] Only a month before, Philip clearly preferred to have money with which to pay mercenaries, but he now was apparently prepared to accept any troops that might help him. His effort to relieve Calais was in vain, however, and the city fell on 4 August.[190] Not only had one French army been destroyed by a relatively small English force, but Philip had allowed that force to remain eleven months more on French territory and capture an important port of entry. Whatever lack of money may have had to do with this failure, the fall of Calais exposed the inadequacies of the government even more than did the battle of Crécy. Within weeks, serious discontent with the monarchy became evident.

4. The Great Subsidy of 1347-1348 and the Black Death

The first, and perhaps strongest, indications of this discontent came from the extreme North, the regions closest to Calais, where the king issued a new call to arms on 1 September 1347.[191] This summons was but another reminder of royal exactions, and for a cause that now appeared lost. By the middle of the month, the barons, prelates, and non-nobles of the province of Reims were demanding the right "to assemble for certain great concerns touching the said [king's] majesty and them[selves], on the matter of the present wars."[192] This request is an important indica-

---

[188] *LC*, no. 192; AD Lot, F 187.   [189] BN Moreau 231, fol. 94r-v.

[190] Perroy, *The Hundred Years War*, p. 120. See *Foedera*, III pt. 1, p. 16, for Edward III's intention to repopulate the town with English settlers. Philip VI diverted some of the funds obtained from the debtors to Lombards, using the money to relieve dispossessed bourgeois from Calais: AN JJ 78, no. 169.

[191] *LC*, no. 193; Guesnon, "Documents," p. 242. This summons was probably limited to a few places which had not paid. The remainder of this chapter is a revised version of my article, "Black Death," pp. 406-416. Reprinted by permission of the editor of *Speculum*.

[192] Texts from AN K 44, no. 12, published by V. de Beauvillé, *Histoire de la ville de Montdidier* (2nd. edn.), Paris, 1875, pp. 510-511.

tion of the king's loss of initiative and also reflects a greater spirit of co-operation among the three Estates of this region than they had displayed in the recent past. Philip did authorize the nobles and clergy to hold an assembly, but his letter was delayed in transmission and the meeting may not have taken place.[193] Two new developments made it less appropriate to hold one.

The first of these developments was an Anglo-French truce, which Edward III was prepared to accept now that he had secured a valuable seaport on the French coast. The papacy was pressing for peace, and in September, Edward empowered proctors to negotiate the truce. On the 28th, it was agreed that hostilities throughout France and the Low Countries would be suspended until 8 July 1348.[194] The second important development occurred on 10 October 1347, when Philip VI summoned the three Estates of the kingdom to meet at Paris on 30 November.[195] Whether or not the king hoped to regain the initiative by this action, the summons may have persuaded the magnates of the province of Reims that their proposed local meeting was no longer necessary.

Cazelles has suggested another political factor of some importance, arguing that disaffected subjects desired an assembly and looked to the heir of the throne, John of Normandy, to lead their drive for reforms.[196] John did obtain considerably more authority at this time, being given personal control of his Norman *apanage* for the first time. He established his own administration, staffed by men who would remain in his service after he became king. He also was given the right to hold assemblies and raise subsidies, and he soon convened an assembly of the Norman Estates in November.[197]

The duke of Normandy celebrated his increased authority as a "joyous accession," and perhaps this fact inspired the Normans to display more generosity than usual.[198] In any case, the assembly granted the extremely large sum of 450,000 pounds, a sum far greater than the war subsidy col-

---

[193] *Ibid.*; Varin, *Reims*, II, 1161, no. 572; Cazelles, *Soc. politique*, p. 215.

[194] *Foedera*, III pt. I, pp. 20-22.

[195] Varin, *Reims*, II, 1161-1162; AN AB xix 2639 (from AM Lille, cartulary 1302); AM Riom AA 31; *INV AM Montferrand*, I, 373 (CC 162). According to Boudet, "Etats d'Issoire," the three Estates of Auvergne met on 27 October 1347, by which time they would have received the summons to Paris. Perhaps the local assembly drew up a list of grievances.

[196] Cazelles, *Soc. politique*, pp. 213-229.

[197] *Ibid.*; Coville, *Etats Norm.*, pp. 344-345.

[198] AN JJ 79A, no. 2, uses this term. For John's exploitation of his "joyous accession" to the kingship three years later, see the next chapter and Henneman, "Black Death," pp. 421f.

lected from the entire kingdom twenty years before. Probably because of the truce, collection would not begin until March, and other significant conditions governed the grant. The tax was expressed in terms of the salaries of troops, with each Norman parish to support one man-at-arms for one year at a daily wage of 6 *sols parisis*. During the year, no other tax was to be levied, not even the tenth on the clergy which had been authorized by the pope. In general, the money was to be raised by a sales tax of 8 *d./l.* (3.3 percent) on merchandise, half payable by the buyer and half by the seller. No exemptions from paying were to be tolerated but no rights or privileges would be prejudiced for the future. In each of the five Norman bailiwicks, a three-man board (one representative from each estate) was to supervise collection, while three men representing the whole duchy were to sit at Rouen and inspect accounts.[199] This action by a Norman assembly provided the rest of the kingdom with a useful model to follow in considering a subsidy for 1348.

The Estates summoned to meet at Paris on 30 November had been enjoined to come with adequate instructions to preclude any "reference back" to localities.[200] The summons did not mention the matters to be discussed, but it must have been evident to all that the kingdom faced a serious fiscal and military situation despite the respite of a truce. When they assembled, the representatives were rather outspoken in criticizing the government for failing to defend the realm adequately despite endless military summonses and numerous unpopular taxes.[201]

As to what transpired while the Estates were in session, we are left with little direct evidence. From the vague account of one chronicler,[202] Vuitry concluded that the assembly confined itself to the utterance of "patriotic sentiments."[203] In fact, however, there must have been considerable bargaining and discussion. For one thing, the representatives were in Paris for a period in excess of two weeks, an unusually long session for this time.[204] In addition, certain clear results emerged from the

---

[199] Coville, *Etats Norm.*, pp. 345-351; Delisle, *Actes norm.*, pp. 356-361. Some of the conditions governing the tax were described in a royal letter of late January 1348, while the rest were published early in March when the collection was to begin.

[200] See Taylor, "1318," pp. 300-302.   [201] Guesnon, "Documents," pp. 242-244.

[202] *Gr. Chron.*, IX, 312, states that the Estates advocated an invasion of England and offered the aid of their persons and property.

[203] Vuitry, *Régime financier*, II, 29.

[204] *INV AM Montferrand*, I, 373 (CC 162), indicates that deputies from this Auvergne community were absent from home for twenty-eight days. According to Petit, *Essai de restitution*, p. 188, the round trip took twelve days. The representatives thus probably spent sixteen days in Paris, a much longer time than that re-

meeting. Already, some new members had been introduced into the royal council, men who were close to John of Normandy. Further changes now took place, including the replacement of the chancellor. These alterations in the personnel of the royal administration reduced the influence of Philip VI's unpopular fiscal experts and provided an important precedent for the more drastic personnel changes to be demanded by the Estates in 1356-1357.[205] Besides these criticisms of the government and the changes in the royal council, the Estates of 1347 seem to have forced the king to halt an incipient return to the coinage debasement which had been so unpopular in past years.[206] In addition, the Estates must have lent their support to the measures taken earlier against Italian moneylenders and their debtors. Where the debt seizure previously may have been restricted to certain companies and certain classes of debtors, it was now made general. In an ordinance of 28 December 1347, the crown ordered collection of the principal and cancellation of the interest on all usurious debts. It was estimated that total outstanding debts amounted to two million pounds, of which 60 percent represented principal.[207]

Of all the developments to emerge from this meeting of the Estates General, the most important one was the early dispatch of commissioners throughout the realm to collect a very large subsidy. By March of 1348, the greater part of the kingdom had agreed to the precise mode of payment, and it seems clear that considerable preliminary agreement had been reached while the Estates were in session. Different regions adopted taxes that differed a good deal in *form*, but all agreed to pay unusually large amounts, and many of the conditions of payment were common to the whole kingdom. Moreover, the specific regional tax agreements were reached rather more promptly than was usual for the reign of Philip VI. Although the king had not persuaded the Estates to grant a tax so binding as to preclude subsequent local discussion, relatively few details must have been left to these local meetings. It is not surprising that regionalism in France was still too strong for the Estates to agree on every detail while they were in session. When such a step was attempted by an assembly eight years later, the tax which followed encountered serious local hostility.[208]

---

quired for the Estates of 1346, although shorter than the period suggested by Cazelles, *Soc. politique*, pp. 224-225.

[205] *Ibid.*, pp. 216f.; Henneman, "Black Death," note 16.

[206] *Ibid.*, note 17. It will be seen in Appendix I, Table I, that the price of a mark of silver was reduced from 9 *l.t.* to 5.5 *l.t.* in January 1348.

[207] *Ord.*, II, 418-420.   [208] See below, Chapter VIII.

A survey of the regional subsidy agreements of early 1348 will make clear the magnitude of the tax and suggest those common characteristics on which some agreement must have been reached at the Paris assembly. Perhaps a week after the Estates General had disbanded, the three orders of the viscounty and provostship of Paris agreed to a large subsidy of 1,500 mounted troops to be paid 6 *s.p.* daily for six months. In return for the 81,000 *l.p.* thus granted, the crown agreed to conditions similar to those already adopted in Normandy, with perhaps minor changes in emphasis. Persons designated (*élus*) by the Estates would superintend the tax; neither the clerical tenth nor any other tax would be collected during the year 1348; and no exemptions from paying would be tolerated.[209] In Vermandois, the three Estates granted a sales tax of 6 *d./l.* (2½ percent) subject to the same conditions. This bailiwick was subdivided into five special fiscal districts, each assigned three *élus*.[210] The two bailiwicks of Auvergne and the Mountains, in a combined assembly of their three Estates, also agreed to a 6 *d./l.* levy.[211] The Bourges district established a sales tax of 8 *d./l.* to meet an assessment of 500 men-at-arms,[212] and there is evidence of the subsidy in the bailiwicks of Senlis, Orléans, Meaux, and Touraine.[213]

In Languedoc, there were more variations as to form of payment and a lower troop salary was used in computing the subsidy. In the seneschalsy of Toulouse, which agreed to support 1,500 men if the truce should end as expected,[214] each *jugerie* demanded special royal concessions of local interest in addition to the basic conditions established throughout the northern bailiwicks. Thus the *jugerie* of Villelongue, while agreeing to maintain eighty-seven of the men-at-arms at a cost of 10,440 *l.t.*, obtained the promise that no *réformateurs* would be sent into

[209] BN *ms. fr.* 8605, fol. 29. This was the only tax grant based on troop salaries for six months. The others were for one year.

[210] Varin, *Reims*, II, 1168-1174. Collections were to be turned over to a receiver general who would then pay the troops. Some receipts and pay orders from later in the year document this process in Vermandois: BN Clairambault 34, no. 14; Clairambault 78, nos. 118, 119, 123, 124.

[211] Boudet, "Etats d'Issoire," pp. 35, 62-65.   [212] *JT Ph. VI*, no. 2010.

[213] For Senlis, Furgeot, *Actes*, II, no. 8916; AN P 2292, p. 115; for Meaux, a 6 *d./l.* sales tax mentioned in *JT Ph. VI*, no. 2457; for Orléans, BN Clairambault 213, no. 3. In Touraine, the local Estates met in February, according to P. Viollet, *Histoire des institutions politiques et administratives de la France*, Paris, 1903, III, p. 236.

[214] *HL*, IX, 610. A document in AD Basses-Pyrénées E 405, no. 124, indicates that inhabitants of the county of Foix and of lands held in *paréage* with the Church were excused from paying. Dated 29 February, it probably belongs to 1348 (1347 old style) rather than to 1341, which is a later archivist's reading of the date.

the region and that violators of monetary ordinances would not be prosecuted.[215] The seneschalsy of Carcassonne chose a hearth tax of 20 *s.t.*, which some communities converted into a lump-sum payment.[216] The Beaucaire district, like that of Toulouse, was assessed 1,500 troops and, in general, adopted a 4 *d./l.* sales tax. Added concessions were demanded by some towns. Nîmes obtained a cancellation of unpaid taxes owed from the previous year by tallageable subjects of the nobles and clergy. In addition, all taxes were to halt if the war should end, and soldiers sent from Nîmes were to be the first ones paid with the money collected from their city.[217] Montpellier promised 6,000 *l.t.* to avoid the sales tax altogether. The royal commissioners promised this town that no more taxes or loans would be sought before mid-1349 and that privileged persons would be required to contribute.[218] For Rouergue, we have only fragmentary evidence of the negotiations at the local level.[219]

From the foregoing evidence, we may conclude that final arrangements for the collection of a large subsidy had been made within three months after the December assembly in Paris and much more promptly in many cases. Compared with most other years of Philip VI's reign, the negotiations had been completed speedily, despite the truce that was in effect. Moreover, the regional agreements had many common characteristics. All described the tax in terms of the salary of mounted troops at a designated daily wage. All were subject to letters of non-prejudice, and all were to be applied exclusively to the support of an army and collected by *élus* of the three Estates of the region in question.[220] In every case, there were to be no exemptions from paying, no other taxes during

[215] BN Doat 81, fols. 99v-119v; BN *Coll. Languedoc* 84, fols. 381r-385v. It is apparent from these figures that the salary scale on which the grant was based was only 6 *s.* 8 *d.* in Languedoc. Consistent with Languedoc's tendency to bargain for more concessions, this rate was 8 *d.p.* lower than that being used in the North.

[216] *INV AM Pézenas*, no. 1640. BN Doat 53, fols. 133-138v, indicates that Narbonne paid 2,200 *l.t.* for its share.

[217] AM Nîmes NN 1, nos. 30-32; Ménard, *Nismes*, II, *preuves*, 135-137.

[218] *Gr. Chartrier*, nos. 2032, 3976.

[219] AM Millau CC 345, fol. 102v and loose booklet inside the register, indicate a series of trips by representatives of the town to work out details of a lump-sum payment.

[220] Exceptions to the general establishment of *élus* may be found in Languedoc, where many of the larger towns paid lump sums to the crown and arranged their own way of raising the money. The practical results were the same as those obtained by using *élus*, except that privileged persons were perhaps in a better position to evade payment. Because lump sums had long been used by the larger southern towns, the *élu* was never regarded there as a great reform and did not achieve permanence. This tradition may explain why Languedoc demanded more concessions and computed the tax on a lower troop salary.

the year. In most cases, the subsidy was not to be levied after the conclusion of peace. These prompt agreements, with so many common features, can only suggest that the Paris assembly had done a good deal more than merely accept the principle of a subsidy. The Estates must have used the Norman grant as a model and agreed to apply similar conditions to the whole kingdom.

Of the few details that were left to be ironed out locally, the most important was the form the tax would take. Variations in form and demands for additional royal concessions were fairly widespread in Languedoc. On the other hand, the Paris assembly must have agreed on the *amount* each district would pay,[221] as well as most of the basic conditions attached to the grant. Of these conditions, the *élu* system was the most important. Generalizing a scheme tried earlier in some localities, it would ultimately become the basis for a new administration to deal with extraordinary revenues. Since 1345, the crown had sought a nationwide grant of men-at-arms with local appointees to collect the taxes. Now, at last, this plan was to be put into effect.

The most striking thing about the subsidy of 1347-1348, however, was its magnitude. Although actual totals are lacking, we know the number of mounted troops which five regions (Normandy, Paris, Bourges, Toulouse, and Beaucaire) intended to support and the salaries at which these troops were to serve. Their annual wages alone would amount to 978,750 *l.t.*, more than triple the receipts of the entire war subsidy of 1328. Yet this total was granted by regions containing only about one-third of the hearths in the kingdom. If taxes were assessed on the rest of the realm at about the same rate, the French kingdom must have expected to pay nearly three million pounds in all during 1348.[222] In the same period, moreover, the papacy resumed its generous loans. Philip VI obtained 12,000 florins at the end of 1347 and another 450,000 during the first five months of 1348. In addition, Clement VI relieved Philip's conscience by canceling a royal debt of 2,800,000 florins representing the many loans and tenths collected by the king and his predecessors for cru-

---

[221] That is, the number of troops each district would supply, and the salary to be used in computing their cost, seem to have been decided upon at Paris. Except for the different salary scale between the Midi and the North, we find great consistency, and there is no evidence that any district balked at all over this point. Local negotiations dealt with the form of the tax and sometimes other matters of purely local interest, but this bargaining was not protracted and does not seem to have dealt at all with the amount of tax.

[222] See Henneman, "Black Death," p. 412, and notes. For the hearth count of 1328, see Lot, "L'état," pp. 15-107.

sades that were never undertaken. The final reckoning, towards 1360, indicated that the Avignon papacy had contributed a total of 3,517,000 florins to the French crown and another 100,000 florins to certain great lords of France.[223] The loans of early 1348 helped keep the crown supplied with funds during the period before significant subsidy collections would be available. The papal contribution augmented the anticipated yield of the subsidy by about 15 percent, and there was thus considerable promise early in 1348 that a reformed royal government would be able to place the crown's finances on a sound footing at last. Supported by the papacy and the Estates of the realm, this development might have had significant consequences if permitted to proceed without interruption. The prestige and effectiveness of assemblies might have been greatly increased. The three Estates had already made substantial progress during 1347 in developing a greater capacity for coordinated action. The trend seemed unmistakably to point towards a more effective role for a central assembly.

It was in this situation that the Black Death made its appearance, reaching Languedoc towards the beginning of Lent 1348.[224] By October, high mortality was being reported as far north as Rouen; towns found their cemetery space inadequate; burghers fled in panic from populated centers.[225] It has long been accepted that the impact on taxation was considerable,[226] but demographic effects varied from one region to another and generalizations are risky. Cazelles has suggested that the death rate in Languedoil was much less than in the Midi, and that the heaviest mortality in the North was among children and the poorer classes of adults. This conclusion suggests that those most able to pay taxes were least affected by the plague. The decline in taxable hearths would thus have been spread over the next decade as France began to feel the loss of the children of 1348.[227] In Languedoc, the case of Albi shows that

[223] Faucon, "Prêts," pp. 573-574. In return for their generosity, the pope and his family were well treated by the king. Assignments of money and fiscal privileges to the count of Beaufort are found in AN JJ 81, nos. 404, 412-414, 417-421; AN K 46, nos. 1-15; K 44, no. 4; AM Alès, 1 S-28. Cf. Faucon, "Prêts," p. 577; Lacoste, *Quercy*, III, 83.

[224] HL, IX, 608-609.

[225] AN JJ 79A, no. 30; Thierry, *Recueil*, I, 544-545; A. Bonal, *Histoire des évêques de Rodez*, Rodez, 1938, II, 579f.; Albe, "Cahors INV," no. 415.

[226] "Taxable material melted like snow in the sun," according to Perroy, *The Hundred Years War*, p. 123.

[227] R. Cazelles, "La peste de 1348-1349 en langue d'oil, épidémie proletarienne et enfantine," *BPH*, 1962, pp. 298-299, 303-305.

towns may have lost three-quarters of their population to the plague but that the urban population recovered somewhat in the next decade. Many of the survivors were better off economically than before, and the number of those too poor to be taxed declined significantly.[228] Perpignan suffered heavy losses among well-to-do, middle-aged people, judging from Emery's statistics for scribes and notaries.[229]

The fate of the scribes and notaries at Perpignan suggests one important result of the plague—a loss of trained administrative personnel. Collection of the subsidy depended on royal officials, tax farmers, and persons named as *élus*. Like scribes and notaries, these were essential persons, but now their ranks were depleted by death and flight, their efficiency impaired by grief and fear.[230] A consequence of this situation is that we have relatively fewer documents for the period from mid-1348 to early 1350. The plague created chaos at the royal court: one-third of the royal notaries perished, as did the queen, the duchess of Normandy, and finally the chancellor. For an extended period, Philip VI traveled from village to village in Brie and Gâtinais, without his chancellor and with the royal council dispersed.[231]

The limited surviving evidence leaves no doubt as to the fate of the large subsidy granted in 1347-1348. The Estates of Senlis begged to have reduced the number of men-at-arms they were committed to support.[232] The Normans, who seem to have increased their earlier grant at a new assembly in May 1348, were unable to convene in a subsequent meeting scheduled for July, and the collectors of taxes began to encounter opposition.[233] In Languedoc, which had been hard-hit by the plague, the effects

---

[228] Prat, "Albi et la peste noire," passim.

[229] R. Emery, "The Black Death of 1348 in Perpignan," *Speculum*, XLII (1967), 614-616.

[230] M. Cazelles has stressed to me in a letter the importance of this administrative chaos. It appears that a number of royal officials had died without rendering their accounts, and the government demanded satisfaction from their executors and heirs: AN PP 117, pp. 629-630, 632, 642.

[231] Bautier, "Chancellerie," pp. 357-359.   [232] AN P 2292, p. 115.

[233] It appears that an assembly at Pont Audemer in May agreed to increase the Norman grant in return for additional royal promises including more effective local control of collection machinery and allocation of one-third of the receipts to local defenses. In the summer, however, collection of taxes began to break down. See Delisle, *Actes norm.*, pp. 369-370; BN Clairambault 212, no. 103; Coville, *Etats Norm.*, pp. 61-62. Some taxes continued to be collected in Normandy, however: BN *ms. fr.* 25699, nos. 75-77; 25998, nos. 487, 491; 25700, no. 34; P. O. 470, *dossier* 10446, no. 2; AN KK 7, fol. 2r.

on taxation were dramatic. Etienne le Galois de la Baume was sent back to Languedoc to resume the post of royal lieutenant which he had held a decade before.[234] In association with a royal councillor, Geoffroi de Charny, he negotiated new arrangements for the subsidy in the seneschalsy of Toulouse, evidence that revenues collected so far were not coming up to expectations.[235] At Cahors, the consuls were struggling to raise money for the rebuilding of local fortifications, and La Baume sought to make the best of a bad situation by urging them to raise funds by fining citizens who had fled the plague and refused to return.[236]

The documents at Montpellier, which are more numerous than elsewhere, reveal the impact of the plague and the difficulties which could arise from slow medieval communications and the rivalries among royal provincial officers. Early in 1348, the town had promised 6,000 l.t. for the support of men-at-arms.[237] Then the arrival of the Black Death disrupted everything, and seven months later, Montpellier still had not been able to pay. The consuls sought relief from Paris, but in October, La Baume's commissioner came to levy a 4 d./l. sales tax since the promised lump sum had not been paid. At length, Montpellier agreed to pay 2,000 pounds, provided that it should be returned if the king canceled the tax because of the plague.[238] At first, Philip merely told La Baume to investigate the mortality at Montpellier and determine what relief ought to be granted, but in December, he took direct action, postponing payment of the subsidy to Easter 1349 and telling the seneschal of Beaucaire not to exert pressure on the town.[239] For several weeks, the consuls were caught

---

[234] Lacoste, *Quercy*, III, 118; Bautier, "Chancellerie," p. 104. On the career of La Baume, see Cazelles, *Soc. politique*, p. 268, note 11; Molinier, *HL*, IX, 498-499, notes.

[235] *HL*, x, cols. 1026-1027, listing the quotas of six *jugeries*, the town of Toulouse, and certain ecclesiastical temporalities. The total tax was over 36,000 l.t., with the share of the *jugerie* of Villelongue to be 7,000 and that of the town of Toulouse to be 4,000. In *HL*, IX, 611, note 2, it is suggested that this tax was in addition to the sums granted earlier in the year. Since the plague reached Languedoc so early, it seems more likely that the July agreement represents a scaled-down subsidy negotiated after the impact of the epidemic had been felt. If so, this document is of great significance, for it indicates a total scarcely more than 20% of the sum needed to support 1,500 men for a year at the salary prevalent in Languedoc. Moreover, the share of the *jugerie* of Villelongue, which had been 5.8% of the sum negotiated during the winter, had risen to 19% of the July grant, while the city of Toulouse was committed to pay only 4,000 pounds, a conservative figure even by the standards prevailing before 1347. One infers that the burden of highly populated Toulouse had been reduced substantially more than that of the less densely populated *jugeries*.

[236] Albe, "Cahors INV," no. 415.   [237] *Gr. Chartrier*, no. 3976.

[238] *Ibid.*, no. 2358.   [239] *Ibid.*, nos. 3977, 3978.

between conflicting orders from La Baume and the seneschal, and in the end they had to make a trip to Paris to clear themselves of disobedience.[240] Finally, on 11 January, they were given a *quittance* for the entire 6,000 pounds, which evidently could not be paid.[241]

Inability to pay the subsidy of 1348 was certainly not limited to Montpellier. At Toulouse, a tax for local fortifications could not be levied, and 17 March 1349, the king authorized the consuls to renew it.[242] Whatever this town's original quota for the subsidy, it had been reduced to 4,000 *l.t.* in July 1348. Early in 1349, La Baume and Charny reduced it to 3,500 *l.t.*, and in March, the king reduced it further, to 2,700 *l.t.*, half to be paid at Easter, the rest late in June.[243]

Limited though it is, this evidence shows unmistakably that the French government was unable to collect more than a fragment of the war subsidy granted during the winter of 1347-1348. The opportunity to regain the military initiative, stabilize royal finances, and capitalize on the cooperation of the Estates was therefore lost. Perhaps the most serious casualty was the development of central representative assemblies. Had the subsidy been collected and the high hopes of early 1348 been realized, the prestige and confidence of central assemblies might have been greatly enhanced, thereby creating the basis for constructive negotiation of taxes on a national level. As it was, however, assemblies representing the entire kingdom now were abandoned. Languedoc began regularly to be treated as a separate region as in 1346, while the Estates of Languedoil were frustrated by new problems when they next attempted to display an initiative comparable to that of 1347.

For Philip VI, the Black Death was the crowning misfortune of a far from happy reign. In the face of many obstacles, both domestic and foreign in origin, he had pursued with considerable tenacity the scheme first developed in 1345—a large grant of men-at-arms from the entire kingdom to replace other taxes and to be financed and collected according to the desires of individual bailiwicks and seneschalsies. Frustrated in 1345 by the absence of an urgent military threat, and in 1346 by the English invasion of Normandy, this plan finally gained the acceptance of his subjects at the end of 1347, only to be frustrated again by a new and greater catastrophe. In the wake of this disaster, the aging monarch was

---

[240] *Ibid.*, nos. 2574, 3979.

[241] For a more detailed discussion of these events, see Henneman, "Black Death," pp. 415-416.

[242] AM Toulouse AA 35, no. 72.

[243] See *HL*, x, cols. 1026-1027, and the discussion above, note 236. The reductions in the town's assessment are in AD Lot F 283.

left without a program. He had been forced to put aside the fiscal experts of the Chamber of Accounts party who had guided his policy since the early years of the war. During the epidemic he lost his queen, on whom he seems to have relied heavily. The initiative had passed from his hands to the duke of Normandy and his followers. In practical terms, the reign of John II may be said to have begun in 1348.[244]

[244] Cazelles, *Soc. politique*, pp. 227-231.

CHAPTER VII

Towards More Uniform Taxation Under John II, 1349-1353

1. Recovery from the Plague

FOLLOWING the plague, every government in Europe faced similar problems in seeking to regain financial stability. The population was reduced and demoralized, yet many had inherited new wealth.[1] The administration was disorganized and the economy dislocated, but costly warfare was temporarily interrupted. In studying the Italian town of Siena, William Bowsky found that the Sienese recouped municipal finances within five years' time by laying heavy emphasis on indirect taxes and forced loans from the wealthy rather than attempting to collect on the basis of households remaining.[2] There are some similarities between Sienese municipal policy and the approach used by the French royal government, especially as regards indirect taxes. Sales taxes had long been the most familiar type of levy in northern and central France. The subsidy granted in 1347-1348 marked their first increase over the 4 *d./l.* which had been common during most of Philip VI's reign. During the decade of the 1350s they would continue to rise, reaching 12 *d./l.* (5 percent) everywhere by 1360. Further generalizations about France, however, are not possible because of the many regional variations in custom and willingness to pay taxes.

The plague also affected England, and a serious resumption of the war was temporarily out of the question. The truce was renewed for one-year periods on 6 August 1348 and 2 May 1349, although frontier skirmishing remained a problem in the Southwest.[3] Although military expenses were fairly low, the monarchy remained unable to live on domaial resources alone, and these resources were subject to the dislocations which followed the plague.[4] The household of the prodigal John of Normandy must have grown more elaborate and costly after he received expanded powers late in 1347. It was not long, therefore, before the government was searching for money once again. John levied a feudal aid in Nor-

---

[1] Prat, "Albi et la peste noire," pp. 19-24.

[2] W. Bowsky, "The Impact of the Black Death upon Sienese Government and Society," *Speculum*, XXIX (1964), 21-22. The first section of this chapter is a revised version of my article, "Black Death," 1968, pp. 416-427.

[3] *Foedera*, III pt. 1, pp. 34, 36, 48-49; H. Denifle, *La désolation des églises, monastères, et hôpitaux en France pendant la guerre de Cent Ans*, Paris, 1899, II, pp. 63-65.

[4] Lewis, *Later Medieval France*, p. 209; Duby, *Rural Economy*, pp. 308f.

mandy during 1349 to meet expenses incurred for the marriage of his daughter, but there are too few documents to determine if much was collected.[5] Another royal expense in 1349 was the purchase of the barony of Montpellier from the king of Majorca for 120,000 pounds. Although it has been argued that the papal loans were applied to this purpose, these loans had stopped suddenly in the spring of 1348, undoubtedly because of the Black Death.[6] The crown was therefore faced with important expenses at a time when papal loans, like subsidies and other revenues, were not available. Collection of Lombard debts did continue in 1349 and 1350,[7] but here again, the chaos following the plague must have kept these receipts below the high expectations of late 1347.

Despite the plague's disastrous effects on royal finances as a whole, the Black Death had one result which the crown could exploit to its profit. There appears to have been a substantial de-hoarding of silver, bringing bullion to the mints in such quantities as to permit the king to claim large *monnayage* receipts. The importance of revenue from this source is illustrated by Fawtier's tabulation of the Journal of the Treasury for the second half of 1349. Given the truce in effect, the low war expenses of 185,648 *l.p.* for this semester seem quite credible. Subsidy receipts, however, were but 27,950 pounds, remarkably small even if we allow for extensive local disbursement of funds by *élus*. It is obvious that revenue from this source was minute when compared with the sums anticipated for 1348. Mint profits, however, were 552,000 *l.p.*, more than 60 percent of the total treasury receipts.[8] To obtain a profit of this size, the crown must have issued close to two million pounds in silver coins during the six-month period. The bullion purchased by the mints for this purpose must have far exceeded what was available in the 1330s, when the mints were starved for silver.[9]

On the collection of subsidies in the two years after the plague, we have very little documentary evidence. In the districts of Poitou and

---

[5] Secousse, *Charles II*, I, 26; BN *ms. fr.* 25999, no. 37; AN AB xix 2638, citing a document in Bibliothèque de Rouen. What is surprising is that John failed to exploit his next opportunity for a feudal aid in 1350. A chronicler reported that after his coronation as king he had his son knighted. See R. Delachenal (ed.), *Chronique des règnes de Jean II et de Charles V*, I, Paris, 1910, 25. Perhaps John was not impressed with the recent tradition of feudal aids and felt that an attempt to levy such a tax at the beginning of the reign would complicate his effort to raise money in 1351.

[6] Faucon, "Prêts," p. 571; Germain, *Commerce*, I, 159-161, 168.

[7] There are twenty-nine entries in *JT Ph. VI* between no. 2473 and 5052 dealing with collections from debtors in 1349 and 1350. See also Henneman, "Italians," note 102.

[8] Fawtier, *Comptes*, p. lxiv.   [9] Appendix I, note 48.

Touraine, a large sales tax of 12 *d./l.* was being levied in the winter of 1349-1350 for men-at-arms. Another imposition was being levied in Maine and perhaps a sales tax at Paris.[10] The Normans held an assembly in February 1349 and in July, a "recently granted imposition" was being collected in the duchy.[11] The crown was also collecting a clerical tenth.[12] The tradition of hearth taxes and the plague's heavy toll created particular problems in taxing Languedoc, but continued raids and reprisals along the Gascon border helped justify requests for subsidies.[13] Guillaume Balbet, a new commissioner with multiple powers, went south in June of 1349, and after lengthy bargaining obtained taxes from Najac, Millau, Martel, Rodez, and Albi by the end of the year.[14] Some southern barons authorized a levy of 20 *s.* per hearth in their lands.[15] In the Beaucaire district, subsidy payments were tiny compared with those of other years: 240 *l.t.* from Alès and 333 from Beaucaire, as opposed to 400 and 1,139 respectively in 1346.[16] The *viguerie* of Uzès offered 270 pounds, also much less than usual, and then this sum was reduced to 190 *l.t.* because of the plague.[17]

These figures suggest that in terms of ability to pay taxes, the French kingdom was virtually prostrate through the end of 1349. Yet it is also clear that the monarchy was determined to collect what it could, once the plague had run its course. Although Montpellier had been excused from paying the 6,000 pounds granted early in 1348, the crown reopened the matter in April 1349 and ordered the consuls to pay 2,000 *l.t.*[18] Later

[10] BN *ms. fr.* 25998, no. 583; Brousillon, *Documents*, p. 53; Petit, *Essai de restitution*, p. 42 (and the discussion in Henneman, "Black Death," note 68).

[11] Coville, *Etats Norm.*, p. 64; Delisle, *Actes norm.*, pp. 398-403; BN *ms. fr.* 25998, no. 532.

[12] Excerpt from BN *ms. fr.* 20691 copied in AN AB xix 2638; BN Moreau 231, fols. 226-227; AN P 2292, pp. 81-91; BN *ms. fr.* 25998, no. 497; AN KK 7, fol. 2v.

[13] *HL*, ix, 618, note 4. The truce was renewed in June of 1350: AN P 2292, pp. 199-219; BN *ms. lat.* 9146, fols. 118r-125v. There were further negotiations and short truces in the summer of 1351 (BN Moreau 699, fols. 231, 235-236), but hostilities on the Gascon frontier sharply increased in the same year: *HL*, ix, 628, note 3.

[14] AD Aveyron E 1364, fol. 73r; 2E 178, no. 8, fols. 4-6; AM Martel CC 4, fols. 5v-7v; AM Millau CC 345, fol. 105r; AM Albi CC 67. Two other documents in AM Millau EE 121 indicate that Millau's subsidy was to support twenty men-at-arms. For Balbet's powers, see *Gr. Chartrier*, no. 3889.

[15] *HL*, ix, 615-616, note 5.

[16] Ménard, *Nismes*, ii, 127; *HL*, ix, 615. The seneschalsy of Beaucaire contributed less than 16,000 *l.t.* in 1349: BN *Coll. Languedoc* 159, fol. 26r.

[17] *HL*, ix, 615.

[18] *Gr. Chartrier*, no. 3982. The crown clearly expected to collect from Montpellier a portion of the tax first granted in February 1348: BN *ms. fr.* 20691, p. 651.

in the year, the town promised the remaining 4,000 pounds as a loan,[19] but again these sums could not be raised, despite coercion of privileged groups who sought to avoid payment.[20]

In the spring of 1350, Bertrand de Pibrac returned to Languedoc, now with the title of *Réformateur Général*. He and Balbet had sweeping powers to raise money from all possible sources.[21] By the end of May, they claimed to have received grants of taxes from the towns of four seneschalsies—Carcassonne, Toulouse, Périgord, and Rouergue.[22] They subsequently levied a subsidy in Quercy also.[23] Details are scanty, but the tax in the Carcassonne district was a *fouage* of 6 *s.* 8 *d.t.*, only one-third of that which had been paid before the plague.[24] Having reached these accords with the southwestern towns, Pibrac wrote to the seneschal of Beaucaire on 28 May 1350, reporting his progress and ordering an assembly of town representatives to meet at Nîmes on 21 June.[25] This assembly made a modest grant which produced 19,000 *l.t.* before the tax was halted by a new truce.[26] Montpellier's share was 1,000 *l.t.*, and we are told that this sum brought the town's total payments since 1345 to 4,500 *l.t.*[27] Thus it had taken Montpellier three years to pay 75 percent of what had originally been promised for one.

In Languedoil, indirect taxes appear to have been rather general in 1350. Early in the year, the districts of Paris, Senlis, Bourges, and Auvergne agreed to pay sales taxes of 4 *d./l.*[28] The bailiwick of Orléans

[19] Germain, *Commerce*, I, 168; *HL*, IX, 615.

[20] BN *ms. lat.* 9174, fols. 230-231. See below for evidence that Montpellier had still not paid the 6,000 pounds in 1350.

[21] AM Toulouse AA 35, no. 82; *HL*, X, cols. 1061-1063.

[22] *Ibid.* In Rouergue, the subsidy was based on a military summons to all nobles and non-nobles (BN *ms. fr.* 25999, no. 26). In addition, this region had to pay a rather large amount for the *commun de paix*, an old tax formerly established by the bishop of Rodez to help maintain order in the diocese. See Cabrol, *Villefranche*, I, 230-231.

[23] Lacoste, *Quercy*, III, 125; AM Martel CC 4, fol. 12r-v; BN *ms. fr.* 23257, fol. 5 (showing that Figeac did not agree to pay until July).

[24] *HL*, IX, 619-620, note 3. The lord of Lautrec, who was to keep one-quarter of the subsidy levied in his lands, received 316 pounds in 1350 (BN *Coll. Languedoc* 159, fol. 56r).

[25] *HL*, X, cols. 1061-1064.

[26] BN *Coll. Languedoc* 159, fol. 26r-v. Collection must have resumed again, for later in the year the inhabitants of Tournon complained about royal commissioners levying a hearth tax or lump-sum equivalent (*HL*, X, cols. 1070-1072). Alès paid the subsidy, evidently a lump-sum for the whole *viguerie*, for there followed a dispute as to which communities should contribute to this (AM Alès 1 S-12, no. 31).

[27] *Gr. Chartrier*, nos. 3890, 3891, 3984, 3989.

[28] AN P 2292, pp. 165-179; BN *ms. lat.* 9146, fols. 109v-115r; BN P.O. 740, *dossier* 16892, no. 2.

paid a tax of 6 *d./l.*,[29] while the Normans convened at Pont Audemer in May and agreed to an imposition of 12 *d./l.* for four months.[30] The militarily vulnerable districts of lower Normandy were paying "*aides* for the war" in the autumn of 1350.[31] There appears to have been a royal wine tax in Picardy,[32] while an imposition was being levied by the crown in Poitou, Limousin, and Touraine.[33] In the North as in the Midi, therefore, the period of paralysis was over by 1350 and taxes of a sort were being levied everywhere. Yet recovery was far from complete, and a diminished population was being assessed at rates which in most cases were barely comparable to those prevailing before 1348. It was not until 1351, that the government succeeded in stabilizing taxes at a significantly higher level and establishing the procedures which would govern royal fiscal policy until late 1355.

Philip VI died late in August 1350, and soon after his coronation, John II began planning assemblies of Estates. These meetings would give the new king an opportunity to receive traditional expressions of loyalty, renew privileges, and rally support for the monarchy and sympathy for its financial needs. Since John planned to visit Avignon at the end of the year, it would be possible for him to convene separate meetings of the northern and southern Estates and attend both assemblies personally.

On 20 November 1350, the barons, prelates, and townsmen were ordered to convene, those of the Midi to meet at Montpellier on 8 January[34] and those of Languedoil to be at Paris on 16 February 1351.[35] At the end of November, John ordered his *réformateur* in Languedoc to

[29] AN PP 117, p. 652.

[30] Coville, *Etats Norm.*, p. 64, has inferred the existence of an assembly from a mutilated account in BN *ms. fr.* 25999, no. 116. There are various indications of the subsidy which resulted. It was a sales tax requiring both buyer and seller to pay $2\frac{1}{2}\%$ on each transaction: BN *ms. fr.* 25700, no. 21; 25998, nos. 1-4; 25999, nos. 4, 25, 64; BN Clairambault 192, nos. 15, 117.

[31] AN K 47, no. 6 *bis*. This tax involved troop salaries and there is no way of determining whether or not it is the same tax cited in the last note. The documents cited there all belong to the bailiwicks of Rouen, Caux, and Gisors. It is possible that the two districts of Caen and Cotentin (lower Normandy) negotiated an entirely separate tax.

[32] Le Maire, *St. Quentin*, II, no. 642.

[33] BN NAF 20026, nos. 22, 23; P.O. 1522, *dossier* 34634, no. 7.

[34] AM Toulouse AA 35, no. 83.

[35] AN P 2292, pp. 249-250; BN NAF 7607, fols. 187-188. Earlier, the day after his accession, John II had written to a list of 344 barons and knights banneret from all parts of the kingdom, telling them to stand by for later instructions, and implying that he would be wanting their advice on some matter: *ibid.*, fols. 159r-173r; BN *ms. fr.* 20691, pp. 943-947.

publicize English truce violations and seek loans from wealthy citizens.[36] This step may have been aimed to prepare the public for a subsidy request, but John evidently did not expect to receive a firm grant at the assemblies he had called. His summons merely expressed a desire to govern well and receive counsel. Expressions like "necessity" and "common profit" which often adorned royal requests for money were conspicuously lacking. The widespread confirmation of privileges, such as took place at the time of the Montpellier meeting in January,[37] might suggest some bargaining, but such grants frequently occurred at the beginning of a new reign. In short, it appears that the two assemblies of the Estates in 1351 were intended primarily to have a propaganda value. They were but one step in a well-planned effort to obtain money at an unpropitious time.

It is certain that the royal desire for a tax was mentioned when the representatives of four southern seneschalsies convened at Montpellier on 8 January 1351.[38] However, the principal negotiations for the subsidy took place *after* the Estates had met, not *during* the central assemblies, as in 1347. In Languedoc, the bargaining process went on for several months and was unusually complicated. The documents reveal two separate but related sets of negotiations. On the one hand, there is evidence of considerable travel back and forth to Paris on the part of town proctors whose errand was to arrange a *finance* with royal fiscal officers. The payment in question was to be a "gift" to the king on the occasion of his "joyous accession." In the meantime, however, Bertrand de Pibrac, the royal *réformateur* in Languedoc, was busily seeking to obtain a war subsidy, justified by the endless military skirmishing in Gascony. In general, his agents requested a sales tax (*gabelle*) in upper Languedoc and a hearth tax (*fouage*) in the districts along the Mediterranean coast. At first glance, it would appear that separate taxes are involved, but in fact this is not the case. The government was proceeding with a rather novel and well-coordinated scheme for exerting pressure on taxpayers. The local authorities in Languedoc could legitimately demand a war subsidy and the demands they now made were extremely onerous. The Beaucaire district was asked to pay a tax of 20 *s.p.* per hearth *juxta antiquum numerum focorum.*[39] Even before the plague, the largest hearth tax ever sought by the crown had been 20 *s.t.* In 1351, the government raised this

[36] *Gr. Chartrier*, no. 1772.

[37] Examples are in *Ord.*, IV, 27-35; *HL*, X, cols. 1072-1073.

[38] *HL*, IX, 624.

[39] BN *Coll. Languedoc* 85, fol. 5 (discussed somewhat inaccurately in *HL*, IX, 627); *Gr. Chartrier*, no. 3893.

rate 25 percent merely by expressing its demand in Paris coinage. With this amount assessed according to pre-plague hearth figures, the burden on the individual taxpayer must have been very heavy. Understandably, there was opposition to such a subsidy and many towns were willing to incur the expense of sending a proctor to Paris to negotiate a *finance*. The account rendered by the royal collectors of this tax states that it was for both the king's accession and the Gascon war. In localities where great poverty made a high hearth tax unfeasible, the commissioners were to substitute a sales tax of 8 *d./l*.[40] We thus discover a coordinated effort to collect as much money as could be squeezed out of Languedoc. The summoning of the Estates, the publicity given to the truce violations, the seeking of "loans," the personal appearance of the king at Montpellier, the exorbitant tax demands of the *réformateur* in Languedoc, and the emphasis on the king's accession as well as the war, were all part of a single money-raising effort.

The results were impressive compared to the subsidy yields of the previous two years. The *viguerie* of Uzès paid a "gift" of 757 pounds for the king's accession; four times what it had paid the year before. Beaucaire contributed 1,900 pounds and felt it necessary to apologize for not producing more.[41] It is possible, but not proven, that the towns of the Beaucaire district were called to a local assembly in February,[42] but negotiation of the subsidy continued well into the spring. On 13 February, Alès empowered a proctor to arrange a fine with the crown at Paris. This step did not deter the royal commissioners in Languedoc, who demanded a few days later that a representative from Alès report to them at Nîmes and arrange payment of a war subsidy before the end of the month.[43] The consuls of Nîmes offered stubborn resistance to paying and were still discussing the matter of 12 April, by which time the seneschal of Beaucaire was beginning to lose patience. His lieutenant arrived at Nîmes on 2 May and ordered the consuls to produce 2,500 pounds.[44]

The consuls of Montpellier, like those of Nîmes, delayed in offering a tax, were summoned before the royal treasurer late in April and agreed

[40] BN *Coll. Languedoc* 159, fol. 26v. Here the hearth tax is frankly described as 25 *s.t.*

[41] BN *Coll. Languedoc* 85, fol. 5.

[42] Bardon, *Alais*, ii, 28, citing no source. Ménard, *Nismes*, ii, 131, mentioned an assembly in March which established a 10 *s.* hearth tax in the Beaucaire district, but also offered no evidence.

[43] AM Alès 1 S-12, nos. 29, 30.

[44] Ménard, *Nismes*, ii, *preuves*, 142-143. Later in the year, there were disputes over whether moneyers were required to contribute to the payment which Nîmes was to make: AM Nîmes NN 1, no. 33.

reluctantly to pay 3,000 *écus* as an installment on whatever *finance* might be negotiated by a representative of the town who was then in Paris.[45] The latter finally agreed to a *finance* of 6,000 florins, and the consuls paid it early in July at the request of local officials.[46] According to a surviving account, the entire seneschalsy paid 72,875 *l.t.*, an impressive sum, although not quite equal to 25 *s.t.* per pre-plague hearth.[47]

The consular accounts of Rodez for 1351 indicate a somewhat similar process. Two consuls attended the Estates at Montpellier in January and returned with a royal letter which presumably dealt with a request for subsidy. One of the consuls then went to Paris to negotiate a *finance*.[48] Meanwhile, Pibrac's officers demanded a *gabelle* from Rouergue to support the war, and an assembly of towns may have been held at Millau in the spring.[49] No agreement having been reached in Paris, Rodez paid Pibrac a provisional subsidy of 320 *l.t.* by the end of September, while a new proctor went to Paris to arrange the desired *finance*.[50] In nearby Quercy, the towns of Figeac and Cajarc are known to have paid a tax, but there are no documents to describe the negotiating process.[51]

Rather than sending proctors to Paris on an individual basis, twenty-two towns of the Carcassonne district sent representatives to the capital in March to negotiate a *finance* on behalf of the entire seneschalsy. Their presence has misled some scholars into believing that the Estates General of the entire kingdom convened at Paris, but in fact these representatives transacted their business some weeks after the Estates of Languedoil had met.[52] Their agreement with the crown was embodied in a royal ordinance of 15 March 1351, according to which the towns "freely and graciously" granted the king 50,000 *l.t.*, to be paid in two installments, one on 5 June and the other on 15 August. In return, they were promised that for a full year they would not be molested by royal officials seeking subsidies or loans. The lesser towns were protected against any effort by the larger communities to fine for less than their share and

---

[45] *Gr. Chartrier*, nos. 3892-3893.

[46] *Ibid.*, nos. 448, 449, 3987. The consuls had to ask royal officers to use force against citizens who were reluctant to contribute.

[47] BN *Coll. Languedoc* 159, fol. 26v.

[48] *A.H. Rouergue*, VI (consular accounts of Rodez), 12-13, 130-131.

[49] *Ibid.*, p. 88, note 1.　　　　　　　　[50] *Ibid.*, pp. 132-134, 141.

[51] AM Cajarc EE supp., a letter of 8 March ordering the town to name proctors to negotiate a subsidy; *ibid.*, CC, no. 89, recording a grant of 90 *l.t.*; BN *ms. fr.* 23257, fol. 6, indicating the tax at Figeac.

[52] Moreau de Beaumont, *Mémoire*, III, 232; Coville, *États Norm.*, pp. 65-66; Vuitry, *Régime financier*, II, 31-32. Cf. Henneman, "Black Death," p. 424 and note 130.

increase the burden of their smaller neighbors.[53] Two weeks later, Narbonne received a special guarantee of its privileges because the consuls had already paid the town's share of the subsidy with a promptness placing Narbonne "ahead of the other towns of Languedoc."[54] Narbonne may also have been early with its share of the August installment, for a document of mid-July mentions a "loan," extended to the royal *réformateur* as Narbonne's quota of the subsidy.[55]

Despite the promise that there would be no further taxation of the Carcassonne towns for a year, the crown soon began calling for crossbowmen to help pacify the troublesome Gascon frontier. The nobles of the viscounty of Narbonne paid a "finance for muster of arms," and the town of Narbonne sent thirty sergeants and a payment of 200 *écus* in addition to its earlier subsidy payment.[56] When still another military summons was issued during the summer, the consuls of Narbonne indignantly refused to pay for any more soldiers, citing the royal promise of 15 March and pointing out that they had already made one additional contribution besides their share of the subsidy.[57]

The assembly of the three Estates of northern and central France, summoned to meet on 16 February 1351, must have convened on schedule. On the 24th, the king dispatched a letter to the bailiff of Gisors, indicating that the clergy had granted a tax while the nobles and towns had expressed a willingess to pay, subject to future local negotiations.[58] The assembly differed from that of late 1347 in that it was shorter and that the second and third estates merely endorsed a subsidy in principle. It has already been argued that this sort of favorable counsel was probably all that the king desired. Actual negotiations of the tax was conducted in a series of subsequent regional meetings.[59]

In his letter of 24 February, John II directed the bailiff of Gisors to summon the townsmen and nobles of his jurisdiction to assemblies at Pont Audemer to be held four days apart in mid-March.[60] The first of these meetings comprised 106 representatives from sixty-three Norman towns. After presenting their grievances and gaining various royal promises, they consented to a sales tax of 6 *d./l.* to run for a year commenc-

---

[53] *Ord.*, III, 674-675; AN JJ 80, no. 229; BN *Coll. Languedoc* 85, fols. 13-14.

[54] *Ord.*, III, 675-676 (from AN JJ 80, no. 351). One suspects that this prompt payment may have enabled Narbonne to escape with a reduced share, contrary to the intent of the documents cited in the last note.

[55] BN Doat 53, fols. 147v-159r.

[56] *Ibid.*; BN *Coll. Languedoc* 85, fol. 22; *HL*, IX, 626.

[57] BN Doat 53, fols. 147v-159r.   [58] Coville, *Etats Norm.*, pp. 351-352.

[59] See Henneman, "Black Death," p. 425.   [60] Coville, *Etats Norm.*, pp. 351-352.

ing on 1 May and to cease if peace should be made. An assembly of thirty-two Norman nobles, meeting several days later, agreed to this levy in their lands, provided that it be collected also in the lands of the royal princes.[61] A lengthy ordinance of 5 April gave royal ratification to this grant and the conditions which would govern the tax.[62] This type of document was to become typical in the 1350s. Many regional tax grants of this period were formally ratified by the king and registered in the chancery or Chamber of Accounts. These "veritable treaties," as Vuitry has called them,[63] form a precedent, at the bailiwick level, for those lengthy ordinances to be issued to the whole kingdom during the turbulent years after 1355. They suggest a growing desire to trade taxes for written guarantees of reform. Royal promises of this nature did not, however, eliminate objections to paying. The Norman subsidy of 1351 encountered opposition when collection started and the government had to apply pressure by issuing a military summons in mid-May.[64]

Parallel to the negotiations in Normandy were comparable developments in the other bailiwicks of Languedoil. Commissioners to redress grievances and negotiate a subsidy were sent to Vermandois and Picardy early in March. By the end of the month, a subsidy of 4 *d./l.* on sales had been obtained from the bailiwick of Amiens, ratified by the king in June, with collection to begin on the 17th of that month.[65] The bailiwick of Vermandois granted a sales tax of 6 *d./l.* at a local assembly in March. Here, as in Normandy, the townsmen and the nobles met separately and concurred in the same basic subsidy, subject to various conditions. It was promised that no rights would be prejudiced and that no other tax would be levied for a year unless an emergency necessitated a general military summons (*arrière-ban*).[66] The bailiwicks of Troyes and Meaux in Champagne similarly granted a 6 *d./l.* sales tax,[67] and the same form of payment was adopted in Anjou and Maine, Senlis, Mâcon, Poitou and Limousin, and Auvergne.[68] On the basis of such evidence, it seems certain that all the districts of northern and central France contributed a subsidy of this sort in 1351. Unlike 1347-1348, the conditions governing

---

[61] *Ibid.*, pp. 66-69. [62] *Ord.*, II, 400-410.

[63] Vuitry, *Régime financier*, II, 35-36.

[64] Coville, *Etats Norm.*, p. 69; AN K 47, no. 10. The money was turned over to war treasurers for military expenses (BN *ms. fr.* 25999, no. 86).

[65] *Ord.*, II, 439-441; AN P 2292, pp. 275, 277.

[66] *Ord.*, II, 391-396, 447; *Ord.*, III, 677; BN NAF 7608, fols. 22-25.

[67] AN P 2292, pp. 301-302.

[68] Vuitry, *Régime financier*, II, 40; Moreau de Beaumont, *Mémoire*, III, 234-235; AN PP 117, p. 659; BN NAF 20026, no. 26.

the grants were different everywhere, although many of these differences were relatively minor. Paris renewed its sales tax in the spring of 1351, subject to a rather detailed list of conditions set forth in the royal ratification of 3 May.[69] It is perhaps no coincidence that just three days before ratifying this agreement, the king confirmed a recent document granting the burghers of Paris exemption from the right of *prise*.[70] The town of Saint-Denis received its own royal letter guaranteeing the conditions under which the subsidy was to be levied.[71]

King John also continued his father's effort to maintain the port of Aigues Mortes, which he visited on his trip to the Midi at the beginning of 1351. The tax levied for the upkeep of the port had produced 3,500 *écus* from March 1348 to March 1349, and in one of his earliest enactments John ordered enforcement of the rule that other communities participate in the payment of this *denier*-per-pound levy.[72] Another source of revenue in 1351 was a settlement with the Genoese concerning the acts of piracy with which their subjects had been charged two decades earlier. The 3 *d./l.* tax on goods imported and exported by Genoese had been in force since 1335 but had not produced the sums needed to compensate French merchants for the damages they claimed. Now, in June 1351, this tax was canceled in return for 40,000 gold florins. This sum went into the royal account at the treasury and further added to the revenues collected in 1351.[73]

Thus by 1351, the crown had managed to accumulate rather sizable revenues and to stabilize taxation following the disaster of the plague. In Languedoil, as we have seen, regional and bailiwick Estates played a prominent part in the royal accumulation of money. These assemblies would proliferate in coming years and in some regions would gradually develop into provincial Estates. They now spread to Languedoc, where assemblies of towns would play an important role in making annual tax grants in the future.

2. The Spread of Regional Assemblies

There is no way of determining exactly how well the actual subsidy receipts of 1351 measured up to receipts of typical years prior to 1347. The shrinkage of population, spiraling prices, and subsequent aggravation of the economic depression must have affected adversely the fiscal

---

[69] *Ord.*, II, 423-426; AN P 2292, pp. 261-270; AN J 384, no. 2.
[70] *Ord.*, IV, 326-333.   [71] AN P 2292, p. 271.
[72] *HL*, IX, 625; AD Hérault A 5, fols. IV-8v; BN *ms. lat.* 9174, fols. 237-239.
[73] *Ord.*, IV, 89; Henneman, "Italians," p. 21, and notes.

position of the crown. It seems certain that domainal revenues, never adequate in the fourteenth century, were diminished after the plague. Perhaps the higher subsidy rates and more regular subsidies which prevailed after 1350 were able to offset the adverse conditions resulting from the plague and bring royal tax revenues back to the average level of the first decade of the Hundred Years' War. However, subsidy receipts in those years were not very great and there is no certainty that even this modest level could be achieved in the 1350s.

It is certain that the government of John II was in acute financial distress in the 1350s despite the higher level of taxation that was reached in 1351. Aside from such extraordinary costs as the payment for the barony of Montpellier, there occurred an inflationary price-and-wage movement which necessitated legislation by the crown.[74] In one of the first comprehensive royal ordinances dealing with military organization and salaries, John had to establish a daily wage of 20 s. for a simple knight, one-third higher than the *grands-gages* rate under Philip VI.[75] In the face of such rising costs, even the higher subsidies of 1351 proved insufficient and on 26 September 1351 the king had to suspend payment of all debts for six months except for alms and fiefs. The same enactment called for the immediate farming of all sales taxes not yet being collected.[76] Further evidence of financial strain affecting both the king and the nobility may be found in early 1352, when it was necessary to instruct war treasurers not to advance salaries to men-at-arms for more than one month.[77]

Against this backdrop of fiscal difficulty, John II reissued in October 1351 the great reform ordinance which had first been issued by Philip IV in 1303.[78] This action may have been aimed at mitigating whatever discontent the higher taxes of 1351 may have generated. It does not seem to be related to any new request for money, despite the contention of Balas that an "Estates General" of the whole kingdom met on 16 November 1351. This writer states that at the supposed assembly the representatives of Vermandois granted a tax while those of Normandy requested a delay.[79] Vermandois did grant a sales tax earlier in 1351 at a bailiwick assembly and renewed it the following summer. Some assembly in the winter of 1352 did grant a sales tax, but it was evidently not attended by representatives of either Normandy or Vermandois.[80] An as-

[74] Perroy, *The Hundred Years War*, pp. 122-123.
[75] *Ord.*, IV, 67-70.
[76] *Ibid.*, II, 449; IV, 6, 498; AN P 2292, pp. 305-309.
[77] *Ord.*, II, 483.   [78] *Ibid.*, pp. 450f.
[79] L. Balas, *Une tentative de gouvernement représentatif au XIVe siècle. Les états-généraux de 1356-1358*, Paris, 1928, p. 24.
[80] See above, note 66, and below, notes 82, 92.

sembly of nobles doubtless did convene in November 1351 when the king instituted a new chivalric order,[81] but there is no trace of any new taxation late in this year.

Aside from the puzzling and undocumented assertion by Balas, all our evidence suggests that taxation in Languedoil in 1352 largely followed the pattern of 1351, but without any central assembly. The *extractus* of the treasury for 1352 indicates the widespread existence of a 6 *d./l.* sales tax such as had been granted in areas of Languedoil in 1351. The bailiwick assembly remained the principal negotiating forum, except that in Normandy the five bailiwicks again convened as a group with the sessions divided into separate meetings of each Estate.

On 9 March 1352 John II wrote to commissioners charged with subsidy negotiations in Normandy, mentioning a recent assembly of clergy, nobles, and townsmen at Paris, where a sales tax of 6 *d./l.* had been granted as a subsidy.[82] There is no indication as to what region was represented at this meeting, nor any reason to infer that Normans had been present. This appears to be the assembly which Balas assigned to the preceding November. Although the king described the meeting as "no small multitude," he did not state or imply that those present represented "our kingdom." They were probably the Estates of one or two bailiwicks who were meeting to discuss a regional tax just as the Normans were. The Estates of Anjou and Maine are known to have met at Paris, and those of the viscounty of Paris or bailiwick of Senlis could have done the same. Hoping that the Normans would follow the lead of the earlier meeting and grant a tax, John II ordered the three Norman Estates to be convened. They met separately at Rouen late in March, the towns on the 25th with the clergy and nobles following at three-day intervals.[83] Coville was of the opinion that the crown expected these assemblies to be short, and came armed with concessions to offer.[84] The formula of the previous year was evidently to be the guide, and no new royal ordinance was needed. A fragmentary account of the bailiff of Caen for Easter 1352 mentioned the meetings at Rouen without giving further information.[85]

Early in June, John II wrote to his officers in Anjou and Maine, instructing them to levy a 6 *d./l.* sales tax which had been granted by the

---

[81] BN NAF 7608, fols. 77r-93v; NAF 7376, fols. 24-27; AN JJ 81, no. 570; *Ord.*, II, 465; Delachenal, *Histoire de Charles V*, I, 62.

[82] Coville, *Etats Norm.*, pp. 354-358.

[83] Coville, *Etats Norm.*, pp. 70, 354-358.   [84] *Ibid.*, pp. 71-72.

[85] *Ibid.*, p. 358. The dowager queen, Joan of Evreux, who held lands in Normandy, permitted levy of the 6 *d./l.* in her lands, subject to a letter of non-prejudice and the right to retain half the proceeds. See *Ord.*, III, 677-678; IV, 121.

barons, prelates, and towns of these districts after "great and mature deliberation" at Paris. It was to be levied for one year following the expiration of a current subsidy.[86] Sales taxes were the usual rule in Languedoil, and as in 1351, most of the bailiwicks agreed to pay 2½ percent. At Paris, we know only of an imposition being levied in September,[87] while in June, the Amiens district granted a new subsidy of unspecified form and amount.[88] In the bailiwick of Bourges, one town paid 400 *écus* in lieu of the sales tax,[89] while the districts of Meaux, Vitry, Chartres, Orléans, Troyes, and Chaumont paid a sales tax of 6 *d./l.*[90] It appears that the consent mechanism in Champagne differed from the Norman procedure. The Norman assemblies were divided according to estate, with each of the three meetings including persons from all five Norman bailiwicks. The four bailiwicks of Champagne appear to have held three separate deliberations, with the three orders meeting together in the one about which we have information, that representing the two bailiwicks of Troyes and Chaumont.[91]

The growing uniformity of taxation in Languedoil should now be obvious, as local assemblies of one or more bailiwicks were beginning to meet annually, authorizing a one-year tax in return for stated royal concessions. This practice had importance for the central assemblies of Estates after 1355 which could draw upon the greater experience in group action and tax negotiating which had been developed in the early 1350s. For the crown, also, these annual bailiwick assemblies must have proven a more satisfactory negotiating forum than the cumbersome procedure of military musters, fines, and various types of coercion and bargaining at a more local level.

Although this more uniform and regular taxation may be viewed as "progress" from the standpoint of both the royal administration and the representative principle, it would be an overstatement to conclude that resistance to taxation was crumbling. To be sure, there was less insistence that all taxation cease while truces were in effect, but this objection had always found fewer adherents in Languedoil than in the Midi. The fairly continuous sales taxes of 1340-1346 had not been interrupted by the occasional truces of that period and they had been allowed in some

---

[86] AN P 2292, pp. 387-401; PP 117, p. 668; D. F. Secousse, introduction to *Ord.*, III, xxv.

[87] AN PP 117, p. 688; P. 2292, p. 403.   [88] *Ord.*, IV, 282-284.

[89] AN P 2292, p. 409, indicates that this district paid a sales tax of 6 *d./l.* The 400 *écu* payment, which must have been in lieu of the sales tax, is mentioned in H. Moranvillé, "Extraits des journaux du trésor," *BEC*, XLIX (1888), 181, no. 133.

[90] AN PP 664; AN P 2292, pp. 337-343.   [91] *Ibid.*, p. 337.

cases to continue for indefinite periods of time. It is true that the taxes of the 1350s were levied at a higher rate and during more extended periods of truce, but the king was now forced to renegotiate them annually. That their renewal was far from automatic will become apparent when one examines the case of Vermandois in 1352.

Once again, the published municipal accounts of Reims make the negotiations in Vermandois our best documented example of this process for 1352. At an assembly of barons, prelates, and towns of Vermandois and Beauvaisis held at Laon on 15 July, royal commissioners made the familiar request that the 6 *d./l.* sales tax granted in 1351 be renewed for another year. The representatives of Reims heard the request, made no commitment, and returned to their city. A new assembly was scheduled for 26 July to hear the reply of the three orders, so Reims was apparently not unique in its noncommittal stance. The second meeting took place but evidently made no grant, postponing the decision for three more days when a new assembly convened at Noyon. Still another week went by, however, before a second Noyon assembly finally agreed to the sales tax.[92] It thus required four bargaining sessions over a three-week period before the grant was renewed. It is possible that other districts, where no detailed documentation has been found, were equally resistant.

A short ordinance of eight articles, drawn up in August 1352, signaled the successful conclusion of the year's subsidy negotiations in Vermandois. Collection of the tax was to begin one week later.[93] Then, on 19 October, there appeared a new, more lengthy, royal enactment which established the conditions under which the subsidy was to be levied and added more generous concessions.[94] This later ordinance probably arose from difficulties encountered in collecting the tax.

The reluctance to grant this tax in Vermandois may relate to a more general difficulty facing town governments in this period. In all probability, the combined effects of war, plague, and economic dislocation left many northern towns in financial difficulty. Towns had incurred debts to put their fortifications in order during the years of recurring military danger on the northern frontier. Additional borrowing was needed in order to provide the king with the money, men, and supplies he continually demanded. The inflationary pressures created by currency debasement and labor shortage may have eased the plight of some debtor communities and increased certain municipal revenues, but the terrible shrinkage of urban population must have undercut other antici-

---

[92] Varin, *Reims*, III, 21-24 (footnote).
[93] *Ord.*, II, 503-505.　　　　[94] *Ibid.*, pp. 505-509.

pated revenues and made it difficult for towns to regain solvency. The continued pursuit of debtors to the Lombards can only have created further embarrassments and made credit more difficult to obtain.[95] The Vermandois town of Saint-Quentin cited a burden of indebtedness and the recent heavy mortality in requesting royal permission to continue levying its municipal wine tax in 1352, and the king authorized a three-year extension.[96] It is likely that the issue of municipal finances played a significant role in subsidy negotiations in northern France. In mid-August, for instance, the crown issued letters noting that Compiègne, having agreed to the royal imposition, was now authorized to levy a four-year municipal tax of its own.[97]

Throughout the 1350s, in fact, municipal finances and royal finances became closely interrelated. In the face of royal weakness, the towns increasingly had to look to their own defenses, and in doing so they assumed many responsibilities which theoretically belonged to the king because "defense of the realm" was involved. Five centuries earlier, the kings' inability to carry out the basic royal function of defending a large realm had led to a breakdown of royal authority as power gravitated to those who could defend their regions. During the Hundred Years' War, the periods of royal incapacity were much shorter, but while they lasted they may well have contributed to the increased local particularism among the towns and the revived power of certain feudal princes. At the same time, however, the same economic and social difficulties which weakened the financial position of the crown were afflicting the finances of the princes and the towns.

If the king encountered difficulty in obtaining a war subsidy from some parts of the royal domain, he failed altogether in his effort to tax Burgundy. Burgundy was currently under royal administration because the duke, Philippe de Rouvres, was then a minor and King John had married his widowed mother, Joan of Boulogne. Under these circumstances, the crown approached Burgundy for a subsidy directly, probably for the first time in a generation. On 2 May 1352, there occurred the

---

[95] *Ibid.*, II, 523-524; IV, 80-82, for John II's renewals of the measures against debtors to Lombards in 1350 and 1353. The collection of the principal of usurious debts was pursued with considerable tenacity through most of the reign (Henneman, "Italians," pp. 38f.), but much more research is needed before the full impact on credit can be determined.

[96] Le Maire, *St. Quentin*, II, no. 655.

[97] AN P 2292, p. 407. The queen, as countess of Boulogne, authorized Arras to levy a local sales tax in the same year, with the countess sharing one-quarter of the proceeds: A. Guesnon (ed.), *Inventaire chronologique des chartes de la ville d'Arras*, Arras, 1862, pp. 97-98.

assembly which is now considered to mark the beginning of the Burgundian provincial Estates. It consisted of five clergy, four nobles, and representatives from thirteen towns. This small group named seven of their number as proctors and empowered them to report to the king their refusal to agree to the 6 *d./l.* sales tax which John had requested. This setback seems to have ended royal efforts to tax Burgundy in 1352.[98]

As in other recent years, taxes were less uniform in Languedoc than in the North, but the use of periodic regional assemblies spread to the Midi in 1352 and was to enjoy a great future there. The prior of Saint-Martin, Bertrand de Pibrac, again assumed direction of the tax-raising effort, his commission as *Réformateur-Général* having been renewed in January.[99] Once again, the southern communities were to pay hearth taxes or a lump sum in lieu of a *fouage*. No royal accession could be invoked as in 1351 and military activity had temporarily subsided, so receipts in the early part of 1352 were generally lower than in 1351.

The Beaucaire district's total contribution of 52,247 *l.t.* suggests a tax of 15 *s.t.* per hearth, although Montpellier paid only 3,000 pounds, probably less than its share.[100] Taxation in this region was troubled by the usual squabbling over who should have to contribute to municipal *tailles*.[101] A *fouage* of 15 *s.t.* was certainly levied in the Carcassonne district.[102] Pibrac spent a busy spring negotiating taxes in Rouergue,[103] while Martel in Quercy, paid 575 pounds as a *finansa* in lieu of a hearth tax (*foguatge*).[104] These scattered documents do not furnish much information about taxes in the first half of 1352, but a change in the military situation brought new demands in the fall.

Despite the more or less continuous renewals of the Anglo-French truce, the first two years of John II's reign had a considerable military history. In general, the English continued to make gains in the North, where the duke of Lancaster (formerly earl of Derby) conducted raids

---

[98] J. Billioud, *Les états de Bourgogne aux XIVe et XVe siècles*, Dijon, 1922, pp. 14-15.

[99] BN *Coll. Languedoc* 85, fols. 30r-31v; *Ord.*, II, 521.

[100] BN *Coll. Languedoc* 159, fol. 27r. I accept the reasoning of Borelli de Serres, *Recherches*, III, 408-410, but believe that the Beaucaire district was probably assessed on a basis of 70,000 rather than 80,000 taxable hearths. The initial payment for the king's ransom in 1358-1360 was clearly based on 70,000 pre-plague hearths. On this basis, 15*s.*/hearth should have produced 52,500 *l.t.*, and this total was very nearly reached. For Montpellier's payment, see *Gr. Chartrier*, D-viii, no. 90.

[101] *Ibid.*, no. 1480; AM Alès 1 S-11, no. 6.

[102] *HL*, IX, 634-635, note 4; X, cols. 1065-1067.

[103] *A.H. Rouergue*, VII, 89; AM Rodez (*cité*) CC 365, no. 67.

[104] AM Martel CC 4, fols. 39r-43v.

from Calais. Guines fell to the English in October 1351.[105] In the West, however, the French made progress, taking Saint-Jean d'Angély in 1351 and generally reversing the English gains of the later 1340s.[106] The tide then turned against France in Gascony, as the English took Saint-Antonin at the end of 1351. Early in the following year, they besieged Agen and captured the *bastide* of Lafrançaise, an important fortress on the Tarn from which they could threaten Toulouse and Albi.[107]

The constable, Charles of Spain, who commanded French forces from Saintonge to Agenais, called upon the nobles and non-nobles of the seneschalsy of Toulouse to help repel the invader.[108] The need for additional armed men was undeniable, but we may assume that those not skilled in warfare were, as always, to pay money instead of serving personally. The count of Foix mobilized his forces to defend Toulouse, but encountered resistance from Pamiers when he asked the town for aid. It was necessary to assure these anxious subjects that no prejudice to town liberties was intended.[109]

Throughout Languedoc, negotiations for the year's second subsidy payment began in the early autumn. It appears that this subsidy was a hearth tax of 10 *s.t.* Although one document reported that the second tax in the Carcassonne district was only five *sols*, we may probably treat this as a scribal error or a special case.[110] Castres paid a *fouage* of 10 *s.* despite some heated debate as to the manner of imposing taxes in the lands of the count of Vendôme.[111] Lodève also contributed,[112] but Albi was excused from paying because the town had spent 30,000 *l.t.* on the hasty repair of its fortifications in the face of the English advance.[113] Having suffered a scare in 1345, Toulouse was better fortified by 1352, and the English lacked the strength to seize this rich prize. The *capitouls*, however, were seriously concerned about the enemy occupation of Lafrançaise and advanced a total of 2,250 *l.t.* to the counts of Foix and

---

[105] Denifle, *Désolation*, ii, 69; *Chron. Jean II*, pp. 33-34.

[106] *Chron. Jean II*, p. 32; Wolff, *Commerces*, p. 37.

[107] *Ibid.*; *HL*, ix, 635-636; Denifle, *Désolation*, ii, 66.

[108] *HL*, ix, 636-637.   [109] BN Doat 93, fols. 196-199v.

[110] The reference to a 5 *s. fouage* is in AM Albi CC 66 and copied in BN Doat 103, fols. 350r-359r, which has since been published in *HL*, x, cols. 1065-1067. Molinier, *HL*, ix, 634-635, note 4, considered it an error.

[111] AM Castres AA 2; *HL*, ix, 634-635, note 4. Cf. BN *Coll. Languedoc* 85, fols. 36r-39v, and AN JJ 81, no. 819, for a lengthy debate over whether Castres should pay a hearth tax or make other financial arrangements.

[112] AM Lodève AA 2, no. 181.

[113] *HL*, x, cols. 1065-1067 (see above, note 110).

Comminges who were directing the French attack upon the place during the fall.[114] The stronghold was soon recaptured.[115]

In the seneschalsy of Beaucaire, the year's second *fouage* gave rise to opposition, particularly at Alès, where the crown sought 800 pounds.[116] Montpellier paid at least 2,500 *l.t.* more after a local royal officer confirmed the cancellation of usury investigations,[117] but Nîmes managed to obtain a reduction in its share.[118] The district finally paid 33,143 *l.t.*, for a total of over 85,000 pounds for the year.[119] The two *fouages* of 1352, amounting to 25 *s.t.*, thus produced 18 percent more than the 25 *s.* hearth tax of 1351. This higher yield reflects the continuing recovery from the dislocation of the Black Death and perhaps also a greater sense of military urgency.

The particular military objective of the French in the winter of 1352-1353 was Saint-Antonin, which Count John of Armagnac was trying to recapture. Subsidy receipts from the second *fouage* of 1352 were largely applied to this siege, but they were not enough. To augment the funds at his disposal, the count had issued commissions on 15 January for the collection of fines for fief alienations in the seneschalsy of Toulouse and in the Albigeois, regions in which this device had long been profitable. It was stated that these fines were to be used for the war,[120] but receipts from this source would take some time to collect. In early March, Armagnac had to conclude a brief truce, halt the siege, and summon the towns of Languedoc to send representatives to Najac to discuss a new subsidy with him.[121]

Six towns of the Beaucaire district sent representatives to Najac who were to speak for the entire seneschalsy. Late in March, these agreed to pay 24,000 *écus*. The sum was based on an average tax of 10 *s.* per hearth but was to be apportioned among the towns, which would be allowed to levy municipal taxes of their own choosing to raise the money and reimburse themselves for the two aids of 1352. The grant was pointedly described as a *don gratuit* which would set no precedent for the future

---

[114] *INV AM Toulouse*, pp. 465, 534 (AA 35, no. 98; AA 45, no. 29).

[115] Wolff, *Commerces*, p. 37.

[116] AM Alès 1 S-16, no. 18; Bardon, *Alais*, ii, 29.

[117] *Gr. Chartrier*, no. 1223. For receipts indicating payments of 1,000 and 1,500 *l.t.*, see *ibid.*, D-viii, no. 64, and D-19, no. 76.

[118] AM Nîmes NN 1, no. 36.   [119] BN *Coll. Languedoc* 159, fol. 27r.

[120] BN Doat 70, fols. 248v-255v.

[121] De Gaujal, *Etude*, ii, 187; Portal, *Cordes*, p. 51. The truce was concluded on 1 March. A general Anglo-French truce, to last until the beginning of August, was concluded on 10 March: *Foedera*, iii pt. i, pp. 82-83.

and would be used exclusively for the seige of Saint-Antonin. No other tax was to be levied during the year for any reason whatsoever. All persons of whatever status would contribute, including nobles who did not serve personally and royal officers. The unpaid parts of the tax would be canceled in the event of peace or truce. The expenses of those appointed by the towns to assess the tax were to be paid from the common receipts. All other crown revenues in Languedoc were to be employed for the prosecution of the military action.[122]

These conditions indicate rather clearly the ideas of the southern towns as to what justified a tax in this period. They were particularly anxious that their money not be diverted to non-military purposes and that the crown make a substantial financial effort of its own. Two final conditions are worth our special notice because they make clear once again the close connection between grants of subsidy and royal missions of investigation and reform. All penalties for violation of monetary ordinances were to be canceled, and other "subsidies, exactions, *fouages*, and loans for the entire said year" were forbidden, whether sought by "*réformateurs*, seneschals, treasurers, or commissioners [presently] appointed or to be appointed [subsequently]".[123] Again it is evident that taxes and their collectors could have many names, forms, or alleged purposes and that they were far from limited to war subsidies per se even when used to pay for a war. This whole transaction was a bargain between the royal government and the municipal governments. Whatever interests the latter represented and whatever abuses or malpractices they may have been guilty of, the crown was approaching them with closed eyes and open hands. Town governments could apportion and manipulate this tax in any way they wished, without fear of prying *réformateurs* or complaints of injustice by the urban populace. This agreement resembled many of the lump-sum arrangements with individual towns during the two preceding generations. From one point of view, the royal government was plying the townsmen with promises and concessions in order to get money quickly. Yet the political opposition within the towns might legitimately view the same transaction from another angle, as an effort by municipal leadership to bribe the government into tolerating without question the status quo in urban affairs.

[122] *HL*, x, cols. 1067-1070, 1094-1096; *Gr. Chartrier*, nos. 2381, 3894; BN *Coll. Languedoc* 159, fol. 27v; 85, fol. 42r; Bardon, *Alais*, II, 32; AM Alès 1 S-13, no. 1. Following the grant by this assembly, representatives of the towns of Vivarais met in April to divide up this region's share of the subsidy. See A. Le Sourd, *Essai sur les Etats de Vivarais depuis leurs origines*, Paris, 1926, p. 24.

[123] *HL*, x, cols. 1067-69.

The Montpellier archives furnish additional information about the levy of this subsidy in the seneschalsy of Beaucaire. The seneschal confirmed an earlier authorization for the municipal taxes at Montpellier to continue for four more years. As promised at the assembly, commissioners on monetary transgressions were ordered to halt their activities but Armagnac had to repeat the order early in June.[124] During the same period, the crown received complaints that as the tax money was being turned over to royal officers, the latter rejected some of it because it was excessively debased. The towns accused the king's men of refusing to accept gold at its current price, and the king now ordered his subordinates to accept the funds.[125] There is not sufficient evidence to determine whether the officers were trying to squeeze a little extra from the taxpayers, or whether the towns, having been excused from penalties for monetary transgressions, had seized upon this concession as an excuse to pay taxes in the most debased money then circulating.

The crown carried out its promise to require nobles and other privileged groups to contribute to the subsidy,[126] but it soon found itself unable to honor its pledge to levy no more money during the remainder of 1353. As early as mid-May, Uzès protested when the lord of Loudun arrived seeking a contingent of crossbowmen. The whole seneschalsy of Beaucaire was being asked to supply 200 men, with the share of Uzès to be ten. In July, both Nîmes and Alès were protesting efforts to levy a tax in addition to that already paid for "the war of Saint-Antonin."[127] Yet Bertrand de Pibrac, now bishop of Vabres, did obtain another grant from this district in July. It produced a total of 22,874 *l.t.*, perhaps representing 7½ *sols* per hearth.[128]

The assembly at Najac in March was not confined to towns of the Beaucaire district, and the basic formula of a 10 *s. fouage* seems to have been the general basis for taxation in Languedoc. Dom Vaissete's statement that this tax was to produce 72,000 pounds in the Carcassonne district[129] seems unfounded, since another text indicates that a 10 *s.* hearth tax was normally expected to yield 50,000 pounds in this seneschalsy.[130]

---

[124] *Gr. Chartrier*, nos. 2372, 2373.

[125] *Ibid.*, nos. 188, 3363; BN *ms. lat.* 9174, fols. 267-268.

[126] *Ibid.*, fols. 255r-v; 269-270; AM Alès 1 S-11, no. 5; AM Nîmes NN 1, no. 37; AD Hérault A 5, fol. 19r-v.

[127] *Ibid.*, fols. 8v-15r; AM Alès 1 S-16, no. 19; Bardon, *Alais*, ii, 33; AM Nîmes NN 1, no. 38.

[128] BN *Coll. Languedoc* 159, fol. 27v.

[129] *HL*, ix, 641-642.

[130] BN *Coll. Languedoc* 85, fols. 36r-39v; AN JJ 81, no. 819.

This latter document sheds some light on the way in which taxes were assessed. The four large towns in the seneschalsy of Carcassonne—Béziers, Carcassonne, Limoux, and Narbonne—regularly paid a lump sum when hearth taxes were granted. In doing so, they must have escaped with a reduced burden because the lesser communities envied this privilege. Those which were subject to the count of Vendôme, resisted the hearth tax on the ground that they too had always paid lump sums. Doubtless they were correct in making this claim, but only because the king chose to take an accommodating position with respect to lands not in the royal domain.[131]

In Rouergue and Quercy, the traditional mode of payment was to grant a tax expressed in sergeants or men-at-arms, and since the siege of Saint-Antonin directly concerned these districts, it was particularly appropriate to ask them for troops in 1353. The town of Rodez may have preferred the hearth tax[132] and the abbey of Bonneval paid the crown 67 *écus*.[133] Millau was asked for troops and sent its contingent to Villefranche, which perhaps was the assembly point for the men of Rouergue. A hearth tax of one-half *écu* was levied at Millau to pay these troops.[134] Cajarc sent men to the siege of Saint-Antonin, while Cahors paid 600 *écus* and was excused from a second tax of 400 *écus*.[135] To raise its share of the subsidy, Albi tried a municipal sales tax but then replaced it with a direct tax, perhaps under pressure from the *populares* of the town.[136] In the viscounty of Lautrec, subjects of the count of Foix were excused from paying anything.[137]

In Auvergne, Montferrand floated a loan to repair fortifications and send "certain people" against the enemy.[138] Then the Estates of the bailiwick met in April to consider a royal request for a 6 *d./l.* sales tax.[139] Expecting an early agreement, John II sent a commissioner to his wife's nearby county of Auvergne, with instructions to collect the same tax granted in royal lands.[140] In May, the crown issued a set of commissions

[131] *Ibid.*

[132] *A.H. Rouergue*, VI, 244.

[133] De Gaujal, *Etude*, II, 187.

[134] *A.H. Rouergue*, VII, 90-93; AM Millau EE 121, no. 134; EE 6.

[135] Dufour, *Cahors*, p. 107, note 3; AM Cajarc EE *supp.*, unnumbered document. Gourdon was approached for money, but then seems to have been excused from paying: AM Gourdon CC 1, no. 19.

[136] AM Albi CC 68, no. 234; *HL*, IX, 642, note 1.

[137] AD Basses-Pyrénées E 490, no. 7.

[138] *INV AM Montferrand*, I, 374 (CC 163, fol. 67). Evidently the town encountered very high interest rates when borrowing the money needed to hire mercenaries to replace the contingent of burghers.

[139] *Ibid.*, p. 375.

[140] *Ord.*, IV, 135; AN P 2292, p. 491.

to collect 6 *d./l.* in many parts of Languedoïl, including Auvergne, and it seems possible to conclude, with Boudet, that the assembly granted the desired subsidy.[141] Montferrand, however, may have resisted, for the town's accounts do not mention this sales tax but do indicate acrimonious debate for the rest of 1353 with royal officers who were demanding troops.[142]

The commissions of mid-May directed that the 6 *d./l.* sales tax be levied in the districts of Touraine, Anjou, Bourges, Orléans, and Chartres as well as Auvergne.[143] The officer sent to Orléans and Chartres obtained agreement to the tax late in July. It was levied in the lands of the duchess of Alençon as well as those of the crown.[144] The government obtained new subsidies from the bailiwicks of Vitry and Chaumont and 500 *l.t.* from the town of Lyon.[145] In Vermandois, an assembly at Noyon in June renewed the 6 *d./l.* tax that was to expire in August.[146] The bailiwick of Amiens, however, was less generous. Asked for 6 *d./l.*, the *échevins* of Amiens and Abbeville agreed to pay only 4 *d./l.*, of which the towns would retain half the proceeds.[147] Ault-sur-Mer also agreed to continue the existing subsidy for another year, but it is not clear how large a tax was involved.[148] In Poitou, the 6 *d./l.* sales tax was in force, with 700 pounds being set aside from the receipts in order to repair the fortifications of Poitiers.[149]

The effort to tax Normandy in 1353 began with a commission of 3 April, one month earlier than those for the rest of Languedoïl.[150] By June, the Normans had agreed to pay the 6 *d./l.* sales tax from July 1353 through June 1354.[151] From a fragmentary account for the collection of this tax at Falaise, we learn that the Norman towns were authorized to levy an additional 2 *d./l.* for local defense.[152] The tax was levied in seigneurial as well as royal lands, for Charles IV's widow, Joan of

---

[141] Boudet, "Etats," p. 35. The commissions are indicated in AN PP 117, p. 674. *Ibid.*, p. 679, states that Guillaume Balbet was sent to tax the county of Auvergne.

[142] *INV AM Montferrand*, I, 375-377 (CC 163).

[143] AN PP 117, p. 674.

[144] *Ibid.*, pp. 674, 678; AN P 2292, pp. 453, 477, 499.

[145] AN PP 117, p. 678; AM Lyon CC 368.

[146] Varin, *Reims*, III, 37, note; *Ord.*, II, 529-532.

[147] *Ord.*, IV, 285; BN NAF 7609, fol. 58r-v.

[148] *Ord.*, IV, 277-279.   [149] *AHP*, XLVI, 149-151.

[150] AN PP 117, p. 674.

[151] Coville, *Etats Norm.*, p. 72; AN P 2292, p. 471; BN *ms. fr.* 20581, no. 24; BN *ms. fr.* 26000, nos. 260, 283.

[152] Coville, *Etats Norm.*, p. 359; BN *ms. fr.* 26000, nos. 235, 299; 20579, no. 39 (this last text indicating that Avranches also retained 500 *l.t.* of the tax).

Evreux, and her nephew, the king of Navarre, both authorized it in their lands in return for letters of non-prejudice.[153] This Norman grant appears to have been general throughout the duchy, but the bailiwicks of lower Normandy which were threatened by the enemy in Brittany held a new assembly in August to discuss measures of defense.[154] Arnoul d'Audrehem, the royal lieutenant, began to assemble an army about the same time,[155] and early in 1354, he convened local assemblies at Saint-Lô and Caen.[156] It thus appears that lower Normandy may have faced a heavier burden than the rest of the duchy.

Despite the evidence that taxes were paid throughout France in 1353 with relatively little resistance, it appears that many of the grants came some months after preceding taxes should have expired.[157] There may have been some reluctance to pay in Languedoil, especially since peace talks were in progress. On 26 July, the Anglo-French truce was renewed until November, pending negotiations which were then in progress at Guines.[158] On 7 November, when the extended truce was soon to expire, John II ordered the provost of Paris to proclaim the *arrière-ban*.[159] This document is our only evidence of taxation at Paris in 1353. The increased level of military activity in some localities, such as at Saint-Antonin and in lower Normandy, may have facilitated taxation of the areas directly affected, but it probably raised the king's expenses more rapidly than his revenue. John therefore turned to other fiscal expedients. For the first time in nine years, the crown began investigating acquisition of fiefs throughout the realm.[160] The coinage was altered several times, and the price of a mark of silver soared to 12.75 *l.t.*, the highest in a decade, before a new reform in the fall.[161]

His weak fiscal position may have made John II receptive to a more enduring peace with England, but the English were in a strong bargaining position, thanks to recent victories and a favorable settlement they had just reached in Brittany. The French candidate for the disputed Breton succession, Charles of Blois, had been an English captive for several years. On 1 March 1353, he concluded an agreement with Edward III whereby he would pay a ransom of 300,000 *écus*, make a marriage alliance with England, and assist the English against France. He would be recognized as duke of Brittany and would help Edward guarantee

---

[153] *Ord.*, III, 677-678; BN NAF 7609, fol. 98r-v.
[154] BN *ms. fr.* 26000, no. 230. Cf. Coville, *Etats Norm.*, pp. 72-73.
[155] AN JJ 82, no. 17 *bis*.   [156] Prentout, *Etats Norm.*, I, 103-104.
[157] AN P 2292, p. 477; PP 117, p. 678.
[158] *Foedera*, III pt. I, p. 86.   [159] AN P 2292, pp. 519-520.
[160] *Ord.*, IV, 134.   [161] See Appendix I, Table I.

that no English or French troops would enter Brittany or Limousin in time of peace.[162] This treaty perhaps was intended to force France to come to the conference table prepared to make concessions.[163] The French position, already unfavorable, was soon to be weakened further by a disastrous quarrel within the royal family.

[162] F. Bock, "Some New Documents Illustrating the Early Years of the Hundred Years' War (1353-1356)," *Bulletin of the John Rylands Library*, xv (1931), 63f., and text published *ibid.*, pp. 84-91.

[163] Perroy, "Franco-English Relations," p. 150.

CHAPTER VIII

The Valois-Evreux Rupture and the Fiscal Crisis of 1354-1356

1. Taxation and Treaty Negotiations, 1354

THE shaky equilibrium in fiscal matters attained by the government of John II in the early 1350s depended upon a low level of warfare, the goodwill of the three Estates of different regions, and the continuation of a fairly reliable income from the clerical tenth and the royal domain. Any disturbance which might increase royal expenses or reduce anticipated revenues could place the monarchy in dire financial straits. Such a disturbance was created in January 1354, when the young constable of France, Charles of Spain, was assassinated by agents of the king of Navarre and his brothers.[1] For the next twenty years, the rich duchy of Normandy experienced a sharp increase in violence and warfare and produced a sharply diminished revenue for the royal treasury. The assassination of the constable thus destroyed the royal financial position which had been achieved with such difficulty in the early 1350s. It was the most important event in the history of French taxation between the Black Death and the battle of Poitiers.

Charles II of Navarre (1349-1387) was the grandson of Louis X on his mother's side and the great-grandson of Philip III on his father's side. Louis X's mother had been the heiress of the counties of Champagne and Brie as well as Navarre, while Louis' daughter, Joan, was the princess excluded from the royal succession in 1316. If a woman could transmit a claim to the French throne, Charles of Navarre had a better claim than Edward III of England. From his father, Philip of Evreux, Charles inherited some highly strategic Norman lands as an *apanage*, and a hostility towards the Valois branch of the Capetian family which went back two generations.[2] Head of the house of Evreux since his teens, Charles II was a formidable figure for dynastic reasons, and John II had married his eldest daughter to the young king of Navarre. Two hundred years later, a Navarrese chronicler christened Charles "El Malo," and French historians mindful of his disruptive role in the fourteenth century quickly embraced the term.[3]

---

[1] Perroy, *The Hundred Years War*, p. 128; Delachenal, *Histoire de Charles V*, i, 83.

[2] Petit, *Charles de Valois*, p. 176; Cazelles, *Soc. politique*, pp. 206-208, indicate earlier phases of the feud.

[3] S. Honoré-Duvergé, "L'origine du surnom de Charles le Mauvais," *Mélanges Halphen*, Paris, 1951, pp. 345-350.

Charles the Bad was more than a powerful Norman lord with a formidable pedigree. He was also a more charismatic figure than his royal father-in-law and perhaps more able as well. He also had strong grievances against the king. In excluding Charles' mother from the French throne, Philip V and Charles IV had retained the lands which she ought to have inherited. Philip VI had hastened to restore Navarre to her, but the monarchy could not afford to surrender the strategic lands of Champagne and Brie, so arranged the substitution of other territories.[4] One of these was Angoulême, which the Evreux later exchanged for other lands. When he married John II's daughter in 1351, Charles the Bad was promised a large dowry which John found increasingly difficult to pay. Despite a series of enactments in 1352 arranging for the payment, the dowry was still largely unpaid at the end of the next year.[5] Meanwhile, Charles and his brothers developed a violent and envious hatred for Charles of Spain, a distant cousin of all the Capetians, who had been the ultimate recipient of the county of Angoulême. John II had conceived an extraordinary affection for Charles of Spain, who had been showered with favors and named constable of France in his mid-twenties.[6]

Charles the Bad was not alone in his feelings about Charles of Spain, for many members of the nobility of northern France had grown increasingly hostile to their king's tendency to let his personal feelings and prejudices influence policy. John's execution of the preceding constable, Raoul of Eu, had been widely condemned, and resentment at this action had been directed towards the youthful favorite who had succeeded Raoul. The smoldering discontent which had appeared a decade earlier had not entirely subsided, and perennial dissidents like the Harcourts now found common cause with the Evreux princes in opposing the king and the constable.[7] The result was the emergence of an important anti-Valois party in Normandy.

Whatever sympathy there may have been for the Evreux brothers when they engineered the assassination, the fact remains that murder of the constable, a spectacular crime in itself, was in this case a deeply personal attack upon the king. A psychological study of the three principals in this drama—the constable, Charles of Navarre, and John II—would, if feasible, make a valuable contribution to our understanding of the politics of the period. Certainly their relationships would have an impor-

---

[4] See Chapter II, note 184.

[5] Secousse, *Charles II*, II, 25; I (*preuves*), 25-27; AN PP 117, p. 665.

[6] Secousse, *Charles II*, II, 29; E. Meyer, *Charles II, roi de Navarre, comte d'Evreux, et la Normandie au XIVe siècle*, Paris, 1898, pp. 32f.

[7] *Ibid.*, pp. 33-35; Secousse, *Charles II*, II, 31; Delisle, *St. Sauveur*, pp. 72f.

tant effect on the constitutional and fiscal history of the later 1350s. We must content ourselves with Perroy's appraisal of John as a man who "lived in a permanent state of panic," who "struck without rhyme or reason at those whom he distrusted, and was incapable of letting these irrational hatreds subside."[8] Charles the Bad he describes as "attractive . . . intelligent and madly ambitious" as contrasted with the "lack-lustre Valois."[9]

Whatever more may be learned about the psychology of these royal princes, one is impressed by the atmosphere of rash and intemperate violence which characterized their relationships. The lack of confidence and insecurity which one finds so often in the aftermath of the Black Death, and in the later Middle Ages generally, were never more evident than in the behavior of John II during the thirty-two months preceding his capture at Poitiers. The French king vacillated between impulsive measures of vengeance and weak appeasement of his enemies. The bizarre conduct of persons such as Charles the Bad, Etienne Marcel, and Robert le Coq in the crisis of 1356-1358 was hardly more erratic than that of John II himself in the years immediately preceding. In fairness to the king, it must of course be remembered that the responsibilities of kingship complicated his position. The fiscal and military situation demanded that he suppress his personal rancors and desire for vengeance when the interests of the kingdom so dictated. Yet this very fact created in John what must have been an unendurable tension, helping to produce that "permanent state of panic" which so aptly characterized his behavior after 1353.

As for Charles of Navarre, he too fell victim to "irrational hatreds." However legitimate his grievances against the Valois, he made remarkably little effort to rally support and gain his ends through legitimate means, even though he was in a position to exert considerable political pressure. Instead, he chose to vent his frustrations by a violent and lawless act. Fortuitous circumstances would in time enable him to attract to his standard a wide variety of malcontents, but he nevertheless remained a renegade. However much the government may have needed reform in these years, the king of Navarre, by engineering the murder of the constable, forever compromised himself as a leader of such reforms. Efforts to overhaul the royal government in 1356-1358, insofar as they were at all sincere or disinterested, would be doomed by the unsavory connection with the house of Evreux. Besides crippling the chances for reform in the succeeding years, Charles the Bad also weakened his own oppor-

[8] Perroy, *The Hundred Years War*, p. 125.   [9] *Ibid.*, p. 128.

tunity to gain redress of legitimate grievances. Henceforth, he must always fear, probably correctly, that his royal father-in-law was plotting vengeance against him. Only the fiscal and military necessities of the English war compelled John II to make concessions to the Evreux. Charles had maneuvered himself into a position where his very security demanded that the international situation remain hostile and disordered. Rather than using his status as a prince of the blood to advance his personal interests, he was compelled from the first to act against the interests of France. Insofar as there existed in these years a desire for peace or a sense of French nationalism, Charles was bound to alienate those who held such sentiments unless he could temporarily deceive them. Writing of Charles the Bad and his murder of the constable, Zacour has aptly observed that "from this moment on his policy, if such it may be called, was to protect himself by exploiting the enmity between the English and the French."[10]

The king of Navarre's persuasive personality was never more in evidence than in his dealings with the pope. Notwithstanding English suspicions of the Avignon papacy, Innocent VI had naturally assumed a major responsibility for efforts to secure an Anglo-French peace in the 1350s. The interests of Charles the Bad were totally opposed to such a peace, yet Innocent seems never to have realized this fact completely. In 1354-1355, he appears to have been utterly persuaded of the king of Navarre's sincerity.[11] In mid-January 1354, Charles seems to have written the pontiff explaining the assassination of the constable in such a way that Innocent VI did not even reproach him for the act.[12] Throughout the remainder of the year, Innocent's correspondence repeatedly urged Charles and John to become reconciled.[13] The pope could hardly have advocated anything else, but one infers that he did not really understand the situation very clearly. His failure to perceive that Charles the Bad could not afford an Anglo-French peace impaired the effectiveness of the pope's role as peacemaker.

From the point of view of the French crown, deteriorating finances and the likelihood of an imminent renewal of the war, compelled John

---

[10] Zacour, *Talleyrand*, pp. 44-45. Cf. G. Mollat, "Innocent VI et les tentatives de paix entre la France et l'Angleterre," *Revue d'histoire ecclésiastique*, x (1909), 738; and Denifle, *Désolation*, II, 172-173.

[11] *Ibid.*, pp. 98-101. Denifle's book is valuable in many respects but is marred by the author's partisanship. He seems to have been even more hostile to Charles II than was Secousse.

[12] *Ibid.*, p. 99, and excerpt of Vatican Register 236 which is published in note 5.

[13] *Ibid.*, pp. 101-102 and notes.

II to suppress his thoughts of revenge and seek some accommodation with the Evreux brothers;[14] for Charles the Bad had immediately sought to protect himself by entering into negotiations with the English, boasting of his responsibility for the murder of Charles of Spain.[15] The nearest important English commander was Henry of Lancaster, who was in Brabant without troops. Despite a second urgent appeal from Charles before the end of January, Lancaster was in no position to intervene on behalf of the king of Navarre. Charles, however, had made no secret of his appeals to England, and John II felt compelled to take a conciliatory position.[16]

Accordingly, on 8 February, John II commissioned the cardinal of Boulogne and the duke of Bourbon to conduct negotiations with the Evreux. They were empowered to satisfy Charles' longstanding demand for lands to compensate for his lost inheritance of Champagne and Brie. They were also to grant any necessary letters of remission for the murder of Charles of Spain.[17] The negotiations culminated in the Treaty of Mantes (22 February 1354) by which the Evreux brothers and their accomplices received their pardon. More important, Charles the Bad was now permitted to add a sizeable part of Normandy to the lands already held by his family: the county of Beaumont-le-Roger and the viscounties of Carentan, Coutances, and Pont Audemer, all to be held directly of the French crown subject to liege homage, and thus on an equal footing with the lands of the duke of Normandy. In return, Pontoise and Beaumont-sur-Oise, less strategic places, were returned to the crown and Charles permanently renounced Champagne.[18] The king of Navarre now controlled virtually the entire Cotentin peninsula and his stranglehold on lower Normandy presented a serious complication to any French plan to repulse the raids launched by English marauders based in Brittany.

[14] Perroy, *The Hundred Years War*, pp. 128-129. Zacour, *Talleyrand*, p. 45, accepts the notion that John II had been "kept in the dark about the extent of Charles' complicity in the murder of Charles de la Cerda." Since, however, the king of Navarre immediately boasted about the deed to the English, John II must have soon learned all the facts. It must have been policy rather than ignorance which caused him to appease his son-in-law during 1354.

[15] R. Delachenal, "Premières négotiations de Charles le Mauvais avec les Anglais (1354-1355)," *BEC*, LXI (1900), 254-255; *Chron. Jean II*, p. 39.

[16] Delachenal, "Premières négotiations," pp. 256-257, 259, 272f. See *Foedera*, III pt. 1, no. 93.

[17] Secousse, *Charles II*, I (*preuves*), 27-32.

[18] *Ibid.*, pp. 33-36, for the treaty, and pp. 37-44, for texts relating to its execution. See also, Denifle, *Désolation*, II, 100; Mollat, "Innocent VI . . . ," p. 738; Meyer, *Charles II*, pp. 42f; *Chron. Jean II*, pp. 40-42.

In addition, the capacity of Normandy to furnish taxes and troops to the king of France now depended utterly on Valois-Evreux relations.[19] These relations remained badly strained and Charles the Bad actually continued his negotiations for English aid until several weeks following the Mantes treaty.[20]

It was in this extremely difficult atmosphere that Arnoul d'Audrehem, as royal lieutenant in the region, convened assemblies in lower Normandy during the early weeks of 1354 to provide for the defense of the land.[21] Whether or not this district had already been forced to supplement the existing sales tax, more resources now were needed. Meeting first at Saint-Lô late in January and perhaps again at Caen some weeks later,[22] the three Estates of Cotentin and adjacent districts agreed that every one hundred hearths would furnish the upkeep for one knight and one archer to serve three months, the money to be used for no purpose other than local military operations.[23] There is no indication as to how the new acquisitions by Charles the Bad in Cotentin affected this grant, but it seems doubtful that he permitted the royal levy in his lands as he had the year before. The general Norman sales tax of 6 *d./l.* ended on 30 June 1354[24] but was evidently renewed, for a royal letter of late July 1354 indicates that a $2\frac{1}{2}$ percent imposition was again in force.[25] In the course of the summer, the king had to order that officers in Normandy apply all available resources to the war.[26]

Meanwhile, it seems that John II decided to call an assembly of the Estates General during the early spring, although the motives which led him to do so are not clear. A document of 18 March reports that the "good towns of the kingdom" were to send the king "two, three, or four wisest and best-advised [persons]" upon receipt of letters sent that day, while a comparable summons went to the barons.[27] On 24 April, a treasury journal entry recorded the remuneration of clerks who had drafted

---

[19] Denifle, *Désolation*, II, 100. The strategically placed Godefroy d'Harcourt supported Charles the Bad.

[20] Delachenal, "Premières négotiations," pp. 261-262. Delachenal saw the treaty of Mantes as unexpected and irritating to the English.

[21] E. Molinier, "Etudes sur la vie d'Arnoul d'Audrehem, maréchal de France (1302-1370)," *Mémoires présentées par divers savants à l'Academie des Inscriptions et Belles Lettres*, 2e sér., VI pt. 1 (1883), 222-223, P.J. 18.

[22] Coville, *Etats Norm.*, p. 74.

[23] *Ord.*, IV, 319-320; BN NAF 7376, fols. 296-298.

[24] BN *ms. fr.* 26000, no. 283.   [25] BN Moreau 233, fols. 50-51.

[26] BN Clairambault 213, nos. 29, 35.

[27] AN P 2292, pp. 537, 539. A summons may have reached Alès. Bardon, *Alais*, II, 34, note 1, certainly knew of the scheduled meeting.

letters close summoning the "barons, bannerets, and good towns of the kingdom" to an assembly of undisclosed time, place or purpose.[28] There is no evidence that such an assembly ever convened, although there were a variety of circumstances which could have prompted John to consider a large-scale consultation. Besides the deteriorating fiscal situation and the rupture with the Evreux family (and in part because of these), the king now had to choose between a disadvantageous peace settlement and an imminent renewal of major hostilities.

The source of the royal dilemma was an extraordinary treaty which his representatives finally concluded with the English on 6 April 1354. This document represented the nadir of French diplomatic fortunes in the fourteenth century. Appropriately enough, the negotiations took place at Guines, former possession of Raoul of Eu, whose execution by the king had provoked a storm of criticism several years before. The treaty of Guines arranged for France to cede to England the regions of Aquitaine, Anjou and Maine, Touraine, Limousin, and Ponthieu, all in *full sovereignty*. It also proposed two Anglo-French marriages, each of which would bring England dowries of 100,000 *écus*. A truce would go into effect until 1 April 1355, pending the ratification of the treaty at the papal court.[29]

The critical questions about this treaty have been posed by Perroy: why did the French give up so much, and what made them change their minds later?[30] It is of course possible that Guy, Cardinal of Boulogne, the principal French negotiator, exceeded his instructions for motives of his own. It is probable, however, that France was in so difficult a position in 1354 that drastic concessions were necessary. They could be modified or repudiated in later negotiations at Avignon if conditions seemed more favorable. The Anglo-Breton treaty of 1353 had given Edward a club to use in forcing concessions from the French, while the murder of the constable and Charles the Bad's appeal to England had been an unexpected blessing of far greater importance. Lacking the finances to fight a major campaign, John II was now confronted with the fact that most of Normandy was held by hostile seigneurs. A renewal of the war at this time might have cost more in the end than did the treaty of Guines.

By nature indecisive and lacking in confidence, John II submitted, for the present, to humiliation at the hands of England, just as he had sub-

---

[28] Moranvillé, "Extraits," p. 206.

[29] Bock, "New Docs.," pp. 71-73, 91-93. The lands were to be granted to the English king *inperpetuum libere et in allodio.*

[30] Perroy, "Franco-English Relations," p. 149.

mitted to a humiliating treaty with Charles the Bad six weeks before. There can be no doubt, however, that he looked forward to the day when he might gain revenge. This fact was not lost upon the Evreux princes and the Harcourts, and no amount of wishful thinking on the part of Innocent VI could alter the atmosphere of hatred and distrust which the assassination of Charles of Spain and subsequent events had engendered.

In the spring and summer of 1354, nothing was said publicly about the treaty, although it was widely known that there would be negotiations at Avignon later in the year for the purpose of concluding a lasting peace. Pending these talks a truce had been proclaimed on 6 April,[31] and John II welcomed this latest respite from the war. He issued circular letters on 1 May announcing this truce and enjoining all his subjects to keep it faithfully.[32] In the light of these diplomatic activities, it seems safe to conclude that the proposed Estates had been contemplated as a fiscal measure in the event that full-scale war resumed. At some unknown date (but surely prior to 6 April), John proclaimed the *arrière-ban*, ordering the "barons, nobles, and good towns of the kingdom" to muster, armed and mounted, at Compiègne on 27 April.[33] The scribes who drafted this order were paid twelve days earlier than those who prepared the letters calling the assembly.[34] In all probability, John hoped to negotiate a subsidy with the Estates and believed that his bargaining position would be strengthened by a prior military summons.[35] Once the truce was announced, it was possible to cancel both orders and resume the practice of negotiating sales taxes with bailiwick assemblies as in the past few years.

Besides the apparent renewal of the 6 *d./l.* sales tax in Normandy,[36] we know of tax agreements with several other districts. All involve the familiar levy of 2½ percent on sales, and although there is less documen-

---

[31] *Foedera*, III pt. 1, pp. 95-96.

[32] BN NAF 7609, fol. 176. The royal finances were somewhat bolstered by the grant of a new clerical tenth by the pope: BN Doat 8, fol. 199f.

[33] AN PP 117, p. 690.   [34] Moranvillé, "Extraits," pp. 203-204.

[35] Letters to the seneschal of Beaucaire early in the spring said that the king had lost all hope of concluding a new truce, and that nobles and non-nobles must therefore be in readiness for a new military summons: BN *ms. lat.* 9174, fols. 263-266v. It appears that all the traditional assumptions still applied, that a tax would still be linked to a call to arms if possible, and that the latter depended on the status of the truce. Presumably the Estates would have served as a propaganda vehicle, before whom the king could stress the urgency of the situation in the hope that a tax would be forthcoming more quickly than was usual when a truce expired (see above, Chapter v, for the experience of 1345).

[36] See above, note 25.

tation for 1354 than for most other years of John's reign, it is probable that this tax was renewed generally in the North. The hesitation over whether to hold a central assembly, and the uncertainties concerning the truce, combined to give the crown a late start in seeking the new grants. In addition, the taxes took longer to negotiate, perhaps because of a growing reluctance to support the ineffectual monarch when a peace treaty seemed about to be ratified. With these delays before the sales taxes were renewed, and with the Evreux party now openly hostile to the king, it seems probable that royal tax receipts declined in 1354. Certainly financial distress would be most evident in the following year.

At any rate, the crown duly issued commissions for the negotiation and levy of a new 6 *d./l.* sales tax in 1354.[37] Notable among the commissioners was Robert le Coq, bishop of Laon, a former royal councillor and bitter enemy of the murdered constable, who had been taken back into the king's service after the treaty of Mantes.[38] Assigned to the bailiwick of Senlis, Le Coq and his associates concluded a subsidy agreement with the Estates of that district in July.[39] Towards the end of August, Philip of Orléans received a letter of non-prejudice for permitting the sales tax to be raised in his lands for another year.[40] By September, the imposition was in force in Poitou.[41] It was December, however, before the bailiwick of Vermandois agreed to renew its contribution of 6 *d./l.* Here, there were bitter complaints about the failure of the crown to enforce its earlier promises restricting the right of *prise*. These requisitions were to be limited to cases of necessity, with a just price to be paid for any property taken. In an ordinance of nineteen articles, the king again promised reform of this abuse, agreed that the sales tax would prejudice no rights, and authorized the continuation of all municipal sales taxes then in force.[42]

2. *Languedoc and the Prince of Wales*

In Languedoc, where Count John of Armagnac remained the king's chief representative, the government continued to rely on frequent short-term grants of men or money to deal with an increasing military threat and a chronic shortage of funds. The result was an almost constant

[37] AN PP 117, pp. 693-694.
[38] On Le Coq, see Cazelles, *Soc. politique*, pp. 256-261.
[39] *Ord.*, II, 557-558.
[40] *Ord.*, IV, 292.   [41] AN P 2292, p. 591.
[42] *Ord.*, II, 567-570; BN Moreau 233, fols. 69r-75v; Varin, *Reims*, III, 59-62; Le Maire, *St. Quentin*, II, no. 662.

round of tax negotiations which must have severely handicapped Armagnac's efforts to prosecute the war. The seneschalsy of Beaucaire had paid two taxes in 1352 and two more in 1353. At the end of 1353, Armagnac may have obtained a third subsidy. It is certain that a new *fouage* was being collected in the Beaucaire district in the first month of 1354. These three taxes appear to have amounted in all to 25 *s.t.* per hearth, thus producing about the same total as the two larger hearth taxes in 1352.[43] One infers that the towns were increasingly reluctant to contribute, yet had to give in when confronted by the military necessity of the Saint-Antonin campaign.[44]

Montpellier's subsidy grant at the beginning of 1354 reflected the growing discontent with the situation. On 7 January, Armagnac accepted a *don gratuit* of 2,000 *écus* to be paid in three widely separated installments, the last being due on 24 June. In return, citizens of Montpellier were excused from monetary violations and no more taxes were to be exacted from the town during 1354 unless the king of England personally came to Gascony.[45] Reacting to Armagnac's inability to limit himself to a single tax in 1353, the consuls of Montpellier thus undertook to define with great precision the circumstances under which they would make another payment. Once again, we find a locality challenging the government's definition of "necessity" and seeking to establish its own criteria for a situation which might justify extraordinary levies of money.

As in the North, a strong reluctance to contribute subsidies persisted, despite the superficial impression of larger, more frequent, and more uniform grants during the 1350s. Royal progress in obtaining taxes, as

[43] BN *Coll. Languedoc* 159, fols. 27v-28r. The two taxes of 1352, discussed in the last chapter, amounted to 15 and 10 *s.t.* per hearth respectively, and produced over 85,000 pounds in the seneschalsy of Beaucaire. In 1353, the first hearth tax had been for 10 *s*. A second one, which produced 22,874 *l.t.* during the summer, averaged about 7½ *s*. per hearth. At the end of 1353, and the beginning of 1354, the crown collected another 22,862 *l.t.*, evidently another 7½ *sols* per hearth. The three *fouages* totaled 25 *s.t.* per hearth, the same amount levied in 1351 in a single tax and in 1352 in two separate levies.

[44] The perseverance of the count of Armagnac was finally rewarded early in 1354 when Saint-Antonin was recaptured. See Darmaillacq, "Prince Noir," p. 6. Also rewarded were the taxpayers of Languedoc who had paid such frequent, albeit small, subsidies. Just as the southern assemblies were proving more effective than those in the North, so also did tax revenues appear to be employed more effectively. These two facts may help to explain the different behavior of the Estates in Languedoïl and Languedoc in the next few years. At the same time, the fall of Saint-Antonin removed the sense of danger, helped contribute to the opposition to taxes found in Languedoc in 1354, and may also have contributed to a sense of false security on the eve of the serious English attack of 1355.

[45] *Gr. Chartrier*, no. 2375; *HL*, IX, 645.

compared with the middle 1340s, was not a reflection of greater compliance, but rather an indication of changing habits. As circumstances compelled a reluctant population to pay higher and more regular taxes out of self-interest, the towns became accustomed to more frequent negotiations and more effective cooperation in bargaining.

The consuls of Montpellier may have had their own troubles in 1354 raising the sum promised to the royal lieutenant. The day before their final payment was due, they obtained permission to levy for an additional month a municipal sales tax currently in force. At the same time, they were accused of charging foreign residents a higher rate than local citizens.[46] The count of Armagnac, meanwhile, was also having difficulties. He appears to have tried to honor his promise to Montpellier regarding further taxation during the year, but it seems clear that he remained in considerable need of funds. He therefore used some ingenuity in finding additional resources, although his methods hardly were new. An assessment of a silver mark on notaries in the seneschalsy of Beaucaire produced a modest sum in May.[47] An attempt to divert to the war effort the proceeds of the 1 *d./l.* still levied to maintain the port at Aigues Mortes encountered resistance from the consuls of Montpellier.[48] Undaunted, Armagnac next attempted to collect unpaid arrears from earlier taxes, a time-honored expedient. It will be recalled that John II at his accession had finally canceled the 1,500 *l.t.* still unpaid from Montpellier's 6,000 *l.t.* subsidy grant in 1348 before the plague. In his fiscal extremity of 1354, Armagnac now tried to collect this sum, but a succession of royal letters in September and October confirmed the earlier remission and therefore thwarted this scheme.[49]

The royal lieutenant naturally did not limit his fiscal activity in 1354 to the seneschalsy of Beaucaire, but the documentation from other places is somewhat limited. At the beginning of the year, the consuls of Pézenas and Agde protested a small hearth tax in their region.[50] It is quite possible that wealthy interests in the Carcassonne district were becoming disenchanted with apportioned hearth taxes by this time, for the subsidy paid in this seneschalsy early in 1354 took the form of a 5 *s. fouage* and a sales tax of 6 *d./l.*[51] Many towns had traditionally levied municipal sales taxes in order to pay their share of a *fouage* and be free of royal tax

---

[46] *Gr. Chartrier*, nos. 2376-2377. [47] BN *Coll. Languedoc* 159, fol. 28r.

[48] *Gr. Chartrier*, nos. 3781, 3784.

[49] *Ibid.*, nos. 3990, 3992, 3993. On Montpellier's earlier grant see above, Chapter vi, and Henneman, "Black Death," pp. 414-417, 419.

[50] *INV AM Pézenas*, no. 1655.

[51] AM Albi CC 68, pcs. 2 and 3; BN Doat 103, fols. 335r-338v; *HL*, ix, 645, note 2.

collectors. However, the resistance of privileged groups and the growing hostility of the *populares* to indirect taxation had increasingly forced town governments to request the help of royal officers in enforcing collection. Perhaps the pressure of internal municipal politics now persuaded town consuls to grant their subsidy (at least in part) as a sales tax. In this way, the royal government rather than the municipality would bear the onus and responsibility for collecting the money.[52] Unfortunately, there is very little evidence to illuminate this question. We learn of this subsidy from the archives of Albi, and other documents in the same series indicate that Albi owed a subsidy of 1,333 *écus* in the summer of 1354 and obtained a reduction to 1,100 *écus*.[53] These latter texts give no indication as to whether this was a second subsidy or a commutation of the earlier hearth and sales-tax combination. During the summer, the crown conducted extensive financial negotiations in Rouergue[54] but because of war damage the king ordered his men to moderate their demands upon Quercy.[55] Among the towns of upper Languedoc, Conques, Najac, and Martel paid *finances* for a hearth tax.[56] The consuls of Agen granted Armagnac 200 sergeants for a siege of Aiguillon and also sent troops to fight the English near La Réole, but soon they had to take emergency measures when Agen itself came under attack.[57] The whole region remained a battleground despite the truce of 6 April.[58]

Despite his financial difficulty, the king never ceased to grant tax concessions to different persons and groups. Inhabitants of the county of Foix were declared exempt from *universa subsidia, tallias, focagia, financias, et impositiones* levied for the war.[59] Three seigneurs who had deserted the English service were given 1,300 *l.t.* annually from the export tax in the Carcassonne district until their lands were recovered.[60] Toulouse may not have paid any subsidy in 1354, for the government needed to maintain its loyalty and its fortifications. The town was permitted to prolong the municipal taxes employed for local defense and received new guarantees of exemption from *franc-fief*.[61]

---

[52] See above, Chapter I, at notes 40-42.

[53] BN Doat 103, fols. 331r-333v; Compayré, *Etudes*, p. 259; AM Albi CC 68, nos. 96, 105, 410, 412.

[54] BN *ms. fr.* 21047, pp. 648-697.

[55] Albe, "Cahors INV," nos. 435, 436; Lacoste, *Quercy*, III, 145.

[56] AD Aveyron 2E 67, no. 22, fol. 10r; 2E 178, no. 8 pt. 2, fols. 2r-4v; AM Martel CC 4, fols. 57v-59r.

[57] AM Agen BB 16.   [58] *HL*, IX, 645-647.

[59] BN Doat 191, fols. 233r-236v.   [60] AN JJ 82, no. 57.

[61] *Ibid.*, nos. 232, 562; *INV AM Toulouse*, pp. 23-24, 466 (AA 3, no. 130; AA 35, nos. 109, 116).

The constant succession of sieges, raids, broken truces, subsidy requests and extortionate expedients made the prospect of a permanent peace very attractive to the inhabitants of Languedoc. Late in the year, the ambassadors of France and England were to convene at Avignon to discuss ratification of the treaty of Guines.[62] Late in August, Edward III issued the necessary powers for his ambassadors,[63] and two months later, he dispatched secret instructions to the duke of Lancaster and earl of Arundel, who were to head the English mission to Avignon. These instructions indicated that the vast territorial concessions of the treaty of Guines were to compensate Edward for abandoning his claim to the French throne. In order to obtain peace, Edward was prepared to abandon some of these lands, and he told his envoys where they might retreat, but he urged them not to let the negotiations be broken off.[64] The treaty was too advantageous to England not to be pursued, but in the months since April, both sides had assumed a more militant stance, which decreased the chances of ratification. Edward seems to have abandoned the Breton treaty of 1353 and was clearly preparing to resume the offensive there.[65] This military build-up and the numerous English truce violations in Agenais had angered the French, who were, in any case, unlikely to go through with the disastrous arrangements made at Guines in April.[66]

France now refused to make the promised cessions of territory in full sovereignty,[67] and any hope of prolonging the negotiations was ruined by Charles of Navarre. The latter had no doubt that John II still plotted revenge against him for the murder of Charles of Spain, and by mid-October even the pope had become aware of the widening breach between the king of France and the Evreux. A barrage of papal letters urged all parties to keep calm and become reconciled,[68] but the kings of France and Navarre were not of a temperament to forgive and forget. In November, Charles the Bad, fearing for his safety, fled to Avignon, where he managed to persuade the pontiff of his sincere intentions while simultaneously reopening negotiations with the English.[69] No longer able

---

[62] Delachenal, *Histoire de Charles V*, I, 89.

[63] *Foedora*, III, pt. I, pp. 100-101; Mollat, "Innocent VI . . . ," p. 739.

[64] Bock, "New Docs.," pp. 75-77, 94-96.   [65] *Ibid.*, p. 80.

[66] Perroy, *The Hundred Years War*, p. 129, says that the French reversed their earlier position on the treaty out of indignation at the continuing Navarrese intrigues and the English build-up in Brittany. I am not persuaded that the French government ever seriously expected to go through with the treaty.

[67] Mollat, "Innocent VI . . . ," p. 741.

[68] Denifle, *Désolation*, II, 102-104, and notes.

[69] Delachenal, "Premières négociations," pp. 269-270; Secousse, *Charles II*, I, 49-50; Zacour, *Talleyrand*, pp. 44-45; Denifle, *Désolation*, II, 102.

to restrain his own fury, John II attempted to seize Charles' Norman possessions, but several important fortresses refused to admit royal troops[70] and thus remained valuable pawns in the continuing Anglo-Navarrese negotiations. An Anglo-French peace would naturally leave Charles the Bad in a highly vulnerable position. By offering the English access to Normandy through Cherbourg, he afforded them an opportunity which sharply diminished their own interest in peace at the very time that France was balking at surrendering sovereignty over ceded territories. Charles now presented a scheme for partitioning France between himself and Edward III which he had prepared some months before. The acceptance of this scheme by Henry of Lancaster marked the end of Anglo-French negotiations and nothing more was heard about the treaty of Guines.[71] Neither Charles nor the English were yet ready to take the offensive, however, so the expiration of the truce was moved from April to late June.[72] This short extension was all that Innocent VI could salvage out of the peace negotiations from which he had hoped so much. It was now all but certain that full-scale hostilities would resume in mid-1355 after nearly eight years of truces and minor skirmishing.

It was Languedoc which was to feel the full force of English power in 1355, just as it had a decade earlier. And despite the continuous state of war which had existed in the Southwest, the inhabitants again failed to make effective resistance, with results even more costly than in 1345. Perhaps Armagnac's recapture of Lafrançaise and Saint-Antonin persuaded the southern population that they were no longer threatened. Certainly, his repeated exactions for these and other projects had left considerable public irritation in their wake.

It is rather difficult to determine precisely what taxes were demanded and obtained in Languedoc during 1355. On 29 December 1354, the king himself took a hand in the matter, doubtless being informed that his lieutenant in the South was running into serious opposition in his efforts to raise money. In a letter to the seneschals of Carcassonne and Beaucaire and the *juge mage* of Toulouse, John II ordered that the towns of these three districts be convened and asked to pay a subsidy amounting to 2 *écus* for every pre-plague hearth (*secundum anticum numerum focorum*) in order to resist the expected Anglo-Gascon assault. Perhaps remembering the condition which Montpellier had attached to its grant a year earlier, John reported that Edward III himself was expected to come to Bordeaux. The royal receivers were to levy this tax even if the

[70] *Chron. Jean II*, p. 47; Denifle, *Désolation*, II, 102.
[71] Delachenal, "Premières négociations," pp. 264-268, 270.
[72] Delachenal, *Histoire de Charles V*, I, 92.

towns did not consent, *cum necessitas leges non habeat*.[73] Our only further information about it, however, comes from old local histories which report that in February, the Beaucaire district granted 48,300 gold *agneaux* while Carcassonne produced 84,000 *agneaux*.[74] Another small sum was obtained from the notaries.[75] Privilege, however, remained a factor, as dependents of the bishop of Valence escaped paying.[76] To maximize collections and obtain more where possible, Armagnac invoked the now familiar and unpopular device of naming *réformateurs*. Although their principal assignment seems to have been legitimate enough (punishment of royal officers for "excesses and crimes"),[77] their extortions aroused such an outcry that in mid-July the count suspended their commissions until the end of September.[78] The plan to assess the population of Languedoc 2 *écus* for every former hearth was extended beyond the three largest seneschalsies once their grants had been made.[79] By April, the towns of Rouergue had assembled and granted 5,000 *écus* payable in three installments.[80] In Quercy, however, Martel seems to have substituted an indirect tax (*gabela*) for the hearth tax paid a year earlier.[81] Besides these various grants, there is some evidence of new demands for men and money in the spring of 1355.[82]

It was the autumn of 1355 before the expected blow fell. On 20 September, Edward the Black Prince, prince of Wales, disembarked at Bordeaux with a force of 4,000 men.[83] He soon began a destructive raid which penetrated to the great towns of the Mediterranean coast. "His intention was not to conquer this region but to ruin it,"[84] and in achieving

---

[73] *HL*, x, cols. 1103-1105; *Gr. Chartrier*, no. 1767; Bardon, *Alais*, ii, 33-34.

[74] Ménard, *Nismes*, ii, 146; *HL*, ix, 649. [75] *Ibid.*

[76] *HL*, x, cols. 1106-1107. [77] *Gr. Chartrier*, no. 1768.

[78] *HL*, ix, 650; BN *Coll. Languedoc* 85, fols. 71r-72v.

[79] AM Millau CC 510, no. 147.

[80] *Ibid.*, CC 510, unnumbered document. [81] AM Martel CC 4, fols. 72v-73v.

[82] *HL*, x, col. 1107, briefly mentions a commission on 11 May to levy a subsidy, marks of silver, and *alie servitute*. It is not clear whether such taxes were those already mentioned here or new levies. A document inventoried in AM Alès 1 S-12, no. 3 concerns an effort to raise crossbowmen in that town in June of 1355 (Cf. Bardon, *Alais*, ii, 36, for a refusal of Alès to send troops to the war in May). *Gr. Chartrier*, D-19, no. 91, is an urgent new subsidy request of 18 May with no indication of the year. The archivist has tentatively assigned this text to 1355. The count of Armagnac requested 600 crossbowmen from the Carcassonne district and may have received some tax in return for canceling this request on 8 June (*INV AM Pézenas*, no. 1660). For feverish construction of fortifications in Languedoc, see *HL*, ix, 653-655.

[83] A. Breuils, "Jean Ier, comte d'Armagnac, et le mouvement national dans le Midi au temps du prince noir," *RQH*, lix (1896), 54; Lehoux, *Jean de France*, i, 47.

[84] *Ibid.*

this goal he was quite successful. Ravaging the hereditary lands of John of Armagnac, Edward spread his devastation past Carcassonne and Narbonne, approached Montpellier and then doubled back past Toulouse, reaching Bordeaux again by early December and leaving the countryside of Languedoc a smoking ruin behind him.[85] Prior to this disaster, the evidence of more regular taxation in Languedoc in the 1350s had been more apparent than real, and we have seen that hostility to royal fiscal and military exactions had been increasing during 1353 and 1354. From this time onward, however, the rapid English gains and the subsequent inroads of the "companies" would create an almost permanent state of "evident necessity" in Languedoc, with a corresponding change, albeit gradual, in the attitude towards taxation.

The appearance of the Black Prince did not give rise to any common reaction in Languedoc, for the scope of the problem varied from one district to another according to the proximity of the enemy. The seneschalsy of Beaucaire, farthest from Gascony, had time to levy a new tax with which to equip more troops. As early as September 1355, the agents of the count of Armagnac were busily seeking a new subsidy.[86] In the face of considerable opposition, he obtained 1,500 *agneaux* from Alès and 4,000 *l.t.* from Montpellier.[87] Early in 1356, the government tried to extort more from Montpellier but the consuls argued that they had supplied troops and were levying special taxes already for their fortifications.[88] The rebuilding of ramparts assumed the highest priority in the badly ravaged Carcassonne district and most taxes there were devoted to this purpose.[89] Rouergue was asked to pay another 2 *s.* per hearth, but having escaped the worst of the English attack, this district was mainly interested in avoiding taxes if other regions failed to pay them. Summoned to Villefranche in December, the towns offered 5,000 *écus* of which Millau's share was to be 441. The consuls of Rodez balked at paying until the whole seneschalsy's assessment was cut in half, to a mere 2,500 *écus*.[90]

[85] H. Hewitt, *The Black Prince's Expedition of 1355-1357*, Manchester, 1958, pp. 43-77; Darmaillacq, "Prince Noir," pp. 13-17, 65-68; Breuils, "Jean Ier," pp. 54-58; Denifle, *Désolation*, II, 85-93; BN *Coll. Languedoc*, 85, fol. 67r; Lehoux, *Jean de France*, I, 48-49.

[86] *Gr. Chartrier*, no. 1769.

[87] *Ibid.*, nos. 1770, 2384; Bardon, *Alais*, II, 37-38; AM Alès I S-16, no. 22.

[88] *Gr. Chartrier*, nos. 1961, 2383.

[89] De Gaujal, *Etude*, II, 190; Mahul, *Cartulaire*, III, 257; BN Doat 53, fols. 226r-242v; Doat 93, fols. 200r-218v. Cf. *HL*, IX, 653-655; Breuils, "Jean Ier," p. 53.

[90] *A. H. Rouergue*, VI, 245-246, note; AM Millau EE 119, no. 112, and EE 8 (tax roll). A ms. inventory in AD Aveyron describes a text in AM Millau CC 516 which is now lost, indicating payment of part of Millau's share of the reduced assessment.

Perhaps disappointed by Armagnac's failure to stop the Prince of Wales, and desiring to bolster royal prestige in Languedoc, the king announced in mid-February 1356 that his son Charles, the seventeen-year-old duke of Normandy and dauphin, would soon become royal representative in Languedoc.[91] A week later, Charles sent word that two special commissioners were heading south to seek a subsidy, and that representatives of the towns were to assemble before them at Toulouse on 26 March.[92] The decisions of this important assembly were promulgated on 4 April 1356. The two special commissioners, Bertrand de Pibrac (now bishop of Nevers) and Jean Chalemard (president of the *Parlement*), were joined by Robert de Clermont, the dauphin's marshal. They presided over a meeting of town representatives from all the seneschalsies of Languedoc. The assembly agreed to a double tax for one year —one *agnel* per hearth and a 6 *d./l.* on sales. The need for taxes was undeniable, but it is probable that those apportioned according to pre-1348 hearth counts were becoming onerous. As urban governments found it increasingly hard to pay for their fortifications and raise their quotas of royal subsidies through municipal taxation, they evidently were prepared to let the crown raise indirect taxes for part of the subsidy. It was stipulated that these taxes would prejudice no rights and would replace all other taxes during the year.[93]

Levy of the new subsidy in Languedoc was also to be conditional upon the actual arrival of the dauphin, for there was some concern that he was not really coming.[94] The attachment of this condition to the grant indicates that Languedoc may have doubted the king's commitment to the defense of the Midi. This region would stand firmly by the crown in later crises, during the king's captivity and again in the 1420s. In early 1356, however, Languedoc suffered from its own crisis. The impression is inescapable that this was a crisis of morale, demanding the presence of a royal lieutenant with more prestige than John of Armagnac; someone who would symbolize a personal involvement in the problems of Languedoc on the part of the Valois family. When the earl of Derby ravaged Languedoc in 1345, the heir to the throne had hurried south to act as royal lieutenant. The southern towns wanted similar reassurance after the more destructive and terrifying campaign of the Black Prince. They

[91] Delachenal, *Histoire de Charles V*, II, *preuves*, 372-373; Ménard, *Nismes*, II, *preuves*, 170; Lehoux, *Jean de France*, I, 51, note 6.

[92] Ménard, *Nismes*, II, *preuves*, 170-171; Bardon, *Alais*, II, 38.

[93] *Ibid.*; HL, x, cols. 1112-1120; *INV AM Pézenas*, no. 1661; Vuitry, *Régime financier*, II, 74-75; Lot and Fawtier, *Institutions*, II, 257.

[94] HL, x, cols. 1112-1120; Lehoux, *Jean de France*, I, 52-54.

had good reason for fearing that the dauphin would not come, for he was diverted by his own problems in Normandy. The king arranged a satisfactory substitute, however, in the person of his second son, John of France, count of Poitiers.[95]

Having granted taxes at Toulouse, the towns of Languedoc then had to arrange for collection, and opposing economic interests seem to have made this task difficult. The consuls of Nîmes debated at length over how to raise 3,000 florins—by a sales tax or by a 5 percent income tax. At length, they borrowed the money, then adopted a slightly graduated income tax to pay off the debt.[96] For its share of the subsidy (700 *agneaux*), Alès levied a high municipal hearth tax of 16 *s.* and a small property tax of .6 percent (12 *s.* per 100 *l.*).[97] Montpellier owed 4,500 *agneaux* for its share of the *fouage*. The crown tried to collect from the townspeople but ran into strong opposition and the consuls paid a *finance* in lieu of the hearth tax. Then they received royal permission to levy a municipal tax on wine for three years.[98] The *finance* did not discharge the 6 *d./l.* sales tax, and the consuls farmed this for four months at 300 *l.t.* after the king's commissioners refused to let them farm it for a year.[99] Pézenas was assessed 476 *agneaux* for the hearth tax and 1,435 pounds for the sales tax and tried to avoid paying.[100] Narbonne also objected, claiming in June, that the crown had not lived up to the conditions of the April grant.[101] Albi used a forced loan to raise its share of the subsidy.[102] At Rodez, the crown began collection of the sales tax in April.[103] The municipal accounts of Najac show that representatives from some towns of Rouergue met in several assemblies during June and July before finally agreeing to a *finance*.[104] Millau decided on its grant somewhat earlier, on 10 June.[105] By midsummer, the threat of new incursions by the Black Prince compelled attention to fortifications and local de-

---

[95] *Ibid.*, pp. 55f.   [96] Ménard, *Nismes*, II, *preuves*, 172-176.

[97] Bardon, *Alais*, II, 37-38, and note 1, p. 38.

[98] *Gr. Chartrier*, nos. 453, 455, 560, 2399, 3313, 3366, 3895.

[99] *Ibid.*, nos. 1788, 1789.

[100] *INV AM Pézenas*, no. 1662. On the *agnel*, which is said to have been worth 25 *s.t.* in 1355-1356, see Appendix I, note 5. This figure, however, is not a very meaningful one because the silver coinage fluctuated so drastically in 1356 that the money of account was very unstable. See the figures in Table I of Appendix I.

[101] BN Doat 53, fols. 248r-261v.   [102] AM Albi CC 68, no. 66.

[103] *A. H. Rouergue*, VI, 184 (note 2) and 251; de Gaujal, *Etude*, II, 191.

[104] AD Aveyron C 1520, no. 5; 2E 178, no. 8, part 3, fols. 3v-6r.

[105] AM Millau EE 119, no. 152. A municipal tax was also levied at Millau for purposes of defense (*ibid.*, EE 111).

fense,[106] and there were misunderstandings between the two marches of Rouergue concerning payment of spies and other war expenses.[107]

Subsequent events suggest that the Estates of Languedoc became established as an important fiscal institution in 1356. As so often in the recent past, the royal government found that the taxes granted in the spring were not sufficient for a full year. To obtain more money, the crown turned increasingly to assemblies of towns or of three estates representing all the districts of Languedoc. By the time the next such meeting could convene, in October 1356, the king had met defeat and capture in the disaster near Poitiers. For the rest of his reign, the fiscal and military régime in Languedoc became almost entirely separate from that of Languedoil.[108] This evolution had its roots in the 1340s, but its culmination in the years after Poitiers would mark a new phase in French administrative history.

3. Languedoil and the Estates General

It is curious that Auvergne remained distinct from Languedoc and continued to be administered from Paris, for this region was, like Languedoc, concerned mainly with the English forces in Gascony and later with the "companies" who ravaged the center and south of France. The arrival of the Black Prince at Bordeaux in 1355 was almost as serious a matter for Auvergne as it was for lower Languedoc. Early in the year, however, this region merely had to deal with a new royal request for 6 *d./l.* Just as he had started seeking taxes from Languedoc at the end of 1354 when no peace settlement seemed likely, so John II must have approached the rest of the kingdom. As early as 4 February 1355, the consuls of Montferrand were conferring with their neighbors at Clermont on the advisability of sending a delegation to the king at Paris to discuss this proposed *gabelle*.[109] Municipal accounts again reveal a succession of local conferences among the consuls of various Auvergnat towns.[110] These culminated in a meeting of the three Estates of Auvergne (perhaps also including representatives from the bailiwick of the Mountains).[111] The assembly was held at Issoire on 11 April[112] and it granted the desired sales tax, subject to conditions embodied in a royal ordinance

---

[106] *Ibid.* See also Moreau, *Recueil*, pp. 292-294, regarding the defenses of Périgueux. Cf. Breuils, "Jean Ier," pp. 59-60.

[107] BN Doat 191, fols. 326r-327r.   [108] Vuitry, *Régime financier*, II, 43.

[109] Boudet, "Etats," p. 34; *INV AM Montferrand*, I, 337 (CC 164).

[110] *Ibid.*, pp. 377-379.   [111] Boudet, "Etats," pp. 35-36.

[112] *Ibid.*, p. 35; *INV AM Montferrand*, I, 378-379.

of nineteen articles. The crown admitted the right of *les trois états* of the region to consent to the subsidy, and it is believed to be the first text which used this expression.[113] A representative left Montferrand for Paris during the assembly, perhaps to arrange a *finance* with the crown.[114] Agreement to the sales tax did not spare Auvergne from further harassments by royal officers, who held musters and caused protests. When the Black Prince arrived in Gascony, the crown made new demands and the towns of Auvergne held new assemblies during the autumn. These were followed by military musters.[115]

In February, when Auvergne was first approached for money, the king sent commissioners throughout Languedoil: to Orléans, Poitou, Champagne, Senlis, and Vermandois, among other places.[116] The results of their efforts are not well documented, but there was a subsidy at Orléans, probably one at Mâcon, and a levy on the subjects of clergy at Amiens.[117] The crown levied a 6 *d./l.* sales tax in Poitou, with 400 pounds being deducted from the receipts in order to pay for maintenance of the fortifications of Poitiers.[118] The inhabitants of Limousin were also much interested in their own defenses in 1355. The Estates of this district granted the crown a subsidy in the spring. The local magnates seem to have taken the initiative in holding this assembly, and the money was to be used exclusively for the construction of a local fortress. Collectors would be accountable to the captain of Limousin and the town of Limoges, and any surplus was to be spent in the district.[119] Farther north, the three Estates of Anjou and Maine also convened in July 1355. Instead of the usual sales tax, they granted a *fouage* to be collected for three months beginning in July.[120] The government also levied a clerical tenth during 1355.[121]

By far our greatest documentation for the next few years is that supplied by Normandy. Because it lay across the channel from England, was adjacent to the Plantagenet bases in Brittany, and extended nearly to the western suburbs of Paris, Normandy was bound to have strategic

---

[113] *Ord.*, III, 678-682; AN P 2292, p. 605; Vuitry, *Régime financier*, II, 41; Delachenal, *Histoire de Charles V*, I, 120.

[114] *INV AM Montferrand*, I, 377.

[115] *Ibid.*, pp. 378-381.   [116] AN P 2292, p. 599.

[117] AN PP 117, p. 701; P 2292, p. 607; BN *ms. fr.* 26000, no. 463. See also Timbal, *Guerre*, pp. 256, 258.

[118] *AHP*, XLVI, 155-156, 158-161.

[119] *Ord.*, III, 684-687; Vuitry, *Régime financier*, II, 42-43.

[120] *Ord.*, III, 7-8, 682-684.

[121] *Ibid.*, no. 325; BN *ms. fr.* 25700, no. 95; Haigneré, *Chartes*, II, no. 1677.

importance. Perhaps in recognition of this fact, two successive heirs to the throne had been named dukes of Normandy. In addition, and of greater immediate importance in 1355, the *apanages* of the Evreux princes lay in Normandy. The king's feud with Charles of Navarre meant that royal tax collectors periodically lost their access to these lands. For the same reason, Normandy was at least potentially accessible to English troops. The fiscal and military situation in Normandy had therefore worsened considerably during 1354. The settlement reached at Mantes early in that year had only temporarily patched up the rupture occasioned by the murder of Charles of Spain. The flight of Charles the Bad to Avignon in November and his later dealings with the English made relations worse than ever. Had John II been able to make good his confiscation of the Evreux fiefs, he might have turned the intrigues of his son-in-law to his own advantage, and strengthened the royal hold on Normandy. So ineffectual, however, was the royal effort to implement this seizure, that John's troops could not take the six important fortresses of Avranches, Cherbourg, Evreux, Gavray, Mortain, and Pont Audemer.[122] Remaining as Navarrese strongholds, these places were in a position not only to afford the English a valuable new *entrée* into Normandy, but also to threaten the environs of Paris itself. A new settlement with Charles the Bad, however distasteful or humiliating, thus became increasingly desirable. For just when troops and money were needed in Normandy more urgently than ever, only a reduced portion of the duchy was in a position to supply them.

At about the same time he had requested new taxes from Languedoc (late December 1354), John II sent commissioners into Normandy for the same purpose. The result was a new sales tax of 6 *d./l.* for the crown and 2 *d./l.* for local defense. This combined tax of 8 *deniers* was levied starting the first of January 1355, at least in the viscounty of Falaise.[123] The quick response and the general nature of the tax throughout Normandy suggests some sort of assembly, but no precise information to this effect has survived. From a wide assortment of pay orders, receipts, and instructions to tax collectors, we learn of this imposition at Harfleur, Eu, Dieppe, and other places, always with 2 *d./l.* retained for local defense measures.[124]

This arrangement was hardly new in 1355, but there seems to have been an unmistakable trend in the direction of local self-help. In part,

[122] Denifle, *Désolation*, II, 102.

[123] BN *ms. fr.* 25700, no. 88; BN NAF 20026, nos. 36-39; AN PP 117, p. 701.

[124] BN *ms. fr.* 25700, nos. 87, 99, 103; BN *ms. fr.* 20581, no. 63.

this trend doubtless reflects a royal realization that communities would pay more willingly when a portion of the money could be applied by them to their own defense. Yet it also suggests a lack of confidence in the crown's ability to discharge its function of defending the realm. Limousin had demanded that all tax money be spent locally, while Languedoc would soon seek reassurance as to the crown's commitment by demanding the presence of a royal prince in the South. Even before the crisis of John's captivity, we find a certain disintegration of effective royal power. The failure to reduce the Evreux strongholds may have shaken the confidence of the Normans. The fragmentation of authority, whereby military and fiscal matters would increasingly be shifted to local responsibility, was already in evidence in Normandy in the year and a half before the battle of Poitiers. This phenomenon would become quite pronounced in the following few years, before the Treaty of Brétigny and the accession of Charles V would permit some restoration of effective centralized authority. The revival in these years of the *élu* scheme previously tried in the later 1340s, would be another symptom of this decentralizing of responsibility for fiscal administration.

The Norman sales tax, collected from the beginning of 1355 was not the only subsidy levied by the crown in the duchy during the year. In March, the dauphin, as duke of Normandy, was sent to his *apanage* accompanied by royal fiscal officers, their errand being to negotiate a second tax with the Norman Estates.[125] Whether these convened in one assembly or two has been debated,[126] but there seems no doubt that the representatives of lower Normandy made a grant for their region, while those from the bailiwicks of Gisors, Rouen, and Caux took action binding only on their districts. The latter grant was for a three-month hearth tax of 5 *sols* to be collected during June, July, and August for the purpose of supporting 2,000 men-at-arms for three months. This tax was collected in the lands of the count of Harcourt, a strong Navarrese sympathizer, but in Charles the Bad's stronghold of Pont Audemer, the money was levied by his officials for his own treasury.[127] The tax was evidently expected to yield a large sum, for the 2,000 troops were to be paid a high scale of salaries: 40 *s.p.* for a knight banneret, 20 *s.p.* for a knight bache-

---

[125] BN P.O. 2777, dossier 61829.

[126] Delachenal, *Histoire de Charles V*, I, 98; Coville, *Etats Norm.*, p. 75; Vuitry, *Régime financier*, II, 75. The documents cited in this argument, BN *ms. fr.* 26000, no. 496, and BN NAF 20075, no. 12, do not really clear up the matter.

[127] BN *ms. fr.* 25947, no. 759. According to *Chron. Jean II*, p. 46, the king became reconciled with the count of Harcourt in July of 1354.

lor, and 10 *s.p.* for a mounted squire.[128] Given the condition of the currency in 1355, this salary scale is understandable, but it represents a significant increase over even the *grands-gages* rate of the preceding decades.

In lower Normandy ("the bailiwick of Cotentin and Saint-Guillaume de Mortain"), the subsidy was expressed by a different formula: each hundred hearths would provide the salary for one man-at-arms and one archer for a given period. This grant for troops by lower Normandy was made in March,[129] while there is no certain evidence of the grant by the other three bailiwicks until May.[130]

A rather elaborate administration was set up to collect the taxes in 1355, at least in upper Normandy, where the Estates named the lord of Saint-Beuve and Martin Evrart, Canon of Rouen, as "commissioners general" (sometimes called "governors general") of the subsidy.[131] They supervised persons called "treasurers general" and "deputies general" who seem to have been virtually identical to the *élus* who appear in documents of later years.[132] Since the Estates General of Languedoil in late 1335 would revive the *élu* idea, it is worth recalling that the last use of *élus*, in 1347-1348, had followed a Norman precedent. Once again Norman practice seems to have pointed the way towards a much wider change in fiscal administration.

Documents mentioning taxes in Normandy during 1355 are abundant. Some speak only of the grant by lower Normandy;[133] others clearly refer to the current tax in the bailiwicks of Rouen, Caux, and Gisors;[134] some

---

[128] BN *ms. fr.* 25947, no. 759. This rate of pay, reflecting the inflationary trend and the drain on seigneurial resources, conformed to the salary scale promulgated in 1351.

[129] *Ord.*, IV, 319; BN NAF 7609, fols. 166r-168v.

[130] Coville, *Etats Norm.*, p. 75; BN NAF 3654, no. 30.

[131] Prentout, *Etats Norm.*, II, 173; BN *ms. fr.*, 26000, nos. 366, 384, 406, 420; 25700, no. 94; 25701, nos. 9, 11; BN NAF 3637, no. 63. Cf. Delachenal, *Histoire de Charles V*, I, 100-102.

[132] Among many references to these officials are BN *ms. fr.* 26000, nos. 352, 354, 355, 357, 359, 364, 366, 367, 369, 371, 373-376, 382, 384, 387, 392, 393, 396-398, 406, 408-414, 418-420, 426, 432, 433, 438, 441, 443-447, 449-451; 25701, nos. 4, 12, 25, 38, 40, 45, 49, 63, 75; 20398, no. 49; P.O. 2130, *dossier* 48319, nos. 6, 7, 9-11; NAF 7609, fol. 232r-v; Clairambault 159, no. 100. The term *élu* is actually used in BN *ms. fr.* 26001, no. 488 and NAF 20075, no. 11.

[133] BN NAF 20075, nos. 12, 14, 15, 19; BN *ms. fr.* 22468, no. 98; BN NAF 7609, fols. 305r-v, 307r-v.

[134] BN *ms. fr.* 25701, nos. 13, 17, 18; NAF 3637, no. 63; 20026, nos. 44, 48, 49, 51.

merely indicate the "subsidy for men-at-arms" granted to the dauphin;[135] while still others specify the sales tax which began in January.[136]

The double tax of 1355 could not prevent a general military summons when the expiration of the truce (24 June) drew nearer. There was indeed every reason to expect military action in Normandy during the summer of 1355 and the king proclaimed the *arrière-ban* on 17 May.[137] Charles the Bad, meanwhile, had spent the months since his departure from Avignon raising troops in Navarre for a planned descent on Normandy. He gained time by deceiving the pope as to his true intentions. Innocent VI, always the peacemaker, kept urging John to await with patience the contrite submission which the pope thought Charles would soon display. Not until May, did Innocent realize that Charles was preparing to pour his troops into Cotentin to assist the anticipated English assault.[138] Demands for a general reconciliation continued to come from Avignon, however, and they were seconded by the efforts to the two queens dowager, Blanche and Joan of Evreux, who urged their kinsman to cease his military plans and receive royal envoys. Leading princes also wrote to Charles, assuring him that he had safe conduct to the royal court.[139]

As it was, all these entreaties fell on deaf ears, and what made possible a new Valois-Evreux accommodation was the failure of Edward III to cross the channel. As we know, it was the Prince of Wales, in Languedoc, who conducted the major English military operations of 1355. Charles the Bad finally reached Cherbourg with 1,000 men in August but then waited in vain for the king of England.[140] With the increasing possibility that he might have to face alone the wrath of the king of France, Charles began to negotiate late in August.[141] The result was the treaty of Valognes, concluded on 10 September 1355, rather more favorable to the

---

[135] In this category are the greatest number of documents, including all those cited above, note 132, and the following: BN *ms. fr.* 20398, no. 60; 26000, no. 321; 26001, no. 485; 25700, nos. 22, 34; 25701, nos. 2, 3, 6, 7, 10, 14-16, 19, 22, 27, 28, 31-33, 37, 42, 57; Clairambault 213, nos. 37, 38, 42, 43, 45.

[136] BN *ms. fr.* 26000, nos. 327-328.   [137] AN K 47, no. 35.

[138] Denifle, *Désolation*, II, 103-105, and notes.

[139] Secousse, *Charles II*, I (*preuves*), 565-576; AD Lot F 31; Denifle, *Désolation*, II, 102, 106.

[140] *Ibid.*; Secousse, *Charles II*, II, 55-56. *Foedera*, III pt. I, p. 109, indicates that Edward III renounced the truce on I June, claiming that he had been deluded by the French. Having made this gesture, Edward did not, however, come to the aid of Charles the Bad.

[141] Secousse, *Charles II*, I, 594; Denifle, *Désolation*, II, 107.

king of France than the earlier treaty of Mantes. To be sure, John repeated his former pardons and restored the lands he had confiscated, but
Charles had to make a public obedience and permit the royal constable
to install a *châtelain* in his principal Norman strongholds.[142] With respect to taxation, the most interesting provisions revolved around the
large sums still owed to Charles for his wife's dowry. Navarrese officers
had sought to claim this sum by confiscating royal subsidy collections in
Norman lands of the Evreux family. John II now undertook to pay the
promised dowry, in return for which it again became possible for the
crown to collect taxes in the Evreux lands.[143]

It was well for the French that a major clash of arms in Normandy
during 1355 had been averted, for the summer tax for men-at-arms was
progressing very slowly. Besides the harassments imposed by the Navarrese officials, the tax was very unpopular (being the second subsidy of
the year), and it encountered such obstacles as local impoverishment
and negligent accounting.[144] During August, tax officials were re-
proached for slow collections, and a conference met at Caen to discuss
ways of speeding the levy in the Navarrese stronghold of lower Normandy. Pay orders from the dauphin (commanding the treasurers general to supply commanders with money for the salaries of their troops),
began to use the expression "all excuses ceasing" by late summer.[145] Thus
this special military subsidy was failing to produce the necessary resources and long delays occurred. As late as October and November, we
still find orders to pay troops from the proceeds of this tax, evidence that
the money was still trickling in slowly.[146] With the Black Prince now
ravaging Languedoc, the king again had to use the *arrière-ban*.[147] Late
in September, the financial position of the crown was so bad that payment of royal debts was suspended for six months.[148]

At the end of his resources, John II finally summoned the three Estates
of Languedoil to meet at Paris on 30 November.[149] This summons
marked the final collapse of the system of taxation employed in northern
France since the aftermath of the Black Death, a system characterized

---

[142] *Ibid.*, p. 108; Secousse, *Charles II*, I, 582-596.

[143] *Ibid.*, pp. 576-579, 582-596. See above, note 127.

[144] Delachenal, *Histoire de Charles V*, I, 103.

[145] Coville, *Etats Norm.*, pp. 75-76; BN *ms. fr.* 25701, no. 42.

[146] BN *ms. fr.* 26001, nos. 485, 488.

[147] Coville, *Etats Norm.*, p. 76. For other measures of military preparedness, see
Ord., IV, 168-170; Varin, *Reims*, III, 73-74.

[148] *Ord.*, III, 15-16.

[149] Delachenal, *Histoire de Charles V*, I, 121, note 1.

by a uniform sales tax renegotiated annually at the bailiwick level in assemblies of the three Estates. Although vastly more efficient than the haphazard local grants of the later 1330s, and no longer dependent on an outright state of war, these regular sales taxes had been at best only a partial victory for the crown. Opposition to paying, far from ending, had begun to grow stronger again after 1352. Moreover, these subsidies were barely adequate to finance the local skirmishing which had characterized the five years following the plague. The rupture with Charles the Bad, the deteriorating military situation in Brittany, and the resumption of major hostilities in 1355, forced the imposition of additional taxes in some areas and exposed the serious fiscal and military weaknesses of the monarchy.[150] There was growing doubt that the crown could defend the kingdom against a new attack, and increasing demand for reform in the government that might eliminate luxury and corrupt officials. Much of this resentment would achieve articulate expression only in the wake of military disaster a year later, but we need not doubt that such sentiments were widespread in the fall of 1355.[151] This discontent was reminiscent of the criticisms expressed on the eve of another great assembly, eight years before.

The conditions of late 1355, however, differed from those of 1347 in significant ways. In 1347, Languedoil had just experienced serious military defeat. The country was not beset by serious internal divisions, but the Estates had had very little experience at working together. In 1355, the North had not suffered any new military disaster but was disrupted by the smoldering feud between the kings of France and Navarre. The Estates, however, were vastly more experienced after five years or more of annual bailiwick assemblies. This experience can only have bred a certain self-confidence which earlier central assemblies had lacked. It must also, however, have helped to produce a revival of local particularism, for these recurrent bailiwick assemblies were calculated to strengthen regional identity and deal with regional problems rather than national ones. The disaffection of northern and western nobles who sympathized with Charles the Bad, the fear that the king could not provide protection for all regions, the growing importance of taxes for local defense, and the tradition of bailiwick assemblies, all point to a revival of that localism which had characterized the first years of the war. The Estates of 1355 therefore possessed greater confidence and experience, were angry at

---

[150] Moreau de Beaumont, *Mémoire*, III, 235, touching on the ineffectiveness of the tax system of the immediately preceding years.

[151] Venette, p. 45.

governmental ineptitude but not chastened by military defeat, and were called upon to offer a national solution to problems which Languedoïl had been accustomed to dealing with at a regional level. Only by understanding these conditions can we interpret the aspirations and failures of the assembly which has been called "one of the most important of the *Ancien Régime* from the financial point of view."[152]

It was on 9 October 1355, that John II issued his letters summoning the Estates General of Languedoïl.[153] By calling this meeting a "necessary consequence of the reopening of hostilities," Delachenal conveys a misleading sense of inevitability to the summons,[154] but in view of the difficulties encountered by the second Norman tax of 1355 and the doubtful loyalty of the king of Navarre, there were surely strong reasons to recommend a large assembly at this time. We may certainly agree with Lot and Fawtier that this meeting opened a period of fifteen years which would be "decisive" in the establishment of regular royal taxation in France.[155] It is clear, however, that this period cannot be treated as a unit. The battle of Poitiers, the treaty of Brétigny, and the crisis of the brigand companies, created new conditions that were not foreseeable late in 1355. All these subsequent events had more impact on taxation than the assembly of 1355, which actually resembled that of 1347 more closely than those of the later 1350s.

Scheduled to convene on 30 November, the Estates did not actually meet until 2 December and they seem to have remained in session no more than a week.[156] Thus the assembly was shorter than that of 1347, even though it gave approval to a lengthy set of reforms and set up a complete fiscal administration. This fact again seems to underscore the greater experience gained by the representatives in the smaller meetings of the early 1350s. The famous ordinance of 28 December 1355 may be seen as an instrument of reform, an expression of grievances, and a major administrative enactment. It belongs in the tradition of the reform ordi-

---

[152] This is the verdict of Balas, *Tentative*, p. 25. As suggested above, Chapter VI, the accomplishments of the Estates of 1347, which have only recently become apparent, suggest that the assembly of 1355 attempted less innovation than once was thought.

[153] Delachenal, *Histoire de Charles V*, I, 121, note 1.

[154] *Ibid.*, p. 120. Vuitry, *Régime financier*, II, 61, was probably more accurate in saying that the king simply hoped that the Estates "would provide more conveniently and more surely for the needs of the government."

[155] Lot and Fawtier, *Institutions*, II, 256.

[156] Delachenal, *Histoire de Charles V*, I, 120. Delachenal and Vuitry, *Régime financier*, II, 61, both base their discussion on the older edition of the *Grandes Chroniques*, later republished by Delachenal as *Chron. Jean II*.

nance of 1303 and those which followed the Estates in 1346.[157] It can also be regarded as a successor to those regional and local ordinances which had followed most of the bailiwick assemblies since 1348. These many enactments of the past decade contained royal promises of reform and set down conditions under which a tax would be levied. Now, in late 1355, the type of ordinance which had become familiar in local negotiations was translated into a uniform measure intended to apply to most of the kingdom.

Of the thirty-three articles of this ordinance, more than three-quarters made up its "reform" section. These provisions were rather commonplace, much like those demanded by the Estates of February, 1346. Thus the crown promised to abolish forced loans and requisitions, restrict extraordinary jurisdictions, and take measures to restore sound money. This last provision had not been necessary in 1346, of course. Of far more significance was an article limiting the power of the *arrière-ban* to the king and his oldest son subject to the counsel of the Estates or their delegates.[158] This amounted to a demand by the assembly to acquiesce in any declaration of "necessity."

Most interesting of all, of course, are those provisions of the ordinance relating to taxation. The assembly broke with the tradition of earlier central Estates and authorized specific taxes which were to be binding on the whole of Languedoil and were to be administered under the direction of the Estates themselves. It has been argued that the assembly did not vote subsidies properly speaking, since it merely promised to raise and maintain an army of 30,000 men.[159] This form, however, was by now a familiar way of expressing subsidies. It was reckoned that the upkeep of such a force for one year would cost 5,000,000 *l.t.*, close to double the sum promised by a larger population just before the Black Death and far larger than any tax previously levied in France. This huge sum was to be raised by means of a sales tax of 8 *d./l.* and a new *gabelle* on salt, restored after being suppressed more than eight years before. There were to be no exemptions from paying these taxes. To administer them, the assembly again adopted the *élu* system tried in 1347-1348 and recently

---

[157] This famous ordinance is in AN JJ 84, no. 400, published in *Ord.*, III, 19-37. Earlier, in May 1355, John had issued an ordinance confirming all but three articles of the reform charter of 1303: AN JJ 84, no. 138. On the frequent reissues of that charter and the reform sentiment in general, see R. Cazelles, "Une exigence de l'opinion depuis Saint Louis: La réformation du royaume," *AB SHF*, 1962-1963, pp. 91-99.

[158] Vuitry, *Régime financier*, II, 66-67, analyzing *Ord.*, III, 19f.

[159] Lot and Fawtier, *Institutions*, II, 257; *Chron. Jean II*, pp. 57-58.

revived in Normandy. The new administration was to consist of a commission of nine "generals-superintendents" (three from each Estate), assisted by two receivers. This supervisory structure at the top would be the ancestor of the future *Cour des Aides*, although the system as first constituted was weakened by the fact that all nine superintendents were required to agree, with disagreements to be resolved not by the Estates, but by the *Parlement* at Paris.[160]

Actual collection of the taxes would be under the direction of *élus*, "upright and solvent men" appointed in the various localities by the three Estates.[161] Neither the *élus* themselves nor the types of taxes enacted can be regarded as innovations. The superintendents were a new departure, at least as regards the whole of Languedoil. The taxes were granted for a year, following the recent precedent of the many bailiwick assemblies. Again no doubt because of recent experience, it was assumed that a new tax would be needed at the end of the year and it was therefore provided that the Estates would reconvene on 30 November 1356. There is no evidence that any of the recent bailiwick assemblies had demanded such a right to reassemble in a year, but in practice they had reconvened and it remains possible that some of them did specifically request to do so. Thus the plan to hold a new assembly in 1356 may have been less of an innovation than it first appears to be. Probably there was little interest in making central assemblies a permanent institution.[162] A definite innovation, however, was the arrangement that during 1356 the Estates would be called into session several times *before* the planned assembly of 30 November. This step became necessary when the Estates decided to supervise the tax they had granted. Perhaps difficulties of collection were anticipated; certainly there was distrust of the royal fiscal machinery and a need to inspect accounts periodically.

It has been rightly observed that the Estates meeting in December 1355 failed to control the government but did get control of the subsidy.[163] The achievement proved to be a somewhat hollow one, and collection of the taxes met great opposition despite the fact that the levies

---

[160] *Ord.*, III, 19-37; Delachenal, *Histoire de Charles V*, I, 121; Lot and Fawtier, *Institutions*, II, 257; Vuitry, *Régime financier*, II, 63-65.

[161] *Ibid.*; G. Dupont-Ferrier, *Les origines et le premier siècle de la chambre ou cour des aides de Paris*, Paris, 1933, pp. 12-13.

[162] Vuitry, *Régime financier*, II, 65.

[163] Lot and Fawtier, *Institutions*, II, 264. Cf. Vuitry, *Régime financier*, II, 64, note 1; G. Picot, *Histoire des Etats-généraux, considerés au point de vue de leur influence sur le gouvernement de la France de 1355 à 1614*, Paris, 1872, I, 43.

took a familiar form. It would seem that the king, however hated his officials and however great the opposition encountered by his tax negotiators, was nevertheless, felt to exercise power more legitimately than
did a central assembly. Long unwilling to entrust representatives with
full freedom of action in assemblies higher than the bailiwick level, much
of the kingdom was not ready to accept the power of such an assembly
to raise a tax on this occasion. The form of the tax itself aroused hostility
also, and there were serious uprisings in Arras and Rouen.[164]

Another serious obstacle to tax raising existed in Normandy, where a
growing band of dissident nobles, led by the Harcourt family, swelled
the ranks of the Evreux faction.[165] In January 1356, the dauphin, now
formally installed as duke in Normandy, assembled the nobles of the
duchy to receive their homage. At this time, Godefroy d'Harcourt sought
and failed to have him first swear to uphold the Norman charters.[166]
There was widespread refusal to pay the tax imposed by the Estates
General, a refusal which doubtless arose partly from that same local particularism which long had motivated the Harcourts. The dauphin appears to have met with the Norman Estates in mid-February at Vau-
dreuil. Aside from the evidence of hostility on the part of the Harcourts,
we do not know much about this meeting.[167] It is probable that the Normans reluctantly ratified the tax granted at Paris in December. The same
collection machinery used in Normandy in 1355 was again in use, and although the Estates General had adopted such a system for all of Languedoil, it is likely that the Norman Estates insisted on retaining control of
collections in the duchy. Because of either separate grants or separate
collection machinery, the Norman documents again make the distinction
between sums levied in lower Normandy[168] and money granted from the
three bailiwicks of Rouen, Caux, and Gisors.[169] Although the Estates
General would reconvene in March and change the form of subsidy, we
have evidence that the earlier *impositions et gabelles* were still being
levied in lower Normandy during April.[170] A hearth tax, however, was

---

[164] *Ibid.*, p. 40 and note 1: Guesnon, *Inventaire des chartes*, pp. 103-105, 110-119;
Chron. Jean II, p. 62; Lot and Fawtier, *Institutions*, II, 257. Cf. Vuitry, *Régime
financier*, II, 67-68. Timbal, *Guerre*, cites 1356 as one occasion on which a community
was prepared to send troops rather than pay the tax.

[165] Picot, *Etats*, I, 38; Denifle, *Désolation*, II, 108.

[166] *Ibid.*; Coville, *Etats Norm.*, pp. 77-78; Delisle, *St. Sauveur*, pp. 78-79.

[167] *Ibid.*; Coville, *Etats Norm.*, p. 78; Prentout, *Etats Norm.*, I, 106-107.

[168] BN *ms. fr.* 26001, nos. 509-513, 515-516, 522; NAF 7609, fol. 286r-v.

[169] BN *ms. fr.* 26001, no. 551, and perhaps also no. 537 (the date of which is
ambiguous).

[170] BN P.O. 539, *dossier* 12144, nos. 2, 9.

substituted in Normandy during the summer. Although some authors have stated that the hostility of the Navarrese party prevented collection of the subsidies in the lands of the Norman barons,[171] it is known that royal receivers were collecting *impositions et gabelles* in the Evreux lands as late as 8 March.[172] It is therefore probable that the lands of the Evreux party were not closed to royal taxation until the precipitate royal coup of early April.[173]

From this evidence, it seems possible to conclude that the Normans refused to accept the decisions of the Paris assembly but were willing to pay some taxes if they could control the collectors directly and limit the subsidy to three months subject to renegotiation at the end of that period. The Norman example shows us that while the Estates General of 1355 had been willing to adopt a single uniform tax structure, unlike their predecessors of 1347, and had even assumed direct responsibility for collecting the promised tax, the kingdom was less willing to follow their lead. The slightly more cautious assembly of 1347 had been followed by rapid agreement in the lesser jurisdictions throughout France. The less inhibited Estates of 1355 assumed sweeping responsibilities at a time when various factors had given new stimulus to local particularism. The national response to a large subsidy for men-at-arms had actually been more favorable in 1348 than in 1356.

In this atmosphere, the Estates General reconvened in March 1356, but without representation from Normandy and Picardy.[174] Aside from the foreseen need to supervise collection of the subsidy, there was now the more urgent requirement that some action be taken to deal with the widespread resistance to paying. It has already been suggested that some regions may simply have denied the tax-raising competence of a central assembly. Another difficulty was the difference of opinion between economic classes as to the desirable form of tax. The towns of Auvergne conferred several times in February for the purpose of sending proctors to Paris who were "to oppose the request which the gentlemen and prelates were to make there."[175] This earliest clear evidence of a rift between the towns and the first two orders is of great interest in view of the action finally taken by the March assembly. It seems apparent that the form of the tax was now at issue, for despite the long tradition of indirect taxation in Languedoil, the new meeting of the Estates General abandoned

---

[171] Coville, *Etats Norm.*, pp. 78-79; Picot, *Etats*, 1, 38-39.
[172] BN *ms. fr.* 26001, no. 526.   [173] See below, note 196.
[174] Picot, *Etats*, 1, 39; Balas, *Tentative*, p. 25.
[175] *INV AM Montferrand*, 1, 379-380, 391 (CC 164, 166).

the earlier impositions in favor of a new and remarkably graduated income tax.

The March Estates embodied their decisions in a royal ordinance of 12 March and supplementary instructions issued on the 20th.[176] The new tax was to be levied on real incomes, pensions, salaries, and other movables according to a regressive scale of rates. A person with an income of ten pounds would pay at a rate of 10 percent (one pound); one with forty pounds would pay at 5 percent (two pounds). For an income of 100 pounds, the tax rate was only 4 percent and each additional hundred pounds of income was assessed at 2 percent, up to incomes of 5,000 pounds for nobles and 1,000 for non-nobles. Additional income over 5,000 and 1,000 pounds, respectively, was, in effect, not taxed at all. The maximum tax any noble would owe was 102 pounds; for a non-noble it was 22 pounds. The *gabelle* would cease immediately and the 8 *d./l.* sales tax at the end of March, with all collections from this latter levy to be returned. The *élu* system was retained, but the superintendents were reduced to a six-man board renamed the deputies-general, and an intermediate board of "deputies-particular" was installed, three such persons in each town. As before, collection was exclusively for the army, and all persons over fifteen, exclusive of monks, would pay the tax, notwithstanding privileges.[177]

The proclamation of this new tax immediately raises certain important questions. What group or class, for instance, should be considered responsible for it? At first glance, such a schedule of rates seems obviously to favor the rich, and it has been suggested that the change was made to accommodate nobles and clergy who were forced to acquiesce in the suspension of their fiscal privileges.[178] Yet it would be a great mistake to judge this subsidy in terms of modern tax structures, and both Picot and Delachenal have rightly criticized earlier historians like Michelet for condemning it too hastily.[179] The indirect taxes adopted in December bore upon sales of merchandise, including certain essential articles of consumption. They clearly weighed most heavily on the poor consumer,[180] and insofar as they reduced the latter's purchasing power, they also affected merchants. The *gabelle* had not been levied for more than eight

---

[176] *Ord.*, III, 24; IV, 171-175; Isambert, IV, 763-768; AN P 2293, pp. 319-326.

[177] *Chron. Jean II*, pp. 59-61; Vuitry, *Régime financier*, II, 68-70.

[178] *Ibid.*, p. 101.

[179] Picot, *Etats*, I, 140, note 2, and p. 141; Delachenal, note 4 to *Chron. Jean II*, pp. 58-59.

[180] Picot, *Etats*, I, 38.

years and the sales tax was one-third higher than what had previously prevailed in most of Languedoil.

Picot attached great significance to the "equality" of these indirect taxes,[181] but as we know there were precedents for requiring that privileged persons pay. His claim that the indirect taxes failed because of the depressed state of commerce is somewhat more plausible, but conditions were no better five years later when even heavier sales taxes for the royal ransom were collected with relatively little opposition.[182]

It is nonetheless quite true that the sales taxes of late December fell miserably short of producing the anticipated sums, and the opposition to these taxes was doubtless obvious when the Estates reconvened at the beginning of March. In all likelihood, these taxes were opposed by three main groups: (1) those leaders of the Estates who had committed themselves to raising a large sum for the army; (2) the small consumer who was hurt by the increase in his cost of living; and (3) the merchants. If the new income tax was devised to meet their objections, it must have been the work of the third Estate, not the clergy or nobility. The inclusion in the new levy of pensions, salaries, and revenues from land, reinforces this conclusion. Moreover, the maximum possible tax was far higher for nobles than for non-nobles, so that large bourgeois fortunes remained virtually untapped. The use of *élus* of the Estates to collect the subsidy excluded from this function seigneurs with high justice, who in the past often levied taxes locally.[183] Finally, the new income tax replaced the tenth paid by the clergy, despite the objections of Innocent VI.[184] If Auvergne's apparent cleavage between the townsmen and the other two orders was typical, we may conclude that the March ordinance, far from being devised to placate nobles and clergy, actually was forced through over their objections.

Another difficult question concerning the new income tax is the matter of where it may have been levied. Delachenal, in dealing with Normandy, has already pointed to ambiguities in the documentation without really resolving the difficulty.[185] Before proceeding to the evidence for Normandy, which is fairly extensive even if equivocal in character, we must first consider Languedoil generally. At Arras, the several corporate bodies making up the municipal government deliberated several times

[181] *Ibid.*, pp. 37, 140.
[182] *Ibid.*, pp. 139, 142. The taxes for the ransom, to be considered in the second volume of this study, are discussed briefly in J. Henneman, "The French Ransom Aids and Two Legal Traditions," to appear in a forthcoming collection.
[183] Vuitry, *Régime financier*, II, 70.   [184] *Ibid.*, p. 208.
[185] Delachenal, *Histoire de Charles V*, I, 173-174.

on whether or not to accept the earlier indirect taxes, then rejected them on 1 March, on the ground that they would create "desolation" in the town.[186] An uprising several days later was probably in response to the efforts of *élus* to collect the taxes anyway. These events occurred while the new assembly at Paris was considering its changes in the form of subsidy. It is not known whether any representatives from Artois attended these Estates, but one may doubt that any collections were possible in Arras before the town government put down the rising and promised reforms in May.[187] The resistance to taxation reported in Normandy and Picardy during early 1356, considered together with the disburbances at Arras, makes it all the more probable that the bailiwicks north and west of Paris had little or no representation at the March assembly and may have sought to negotiate and control their taxes locally as in the recent past.[188] There is also uncertainty about Auvergne, although this region did participate in the assembly at Paris in March. We find no hint that the new income tax was levied in Auvergne, aside from the negative evidence that nothing more is heard about any *gabelle*. However, the Auvergnat towns were busily occupied during the spring and summer of 1356 with raising troops to deal with the latest *chevauchée* of the Black Prince.[189] Perhaps this English raid interrupted the income tax before any collection could begin; such external interruptions were certainly not unknown in the annals of French taxation. In any case, it appears that Auvergne raised its own troops under the supervision of local commanders and the royal bailiff, levying municipal and local taxes to finance these forces, all without reference to the income tax established in Paris.

By the spring of 1356, therefore, the impressive program of the previous December had fallen far short of expectations. If the Estates General were finally ready to make a binding grant and supervise tax collections, their constituents were less ready than in 1348 to accept the arrangements of a central assembly. The taxes ordained in December 1355 could not, in any case, produce the sums desired and they provoked violent opposition from the bourgeoisie. The new income tax proposed in March shifted a slightly greater burden to the wealthy, but the assembly arranging this levy may have represented only a fraction of Languedoil and its tax may not have been collected in all the regions that were

---

[186] Guesnon, *Inventaire de chartes*, pp. 103-105.

[187] *Ibid.*, pp. 110-119; *Chron. Jean II*, p. 66.

[188] In the case of Picardy, see *Ord.*, iii, 68-69; Thierry, *Recueil*, i, 574-575; Vuitry, *Régime financier*, ii, 72; Picot, *Etats*, i, 41.

[189] *INV AM Montferrand*, i, 392-393 (CC 166); *Chron. Jean II*, pp. 69-71.

represented. The Estates met for a third time, on 8 May, and made still another adjustment to the tax structure, retaining the income tax but making the rate scale less sharply regressive.[190] This second change in the direction of an increased burden for the wealthy, may reflect the continued inadequacy of subsidy collections and the increasing strength and influence of the bourgeoisie in the Estates. At the same time, the royal ordinance of 26 May 1356 seemed to admit that the effort of the Estates to tax the kingdom had degenerated into utter confusion. To retrieve the situation, the government surrendered to the local particularism of bailiwicks wishing to supervise their own taxes, and merely directed that each district pay either the indirect taxes ordered in December or the revised income tax. The latter was to be payable in two installments, on 24 June and 15 August.[191] This concession may have eased the situation and improved the speed of collection. A letter of non-prejudice issued in June, offers the year's first evidence of any collection from the recalcitrant towns of Picardy.[192] From Auvergne, on the other hand, we continue to hear only of locally equipped troop contingents.[193]

In Normandy, political and fiscal matters continued to reflect the ambiguous position of Charles the Bad. It has already been pointed out that the Normans refused to acquiesce in the actions of the Estates General but apparently agreed in February 1356 to the levy of the 8 *d./l.* and salt *gabelle* for three months, subject to local supervision (including separate administrations for upper and lower Normandy). Continuing disaffection among the Norman baronage produced a Navarrese party of increasing strength, but this hostility to the crown probably did not hinder taxation seriously before April, since the crown was able to collect the subsidy even in the Evreux lands.[194]

The Norman situation, however, experienced a radical change early in April. For two years, John II and the king of Navarre had remained on mutually hostile terms despite the two nominal settlements of Mantes and Valognes. An added grievance for King John had been provided late in 1355 when the dauphin himself had become involved in an obscure intrigue engineered by Navarrese partisans, whereby the young prince was to seek the emperor's aid in forcing John to dismiss certain unpopu-

[190] Picot, *Etats*, I, 41; Vuitry, *Régime financier*, II, 71.

[191] *Ibid.*; *Ord.*, III, 53-55; Isambert, IV, 769-770.

[192] *Ord.*, III, 68-69; Thierry, *Recueil*, I, 574-575.

[193] *INV AM Montferrand*, I, 393. A receipt in BN NAF 20026, no. 57, may, however, indicate collection of the war subsidy in Auvergne, Touraine, and other regions of central France.

[194] See above, note 172.

lar officers in the government. Although he had pardoned his son and son-in-law for involvement in this conspiracy, the French king was nearing the end of his patience.[195] Strategic and political considerations, as well as personal and fiscal ones, had long suggested the need for a decisive stroke against Charles the Bad, but John characteristically waited too long and then acted with clumsy savagery. While the dauphin and the king of Navarre were dining together at Rouen on 5 April, John arrived suddenly, arresting Charles the Bad and ordering the summary execution of several Navarrese partisans including the count of Harcourt. For the next nineteen months, Charles of Navarre would remain a political prisoner around whose cause would rally a large and diverse body of malcontents. This abrupt stroke aroused widespread criticism from the chivalry of France.[196] John II was doubtless guilty of handling the matter badly, but from the royal point of view, Charles had furnished ample provocation, notwithstanding Edward III's later declaration to the pope that he had never conspired with Charles against France.[197]

For the historian of French taxation, these events are important because they plunged Normandy into a civil war which was to last for the better part of a decade. Leadership of the Evreux family was assumed by Philip of Navarre, Charles' brother, who promptly fortified the castles in his family's territory and asked Edward III to send aid from Brittany, where the duke of Lancaster had been acting as English commander since the fall of 1355. Not only was this English aid forthcoming, but Philip was joined by various Norman nobles, headed by Godefroy d'Harcourt, lord of Saint-Sauveur.[198] It goes without saying, that the events of 5 April closed the extensive Evreux territories to French tax collectors, and with them the lands of those barons sympathetic to the Navarrese party.[199]

Where taxes could be collected, they seem to have been the imposition and *gabelle* authorized by the Normans in February. In May, however, the French captured Evreux and the dauphin held assemblies to authorize a new tax. In lower Normandy, which was most vulnerable to Anglo-

---

[195] See Secousse, *Charles II*, i, 45-55.

[196] *Chron. Jean II*, pp. 62-66; Delisle, *St. Sauveur*, pp. 77, 80f.; Denifle, *Désolation*, ii, 109.

[197] *Ibid.*, p. 104. The pope named another peace mission on 8 April: Zacour, *Talleyrand*, p. 45.

[198] *Foedera*, iii pt. 1, pp. 123, 128-129; Delisle, *St. Sauveur*, p. 84; Denifle, *Désolation*, ii, 109.

[199] Coville, *Etats Norm.*, pp. 78-79.

Navarrese ravages, a sizeable sales tax of 5 percent (12 *d./l.*) was granted, half of it to be applied to the royal army and the other half to local defense. This subsidy, evidently superseding the earlier indirect taxes, was to run for a year beginning in June.[200] It illustrates the recent trend in royal taxation—a steadily increasing tax burden and a comparable increase in the proportion of the receipts which were earmarked for local employment. This trend was always most pronounced in those districts facing the gravest military threat. Not long afterwards, the Estates of all Normandy convened and granted a special hearth tax of 10 *s.* for the three months of June through August.[201] It was levied in lower Normandy[202] as well as elsewhere and many receipts and pay orders indicate the activities of the collectors.[203] Once again, the Normans as a whole preferred to grant a temporary levy, which in the bailiwick of Cotentin was concurrent with the sales tax.

It is interesting to note that Normandy, now faced with the kind of permanent warfare which had long troubled Languedoc, was beginning to adopt the system of frequent short-term taxes which, as we have seen, had been used in the Midi for several years. That there was growing dissatisfaction with the traditional forms of subsidy throughout the realm is demonstrated by the events of 1356. Languedoc made one of its rare experiments with a sales tax; Normandy tried a hearth tax; and the Estates of Languedoil were trying to levy an income tax. Despite one document which seems to indicate the levy of this income tax in Normandy in July, it does not seem credible that the Normans were paying that tax on top of their self-imposed local assessments. Throughout 1356, they seem to have acted quite independently of the general Estates.[204]

---

[200] For the capture of Evreux, Secousse, *Charles II*, 1, 60-61. For the tax, Coville, *Etats Norm.*, pp. 80-81, 360-361; BN *ms. fr.* 25701, no. 88; 26001, nos. 577, 578, 584; P.O. 470, *dossier* 10446, no. 3; Clairambault 213, no. 69.

[201] BN *ms. fr.* 25701, nos. 83, 86, 90; P.O. 2886, *dossier* 64120, nos. 3, 4.

[202] Texts indicating collection in lower Normandy are BN *ms. fr.* 20026, no. 56; 20402, no. 19; 22468, nos. 6, 7, 74; 26001, nos. 577, 578, 584, 605, 624.

[203] Texts indicating collection in upper Normandy or throughout the duchy are BN *ms. fr.* 25701, nos. 76, 77, 80-83, 90, 93; 20402, nos. 15-18, 20; 26001, nos. 554, 560, 566, 571, 586, 588, 603, 608, 620-623, 625, 626, 631, 641, 643, 644, 646 663, 672; NAF 7609, fols. 339r-340v; NAF 20075, no. 18; P.O. 2286, *dossier* 64120, no. 7; BN Clairambault 213, nos. 62, 63, 65, 68, 71, 74.

[204] BN P.O. 108, *dossier* 2264, no. 2, mentions a commissioner assigned to collect the subsidy granted in March, which presumably was the income tax established at Paris. The document, however, is only a receipt indicating that the officer in question received some money from one of the treasurers general. The latter was probably collecting the Norman subsidy granted in May. According to Coville, *Etats Norm.*, p. 84, collection of this tax proceeded only with difficulty. It is un-

Although the clergy as well as laymen were expected to share in the taxes authorized by the successive assemblies of the Estates General, it is not entirely clear whether they did. Officers of the bishop of Paris resisted taxation on the basis of their privileges, thus challenging the ordinance which had ordered collection despite privileges.[205] A cleric of Senlis claimed exemption from paying a *taille* aimed at supporting troops sent to Picardy in response to the *arrière-ban*.[206] The bishop of Laon did furnish troops but obtained a letter of non-prejudice.[207] In one diocese, that of Rouen, it is certain that the clerical tenth was in force during 1356.[208]

The difficulties surrounding tax collections in 1356 must not obscure the basic concern of the monarchy, which of course was the war itself. All of western France was ablaze with conflict in the summer of 1356, as the English, already strong in Brittany, now took advantage of the Franco-Navarrese hostilities and moved into lower Normandy. On 18 June, the duke of Lancaster, the count of Montfort, and Robert Knolles landed in Cotentin with over 2,000 men.[209] A month later, the lord of Saint-Sauveur, Godefroy d'Harcourt, completed his break with France by making Edward III the heir to his *seigneurie*. Philip of Navarre rendered homage to Edward as king of France and duke of Normandy.[210] Harcourt would be killed in battle later in the fall, but English and Navarrese forces would ravage Normandy for years from Saint-Sauveur.[211] The long Norman struggle invited the participation of freebooters of every kind. Within a year, two of the most feared captains of the 1360s, both of them former partisans of Charles of Spain, had made their appearance in Normandy to fight the Navarrese. Their names were Arnaud de Cervole and Bertrand Du Guesclin.[212]

The *arrière-ban* was proclaimed in France on 26 June in order to resist Lancaster's forces in Normandy.[213] John II's troops had regained Breu-

---

proven, and most unlikely, that the Normans were also contributing to the levy ordered by the Estates General in March.

[205] BN NAF 7609, fols. 343-344. [206] Timbal, *Guerre*, p. 53.

[207] BN Moreau 233, fol. 145. [208] BN *ms. fr.* 26001, no. 579.

[209] Delisle, *St. Sauveur*, pp. 86-89; Denifle, *Désolation*, ii, 110.

[210] *Ibid.*, p. 111; *Foedera*, iii pt. 1, p. 124. On Edward III's claim to be both king and duke, see J. Le Patourel, "Edward III, 'roi de France et duc de Normandie,' 1356-1360," *RHD*, xxxi (1953).

[211] Delisle, *St. Sauveur*, pp. 91-99, 142-143.

[212] A. Cherest, *L'Archiprêtre: épisodes de la guerre de cent ans au XIVe siècle*, Paris, 1879, p. 21; R. Cazelles, "Du Guesclin avant Cocherel," *Actes du Colloque International de Cocherel* (1964), p. 35f.

[213] Varin, *Reims*, iii, 78.

teuil and were besieging Pont-Audemer in mid-August when word was received that the Prince of Wales had marched out of Gascony and was now in Poitou.[214] The Black Prince, who had virtually conquered Quercy the year before and had taken Périgueux early in February,[215] apparently now sought to join the English forces in Normandy for concerted operations. To prevent such a junction, John II determined to move against the Black Prince who was farther from his base and had no Navarrese allies to support him. At the end of August, the prince was at Issoudun, ravaging Auvergne, while John had collected French forces at Chartres.[216] In the face of superior opposition, Edward began to fall back on Gascony, only to be overtaken in mid-September by the royal army in Poitou.

Outnumbered and lacking supplies, the English appeared to be in serious straits. Papal legates on a peace mission obtained a brief delay in the hostilities. Edward may have interpreted this as an effort by French cardinals to weaken him further,[217] but one French historian sees the affair in a different light, since it may have afforded the prince a chance to deploy his forces more effectively. Whatever the intentions of the papal legates, the ensuing encounter near Poitiers on 19 September 1356 was a great French disaster. Victimized by poor tactics and English archery, the French knights were slaughtered and John II captured.[218]

The Battle of Poitiers was an event equaled only by the Black Death in its ultimate impact on royal taxation in France. Its immediate effect was to precipitate a political crisis at Paris and introduce a new phase in the complex duel between the House of Valois and the partisans of Charles the Bad. It would also introduce a new era in the kingdom's fiscal history. For more than half a century, royal efforts to develop a system of taxation had revolved around the war subsidy. Now there would begin to emerge a new fiscal regime, the *aides*, *gabelles*, and *tailles* which were to remain the basic royal taxes for centuries. These levies doubtless retained their importance because of military needs, but they were instituted to meet the special crisis created by Poitiers, the captivity of the king of France. The traditional feudal aid for ransoming one's lord now was merged with the more recent concept of "evident necessity." For the next decade, the vital factor, which would sharply alter the scope of royal taxation, was the ransom of John II.

---

[214] *Chron. Jean II*, pp. 67-69, describes these campaigns of 1356. Cf. Denifle, *Désolation*, II, 112.

[215] *Ibid.*, p. 115.   [216] *Ibid.*, p. 118.   [217] Zacour, *Talleyrand*, p. 52.

[218] Perroy, *The Hundred Years War*, pp. 130-131.

CHAPTER IX

A Half-Century of Royal Taxes: Major Conclusions

1. The Age of the War Subsidy

IN THE history of French taxation, the period from the outbreak of Anglo-French hostilities in 1294 until the capture of John II at Poitiers, can properly be called the age of the war subsidy. Taking many forms and obtained in various ways, the war subsidy was by far the most important tax in this period. Prior to 1356, only military emergency could justify an extraordinary tax, and taxpayers often defined "necessity" rather narrowly. Thereafter, the "common profit" would not be tied so strictly to war or invasion and the "aids for the deliverance" of the king would gradually form the basis for regular taxation.[1]

We have been concerned here with the second half of the age of the war subsidy, beginning with the Anglo-French war of 1324-1325. In part because the sources are not easily accessible, scholars have neglected these years and have been too ready to dismiss them as a period in which few significant developments occurred. Even Robert Fawtier saw the forty years after 1314 as mere repetition of earlier experiences and claimed that "it would be wearisome to follow the monotonous detail."[2] Yet this detail is worth examining, for it shows that taxation evolved gradually but steadily. Just as Philip IV no longer is considered a dramatic innovator, so his successors may now be regarded as capable of innovation. Each succeeding king practiced innovation in the only way the Middle Ages could accept—by adapting earlier precedents to new conditions.

These years were important ones for representative assemblies. After considerable experimentation with such meetings in the years 1315-1321, the crown abandoned large fiscal assemblies for two decades. Yet the central assemblies of the 1340s and the regional ones of the early 1350s were of great significance for French institutional growth. In both its initiatives and its failures, the Estates General of 1355 represented the

---

[1] Vuitry, *Régime financier*, II, 108-113; Esmein, *Cours*, p. 568; Lot and Fawtier, *Institutions*, II, 259. In my forthcoming article, "The French Ransom Aids and Two Legal Traditions," it is pointed out that the circumstances of the king's captivity had the effect of making his ransom a matter of "evident necessity." Therefore, these aids combined the feudal tradition with the Romano-canonical doctrine of paying taxes for the common profit to uphold the *status regni*.

[2] Lot and Fawtier, *Institutions*, II, 222.

culmination of the experiences of a decade. This famous meeting resembled more closely its predecessor of 1347 than the celebrated assemblies which followed the king's capture.

By 1322, the French crowns had gained important experience in obtaining extraordinary taxes. It had learned that appeals to Romano-canonical principles like "evident necessity" and "defense of the realm" did not always produce a satisfactory response, and that it was necessary to dramatize the need for money by using propaganda and calling out the army. The government had discovered that representatives with full powers would still evade making binding commitments, that there was a deeply ingrained distrust of taxation if a genuine war was not in progress, and that certain kinds of fiscal expedient could yield large profits on occasion without directly challenging sensitive privileges. Yet the crown had also learned that a justifiable war subsidy might produce very large sums, even if a strenuous effort was required to collect it. Charles IV and his successors built upon this experience, but their policies were inevitably determined by the political, military, and diplomatic conditions of the moment, factors which often were beyond their control.

The political realities of 1322, even more than his personal inclinations, compelled Charles IV to adopt a more cautious approach to taxation than that of his brother Philip. Charles levied subsidies only when his reasons for doing so were unassailable, and he strictly observed the principle of *cessante causa cessat effectus*. This policy forced him to resort to borrowing, extortion, and other fiscal expedients, but these actions were based on unquestioned royal rights and could, in the short run, be carried out with a minimum of controversy. The king's conservatism and his short, victorious campaigns made his reign a success. He did not precede his tax requests with a general *arrière-ban*, but still tied them rather closely to the obligation of military service. His opportunity for a master stroke came in the winter of 1326-1327, when he seemed ready to put into effect his advisers' plan for conquering Gascony. Yet when his nephew seized the English throne, he reverted to form and chose the path of prudence and peace. The kingdom seemed more confident and contented in 1328 than in 1322, but Charles left his successor unsolved problems in Flanders and Gascony, as well as an unpopular coinage policy.

It is tempting to dismiss Philip VI as a mediocrity, but he seems to have had greater competence and stability than his son. His serious defeat at Crécy was balanced by the earlier victory at Cassel. His usual military policy was perhaps too cautious for the tastes of the French nobility, but it would be vindicated by subsequent events. Philip relied heavily on advisers but was not dominated by them.[3] His great weakness seems to have been self-doubt. The centuries of unbroken royal succession from one Capetian to the next had created a very strong sense of legitimacy in France. The crown once worn by St. Louis conveyed title to a sacred office, yet Philip's right to it was uncertain. He was careful not to use the Great Seal until after his coronation. He treated the magnates with excessive deference and was easily embarrassed by their factional rivalries. He ordered the return of a feudal aid when it occurred to him that its collection might have aroused divine wrath. He went to great lengths to assure that Edward III's homage met precise legal standards, but the effort availed him little when Edward proclaimed himself king of France. Whatever Edward's motives in claiming the throne, it was a shrewd maneuver to use against a man like Philip.[4]

Even more than Charles IV, therefore, Philip VI felt it necessary to proceed with caution in the financial sphere. He agreed to abandon mint profits and restore the fabled sound money of St. Louis. In tying his subsidies to the obligation of military service, he employed the *arrière-ban* in 1328 and in the first four years of the Hundred Years' War. Regional military summonses were used on many other occasions. He too was scrupulous about *cessante causa*, ordering a quick return of taxes in 1329 when Edward's homage prevented war with England. In 1338, he went further and accepted the southern towns' definition of war as outright invasion, in the absence of which a tax was unjustified.

Philip's own policies before 1340 had much to do with his difficulties after that year. Frequent truces made it harder to justify war subsidies, and declining revenues from this source could not be made up by the newly imposed *gabelle*. Moreover, Philip had exhausted many of the irregular sources of money which had often served as stop-gap expedients. The moneylenders and their debtors, victimized by three royal seizures between 1331 and 1340, could not be tapped again immediately. Coinage alterations, resumed in 1337, were stepped up in 1340, but the ensuing outcry forced a new reform in 1343.

Persistent financial troubles forced the crown to seek new policies. Philip and his advisers pursued this task with considerable tenacity and some imagination. The Estates of 1343 opened a new era of representative assemblies. For the next sixteen years, they would occur frequently

---

[3] See Cazelles, *Soc. politique*, pp. 404-436.

[4] This is the position of Lewis, *Later Medieval France*. See above, Chapter 1, note 35.

at the national level, while some of the provincial Estates began to flourish in the same period. In 1343, Philip offered the Estates a specific proposal: revaluation of the coinage in return for a sales tax of 1⅔ percent for one year. Advance notification of this plan enabled the towns to do what they had not done before—send proctors with sufficient instructions to make a firm commitment. Some of these proctors were instructed to oppose the plan, but most agreed, subject to formal ratifying charters for the towns of Languedoc. This meeting marked the only occasion on which Philip VI or his son asked the Estates to consent to a specific proposal announced in advance.

Philip VI's government did not develop a comprehensive policy on war taxation until 1345. For the next three years, however, the king made every effort to put into effect a plan which would finance annually a national army of specified size. He was prepared to let his subjects choose the form of tax and name the persons who would collect the money and pay the troops. This plan, tenaciously pursued in the face of many obstacles, was probably the most important fiscal initiative of Philip VI's reign. It revived the principle that all were obliged to contribute to the defense of the realm without the cumbersome formality of a general call to arms. Until war subsidies were freed from dependence on the *arrière-ban*, there could be no possibility of expanding the sense of common profit to include times of peace. Philip VI was willing to accept local variations and abandon direct control of the tax receipts if these concessions would bring him the resources he needed so badly.

The proposed tax in men-at-arms failed to win wide support in 1345, partly because the kingdom did not perceive a serious military threat, and perhaps also because the king had not taken adequate counsel before proceeding. This reversal may explain why Philip did not advertise a specific plan when he summoned the Estates in 1346. He wanted endorsement of the plan itself before seeking consent to a definite tax. Having received favorable counsel, he was ready to implement the plan, when the English invasion, the Crécy debacle, and the Calais campaign successively jolted the monarchy and frustrated systematic policy making. In Languedoc, moreover, the royal scheme was less relevant, and Philip was handicapped by his ignorance of particular circumstances in the Midi. Nevertheless, he had effectively "sold" his proposal to the kingdom, and it was taken over by the Estates General late in 1347. The Black Death then intervened to ruin prospects for collecting a very large subsidy, but the Estates would revive Philip's plan late in 1355. A nationwide tax computed in men-at-arms never succeeded in producing the desired army, but it did lead to the establishment of *élus,* and these formed the basis for the special administration for extraordinary taxes which finally developed after 1356. Even more important, it helped to divorce war financing from the *arrière-ban* and paved the way for the growth of bailiwick assemblies in the 1350s. These bodies regularly granted taxes in return for royal concessions, even when a truce was in effect.

John II, a much less stable personality, was the effective ruler of the kingdom for eight years, from 1348 to 1356. In the first half of this period, French finances recovered gradually from the impact of the plague, but John weakened his position by antagonizing important interests. His dramatic feud with his equally erratic relative, Charles of Navarre, proved to be a serious blow to the royal fiscal position. Aside from the political questions involved, this struggle undermined royal power and public order in the wealthy province of Normandy. It is hard to over-estimate the importance of this duchy, which had played a pivotal role in the history of royal finances since its acquisition by the crown. In 1339, 1347, and 1355, the Norman Estates granted sizeable taxes and established models which the rest of the kingdom followed.

The Estates General of 1347 and 1355 both followed the Norman lead, but the latter assembly attempted more than was justified by practical politics and economics. Had the Estates of 1355 and early 1356 delivered the promised taxes, their demands for governmental reform would have been irresistible, but local particularism thwarted collection and the failure to produce the needed money weakened the effectiveness of the Estates.

As long as John II was present and in need of funds, there was still a strong possibility that the Estates might effect permanent changes in the government. With John's capture, however, the reform movement was ruined because the Estates were exploited by self-seeking adventurers. Assemblies became discredited, the kingdom rallied to the monarchy as the only hope for restoring order, and the king's ransom necessitated taxes which were not subject to negotiation.[5] Thus the capture of John II ultimately served the cause of royal absolutism. Although it was not apparent at the time, the age of the war subsidy was over, and the history of French taxation entered a new period on 19 September 1356.

[5] On the desire of the kingdom to be ruled by a strong hand, see Cazelles, *Soc. politique,* p. 430. Lewis, *Later Medieval France,* p. 80, observes that "the very misfortunes of France reinforced the image of the saviour of France."

2. The Low Level of Taxation: Privilege and Politics

When one surveys the taxes levied in France during the age of the war subsidy, it soon becomes apparent that they were actually very light. Not until the end of 1347, do we find a sales tax as high as 2½ percent (6 *d./l.*), and the relatively rare income taxes did not exceed 2½ percent before 1356. The light taxation is harder to document when one deals with hearth taxes, but the heaviest such tax before the Black Death was 20 *s.* and many *fouages* were much smaller. After the plague, 20 or 25 *s.* hearth taxes became more common and because these were based on pre-plague hearths until well into the 1360s, the burden on the individual must have been greater.

Our best means of determining the weight of taxation is to compare tax receipts and other revenues in different years. Scanty documentation and the complex problems caused by the coinage changes make any absolute figures very suspect, however. In Appendix 1, some effort has been made to resolve these difficulties sufficiently to permit utilization of such treasury documents as do remain. The figures evolved in Appendix 1 do not inspire absolute confidence but they permit some observations about the relative importance of subsidies and other revenues in the royal financial structure. Because of coinage changes, it has been necessary to convert treasury receipts to silver marks. Although the crown could regularly expect a certain amount of income from fines, forfeitures, customs duties, and regular taxes on Italians, we have seen that revenue from these sources sometimes was sharply increased as a fiscal expedient. Because they experienced such fluctuations, these revenues have been classified as "extraordinary," along with loans, subsidies, "gifts," coinage profits, and the clerical tenth. As a result, the king's "ordinary" revenues have been defined rather strictly as net profits from the domain and such things as chancery fees which formed a regular part of the king's income and experienced few fluctuations. Even with "ordinary" revenues so narrowly defined, the king's income from this source remained very important, a fact which lends some substance to the perennial demand that he should live within these revenues.

Treasury receipts from ordinary revenues averaged slightly less than 74,000 marks in the first four years of Charles IV's reign and slightly less than 108,000 marks in the first four years of Philip VI's reign. The increase under Philip VI was due in part to the acquisition of the Valois *apanage*, but mainly to the revenue from Agenais and other regions conquered from English Guyenne by Charles IV.[6] In the first years of both reigns, the clerical tenth averaged somewhat more than 44,000 marks annually. As for war subsidies, that of 1328 seems to have produced 57,000 marks; slightly higher totals may have been obtained in 1339 and 1340. Strayer's estimate for the subsidy of 1304 is equivalent to about 110,000 marks, while the sum granted but not collected in 1347-1348 may have approximated 530,000 marks. By way of comparison, the coinage profits for the second half of 1349 amounted to around 100,000 marks.[7]

These figures suggest that total war subsidy receipts in a given year did not equal the king's ordinary revenues, or even the net profits of the bailiwicks and seneschalsies, which averaged nearly 83,000 marks the first four years of Philip VI's reign. It seems equally certain that no tax actually collected in the period considered here came close to that which Philip the Fair had collected in 1304. At the same time, the magnitude of the subsidy promised in 1347-1348 is reaffirmed. The tax so optimistically envisioned by the Estates of late 1355 would have been larger still. It should be added, of course, that our figures for domainal receipts belong to the early years of Philip VI's reign, when the depression had not yet become serious. After the Black Death, these receipts must have declined significantly, and it is likely that receipts from Normandy experienced another decline when the Valois-Evreux feud broke out in 1354.[8] Receipts from the tenth must also have been diminished in the course of the century, since clerical revenues suffered a serious decline.[9] Since rates of taxation gradually increased after 1347, it is probable that extraordinary taxes became increasingly important in the royal budget while the domain and the tenth declined in relative importance.

With regard to the form of taxation, the regions which were coming to be known as Languedoil usually preferred sales taxes, while Langue-

---

[6] The figures in AN KK 2, fols. 23r-24v, 44r-47v, show that in 1328 the domainal receipts from Languedoc were very sizeable. The *net* revenues of the seneschalsy of Toulouse came to 295,490 *l.t.*, almost 20% of the year's total treasury receipts. Three other southern districts which profited from the gains made in Aquitaine were those of Agen, Carcassonne, and Saintonge. They produced nearly 40,000 pounds, while Valois yielded only 822 pounds.

[7] The basis for the conversion into marks, described in Appendix 1, is column 2 of Table 1. For the foregoing discussion of relative totals, see Tables 2-4 of the same appendix.

[8] See Lewis, *Later Medieval France*, p. 209, on the shrinkage of ordinary royal revenues.

[9] J. Favier, "Temporels ecclésiastiques et taxation fiscal: le poids de la fiscalité pontificale au XIVe siècle," *Journal des Savants* (1964), p. 109.

doc normally paid hearth taxes.[10] The latter were generally apportioned among the communities of a given district with the larger towns almost invariably paying a lump sum for their share and raising the money by means of municipal taxation. In the first half of our period, however, there were so many exceptions to this general rule that it is difficult to point to any discernible pattern. Towns in the North as well as those in Languedoc resorted to lump-sum payments. Paris regularly computed its tax grants in men-at-arms, and the communities of Périgord, Quercy, and Rouergue expressed their subsidies as "a certain number of sergeants" in most cases. Taxes were often concealed by other names—loans, fines, and "compositions" with *réformateurs*. Somewhat more uniformity may be detected after 1340, and especially after 1350, but it is really not possible to make a meaningful classification of taxes according to their form. In 1356, everybody seemed discontented with the status quo. Normandy tried a hearth tax, Languedoc a sales tax, and the Estates General of Languedoil a tax on incomes. On the rare occasions when nobles made a special grant, as in 1340 and 1347, the tax was on revenues. Normally, however, the nobility was being generous if it allowed collection of other taxes from tallageable subjects.

Despite the great variety in the forms of tax, subsidies throughout France tended to favor the rich. Sales taxes, especially on articles of consumption, were widespread in the North, and these naturally bore most heavily on the poor consumer. Lump-sum payments by towns, widely used in the South, permitted the municipal governments to tax their own citizens more or less as they chose. Insofar as the crown tapped the resources of the wealthy, it was mainly through indirect methods such as coinage alterations, fines for acquiring fiefs, and confiscation of debts to Lombards. The frequent use of such expedients is no doubt partly explainable by the fact that it afforded the government a way of taxing the rich. Fines in lieu of military service, when not bought off by lump sums, also served this purpose. The sharp decline in royal revenues in 1341, despite the widespread imposition of indirect taxes, shows that the crown was seriously handicapped in periods when a truce precluded the fiscal use of the *arrière-ban*.

The opportunities for the rich to escape taxation were increased by the

[10] Lot and Fawtier, *Institutions*, II, 223, following Viard's erroneous statement that a 20 s. hearth tax was levied throughout the realm in 1342, give the misleading impression that the *fouage* became common in the North after this date. Actually, our first clear indications of hearth taxes in the North belong to 1355 and 1356. After a few more experiments in the late 1350s, a general *fouage* was finally established in Languedoil at the end of John II's reign.

existence of numerous privileges, some of which appeared to include tax exemptions. Theorists, of course, had long argued that an emergency suspended private rights. According to Baldus, a tax for the public utility touched all equally and could be levied in proportion to wealth in immovable property, livestock, and money.[11] It was difficult to apply this theory, however, because all such taxes were not collected by the crown. Many taxpayers paid their royal subsidies by means of municipal taxes. Both royal and municipal taxes were challenged at times on the grounds that they were not really for the common profit. This kind of argument could have great importance if the common profit alone could override privilege.

Privilege was therefore a complex matter which the historians of taxation must consider carefully. Not only were there innumerable customary rights, but many other privileges were granted by the kings, especially the first two Valois, for reasons of generosity or expediency. When the king was in political difficulty, he may have been encouraged to grant additional favors, often when the treasury was least able to afford them.

Certain categories of person were normally excused from paying taxes, although there were always enough exceptions to the rules to permit considerable acrimony and litigation. Royal moneyers, for instance, were forced to pay municipal *tailles* in the early years of Philip VI's reign,[12] but thereafter they established their exemption from taxes, which the *Parlement* upheld.[13] When municipal governments in the Beaucaire district tried to tax them in 1350, John II held that they could be taxed only if they were not practicing their trade.[14] Clerks of the Chamber of Accounts were excused from paying the tenth on their ecclesiastical benefices.[15] Royal sergeants and notaries also claimed exemptions from most taxes, although the king periodically assessed them for marks of silver. They obtained recognition of their exemption at Toulouse in 1342[16] but in the same year were required to pay *tailles* at Agen, and throughout Languedoc the crown usually ordered them to pay.[17] Doctors and lawyers

---

[11] Post, *Studies*, p. 18.

[12] *Gr. Chartrier*, nos. 1476-1478; BN Doat 87, fols. 88r-89v.

[13] Timbal, *Guerre*, p. 49; *Ord.*, II, 339; Furgeot, *Actes*, I, no. 3764; II, no. 9403.

[14] *Gr. Chartrier*, nos. 1548, 1549. In the summer of 1350, the consuls of Lunel brought suit against moneyers who refused to pay *tailles*: AM Lunel CC 60, no. 2222.

[15] J. Viard, "La chambre des comptes sous le règne de Philippe VI de Valois," *BEC*, XCIII (1932), 346-347.

[16] *INV AM Toulouse*, p. 81 (AA 5, no. 158); AD Hérault A 1, fols. 94v-95r.

[17] Tholin, *Agen*, pp. 53-54, 61-62; BN Doat 52, fol. 59r-v; ANP, XLVI, pp. 152-153; *Gr. Chartrier*, no. 3249; *INV AM Toulouse*, p. 33 (AA 3, no. 216).

also claimed exemption, but as we have seen, they were also sometimes subject to special occupational taxes.[18] After the king's capture, all forms of privilege were increasingly overruled, and in August 1362, John II clarified the rights of lawyers, notaries, sergeants, and moneyers: they were not to be taxed on the emoluments of their offices but any property they owned was subject to taxation.[19]

The categories of privileged persons discussed so far formed only a tiny part of the population who owed their privileges to special functions which they filled in the administration of the kingdom. Of far greater importance are the privileges which were claimed by towns, the clergy, and the nobles—the three estates of society. The towns stood very little chance of being excused from a war subsidy, although it was sometimes possible to resist taxation if their privileges included exemption from military service. A town might also seek to avoid paying if it was not directly subject to the crown, but this tactic rarely succeeded except in the case of feudal aids. Towns like Montpellier and Rodez objected to paying their own lords as much as they did to royal taxation. Their resistance seems to have diminished as years went by, partly no doubt because of a heightened sense of "necessity" but perhaps also because they became accustomed to the unhappy reality of paying subsidies.

Although communities often challenged the legitimacy of a subsidy demand and frequently negotiated lump-sum payments which reduced the amount of a tax, there were really only two situations in which towns could get excused from paying. Both of these were cases in which tax exemption could be justified on grounds of evident necessity—cases of extreme hardship resulting from natural disaster or military devastation, and location near an important frontier.[20]

Within the towns, municipal governments faced many of the same fiscal difficulties encountered by the crown, especially in the years following the Black Death.[21] Because so many municipal taxes were shared with the crown, were used to pay war subsidies, or were employed for royal purposes such as defense, the king was necessarily interested in the

[18] Ménard, *Nismes*, II, *preuves*, 67-69. See above, Chapter IV, note 75.

[19] *Gr. Chartrier*, no. 2571.

[20] From the early 1340s onwards, Périgueux was excused from royal taxation because it had suffered at the hands of the enemy or needed to repair its walls. See above, Chapter V, for this exemption in 1342. For the tax reductions granted to various communities in the wake of the Black Death, see the relevant portions of Chapters VI and VII. On frontier towns, see Chapter I, note 51. Viard, in AN AB xix 2636, cited a text which gave Agen fiscal privileges precisely because of its frontier location.

[21] See the comments above, in Chapter VII, part 2.

efforts of town governments to enforce collection. All the privileged groups made efforts to avoid municipal taxation, but there was also opposition from certain groups of non-noble laymen who could not claim privileges. Among these were the *populares* who claimed inequities in the assessment of taxes,[22] those who lived in one town but had property in another,[23] and the inhabitants of suburban parishes outside the walls.[24] Although the royal government sometimes found it useful to threaten municipalities with investigation of their complaints, it usually ordered these persons to contribute. A special problem was presented by those bourgeois who were required to repair or destroy (for reasons of local defense) buildings or ramparts which they owned.[25] This action might be equivalent to paying a tax for local defense and it might be resisted.

In general, however, we may say that towns, whoever their direct seigneur, were not excused from paying war subsidies except in most unusual situations, and that the bourgeois inhabitants were unable to make good individual exemptions from paying royal or urban taxes. It was the other classes of society which were most concerned with privileges and exemptions, while the towns normally found it desirable to oppose these claims wherever possible.

The clergy also found it difficult, in practice, to escape paying taxes, although they had well-defined privileges which they continuously sought to invoke. Except for brief periods in 1336-1337 and 1347-1348, the French clergy regularly paid a tenth granted to the king by the pope.[26] In principle, however, clerics were supposed to be exempt from other taxation. This exemption, asserted in canon law and affirmed by Beaumanoir in the thirteenth century, spared clerics from paying *tailles, banalités*, and internal tolls.[27] By the end of Philip III's reign, however, the French government was attacking clerical immunities, and the papacy did not always choose to defend them insofar as taxation was

[22] *Gr. Chartrier*, nos. 3299, 3531.

[23] A. Magen and G. Tholin (eds.), *Archives municipales d'Agen, Chartes, première série (1189-1328)*, Villeneuve-sur-Lot, 1876, pp. 299-301; AD Gard, ms. inventory of AM Beaucaire, fol. 151r; BN *Coll. Languedoc* 84, fol. 322.

[24] Magen and Tholin, *op. cit.*, pp. 299-301; Moreau, *Recueil*, pp. 87-88; Timbal, *Guerre*, pp. 248-249; Furgeot, *Actes*, II, nos. 4612, 8561.

[25] Le Maire, *St. Quentin*, II, no. 569.

[26] Grants of tenths after 1328 are summarized in Vuitry, *Régime financier*, II, 206f.

[27] G. Campbell, "Clerical Immunities in France during the Reign of Philip III," *Speculum*, XXXIX (1964), 418.

concerned.[28] Both royal and papal positions were due in part to the fact that there were many different grades of clergy. Those in lesser orders who were married and/or engaged in commerce were not considered to be "living clerically."

Whereas a noble claimed tax privileges because he was supposed to render personal military service, the basis for a cleric's privileges was his immunity from personal military service. As early as Philip III's reign, the crown had sought to extend to all clergymen, of whatever grade, the taxes levied on laymen for the "common good."[29] Moreover, even when the basis for taxation was shifted to the *arrière-ban*, the immunity from personal service did not excuse the clergy from obligations arising from their position in the feudal structure.[30] Since the tenth was regularly granted by the pope in the fourteenth century, these considerations apply mainly to the occasions when the crown sought additional money from the clergy directly, as it did in 1337, 1340, 1346, 1348, 1351, and 1355.[31] At these times, letters of non-prejudice and other guarantees sometimes left the rights of the clergy intact.

Clerical privileges were not a great issue when the king approached the French church for a subsidy, because canon law recognized the principle of "defense of the realm." At the local level, however, the conflicts and litigation were almost continuous. Once again, the issue was usually municipal taxation. Taxes levied by a town to pay a war subsidy often met with clerical resistance. The clergy, as local residents, were in a position to profit from improved fortifications, and in some towns they would pay taxes only for this purpose.[32] More frequently, however, they opposed all municipal levies whatsoever and had to be ordered to pay by the royal government.[33] In the face of persistent clerical opposition to municipal taxes for purposes other than town defenses, the crown repeatedly backed the town governments. We may cite examples from many widely scattered towns during the period 1320-1347.[34] Sometimes

---

[28] *Ibid.*, p. 419.   [29] *Ibid.*   [30] *Ibid.*, p. 421.

[31] These occasions have all been discussed previously. Among the relevant sources are Coville, *Etats Norm.*, pp. 351-352; Prentout, *Etats Norm.*, III, 63-67; BN Doat 109, fols. 303v-319; BN Moreau 229, fols. 124, 192; BN *Coll. Languedoc* 84, fols. 125r-128. The whole question of clerical exemption in the period immediately following 1356 is dealt with in Dupont-Ferrier, *Institutions*, II, 166-167.

[32] F. Humbert, *Les finances municipales de Dijon du milieu du XIVe siècle à 1477*, Paris, 1961, pp. 73f.

[33] Timbal, *Guerre*, pp. 51-53, 233, 238, 240; G. Guigue, *Les Tards-Venus en Lyonnais, Forez, et Beaujolais*, Lyon, 1886, pp. 3-5.

[34] From Agen, Toulouse, and Montpellier in the South to Eu and Provins in the North, clergy were regularly forced to contribute: Boutaric, *Actes*, II, nos. 5983,

the issue was restricted to clerics who were married or engaged in trade. The crown always required these to pay taxes.[35]

Sometimes a certain category of clergy would be exempt and other persons would try to take advantage of that exemption. At Saint-Quentin, for instance, the dean and chapter were considered exempt from the *maltôte* and from local defense obligations, but when certain lawyers claimed exemption and servants of the church choir tried to avoid garrison duty, they were unsuccessful.[36] In Paris, the various disputes between the town and cathedral chapter led to a statement in 1343 that the payment of a tax would not prejudice the chapter's rights. All other Parisians were to contribute, however.[37]

Although the crown usually ordered the clergy to contribute, it did not invariably require them to do so. It will be recalled that in 1337, ecclesiastics in Languedoc were specifically excluded from paying the subsidy in places where they held *roturier* property but did not reside.[38] In this case, however, the government hoped to obtain a special subsidy grant from the clergy as a class. In 1321, when Périgueux sought to make the clergy contribute to a local *taille* for repurchasing suspended privileges from the crown, the *Parlement* forbade the consuls to force payment from clerks living clerically.[39] Hospitals caring for the sick received the privilege of exemption from subsidies and *amortissement*.[40] As individuals or as corporate bodies, the clergy, like the nobility, could be seigneurs whose tallageable dependents were a valuable source of revenue. On some occasions, the king heeded clerical demands that these persons not be forced to pay taxes.[41] The long debate over the taxable status of the Paris chapter's serfs was ultimately resolved in favor of the chapter.[42]

7490; Furgeot, *Actes*, I, no. 4548; II, nos. 5145, 5212, 6072, 6361, 7771; Timbal, *Guerre*, pp. 51-54; Tholin, *Agen*, pp. 20-21, 50-52; *Gr. Chartrier*, nos. 3295-3297; *INV AM Riom*, pp. 62-63; BN Doat 53, fol. 62; Doat 119, fols. 62r-63v; *A.H. Rouergue*, VII, 78; AD Hérault A 4, fol. 134; *INV AM Toulouse*, p. 31 (AA 3, no. 183); A. Le Gris (ed.), *Le Livre Rouge d'Eu, 1151-1454*, Rouen and Paris, 1911, pp. 203-204.

[35] *Gr. Chartrier*, no. 3207; Furgeot, *Actes*, II, no. 6742; Le Maire, *St. Quentin*, I, no. 274.

[36] *Ibid.*, II, nos. 570, 590.

[37] AN AB xix 2636, copied from AD Côte-d'Or B 11477, no. 1905.

[38] AD Hérault A 4, fols. 86v, 88 v.   [39] Boutaric, *Actes*, II, no. 6489.

[40] Sibertin-Blanc, "Levée," p. 332; BN Moreau 230, fol. 180r; BN NAF 7605, fols. 139-140.

[41] BN *ms. fr.* 25698, no. 69; *HL*, x, cols. 968-969.

[42] Timbal, *Guerre*, pp. 56-57; AN K 42, no. 43. The *échevins* of Saint-Quentin were prepared to admit the exemption of the dean, canons, and domestic clerks of the chapter there: Le Maire, *St. Quentin*, II, note to no. 534.

The extensive temporal privileges claimed by the bishop of Mende were upheld in 1339.[43] In Velay, the clergy at first were so successful in resisting taxation of their men that some persons even falsely declared themselves to be tallageable by the bishop of Le Puy in order to escape subsidy payments. By the 1340s, however, the clergy of this region were no longer able to make good their claims.[44] Elsewhere, a monastery in Compiègne had to allow the levy of a sales tax on its lands in 1341.[45] A year later, the subjects of the bishop of Chartres contributed to a fiftieth.[46]

We may conclude from these different examples, that although the clergy sometimes succeeded in invoking privileges to escape taxation, they had to pay in the great majority of cases. As with the towns, therefore, privilege does not seem to have permitted many clergy to avoid paying subsidies.

The nobles, however, were another matter entirely. It was they who were especially involved when there was a question of whether the common profit could override private rights. The nobility could claim exemption from taxation on the basis of their traditional obligation to render personal military service. The revival of the *arrière-ban* and the development of war subsidies turned the nobles' obligation of military service into an important right, for those who served personally would naturally not pay a tax based on the commutation of service. If they served for a time at their own expense, the revenues of their fiefs supported such service, and a royal tax on their tallageable subjects would pose a threat to those revenues. The crown, on the other hand, preferred to tax these subjects and hire trained mercenaries with the funds. Herein lay the main conflict over noble exemptions.[47]

In Languedoc, where more nobles lived in towns and were subject to the municipal *tailles,* the issue was more complicated. Were they to contribute to *tailles* to raise a war subsidy if they also rendered personal service? This sort of double taxation was protested in 1337.[48] If munici-

---

[43] BN *Coll. Languedoc* 83, fol. 132; AD Hérault A 4, fols. 87v-88r.

[44] Delcambre, *Etats Velay*, pp. 51-52.

[45] Furgeot, *Actes*, I, no. 3317.   [46] BN Clairambault 473, pp. 15-25.

[47] Dupont-Ferrier, *Institutions*, II, 175; Timbal, *Guerre*, p. 19; *INV AM Cordes,* p. 251 (FF 62). In 1346, those who served as men-at-arms under the viscount of Narbonne were excused from paying the subsidy, as were those who contributed to their maintenance (BN *Coll. Languedoc* 84, fol. 330). Another basis on which nobles claimed and sometimes received exemption from paying subsidies was the possession of high justice. See Timbal, *Guerre*, pp. 231-232; Ménard, *Nismes*, II, *preuves*, 107. BN NAF 3653, no. 67.

[48] See above, Chapter IV, notes 13-14. Cf. *HL*, x, *col.* 770, for the royal order to collect taxes in royal and church lands before levying them in noble lands. The

pal taxes, for whatever purpose, were based on property or income, were the nobles to be assessed for all their property, even that located in the country? This question was resolved by developing the distinction between noble and *roturier* lands. The latter was urban property, traditionally taxable by municipal governments, while the former comprised rural fiefs. It appears that liability to taxation depended more on the status of the property than the status of the owner.[49] On a number of occasions, nobles were forced to pay municipal taxes when they sought to avoid them.[50] It will be recalled, however, that the nobility of Languedoc received a sweeping reaffirmation of their privileges in 1338 and were promptly relieved of fiscal exactions when they complained in 1340.[51] Some of them also escaped paying for the coinage reform of 1343-1344, even though this tax had nothing to do with military obligations and the reform was one which should have been especially beneficial to nobles.[52] Tallageable subjects were declared exempt from paying in other regions besides Languedoc.[53]

There were two other forms of noble fiscal privileges, although both were somewhat specialized in character. One of these involved the greater magnates, mainly those who held *apanages* or peerages. The territory and subjects of these lords do not seem to have been taxable by the crown under normal circumstances. The king therefore had to work out special tax-sharing arrangements with men like the duke of Burgundy and count of Blois.[54] A second type of special fiscal privilege was that employed by Philip VI when dealing with seigneurs to whom he was particularly indebted. The king might share subsidy receipts with such a lord, or exempt his lands from the subsidy, or permit him to collect the subsidy for his own benefit. In this way, the king sought to repay debts to the count of Foix, reward his seneschal of Toulouse, and favor other members of the aristocracy.[55]

---

careful handling of the nobility in 1337 was probably dictated more by practical politics than by privileges.

[49] AD Hérault A 4, fols. 36v, 140r-v, 158v-159r. As pointed out by Timbal, *Guerre*, p. 24, the exclusion of all noble property from taxes based on land would have created impossible difficulties.

[50] *Gr. Chartrier*, no. 3241; BN Doat 253, fol. 874v; Bibliothèque de Lunel, ms. *INV AM Lunel*, fols. 28r, 31v.

[51] See above, Chapter IV; *Gr. Chartrier*, no. 3354; Delcambre, *Etats Velay*, pp. 50-51, 58; AD Hérault A 4, fols. 144r-v, 226v-227v, 229v-231r; *Ord.*, II, 122.

[52] AD Hérault A 4, fol. 203.

[53] For Champagne, see above, Chapter IV, and AN P 2291, p. 483.

[54] Billioud, *Etats Bourgogne*, p. 154; Chapter II, note 218; Chapter V, notes 119-122.

[55] See above, Chapter IV, notes 60-63.

It thus appears that the feudal nobility found its privileges more valuable than any other group in seeking to escape taxation. Yet the nobility was by no means completely tax exempt, and the unfavorable pressure of public opinion enabled the king to override their privileges more frequently in the last ten years of our period. In 1345, the lords of Languedoc could no longer gain tax exemption for their tallageable subjects unless they personally went to the army.[56] In 1347 and 1348, subsidy grants explicitly stated that all persons must contribute to the tax, regardless of their privileges.[57] In 1351, John II's military ordinance weakened traditional vassal ties by establishing more up-to-date military units and no longer requiring nobles to render personal service under their own lords.[58] Finally, the income taxes ordered in 1356 clearly aimed at tapping the resources of the nobles to a greater degree than in the past.[59] Moreover, the privileges conferred by nobility seem to have been somewhat ill-defined. The concept of "living nobly" and refraining from trade lagged far behind the concept of "living clerically."[60]

We may summarize the subject of privilege by saying that it was probably not of decisive importance in the age of the war subsidy. The nobles and clergy in particular, and others to a lesser extent, continually invoked privilege in hopes of avoiding taxation. They created delays, reduced receipts, and complicated the tax-raising process, but the government increasingly overruled their appeals. Privileges "did not, like a talisman, protect the recipients for evermore."[61] Clerical privileges usually were disallowed and even the nobles were losing ground by mid-century in their effort to escape taxes. Low tax receipts in this period were due partly to the failure to exploit the wealthy, but formal privileges did not play the major role in this failure. Notwithstanding the notoriety given to privilege by liberal critics of the *ancien régime*, we must look elsewhere to explain the low taxes in France prior to 1356.

A more acceptable explanation for the tax structure in this period may be found by considering the question of practical politics. The "political society" at the French court described by Raymond Cazelles, was determined by such things as regional groupings, personal loyalties, family

---

[56] AD Hérault A 4, fol. 226r-v.

[57] See above, Chapter VII. Dupont-Ferrier, *Institutions*, II, 162f., lists a number of instances from the late 1340s onward, in which nobles and all other privileged persons were required to contribute to subsidies. For the case of 1353, see Chapter VII.

[58] *Ord.*, IV, 67-70.

[59] See Chapter VIII, part III, especially at note 179.

[60] Timbal, *Guerre*, pp. 342-343.   [61] Lewis, *Later Medieval France*, p. 98.

connections, and bureaucratic rivalries within the government. This aspect of political power in the late medieval monarchies deserves more study than it has received. In terms of governmental policy, Cazelles has argued that the use of representative assemblies varied according to which faction dominated the council. Those associated with the Chamber of Accounts used assemblies for fiscal purposes but rarely for other things. The opposing faction made considerable use of consultive assemblies but not for fiscal purposes.[62] This analysis is not entirely satisfactory, but in general, it appears valid. Fiscal assemblies were important under Philip V, then went into eclipse until revived in the 1340s when Mile de Noyers was back in power. After Crécy, the Chamber of Accounts again lost influence, but this time the crown did not abandon central assemblies. Yet the important Estates of 1346, 1347, and 1355 were not really the product of royal initiative but were, in a sense, forced on the king by circumstances.

It is probable that personnel changes in the royal council led to reorientations of royal policy, but there were other important ways in which practical politics influenced taxes. The great landed interests were always influential, but Philip VI had special political reasons for favoring the magnates who had made him king. Their influence brought about deflationary coinage "reforms" when such measures were not economically sound. They must have played a considerable role in determining the regressive forms of taxation employed in Philip's reign. Once the nobles were weakened by the disgrace at Crécy, the crown did not hesitate to confiscate their debts to moneylenders and negotiate subsidy grants which required the nobles to pay their share. Their declining attendance at the successive assemblies of 1355-1356 may be regarded as both a cause and an effect of the successive changes in the rates of the taxes. These changes shifted the burden of taxation increasingly towards the wealthy, especially the wealthy nobles.

On a more local level, we find that political considerations also affected taxation of the towns. Competing communities, factions, or economic interests determined local political conditions. The debate over the Carcassonne cloth *gabelle* in 1330-1333 and the crown's unsuccessful effort to improve Mediterranean port facilities in 1336, were both affected by competition among economic interests. Local jealousies led towns to make subsidy grants conditional upon similar grants from the other towns. The politics of individual communities, pitting patricians against *populares*, unquestionably affected the form and size of royal

---

[62] See Cazelles, *Soc. politique*, p. 128, on the shifting use of assemblies.

subsidies. Moreover, these political conditions gave the king's officers their opportunity to exploit multiple fiscal powers. The threat of investigation by *enquêteurs-réformateurs* sometimes induced municipal governments to pay impressive sums. These investigations were not limited to abuses of power by the patricians. They also focussed on coinage violations, fief acquisitions, and usury. Potentially, the fines were lucrative, and the local dislike of them suggests that they were a useful form of pressure to employ against the wealthy.

In short, it appears that the form and direction of taxation in our period were constantly affected by the political position of various interests. If specified privileges played a relatively minor role, actual power, influence, and rivalries could be very important. The relatively low level of taxation and the extremely light burden assumed by the wealthy are in part a reflection of these political realities.

3. Necessity and Localism: Theory and Practice

Among the factors which conditioned practical politics in fourteenth century France, local particularism was very significant. The interests and ties of the great magnates and urban patricians were usually not national, but were oriented around a given region with its own legal and cultural tradition. It is true that a common loyalty to the king and the emergent belief in the sacred soil and chosen people of France were impressive unifying factors.[63] Nevertheless, we have seen that regional parochialism remained strong and affected royal taxation. It played an important role in determining the French attitude towards assemblies of Estates and Romano-canonical theories of "evident necessity."

The basic principles of royal sovereignty as expounded by the legists have been summarized in Chapter 1, where it was pointed out that they had not been fully applied in practice at the beginning of the fourteenth century. We may now conclude that in the period up to 1356, these theories gained only a partial and uneven acceptance in France. The most frequently encountered legal maxim was that involving the common profit, the necessity which "knows no law." The king attempted to justify a number of policies on this basis, and there is reason to believe that the kingdom was prepared to accept the doctrine that necessity could override traditional rights and privileges.[64] Yet taxes still ran into

[63] Strayer, "France," passim.

[64] Many appeals to necessity and the common profit are found in the *Ordonnances*. I am indebted to the research of J. Greenlee, "French Royal Propaganda from Philip the Fair to Louis XI (1300-1483)," unpublished M.A. essay, McMaster University, Hamilton, 1969. The assertion of Coville, *Etats Norm.*, pp. 54-55, that the

opposition, and the complaints and appeals against taxation are valuable indications of the degree to which the claims of the legists were accepted, rejected, or modified.

A variety of reasons were advanced by those who hoped to escape taxation. In 1321, when the king sought a tax in peacetime for reforms which he declared were for the common profit, the towns denied that the reforms were justified. In 1325, Narbonne declared that expiration of a truce did not imply a state of war or justify a tax. In 1328, Montpellier resisted paying on the grounds of local poverty, and Narbonne used a similar argument in 1343. The feudal aids of the 1330s were generally opposed on the basis of precedent or privilege. The tax for restoring the harbor at Aigues Mortes was resisted in 1336 by communities distant from the port, who claimed that it did not serve the common profit. In 1337, opposition to the war subsidy took several forms. Nobles invoked privilege; the consuls of Narbonne claimed they had not consented; and those of Montpellier claimed they were not directly subject to Philip VI. In 1338, the southern towns denied the existence of a war because no invasion had occurred.

A year later, the attitude towards royal taxation depended on geographical location. The Normans were generous in subsidizing a proposed invasion of England, but some towns of lower Languedoc bitterly resisted a military summons to distant Picardy. A similar pattern prevailed in the next two years, as the regions most threatened by English attack agreed rather promptly to subsidies while those in safer locations were more reluctant to pay. Following the end of a truce in 1342, the crown collected taxes on a fairly broad basis, apparently without seeking consent first, but a new truce in 1343 brought immediate resistance to subsidies in Languedoc. In 1345, the imminent end of this truce was not regarded by the towns of Languedoc and Vermandois as sufficient justification for a new tax. Thereafter, the willingness to pay taxes seemed to depend on the military situation. Languedoc was prepared to pay in 1346, during the siege of Saint-Antonin in 1352-1353, and after the raid of 1355, but was decidedly reluctant to do so in 1347 and 1354. In the North, high taxes were promised between the fall of Calais and the Black

---

Estates General of the 1350s borrowed the doctrine of necessity from the earlier Norman charter is very misleading, for as Post, *Studies*, passim, makes very clear, the expression had long been familiar. Philip VI invoked necessity in seeking a clerical tenth in 1340 (LC, no. 119). Twenty years earlier, the crown allowed Tournai to continue the levy of a municipal tax because of evident necessity. See d'Herbomez, "Notes," p. 696, note 1. In 1354, John II explicitly appealed to necessity when seeking a tax from Languedoc (Chapter VIII, note 73). A wide variety of other examples could be cited.

Death, but from 1352 to 1356, taxes were unpopular except in particular localities facing a military danger.

It is hardly surprising that subsidies were paid more willingly by regions feeling threatened by the war. Yet this fact is significant, for it shows the French population did agree that "necessity" could justify taxation. When people believed that an emergency existed, there were few appeals based on precedent or privilege, for an emergency could override these. During truces or lulls in the fighting, however, taxes often were opposed because of precedent or privilege, and we may infer that the appellants did not believe that a real emergency was involved. Most opposition to royal taxes in France during this period was based on the conviction that they were not justified by "evident necessity."

One doctrine of legal theory, therefore, was clearly accepted in practice: the principle that "necessity knows no law." On the other hand, royal subjects often challenged the competence of the king and his council to define this necessity and declare when the common profit was at stake. They were not prepared to agree that "what pleases the prince" was binding upon them. It was on this point that localism tended to restrict the authority conferred on the king by the legists. In expressions like *pro patria mori*, the average bourgeois of Philip VI's reign seems to have equated *patria* with *pays* in the local sense. No doubt the war was helping to develop the broader view of the *regnum* as *patria communis,* but this idea was not much in evidence among ordinary Frenchmen before the disaster at Poitiers.

Royal subjects agreed in associating the common profit with war only, and the king himself sometimes seemed to share this view even though his lawyers held otherwise. Yet there were many different ideas as to what constituted necessity. The efforts of some communities to define the situations justifying a tax are valuable evidence of popular thinking about the common profit. The city of Paris regularly demanded that the king or his heir lead the army personally if it contributed a subsidy in men-at-arms. Perhaps the Parisians felt a stronger loyalty to the royal person than to the realm. It is likely, however, that they established this condition because they had grown suspicious of declarations of emergency. In a genuine crisis, the king would be at the scene of action and his presence would leave no doubt that he took the danger seriously. His absence would create suspicions that appeals to patriotism were but a fiscal expedient.[65]

[65] The Parisians were not alone in regarding the king's presence with the army as a criterion for paying war subsidies. A text of 1361 indicates that this requirement

The towns of Languedoc also tried to define necessity and establish rules for the justification of a subsidy. We have noted Narbonne's argument in 1325, that the end of a truce was not ipso facto the occasion for a war subsidy.[66] In the same year, Cordes agreed to pay as long as the king maintained in the field an army of specified size.[67] In 1338, it was argued that only an outright invasion justified a tax, and the king himself acquiesced in this principle.[68] In 1354, Montpellier applied a curious modification of the rule which Paris followed: the town would pay a second tax only if Edward III personally led the English army in Gascony.[69]

In all these cases, the towns were trying to define with precision the "necessity" which would justify extraordinary taxation. These efforts suggest that the common profit, as understood by most Frenchmen, was judged in very local terms and was not really synonymous with "defense of the realm." It is also evident that the principle *cessante causa* had gained wide acceptance in France, not only among royal subjects but by the king himself.[70] The insistence that emergency measures must be terminated abruptly when the emergency was over tended to encourage people to define emergencies in local terms.

This skeptical and parochial reaction to royal assertions of "necessity" can be attributed in part to the government's own methods in the first third of the century, when the crown began to abuse the *arrière-ban*. Philip IV had found that military summonses were more acceptable to the kingdom as a basis for taxation than a mere declaration that the realm was in danger. Having learned this, however, kings overworked the *arrière-ban*, which was used so frequently that it was no longer taken as clear proof that the kingdom was threatened. After the disaster at Crécy, however, the danger was unmistakable, and it is interesting to find a new expression appearing in 1347—*arrière-ban après bataille*.[71] Communities had sometimes promised subsidies on condition that no other tax be levied in the same year except the *arrière-ban*. They doubtless had in mind a major emergency, but the king was tempted to use a military summons whenever he needed more money. In the aftermath of

---

was written into the list of services and taxes owed by an ecclesiastical establishment in time of war: AN JJ 91, no. 509.

[66] See above, Chapter II, at note 65.   [67] AM Cordes CC 29, no. 267.
[68] See above, Chapter IV, note 101.   [69] See above, Chapter VIII, at note 45.
[70] See Brown, "*Cessante causa*." Another example of narrow localism is found in *INV AM Toulouse*, p. 463 (AA 35, no. 70), where the *capitouls* of Toulouse, asked to swear to uphold a Franco-Castilian treaty in 1347, had to be promised that the treaty would not require them to aid Castile with troops.
[71] See above, Chapter VI, note 175.

Crécy, however, the modifying words *après bataille* left no doubt as to the magnitude of the crisis which would justify a second tax.

A new sense of urgency in the kingdom after the defeats of 1345-1347, made tax collection less controversial for a while, but localism and resistance to taxes began to appear again after 1352. This time they were compounded by a distrust of the royal government's effectiveness and a concern over the state of local finances. If the king's subjects accepted their obligation to contribute to the defense of the realm, was the king willing and able to defend them in return? Many people were not sure. In granting a subsidy in 1355, the Normans reserved 25 percent of it for local defense. In the same year, the Estates of Limousin demanded that all money from their taxes be spent locally. A year later, Languedoc felt sufficiently uncertain of the king's interest in defending the Midi to demand that he send his son to the South as royal lieutenant.[72] The growing doubts about the government's effectiveness were paralleled by increased local initiative in the area of self-defense, and more frequent requests for permission to levy special local taxes. When the crown asked for subsidies based on necessity, people countered with questions: was the emergency genuine? Would the measures taken to deal with it be terminated when it was over? Would the crown make these measures truly effective if supplied with funds? As regional and bailiwick assemblies became more and more frequent, these questions were asked by representatives who were more experienced and confident, yet increasingly oriented towards the interests of their particular region.

Thus the king's power to levy taxes for the general welfare in time of necessity was limited, in practice, by his subjects' concern for the local welfare. The tendency to view the common profit in local terms was encouraged by the widespread acceptance of *cessante causa*. The threat to the kingdom might continue long after a given locality was out of danger. In treating necessity as a regional matter, such a locality could hope to shorten the duration of a tax by claiming that the emergency was past.

On the other hand, the royal taxing power was not significantly limited in practice by the idea of consent as expressed by *quod omnes tangit ab omnibus approbetur*. Those who opposed taxes rarely invoked this principle, although they were certainly familiar with it. In Languedoc, where Roman law was best known, Narbonne claimed the right to consent in 1337, and many towns did so four years later when the *gabelle* was imposed. The northern bailiwicks showed some concern about this right in

---

[72] See above, Chapter viii, at notes 94-95, 119, 124.

1346 and in 1352-1353. In the overwhelming majority of cases, however, opposition to taxes did not focus upon a legal need for consent.

In practice, of course, the king usually obtained it. Consent of a sort was implicit in those local negotiations which culminated in lump-sum payments of subsidies, and as we have seen, it was needed as a practical matter to facilitate collection.[73] Yet even when consent was given locally, the levy of taxes often encountered opposition. Moreover, there were many occasions when taxes seem to have been imposed without any effort to grant a hearing to those whose rights were touched. At these times, the resistance to paying was not noticeably greater and could even be less if a manifest emergency (by local definition) was involved. In 1328, 1337-1338, and 1342, the crown taxed many parts of France without appearing to have sought even a *pro forma* procedural consent, and the same was true for Languedoil, at least, in 1325, 1326, and 1344. On the other hand, the Estates General of 1355 decidedly did consent to a subsidy but the tax encountered widespread resistance. In short, the principle of consent was not, in practice, taken very seriously by the French taxpayer. If he believed his interests to be threatened by an emergency, he paid taxes whether or not the king had obtained consent. If he perceived no case of evident necessity, he opposed taxation, citing precedent or privilege but not *quod omnes tangit*.[74]

This attitude may also shed light upon the development of central assemblies, where *plena potestas* failed to produce representatives who were willing to take decisive action. Proctors with full powers were necessary if an assembly was to give consent to a royal proposal and make it binding on constituent communities. Charles Taylor noted that the early fourteenth century assemblies did not make binding commitments, and suggested that proctors needed other, less formal instructions to supplement their full powers.[75] Gaines Post contended that in the procedures of a court of law, *plena potestas* implied all the instructions that were necessary.[76] It is not certain, of course, that Frenchmen viewed assemblies of Estates as comparable to a judicial proceeding,[77] and even

[73] See above, Chapter I, note 67.

[74] This was not entirely inconsistent with legal theory, for some French legists argued that in a genuine crisis the king could impose taxes even if consent was refused: Post, *Studies*, pp. 477-478.

[75] Taylor, "1318," p. 300.

[76] Post, *Studies*, pp. 91-162. See above, Chapter I.

[77] Hoyt, "Recent Publications," p. 370. We might recall the distinction in Latin terminology described by Langmuir, "Politics and Parliaments," pp. 53-58. In the early thirteenth century the French seem to have kept large political assemblies (*concilia*) separate from judicial ones (*curiae*). See Chapter I, at note 70.

proctors with full powers could be limited by instructions confining them to the matter for which they had been summoned.[78]

Whatever *plena potestas* did or did not imply in practice, the really significant fact is that Philip VI and John II do not seem to have requested such powers when summoning central assemblies. Only once, in 1343, did they attempt to inform constituents by advertising in advance a specific proposal. On that occasion, proctors came to Paris with instructions to deal with the proposal and most of them gave a prompt and favorable response. Yet the crown never tried to advertise a proposed war subsidy in such a specific way, nor was the technique used in 1343 repeated subsequently, despite the apparent success of that assembly from the royal viewpoint. As a rule, the king used vague generalizations to describe the business to be discussed, and then asked merely for representatives who were "sufficiently instructed and advised." This was true even in 1347 when the summons made it clear that the government did not want "reference back" to create delays.[79]

Up to 1321, however, the crown had usually asked for full powers, even though it did not press assemblies for binding commitments. Taylor implied that the kings were merely practicing the art of the possible, and that they would have been happy to obtain consent to taxes from the Estates if the latter had come with adequate instructions. The brief memorandum submitted to the king in 1339 certainly suggests that the government would have preferred to negotiate taxes with assemblies rather than doing so locally.[80] Nevertheless, the king and his lawyers must have known what was needed to obtain proctors with sufficient authority to give consent. The government had to issue a summons describing the business to be considered and requiring the representatives to have full powers. The fact that it did not do so leads one to conclude that the crown did not call central assemblies of Estates for the purpose of obtaining consent.

In all probability, the king's subjects did not view them as consenting bodies either. Roman lawyers claimed that the king had the power to define an emergency but that he had to obtain consent to any tax which might be required. In fourteenth century France, however, public opinion virtually reversed this theory. Even when their rights were affected,

[78] See above, Chapter 1, note 61.

[79] The essential words, from Varin, *Reims*, II, 1161-1162, are quoted and commented upon by Taylor, "1318," p. 302. The representatives were merely to be "instructed, counselled and advised."

[80] Jusselin, "Comment la France . . . ," pp. 229-230. Taylor's views may be inferred from all his articles, but see especially "1318," pp. 299-301.

people did not insist on consenting to taxes if convinced an emergency existed, but they often wanted to join in judging the emergency.[81] It sometimes behooved the king to seek agreement from his subjects before declaring that the common profit was at stake. This kind of agreement was not consent but counsel. The legal writer who described the realities of fourteenth century France actually was Beaumanoir, who said that the king had to act *par grant conseil*.[82] Central assemblies could be a useful device for taking counsel, even if not used to obtain consent. The role of counsel was apparent in the reign of Philip V. Assemblies in 1319 gave favorable counsel, agreeing that a tax would be needed. A war subsidy then could be negotiated locally. Assemblies in 1321, however, gave *petit conseil*, denying that the common profit justified a program which would entail a peacetime subsidy.[83]

If both the king and his subjects regarded central assemblies as a vehicle for counsel rather than consent, the representatives did not need to have full powers. They only had to be respected and well-informed persons whose counsel would carry weight. Studying the thirteenth century, Langmuir found that counsel was sought far more frequently than consent.[84] In the context of the Hundred Years' War, however, counsel was needed mainly to verify the existence of an emergency and endorse the royal measures for dealing with it, whereas consent should have been required for every tax if the French had taken *quod omnes tangit* as seriously as the English did. Under such circumstances, the frequent taxes requiring consent could have given birth to frequent central assemblies. Since, however, neither king nor subjects viewed central assemblies as consenting bodies, the continuity of these Estates depended on the need for counsel, and the circumstances requiring counsel were of such a character as to discourage frequent meetings at the national level.[85] If

---

[81] The kings' repeated concessions to the principle of *cessante causa*, as in 1313, 1329, and 1338, may be seen as an indication that they took seriously their subjects' views of what justified emergency taxation. If the royal devotion to *cessante causa* impressed taxpayers as an adequate guarantee of their rights, it may have reduced their interest in the right of consent and retarded the practical application of *quod omnes tangit* in France. In her forthcoming article on *cessante causa*, Elizabeth Brown will explore the question more fully and express some perceptive thoughts on this subject.

[82] See above, Chapter 1, note 69.

[83] See above, Chapter 1, at notes 95 and 103-107.

[84] See Chapter 1, note 68, for the statement of Langmuir's position.

[85] It should be stressed that we are considering *central* assemblies of Estates, such as those representing all of Languedoil. Regional assemblies often did give consent, taking over the function which had often been performed at the town or *viguerie* level in the early years of our period. The development of regional assemblies as

the emergency was so obvious as to be beyond dispute, the king could dispense with the counsel of an assembly without arousing criticism. If, however, only part of the kingdom appeared directly threatened, the king might find a central assembly inappropriate and prefer to seek taxes locally from those whose sense of common profit might persuade them to pay. In the absence of a firm commitment to the principle of consent, the general Estates could be useful only in certain types of situation where counsel on a national basis was called for. At times, no doubt, the crown showed questionable judgment in failing to call an assembly when its counsel might have facilitated tax collections. As time went on, how-ever, and localism began to lose ground, there would be less disagree-ment over "necessity" and less need for counsel on this subject. An ex-tended period of manifest emergency would only serve the cause of royal taxing power at the expense of the Estates.

These considerations help to explain when and why central assemblies were summoned. Once convened, however, the Estates briefly acquired an identity of their own. On such occasions, their actions depended heavily on the politics of the moment, and especially on the interplay between local particularism and national danger. In this connection, two assemblies were noteworthy—the Estates General of December 1347 and of December 1355. The successes of the former remain conjectural be-cause of the appearance of the Black Death. The failures of the latter can be measured by the documents of 1356.

In 1347, an assembly was in demand following the recent military defeat. In 1355, the Estates met in an atmosphere of fiscal and dynastic crisis, but without a recent military disaster. These latter Estates were more experienced, however, for assemblies had been widespread as the local level for about a decade, whereas they had had only a short recent history in 1347. On each occasion, the Estates General followed a recent Norman precedent by granting a large number of men-at-arms and pro-viding that taxes would be collected by *élus* rather than royal officials. In 1347, the Estates obtained changes in the personnel of the government and a few reforms, and then authorized a tax. Local assemblies, however,

---

consenting bodies in lieu of individual localities was another reason why central Estates seemed less necessary. This development, in the 1350s and 1360s, marked the beginning of most of the provincial Estates in France. Many of those bodies survived precisely because they were usually able to deliver the taxes they granted, like the Estates of Languedoc after 1346 but unlike the Estates General of Languedoil in 1355-1356. It should be noted, however, that even consent by regional assemblies was not always treated as binding by specific localities which did not feel im-mediately threatened.

were to decide on the form of the tax and appoint the *élus*. The Estates of 1355 represented only Languedoil and apparently felt no need to consider local viewpoints. Obtaining an impressive list of reforms, the assembly consented to a specific tax and proposed to name its own *élus*.

This failure to respect localism proved to be a blunder. The emergency was less evident than it had been following Crécy and Calais, while localism had experienced a resurgence owing to recurrent bailiwick assemblies and growing doubts about the king's capacity to defend the realm. Taxes were resisted in 1356 until local assemblies adopted them or devised acceptable substitutes. Whereas only the Black Death seems to have prevented collection of the subsidy of 1347-1348, local opposition doomed the taxes granted by the Estates of 1355. Most people did not feel bound by the action of this assembly, even though it had consented to taxation.

In the fall of 1356, the French continued to hold the views which had been common for several decades: emergencies justified the suspension of rights and privileges for the common good, but they had to be legitimate emergencies. Consent might be a practical requirement at the local level but usually was not demanded by the holders of private rights if they accepted the existence of an emergency. Central assemblies were helpful ways of giving counsel and pronouncing on the validity of an emergency, but they were not normally used to obtain consent. When they gave consent, it was not considered binding by those who defined common profit in largely local terms. The main issue throughout France remained "necessity," and only after the king was a captive would it be truly "evident."

APPENDIX I

Coinage Problems and Their Effect on Fiscal Documents

The royal policy regarding the currency is important to the study of French taxation for several reasons. In the first place, the coinage yielded the crown mint profits, or *monnayage*, a revenue which could be very large. Miskimin has called it the largest tax paid by Frenchmen in the fourteenth century,[1] although we have not treated it here as a tax, strictly speaking. Another reason for the importance of the currency is that alterations of the coinage had economic effects which could be translated into political action or reaction. Insofar as debasement was inflationary, it could hurt those who were creditors or depended largely on fixed rents and manorial dues. Insofar as a return to "sound money" was deflationary, it must have aggravated the economic depression, especially among debtors. A final reason for considering coinage problems here is that figures in the crown's surviving financial records cannot be utilized without some adjustment to compensate for changes in the currency.

The French had experimented with gold coins in the 1260s and had minted gold fairly regularly since the 1290s. The currency, however, was still based on a silver standard, supplemented by gold coins which were generally reserved for large transactions such as those of an international nature.[2] As pointed out in Chapter 1, the money of account was expressed in either *livres tournois* or *livres parisis*, five of the former equaling four of the latter. The coins which actually circulated had many names, and their value in money of account rarely remained constant very long. The silver coin of largest denomination was the *gros tournois*, which for a long time equaled one *sol* (twelve *deniers*) *tournois*, although seriously overvalued for a time by Philip IV and again in the period 1337-1343. After 1343, it was usually valued at one *s.p.* (15 *d.t.*). The silver penny or *parisis* remained consistent with money of account for most of our period (at $1\frac{1}{4}$ *d.t.*), as did the *double parisis* and *double tournois* (2 *d.*). These were the most important of many silver coins.[3]

---

[1] Miskimin, *Money*, p. 46. Lot and Fawtier, *Institutions*, II, 215, suggest that people were more willing to pay this kind of tax than other forms.

[2] Miskimin, *Money*, pp. 30-33.

[3] Another small coin was the halfpenny, called a *maille* or *obole*. For different types of coins, see N. de Wailly, "Mémoire sur les variations de la livre tournois depuis le règne de Saint Louis jusqu'à l'établissement de la monnaie decimale," *Mémoires de l'Institut Imperial de France*, XXI (1857), pt. 2, pp. 296f. Cf. J. La-

Up until the Black Death, the value of gold coins in money of account fluctuated much more than that of the silver ones because of the unstable ratio between the two metals.[4] Coins like the *écu*, *royal*, *agnel*, and *mouton* were all intended, ideally, to correspond to one pound *tournois* or 20 *gros*, but rarely did they actually equal either. Then, from 1349 to 1360, the crown's frequent alterations of the silver coinage created such monetary anarchy that the gold coins were relatively more stable and much less debased. It became so difficult to determine the value of silver coins that administrative documents, instead of using money of account, often expressed large sums in *écus* or some other gold coin. Only with the reign of John II, do we need to be concerned seriously with the real coinage as opposed to the money of account.[5]

In determining the intrinsic value of the silver coinage, the standard was the mark of Troyes, containing 4,608 grains of silver. Metal used for the coinage (*argent-le-roi*) was supposed to have a fineness of .958 (23/24), although precisely accurate measurement was not possible.[6] Beginning with Charles IV, the crown described its currency by using an expression called the *pied de monnaie*. The *pied*, expressed in the documents as an ordinal numeral, was derived from a formula which took into account three important characteristics of a given coinage: the *prix*, *taille*, and *titre*. The *prix* was the official value of the coin in money of account as set by the king. The *taille* was the number of coins minted from a mark. The *titre* was the alloy or silver content of the coin, expressed in *deniers* of 24 grains each. The king could alter the currency by changing any one of these.[7] For our purposes, it is necessary only to note that the *pied*

---

faurie, *Les monnaies des rois de France, Hugh Capet à Louis XII*, Paris, 1951, pp. 27-60 and corresponding plates.

[4] Watson, "Gold and Silver," pp. 11-25.

[5] De Wailly, "Variations," pp. 234f., has published tables which indicate some of the following values for gold coins in *livres tournois*: *écu* – 18 *s.* 9 *d.* (1348 and 1350-1351), 25 *s.* (1349), 15 *s.* (1352-1353), 12½ *s.* (1354); *agnel* (*mouton*) – 15 *s.* (1346), 25 *s.* (1355-1356, 1359-1360), 30 *s.* (1356-1359); *royal* – 25 *s.* (1356-1359), 40 *s.* (1359-1360), 16 *s.* 8 *d.* (1360-1361). These figures illustrate the frequent fluctuations, but they are very suspect otherwise. In 1353 (see above, Chapter VII, note 122), a grant of 24,000 *écus* in the Beaucaire district was supposed to be equivalent to a 10 *s.* hearth tax, but if so, the *écu* at that time must have been reckoned at 30 *s.t.*, double de Wailly's figure.

[6] Miskimin, *Money*, p. 31.

[7] L.F.J.C. de Saulcy, *Recueil de documents rélatifs à l'histoire des monnaies frappées par les rois de France*, I, Paris, 1879, xiv; cf. the discussion of Miskimin, *Money*, pp. 32-36. For further clarification of this formula, I am indebted to Thomas Prest of the University of Iowa, who is undertaking intensive research into royal coinage policies in this period. In effect, one calculates the *pied* by multiplying the

divided by four equaled the official value, in pounds *tournois*, of coins minted from one mark of silver. To put this another way, for any given coinage issued by a mint, we may determine the value of the silver mark in pounds *tournois* by dividing the *pied* of that coinage by four. Since most financial documents expressed figures in money of account, it should, in theory, be possible to convert these to marks and have a standard basis for comparing figures from periods of debasement with those from periods of sounder currency. So few financial documents have survived, however, that we cannot rely on this computation with complete assurance.

In attempting a conversion into marks for purposes of comparison, we encounter certain obstacles. For one thing, different mints might simultaneously be producing coins of a sharply different *pied*. Moreover, some issues were of short duration and were soon replaced by coins of different *pied*.[8] Thus even if financial accounts were based on the current *pied* or official price of silver coins, it is not always clear what figure should be used when converting into marks. Fortunately, the price of silver was reasonably consistent during those years for which treasury records have survived.

A second problem is suggested by fluctuations in the *monnayage*. When money was minted, the crown circulated coins with an official value that exceeded the actual cost of the metal. The difference represented the *monnayage*. One part, called the *brassage*, was relatively consistent; its purpose was to defray mint costs. The other, more variable, and often much larger part of the *monnayage* was the royal profit strictly speaking, known as *seigneuriage*.[9] Between them, these two components of the *monnayage* reflected a fluctuating difference between the mint price of a silver mark and the value established by the king.

For example, if the coinage was on the 24th *pied*, the mark would be valued at six *livres tournois* (120 *sols*) in coins put into circulation. Thus if the mints were issuing silver *gros* valued at one *s.t.* each, they would strike 120 of these coins from each mark of silver. If, however, the metal had actually cost the crown only 5 *l.t.* per mark, each of the *gros* would actually contain only 10 *d.* worth of silver. The *monnayage* taken by the

---

number of coins cut from the mark (*taille*) by the *prix* of the coin in *deniers tournois* and dividing the result by five times the alloy (*titre*) of the coin as expressed in *deniers* and grains of *argent-le-roi*.

[8] See the tables in Miskimin, *Money*, pp. 161f., and especially pp. 181-187, for examples of short-lived and/or simultaneous coinages of different *pieds*.

[9] A. Landry, *Essai economique sur les mutations des monnaies dans l'ancienne France de Philippe le Bel à Charles VII*, Paris, 1910, pp. 30-31.

government would amount to 2 *d.* per *gros* or 16.7 percent.[10] At such a rate the king would collect 25,000 *l.t.* from an issue of coins amounting to 150,000 *l.t.* Such was the case in 1339, for instance, when there were many silver coinages, all on the 24th *pied.* For the first half of that year the price of a mark of silver was reported as 100 *s.t.* (five pounds), and during this period the mints issued silver coins valued at more than 150,000 *l.t.*[11] Unfortunately, we are only rarely informed as to the actual amount coined in a given year. For the reigns of Charles IV and Philip VI, these figures are available only for 1338-1339. There is thus no way of estimating total *monnayage* receipts unless a treasury document itemizing royal receipts has survived for a full year. We do, however, possess fairly extensive figures for the changing price of silver and the changing *pied de monnaie,* and a comparison of these should suggest the periods in which the king collected an unusually high or low rate of *monnayage.* The actual price of silver and the *pied* followed different curves in their fluctuations. The first of these sets of figures appears preferable for converting receipts into marks, for the *pied* reflected royal edict rather than actuality and sometimes applied to a very small issue of coins.

Royal policy towards changes in the *pied* was affected by many factors, but when these changes threatened particular interests, the ensuing debate inevitably raised the question of whether the king had the right to alter the currency. For centuries prior to 1300, the coinage had been seen as a seigneurial right, just as weights and measures were. According to this "feudal" theory, the currency was part of a lord's property or domain.[12] As Bridrey pointed out, this theory was compatible with medieval economic conditions and would not have lasted so long otherwise. Although the revival of international commerce undermined the lords' ability to fix the value of their coinage, their financial needs underscored the value of their rights over the currency.[13] As royal authority expanded in the thirteenth century, the number of seigneurial coinages diminished rapidly, however, and Louis IX declared that while royal coins could circulate throughout the realm, those of a baron could only be used in his own *seigneurie.* In time, the barons were also prohibited from debasing their coins; their minting of coins was suspended briefly in 1313 and 1320, and Philip V was able to buy up some coinage rights before his

[10] As Prof. Miskimin has pointed out to me, this example is oversimplified, since it assumes that the mints paid for the silver in the same coinage being struck.

[11] Miskimin, *Money,* pp. 167-168; de Saulcy, *Documents,* p. 11.

[12] E. Bridrey, *La théorie de la monnaie au XIVe siècle, Nicole Oresme,* Paris, 1906, pp. 107-113.

[13] *Ibid.,* pp. 142-143, 159-161.

reversal in 1321.[14] Gresham's law worked against the remaining baronial currencies if the king alone was able to debase his coins, and raising the *pied* permitted the king to offer a higher price for silver and attract it away from other mints.

The relative importance of the royal coinage among the currencies in France had thus increased greatly by 1322 and the king's rights over his coinage became increasingly lucrative. By the 1290s, royal fiscal needs had led to alterations in the *pied*.[15] Whether reflecting debasement as such or overvaluation, such changes could afford the king temporary advantage, since money received in sound currency might be reminted in coins of the higher *pied*. The real profit, however, was derived not so much from this practice as from adjusting the rate of *seigneuriage*.

Coinage manipulation offers an example of the way in which "ordinary" revenues could be stretched to extraordinary lengths. The profits for the crown could be very considerable, and in the second half of 1298, Philip IV collected over 555,000 *l.p.* in *monnayage*, nearly two-thirds of the treasury's receipts.[16] Both high *monnayage* and frequent changes in the *pied* were unpopular, and even in the thirteenth century, the influential inhabitants of certain regions had persuaded the king or local lord to accept some fixed alternative tax in lieu of his right to alter the currency.[17]

Space does not permit consideration of the vast legal and theoretical literature dealing with the coinage. Suffice it to say that there were growing criticisms of the old idea that the currency was a seigneurial right which could be treated as private property. Alterations in the *pied* now affected so many people that they were coming to be seen as a matter of the public welfare, and even those writers who still clung in part to the seigneurial view of the coinage began to argue that changes in the *pied* required the consent of those who were affected.[18] Philip IV himself is said to have had some doubts about his right to alter the coinage, and under heavy pressure from the prelates and other influential interests, he restored sound money in 1306.[19] A similar pressure compelled Philip

[14] Landry, *Essai*, pp. 2-7; Miskimin, *Money*, pp. 50-51.

[15] Bridrey, *Théorie*, pp. 159-165. [16] See the table in Miskimin, *Money*, p. 43.

[17] P. Spufford, "Assemblies of Estates, Taxation, and Control of the Coinage in Medieval Europe," *SPIC*, XXXI (1965), 117-118. One such tax was a *fouage* levied in Normandy.

[18] *Ibid.*, p. 119; Bridrey, *Théorie*, pp. 165, 176. See also P. Michaud-Quantin, "La politique monétaire royale à la Faculté de Theologie de Paris en 1265," *MA*, LXVIII (1962), 137-151.

[19] Cazelles, "Quelques réflexions," pp. 85-86.

VI to reform the currency in 1329-1330. The growing body of theoretical literature culminated in the work of Nicholas Oresme who, in the later 1350s, expanded on the earlier writings and attacked root and branch the whole concept of the coinage as a property right.[20] Yet even the great reform of 1360, presumably carried out under Oresme's direct influence, coupled the restoration of stable currency to the establishment of regular, and rather heavy, royal taxes.[21]

While opposition was gradually mobilizing, first to the royal practice of coinage alteration and then to the theory on which it was based, a number of very important economic considerations had entered the picture. For several centuries, the population and the volume of trade had been growing, thereby creating a need for a larger money supply and for coins of a larger denomination. The long range trend towards debasement, the minting of silver coins larger than a penny (such as the *gros tournois*), and ultimately the revival of gold coinage itself, can all be seen as responses to this situation. Silver remained the essential precious metal for the great bulk of domestic transactions, and a recent study has shown that the fourteenth century witnessed a serious silver shortage in western Europe.[22] For two years in the middle 1330s, the French mints were closed because of a lack of silver.[23] Although the matter has been debated, it is possible that increases in the price of silver (by raising the *pied de monnaie*) were needed to attract silver to the mints and prevent it from leaving the kingdom.[24]

Moreover, some economic interests were not hostile to inflation, however much they may have opposed chronic instability in the coinage. In the early 1320s, when an assembly of coinage experts submitted recom-

[20] Bridrey, *Théorie*, pp. 45-54, 183-297; Spufford, "Assemblies," p. 127; H. Estrup, "Oresme and Monetary Theory," *Scandinavian Economic History Review*, XIV (1966), 97-116. Oresme, of course, did not invent his theory completely, but he turned many earlier ideas of a piecemeal nature into a comprehensive doctrine that was well oriented towards practical application. Oresme's most important principle was that coinage belongs to the community, not to the prince or seigneur, and that alteration of the coinage is desirable only under peculiar circumstances of necessity.

[21] Bridrey, *Théorie*, pp. 449f., 561-652.

[22] Watson, "Gold and Silver," pp. 15-16. On the connection between the bullion shortage and coinage alteration, see Lewis, *Later Medieval France*, pp. 56-57.

[23] De Saulcy, *Documents*, p. 219.

[24] Landry, *Essai*, pp. 6f., 122f. Miskimin differs strongly with Landry on this point (see, for instance, *Money*, pp. 43-44). Oresme regarded shortage of specie as one of the things which might justify coinage alteration (Bridrey, *Théorie*, p. 277). Shortage of bullion for the mints seems to have been behind an increase in the *pied de monnaie* in 1333, judging from *Ord.* II, 83-88. Cf. Cazelles, "Quelque réflexions," p. 88, regarding 1322.

mendations to Charles IV, their proposals suggested that there was doubt in some quarters as to the virtue and feasibility of returning to the much-praised coinage of St. Louis.[25] Yet at that time, such a step would have entailed only about a 26 percent reduction in the price of silver, from 78½ to 58 *s.t.* per mark. In 1343, however, when revaluation did take place, it was far more drastic, amounting to a 76 percent reduction. Philip VI hoped to minimize the deflationary effects by completing the change in several steps, but when profiteers began stockpiling goods for later sale it was decided to complete the entire reform at once. The measure thus had an immediate and severe impact, arousing widespread discontent, as many people believed themselves to have been impoverished by the dramatic decrease in the value of silver and the accompanying decline of prices generally. This large and sudden revaluation was what really ended the long period of nostalgia for the coinage of St. Louis.[26] Thereafter, the criticism was less against debasement than against alterations per se. Stability was what was desired, and most people feared chronic changes in the coinage more than inflation. This sentiment became clear late in 1356, when the government was in turmoil and a growing party endorsed Oresme's demands for monetary reform. The dauphin encountered the bitter opposition of Etienne Marcel and the Parisians when he ordered a coinage change which actually improved the alloy of the currency, reducing it from the 60th to the 48th *pied*. It was alteration as such, not the form it took, which now drew the ire of the critics.[27]

In short, it is clear that there were economic interests and legal arguments both for and against coinage debasement, and a more sophisticated approach to the problem was developing. Even without dwelling

[25] P. Guilhiermoz, "Avis sur la question monétaire données aux rois Philippe le Hardi, Philippe le Bel, Louis X, et Charles le Bel," part 7, *Revue Numismatique*, xxx (1927), 96-110. These undated documents from AN J 459 have been assigned to various years between 1314 and 1324 by different modern scholars, with Guilhiermoz himself preferring 1324. Prof. Elizabeth Brown informs me that documents in the Martel archives offer some support to Guilhiermoz, but the texts also seem to fit the context of 1322, since they indicate an assembly on 8 July to discuss the coinage, such as is known to have occurred in 1322. In any case, there seems little doubt that the texts belong to the first half of the reign of Charles IV.

[26] Cazelles, "Quelques réflexions," pp. 94-95, 257-260. As to the question of whether or not prices generally followed changes in that of silver, it is the argument of Miskimin, *Money*, passim, that they followed the coinage rather closely. This thesis cannot be considered really proven, given the limited evidence with which Miskimin had to work and the attacks on his sources and methodology made by critics like D. Herlihy (*Speculum*, 1964, pp. 328-330). Nonetheless, a coinage change like that of 1343 could only have been dramatically deflationary.

[27] Bridrey, *Théorie*, pp. 485-488.

on the important treatise of Oresme, we may note a growing awareness that sudden changes could create havoc at times of great commercial activity, as Cazelles has pointed out.[28] Even with the progress in grasping the economics of coinage mutation, the practice remained a major issue prior to 1360. Potentially an explosive matter when important interests were involved, the coinage presented the king with an almost impossible dilemma. Exploitation of coinage rights to obtain fiscal advantages might seriously jeopardize the monetary system as well as arousing political opposition.[29] Yet the temptation to balance the budget with high *monnayage* revenues was all but irresistible.

The principal coinage alterations which took place up to 1356 are outlined in Table 1. It is not an exhaustive list of available figures, but it does tabulate the major values of the silver mark for different coinages (one fourth of the *pied*) and the prices of silver brought to the mint. The difference, expressed as a percentage of the former figure,[30] offers some indication of the way in which royal mint profits fluctuated. As already explained, part of this percentage is not profit, strictly speaking, but *brassage*, yet it is not known how great this component of *monnayage* was. Although less subject to fluctuation than *seigneuriage*, it was probably not constant. Oresme, somewhat arbitrarily, proclaimed 3⅓ percent (8 *d./l.*) to be a fair *brassage*,[31] but in 1330, when Philip VI had promised not to take any profit from the coinage reform completed in that year,[32] the coinage was valued at 7.3 percent over the mint price of silver. It is not entirely clear, however, whether this figure represented the rate of *brassage*. Whatever the *brassage*, we are certainly safe in saying that any difference of more than 10 percent was *seigneuriage* and therefore clear royal profit. These percentages cannot, of course,

[28] Cazelles, "Quelques réflexions," pp. 262-263, pointing out that revaluations tended to be ordered during periods of light commercial activity such as the period between October and March. For the illustration of this practice in years like 1343, 1353, 1354, see Table 1.

[29] Estrup, "Oresme," p. 97.

[30] It might appear more logical to express the difference as a percentage of the actual price of silver, since this was the lower figure, and Miskimin does so (*Money*, p. 42). I prefer, however, to treat *monnayage* as the percent the king collected on the coins he actually issued (see the illustration, given earlier in this appendix, based on the figures for 1339). This percentage is naturally lower than one based on the price of silver, but as Table 1 indicates it still could exceed 40%. Oresme's suggested fair rate for *brassage* (see next note) seems extremely low. Since it would be still lower if computed on the actual price of silver, I am inclined to think he had in mind a percentage based on the king's valuation, not the actual price.

[31] Bridrey, *Théorie*, p. 215.   [32] Cazelles, "Quelques réflexions," p. 90.

be translated into total *monnayage* receipts except in the rare instances when we know the total amount of silver coinage issued. Unfortunately, such figures are lacking for those years in which surviving treasury documents report *monnayage* receipts.

It has been impossible to avoid the expression "sound money," although the words imply an unintended value judgment and represent only a relative standard. However, the term does have some meaning, for at least until the mid-1340s, sound money referred to the coinage of St. Louis which had long been the object of nostalgic admiration. His currency valued the mark at 58 *s.t.*, and for seventy years or more after his death, sound money meant slightly under three pounds per mark. Thereafter, however, this figure was no longer realistic, and the reform of 1360 stabilized the currency at double the *pied* of St. Louis, valuing the mark at 6 *l.t.*

TABLE 1

FLUCTUATIONS IN THE SILVER COINAGE

Date	Value of silver mark established by the king[a] (¼ of pied)	Price of silver brought to the royal mints[b]	Percentage of difference
Reign of Louis IX	2.9 *l.t.*[c]	2.7 *l.t.*[c]	7
1304		6.2–7.2	
1306		8.5	
1307	2.71–3.01	2.78	
1308	2.89–3.03	2.95	
1309-1310	2.91–3.01		
1311-1312	3.75	3.5–3.75	
1313-1317	3.86–3.95	2.7	30.8
1318-1321	3.86–3.95	3.38	11.5
1322	3.63–3.86		
Oct. 1322-May 1323	4.43–4.52	4[d]	11
May 1323-July 1326	4.09 & 5.43[e]	4	?[e]
July-Dec. 1326	6	4.5	25
1327	6	5	16.7
1328 (to Nov.)	6	5.4	10
Nov. 1328-Dec. 1329	6	5.55	7.5
Dec. 1329-Apr. 1330	4.59	4.2	8.5
Apr.-Sept. 1330	3.13	2.78	11
Sept. 1330-Jan. 1332	3	2.78	7.3
Jan. 1332-June 1333	3	2.88	4
June 1333-Mar. 1335	4.15	2.88 (?)[f]	32.7 (?)[f]
Mar. 1335-Feb. 1337	(Mints closed because of lack of silver)		
1337	4.5	3.63	17.8
1338	4.5	4	11

TABLE 1 (*continued*)

FLUCTUATIONS IN THE SILVER COINAGE

Date	Value of silver mark established by the king (¼ of pied)	Price of silver brought to the royal mints	Percentage of difference
Dec. 1338	6 *l.t.*	4.8 *l.t.*	20
Jan.-Aug. 1339	6	5	16.7
Aug. 1339-Feb. 1340	6	5.25	12.5
Feb.-Apr. 1340	7.5	6.25	16.7
Apr.-Aug. 1340	9	6.75	25
Aug.-Dec. 1340	9	7	22
Dec. 1340-Feb. 1341	10.5	7.5	28.6
Feb.-May 1341	12	9.2	23.3
May-Aug. 1341	12	9.6	20
Aug.-Dec. 1341	12	10	16.7
Dec. 1341-Mar. 1342	12	10.5	12.5
Mar.-June 1342	12	11	8.3
June-Sept. 1342	15	12.5	16.7
Sept. 1342-Apr. 1343	15	13	13.3
Apr.-Sept. 1343	15	13.5	10
Sept.-Nov. 1343	11.25[g]	9.6	14.6
Nov. 1343-Feb. 1345	3.75[g]	3.2	14.7
Feb. 1345-Apr. 1346	3.75	3.4	9.3
Apr.-July 1346	3.75	3.53	3.2
July 1346-Jan. 1347	6	4.5	25
Jan.-Mar. 1347	6	5	16.7
Mar.-July 1347	9[h]	6.75	25
July 1347-Jan. 1348	9	7.5	16.7
Jan.-Aug. 1348	5.5	4.8	12.7
Aug.-Dec. 1348	5.89-6.03	5	16.7
1349	9	6.5 (?)[i]	27.8
Jan.-Apr. 1350	9	7.5	16.7
Apr.-Aug. 1350	6	4.75	20.8
Aug.-Nov. 1350	9	5.2	42.2
Nov. 1350-Feb. 1351	9	5.6	37.8
Feb.-Mar. 1351	9	6	33.3
Mar.-June 1351	12	6.4	46.7
June-Aug. 1351	12	7.4	38.3
Aug.-Sept. 1351	12	8.2	31.7
Sept.-Dec. 1351	13.5	9.5	29.6
Dec. 1351-Jan. 1352	13.5	10	25.9
Jan.-Feb. 1352	13.5	11	18.5
Feb.-Mar. 1352	7.5	4.2	44
Mar.-July 1352	7.5	4.8–5.2	33.3
July-Oct. 1352	9 & 10[j]	5.6–6	about 39
Oct.-Nov. 1352	9 & 10	6.4	about 33
Nov.-Dec. 1352	12	7.5	37.5
Dec. 1352-Feb. 1353	12	8.5	29.2

TABLE 1 (*continued*)

Date	Value of silver mark established by the king (¼ of pied)	Price of silver brought to the royal mints	Percentage of difference
Feb.-Apr. 1353	12 *l.t.*	9.2 *l.t.*	23.3
Apr.-July 1353	16	11	31.3
Aug. 1353	16	11.75	26.5
Sept.-Oct. 1353	16	12.75	20.3
Nov. 1353-Feb. 1354	8.13[k]	4.5[k]	44.6
Feb.-Mar. 1354	8.13	5.5	32.3
Apr. 1354	8.13	6.2	23.7
May 1354	12	6.2	48.3
June 1354	16	9.1	43.1
July-Aug. 1354	16	10.6	33.8
Sept.-Nov. 1354	16	11.4	28.8
Nov. 1354-Jan. 1355	6[l]	4.2	30
Feb.-Mar. 1355	8[l]	4.8	40
Apr.-May 1355	10[l]	5.3	47
May-July 1355	12[l]	6.5	45.8
July-Aug. 1355	16[l]	10	37.5
Sept. 1355	18[l]	11	38.9
Sept.-Oct. 1355	20[l]	12.5-14	about 35
Oct.-Nov. 1355	25	16	36
Nov.-Dec. 1355	30	18	40
Jan.-May 1356	6	4.75	20.8
May-Aug. 1356	12	4.75	60.4
Aug.-Sept. 1356	12	6.5	54.2
Sept.-Oct. 1356	15[m]	7.25	51.7

[a] This column reproduces figures tabulated in Miskimin, *Money*, pp. 161-190, with certain corrections and the omission of minor coinages or those whose *pied* differed only slightly from the prevailing one. Our purpose is to give a simplified representation of the royal valuation of the mark which prevailed at any given time. Miskimin's figures are derived from the documents of de Saulcy.

[b] De Saulcy, *Documents*, pp. 10-14 published an excerpt from BN *ms. fr.* 18500 entitled *valor marche argenti*, from which the figures in this column are taken. Several similar documents published by de Saulcy in subsequent pages have been used for making a few minor corrections. L. Borrelli de Serres, "Les variations monétaires sous Philippe le Bel," *Gazette numismatique française*, 1901, pp. 245-367; 1902, pp. 9-67, has published figures which largely concur with those of de Saulcy but which furnish some additional information for the reign of Philip V which has also been utilized here.

[c] These figures are not taken from the sources indicated in the last two notes but are from N. de Wailly, "Recherches sur le systeme monétaire de Saint Louis," *Mémoires de l'Institute Imperial de France*, xxi (1857), 118-119.

[d] Cazelles, "Quelques réflexions," p. 88, note 20, states that the price of the mark did not rise to 4 *l.t.* until early 1323, whereas de Saulcy places it in 1322.

Footnotes to Table 1, Appendix I (*cont.*)

^e Miskimin, *Money*, p. 43, reproduces figures which were tabulated by Fawtier, *Comptes*, pp. lix f. These are derived from royal treasury registers which show *monnayage* (in *l.p.*) increasing from about 6,600 pounds in 1323 to over 70,000 in 1324 and 108,000 in 1325. These permit us to conclude that most coins issued in 1323 were those valuing the mark at 4.09 *l.t.*, from which little *monnayage* could be expected. In the two following years, however, an increasing proportion of the coins must have been those at the higher *pied*.

^f In late March 1333, Philip VI convened an assembly to discuss the coinage and probably other fiscal matters also (see Chapter III, part 2). Some weeks later, the king raised the *pied*, valuing the mark at 4.15 *l.t.*, but there is no evidence of any rise in the mint price of silver. Ordinarily this would be an indication that the crown was collecting sharply increased *monnayage*. In this case, however, Philip was clearly trying to attract bullion to the mints, and in *Ord.*, II, 83-88, he promised to charge no more than the necessary *brassage* if people would bring a portion of their silver to the mints. If he really did collect a higher *monnayage* after June 1333, he was going back on this promise and thereby hastened the bullion crisis which occurred in 1335. It seems unlikely that he did this, particularly at a time when he was suffering pangs of conscience about the feudal aids and the crusade. In compiling Table 4, therefore (see note ^e to Table 4), I have proposed a second set of figures based upon a hypothetical and completely undocumented rise in the price of silver to 3.88 *l.t.* Such an increase might well have been authorized by the assembly as a last resort if bullion could not be attracted to the mints by other means. If put into effect, it would yield the crown a 6.6% *monnayage* in the period 1333-1335, slightly less than that of 1330-1332, when Philip had also promised not to take any unnecessary profit.

^g Miskimin, *Money*, pp. 168-169, has indicated simultaneous coinages of a higher *pied*, putting the mark at 13.75 *l.t.* in the fall of 1343 and 6.11 *l.t.* from November 1343, to July 1346. A reading of the texts printed by de Saulcy, *Documents*, pp. 245-247, suggests that the second of these figures was actually 5.5 *l.t.* The values indicated here in Table 2 are based on the *pied* of the *gros tournois*, usually the most important silver coin. The higher values reflect the *pied* of the *deniers parisis* minted during the same period.

^h In April 1347, Philip VI ordered a new coinage that would be on the 22nd *pied* and reduce the price of silver to 4.8 *l.t.* There is no evidence that these orders were put into effect before January 1348, when they were reissued following the Estates. Interestingly, the king had also been negotiating with assemblies in April 1347 (see above, Chapter VI and de Saulcy, *Documents*, p. 253).

ⁱ The document published in de Saulcy, *Documents*, pp. 10-14, gives several changes in the price of silver during 1349, ranging upwards from 6 to 6.75 *l.t.* Other texts, *ibid.*, p. 266, give a different sequence of price changes, ranging from 6.25 to 6.52 *l.t.* The mean figure (and that which prevailed during the months when commercial activity was normally greatest) was 6.50 *l.t.*

^j Miskimin, *Money*, p. 170, reports the two coinages of this period as valuing silver at 8.25 and 10 *l.t.*, but his lower figure seems to be a miscalculation. Evidence from de Saulcy, *Documents*, pp. 304-305, indicates that the two values should be 9 and 10 *l.t.*, respectively.

^k In October 1353, the king ordered a new coinage at the 26th *pied* (6.5 *l.t.* per mark). By 3 November, the price of silver had dropped to 4.5 *l.t.* and on the ninth, the mints started striking the coinage at the higher value of 8.13 *l.t.* per mark. It is not clear that any coins were actually struck at the 26th *pied*.

Footnotes to Table 1, Appendix I (*cont.*)

[1] In all these periods, the mints were issuing coins of a lower *pied*, which in general valued silver at about two pounds less than the figures given here. In each of these cases, however, the tables in Miskimin, *Money*, pp. 172-175, indicate that vastly more coins were struck at the higher *pied*, so I have discarded the lower figure in preparing my table.

[m] After this date (the battle of Poitiers), completely separate coinage policies prevailed in Languedoc and Languedoil for about four years, with the *pied* often radically different between the two regions.

The first major departure from the currency of St. Louis was that of Philip the Fair, under whose reign the price of silver rose 300 percent until Philip restored sound money in the fall of 1306. There followed five years of stability, followed by a fairly minor, though controversial debasement in 1311, after which another decade of relative stability ensued. Charles IV, facing a bullion shortage and a kingdom hostile to taxation, raised the *pied* in 1322 but collected no significant *monnayage* until 1324. By the summer of 1326, the mark was raised in value to 6 *l.t.* and the monarchy realized impressive *monnayage* receipts.[33]

The mark continued to be valued at six pounds until the end of 1329. Then Philip VI restored sound money by Easter 1330. Following the assembly of March 1333, the *pied* was raised 38 percent, but if this measure was intended to attract specie to the mints it failed to prevent their having to close in 1335 for lack of silver.

When the mints were reopened in February 1337, the fiscal pressures of the Hundred Years' War began to force the king into new alterations of the *pied*. By 1343, it had risen 500 percent in a decade, creating the discontent which led to the assembly of that summer and the ensuing reform. The precipitous drop in the value of the mark in the fall of 1343 was followed by a new period of stability, but in 1346-1347, debasement resumed. When, in March of 1347, the mark again reached 9 *l.t.*, seigneurial discontent seems to have forced the king to order a revaluation to 5.5 *l.t.* This change, if put into effect at all, was short-lived, but it was re-enacted at the beginning of 1348, following the Estates General of the preceding month. This new reform, however, could not long survive the fiscal crisis created by the Black Death. In 1349, the mark was again at

[33] Referring again to the table cited above, note e to Table 1, there are no figures for *monnayage* receipts in 1326 when the rate was highest, but for the first ten months of 1327 they came to 314,691 *l.p.*, nearly triple the total for 1325 and nearly two-thirds of the total treasury receipts for that accounting period. The same table indicates very small coinage profits in the first two years of the reign and these figures have been reproduced here in Table 2.

9 *l.t.* and the crown collected extremely large profits from inflating the *pied*.[34]

A dramatic increase in *seigneuriage* rates marked the accession of John II in August 1350, and for most of his reign this unfortunate prince exploited the currency far more than any of his predecessors. Although Table 1 lists only the more prominent changes and makes no pretense to being exhaustive, the most cursory glance at its figures suggests why the clamor of the reformers was being directed more against instability than against inflation as such. Despite occasional efforts at revaluation, the trend was towards an ever higher *pied*. The crown's grave fiscal difficulties of 1355 are reflected in the coinage figures. The attempt to placate the Estates with a revalued currency at the beginning of 1356 foundered when it became evident that the assemblies could not deliver the taxes they had promised.

If we regard the last column of Table 1 as relative measurement of the rate of *monnayage*, it is possible to summarize the periods in which the kings seem to have made the greatest use of this source of income. The first such period came under Charles IV, in 1326-1327. Under Philip VI, the highest rates came in the summer of 1340, when the first serious military action of the Hundred Years' War strained the crown's finances; 1341, when the existence of a truce made for sharply reduced subsidy receipts; and (1346-1347), when the English were besieging Calais. Above all, of course, there was 1349, the year after the plague. The large *monnayage* known to have been collected in the second half of that year suggests that the output of the mints in that period may have approached two million *l.p.*[35] Under John II, the *monnayage* rates reached their peak in 1356 when they seem to have exceeded 50 percent. Throughout our period, they seem to provide a sort of barometer for measuring the financial malaise of the monarchy. In short, the figures of Table 1 make it clear that fiscal, political, and military factors exerted an important influence on royal coinage policy.

Our immediate concern is the degree to which coinage changes com-

[34] Fawtier, *Comptes*, p. lxiv; Miskimin, *Money*, p. 43. The *monnayage* of over 552,000 *l.p.* amounted to more than 70% of the treasury receipts in this half-year.

[35] *Ibid.* The figure of 27.8% given in Table 1 is not very reliable because the mint price of silver did not remain constant in that year (see note i to Table 1). If, however, we assume a *monnayage* of 27.8%, it would have required an output of nearly two million *l.p.* in coins to produce the *monnayage* receipts collected in this half-year period. Large amounts of silver must have come to the mints, and one infers a substantial de-hoarding in the wake of the Black Death.

plicate the task of interpreting the royal financial records. These were of several different types, but only a few samples of each have survived the eighteenth century. For a long time, the king's finances had been entrusted to the Templars, and even after the treasury was established at the Louvre, it long retained the structure of a bank. The king's account there, while the largest and most active, was not the only one. Most important royal officers who drew salaries and incurred expenses also maintained accounts at the treasury. The cashier of the treasury was the *changeur*, and the Book of the Changer (*Livre du Changeur*) can be viewed as the king's monthly bank statement. One of these has survived for the period 1335-1343, and Viard has tabulated its figures by month and year.[36] The actual register does not furnish much detailed information, since most entries merely indicate sums credited to the royal account by various financial officials.

The Book of the Changer had a rather specialized function and its figures were arranged accordingly. It was derived, however, from a much more detailed and valuable register, the Journal of the Treasury. The surviving treasury journals[37] are a mine of information, although utilization of them encounters the inevitable obstacles. This journal was a daily register of all treasury transactions as they occurred, indicating receipts, expenditures, and shifts of funds from one account to another, all in chronological order without any arrangement of the transactions as to type. The Book of the Changer was compiled from this register simply by extracting and regrouping, month by month, those entries which pertained to the king's own account.

A third major financial record was the Book of Common Receipts and Expenditures.[38] Like the Book of the Changer, it was evidently derived from the treasury journal. This register was compiled semiannually, at St. John's (24 June) and Christmas. It classified treasury receipts and expenditures for each half-year accounting period according to type of revenue. As such, it is an extremely valuable source and the failure of an extended series to survive is most regrettable.

[36] Based on AN KK 5, the figures are published in *JT Ph. VI*, pp. xli-xlvii.

[37] The two important surviving registers, AN KK 1 (1322-1326) and AN KK 6 (1349-1350) have been published by Viard (*JT Ch. IV* and *JT Ph. VI*). Other important fragments have been published by H. Moranvillé, "Extraits des journaux du trésor," in *BEC*, XLIX (1888), pp. 149-214, 368-452.

[38] For the period covered by this book, only one of these registers has survived: AN KK 2 (1327-1330). Fawtier, *Comptes*, p. lix f., has published those portions which carry both receipts and expenditures for a full accounting period, notably the first ten months of 1327 and the entire year 1329.

Other types of financial records[39] have been utilized where appropriate in the foregoing chapters, but we are concerned here only with the three kinds of register just described, or more precisely, those parts which deal with receipts. We may supplement them with several memoranda indicating total receipts (actual or projected) for certain years of Philip VI's reign.[40] These classify the figures according to category of revenue as do the Common Receipts.

The study of taxes in this period would obviously be more meaningful if we could compare the receipts for a succession of years, in terms of both totals and types of revenue. We have available complete treasury journals for 1322-1325 and Common Receipts for 1328-1330, plus rather cryptic budget memoranda for 1331, 1332, 1335, and 1344, and complete Books of the Changer for 1336-1342. Documents covering less than a full accounting year must be excluded because extrapolating their figures would create an excessive possibility of error. Nevertheless, we are left with figures of a sort for eighteen years in a twenty-three-year period, and it seems incumbent upon the historian to try and exploit them in some meaningful way.

As pointed out in an earlier study, the effort to compare these figures encounters serious obstacles.[41] For one thing, treasury receipts were not the same as total revenues. Taxes collected by *élus* were supposed to be turned over directly to military paymasters, but long before the introduction of *élus*, it is probable that subsidy receipts were often applied to the local war effort without being sent to Paris. Few receipts from subsidies appeared in the treasury journal of 1325, and Fawtier did not even list them under a separate heading when tabulating the figures in the register.[42] Much the same is true of domainal receipts. These were to go to Paris after deductions for local expenditures, but it is likely that in wartime many of the profits of the domain were diverted to military

---

[39] These included the *Comptes du trésor*, of which none have survived between 1316 and 1384; the *extractus*, a very useful abridged summary of the Common Receipts and Expenditures of which some surviving fragments have been published by Moranvillé, *loc. cit.* above, note 37; and the *Ordinarium*, a list of salaries and annuities of which the only surviving example has been published by Viard at the end of *JT Ph. VI*, pp. 857-930. The foregoing discussion of these different treasury documents has been based on Viard's introduction to *JT Ph. VI* and Rey, *Domaine*, pp. 77f.

[40] These budget memoranda have been published by A. de Boislisle, "Le budget et la population de la France sous Philippe de Valois," *AB SHF*, xii (1875) and Boislisle, "Note sur des rapports financiers addresses à Philippe VI," *BEC*, liii (1892); and H. Moranvillé, "Rapports à Philippe VI sur l'état de ses Finances," *BEC*, xlviii (1887).

[41] Henneman, "Financing," pp. 295-297. [42] Fawtier, *Comptes*, pp. lix f.

expenses in the bailiwicks and seneschalsies. Even in the relatively less troubled years before the Black Death, changing economic and military conditions must have caused fluctuations in the net domainal revenues which reached the treasury.

Yet for all the uncertainties about local disbursements, a comparison of treasury receipts may still be useful if the obstacles caused by currency changes can be overcome. When considering this problem in connection with the taxes of 1340, I explored the possibility of converting treasury figures to marks, using the *pied de monnaie*. This conversion produced such great inconsistencies in domainal revenues that I concluded that the treasury journals and the Book of the Changer were based on figures other than current money of account.[43] This reasoning was incorrect, for the inconsistencies can be eliminated by using the actual mint price of silver rather than the *pied*. Additional data from the Common Receipts of 1328 and 1330 helped to clarify the matter, and the resultant conversion of treasury receipts into marks of silver is indicated in Table 2.

Very clearly, the Book of Common Receipts used money of account at the current price of silver, usually *l.p.*, sometimes *l.t.* Entries for the St. John semester of 1330 are recorded separately for the periods before and after Easter, when the coinage was revalued.[44] In the case of the treasury journals, the same currency must logically have been used. Revenues received in real money (*écus, gros,* etc.) were converted into money of account for entry in the royal registers. There is now no basis for supposing that they were first converted into some unchanging but fictitious currency like the sound money of Louis IX. Borrelli de Serres cited various entries in the treasury journals showing that figures were corrected to reflect the price of silver current at the time the journal was prepared.[45] Under these circumstances, the Book of the Changer must also have been based on current money. With more extensive records available for the reign of Charles VI, Maurice Rey found that the totals in this type of register roughly paralleled the Common Receipts but tended to be 15-18 percent lower.[46] This conclusion reinforces the view that the same currency was used in compiling both, and it offers a means of correcting Book of the Changer totals for 1336-1342 to bring them into rough conformity with the Common Receipts of other years for purposes

[43] Henneman, "Financing," pp. 296-297, and notes. Both the figures and the reasoning given here in note 134 now seem very questionable.

[44] AN KK 2, fol. 132r.

[45] Borrelli de Serres, *Recherches,* III, 458-459.   [46] Rey, *Domaine,* pp. 79-80.

TABLE 2
Tabulation of Treasury Figures
1322-1325 and 1328-1331[a]

	1322	1323	1324	1325	1328	1329	1330	1331
(in livres parisis)								
Subsidies, gifts, impositions, etc.					150,250[b]	149,266[b]	70,152[b]	18,000[b]
Monnayage	546	6,603	70,454	108,013	185,104	45,106	12,240	?[g]
Clerical tenth	101,456	173,564	175,866	106,043	195,370	139,299	129,418	10,000
Fines	56,871	66,095	28,266	27,111	5,048	25,065	9,765	
Confiscations, finances, forfeitures	2,731	8,652	52	58,295	53,290	46,968	18,564	37,000
Loans & extortions	91,738	101,031	50,015	89,882	116,076[c]	4,824	148,926[d]	
Total EXTRAORDINARY revenues	253,342	355,945	324,653	389,344	705,138	410,588	389,065	65,000
Bailiwicks & seneschalsies	131,159	164,941	177,525	169,650	370,581	332,218	222,273[d]	229,297
Other ordinary revenues	92,864	77,066	36,204	51,067	104,067	96,730	97,405	63,419
Total ORDINARY revenues	224,025	242,107	213,729	221,093	474,648	428,948	319,678	292,716
Total receipts	477,367	598,052	538,382	610,437	1,179,786	839,536	708,743	357,716[g]
(in marks)[h]								
Total receipts	176,803	186,891	168,245	190,762	268,133	189,079	268,297[e]	145,462[g]
Ordinary revenues	82,972	75,655	66,890	69,092	107,875	97,488	109,986[e]	116,110[f]
Bailiwicks & seneschalsies	48,577	51,544	55,477	53,016	84,223	75,504	82,103[e]	87,599[f]
Clerical tenth	37,521	54,239	54,938	33,138	44,402	31,364	56,530[e]	?[g]

Footnotes to Table 2, Appendix I

ᵃ The figures for 1322-1325 are ultimately derived from Viard's published text of *JT Ch. IV* (AN KK 1), and are adapted from the tables printed by Fawtier, *Comptes du trésor*, pp. lix-lx. The figures for 1329 are adapted from Fawtier's tabulations from AN KK 2, fols. 72-119, published *ibid.*, pp. lxii-lxiii. Those for 1328 and 1330, I have tabulated from AN KK 2, fols. 21-71, 120-160. The figures for 1331, much less detailed, are based on a budget memorandum published by Moranvillé, "Rapports," pp. 382-383. All figures in marks are obtained by utilizing column 2 of Table 1 above.

ᵇ Included are "gifts," export taxes, and minor impositions as well as war subsidy receipts, plus the indemnity being paid by the Flemings following their defeat in 1328. The latter figure exceeded 46,000 *l.p.* in 1330. Actual war subsidy receipts were roughly 250,000 *l.p.*, or about 57,000 marks, distributed equally between 1328 and 1329.

ᶜ This figure includes 42,302 *l.p.* listed in the register under miscellaneous receipts. It was obtained from a former receiver of Carcassonne, and if not an extortion or fine, strictly speaking, it certainly belongs with extraordinary revenues.

ᵈ Here again, certain large sums recorded under miscellaneous or "common" receipts ought to have been listed under another heading and have therefore been reclassified in this table. Several collections from the receivers of certain seneschalsies clearly belong in the section on domainal profits. Certain other large sums collected from delinquent royal officers and some important prelates should be grouped with the extraordinary revenues, although it is not clear which should be called loans or gifts and which should be considered *finances* or confiscations.

ᵉ Conversion into marks in the case of 1330 is a complex operation, but it is feasible because register KK 2 carefully separates receipts before and after Easter when the price of silver fell from 4.2 to 2.78 *l.t.* (see above, note 44).

ᶠ The figures for 1331 are in a budget memorandum of 1332. Apparently lacking a complete record, the compiler drew on some figures for 1330 and even 1329 in order to complete his estimate of bailiwick and seneschalsy profits. The total given here in pounds reflects the total in the document, but when converting to marks, I have first changed all figures to 1331 pounds.

ᵍ No figures for the clerical tenth having been estimated for 1331, we may assume hypothetical receipts of around 44,500 marks, the average sum from this source in 1322-1330. In this case, total receipts in 1331 would have been around 190,000 marks.

ʰ 5/4 x 1/n, where n is price of silver from Table 1, column 2.

TABLE 3

COMPARISON OF TWO REIGNS

Revenue (*marks*)	Charles IV	Philip VI	Rate of Change (*percent*)
Average clerical tenth	44,964	44,099	negligible decline
Average ordinary revenues	73,652	107,865	46.4
Average bailiwicks & seneschalsies	52,153	82,714	58.4
Other ordinary revenues	21,499	25,379	18

TABLE 4

SUGGESTED COMPARISON OF TREASURY RECEIPTS, 1322-1344

Year	Receipts (in l.p.)	Receipts (in marks)	Sum of net ordinary revenue + clerical tenth (in marks)	Extraordinary revenues other than clerical tenth (in marks)
1322	477,367	176,803	120,493	56,310
1323	598,052	186,891	129,894	56,997
1324	538,382	168,245	121,978	46,517
1325	610,437	190,762	102,230	88,532
1328	1,179,786	268,133	152,277	115,856
1329	839,536	189,079	128,852	60,227
1330	708,743	268,297	166,516	101,781
1331[a]	456,700	190,000[d]	160,610	29,390
1332[a]	405,525	176,315	(151,964)[c]	
1335[a]	542,160 or [e]	244,417 or [e]	198,978 or [e]	
	586,660	189,245	158,371	
1336[b]	208,656[f]			
1337[b]	546,689	188,513	(107,864)[c]	80,648?
1338[b]	521,560	162,988	(151,964)[c]	11,024?
1339[b]	899,504	219,390	(151,964)[c]	67,426?
1340[b]	1,261,327	233,579	(151,964)[c]	81,615?
1341[b]	933,726	121,384	(151,964)[c]	?
1342[b]	1,129,283	112,928	(151,964)[c]	?
1344[a]	543,860	212,545		

[a] In these years, budget memoranda omit the clerical tenth. An estimated tenth of 44,500 marks (the average, 1322-1325, 1328-1330) has been added.

[b] Receipts for these years are Book of the Changer totals augmented by 20%.

[c] This figure represents the average total of the tenth and net ordinary revenues collected in the first four years of Philip VI's reign, except in the case of 1337 when no tenth was collected.

[d] See note [g] to Table 2.

[e] See note [f] to Table 1 for the problem of determining a price of silver in the period 1333-1337. Two sets of figures are presented in Table 4, the first based on the price of 2.88 *l.t.* prevailing in 1332-1333, the second based on a hypothetical price of 3.88 *l.t.* which assumes that the mint price increased when the *pied de monnaie* was raised in June 1333. There is, of course, no documentary evidence of any increase, much less the precise one suggested here. However, the figures based on the higher price are much more plausible. The sum of 158,371 marks for ordinary revenues and the tenth is quite compatible with the same figures for 1328-1331. The figures for 1335 are hypothetical for another reason. They are derived from a budget memorandum (*AB SHF*, 1875, pp. 91-93) which estimates total receipts at over 656,000 *l.p.* The subsequent analysis of this total makes it clear that it represents gross ordinary revenues but includes very few of those revenues we have classified as extraordinary. After making adjustments to bring the figures into conformity with the ordinary-extraordinary classification employed in Table 2 we

Footnotes to Table 4, Appendix I (*cont.*)

can deduct the domainal profits disbursed locally and arrive at net domainal receipts of 353,000 *l.p.* and total receipts of 414,000 *l.p.* before the addition of the estimated clerical tenth.

[f] The extremely low figure for 1336 (which appears in the monthly breakdown as well as the total for the year) is completely incompatible with all the other figures in this table. Given the additional problem of determining the price of silver (see last note), no conversion to marks seems worth attempting. There are three explanations for the tiny receipt figures for 1336: (1) increased military preparations which may have caused much greater local disbursement of domainal profits, (2) the cancellation of the clerical tenth by the pope, and (3) the king's decision to return all sums collected for feudal aids in 1333-1335 which also drained the domain's profits at the local level. Philip VI's treasury usually received about 125,000 marks annually from the tenth, the bailiwicks, and the seneschalsies. Little if any money from these sources could have reached Paris in 1336.

of comparison. Thus in Table 4, the Changer's totals have been augmented by 20 percent, on the hypothesis that the difference discovered by Rey held equally true seventy years earlier.

To summarize, it appears that the documents suggesting treasury receipts in the period 1322-1344 were all compiled using current money of account. Conversion of the figures into marks for purposes of comparison is feasible if certain caveats are kept in mind: (1) the uncertain fluctuations in revenues disbursed locally, (2) the problem of finding a suitable price of silver for making the conversion, and (3) the very limited evidence to justify our augmentation of the Book of the Changer figures. None of these three difficulties poses a problem in compiling Tables 2 and 3. We have figures for four consecutive years of Charles IV's reign and four consecutive years at the beginning of Philip VI's reign, each period being disturbed by one minor war. In Table 4, however, the figures are much less meaningful because they depend so much on conjecture. The fluctuating level of warfare may have caused sharp variations in local disbursements. The frequent coinage changes in 1340-1342 compel us to select a "best price" for converting into marks.[47] Finally, the figures taken from the Book of the Changer may be compared with each other, but whether they may validly be compared with the totals of 1322-1331 remains largely speculative.

[47] Three prices given in Table 1 for 1340 between February and December average 6.67 *l.t.* However, during the period when most taxes were being collected the price was either 6.75 or 7. Our "best price" for 1340 should thus probably be somewhat higher than the average, and I have selected 6.75 *l.t.*, the price which actually prevailed between April and August, as the basis for a conversion into marks. By a similar process, 9.6 *l.t.* has been chosen as the best price for 1341 and 12.5 *l.t.* as the price for 1342 (see Table 4).

Tables 2, 3, and 4 furnish the basis for much of the tabulation of royal taxes and revenues in Appendix II. Some of the information derived from these tables deserves additional comment. It appears that domainal receipts and ordinary revenues as a whole remained rather consistent within each of the two reigns and were relatively unaffected by the wars of 1324-1325 and 1328. They increased nearly 60 percent from Charles' reign to Philip's, the rise being largely due to the increased profitability of the domain. The acquisition of the extensive Valois lands, while important, actually contributed less to this increase than did the conquests in Guyenne during the second half of Charles IV's reign.[48] The clerical tenths fluctuated from year to year because of delinquent payments and the irregular timing of papal grants. Yet the average annual receipts in marks were remarkably consistent between the two reigns.

Table 2 also shows that there were important fluctuations in those revenues we have called "extraordinary." The conservatism of Charles IV at the beginning of his reign is quite apparent here: the emphasis being on loans and judicial fines rather than the more controversial revenues like subsidies and *monnayage*. The latter two were more acceptable politically when the kingdom was at war. An illustration of this fact is afforded by the years 1328 and 1330 when extraordinary revenues were roughly equal and were unusually high. In 1328, a war year, subsidies and *monnayage* were their main component, while in 1330, these were insignificant and large loans or extortions from individuals predominated.

Tables 2 and 4 (the latter admittedly a source of dubious value) also suggest that total annual treasury receipts prior to the Black Death usually amounted to around 175,000 to 190,000 marks unless the extraordinary revenues were particularly inflated. The relative importance of the domain was greater in the first half of Philip VI's reign, as 45 percent of the total receipts in 1328-1331 came from this source as opposed to 41 percent in the period 1322-1325. It is probable that domainal receipts were of even greater relative importance in the peaceful years of the mid-1330s.

The main value of Table 4 lies in the internal comparison of the receipt totals for 1337-1342. The figures for 1336 seem to reflect the cancellation of the clerical tenth and the return of the knighting aid, explaining in part the difficult financial position of the monarchy at the beginning of the Hundred Years' War. The receipts in the early years of the war

[48] Thus the districts of Agen, Saintonge, and Toulouse produced important profits in 1328 and 1330, considerably more than the former Valois lands. AN KK 2, as cited above, Chapter IX, note 6.

make abundantly clear what was suggested in an earlier study: treasury receipts peaked in 1340 and then fell precipitously before achieving a more modest level in the middle years of the decade.[49] Because of the high rate of *monnayage* prevailing in 1340 and the extortion from the Italians in that year, it is entirely possible that the highest *subsidy* receipts of this period were in 1339. The last column in Table 4, hypothetical though it is, suggests that the subsidy of 1339 may have come to around 60,000 marks. This figure compares with the subsidy of roughly 57,000 marks in 1328. By contrast, Strayer's estimate of the subsidy receipts of 1304 yields a total of slightly under 110,000 marks,[50] doubtless the largest subsidy actually collected up to 1356.

[49] Henneman, "Financing," pp. 297-298.
[50] Strayer and Taylor, *Studies*, p. 74, where Strayer suggests minimum subsidy receipts of 735,000 *l.t.* in a year when the price of silver was between 6.2 and 7.2 *l.t.*

TABULATION OF MAJOR TAXES AND EXTRAORDINARY ROYAL REVENUES, 1322-1356

Year	Subsidies	General Remarks
1322	None	Negligible coinage profits; heavy fine on Jews and other large judicial fines; heavy royal borrowing
1323	None	Increased, but still minor coinage profits; even greater revenue from fines and borrowing than in 1322 (28% of total treasury receipts)
1324	Sergeants levied in regions nearest to Gascony	Significant decline in fines and borrowing, largely offset by increased *monnayage*
1325	Subsidy throughout kingdom: 1 *d./l.* sales tax in North; sergeants in upper Languedoc; lump sums from towns of lower Languedoc. Collections interrupted by peace in June and most receipts disbursed locally	Introduction of 4 *d./l.* export tax; heavy *finances* and gifts from Italians; another sharp increase in *monnayage*; 40% increase in revenue from loans and extortions; heavy fines for fief acquisitions and violations of royal ordinances, sometimes combined with subsidy payments
1326	Subsidies following general format of 1325. Some regions paid two taxes. Receipts probably much greater than in 1325	Slackening of fines levied by *enquêteurs*; continuing increase in *monnayage*
1327	Some taxes collected and others negotiated, but all halted in March when peace concluded	High *monnayage*; important judicial fines and levies for *franc-fief* and *amortissement*
1328	War subsidy in second half of year, generally in the form of lump-sum payments or apportioned income taxes for the support of troops	Substantial *monnayage*; heavy fines, borrowing, confiscations; much greater domainal receipts than in previous reign
1329	Continued collection of arrears from subsidy of 1328	Sharp decline in borrowing, coinage profits, and extraordinary revenues generally
1330	None, except for a few arrears	War indemnity from Flanders; minor coinage profits; very heavy borrowing and extortions
1331	Minor levy of sergeants for Saintes expedition	Continued investigation of fief alienations; major extortion from Italians and their debtors
1332	None	Continued collection from Italians and their debtors; probable decline in other extraordinary revenues

Year	Subsidies	General Remarks
1333	None	End of export tax and collections based on usury; beginning of collection of feudal aid
1334	None	Continuing collection of knighting aid and a few large fines
1335	Minor levy in Southeast for Sainte-Colombe expedition	Levy of knighting aid in first half of year, followed by return of some receipts from this source; beginning of effort to collect crusading aid; a few large judicial fines
1336	Local subsidies for port repairs and naval defense	Some receipts for crusading aid; treasury receipts drastically reduced by return of knighting aid and cancellation of clerical tenth
1337	Fines in lieu of military service; lump-sum payments from certain towns; unsuccessful effort to generalize 20 s. hearth tax in Languedoc where payments finally averaged about half that much	No clerical tenth; new investigation of fief transactions and usury; confiscation of debts to usurers; resumption of coinage profits; probably resumption of export tax
1338	Fines in lieu of service; large lump sums from towns of Toulousain, less from other southern towns	Resumption of clerical tenth; continuing revenue from coinage and investigation of fiefs and usury, but drastic decline in extraordinary receipts as result of return of subsidy in lower Languedoc
1339	Fines in lieu of service and indirect taxes in the North; large grant for troops in Normandy; lump-sum payments and contingents from Languedoc despite opposition. Largest subsidy receipts since 1328 and perhaps largest for entire reign	Continuing overvaluation of silver coinage and probable increase in *monnayage*
1340	Subsidies everywhere in wide variety of forms; lump sums and sergeants from Languedoc; 4 *d./l.* sales tax in many parts of North; 2% income tax from nobles of many regions	Increased coinage alterations and probably high *monnayage*; forced loans; export tax; new clerical tenth; new confiscation of debts to Lombards. Extraordinary revenues and treasury receipts at highest level of reign
1341	Sharp decline in subsidy receipts because of truce, but continuation of 4 *d./l.* sales tax in much of Languedoil	High rate of *monnayage*; *gabelle* on salt instituted; sums collected from Florentines. Total treasury receipts down by nearly 50%

355

Year	Subsidies	General Remarks
1342	Continuation of 4 *d./l.* sales tax in North; hearth tax of 15 *s.* or 20 *s.* levied in South, sometimes commuted to lump sums	Continued coinage manipulation; probable increase in *gabelle* revenues
1343	New subsidies in South halted because of truce. Northern sales tax renewed in return for coinage reform; Languedoc, following August assembly, pays lump sums in lieu of sales tax for coinage reform	Probable increase in *gabelle* receipts owing to improved administration. Probable sharp decline in coinage profits
1344	Few subsidy receipts other than arrears and continuation of sales tax in North	Fiscal expedients including new round of *franc-fief* investigations; new clerical tenth; *gabelle* continues
1345	Modest subsidies in Languedoil, where some districts offered maintenance of men-at-arms and others continued the old 4 *d./l.* sales tax. Little taxation in Languedoc until late in the year, when most regions paid a 10 *s. fouage* or lump sum in lieu of it	New extortion from Italians; continuation of *gabelle*. Few coinage profits and probable decline in domanial receipts owing to English conquests
1346	Parts of Languedoil grant tax to support troops; others pay 4 *d./l.* sales tax or fines in lieu of service during Crécy campaign. Two 10 *s.* hearth taxes in Languedoc	*Gabelle* canceled in some regions. Increased *monnayage* late in the year. Heavy borrowing from pope
1347	Scattered subsidies in northern France for troops; ad hoc arrangements elsewhere with little evidence of general tax	Increased coinage profits but *gabelle* canceled everywhere. New confiscation of debts to Lombards
1348	Extremely large subsidy ratified locally after assembly of Estates, with collection to begin in March; receipts only minor after arrival of Black Death	Generalization of debt confiscation; 1,200,-000 pounds anticipated from debtors to usurers. Negligible *monnayage* but heavy papal loans
1349	Scattered light taxes where conditions in wake of plague permit collection	Continued collection of debts to usurers where conditions permit; drastic increase in *monnayage*
1350	Increased and more general taxation but receipts still low	Continued pursuit of Lombard debtors; increased rate of *monnayage*

Year	Subsidies	General Remarks
1351	Substantial increase in taxes: 6 *d./l.* sales tax through most of Languedoil; *fouage* amounting to 25 *s.t.* in much of Languedoc (for war and king's accession)	Forced loans and continued high level of *monnayage*
1352	Two southern hearth taxes totaling 25 *s.t.*; 6 *d./l.* sales tax in North	Sounder currency but *monnayage* rates exceed 40%
1353	Renewal of nothern sales tax despite rising opposition; three *fouages* in Languedoc totaling 25 *s.t.*	Possible decrease in coinage profits; new fines for fief alienations
1354	Sharply lower *fouage* in Languedoc; continued sales tax in most of North but some disruption in Normandy	New coinage debasement and high rate of *monnayage*. Probable decline in domainal receipts in Normandy
1355	Possible 20 *s. fouage* in Languedoc but little evidence of collections until after English raid. Heavy emphasis on local defense measures. Parts of Languedoil grant subsidies to be used mainly for regional defense. Collapse of general taxation	Wildly fluctuating coinage; evidence of general royal bankruptcy; probable drastic loss of domainal revenues in Southwest and parts of Normandy
1356 (to 19 Sept.)	8 *d./l.* sales tax and restored *gabelle* granted by Estates but widely opposed. All regions try new forms of tax and determine to control collections locally. Successive income taxes in North and heavy sales tax in South	Rate of *monnayage* exceeding 50%. Few domainal receipts probably reaching Paris. Civil war in Normandy

357

Bibliography and Index

Bibliography

I. MANUSCRIPT SOURCES

PARIS: ARCHIVES NATIONALES

Inventories: Series 1, numbers 33-41 (Godefroy and Dupuy), 62-68 (Curzon).
Series 2, numbers 57 *bis*, 58 *bis*, 59 *bis*.
Series AB xix: numbers 2635-2643.
Series F 2: 1, numbers 1464, 1465.
Series J: numbers 210, 377, 384, 388, 404, 623.
Series JJ: numbers 52, 53, 54A, 58, 61, 62, 64, 65A, 65B, 66-78, 79B, 80-89.
Series K: numbers 41-48, 497-499.
Series KK: numbers 2, 5, 7, 394.
Series P: numbers 2288-2293.
Series PP: number 117.
Series X 2a: number 5.

PARIS: BIBLIOTHÈQUE NATIONALE

Manuscrits français: numbers 6739, 7222, 7323-7344, 7346, 7350, 7357-7359, 7858, 7877, 7878, 8605, 16200, 16647, 20398, 20402, 20410-20413, 20579, 20581, 20683-20685, 20691, 21023, 21040-21043, 21047, 22295, 22468, 23256, 23257, 24120, 25697-25701, 25902, 25993-26003.
Nouvelles acquisitions françaises: numbers 1433, 1481, 3637, 3653, 3654, 7373-7376, 7389, 7416, 7430, 7599-7609, 7990, 20025, 20026, 20075, 21155, 21857.
Pièces originales: numbers 60, 93, 108, 225, 268, 470, 524, 539, 650, 651, 1522, 1675, 2130, 2169, 2268, 2286, 2477, 2777, 2886.
Manuscrits latin: numbers 9046, 9146, 9174, 9175, 9192, 9194, 11016.
Nouvelles acquisitions latines: number 185.
Collection Baluze: numbers 87, 390.
Collection Clairambault: numbers 11, 12, 29-31, 33, 34, 78, 108-110, 125, 157, 159, 192, 193, 210-214, 228, 229, 470-473.
Collection Colbert (Cinq Cents): number 64.
Collection Doat: numbers 8, 51-53, 60, 64, 70-73, 81, 87, 93, 109, 116, 119, 125, 127, 132, 145-147, 149, 157, 164, 182-192, 243, 249-255, 257.
Collection Dupuy: numbers 533, 673.
Collection Fontanieu: see Nouvelles acquisitions françaises, nos. 7599-7609.
Collection Languedoc: numbers 82-85, 159.
Collection Moreau: numbers 221-235, 699.

ARCHIVES MUNICIPALES/COMMUNALES

Agen: Series BB, numbers 15, 16.
Albi: Series AA, number 44; series CC, numbers 54, 58, 60, 61, 64, 65, 67, 68.
Alès: 1 S, series 3, 11, 12, 16, 23.
Cajarc: Series CC, CC *supp.*, EE, EE *supp.* (many individual parchments).
Castres: Series AA, numbers 2, 4; series CC, no. 1.
Cordes: Series CC, numbers 29-32.
Gourdon: Series AA, number 2; series BB, numbers 20, 21; series CC, numbers 1, 47, 48; series EE, number 1.
Lodève: Series AA, number 2.
Lunel: Series CC, number 60.

Lyon: Series AA, number 2; series BB, number 368; series CC, numbers 288, 340, 368.

Martel: Series BB, number 3; series CC, numbers 3, 4.

Millau: Series CC, numbers 60, 63-65, 345-349, 505, 508-510, 512, 516; series EE, numbers 1-6, 8, 11, 111, 118, 119, 121; series ee, numbers 9, 32; *archives non classées*, one *liasse*, two registers.

Montpellier: *Armoire* B, *cassette* 2; *armoire* G, *cassettes* 1, 2, 5, 6; *armoire* H, *cassette* 6.

Narbonne: AA 172.

Nîmes: Series CC, number 1; series LL, number 1; series NN, number 1; series RR, number 1.

Périgueux: Series CC, numbers 47-50, 58.

Pézenas: *Armoire* B, *layette* 3.

Riom: Series AA, numbers 15, 16, 21, 31; series CC, numbers 7-10, 13, 14.

Rodez: *Bourg*, series CC, number 125; *Cité*, series CC, numbers 361, 365, 371.

Toulouse: Series AA, numbers 6, 35, 36, 45; series CC, number 1845.

ARCHIVES DÉPARTEMENTALES

Aveyron: Series C, numbers 1364, 1519, 1520; series E, number 1594; series 2E, numbers 12, 67, 157, 178, 212; series G, numbers 10, 28, 31, 473, 492, 965 *bis*.

Gard: two unsigned eighteenth century inventories of the Beaucaire municipal archives.

Hérault: Series A, numbers 1, 4, 5.

Lot: Series F, numbers 3, 5, 6, 10, 11, 14, 20, 21, 31, 35-37, 114, 152, 174, 187-189, 208, 229, 271, 283.

Pas-de-Calais: Series A, numbers 530, 563; *Collection Rodière*, ms. 106.

Basses-Pyrenées: Series E, numbers 404-406, 408, 490.

Tarn: Series E, numbers 1402, 2298.

Tarn-et-Garonne: Series A, number 207.

II. ARCHIVE INVENTORIES

Affre, H. *Inventaire sommaire des archives communales de Rodez.* Rodez, 1878.

Albe, E. "Cahors: Inventaire raisonné et analytique des archives municipales," *2e partie, Bulletin de la Société des Etudes Litteraires, Scientifiques et Artistiques du Lot*, XLI (1920), pp. 1-48; XLIII pt. 2 (1922), pp. 1-28; XLV pt. 2 (1924), pp. 28-99.

Berthelet, J. *Archives de la ville de Pézenas, Inventaires et documents: Inventaire de F. Ressequier.* Montpellier, 1907.

⸺. *Repertoire numerique des archives de l'Hérault, série E supplement.* Montpellier, 1925.

Berthelet, J. and Castets, F. *Archives de la ville de Montpellier, Inventaires et documents: Inventaire du Grand Chartrier.* I. Montpellier, 1895-1899.

Bousquet, H. *Inventaire des archives du château de Vezins.* 3 vols. Rodez, 1934-1939.

Boyer, F. *Ville de Riom: Inventaire sommaire des archives communales antérieures à 1790.* Riom, 1892.

Chomel, V. *Repertoire numerique des archives communales de la ville de Limoux antérieures à 1790 (Archives départementales, Aude, sous-série IV-E).* Carcassonne, 1958.

Combarieu, L. *Inventaire sommaire des archives départementales antérieures à 1790: Lot.* Vol. III. Cahors, 1900.

Dainville, O. de. *Archives de la ville de Montpellier, Inventaires et documents.* II. Montpellier, 1955. This work supplements that of Berthelet and Castets listed above, and together the two volumes make up the inventory of the *Grand Chartrier* cited in the notes.

Desjardins, G. and Affre, H. *Inventaire des archives de la commune de Saint-Affrique.* Saint-Affrique, 1886.

Durand, G. *Ville d'Amiens, inventaire sommaire des archives communales antérieures à 1790.* I. The series of Amiens inventories consists of seven volumes. Amiens, 1891-1925.

Esquier, G. *Inventaire des archives communales de la ville d'Aurillac antérieures à 1790.* 2 vols. Aurillac, 1906-1911.

Estienne, C. and Lempereur, L. *Inventaire sommaire des archives départementales antérieures à 1790: Aveyron, Archives ecclésiastiques.* 3 vols. Rodez, 1934.

Fawtier, R. *Registres du Trésor des Chartes: Inventaire Analytique.* I. Paris, 1958.

Guerout, J. *Registres du Trésor des Chartes: Inventaire Analytique.* II, pt. I. Paris, 1966.

Hardy, M. *Ville de Périgueux, Inventaire sommaire des archives communales antérieures à 1790.* Périgueux, 1897.

Jolibois, E. *Inventaire sommaire des archives communales antérieures à 1790, ville d'Albi.* Paris, 1869.

Lempereur, L., de Gaulejac, B., and Bousquet, J. *Archives de l'Aveyron, Inventaire sommaire, série G, 2G, 4G.* IV. Rodez, 1958.

Mouynès, G. *Ville de Narbonne, Inventaire sommaire des archives communales antérieures à 1790, série AA.* Narbonne, 1877.

Portal, C. *Inventaire sommaire des archives communales antérieures à 1790, ville de Cordes.* Albi, 1903.

Redet, et al. *Table des manuscrits de D. Fonteneau conservés à la bibliothèque de Poitiers.* I. Poitiers, 1839.

Richard, J. M. *Inventaire sommaire des archives départementales antérieures à 1790: Pas-de-Calais, Archives civiles, série A.* 2 vols. Arras, 1878-1887.

Roschach, E. *Ville de Toulouse, Inventaire des archives communales antérieures à 1790, série AA.* Toulouse, 1891.

Rossignol, M. and Garnier, J. *Inventaire sommaire des archives départementales antérieures à 1790: Côte-d'Or, Archives Civiles, série B.* 6 vols. Paris, 1863-1864; Dijon, 1873-1894.

Teilhard de Chardin, E. *Inventaire sommaire des archives communales antérieures à 1790, ville de Clermont-Ferrand: Fonds de Montferrand.* 2 vols. Clermont-Ferrand, 1902-1922.

III. CHRONICLES AND PRINTED SOURCES

Archives historiques du Poitou. Poitiers, 1872-. Vols. XI, XIII, XVII, XLIV, XLVI, and LII used here.

Archives historiques du Rouergue. Rodez. Vols. V-VII, XII and XVII used here.

Artières, J. *Annales de Millau.* Millau, 1894-1899.

————. *Documents sur la ville de Millau* (*Archives historiques du Rouergue.* VII). Millau, 1930.

Baillaud, E. (ed.). *Coutumes et privileges de Rouergue.* 2 vols. Toulouse, 1910.

Barthélemy, L. *Inventaire chronologique et analytique des chartes de la maison de Baux.* Marseilles, 1882.

Beaumanoir, Philippe de. See below, Salmon.

Beaurepaire, C. de (ed.). *Chronique normande de Pierre Cochon.* Rouen, 1870.

Bock, F. "Some New Documents Illustrating the Early Years of the Hundred Years' War (1353-1356)," *Bulletin of the John Rylands Library*, xv (1931), pp. 60-99.

Boislisle, A. de. "Le budget et la population de la France sous Philippe de Valois," *Annuaire Bulletin, Société de l'Histoire de France*, xii (1875), pp. 86-94, 181-190, 199-207, 232-240.

——. "Note sur des rapports financiers addressés à Philippe VI," *Bibliothèque de l'Ecole des Chartes*, liii (1892), pp. 111-114.

Boudet, M. "Nouveaux documents sur Thomas de la Marche, seigneur de Nonette et d'Auzon, bâtard de France (1318-1360)," *Le Moyen Age*, xvi (1903), pp. 283-302.

Boutaric, E. *Actes du Parlement de Paris, première série.* 2 vols. Paris, 1864-1867.

Brandt, W. (ed. and trans.). *The Recovery of the Holy Land*, by Pierre Dubois. New York, 1956.

Brousillon, B. de. *Documents inédits pour servir à l'histoire du Maine au XIVe siècle (Archives historiques du Maine. v).* Le Mans, 1905.

Cazelles, R. (ed.). *Lettres closes, lettres "de par le roi" de Philippe de Valois* (extrait de l'*Annuaire Bulletin, Société de l'histoire de France*). Paris, 1958.

Chaplais, P. (ed.). *The War of Saint-Sardos (1323-1325): Gascon Correspondence and Diplomatic Documents.* London, 1954.

Chassaing, A. *Spicelegium Brivatense. Recueil de documents historiques relatifs au Brivadois et à l'Auvergne.* Paris, 1886.

Compayré, C. *Etudes historiques et documents inédits sur l'Albigeois, le Castrais, et l'ancien diocèse de Lavaur.* Albi, 1841.

Constans, L. (ed.). *Le livre de l'épervier, cartulaire de la commune de Millau.* Montpellier, 1882.

Coville, A. "Les Etats de 1332 et de 1357," *Le Moyen Age*, vi (1893), pp. 57-59.

Cuttino, G. P. (ed.). *The Gascon Calendar of 1322.* Camden Society, lxx. London, 1949.

Decrusy, Isambert, F., Jourdan, A. (eds.). *Recueil général des anciennes lois françaises depuis l'an 420 jusqu'à la Révolution de 1789.* 27 vols. Paris, n.d. [18th century-1827].

Delachenal, R. (ed.). *Chronique des règnes de Jean II et de Charles V.* 2 vols. Paris, 1910.

Delisle, L. (ed.). *Actes normands de la chambre des comptes sous Philippe de Valois.* Rouen, 1871.

Dubois, P. See Brandt, above.

Dumas de Rauly, C. "Documents inédits sur Saint-Antonin pendant la guerre de Cent Ans, extraits de l'inventaire-sommaire des archives de cette ville," *Bulletin archéologique et historique de la Société Archéologique de Tarn-et-Garonne*, ix (1881), pp. 273-301.

Dureau de la Malle. "Document statistique inédit (quatorzième siècle)," *Bibliothèque de l'Ecole des Chartes*, ii (1840-1841), pp. 169-176.

Faucon, M. "Prêts faits aux rois de France par Clément VI, Innocent VI et le comte de Beaufort," *Bibliothèque de l'Ecole des Chartes*, xl (1879), pp. 570-578.

Fawtier, R. (ed.). *Comptes du trésor. Documents financiers.* ii. Paris, 1930.

——. "Une compte de menues dépenses de l'hôtel du roi Philippe VI de Valois pour le premier semestre de l'année 1337," *Bulletin de philologie et d'histoire*, 1928-1929, pp. 183-239.

Froissart. See below, Kervyn de Lettenhove.

Furgeot, H. *Actes du Parlement de Paris, deuxième série.* 2 vols. Paris, 1920-1960.

Gasnault, P. "Nouvelles Lettres Closes et 'de par le roy' de Philippe VI de Valois," *Bibliothèque de l'Ecole des Chartes*, cxx (1962), pp. 176-179.

Géraud, H. (ed.). *Chronique latine de Guillaume de Nangis de 1113 à 1300 avec les continuations de cette chronique de 1300 à 1368.* 2 vols. *Société de l'histoire de France*, Paris, 1843.

Guérin, P. *Recueil de documents concernant le Poitou.* . . . See above, *Archives historiques du Poitou.* xi, xiii, xvii.

Guesnon, A. (ed.). "Documents inédits sur l'invasion anglaise et les états au temps de Philippe VI et de Jean le Bon," *Bulletin de philologie et d'histoire*, 1897, pp. 232-246.

———— (ed.). *Inventaire chronologique des chartes de la ville d'Arras.* Arras, 1862.

Guilhiermoz, P. "Avis sur la question monétaire donnés aux rois Philippe le Hardi, Philippe le Bel, Louis X, et Charles le Bel," part 7, *Revue Numismatique*, xxx (1927), pp. 96-110.

Haigneré, *Les Chartes de Saint-Bertin.* 4 vols. Saint-Omer, 1886-1899.

Hellot, A. (ed.). "'Chronique parisienne anonyme de 1316 à 1339," *Mémoires de la société de l'histoire de Paris*, xi (1885), pp. 1-181.

d'Herbomez, A. "Notes et documents pour servir à l'histoire des rois fils de Philippe le Bel," *Bibliothèque de l'Ecole des Chartes*, lix (1898), pp. 497- 532, 689-711.

Higounet-Nadal, A. *Les comptes de la taille et les sources de l'histoire démographique de Périgueux au XIVe siècle.* Paris, 1965.

Honoré-Duvergé, S. "Un fragment de compte de Charles le Mauvais," *Bibliothèque de l'Ecole des Chartes*, cii (1941), pp. 292-297.

Huilliard-Breholles, A. *Titres de la maison ducale de Bourbon.* 2 vols. Paris, 1867-1874.

Isambert, F. See above, Decrusy.

Jacotin, A. (ed.). *Preuves de la Maison de Polignac.* 5 vols. Paris, 1898-1906.

Jassemin, H. "Les papiers de Mile de Noyers," *Bulletin de philologie et d'histoire*, 1918, pp. 174-226.

Jusselin, M. "Comment la France se préparait à la guerre de cent ans," *Bibliothèque de l'Ecole des Chartes*, lxxiii (1912), pp. 209-236.

Kervyn de Lettenhove, H. (ed.). *Oeuvres de Froissart.* 18 vols. Brussels, 1876-1877.

Langlois, C. V. (ed.). *Inventaire d'anciens comptes royaux dressé par Robert Mignon. Documents financiers.* 1. Paris, 1899.

————. "Registres perdus de la chambre des comptes," *Notices et Extraits des Manuscrits*, xl (1917), pp. 33-398.

Le Gris, A. (ed.). *Le Livre Rouge d'Eu 1151-1454. Société de l'histoire de Normandie.* Rouen-Paris, 1911.

Le Maire, E. (ed.). *Archives anciennes de la ville de Saint-Quentin.* 2 vols. Saint-Quentin, 1888-1910.

Lemoine, J. (ed.). *Chronique de Richard Lescot, moine de Saint-Denis (1328-1344). Continuation de cette chronique (1344-1364).* Paris, 1896.

Longnon, A. (ed.). *Documents rélatifs aux comtés de Champagne et de Brie.* 3 vols. *Collection des documents inédits.* Paris, 1901-1914.

Luce, S. (ed.). *Chronique des quatre premiers Valois (1327-1393). Société de l'histoire de France.* Paris, 1862.

Magen, A. and Tholin, G. (eds.). *Archives municipales d'Agen, Chartes, première série (1189-1328).* Villeneuve-sur-Lot, 1876.

Mahul, A. (ed.). *Cartulaire et archives des communes de l'ancien diocèse et de l'arrondisement administratif de Carcassonne.* 6 vols. in 7. Paris, 1857-1882.

Maillard, F. (ed.). *Comptes royaux 1314-1328. Documents financiers.* iv. Paris, 1961.

Martin, E. *Cartulaire de la ville de Lodève*. Montpellier, 1890.

Martin-Chabot, E. *Les archives de la cour des comptes, aides, et finances de Montpellier (avec un essai de restitution des premiers registres de la sénéchausée)*. Paris, 1907.

Mignon. See above, Langlois.

Miret y Sans, J. "Lettres closes des deniers Capetiens directs," *Le Moyen Age*, XVIII (1915), pp. 35-57.

———. "Lettres closes des premiers Valois," *Le Moyen Age*, XX (1917-18), pp. 53-88.

Molinier, A. and Molinier, E. (eds.). *Chronique normande du XIVe siècle. Société de l'histoire de France*. Paris, 1882.

Moranvillé, H. "Extraits des journaux du trésor," *Bibliothèque de l'Ecole des Chartes*, XLIX (1888), pp. 149-214, 368-452.

———. "Lettres privées adressées à un trésorier de France au XIVe siècle," *Bibliothèque de l'Ecole des Chartes*, XCIX (1938), pp. 297-312.

———. "Notes de statistique douanière sous Philippe VI de Valois," *Bibliothèque de l'Ecole des Chartes*, LXIV (1903), pp. 567-576.

———. "Rapports à Philippe VI sur l'état de ses finances," *Bibliothèque de l'Ecole des Chartes*, XLVIII (1887), pp. 380-395.

Newhall, R. (ed.). *The Chronicle of Jean de Venette* (tr. J. Birdsall). New York, 1953. See also above, Géraud. This chronicler has been generally treated as a late continuer of Guillaume de Nangis (1340-1368) and the Latin version is included in Vol. II of that edition.

Ordonnances des roys de France de la troisième race recueillies par ordre chronologique. (Many editors, 21 vols.). Paris, 1723-1849. The principal editors of concern in this study are Laurière and Secousse.

Petit, J., Gavrilovitch, M., et al. (eds.). *Essai de restitution des plus anciens mémoriaux de la chambre des comptes de Paris*. Paris, 1899.

Portal, C. *Extraits de Registres de Notaires, documents des XIVe-XVIe siècles concernants principalement le pays Albigeois (Extrait de la Revue du Tarn)*. Albi, 1901.

Prou, M. and d'Auriac, J. (eds.). *Actes et comptes de la commune de Provins*. Provins, 1933.

Richard, J. M. "Instructions données aux commissaires chargés de lever le rançon du roi Jean," *Bibliothèque de l'Ecole des Chartes*, XXXVI (1875), pp. 81-90.

Rigal, J. L., and Verlaguet, P. A. *Notes pour servir à l'histoire de Rouergue*. 2 vols. Rodez, 1913-1926.

Rymer, T. (ed.). *Foedera, conventiones litterae et cujuscunque generis acta publica inter reges Angliae et alios quosvis imperatores, reges, pontifices, principes vel communitates* (3rd edn.). 9 vols. The Hague, 1739-1745.

Saulcy, L.F.J.C. de. *Recueil de documents relatifs à l'histoire des monnaies frappées par les rois de France*. 4 vols. Paris, 1879-1892.

Salmon, A. (ed.). *Livre des Coutumes et des Usages de Beauvaisis par Philippe de Rémi, sieur de Beaumanoir*. 2 vols. *Société de l'histoire de France*. Paris, 1899-1900.

Secousse, D. F. *Recueil de pièces servant de preuves aux Memoires sur les troubles excités en France par Charles II dit le Mauvais, roi de Navarre et comte d'Evreux*. Paris, 1755.

Tardif, J. *Monuments historiques*. Paris, 1866.

Thierry, A. (ed.). *Recueil des monuments inédits de l'histoire du tiers état, première série*. 4 vols. *Collection des documents inédits*. Paris, 1850-1859.

Tholin, G. (ed.). *Chartes d'Agen se rapportant au règne de Philippe de Valois*. Bordeaux, 1898.

Varin, P. (ed.). *Archives administratives de la ville de Reims*, 4 vols. *Collection des documents inédits*. Paris, 1843.

Verlaguet, P. A. *Cartulaire de l'Abbaye de Bonnecombe (Archives historiques du Rouergue)*. Rodez, 1918-1925.

———. *Cartulaire de l'Abbaye de Bonneval en Rouergue (Archives historiques du Rouergue)*. Rodez, 1938.

Viard, J. (ed.). *Documents parisiens du règne de Philippe VI de Valois extraits des registres de la chancellerie*. 2 vols. Paris, 1899-1900.

———. *Les grandes chroniques de France*. 9 vols. *Société de l'histoire de France*. Paris, 1920-1937.

———. *Les journaux du trésor de Charles IV le Bel. Collection des documents inédits*. Paris, 1917.

———. *Les journaux du trésor de Philippe VI de Valois suivis de l'ordinarium thesauri de 1338-1339. Collection des documents inédits*. Paris, 1899.

Viard, J. and Déprez, E. (eds.). *Chronique de Jean le Bel*. 2 vols. *Société de l'histoire de France*. Paris, 1904-1905.

IV. SECONDARY WORKS CITED IN THE FOOTNOTES

Anon. *Nouvelles recherches pour servir à l'histoire de la ville de Beaucaire*. Avignon, 1836.

Atiya, A. S. *The Crusade in the Later Middle Ages*. London, 1938.

Balas, L. *Une tentative de gouvernement représentatif au XIVe siècle. Les états-généraux de 1356-1358*. Paris, 1928.

Bardon, A. *Histoire de la ville d'Alais*. 2 vols. Nîmes, 1891-1896.

Barroux, R. "Procès des évêques de Mende avec la royauté (1336-1369) au sujet de la réparation du port d'Aigues Mortes," *Bibliothèque de l'Ecole des Chartes*, LXXXV (1924), pp. 79-109.

Bautier, R.-H. "Recherches sur la chancellerie royale au temps de Philippe VI," *Bibliothèque de l'Ecole des Chartes*, CXXII (1964), pp. 89-176; CXXIII (1965), pp. 311-459.

Bayley, C. "Pivotal Concepts in the Political Philosophy of William of Ockham," *Journal of the History of Ideas*, X (1949), pp. 199-218.

Beauvillé, V. de. *Histoire de la ville de Montdidier* (2nd edn.). Paris, 1875.

Bertin, P. *Une commune flamande-artésienne: Aire-sur-la-Lys, des Origines au XVIe siècle*. Arras, 1947.

Bertrandy, M. *Etude sur les chroniques de Froissart: Guerre de Guienne, 1345-1346*. Bordeaux, 1870.

Bigwood, G. "La politique de la laine en France sous les règnes de Philippe le Bel et de ses fils," *Revue belge de philologie et d'histoire*, XV (1936), pp. 79-102, 429-457; XVI (1937), pp. 95-129.

Billioud, J. *Les états de Bourgogne aux XIVe et XVe siècles*. Dijon, 1922.

Bisson, T. N. *Assemblies and Representation in Languedoc in the Thirteenth Century*. Princeton, 1964.

Boislisle, A. de. "Projet de croisade du premier duc de Bourbon," *Annuaire-Bulletin, Société de l'Histoire de France*, XIV (1877), pp. 230-236, 246-255.

Bonal, A. *Histoire des évêques de Rodez* (ed. J. Rigal). 2 vols. Rodez, 1935-1938.

Borrelli de Serres, L. "Les variations monétaires sous Philippe le Bel," *Gazette numismatique française*, 1901, pp. 245-367; 1902, pp. 9-67.

———. *Recherches sur divers services publics du XIIIe au XVIIe siècle*. 3 vols. Paris, 1895-1905.

Boudet, M. "Les états d'Issoire de 1355 et leurs commissaires royaux," *Annales du Midi*, xii (1900), pp. 33-66.

Bowsky, W. "The Impact of the Black Death upon Sienese Government and Society," *Speculum*, xxxix (1964), pp. 1-34.

Bréquigny, L. de. "Mémoire sur les differends entre la France et L'Angleterre sous le règne de Charles le Bel," in C. Leber, *Collection des meilleurs dissertations, notices, et traités particuliers rélatifs à l'histoire de France.* xviii, Paris, 1838.

Breuils, A. "Jean Ier, comte d'Armagnac, et le mouvement national dans le Midi au temps du prince noir," *Revue des questions historiques*, lix (1896), pp. 44-102.

Bridrey, E. *La théorie de la monnaie au XIVe siècle, Nicole Oresme.* Paris, 1906.

Brown, E. "*Cessante Causa* and the Taxes of the Last Capetians: The Political Applications of a Philosophical Maxim," unpublished paper to appear in a forthcoming collection.

————. "Charters and Leagues in Early Fourteenth Century France: The Movement of 1314 and 1315" (doctoral dissertation, Harvard University). Cambridge (Mass.), 1960.

————. "Philip the Fair, '*Plena Potestas*,' and the *Aide pur fille Marier* of 1308," *Representative Institutions in Theory and Practice: Historical Papers Read at Bryn Mawr College, April 1968. Studies Presented to the International Commission for the History of Representative and Parliamentary Institutions* xxxix (1970), pp. 1-27.

————. "Politics, Taxation, and Discontent: Philip the Fair's Legacy to his Sons" (unpublished paper presented before the Society for French Historical Studies). Ann Arbor, 1966.

————. "Subsidy and Reform in 1321: The Accounts of Najac and the Policies of Philip V," forthcoming in *Traditio*, xxvii (1971).

————. "Assemblies of French Towns in 1316: Some New Texts," forthcoming in *Speculum*, xlvi (1971).

————. "Taxation and Morality in the Thirteenth and Fourteenth Centuries" (paper presented before the American Historical Association). Washington, 1969.

Brundage, J. *Medieval Canon Law and the Crusader.* Madison, 1969.

Cabrol, E. *Annales de Villefranche de Rouergue.* i. Villefranche, 1860.

Callery, A. *Histoire du pouvoir royal d'imposer depuis la féodalité jusqu'au règne de Charles V.* Brussels, 1879.

Campbell, G. "Clerical Immunities in France during the Reign of Philip III," *Speculum*, xxxix (1964), pp. 404-424.

Carpentier, E. "Autour de la peste noire: Famines et épidémies dans l'histoire du XIVe siècle," *Annales: Economies, sociétés, civilisations*, xvii (1962), pp. 1062-1092.

Carreau, M.-E. *Les commissaires royaux aux amortissements et aux nouveaux acquêts sous les Capetiens (1275-1328)* (unpublished Ecole des Chartes thesis). Paris, 1953.

Cazelles, R. "De Guesclin avant Cocherel," *Actes du Colloque International de Cocherel*, 1964, pp. 33-40.

————. "Une exigence de l'opinion depuis Saint Louis: La réformation du royaume," *Annuaire-Bulletin, Société de l'Histoire de France*, 1962-1963, pp. 91-99.

————. "Les mouvements révolutionnaires du milieu du XIVe siècle et le cycle de l'action politique," *Revue historique*, ccxxvii (1962), pp. 279-312.

————. "La peste de 1348-1349 en langue d'oil, épidémie proletarienne et enfantine," *Bulletin philologique et historique*, 1962, pp. 293-305.

————. "Quelques réflexions à propos des mutations de la monnaie royale française (1295-1360)," *Le Moyen Age*, lxxii (1966), pp. 83-105, 251-278.

————. *La société politique et la crise de la royauté sous Philippe de Valois.* Paris, 1958.

Chaplais, P. "English Arguments Concerning the Feudal Status of Aquitaine in the Fourteenth Century," *Bulletin of the Institute of Historical Research*, XXI (1948), pp. 203-213.

————. "Règlements de conflits internationaux franco-anglais au XIVe siècle, 1293-1327," *Le Moyen Age*, LVII (1951), pp. 269-313.

Cherest, A. *L'Archiprêtre: episodes de la guerre de cent ans au XIVe siècle.* Paris, 1879.

Cheruel, A. *Histoire de Rouen pendant l'époque communale, 1150-1382.* 2 vols. Rouen, 1843-1844.

Compayré, C. *Etudes historiques et documents inédits sur l'Albigeois, le Castrais, et l'ancien diocèse de Lavaur.* Albi, 1841.

Congar, Y. "Quod omnes tangit ab omnibus tractari et approbari debet," *Revue historique de droit français et étranger, 4e série*, XXXVI (1958), pp. 210-259.

Coville, A. *Les états de Normandie, leurs origines et leur développement au XIVe siècle.* Paris, 1894.

————. in *Histoire de France*. Vol. IV pt. 1. See Lavisse.

Cuttino, G. *English Diplomatic Administration, 1259-1339.* London, 1940.

————. "The Process of Agen," *Speculum*, XIX (1944), pp. 161-178.

Darmaillacq, B. "Le prince noir contre le comte d'Armagnac, expedition de 1355," *Revue de Gascogne*, LV (1914), pp. 5-17, 66-72.

Declareuil, J. *Histoire général du droit français des origines à 1789.* Paris, 1925.

Delachenal, R. *Histoire de Charles V.* 5 vols. Paris, 1909-1931.

————. "Premières négotiations de Charles le Mauvais avec les Anglais (1354-1355)," *Bibliothèque de l'Ecole des Chartes*, LXI (1900), pp. 253-282.

Delaville le Roulx, J. *La France en l'Orient au XIVe siècle.* 2 vols. Paris, 1886.

Delcambre, E. *Les états du Velay des origines à 1642.* Saint-Etienne, 1938.

————. "Le paréage du Puy," *Bibliothèque de l'Ecole des Chartes*, XCII (1931), pp. 121-169, 285-344.

Delisle, L. *Histoire du château et des sires de Saint-Sauveur-le-Vicomte.* Valognes, 1867.

Denifle, H. *La désolation des églises, monastères et hôpitaux en France pendant la guerre de Cent Ans.* 2 vols. Paris, 1899.

Déprez, E. *Les préliminaires de la guerre de Cent Ans: La papauté, la France, et l'Angleterre (1328-1342).* Paris, 1902.

Dognon, P. *Les institutions politiques et administratives du pays de Languedoc du XIIIe siècle aux guerres de religion.* Toulouse, 1895.

Duby, G. *Rural Economy and Country Life in the Medieval West* (English edn., tr. C. Postan). London, 1968.

Dufour, E. *La commune de Cahors au Moyen Age.* Cahors, 1846.

Dupont-Ferrier, G. *Etudes sur les institutions financières de la France à la fin du moyen âge.* 2 vols. Paris, 1930-1932.

————. "Ignorances et distractions administratives en France aux XIVe et XVe siècles," *Bibliothèque de l'Ecole des Chartes*, C (1939), pp. 145-156.

————. *Gallia Regia, ou etat des officiers royaux des bailliages et des sénéschausées de 1328 à 1515.* 6 vols. Paris, 1942.

————. *Les origines et le premier siècle de la chambre ou cour des aides de Paris.* Paris, 1933.

Ehler, S. "On Applying the Modern Term 'State' to the Middle Ages," *Medieval Studies Presented to Aubrey Gwynn.* Pp. 492-501. Dublin, 1961.

Emery, R. "The Black Death of 1348 in Perpignan," *Speculum*, XLII (1967), pp. 611-623.

Esmein, A. *Cours élémentaire d'histoire du droit français.* Paris, 1903.

Espinas, G. "Les finances de la commune de Douai des origines au XVe siècle," *Nouvelle revue historique de droit français et étranger,* 1901, pp. 410-443.

Estrup, H. "Oresme and Monetary Theory," *Scandinavian Economic History Review,* XIV (1966), pp. 97-116.

Favier, J. *Un conseiller de Philippe le Bel, Enguerran de Marigny.* Paris, 1963.

———. "Temporels ecclésiastiques et taxation fiscal: le poids de la fiscalité pontificale au XIVe siècle," *Journal des Savants,* 1964, pp. 102-127.

Fawtier, R. *The Capetian Kings of France* (English edn., tr. L. Butler and R. Adam). London, New York, 1960.

Félibien, M. & Lobineau, G. *Histoire de la ville de Paris.* 5 vols. Paris, 1725.

Fesler, J. "French Field Administration: The Beginnings," *Comparative Studies in Society and History,* V (1962), pp. 76-111.

Fourquin, G. *Les campagnes de la région parisienne à la fin du moyen âge.* Paris, 1964.

Funck-Brentano, F. *Philippe le Bel en Flandre.* Paris, 1897.

Garnier, E. "Biographie de Robert de Fiennes, connétable de France (1320-1384)," *Bibliothèque de l'Ecole des Chartes,* XIII (1852), pp. 23-52.

Gaujal, M. de. *Etudes historiques sur le Rouergue.* 4 vols. Paris, 1858-1859.

Germain, A. *Histoire de la commerce de Montpellier antérieurement à l'ouverture du port de Cette.* 2 vols. Montpellier, 1861.

Gierke, O. *Political Theories of the Middle Age* (ed. and trans. F. Maitland). Beacon edn. Boston, 1958.

Greenlee, J. "French Royal Propaganda from Philip the Fair to Louis XI (1300-1483)" (unpublished M.A. essay, McMaster University). Hamilton, 1969.

Guenée, B. "Etat et nation en France au moyen âge," *Revue historique,* CCXXXVII (1967), pp. 17-30.

Guessard, F. "Etienne de Mornay, chancelier de France sous Louis Hutin," *Bibliothèque de l'Ecole des Chartes,* V (1843-44), pp. 373-396.

Guigue, G. *Les Tards-Venus en Lyonnais, Forez, et Beaujolais.* Lyon, 1886.

Guilhiermoz, P. *Essai sur l'origine de la noblesse en France au moyen âge.* Paris, 1902.

Heers, J. *L'Occident aux XIVe et XVe siècles: Aspects economiques et sociaux.* Paris, 1963.

Henneman, J. "The Black Death and Royal Taxation in France, 1347-1351," *Speculum,* XLIII (1968), pp. 405-428.

———. "*Enquêteurs-Réformateurs* and Fiscal Officers in Fourteenth Century France," *Traditio,* XXIV (1968), pp. 309-349.

———. "Financing the Hundred Years' War: Royal Taxation in France in 1340," *Speculum,* XLII (1967), pp. 275-298.

———. "The French Estates General and Reference Back to Local Constituents, 1343-1355," *Representative Institutions in Theory and Practice: Historical Papers Read at Bryn Mawr College, April 1968. Studies Presented to the International Commission for the History of Representative and Parliamentary Institutions,* XXXIX (1970), pp. 29-52.

———. "The French Ransom Aids and Two Legal Traditions," unpublished paper to appear in a forthcoming collection.

———. "Taxation of Italians by the French Crown, 1311-1363," *Mediaeval Studies,* XXXI (1969), pp. 15-43.

Herbomez, A. d'. "Philippe de Valois et la maletôte à Tournai," *Le Moyen Age,* XX (1907), pp. 57-81.

Hervieu, H. *Recherches sur les premiers états généraux et les assemblées réprésenta-tives pendant la première moitié du XIVe siècle.* Paris, 1879.

Hewitt, H. *The Black Prince's Expedition of 1355-1357.* Manchester, 1958.

Hirschauer, C. *Les états d'Artois.* 2 vols. Paris, 1923.

Honoré-Duvergé, S. "L'origine du surnom de Charles le Mauvais," *Mélanges d'his-toire du Moyen Age dédiés à la mémoire de Louis Halphen.* Pp. 345-350. Paris, 1951.

Hoyt, R. S. "Recent Publications in the United States and Canada on the History of Representative Institutions before the French Revolution," *Speculum,* XXIX (1954), pp. 356-377.

Humbert, F. *Les finances municipales de Dijon du milieu du XIVe siècle à 1477.* Paris, 1961.

Jenkins, H. *Papal Efforts for Peace under Benedict XII.* Philadelphia, 1933.

Johnstone, H. "France: The Last Capetians," *The Cambridge Medieval History.* VII, pp. 305-339. Cambridge (Eng.), 1932.

Kantorowicz, E. *The King's Two Bodies: A Study in Medieval Political Theology.* Princeton, 1957.

Lacoste, G. *Histoire générale de la province de Quercy.* 4 vols. Cahors, 1873-1876.

Lafaurie, J. *Les monnaies des rois de France de Hugh Capet à Louis XII.* 2 vols. Paris, 1951-1956.

Lagarde, G. de. "La philosophie sociale d'Henri de Gand et Godefroid de Fon-taines," *Archives d'histoire doctrinale et littéraire du Moyen Age,* XVIII (1943-1945), pp. 73-142.

Lagrèze-Fossat, A. *Etudes historiques sur Moissac.* 3 vols. Paris, 1870-1874.

Landry, A. *Essai economique sur les mutations des monnaies dans l'ancienne France de Philippe le Bel à Charles VII.* Paris, 1910.

Langlois, C. V. in *Histoire de France.* Vol. III pt. 2. See Lavisse.

Langmuir, G. "Concilia and Capetian Assemblies, 1179-1230," *Album Helen Maud Cam,* II, pp. 27-63. *Studies Presented to the International Commission for the History of Representative and Parliamentary Institutions,* XXIV (1963).

——. "Counsel and Capetian Assemblies," *Studies Presented to the International Commission for the History of Representative and Parliamentary Institutions,* XVIII (1958), pp. 21-34.

——. "Politics and Parliaments in the Early Thirteenth Century," *Studies Pre-sented to the International Commission for the History of Representative and Parliamentary Institutions,* XXIX (1966), pp. 47-62.

Larenaudie, M. "Les famines en Languedoc aux XIVe et XVe siècles," *Annales du Midi,* LXIV (1952), pp. 23-39.

Lavisse, E. (ed.). *Histoire de France.* 9 vols. Paris, 1900-1911.

Lehoux, F. *Jean de France, duc de Berri: Sa vie, son action politique (1340-1416).* 3 vols. Paris, 1966-1968.

Lehugeur, P. *Philippe de Long, roi de France 1316-1322: Le mécanisme du gouverne-ment.* Paris, 1931.

Le Patourel, J. "Edward III and the Kingdom of France," *History,* XLIII (1958), pp. 173-189.

——. "Edward III, 'roi de France et duc de Normandie,' 1356-1360," *Revue his-torique de droit français et étranger, 4e série,* XXXI (1953).

Le Sourd, A. *Essai sur les Etats de Vivarais depuis leurs origines.* Paris, 1926.

Lewis, P. S. *Later Medieval France: The Polity.* London & New York, 1968.

Lopez, R. and Miskimin, H. "The Economic Depression of the Renaissance," *Eco-nomic History Review,* XIV (1962), pp. 408-425.

Lot, F. *L'art militaire et les armées au moyen âge.* 2 vols. Paris, 1946.

———. "L'état des paroisses et des feux de 1328," *Bibliothèque de l'Ecole des Chartes,* xc (1929), pp. 51-107.

Lot, F. and Fawtier, R. *Histoire des institutions françaises au moyen âge.* 3 vols. Paris, 1957-1963.

Lot, M. "Projets de croisade sous Charles le Bel et sous Philippe de Valois," *Bibliothèque de l'Ecole des Chartes,* xx (1859), pp. 503-509.

Lucas, H. "The Great European Famine of 1315, 1316, 1317," *Speculum,* v (1930), pp. 343-377.

———. *The Low Countries and the Hundred Years' War (1326-1347).* Ann Arbor, 1929.

Lyon, B. *From Fief to Indenture: The Transition from Feudal to Non-Feudal Contract in Western Europe.* Cambridge (Mass.), 1957.

Marongiu, A. "Q. o. t., Principe de la démocratie et du consentement au XIVe siècle," *Album Helen Maud Cam,* II, pp. 101-115. *Studies Presented to the International Commission for the History of Representative and Parliamentary Institutions,* xxIV (1961).

McFarlane, K. "England and the Hundred Years War," *Past and Present,* xxII (1962), pp. 3-13.

Ménard, L. *Histoire civile, ecclésiastique, et littéraire de la ville de Nismes, avec des notes et des preuves.* 7 vols. Paris, 1744-1758.

Meyer, E. *Charles II, roi de Navarre, comte d'Evreux, et la Normandie au XIVe siècle.* Paris, 1898.

Meynial, E. "Etudes sur la gabelle du sel avant le XVIIe siècle en France," *Tijdschrift Voor Rechtsgeschiedenis,* III (1922), pp. 119-162.

Michaud-Quantin, P. "La politique monétaire royale à la Faculté de Theologie de Paris en 1265," *Le Moyen Age,* LXVIII (1962), pp. 137-151.

Millerot, T. *Histoire de la ville de Lunel depuis son origine jusqu'en 1789.* Montpellier, 1879.

Miskimin, H. *Money, Prices, and Foreign Exchange in Fourteenth Century France.* New Haven, 1963.

Molinier, A. See Vic, C. de, and Vaissete, J.

Molinier, E. "Etudes sur la vie d'Arnoul d'Audrehem, maréchal de France (1302-1370)," *Mémoires presentées par divers savants à l'Academie des Inscriptions et Belles Lettres, 2e série,* VI pt. 1 (1883), pp. 1-359.

Mollat, G. "Clément VI et le chancelier Firmin de Cocquerel," *Bibliothèque de l'Ecole des Chartes,* cxxII (1964), pp. 257-261.

———. "Innocent VI et les tentatives de paix entre la France et L'Angleterre," *Revue d'histoire ecclésiastique,* x (1909), pp. 729-743.

Moreau, J.-N. *Mémoire la constitution politique de la ville et cité de Périgueux, avec Recueil de titres et autres pièces justificatives employés dans le Mémoire sur la constitution politique.* 2 vols. in one. Paris, 1775.

Moreau de Beaumont, J.-L. *Mémoire concernant les impositions et droits en Europe* (2nd edn.). 5 vols. Paris, 1787-1789.

Nortier, M. "Le sort des archives dispersées de la Chambre des Comptes de Paris," *Bibliothèque de l'Ecole des Chartes,* cxxIII (1965), pp. 460-537.

Pegues, F. *The Lawyers of the Last Capetians.* Princeton, 1962.

Perousse, G. "Etude sur les origines de la gabelle et sur son organisation jusqu'en 1380," *Positions des thèses, Ecole des Chartes,* 1898, pp. 89-98.

Perroy, E. "Franco-English Relations, 1350-1400," *History,* xxI (1936-1937), pp. 148-154.

————. "La fiscalité royale en Beaujolais aux XIVe et XVe siècles," *Le Moyen Age*, XXXIX (1928), pp. 5-47.

————. *The Hundred Years War* (English edn., tr. W. B. Wells). London, 1951.

Petit, J. *Charles de Valois (1270-1325)*. Paris, 1899.

Picot, G. *Histoire des Etats-généraux, considerés au point de vue de leur influence sur le gouvernement de la France de 1355 à 1614*. 4 vols. Paris, 1872.

Piton, C. *Les Lombards en France et à Paris*. 2 vols. in one. Paris, 1892.

Plancher, U. *Histoire générale et particulière de Bourgogne, avec des notes, des dissertations, et les preuves justificatives*. 4 vols. Dijon, 1739-1781.

Port, C. *Essai sur l'histoire du commerce maritime de Narbonne*. Paris, 1854.

Portal, C. *Histoire de la Ville de Cordes 1222-1799*. Albi, 1902.

Post, G. *Studies in Medieval Legal Thought: Public Law and the State, 1100-1322*. Princeton, 1964.

Poux, J. "Essai sur le commun de paix ou pezade dans le Rouergue et dans l'Albigeois," *Positions des thèses, Ecole des Chartes*, 1898, pp. 107-116.

Powicke, F. M. "Reflections on the Mediaeval State," *Transactions of the Royal Historical Society*, XIX (1936), pp. 1-9.

Prarond, E. *Histoire d'Abbeville avant la Guerre de Cent Ans*. Paris, 1891.

Prat, G. "Albi et la peste noire," *Annales du Midi*, LXIV (1952), pp. 15-25.

Prentout, H. *Les états provinciaux de Normandie*. 3 vols. Caen, 1925-1927.

Renouard, Y. "Les Papes et le conflit franco-anglais en Aquitaine de 1259 à 1337," *Mélanges d'archéologie et d'histoire*, LI (1934), pp. 258-292.

Rey, M. *Le domaine du roi et les ressources extraordinaires sous Charles VI, 1388-1413*. Paris, 1965.

Richard, J. "Finances princières et banquiers au XIVe siècle: L'affaire des Bourgeoise et la Réformation de 1343 en Bourgogne," *Annales de Bourgogne*, XXVII (1955), pp. 7-32.

Richard, J.-M. *Une petite-nièce de Saint-Louis, Mahaut comtesse d'Artois et de Bourgogne (1302-1329)*. Paris, 1887.

Riesenberg, P. *Inalienability of Sovereignty in Medieval Political Thought*. New York, 1956.

Robinson, W. "Money, Population, and Economic Change in Late Medieval Europe," *Economic History Review*, XII (1959), pp. 63-76.

Rogozinski, J. "The Counsellors of the Seneschal of Beaucaire and Nîmes, 1250-1350," *Speculum*, XLIV (1969), pp. 421-439.

————. "Social Conflict in the Urban Communities of Lower Languedoc during the Fourteenth Century," unpublished paper presented at the Midwest Medieval History Conference. Omaha, 1967.

Roover, R. de. *Money, Banking, and Credit in Mediaeval Bruges*. Cambridge (Mass.), 1948.

Secousse, D. F. *Mémoires pour servir à l'histoire de Charles II, roi de Navarre et comte d'Evreux, surnommé le Mauvais*. 2 vols. Paris, 1758. (For first volume, *preuves*, see Section III of bibliography.)

Sibertin-Blanc, C. "La levée du subside de 1337 en Rouergue et l'Hôpital d'Aubrac au début de la guerre de Cent Ans, à propos d'un mandement inédit de Philippe de Valois," *Bulletin philologique et historique*, 1953-1954, pp. 301-338.

Spufford, P. "Assemblies of Estates, Taxation, and Control of the Coinage in Medieval Europe," *Studies Presented to the International Commission for the History of Representative and Parliamentary Institutions*, XXXI (1965), pp. 115-130.

Stephenson, C. *Mediaeval Institutions: Selected Essays* (ed. B. Lyon). Ithaca, 1954.

Strayer, J. R. "Defense of the Realm and Royal Power in France," *Studi in onore di Gino Luzzatto.* I, pp. 289-296. Milan, 1950.

———. "France: The Holy Land, the Chosen People, and the Most Christian King," *Action and Conviction in Early Modern Europe* (ed. T. Rabb and J. Siegel). Pp. 3-16. Princeton, 1969.

———. "Italian Bankers and Philip the Fair," *Explorations in Economic History,* VII (1969), pp. 113-121.

———. "Laicization of French and English Society in the Thirteenth Century," *Speculum,* XV (1940), pp. 76-86.

———. "Normandy and Languedoc," *Speculum,* XLIV (1969), pp. 1-12.

———. "Pierre de Chalon and the Origins of the French Customs Service," *Festschrift Percy Ernst Schramm zu seinem siebzigsten Geburtstag von Schülern und Freunden zugeeignet.* I, pp. 334-339. Wiesbaden, 1964.

———. "Viscounts and Viguiers under Philip the Fair," *Speculum,* XXXVIII (1963), pp. 242-255.

Strayer, J. R., and Taylor, C. H. *Studies in Early French Taxation.* Cambridge (Mass.), 1939.

Taylor, C. H. "An Assembly of French Towns in March, 1318," *Speculum,* XIII (1938), pp. 295-303.

———. "Assemblies of French Towns in 1316," *Speculum,* XIV (1939), pp. 275-299.

———. "The Composition of Baronial Assemblies in France, 1315-1320," *Speculum,* XXIX (1954), pp. 433-459.

———. "French Assemblies and Subsidy in 1321," *Speculum,* XLIII (1968), pp. 217-244.

Timbal, P., et al. *La guerre de Cent Ans vue à travers les registres du Parlement (1337-1369).* Paris, 1961.

Ullmann, W. *The Medieval Idea of Law as Represented by Lucas de Penna.* London, 1946.

Vaissete, J. See below, Vic, C. de.

Viard, J. "La campagne de Crécy, juillet-aôut 1346," *Le Moyen Age,* XXXVII (1926), pp. 1-84.

———. "La chambre des comptes sous le règne de Philippe VI de Valois," *Bibliothèque de l'Ecole des Chartes,* XCIII (1932), pp. 331-359.

———. "La France sous Philippe VI de Valois. Etat géographique et militaire," *Revue des questions historiques,* LIX (1896), pp. 337-402.

———. "La guerre de Flandre (1328)," *Bibliothèque de l'Ecole des Chartes,* LXXXIII (1922), pp. 362-382.

———. "Itineraire de Philippe de Valois," *Bibliothèque de l'Ecole des Chartes,* LXXIV (1913), pp. 74-128, 524-592; LXXXIV (1923), pp. 166-170.

———. "Philippe de Valois avant son avènement au trône," *Bibliothèque de l'Ecole des Chartes,* XCI (1930), pp. 307-325.

———. "Philippe de Valois. Le début du règne," *Bibliothèque de l'Ecole des Chartes,* XCV (1934), pp. 259-283.

———. "Les projets de croisade de Philippe de Valois," *Bibliothèque de l'Ecole des Chartes,* XCVII (1936), pp. 305-316.

———. "Les ressources extraordinaires de la royauté sous Philippe VI de Valois," *Revue des questions historiques,* XLIV (1888), pp. 167-218.

———. "Le siège de Calais," *Le Moyen Age,* XL (1929), pp. 129-189.

Vic, C. de, and Vaissete, J. *Histoire générale de Languedoc avec des Notes et les pièces justificatives* (new edn., ed. A. Molinier et al.). 16 vols. Toulouse, 1872-1904.

Viollet, P. *Histoire des institutions politiques et administratives de la France.* 3 vols. Paris, 1890-1903.

Vuitry, A. *Etudes sur le régime financier de la France avant la Révolution de 1789, nouvelle série.* 2 vols. Paris, 1878-1883.

Wailly, N. de. "Mémoire sur les variations de la livre tournois depuis le règne de Saint Louis jusqu'à l'établissement de la monnaie decimale," *Mémoires de l'Institut Imperial de France,* XXI (1857), pp. 177-427.

―――. "Recherches sur le system monétaire de Saint Louis," *Mémoires de l'Institut Imperial de France,* XXI (1857), pp. 114-176.

Watson, A. "Back to Gold—and Silver," *Economic History Review,* XX (1967), pp. 1-34.

Wilks, M. *The Problem of Sovereignty in the Later Middle Ages.* Cambridge (Eng.), 1963.

Wolff, P. *Commerces et marchands de Toulouse (vers 1350-vers 1450).* Paris, 1954.

―――. "Les luttes sociales dans les villes du Midi française, XIIIe-XVe siècles," *Annales: Economies, sociétés, civilisations,* II (1947), pp. 443-454.

Wood, C. "*Regnum Francie*: A Problem in Capetian Administrative Usage," *Traditio,* XXIII (1967), pp. 117-147.

Zacour, N. *Talleyrand: The Cardinal of Périgord (1301-1364). Transactions of the American Philosophical Society,* L pt. 7. Philadelphia, 1960.

Henri de Sully, butler of France,
34, 36, 55
Hervieu, Henri, 172, 194
Hesdin, 150
high justice, 210
Holland, 58, 113
Holy Land, 105
Holy Roman Empire, 8
hommes de corps, 210
Hugues de la Celle, 34
Humbert II, dauphin of Viennois, 109
Hundred Years' War, 79, 81, 87, 115,
210, 250, 254, 305, 327, 344, 349

Ile-de-France, 11, 127, 224-26
imperial fisc, 17
income tax, 295, 297, 300
Innocent VI, 267, 271, 277, 287, 296
Isabella, queen of England, 41, 52,
55, 57, 66
Issoire, 282
Issoudun, 302
Italians, 13, 18, 29, 39, 46, 56, 76, 81,
82, 100n, 153, 189, 221, 230, 308,
349, 354, 356

Jean Chalemard, 280
Jean de Marigny, bishop of Beauvais,
135, 137, 143, 145n, 146, 159, 162-65,
167-69, 174, 202, 204, 206, 213
Jean de Nesle, 221n
Jews, 13, 14, 18, 29, 30, 38, 46, 48-50,
82, 83, 174, 354
Joan of Boulogne, queen of France, 254
Joan of Evreux, queen dowager of
France, 251n
Joan of Evreux, queen of Navarre,
viii, 69, 170, 172, 261, 262, 264, 287
Joan of France, duchess of Burgundy
and countess of Artois, 88
John I, posthumous king of France, 15
John II, 3, 238, 240, 243, 247, 249-51,
254, 255, 260, 262, 264-72, 274,
276, 277, 282, 284, 287, 288, 290,
291n, 298, 299, 301-303, 307,
310-12, 318, 326, 332, 344
John XXII, 41, 92, 103, 104
John I, count of Armagnac and Rodez,
viii, 120, 159n, 212-14, 257, 259,
272-75, 277-80
John of France, duke of Normandy,

93, 97, 101-103, 140, 181, 192,
201-14, 228, 230, 239. *See also* John II
John of France, count of Poitiers, 281
John of Luxembourg, king of Bohemia,
88, 91, 134
journal of the treasury, 240, 345, 346
"joyous accession," 39, 228, 244
jugerie (in seneschalsy of Toulouse),
11, 72, 119, 174; of Albigeois, 47,
84, 128, 144, 167, 168, 186, 257;
of Lauragais, 47; of Rieux, 128; of
Rivière, 47, 67; of Verdun, 67, 128;
of Villelongue, 47, 128, 231, 236n

knight bachelor, 21, 132, 285
knight banneret, 21, 99, 243n, 285
knighting aid, 106, 107, 112, 178, 349,
355. *See also* feudal aids

La Charité, prior of, 47, 71
Lafrançaise, 256, 277
La Marche, county of, 51, 57, 181
Lancaster, Henry, duke of, 255, 268,
276, 277, 299, 301. *See also*
Derby, earl of
Langmuir, Gavin, 26, 35n, 327
Languedoc, 5, 6, 10, 11n, 15, 27,
37, 38, 53, 56, 86, 102, 123, 141n,
171, 177-80, 188, 220, 235-37, 248,
249, 276, 285, 287, 300, 306, 309-11,
317, 318, 321, 323, 324, 354-57;
English raids against, 185, 278, 279;
feudal aids in, 98-100; *gabelle du sel*
in, 156, 158, 159; port facilities in,
110; tax for coinage reform in, 173,
175, 176
  Estates of Languedoc: 273n, 328n;
in 1346, 191, 202-205, 207, 208, 210,
211; *in 1351*, 243, 244, 246; *in 1353*,
257, 258; *in 1356*, 280-82
  *taxes and subsidy negotiations in
Languedoc: in 1324*, 45; *in 1325*, 46,
48-50; *in 1326*, 62; *in 1328*, 71; *in 1337*,
116, 117, 119, 121; *in 1338*, 127,
130, 132; *in 1339*, 134, 135; *in 1340*,
143; *in 1341*, 160, 161; *in 1342*, 162,
163, 165; *in 1343*, 167-69; *in 1345*,
183-87; *in 1346-47*, 208-16; *in 1348*,
231, 234; *in 1349-50*, 241, 243; *in 1351*,
244, 245, 247; *in 1352-53*, 255-58;
in 1354, 272, 273n, 275; *in 1355-56*,
277-82